# Prentice Hall

# Drive Right

## UPDATED TENTH EDITION

**Authors**

Margaret L. Johnson

Owen Crabb

Arthur A. Opfer

Randall R. Thiel

**Consulting Author**

Frederik R. Mottola

PEARSON

Prentice Hall

Boston, Massachusetts
Upper Saddle River, New Jersey

## About the Authors

### Authors

**Margaret L. Johnson** is a former supervisor of Driver, Consumer, and Health Education at Glenbrook North High School, Northbrook, Illinois. She also was an instructor of Traffic Safety and Driver Education at Northeastern Illinois University in Chicago.

**Owen Crabb** is Driver Education Specialist with the Maryland State Department of Education. He also has assisted several states in developing driver education programs.

**Arthur A. Opfer** has taught driver education at both the high school and college levels. He is a former Regional Traffic Coordinator for the Superintendent of Public Instruction at Educational Service District 105, Yakima, Washington.

**Randall R. Thiel** is Education Consultant for the Alcohol-Traffic Safety Program for the Wisconsin Department of Public Instruction. He has taught driver eduction at the

high school level and has been involved in teacher preparation programs at universities in Texas, Pennsylvania, and Indiana.

### Consulting Author/Teacher's Edition Writer

**Frederik R. Mottola** is Professor Emeritus of Public Health at Southern Connecticut State University and Executive Director of Driver Behavior Institute. He is the creator of the Zone Control System of Space Management and Reference Point Visualizations. He is a consultant and educator for traffic safety education programs for teachers, students, and drivers on local, national, and international levels.

### Special Needs Contributor

**John F. Knippel** is a Traffic Safety Educator at Bloomington High School, Colton Joint Unified School District, Bloomington, California.

**DISCLAIMER**

Driving any vehicle safely is the responsibility of the driver and all drivers operate their cars at their own risk. The techniques, suggestions and ideas contained herein are of broad general usefulness and not intended to replace actual driving experience, driving skills or a valid license. The techniques, suggestions and ideas contained herein cannot be considered absolute recommendations.

Federal, state, local and other applicable regulations and guidelines concerning road safety and driving practices change rapidly. The reader should note, therefore, that the development of new regulations, guidelines and practices may require changes in some techniques, suggestions and ideas contained in this material.

While the information contained in this book has been compiled from sources believed to be reliable and correct at the time of original publication, neither the publisher nor the author make any warranty, express or implied, with respect to the use of any techniques, suggestions and ideas disclosed in this book. The publisher and author disclaim any and all liability for any damages of any kind or character, including

without limitation any compensatory, incidental, direct or indirect, special, punitive, or consequential damages, loss of income or profit, loss of or damage to property or person, claims of third parties, or other losses of any kind or character arising out of or in connection with the use of this book or the accuracy of the information contained herein, even if the publisher or author has been advised of the possibility of such damages or losses.

**Copyright © 2007 by Pearson Education, Inc., publishing as Pearson Prentice Hall, Boston, Massachusetts 02116.** All rights reserved. Printed in the United States of America. This publication is protected by copyright, and permission should be obtained from the publisher prior to any prohibited reproduction, storage in a retrieval system, or transmission in any form or by any means, electronic, mechanical, photocopying, recording, or likewise. For information regarding permission(s), write to: Rights and Permissions Department, One Lake Street, Upper Saddle River, New Jersey 07458.

ISBN-0-13-131609-5

4 5 6 7 8 9 10   11 10 09 08

PEARSON
Prentice
Hall

## Contents

## Kaywood Award Recipients

The Richard Kaywood Award is presented annually to an individual who has made a significant national or international contribution to traffic safety education. It was established in 1985 as a living memorial to Dr. Richard Kaywood. The award honors his outstanding contributions to driver and traffic safety education, including his twenty-five years as co-author of the *Drive Right* program. The Richard Kaywood Award was created as a result of a cooperative effort between the American Driver and Traffic Safety Education Association (ADTSEA) and Scott Foresman. The award is presented at the annual ADTSEA Conference. The first award was presented in 1985, one year after Dr. Kaywood's untimely death.

Dick Kaywood had a long and productive career, beginning with his work in safety education as an assistant professor of health and physical education at the University of California at Santa Barbara. In 1956 he became the multischool chairman of driver education in the Anaheim Union High School District. In 1965 he became an associate professor of driving and traffic safety education at California State University at Long Beach. He went on to become a full professor and coordinator of safety and driver education. During his last three years, he also served as interim chairman of the health science department.

He was a charter member of the California Driver Education Association (later called the California Association for Safety Education) and an early member of ADTSEA. In 1959 Dick became editor of the California Association's CALDEA Calendar. In succeeding years, he developed it into a nationally recognized publication. In 1970 it became the official journal of ADTSEA, and the name was changed to the *Journal of Traffic Safety Education.* This was the only national journal dedicated to driver and traffic safety education. Dick had just started his twenty-fifth year as editor when he died in 1984. In addition to his work with the journal and *Drive Right,* Dick wrote extensively—with over one hundred articles, research reviews, editorials, and reports in driver and traffic safety education to his name.

In addition to his teaching and writing, Dick served as a member of the Transportation Research Board's Driver Education Committee from 1979 to 1983. He was one of the originators and coordinators of the First National Conference on Driving Simulators in 1977.

Retirement enabled Dick to devote more time to other professional activities. Just prior to his death, he had completed an issue of the journal, was participating in a revision of *Drive Right,* and was serving as editor of the Orange County Trauma Society's Newsletter.

Throughout his life, Dick was a tireless worker and strong advocate for quality driver and traffic safety education programs. Dick Kaywood's life exemplifies the spirit of the words inscribed on the Richard Kaywood Award medallion: Outstanding Contributions—Driver and Traffic Safety Education.

The **best** Driver Education Program in America **just got better!**

**Drive Right made the changes instructors wanted to see!**

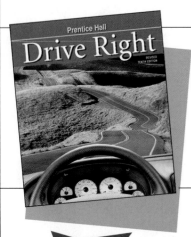

**Revised 10th Edition**

## Features you've loved:

- Solid content emphasizing the IPDE Process
- Easy-to-read Teacher's Edition with a focus on helpful teaching suggestions
- Useful student and teacher print support materials

## Features you've wanted:

- Updated content incorporating the latest trends in driver education
- Improved Teacher's Edition with more classroom activities
- Increased support with new videos

# Better,

Challenging questions start students thinking before they get behind the wheel.

**What Do You Think?**

Some vehicles now come with daytime running lights. Should daytime running lights be mandatory equipment on all vehicles?

manner. Avoid locking the brakes in an emergency stop. Locked brakes make steering impossible because wheels must be turning to provide traction for steering. Some newer vehicles have an antilock braking system. Such a system helps prevent loss of steering control. An antilock braking system, through the use of computers, helps brake your vehicle in an emergency. All you need to do is to apply the brakes hard, continually. No pumping action is needed.

As the driver of the car in the picture below enters the intersection, the white car from the right makes a right turn and enters the driver's path. The driver avoids locking the brakes so as not to lose steering control. Locking the brakes could have caused the car to slide and result in a conflict.

**Steer** When you decide to steer away from a possible conflict, execute just the amount of steering needed. Oversteering can cause you to lose control of your vehicle, especially at higher speeds. Higher speeds also require more space for your maneuver.

Understeering can also present a problem. Try to steer just enough to avoid a conflict without making jerky or sudden movements. Drivers who keep space cushions around their vehicles usually have an escape path to steer into, thus reducing risk.

**Communicate** In many instances your only action will be to communicate. When you do communicate, you must do it early enough so other users know your intentions. Communicate by using the following:

- **Headlights, taillights, and brake lights** Use headlights during

**You Are the Driver!**
What procedures would you follow to avoid conflict? Assume that your vehicle has an antilock braking system.

80 Unit 1 The Driving Task

...UNT BRAKE LIG...
...es in the United...
...gh-mount brake...
...g drivers an ae...
...y are effective...
...d those further...
...xperience up to...

...ning to drive...
...e the IPDE...
...fully...

...has closed...

...g a line-of-...

...avy load o...

...s unsure...
...torcycle.

...e Ahead...
...e tech-...
...other...
...gh, and...
...lowing.
...of...
...y...
...d. Be...
...high-...
...the...
...o...
...s

Behind-the-wheel photos and questions prepare students for situations they may encounter on the road.

# more up-to-date content

Interesting facts and information appeal to teens and help deepen their understanding of the rules of the road.

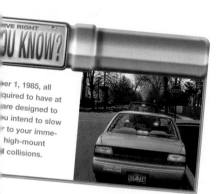

**OU KNOW?**

er 1, 1985, all quired to have at are designed to u intend to slow r to your imme- high-mount collisions.

in response to a changing on.

**dden Stops**

eas where sudden stops ree high-risk areas zones and sudden stops re ns where drivers o stop for traffic or s o parked vehicles iveways with high- fic

**Away**

in an unfamiliar area g for an address. If way from the road ead stops suddenly, ake these steps to is mistake: zone ahead is n. If you are her vehicle, ollowing

Chapter 9  Driving in Urban Traffic  **179**

Driving tips prepare students for their experience behind the wheel.

owed with a yellow arrow as a g. Watch for oncoming drivers ight proceed, thinking your rrow is their green light.

**d Green Light** A delayed ght indicates that one side tersection has a green light e light for the oncoming emains red. This light allows om one side to turn or go before the light for oncom- ic turns green. Obey your ly. Do not assume that proceed when oncoming roceeds.

**n Red**

and the District of Columbia nit turns on red. A few local ents may not. Watch for signs at prohibit turning on red.

**Red** Before turning right ight, come to a full stop as d at a STOP sign. Move to where you can see clearly. e front zones for openings. yield the right of way to any pedestrian in, or approach-

**SAFE DRIVING**

**TIP**

When a light turns yellow as you approach an intersection, prepare to stop. Do not speed up to try to get through the intersection.

pear with the normal red, yellow, and green signals. In many places the green arrow simply turns off to indicate the protected turn has ended. Others

Where should you search for vehicles and pedestrians when turning right on red?

Chapter 7  Negotiating Intersections  **137**

**IPDE PROCESS**

**1** Identify
**2** Predict
**3** Decide
**4** Execute

## More Emphasis on Managing Risk

From cover to cover, *Drive Right* stresses the IPDE Process while incorporating the Zone Control and Smith Systems to put your students on the road toward low-risk driving.

**New** Student Edition **Features!**

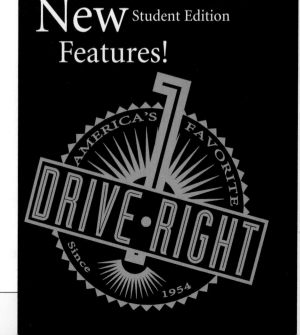

AMERICA'S FAVORITE

DRIVE·RIGHT

Since 1954

...e boards and illustrations clearly demonstrate **driving maneuvers and safety concepts.**

# Better

## The revised Teacher's Edition with wraparound

### Focus:

Summaries, along with key vocabulary terms, help you prepare for the lesson.

### Teach:

- Discussion questions
- Explanations for difficult-to-teach concepts
- Demonstration activities
- Content application activities

---

**9.1**

## Adjusting to Urban Traffic

### 1 Focus

#### Summary

This lesson highlights the main factors that make city driving difficult and how to use the IPDE Process in urban traffic.

#### Vocabulary

**Review:** *closed zone, decide, execute, identify, line-of-sight restriction, predict*

### 2 Teach

#### Discuss

Ask: How often do you expect to drive in an urban setting? (Answers will vary depending on the communities where students live. If your school is in rural area, ask students how often they expect to drive in the closest urban area.)

#### Demonstrate

Use **Video 2** Segment on the IPDE Process in Urban Traffic to show how to respond to urban traffic situations.

---

### Objectives

1. Name two factors that can make driving difficult in city traffic.
2. Describe how to use the IPDE Process for city driving.

**9.1**
## Adjusting to Urban Traffic

Once you are comfortable making basic maneuvers and using the IPDE Process, you will be ready to start driving in city traffic. City driving will test your best abilities.

#### Traffic Complexity

When you drive on a little-used rural road in good weather at a moderate speed, you probably will encounter few critical hazards. However, driving in heavy, fast-moving, city traffic is different and more challenging.

Two main factors make city driving difficult:

- Traffic is more dense in urban areas than it is in rural areas. There are more cars, buses, trucks, and pedestrians per mile.
- City traffic hazards are closer to you than they are in rural areas. Those hazards can quickly block your path.

In rural driving situations, the number of hazards per mile is low; you usually have an adequate "space cushion." You have time to adjust to the traffic scene. However, in city driving you may have to respond to several close hazards and possible conflicts at the same time.

**Number of Hazards** Mile for mile, city roads have the highest number and variety of hazards. Compare the two pictures of the same location on this page. Which situation is harder to handle. Why?

**Time, Distance, and Speed** As you drive, remember it takes time to use the IPDE Process. You will have to contend with many situations with closed zones and line-of-sight restrictions. If you cannot increase the distance between your vehicle and a hazard, you must change your lane position, slow, or stop to give yourself time to solve the conflict.

**Using the IPDE Process**

Heavy urban traffic will test your driving skills. Focus your attention on driving to avoid conflicts and distractions. You might see other

The number of urban hazards can vary dramatically.

176 Unit 3 Driving in Different Environments and Situations

---

### Teacher's Resources

**Resource Book**
Overheads, pages 45–46
**Demonstration Overheads**
Overhead B
**Video 2**
Segment on the IPDE Process in Urban Traffic

### Background

**The IPDE Process and City Driving**
The IPDE Process with the Zone Control System is particularly important in urban situations. In a situation with few hazards, traveling the speed limit probably is safe. The same street with more hazards, such as rush-hour traffic, might demand a lower speed. Lowering the speed gives drivers more time to make identifications and decisions. The IPDE Process provides a standard of acceptable performance during any traffic situation.

---

### Teacher's Resources:

A listing of ancillary items appropriate for use with each lesson

# support with more activities

teacher notes provides everything you need when you need it.

...ed to slow when your left- and right-front zones are closed.

...s using cellular phones. You
...ill see aggressive drivers who
...essly increase the risk in a situ-
...by challenging other drivers.
...extremely angry or thoughtless
...s will actually charge at others
...ugh they are in a rage. In "road
...situations, be cool and drop
...Give the angry, distracted, or
...-minded driver distance. You
...ontrol these situations by
...ng them.
...udy the picture above and
...about how you would apply
...DE Process. As you drive, focus
...e IPDE Process in these ways:
...**entify** Be vigorous in using
...ur visual skills. "Aim high" and
...ok well ahead to your target
...ea. Check your searching
...nges to make sure your front
...ne is open and you have time
...spot things like a line-of-sight
...striction.

- **Predict** Predict possible points of conflict quickly and gain valuable time to respond.
- **Decide** Always be ready to communicate or adjust your vehicle position by changing speed and/or using distance effectively.
- **Execute** Be ready to use your vehicle's controls to make smooth low-risk maneuvers in traffic.

### Review It
1. What two factors can make city driving difficult?
2. How can you best use the IPDE Process in city driving?

### SAFE DRIVING

Studies have shown that using a cellular phone while driving can increase the risk of collision. Drivers should not split their attention between driving and other attention-intensive activities.

Chapter 9  Driving in Urban Traffic **177**

## Demonstrate

Use **Demonstration Overhead B** and **Resource Book,** page 46 to illustrate how reducing speed helps you see more elements in a congested urban traffic situation. Tell students that they have six seconds to view a traffic scene. Show **Overhead B** with three vehicles (see **Resource Book,** page 46) for six seconds. Turn the projector off and ask which vehicle is most at risk and why. Show **Overhead B** with six vehicles for four seconds. Turn off the projector and ask which vehicle is most at risk and why. Show **Overhead B** with nine vehicles for two seconds. Turn off the projector and ask which vehicle is most at risk and why.

Fewer students will have the correct response for the third scene than the first two. Ask them if they know why. (Some students will tell you that they did not have enough time to see the scene.) This gives you the opportunity to discuss how reduced speed provides more time to see problems in congested situations.

### 3 Assess

### Answers to Review It

1. High-density traffic and having hazards closer to you are the two main factors that make urban driving difficult. (p. 176)
2. Identify hazards with vigorous visual skills, predict points of conflict early, be ready to communicate or adjust your vehicle speed and/or position, and be ready to execute smooth low-risk maneuvers. (p. 177)

Chapter 9 | Driving in Urban Traffic | **177**

## Activity

**Class Activity** The first part of this activity will help students understand ...s a limit to how much information can ...ed at one time. The second part will ...nts understand the need to limit what ...oking for. You will need an overhead ...nd can make an overhead from the **Resource Book,** page 45.
...ch number on the transparency give ...e second to look and then ten sec-...te down what they can remember. ...he smallest number and progress to

the greatest. Read off the numbers and see how many students recalled them correctly. Point out that most people's ability to recall the number decreases as the number of digits increases. Just as you can be overloaded with numbers, you can be overloaded with information in urban traffic.

Tell students that you will show them the four numbers again, but this time they are to write down how many times the numeral 4 appears in each number. Provide the correct answers and point out that the second activity was easier because the search was limited.

## Assess:

Answers to the review questions located at the end of each section.

## Additional Support:

- Strategies for Special Needs
- Cross-Curricular Connections
- Background Notes
- Facts and Figures

# Revised
Teacher's Edition with
## Wraparound
## Notes!

AMERICA'S FAVORITE
**DRIVE·RIGHT**
Since 1954

## Activities:

Different learning activities are provided for the whole class,
small groups, or in-class driving rehearsals.

## Teaching Resources

This kit contains all the black-line masters you need, neatly organized in a sturdy file.

- **Tests and Activities**
  Blackline masters of Chapter Activity worksheets; Chapter Tests, Unit Tests, Final Tests, and Sample Questions for Written Driving Test

- **In-Car Checklists**
  Blackline masters of check-lists for in-car instruction

- **Resource Book**
  Activity masters for the Teacher's Edition, information sheets, and a listing of audio-visual and computer resources

- **Skills and Applications Workbook Teacher's Edition**

- **Companion Student Edition and Teacher's Edition**
  Workbook for students who need more language support

- **Spanish Handbook**
  Translations of chapter main ideas, glossary, and in-car procedures

- **Parent Guide**
  Tips for conducting practice driving sessions

- **Posters**
  Full-color posters to highlight key concepts

- **Lesson Plans**
  Available for each section of every chapter

# Better

**Two Videos!**

## Video 1: The Driving Task and Vehicle Control
## Video 2: Driving in Different Environments

Animated simulations demonstrate key driving maneuvers and procedures for avoiding collisions. Includes Teacher's Guide.

# ways to *liven* up your lessons!

## Demonstration Overhead Transparencies

Color overheads with manipulative vehicles help you demonstrate driving maneuvers.

### Plus!

## Content Overhead Transparencies

Color pictures, diagrams, and graphs help you teach key driving concepts.

## Computer Test Bank

Save time preparing tests! This CD-ROM package makes it easy to print out ready-made tests with extensive customization options. Includes 50 test questions per chapter. Formatted for both Windows and Macintosh.

## Skills and Applications Workbook

Student worksheets reinforce concepts, vocabulary, and skills content from each chapter. Teacher's Edition available separately or in the Teaching Resources.

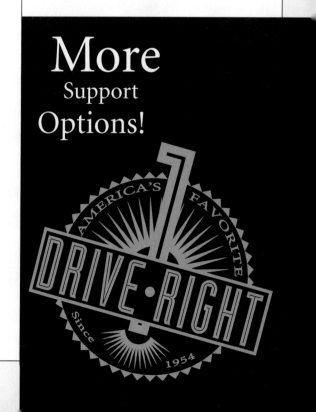

# To order *Drive Right,* call 1-800-848-9500

| | |
|---|---|
| Student Edition, hardcover With Go Driver CD-ROM | 0-13-251279-3 |
| Student Edition, softcover With Go Driver CD-ROM | 0-13-251278-5 |
| Teacher's Edition | 0-13-131609-5 |
| Teaching Resources Package (Includes ancillary products*) | 0-13-251277-7 |
| Skills and Applications Workbook SE | 0-13-068328-0 |
| Skills and Applications Workbook TE* | 0-13-068329-9 |
| Resources Book* | 0-13-068320-5 |
| Tests and Activities* | 0-13-068331-0 |
| In-Car Checklists* | 0-13-068336-1 |
| Companion* | 0-13-068332-9 |
| Companion Answer Key* | 0-13-068333-7 |
| Spanish Handbook* | 0-13-068335-3 |
| Parent Guide* | 0-13-068334-5 |
| Lesson Plans* | 0-13-036223-9 |
| Computer Test Bank With CD-ROM* | 0-13-251269-6 |
| Poster Package* | 0-13-068337-X |
| Demonstration Overhead Transparencies | 0-13-068338-8 |
| Content Overhead Transparencies | 0-13-068330-2 |
| Video Package | 0-13-068346-9 |

*Included in Teaching Resources Package and also available separately*

PEARSON

Prentice Hall

The *Drive Right* program is designed to help novice drivers develop the knowledge, skills, and attitudes necessary to become safe, low-risk, responsible drivers—and to DRIVE RIGHT. Since the driving task is primarily a thinking task, an organized decision-making process is necessary for drivers to manage the many risks they will encounter on the roadway. *Drive Right* uses the IPDE Process as the basis of instruction. The IPDE Process is an organized system for seeing, thinking, and responding. Students learn how to identify, predict, decide, and execute in a manner that develops the behaviors and the mental skills necessary to manage risk. *Drive Right* also teaches students how to use the Smith System and the Zone Control System to help them apply the IPDE Process more effectively for low-risk driving.

The *Drive Right* text begins with an overview of the driving task and skills needed to navigate the complex highway transportation system (HTS) and the responsibilities involved in obtaining a driver's license and becoming a safe driver. It then begins teaching the concepts and basic maneuvers necessary to develop the knowledge and the physical skills of driving. This sequence puts students behind the wheel prepared to develop the necessary mental skills and attitudes for low-risk driving. Throughout the text students will learn many concepts and driving maneuvers. They will learn how to use the IPDE Process, along with the Smith System and Zone Control System, to process and apply the concepts into safe driving behaviors.

*Drive Right* teaches students the Smith System and the Zone Control System along with the IPDE Process to help students develop sound habits of searching and managing space. The Smith System's five rules help students develop good seeing habits. The Zone Control System helps students manage the six zones around their vehicle and see and respond to changes in the traffic environment at a time when best control can be achieved. Incorporating the Smith System and Zone Control System into the IPDE Process will put students on the road toward developing low-risk driving behaviors. With continual practice, these behaviors will become habits for a lifetime of safe driving.

Throughout the *Drive Right* text, students learn how to apply the IPDE Process to different driving environments and conditions. Procedures are presented in a step-by-step method for easy learning and are illustrated in diagrams, traffic boards, and photographs. Students are continually involved in the decision-making process with questions to analyze situations and conditions in the photographs. They continue to be involved through application questions in the assessment components and the *Skills and Applications Workbook*. Teachers have the opportunity to help students practice decision-making with active learning activities provided in the Teacher's Edition.

*Drive Right* also prepares students to use the IPDE Process to help them make responsible decisions about driving-related behaviors. They learn how to use the decision-making process in a manner to control their own emotions as they deal with aggressive and irresponsible drivers. They learn how to use this process to cope with peer pressure to engage in high-risk driving activities such as speeding, "showing off," and driving after drinking alcohol or using other drugs. Thus students develop responsibility for safe driving.

Drivers trained in the IPDE Process will develop low-risk driving behaviors. They will be more likely to correctly identify and predict traffic information, make sound decisions, and execute safe driving maneuvers. They will manage the space around their vehicle to maintain a safe path of travel. With practice, these safe driving behaviors will become habits so that they can DRIVE RIGHT for a lifetime of low-risk, low-stress driving.

## How to Use the Drive Right Program

The *Drive Right* program provides a complete package that will enable you to teach driving in an effective manner with a minimum of preparation. The program provides a balance between the teaching of concepts and the development of skills. The Teacher's Edition and ancillaries provide options that enable you to customize the program to your particular teaching style and the learning needs of your students.

### Student Text

Each chapter opens with the *You Are the Driver!* feature. Students are asked questions about the situation in the picture to help them begin to explore issues for new drivers that will be presented in the chapter. Additional *You Are the Driver!* questions appear on photographs throughout the chapter. Students are directed to www.PHSchool.com/driveright, where they will find chapter activities, self-quizzes, and resource Web links.

The up-to-date, easy-to-read text provides students with all the information they need to become safe, responsible, low-risk drivers. Students know exactly what they are supposed to learn since lesson *Objectives* are listed right on the student page at the beginning of each section. The many behind-the-wheel photographs and traffic boards are integrated with the text to make the content come alive and to help students learn driving maneuvers and how to react to driving situations. Some photographs include *You Are the Driver!* questions to develop students' decision-making skills. *Review It* questions at the end of each section help students assess their mastery of lesson objectives. Vocabulary words appear in bold type and are defined and used in context.

Sidebar features expand text content and bring important issues to students' awareness.

- *Did You Know?* enhances students' interest and knowledge with interesting facts and information about the past, present, and future of traffic safety and related topics.
- *What Do You Think?* stimulates discussion or debate of issues related to traffic safety.
- *Safety Tips* and *Consumer Tips* highlight safe driving behaviors and ways to be a smart consumer of driving-related products and services.

The three-page *Chapter Review* provides a variety of ways for students to review and apply key concepts. Page references are provided so that students can find the answers to check themselves and identify what they need to study further. A variety of individual and group *Projects* can be assigned at the beginning of the chapter and then be discussed in class or assigned as homework. The *Chapter Test* provides objective and essay questions to assess knowledge and understanding. *Decision Making* presents four illustrations for students to analyze and apply what they have learned to make decisions about driving and other situations—in class discussion or as homework.

### Teacher's Edition

The *Drive Right* Teacher's Edition has been developed to help you bring the excitement of discovery, problem solving, and decision making to the students during their classroom experiences.

A *Chapter Planning Guide* precedes each chapter to help you prepare for teaching. The planning guide identifies for each section features in the Student Text for discussion as well as demonstrations and activities in the Teacher's Edition so that you can decide which ones you want to use in teaching the chapter and gather any necessary materials. The guide identifies any ancillary materials available for use with each section. In addition, other resources are suggested for use with the chapter—videos, software, kits, equipment, and PHSchool.com/driveright.

All of the teacher notes wrap around the Student Text pages. At the beginning of each chapter you will find a chapter overview, a list of vocabulary words, strategies for introducing the chapter and for the *You Are the Driver!* feature, and suggestions for teaching special needs students.

For every section, wraparound notes on the side provide the core teaching strategies in a three-step lesson plan. Other teaching options appear below the Student Text pages—various activities and background information, as well as a listing of teacher's resources from *Drive Right* ancillaries to use with the section.

## Lesson Plan

The three-step lesson plan in the side notes provides a variety of teaching strategies for each section.

**1. Focus** A summary of lesson content is provided along with a list of new vocabulary words (in bold on student pages) and review words introduced in earlier chapters.

**2. Teach** Four types of teacher notes are provided. *Discuss* highlights lesson concepts and features for class discussion. *Explain* suggests concepts to emphasize and presents information to share with students to expand their knowledge and understanding. *Demonstrate* provides activities to demonstrate concepts and driving procedures using the Demonstration Overheads and other techniques. *Apply* provides strategies to help students apply concepts they have learned.

**3. Assess** The answers to all questions are provided.

## Activities

Because this is a textbook about driving, the final use of concepts within this book will be in the quality of decisions the students will make while driving. Therefore, the Teacher's Edition provides several types of activities in each chapter. Some of these activities give students an opportunity to do in the class-

room—as close physically and mentally as possible—the performance expected from them during in-car lessons. Other activities provide opportunities for students to gain a better understanding of concepts and explore topics in a variety of ways. These activities can add fun and interest for both you and the student as you make the concepts within the text come alive.

There will be more activities than you may have the time to conduct, but they provide you with choices to get students involved in the learning process. You will need to look at the Activity options before you teach a chapter to decide which ones you want to use and what advance preparation will be needed to gather supplies and make copies of sheets from the Resource Book.

Four types of *Activities* provided in the Teacher's Edition are described below. The first two involve in-class practice of driving procedures.

**Model Car Activity** Students use Matchbox model cars, or other cars the same size, along with *Model Roadway* sheets (found in the Resource Book). Students work in small groups to demonstrate the proper steps for driving procedures and behavioral patterns for the IPDE Process. See pages T18–T19 for detailed instructions.

**In-Car Driving Rehearsal** Students simulate procedures for various driving situations in the classroom to help them become mentally and physically prepared for in-car instruction. In some activities students walk around the room or use their desks as vehicles and a simulated steering wheel—a plastic or paper dinner plate or a cardboard pizza round—to practice use of visual skills with driving maneuvers. In other activities students do tasks that are physically equivalent to driving tasks, such as accelerating and braking.

**Small Group Activity** Students work in groups of four to six to explore topics. Note that some of these activities involve research outside the classroom that needs to be assigned in advance of discussion in class. Some require each student to take on a role or to explore one aspect of the topic. Others involve use of activity sheets provided in the Resource Book. Some of these activities can be adapted for class discussion instead of small groups.

**Class Activity** A variety of types of activities are suggested for use with the entire class. These include discussion of situations portrayed in photographs in the Student Text, debate of issues, and demonstrations to stimulate discussion.

### Other Options

Other options for special types of activities and for background information appear below the Student Text pages.

**Special Needs** A variety of strategies are provided for teaching students with special needs in the classroom.

**Cross-Curricular** These activities connect driver education to other subjects in the school curriculum.

**Background** Additional background information expands on concepts in the lesson or extends content to related topics.

**Facts and Figures** Statistical information and interesting facts related to lesson concepts are presented.

### Ancillaries

The *Drive Right* program provides a variety of ancillary products to help you use the teaching strategies and activities presented in the Teacher's Edition, to help students understand the key concepts and apply them, and to assess students on what they have learned.

### Skills and Applications Workbook

This workbook contains four pages for each chapter. First, all vocabulary words and other key terms are reviewed along with key concepts. Then students are provided a variety of questions to apply concepts and skills they have learned. The Teacher's Edition provides the answers printed in red on the student pages.

### Teacher's Resource File

All the support you need comes in a Teacher's Resource File. Reproducible blackline masters are organized into booklets by topic so that you can choose what you want to use. Tabbed dividers allow you to file masters by type or by unit, or you could file the masters in a 3-ring binder.

**Resource Book** Support materials for the Teacher's Edition are provided. Find special instructions for activities, masters to reproduce for student use or to make overhead transparencies, and information sheets to provide additional teaching materials on reference points, what to do in a collision, and other topics.

**Tests and Activities** For each chapter there are two tests with multiple choice questions plus one essay question and two activities to review vocabulary and to review and apply concepts. Four unit tests, a final test, and a sample written driving test are also included.

**In-Car Checklists** The 40 In-Car Checklists provide step-by-step driving procedures to use during in-car instruction and for performance assessment.

**Companion** This workbook will help ESL students or those who have difficulty reading to better understand the *Drive Right* text. It is a self-study guide designed for the students to use along with *Drive Right* through pre-reading activities and the presentation of a glossary of words in simple terms. Answers reading activities and the presentation of a glossary of words in simple terms. Answers are provided in a separate Teacher's Edition, which can be given to students to check their own work.

**Spanish Handbook** To help Spanish-speaking students use *Drive Right* more easily, this book contains Spanish translations of the main ideas of each chapter, the glossary, and the In-Car Checklists.

**Lesson Plans Book** This book will help you plan ahead for teaching each lesson in *Drive Right*. It provides teacher's notes in a 3-step lesson plan and lists activity options.

**Parent Guide** This book provides parents with tips for conducting practice driving sessions and the In-Car Checklists to use when students are practicing procedures in the car.

**Posters** Use the four posters for bulletin board display as well as a way to motivate students and elicit discussions. Poster topics include signs, the IPDE Process, controlling emotions, and the costs of driving under the influence of alcohol.

**Demonstration Overheads** Various traffic board roadways and intersections can be used with manipulative vehicles to demonstrate driving maneuvers. Suggestions for using these overheads are provided in the Teacher's Edition.

**Content Overheads** Illustrations, diagrams, and graphs are provided as overhead transparencies to help you discuss key concepts with the class.

**Computer Test Bank** A CD-ROM (in IBM or Macintosh format) allows you to generate an infinite supply of customized tests. The package comes with a *Program Guide* with instructions and a *Testbank Guide* that lists the questions for each chapter.

**Videos** Two videotapes present realistic animations to demonstrate key driving procedures and concepts. A Teacher's Guide comes in the package with the two videos.

**PHSchool.com/driveright** The Prentice Hall Web site for *Drive Right* provides students with activities using the Internet and self-quizzes to use with each chapter. Teacher's notes for activities and quiz answers are provided for teachers. Resource Web links are provided for both students and teachers.

Most behaviors required of the student in the car can take place in some form during classroom sessions. The *Drive Right* Teacher's Edition provides two types of activities—the Model Car Activity and the In-Car Driving Rehearsal—that will give the students preparation in the classroom for successful in-car performance.

Through the use of these activities, you will be able to save hours of instructional in-car time. For example, suppose you have a class of 30 students and you spend 20 minutes during a class session having the students practice a particular concept or behavior. This saves spending time individually with each student in the car. It could save you 10 hours (600 minutes) of in-car time by merely using one activity. Both you and the students will gain. You save time, and the students are more likely to experience success in the car after practicing in the classroom.

Teaching these activities will require some advance preparation and an understanding of how to conduct the activities. The instructions below are repeated in the *Drive Right* Resource Book, which also contains sheets for reproduction to use with the activities.

## Model Car Activities

The Model Car Activity requires the students to "drive" a model car on roadway sheets to demonstrate the proper steps of a procedure, and to demonstrate numerous behavioral patterns that apply to searching techniques and space management. Students will work in groups of three, with each student taking on a different role.

The Model Car Activity helps the student get a mind-set for performing driving tasks in the car. If a student doesn't understand a proper procedure while doing the modeling, he or she more than likely will not know it any better when in the driver education car.

## Preparation for the Model Car Activity

You will need to gather and prepare materials to use for these activities. Once gathered, however, the same materials can be used for all of the Model Car Activities.

**Roadway Sheets** A set of eight roadway sheets are provided in the Resource Book for duplication for student distribution. Each Roadway sheet needs to be prepared from two 8 1/2-by-11 master sheets (labeled A and B) to make one 11-by-17 sheet. You can either photocopy the two sheets and then tape them together or photocopy them side-by-side onto an 11-by-17 sheet of paper, making sure they align properly. You will need one copy for each group of three students, and you should collect them after each class for future use. The eight roadway sheets are:

1. two-lane roadway
2. four-lane roadway
3. four-way intersection
4. T-intersection
5. curve with large radius
6. curve with small radius
7. cloverleaf exit ramp
8. parking lot with three types of parking spaces

**Model Cars and Wild Cards** For every group of three students, you will need two Matchbox model cars or other model cars the same size. For each group you will also need a piece of wood (approximately a 1-inch cube) or other small object to be used as a wild card item for problem-solving.

## Conducting the Model Car Activity

Divide the class into groups of three with the three student desks in a row butting against each other. It is desirable to have all students view the roadway sheets from the same perspective. Give the center student the roadway sheet and necessary cars and objects to represent the wild card (pieces of wood or other object) for the problem-solving situation.

When solving space management problems, you will tell students to use the wild card to create various restrictions in their line of sight and path of travel (depending on the lesson topics). For an example of using wild cards, see the Activity on page 72.

There are three roles the students perform: the driver, the instructor, and the supervisor. All three students rotate into all three roles for each problem or task to be performed. Each role has a specific responsibility:

**Instructor** The instructor gives the driver a problem to solve or a task to perform. It is best for students to learn to perform single behaviors rather than to memorize all the steps of a procedure. Therefore, the instructor should tell the student what the step is and ask him or her to demonstrate its correct behavior. After one step is performed, the instructor states whether or not the driver's performance was correct. When performance is not correct, the instructor coaches the driver for correct performance.

**Driver** The driver moves the car as it would appear from an outside view, explains the actions he or she would be taking, states what the view would be from the driver's seat, and, when possible, demonstrates the physical action to be taken.

**Supervisor** The supervisor double-checks on the instructor to be certain that the activity is being conducted correctly and that proper feedback is being given.

As the students work in their groups solving the problems, you can walk about the classroom monitoring what is being correctly or incorrectly performed and answering questions. After all members of each group state that they are able to perform correctly, you may want to review the problem with the total class by using overhead transparencies or doing it on the chalkboard. You can call upon one student for the first step, another for the second, etc., until the procedure or problem-solving situation is completed. If you use overhead transparencies, you can use the *Drive Right* Demonstration Overheads with manipulative cars. If you use a chalkboard, it is best to use a 1:24 scale model car or larger. To draw accurate scale roadways, figure the width of your car as 6 feet and a standard travel lane as 12 feet, or two car-widths wide.

## In-Car Driving Rehearsal

The In-Car Driving Rehearsal activity has students simulate behaviors and procedures for various driving situations in the classroom to help them become mentally and physically prepared for in-car instruction. For many of these activities you will need to provide a simulated steering wheel for each student in the class. You can use 10-inch plastic or paper picnic plates or cardboard 10-inch pizza rounds (donated or purchased from a local pizzeria). It is possible to use a piece of paper 8 1/2-by-11 (held horizontally), but the plate or pizza round works best and can be reused throughout the course.

Student chairs can be arranged to represent various types of roadways. To form travel lanes, move rows of chairs to clear pathways of at least 4 feet wide per lane width. A two-lane roadway will require at least 8 feet of aisle width. You can use duct tape or masking tape to create pavement markings for lane seperation.

To form intersections, cluster chairs into a group of a minimum of four. Each chair can represent a vehicle, with some occupied by students and others not. You can have students standing alongside the roadway to represent line-of-sight restrictions. Curves in the roadway can also be formed by arranging the chairs as such.

## Pacing Guide

There are many ways to set up the classroom phase of your driver education program. Each school will set up the program that fits state or district requirements and works best in the school's particular schedule of class periods. Some suggestions for organization and a pacing guide are provided here for developing a schedule for the classroom phase of your *Drive Right* program.

The *Drive Right* program is organized to provide flexibility. You can teach the chapters in any order or omit some chapters. Each chapter is independent of the others except for chapters following Chapter 4; students need to be taught how to use the IPDE Process before proceeding to Chapters 6–11.

*Drive Right* is organized into 18 chapters, which allows for an easy schedule of one chapter a week for eighteen weeks or two chapters a week for nine weeks. However, the amount of time needed to teach each chapter varies because of length and content. Therefore, two pacing guides are provided to fit different classroom time periods for 30 hours of instructions. The majority of states require a minimum of 30 hours of classroom instruction, with additional instruction in the car, driving range, and/or simulator.

Many schools have 45-minute sessions scheduled four or five times a week for nine weeks or two or three times a week for eighteen weeks. The first pacing guide suggests a plan for thirty-six classroom sessions of about 45 minutes each.

### Pacing Guide for 45-Minute Classroom Sessions

| Chapter in Drive Right | Classroom Sessions |
|---|---|
| 1 You Are the Driver | 1 |
| 2 Signs, Signals, and Roadway Markings | 2 |
| 3 Basic Car Control | 2 |
| 4 Managing Risk with the IPDE Process | 3 |
| 5 Natural Laws and Car Control | 2 |
| 6 Performing Basic Vehicle Maneuvers | 2 |
| 7 Negotiating Intersections | 2 |
| 8 Sharing the Roadway | 3 |
| 9 Driving in Urban Traffic | 2 |
| 10 Driving in Rural Areas | 3 |
| 11 Driving on Expressways | 3 |
| 12 Driving in Adverse Conditions | 2 |
| 13 Handling Emergencies | 2 |
| 14 Effects of Driver Condition | 2 |
| 15 Alcohol, Other Drugs, and Driving | 2 |
| 16 Buying and Owning a Vehicle | 1 |
| 17 Maintaining Your Vehicle | 1 |
| 18 Planning Your Travel | 1 |

Some schools have block scheduling with 90-minute classroom sessions meeting once or twice a week. The second pacing guide suggests a plan for eighteen 90-minute classroom sessions. This pacing guide can be adapted for summer school and after-school programs that meet for 90 minutes or more for a varying number of days per week.

These pacing charts are just a guide. If your driver education program meets more often or has longer classroom sessions, you can increase the teaching time for chapters by using more of the activities and teaching strategies provided in the Teacher's Edition and providing more in-class time for review and assessment using ancillary materials. You also may want to eliminate the last three chapters from your program to allow more time to teach driving maneuvers in the classroom for Chapters 3–11.

## Pacing Guide for 90-Minute Classroom Sessions

| Chapter in Drive Right | Classroom Sessions |
|---|---|
| 1  You Are the Driver | |
| 2  Signs, Signals, and Roadway Markings | 1 |
| 3  Basic Car Control | 1 |
| 4  Managing Risk with the IPDE Process | 2 |
| 5  Natural Laws and Car Control | 1 |
| 6  Performing Basic Vehicle Maneuvers | 1 |
| 7  Negotiating Intersections | |
| 8  Sharing the Roadway | 3 |
| 9  Driving in Urban Traffic | 1 |
| 10  Driving in Rural Areas | |
| 11  Driving on Expressways | 3 |
| 12  Driving in Adverse Conditions | 1 |
| 13  Handling Emergencies | 1 |
| 14  Effects of Driver Condition | 1 |
| 15  Alcohol, Other Drugs, and Driving | 1 |
| 16  Buying and Owning a Vehicle | |
| 17  Maintaining Your Vehicle | |
| 18  Planning Your Travel | 1 |

Students for whom English is a second language (ESL students) are fluent in their own native language but may be limited in their use of the English language. The *Drive Right* program provides several ways for you to easily help these students.

### Characteristics of ESL Students

ESL students are similar to other students in the classroom. Most are intellectually capable of doing the work at their grade level and eager to learn. However, ESL students often experience great frustration because their difficulties with English keep them from understanding what is going on. This frustration often results in low self-esteem and may lead to behaviors that interfere with the learning process. Such behaviors may include reluctance to speak in class, lack of attention, acting up, poor attendance, and assignments that are incomplete or not turned in. Students may fear being ridiculed for doing or saying something incorrectly.

Most ESL students are eager to improve their English, although they may have trouble doing so. They also are eager to learn to drive, and the driver education teacher can help them in both areas. You do not need any special training to help these students, just implement some of the following suggestions and use the *Drive Right Companion,* a workbook designed specifically for ESL students.

### Using the Drive Right Companion

The *Drive Right Companion* was developed to help the ESL student understand and use the *Drive Right* textbook. The *Companion* is designed to be used before and while students read the *Drive Right* textbook to help them understand the concepts. It contains a combination of simplified vocabulary and activities to reinforce vocabulary and concepts. The *Companion* is designed for the students to use on their own and not as a test. You can give students the answers from the *Companion Teacher's Edition* to check their own work or check the work quickly yourself so that students get immediate feedback on whether they understood the material.

The *Drive Right Companion* follows the structure of the *Drive Right* textbook. It is organized by chapters, which are divided by sections that correspond with those in the textbook. The chapters in the *Companion* include the following sections.

**Words and Ideas** This section provides simplified definitions and explanations for vocabulary and concepts in the textbook. This material is not intended to replace the textbook, but rather help the students understand it. Common terms as well as technical terms are covered. If a word or concept is clearly presented in the textbook, it may not be covered in the *Companion.*

**Figure It Out** This activity asks students to use information found in the textbook or the *Companion* to answer questions.

**Think About It** These activities provide opportunities for students to use their background knowledge and common sense, think critically, and use the English they have just learned. These activities often do not require going back into the textbook; rather, they are designed to stimulate the student to think in English.

**Double Trouble** This section helps students with idiomatic usage, figurative speech, and words that have multiple meanings. As in the other sections and activities, the goal is to present information in an interactive format and to make use of the student's own experience and knowledge where possible.

### Classroom Strategies

ESL students learn best when they can experience directly what they are learning—see a visual, touch an item, or interact with some thing. In this respect, driver education is an excellent subject to teach to ESL students because it is so practical and experience-oriented. The *Drive Right* textbook uses pictures extensively to teach concepts, which helps ESL students. The Teacher's Edition has many demonstrations and activities that will help ESL students learn key concepts and driving procedures through active learning.

The following strategies can facilitate learning by ESL students.

- Provide a classroom environment that reduces anxiety, encourages participation, reinforces positive responses, and does not punish or ridicule mistakes. Give positive feedback to students to let them know they are on the right track. Do not correct language errors; rather, model correct language use. Encourage students to ask questions when they don't understand.

- Do not assume that a lack of participation indicates a lack of interest. Beginning language learners often go through an active listening period called the "silent period."

- Provide visual aids and concrete examples to explain the meanings of words whenever possible. Involve other senses, such as hearing and touch. The driving simulator can be particularly useful in this way.

- To help students learn new vocabulary, have someone pronounce each word, or make a tape recording of new vocabulary for the students. Have students make flash cards, with a term on one side and a drawing or explanation on the other. The in-car

sessions are excellent opportunities to present and explain new vocabulary and engage the ESL student in conversation.

- Provide opportunities for oral participation in a low-risk atmosphere. Cooperative learning activities and small group discussions, as provided in the Teacher's Edition, are all helpful. Choose topics that students can discuss from personal experience rather than book learning. The chapter opener photographs and the decision-making feature at the end of each chapter in *Drive Right* are particularly useful.

- Develop lessons that go from simple to complex, concrete to abstract. Start instruction from things that the student already knows and has experience with. Continue instruction with as much hands-on, experience-based, concrete material as possible.

- Be sensitive to the ESL student's concern about being different from the others. Some will not want other students to know that they are getting special help or are having to do special assignments.

- Students will benefit from appropriate field trips. A useful trip would be to the office that issues drivers' licenses. Before going, discuss what students will observe and learn from the trip. Discussion topics may include what kinds of services are provided at the office, who can help you if you have questions, and options for oral or foreign language forms.

The *Drive Right* program provides you with many strategies for dealing with special needs students in the driver education class. In the Teacher's Edition strategies are highlighted for teaching concepts and driving skills to special needs students at the beginning of each chapter and throughout. Also, many of the other activities and demonstrations in the Teacher's Edition employ active learning, which will be of value for the special needs student as well as others. The multiple intelligence theory of varying learning styles is the basis for these activities. In addition, an ancillary book, the *Drive Right Companion,* is designed to help poor readers and those not proficient in English better understand the *Drive Right* textbook with simplified vocabulary and activities.

The focus of *Drive Right* on visual and space-management skills and risk-reducing strategies should work in favor of all students whether they have been identified as special needs or not. The activities in the Teacher's Edition that help prepare students for in-car instruction will be especially helpful for special needs students. By learning procedures and practicing them in the classroom first, they are more likely to be successful in the car.

### Special Needs Students

The number of students identified as having special needs has increased in recent years partly due to full inclusion and partly due to a broadening of the concept to include students with a wide variety of problems. Special needs students include those with physical disabilities, learning disabilities, emotional disabilities, or a combination of disabilities.

Many special needs students are identified early in their school careers and are placed in special education programs. These students are usually in full-time special education classes. Some are in regular classes but are pulled out periodically for special education

and tutoring. Some students, because of full inclusion and parents' desires, are in regular classes all day long. Advances in technology and in teaching methods have enabled many students with disabilities to learn to drive safely.

You may also have in your classes students who have special needs but have not been identified as needing special education services. The following clues might help to identify students with special needs:

- Student's assignments are incomplete, poorly done, or not the student's own work.
- Student is a poor reader.
- Student is excessively absent.
- Student does not participate in group activities well or at all.
- Student is not accepted by peers.
- Parents or other teachers show concern about student's performance.
- Student demonstrates a lack of perseverance, concentration, or attention.
- Student does not express self well, or rarely expresses self, or has a speech problem.
- Student has poor coordination.
- Student is easily discouraged or shows low levels of motivation.
- Student is overly active.

If you think that a student might benefit from special education services and has not been formally identified, notify the special education teacher or department. A specialist can often determine whether the student learns slowly or has a specific learning disability.

### Working with Special Needs Students

When working with special needs students, you need to consider their learning needs emotional needs, and physical needs.

**Learning Needs** Special needs students often get frustrated during their attempts to learn new material. Their frustration is often compounded by feelings of discouragement or embarrassment, especially when others become aware of the situation. Learning difficulties include not immediately knowing right from left, not understanding new concepts quickly, and poor reading and comprehension. Giving these students special assignments, such as reading the *Drive Right Companion,* can help them learn more easily. Be alert to the fact that some students might not want peers to know about any special assignments.

Another way of avoiding embarrassment for them is to assign every student in class a partner or "buddy" to do activities and to study together both in class and out of class. Don't let the students pick their own buddy. During the first two weeks of class, you should match up the most compassionate good students with your special needs students, and then match the brightest students with those having the most difficulty reading and getting assignments done.

**Emotional Needs**  Poor self-esteem and a lack of self-worth can be detrimental to a young person's attitude toward driving and can also affect driving ability. Provide positive feedback and encouragement often. Help timid or passive students become more aware of their rights as well as methods of safe assertion in traffic.

Listen carefully for clues to fear of certain driving situations. Many situations can be frightening—for example, entering an expressway or starting forward from a stop on a very steep hill. You can help students rehearse driving maneuvers by preparing slides or videos of traffic situations in your community. Use the activities in the Teacher's Edition for In-Class Driving Rehearsal and Model Car Activities to help students learn and practice driving procedures. Then they are more likely to experience less stress and more success during in-car sessions.

Be alert to the overly aggressive student who needs to develop a greater understand

ing of, and sympathy for, the rights of other roadway users. The student might be skillful physically but lack mature judgment. Help such students learn that responsible behavior in traffic involves developing a cooperative attitude, overcoming the tendency to push oneself and one's vehicle past safe limits. This is especially important with the increase in aggressive driving and road rage. Group activities and the use of partners can help you spot students with emotional problems and help them work through the lack of control.

A driver education class might provide the first opportunity for a student to learn how to deal effectively with emotions that could interfere with driving judgment. When leading class discussions on emotions and attitudes, select guidelines and topics carefully. Direct the topic toward problem solving. Role playing can be useful in this area.

**Physical Needs**  When assigning seats, consider students' visual or hearing disabilities and seat them accordingly. For students with metabolic or emotional conditions, discuss the importance of nutrition to a driver (the importance of breakfast, frequency of meals, type of foods eaten, and food allergies). Be aware of students who must take prescribed medication. When the medication is not taken or taken at the wrong time, adverse reactions can occur. Be sure to discuss special equipment or driving techniques and strategies with students with physical disabilities.

### In-Class Instruction

The instructional strategies described below can facilitate student learning and comprehension.
- Select materials that incorporate other learning modalities for the student who is primarily a visual or aural learner.
- Use sequential learning activities to help the student achieve success on basic con-

cepts and to increase self-confidence before proceeding to more difficult work.

- Separate complex learning tasks into single-concept tasks.
- Avoid assuming that all students understand the basic information. Special needs students might have difficulty with concepts, such as judging an approaching vehicle's speed and distance or determining which direction to turn the wheels when parking on a hill. Suggestions to handle these situations are given in the special needs notes in each chapter.
- Substitute simple words for the student who has a limited vocabulary, or has difficulty understanding terminology. The *Drive Right Companion* provides such strategies. You can also ask students to explain what they do understand. Then listen carefully to their word choice and explanation to calculate how to rephrase the concept. Techniques for ESL students described on pages T22–T23 can help any student with language difficulties.
- Use audio cassettes of written material as supplements for the student with low reading ability.
- Use slides and videos for teaching concepts and for scanning techniques to help increase eye movement.
- Create games for learning and reviewing terms and concepts. Use common games such as Bingo, Fish, War, and Jeopardy.
- Extra time in a driving simulator can provide additional hands-on experience, as well as the In-Class Driving Rehearsal activities in the Teacher's Edition.

### In-Car Instruction

Many special needs students have never been in the driver's seat prior to the first in-car lesson. Procedures might not be remembered the day after the in-car lesson. Even simple turns might prove difficult. Be especially alert for inappropriate—even hazardous—

student responses during in-car instruction. Include sincere compliments, even for minor successes.

Driving straight can provide the opportunity to develop confidence, which can provide the foundation for developing other skills. Should the student become frustrated with a certain skill, such as backing, practice that skill for a limited time rather than for an entire driving period. Determine which skills are most critical and review them often as a confidence builder.

Review skills periodically. Use home assignments before and after in-car lessons to prepare and reinforce learning. Question students before starting a new lesson to be sure they completely understand the task to be practiced.

### Resources

Ask for assistance from your school's special-education teacher, aide, school psychologist, social worker, speech therapist, or driver education teacher specializing in instruction for students with disabilities. Enlist parent participation in finding strategies for motivation. Use resource center materials to enable the student, parents, special-education teacher, and aide to coordinate efforts for maximum student learning.

Your state or regional Department of Education, as well as national and regional teacher associations for driver education, can provide additional information on teaching special needs students. Your state department of motor vehicles may publish a special-driver guide to traffic laws and procedures. Many states offer a special oral examination for people who have learned the driving laws but have low-level written test abilities.

John F. Knippel
Traffic Safety Educator
Bloomington High School,
Colton Joint Unified School District
Bloomington, California

## Resources

### Distributors of Audiovisual, Software, Kits, Equipment, and Other Resources

Suggestions are provided in the Chapter Planning Guides for videos, software, kits, equipment, and other driver education resources. These resources are suggestions only. You might want to preview unfamiliar items for appropriateness to your curriculum. Contact the distributors listed below for ordering information and to learn more about the products.

**AAA Foundation for Traffic Safety**
1440 New York Avenue, N.W.
Washington, D.C. 20005
(800) 305-SAFE
http://www.aaafts.org

**American Automobile Association (AAA)**
AAA Traffic Safety and Engineering
1000 AAA Drive
Heathrow, FL 32746-5063
(407) 444-7960
http://www.aaa.com

**ABS Alliance**
P.O. Box 13966
10 Laboratory Drive
Research Triangle Park, NC 27709
(919) 549-4800
http://www.abs-education.org

**Drunk Busters of America**
W6279 County Road F
Brownsville, WI 53006
(920) 583-2491
http://www.drunkbusters.com

**Innocorp, Ltd.**
P.O. Box 930064
Verona, WI 53593
(800) 272-5023
http://www.fatalvision.com

**Insurance Institute for Highway Safety, Inc.**
1005 N. Globe Road
Arlington, VA 22201
(703) 247-1500
http://www.iihs.org

**Interactive Driving Systems, Inc.**
P.O. Box 98
Cheshire, CT 06410
(203) 272-9391
e-mail: frmottola@aol.com

**Meridian Education**
P.O. Box 911, 12 Perrine Road
Monmouth Junction, NJ 08852
(800) 727-5507
http://www.meridianeducation.com

**Motorcycle Safety Foundation**
2 Jenner Street, Suite 150
Irvine, CA 92618-3806
(800) 446-9227 or (949) 727-3227
http://www.msf-usa.org

**National Commission Against Drunk Driving**
8403 Colesville Road, Suite 370
Silver Spring, MD 20910
(240) 247-6004
http://www.ncadd.com

**National Safety Council**
1121 Spring Lake Drive
Itasca, IL 60143
(800) 621-7619 or (630) 285-0797
http://www.nsc.org

**Operation Lifesaver, Inc.**
1420 King Street, Suite 401
Alexandria, VA 22314
(800) 537-6224
http://www.oli.org

**3I Company**
P.O. Box 752
Oshkosh, WI 54902
(920) 233-5440
http://3icompany.com

## Associations and Organizations

**American Association of Motor Vehicle Administrators (AAMVA)**
4301 Wilson Blvd. Suite 400
Arlington, VA 22203
(703) 522-4200
http://www.aamva.net

**American Driver and Traffic Safety Education Association (ADTSEA)**
Highway Safety Center
Indiana University of Pennsylvania
Indiana, PA 15705
(800) 896-7703 or (724) 357-4051
http://adtsea.iup.edu

**Association of Driver Rehabilitation Specialists (ADED)**
P.O. Box 49
Edgerton, WI 53534
(608) 884-8833
http://www.driver-ed.org

**Driving School Associations of the Americas (DSAA)**
8511 W. Lincoln Ave.
West Allis, WI 53227
(800) 270-DSAA
http://www.autodrivingschools.com

**National Highway Traffic Safety Administration (NHTSA)**
The Office of Public and Consumer Affairs
Department of Transportation
400 Seventh St., SW
Washington, D.C. 20590
(202) 366-9550
http://www.nhtsa.dot.gov

**National Sleep Foundation**
1522 K Street, N.W., Suite 500
Washington, D.C. 20005
(202) 347-3471
http://www.sleepfoundation.org
http://www.drowsydriving.org

**National Student Safety Program**
Highway Safety Center
Indiana University of Pennsylvania
Indiana, PA 15705
http://www.adtsea.iup.edu/nssp

**Prentice Hall**

# Drive Right

## UPDATED TENTH EDITION

**Authors**

Margaret L. Johnson

Owen Crabb

Arthur A. Opfer

Randall R. Thiel

**Consulting Author**

Frederik R. Mottola

PEARSON

Prentice Hall

Boston, Massachusetts

Upper Saddle River, New Jersey

## About the Authors

**Margaret L. Johnson** is a former supervisor of Driver, Consumer, and Health Education at Glenbrook North High School, Northbrook, Illinois. She was also an instructor of Traffic Safety and Driver Education at Northeastern Illinois University in Chicago.

**Owen Crabb** is a former Driver Education Specialist with the Maryland State Department of Education. He has also assisted several states in developing driver education programs.

**Arthur A. Opfer** has taught driver education at both the high school and college levels. He is a former Regional Traffic Coordinator for the Superintendent of Public Instruction at Educational Service District 105, Yakima, Washington.

**Randall R. Thiel** is Education Consultant for the Alcohol-Traffic Safety Program for the Wisconsin Department of Public Instruction. He has taught driver education at the high school level and has been involved in teacher preparation programs at universities in Texas, Pennsylvania, and Indiana.

**Frederik R. Mottola** is Professor Emeritus of Public Health at Southern Connecticut State University and Executive Director of Driver Behavior Institute. He is the creator of the Zone Control System of Space Management and Reference Point Visualizations. He is a consultant and educator for traffic safety education programs for teachers, students, and drivers on local, national, and international levels.

### DISCLAIMER

Driving any vehicle safely is the responsibility of the driver and all drivers operate their cars at their own risk. The techniques, suggestions and ideas contained herein are of broad general usefulness and not intended to replace actual driving experience, driving skills or a valid license. The techniques, suggestions and ideas contained herein cannot be considered absolute recommendations.

Federal, state, local and other applicable regulations and guidelines concerning road safety and driving practices change rapidly. The reader should note, therefore, that the development of new regulations, guidelines and practices may require changes in some techniques, suggestions and ideas contained in this material.

While the information contained in this book has been compiled from sources believed to be reliable and correct at the time of original publication, neither the publisher nor the author make any warranty, express or implied, with respect to the use of any techniques, suggestions and ideas disclosed in this book. The publisher and author disclaim any and all liability for any damages of any kind or character, including without limitation any compensatory, incidental, direct or indirect, special, punitive, or consequential damages, loss of income or profit, loss of or damage to property or person, claims of third parties, or other losses of any kind or character arising out of or in connection with the use of this book or the accuracy of the information contained herein, even if the publisher or author has been advised of the possibility of such damages or losses.

ISBN 013-131607-9 (hardcover)
ISBN 013-131610-9 (softcover)

1 2 3 4 5 6 7 8 9 10    10 09 08 07 06

**PEARSON**
Prentice Hall

## Consultants and Reviewers

### Consultants

**Leon Butorac**
Former Traffic Safety Teacher
Auburn High School
Auburn, Washington

**Jerry L. Gaines**
Driver Education Coordinator
Palos Verdes Peninsula Unified
School District
Palos Verdes Estates, California

**Terry Kline**
Assistant Professor
Traffic Safety Institute
Eastern Kentucky University
Richmond, Kentucky

**Gregory Schitkovitz**
Teacher, Driver Education
Glenbrook North High School
Northbrook, Illinois

**Elizabeth A. Weaver**
Driver Education Specialist
Department of Education
Boise, Idaho

### Reviewers

**Barbara E. Brody**
Coordinator, Driver Education
Improvement Program
Minnesota Highway Safety Center
St. Cloud State University
St. Cloud, Minnesota

**Paul Cram**
Teacher, Driver Education
Washington High School
Washington, Illinois

**Alex Hansen**
Department Chair, Traffic Safety
Education
Lakes High School,
Clover Park School District
Lakewood, Washington

**Sally Ann Holland**
Instructor/Owner
Drivers Edge
Glenburn, Maine

**David J. Holloway**
Teacher, Driver Education
Windsor High School
Windsor, Vermont

**James M. Lewis**
Department Chair, Driver Education
Simi Valley High School
Simi Valley, California

**Edward McEvoy**
Department Chair, Driver Education
Hempstead High School
Dubuque, Iowa

**William G. Robbins, Sr.**
Instructor/Owner
Rocky Mountain Driving Academy
Lakewood, Colorado

**Major Thompson**
Department Chair, Driver Education
Fayette County Community School
Fayettville, Georgia

**C.E. Welch**
Department Chair,
Driver Education
Southeast High School
Springfield, Illinois

# Contents

## Unit 1
## The Driving Task

1

# Unit 2
# Controlling Your Vehicle 88

**Unit 3**
# Driving in Different Environments *172*

Unit 1
The Driving Task

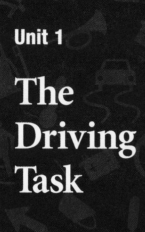

## Unit 1

# The Driving Task

# The Driving Task

### Unit Overview

This unit introduces students to the driving task, which includes social, physical, and mental skills. They will learn the meanings of various traffic signs, traffic signals, and roadway markings. They will also learn the purpose of vehicle instruments, devices, and controls; proper procedures for starting, moving, and stopping a vehicle; and ways to use the IPDE Process with the Zone Control System and the Smith System to increase driving safety.

### About the Photograph

This scene illustrates one of many different kinds of driving environments. Beginning drivers might be confused and intimidated by the idea of driving on curves and highways. Explain that by learning how to use good visual and decision-making skills, new drivers will soon be able to negotiate this driving environment.

# Chapter 1   Planning Guide

 **Student Features**

 **Teacher's Edition**

| | Student Features | Teacher's Edition |
|---|---|---|
| **Chapter 1**<br>**You Are the Driver** | You Are the Driver! *p. 3* | Projects *p. 2*<br>Special Needs *p. 3* |
| **1.1   You Are Part of the System** *pp. 4–5*<br>• Describe the three parts of the highway transportation system (HTS).<br>• Tell how the HTS is regulated. | | Activity *pp. 4, 5*<br>Special Needs *p. 3* |
| **1.2   Your Driving Task** *pp. 6–7*<br>• Explain how social, physical, and mental skills work together in your driving task.<br>• Name the four steps in the IPDE Process. | | Activity *pp. 6, 7* |
| **1.3   Your Driving Responsibilities** *pp. 8–10*<br>• Explain how your attitude will affect your driving.<br>• List some examples of HTS breakdowns.<br>• Describe several major causes of collisions.<br>• Explain how drivers can help protect our environment. | What Do You Think? *p. 9* | Demonstrate *pp. 9, 10*<br>Activity *pp. 8, 9, 10* |
| **1.4   Your Driver's License** *pp. 11–14*<br>• Explain how a graduated driver licensing program can help you drive more safely.<br>• List some of the main concepts stressed in a quality driver education program. | Safe Driving Tip *p. 14*<br>What Do You Think? *p. 12*<br>Did You Know? *p. 13* | Demonstrate *p. 11*<br>Activity *p. 14* |
| **Assessment** | Reviewing Chapter<br>  Objectives *p. 15*<br>Projects *p. 15*<br>Chapter Test *p. 16*<br>Decision Making *p. 17* | Answers pp. *16–17* |

## Teacher's Resource File

## Videos, Overheads, and Software

**Companion** *pp. 4–9*
**Spanish Handbook** *pp. 3–4*

---

**Resource Book**
Classroom Activity,
 *pp. 21–22*

---

**Resource Book**
Classroom Activity,
 *pp. 21–23*

**Content Overhead 1**

---

**Resource Book**
Classroom Activity,
 *pp. 24–25*
Information, *pp. 67–68*

**Content Overhead 2**

---

**Skills and Applications**
**Workbook**, *pp. 1–4*
**Tests and Activities**
Chapter 1 Activities 1-1
 and 1-2, *pp. 3–4*
Chapter 1 Test A and Test B,
 *pp. 5–8*

**TestWorks CD-ROM**
 Chapter 1 Test

## Technology Resources

AAA Foundation for Traffic Safety, *Heavenly Debate,* video, 7 minutes

Insurance Institute for Highway Safety, *Young Drivers: The High-Risk Years,* video, 9 minutes

## Kits, Equipment, and Other Resources

Interactive Driving Systems, Inc., *Risk Factor Kit*

**Go Online**
PHSchool.com
For: Chapter 1 online activities
Visit: PHSchool.com
Web Code: cak-9999

# Chapter 1

## You Are the Driver

### Chapter Overview

Chapter 1 introduces students to the highway transportation system and the driving task. The chapter describes the driving task as a complex set of skills conducted in a complex highway transportation system and presents the results of system breakdowns. It explains how a driver education course, driving practice, and the licensing process work together to produce better drivers.

### Chapter Vocabulary

*collision, defensive driving, driving task, graduated driver licensing program, highway transportation system, IPDE Process, risk, Smith System®, vehicle code, Zone Control System*

2

## Teacher's Resources

For students to use as they read the chapter:

**Companion**
pages 4–9

**Spanish Handbook**
pages 3–4

## Projects

Review the projects described on page 15. Some of the projects can be assigned at any time while others are more closely tied to the content presented in the student text.

# CHAPTER 1
## You Are the Driver

**1.1** You Are Part of the System

**1.2** Your Driving Task

**1.3** Your Driving Responsibilities

**1.4** Your Driver's License

## You Are the Driver!

Imagine you have just received your driver's license. You've worked hard to get this far, and now it's time to celebrate. Your driving privilege is one of the things that makes this moment possible. Beyond this moment, driving will play an important part in your life. How important do you think it is to maintain a good driving record?

This chapter introduces you to driving and the responsibilities that go along with it. You will also learn how driver education and driver's licensing programs can help you become a responsible, low-risk driver.

**Go Online**
PHSchool.com
**For:** Chapter 1 online activities
**Visit:** PHSchool.com
**Web Code:** cak-9999

3

# You Are Part of the System

## Focus

### Summary

This lesson introduces students to the highway transportation system and the driving task.

### Vocabulary

*highway transportation system, risk, vehicle code*

## Teach

### Discuss

Ask students to brainstorm to develop a list of behaviors and situations that might increase the risk for collisions. After brainstorming, ask: How do you think peer pressure, self-image, and ego affect risk factors? What can drivers do to minimize such risk?

### Discuss

Place these headings on the chalkboard to form three columns: People, Vehicles, Roadways. Have the class brainstorm at least ten risk factors for each category. Then discuss how each can contribute to the risk of driving.

### Objectives

1. Describe the three parts of the highway transportation system (HTS).
2. Tell how the HTS is regulated.

You are about to take a driver education course, apply for your driver's license, and join the millions of others who share our country's roads. If you grow to meet this challenge, you will have a lifetime filled with many new opportunities. Your key to this exciting future will be your ability to master the new skills needed to manage the conflicts and risks associated with driving.

In everyday life, there are many types of conflicts and risks. But, the main **risk** in driving is the possibility of having a conflict that results in a collision.

### The Highway Transportation System

When you drive, you will become part of a massive system called the **highway transportation system,** or HTS. The HTS has three parts: people, vehicles, and roadways. The purpose of the HTS is to move people and cargo from one place to another in a safe, efficient, and economical manner.

Of all transportation systems, the HTS is the most complex. It has the greatest variety of users, including drivers, passengers, motorcyclists, bicyclists, and pedestrians. The HTS has a wide range of roadways from simple rural lanes to complex multilane urban roads and expressways.

### People

The people who use the HTS by walking, driving, or riding are

called *roadway users.* Roadway users vary greatly in their ability to use the system.

While most individuals consistently drive in a safe, low-risk, responsible manner, others do not. Drivers with good skills sometimes operate their vehicles when they are overly distracted, tired, ill, or impaired by alcohol. To protect yourself and others in these situations, you will have to be the one to take responsibility for avoiding trouble.

### Vehicles

Think about the wide range of vehicles that use the HTS. Mopeds and motorcycles are small and have little protection. At the other extreme is the tractor-semitrailer weighing tons. In between are cars, vans, small trucks, buses, campers, farm vehicles, and construction equipment. During this course, you will be called on to develop special skills to lower risk and avoid conflicts when interacting with these vehicles.

### Roadways

Roadways of the HTS vary from dirt lanes to complex multilane expressways. Common conditions such as rain, nighttime, or rough pavement, can become major problems. It is up to you to maintain control of your vehicle at all times and in all conditions.

4  Unit 1  The Driving Task

## Teacher's Resources

### Resource Book
Classroom Activity, pages 21–22

## Activity

**Small Group Activity**  Divide the class into groups of three. Give each member of the group a copy of the Partial Risk Factors sheet located in the **Resource Book,** pages 21–22. Ask each group to evaluate the risk factors under one of the three components of the highway transportation system. After adequate time, have one person from each group report their findings to the class.

The highway transportation system consists of a complex mix of people, vehicles, and roadways.

## Regulating the HTS

Drivers who operate their vehicles in a responsible, low-risk manner are the most important part in the HTS. To make sure this happens, all states grant individuals the privilege of driving on their roads by issuing them a driver's license. By passing a licensing exam, you agree to obey traffic laws in exchange for the privilege of operating a motor vehicle on public roads.

Many federal, state, and local government agencies help regulate the HTS. The federal government has established the National Highway Safety Act with a set of traffic-safety guidelines. Federal, state and local governments in turn enforce these national guidelines:

- Laws are passed to make up the **vehicle code.**

- Enforcement agencies assure that laws are obeyed.
- Motor vehicle departments set rules to assure that driver and vehicle standards are met.
- Courts decide whether drivers charged with violating the laws are guilty or innocent.
- Highway traffic engineers plan, build, and maintain the complex system of roadways.

### Review It

1. What are the parts and purpose of the HTS?
2. How is the HTS regulated?

## ③ Assess

### Answers to Review It

**1.** The highway transportation system (HTS) is made up of roadway users, vehicles, and roadways. The purpose of the HTS is to move people and cargo from one place to another in a safe and efficient manner. (p. 4)
**2.** Drivers who use the HTS are the most important element in making sure the HTS is safe and efficient. Federal, state, and local government agencies help regulate the HTS. (p. 5)

## Activity

**Class Activity** Give each student a copy of the Partial Risk Factors sheet located in the **Resource Book,** pages 21–22. Ask students to read all the risk factors. Have them classify which risk factors they, as responsible drivers, will be able to eliminate or minimize. Place an X next to each factor that could be eliminated and an M next to each factor that could be minimized. Ask them to also add five risk factors to each of the three components. After this assignment is completed, have students form groups of three to compare their responses.

## Special Needs

Some students benefit from being involved in activities where they can express themselves artistically. Invite a small group of students to develop a bulletin board display about licensing requirements for drivers in your state.

# Your Driving Task

## Focus

### Summary

This lesson describes the driving task as a complex set of social, physical, and mental skills conducted in a complex highway transportation system.

### Vocabulary

*defensive driving, driving task, IPDE Process, Smith System, Zone Control System*

## Teach

### Discuss

Ask: What are some of the basic social skills used in everyday life? After some discussion, ask: How do these basic social skills translate into valuable skills for driving?

### Discuss

Hold up a $20 bill and ask: Which would you feel better, to give someone $20 or to have someone steal $20 from you? Then make the point that when you are courteous, you are giving others a gift, and they cannot steal it from you. That puts you in a win-win situation because you are in control. Some individuals set themselves up for a lose-lose situation by not giving anyone a break, which often causes high risk and stress.

### Objectives

1. Explain how social, physical, and mental skills work together in your driving task.
2. Name the four steps in the IPDE Process.

The **driving task** includes all the social, physical, and mental skills required to drive. To perform the driving task with low-risk results, you must develop habits for

- using knowledge and visual skills, as shown in the picture
- obeying traffic laws
- judging time and space
- anticipating how your car will respond under normal and emergency conditions

### Social Skills

Like other social tasks, driving requires you to interact successfully with people. If you are a courteous driver, you not only obey traffic laws, but you make an extra effort to work with other drivers. Without courtesy and cooperation, low-risk driving is impossible.

All drivers bring their own problems and skill levels to your shared driving world. A big part of your driving task will be applying your social skills to these types of situations so that everyone avoids conflicts.

### Physical Skills

You must learn the physical skills of driving so well that they become natural habits. Then you can focus your attention on the social and mental tasks of driving. Beginning drivers often need to concentrate heavily on the physical skills of driving. After extended practice, these drivers acquire the ability to control their vehicle. They can then focus their attention on the social and mental aspects of driving.

### Mental Skills

Safe, low-risk driving is primarily a mental task that involves decision making. Physical skills are minor when compared to the necessary decision-making skills.

### The IPDE Process

The **IPDE Process** is a process of seeing, thinking, and responding. The four steps of this process are pictured on the opposite page.

- **Identify** important information in the ongoing driving scene.
- **Predict** when and where possible points of conflict will develop.
- **Decide** when, where, and how to communicate, adjust speed, and/or change position to avoid conflict.

Mental and visual skills are critical to your driving task.

## Teacher's Resources

No *Drive Right* resources are needed for teaching Section 1.2.

## Activity

**Small Group Activity** Divide the class into groups of five. Have each group list ten possible driving errors that annoy or irritate other drivers. Have the groups discuss why these errors are annoying or irritating. Then have each group list ten different ways that a driver can be courteous to others.

**Identify** the oncoming car, turn signal, and driveway.

**Predict** that your path of travel and the oncoming vehicle's path of travel will conflict.

**Decide** to slow or stop.

**Execute** speed reduction decision by taking foot off accelerator and gently braking.

• **Execute** the right action(s) to prevent conflict.

Two other systems will help you use the IPDE Process. The **Smith System** is an organized method designed to help drivers develop good seeing habits. In addition, the **Zone Control System** is a method for managing the space around your vehicle. These systems will help you apply the IPDE Process for effective, low-risk driving.

Once you have mastered the IPDE Process, you will be able to drive in a way that reduces conflicts.

This ability, called **defensive driving,** lowers the risk of conflict by protecting you and others from dangerous driving situations.

### Review It

1. How does the driving task require a blend of social, mental, and physical skills?
2. What are the four steps in the IPDE Process?

# Your Driving Responsibilities

## 1 Focus

### Summary

This lesson emphasizes the responsibilities associated with driving. It also presents the importance of emotions and the results of system breakdowns.

### Vocabulary

*collision*

## 2 Teach

### Explain

Stress that collisions can have multiple causes. Point out that the removal of one of these causes might prevent a collision.

### Discuss

Ask: How do you think television programs, movies, and car commercials influence driving behavior? Are driving scenes realistic? Are the outcomes of dangerous driving and collisions realistic? How is the use of safety belts portrayed?

### Discuss

Draw students' attention to the *You Are the Driver!* photograph and ask: How can you use these techniques to say "no"? (Ask questions. State the problem. State consequences. Suggest alternatives. Leave and encourage others to join you.)

### Objectives

1. Explain how your attitude will affect your driving.
2. List some examples of HTS breakdowns.
3. Describe several major causes of collisions.
4. Explain how drivers can help protect our environment.

When you earn your first driver's license, the state you live in will extend you the privilege to drive. Driving is a privilege—not a right. The driving privilege is based on the assumption that you will be a responsible traffic citizen and obey all traffic laws. Driving also is a major responsibility. If you assume it and respect it, you will enjoy a lifelong adventure of safe, low-risk, low-stress driving. If you do not handle this responsibility, you have the power to ruin your life and the lives of others.

### Attitude

Your attitude toward life and driving affects your willingness to learn and to effectively use safe-driving habits. For many, reckless driving is a way of getting attention. What they don't realize is that they are getting noticed in a negative way.

Road rage shows an extremely negative attitude toward driving. The driver who is in a rage is likely to do anything. Your best defense is to put distance between yourself and the enraged driver. Don't challenge an enraged driver. Instead, give way. Be extremely cautious at intersections because some drivers simply refuse to obey red traffic lights. In extreme situations, alert police if possible.

Other drivers drive in a responsible low-risk way day after day, year after year. They know their low-risk driving eventually will gain them respect. Getting quick attention is easy. Earning respect over the long haul takes time and effort.

Your attitude will guide you as you manage your relationships with others. There will be times when others will try to get you to do things you normally would not do. They will push you to drive in a way you shouldn't. Saying no—especially to a friend as shown in the picture—isn't easy.

**You Are the Driver!**
How can you use these techniques to say "no"?
- Ask questions.
- State the problem.
- State the consequences.
- Suggest alternatives.
- Leave and encourage others to join you.

8 Unit 1 The Driving Task

## Teacher's Resources

**Resource Book**
Classroom Activity, pages 21–23

**Content Overheads**
Overhead 1

## Activity

**Class Activity** Have students use the library or Internet to locate newspaper or magazine articles about a celebrity making bad decisions related to driving. The articles should include information about the initial incident and the subsequent outcomes. Students can choose local, national, or international celebrities. Have each student prepare a short oral report describing what happened and how the celebrity's life was affected. Also include information about how the lives of other's were affected, including other drivers, passengers, and pedestrians.

## Breakdowns in the HTS

A breakdown in the HTS occurs when any part of the system does not work well. Traffic tie-ups and collisions are two examples of HTS breakdowns. Your ability to drive responsibly will be the major factor in helping you avoid being part of these breakdowns.

A **collision** occurs when a vehicle conflicts with and hits another object. Collisions are a major cause of injury and death.

### Collision or Accident?

*Collision* is a more accurate term than *accident*. Why? Because *accident* implies that something just happens by chance. In reality, almost every collision is the product of a predictable cause. The drunk driver hit the pole. The speeding driver ran off the road. The careless driver didn't wear a safety belt or tuned a radio at the wrong time and hit a tree.

Over the years our national driving record has steadily improved. This is the result of an ongoing highway safety effort involving engineering, enforcement, and education. Still we should not be lulled into a false sense of security. Check the chart on this page and compare your chance of dying in a car crash versus other events.

**Causes of Collisions** Of all the possible causes of collisions, driver error is by far the most common. Frequent errors include breaking various laws, not slowing in adverse weather conditions, and operating a defective vehicle. Other serious driver errors are

- following another vehicle too closely

- driving too fast for conditions
- not wearing safety belts
- driving after drinking or using drugs
- driving while very tired

Like most complex events, traffic collisions usually have more than one cause. For example, a vehicle skids off a slippery turn and collides into a tree. The initial report might list the cause as driving too fast for conditions. But a close inspection might reveal that the road was abnormally slick and the tires on the vehicle were very smooth. The slick roadway and the smooth tires added to the problem. Even though the primary cause of the collision was driving too fast, you must know all the factors involved to really understand why the collision happened. If you had been the driver in this collision, what aspects could you have controlled?

**Causes of Death** The chart on the next page compares traffic collisions with other major causes of death for young people. Why is driving such a high-risk activity? Lack of experience is a major factor for this poor driving record. Other factors include increased exposure to night driving, increased risk taking, susceptibility to peer pressure, and mixing drinking and driving.

Does this mean all young drivers are bad? Absolutely not! All drivers can learn to apply the principles of responsible low-risk driving with good results.

Look at the chart below comparing the odds for deaths. Why do you think air travel is so much safer than driving?

**Compare the Odds**

You will be killed in an air crash

1 in 4,600,000

You will die in a fire

1 in 40,000

You will die in a car crash

1 in 125

Driving a car is still the most dangerous way to travel.

---

## Activity

**Small Group Activity** Divide the class into teams of five. Have students write nine numbers between the range of 1 to 180 on a piece of paper. Then give them a copy of the Partial Risk Factors sheet from **Resource Book** pages 21–22. Have them locate the risk factor represented by each of the nine numbers and write them next to the numbers on their paper. Ask: What is the likelihood of a collision occurring if all those risk factors were to take place at the same time?

Explain that multiple risk factors are present when a collision occurs. There is always more than

one thing that goes wrong. Have all the students in the group share their nine risk factors with each other. Ask: How many different combinations of nine can be made from the list of partial risk factors? Explain that there will always be risk factors. To counteract them, a driver needs to eliminate as many as possible and to form good habits to prevent additional risk factors.

---

## Explain

Emphasize the use of the word *collision* rather than *accident*. Review the causes of collisions.

## Demonstrate

Demonstrate how multiple risk factors make the driving task more difficult. Write each of the following risk factors on a separate sheet of paper: left curve, sand on road, raining, tired driver, traveling 15 mph over the speed limit, low tire pressure, worn tires, faulty windshield wipers. Have a volunteer come to the front of the class to catch some paper balls that you will throw. Read one of the risk factors, then crumple the paper into a ball, and throw it to the volunteer. Repeat this process until all eight have been thrown. Most likely the volunteer will catch all eight. Gather up all eight risk factors and throw them all at once at the student. Most of them will not be caught. Ask: What was the difference between the first and second time the risk factors were thrown? (The first time the volunteer had time to deal with each factor. The second time all factors came at once.) Explain that if a driver is confronted with several factors, it may be beyond the driver's capability to cope with the situation.

## Discuss

Discuss the *What Do You Think?* question. Ask: Why do you think air travel is so much safer than driving? (The air-travel system is more strictly controlled. Standards for pilots and airplanes are tougher. Also, there are many more people traveling in vehicles than in planes.)

## Demonstrate

Use the graph or **Content Overhead 1** to illustrate the relationship between motor vehicle collisions and all other causes of death for youth. Discuss the reasons for the high number of deaths from motor vehicle collisions.

## Explain

Because transportation consumes a major part of our energy resources, a 10 percent reduction in transportation-related fuel consumption will generate larger savings than a 10 percent reduction in other small areas of fuel consumption.

## Discuss

Discuss with the class what environmental responsibility is and why it is good for our planet.

 **3 Assess**

## Answers to Review It

**1.** Your attitude will guide you as you enter into and adjust to new driving and social situations. (p. 8)

**2.** Collisions and traffic jams are examples of breakdowns in the HTS. (p. 9)

**3.** Three major causes of collisions are breaking traffic laws, not slowing in adverse weather conditions, and operating a defective vehicle. (p. 9)

**4.** Students should list some of the environmental actions on page 10.

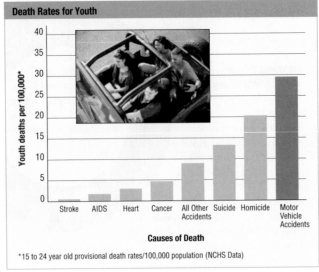

**Death Rates for Youth**

*15 to 24 year old provisional death rates/100,000 population (NCHS Data)

More young people die from vehicle collisions than from any other single cause.

**Social and Economic Loss** Collisions have tremendous social and economic effects. Traffic collisions cost our nation billions of dollars each year in property damage, time away from work and school, medical fees, and insurance premiums. The cost of mental anguish and physical suffering simply cannot be measured.

### Other Responsibilities

In addition to driving, all drivers have additional responsibilities. These include financial and environmental responsibilities.

### Financial Responsibility

As a driver, you are responsible for your share of driving-related costs. Vehicle-related costs include fuel as well as maintaining and insuring your car. You also are financially

responsible by law for any damage or injuries that you cause.

### Environmental Responsibility

Our nation's demand for transportation has created many threats to our environment, including
- air pollution
- water pollution
- chemical spills
- land pollution through thoughtless disposal of vehicle-related products

How can transportation-related environmental problems be managed? All drivers should act responsibly by
- buying and maintaining fuel-efficient vehicles
- using fuel-efficient driving habits
- recycling used materials
- reducing driving through car pools and the use of public transportation when possible
- working for strong national, state, and local policies that encourage the use of energy-efficient driving

### Review It

1. How do attitudes affect driving?
2. What are some examples of breakdowns in the HTS?
3. What are the three major causes of collisions?
4. What are some actions drivers can take to protect our environment?

## Activity

**Class Activity** This activity will give students an opportunity to see how a filtering process for making responsible decisions can be of value. Give each student a copy of the Decision-Making Filters sheet from **Resource Book** page 23. Have students read the eight steps of the filter. Ask students to describe situations when the decision-making filters would be helpful for making responsible decisions. (Such decisions may deal with being honest, avoiding use of tobacco products, being kind to people, not using drugs and alcohol, etc.)

**O**nce you start driving, everyone will want you to become a safe driver. Your family will support you. Your friends will encourage you. Government and private industry will try to help you through licensing and education programs. Still, driving is one of the most dangerous activities you will ever do. For young people, the risk is even higher. Look at the graph on this page to see just how deadly driving can be.

Why is the highway death rate among teens so high? Most of the time, young drivers simply make mistakes from inexperience. *Forty-one percent of the young people who were killed in these collisions died in single-car collisions.*

### Licensing Process

The purpose of a comprehensive driver licensing program is to make sure only safe drivers are allowed

on public roads. Most licensing programs require applicants to take written, physical, and driving exams.

### Graduated Driver Licensing

Structured practice-driving time for new drivers works. As you ride with other drivers, you pick up some good and bad driving habits.

To help young drivers adjust to driving, many states have a **graduated driver licensing program**, which requires young drivers to progress through a series of licensing stages. Typically these programs have three stages.

**Learner's Permit Stage**  Supervised conditions include

- The learner receives a permit to drive when supervised by an adult, licensed driver.
- The permit must be held for a minimum period of violation-

### Objectives

1. Explain how a graduated driver licensing program can help you drive more safely.
2. List some of the main concepts stressed in a quality driver education program.

---

**Driver Fatality Rate by Age**

Deaths per 100 million (y-axis: 0, 2, 4, 6, 8, 10)

Driver's age (x-axis: 16, 17–18, 19–24, 25–39, 40–59, 60–69, 70–74, 75–79, 80–84, 85+)

The main reason that the death rate for 16-year-old drivers is so high is lack of driving experience.

## Teacher's Resources

**Resource Book**
Classroom Activity, pages 24–25
Information, pages 67–68

**Content Overheads**
Overhead 2

1.4

# Your Driver's License

## **1** Focus

### Summary

This lesson explains how a driver education course, driving practice, and the licensing process work together to produce better drivers.

### Vocabulary

*graduated driver licensing program*

## **2** Teach

### Explain

Provide information on the licensing process in your state. Include information about license renewal.

### Demonstrate

Use the graph or **Content Overhead 2** to illustrate the fluctuation in the number of deaths at various ages.

Ask: What does the information in the graph tell you about the death rate for you and your peers? How can you explain the higher death rate for younger drivers?

## Discuss

Discuss the *What Do You Think?* question. Ask: How do you think teen drivers will receive a graduated driver licensing program? If your state has a graduated driver licensing law, discuss it with the class. Ask what they like or dislike about it. If there isn't one, ask students what they think about one being passed. Ask: What other ways can you think of to reduce the high rate of teen collisions?

## Discuss

If your state doesn't have a graduated driver licensing law, ask the class how many would volunteer to go through the same stages as described in the text. Ask: How would you feel if your parents imposed those stages upon you?

## Discuss

Read this statistic from the Insurance Institute for Highway Safety to the class: "Forty-three percent of teenage motor vehicle deaths in 1996 occurred between 9 P.M. and 6 A.M." Ask: Why do you think such a high percentage of teenage fatalities occurs during these hours?

free and collision-free driving (usually six months).
- Safety belts must be worn by all occupants.
- Other licensed drivers, such as family members, may be asked to provide a minimum number of hours of practice driving.

**Intermediate License Stage**

The learner drives under the following restrictions during this stage:
- The learner must have successfully completed the learner's permit stage and an approved driver education course.
- Supervised driving may be continued to meet the required hours.
- Safety belts must be worn by all occupants.
- Night driving, especially late night driving, is restricted.

- Passengers can be limited in age and/or number.
- The intermediate license must be held for six months or more of collision-free and violation-free driving. If the learner has a violation or collision, the intermediate license "clock" is set back to zero.
- Penalties for violations are increased. Many times violators are required to go to traffic school.

**Full-Privilege License Stage** To graduate to this full unrestricted license stage, the learner must
- successfully complete the intermediate stage violation-free and collision-free
- in some states, complete an advanced driver education course

Do these graduated driver licensing programs work? Yes! In New Zealand, Australia, Canada, and

Graduated driver licensing programs have three basic stages.

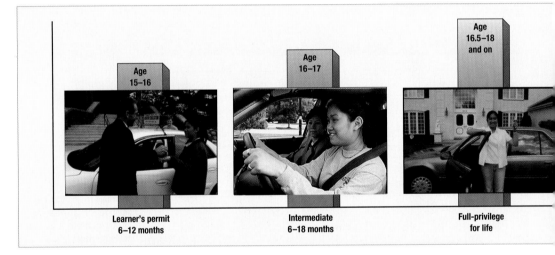

Age 15–16 | Learner's permit 6–12 months

Age 16–17 | Intermediate 6–18 months

Age 16.5–18 and on | Full-privilege for life

## Facts and Figures

According to the Insurance Institute for Highway Safety, 63 percent of teenage passenger deaths in 1996 occurred in collisions in which another teenager was driving. Twenty percent of passenger deaths of people of all ages in 1996 occurred when a teenager was driving. Death rates were higher in 1996 among male teenage drivers than among females—13 per 100,000 people compared with 6 per 100,000.

The rate of nighttime fatal crashes per 100 million miles traveled in 1996 by male drivers 16–19 years old was about four times the rate for 30–54 year old male drivers. Among teenage drivers (16–19 year old), 21 percent of fatally injured male drivers, and 9 percent of fatally injured female drivers in 1996 had blood alcohol concentrations at or above 0.10 percent. Male teenage drivers with blood alcohol concentrations in the 0.05–0.10 percent range are 18 times more likely than sober teenagers to be killed in single-vehicle collisions. The corresponding comparison for females is 54 times more likely. Forty-three percent of teenage motor vehicle deaths in 1996 occurred between 9 P.M. and 6 A.M.

more recently in the United States, they have demonstrated their worth.

Even if your state does not have a formal program, you can follow the stages of these graduated licensing programs to obtain similar results. Just remember that good drivers never stop learning.

### Organ Donor Program

You may indicate your desire to be an organ donor by filling out an organ donation declaration on your driver's license or by signing an organ donor card. Remember that the most important step in considering organ donation is informing your family and other loved ones of your decision. This will ensure that your wishes are carried out.

### Implied Consent Programs

In most states you may be asked to sign a statement when you get your driver's license saying that you agree to take an alcohol test on request. If you refuse to take the test, you will lose your driver's license.

**EARLY DRIVER EDUCATION** Dr. Amos E. Neyhart taught one of the first high school driver education courses in 1933. He taught the course free, in his own car. Dr. Neyhart explained that before his class was offered, people learned to drive from the people who sold cars. They would teach how to start, steer, and stop. But once the buyer got moving and steering, the salespeople would jump out!

### Driver Education and Your License

As you begin this course, you probably are thinking of the advantages of your new driver's license. You should be equally interested in learning the skills you need to become a responsible, low-risk driver. The driving situation shown here and on the next page is an example of a lesson to be learned.

**You Are the Driver!**
What would you predict might be around the curve?

Chapter 1 You Are The Driver **13**

## Discuss

Draw students' attention to the *You Are the Driver!* photograph. Ask: What would you predict might be around the curve? After students give their predictions, have them turn the page for a situation they could have predicted.

## Discuss

Discuss the importance of the organ donation program. See **Resource Book** pages 67–68 for additional information. If possible, invite a guest speaker to address your class about organ and tissue donation.

## Cross Curricular

**Health** Have students research organ and tissue donation. Ask them to investigate what organs and tissue are most needed and how long potential recipients usually wait. Also ask them to report on the process for letting others know that you wish to be a donor.

Draw students' attention to the *You Are the Driver!* photograph. Ask: Would you be ready to avoid the hikers? How? (You could have predicted that something might be in your lane around the curve.)

## Discuss

Have students do the Activity below. A discussion of the different results of this activity will help them realize that if they know where to look and what to look for, they are more likely to be successful in finding it. Help students realize that an orderly visual search pattern for driving will help them achieve success. Tell students that in this class they will learn how to use the IPDE Process to help them make safe driving decisions. They also will learn how to use an orderly visual search pattern to help them know where to look and what to look for as they drive.

## 3 Assess

## Answers to Review It

1. The graduated driver's license program gives you an advantage by providing more systematic quality practice driving time. (pp. 11–12)

2. The key driving concepts in the *Drive Right* driver education program are: driving is a decision-making process based on the IPDE Process; your driving will be greatly influenced by your attitude; safety belts must be worn; never drink and drive. (p. 14)

**You Are the Driver!**
Would you be ready to avoid these hikers?

You will have a wide range of classroom and on-road experiences in this course. Under the professional guidance of an instructor, you will learn the skills and develop the habits needed to become a low-risk driver.

**TIP**

**SAFE DRIVING**

Be sure to include night driving and bad weather in your supervised driving experiences.

### Your Beginning

The *Drive Right* program is your start toward becoming a responsible low-risk driver. The course you are about to take is based in part on the following key concepts

- Driving is a mental decision-making process. In this program, you will learn how to use the IPDE Process to become a responsible low-risk driver.
- Your driving will be greatly influenced by your attitude.
- Safety belts and other restraints must be used at all times.
- The statistics arguing against drinking and driving should convince you to never drink and drive.

Once you pass your driver education program, you should take at least one year to ease into full-time driving responsibilities. After you have driven well under a wide variety of road and traffic situations, you can start to think of yourself as an accomplished new driver.

### A Continuous Process

This driver education course will help start you on your personal lifetime driving adventure. It cannot teach you about everything you will encounter when driving. As long as you drive, you will need to use and improve your skills in a systematic way. Good drivers never stop learning.

### Review It

1. How can a graduated driver licensing program help you?
2. What are the key concepts in a quality driver education program?

## Activity

**Class Activity** This activity will help students experience how effective an orderly search pattern is to driving. Duplicate enough copies of the two Test Your Perception activity sheets from **Resource Book**, pages 24–25, to give three copies of sheet A to half of the students and three copies of sheet B to the other half. Tell students this is an eye-hand coordination exercise and they are to work as fast as possible to connect the numbers, beginning with 1. Give them 60 seconds. After 30 seconds begin telling students the lapse time every 5 seconds.

When time is up, tell them to circle the highest number reached. Then repeat this process with the remaining two copies. After the third trial, ask students to write on the sheet a sentence describing how they felt about doing this exercise. Then have students share their comments and show their results. (The students with sheet A will have progressive success with each trial and will draw a tennis player. Students with sheet B will not improve and may even regress, and their drawing will be a scribbled mess of lines. (See Discuss above.)

## Reviewing Chapter Objectives

### 1. You Are Part of the System

1. What are the three parts of the highway transportation system (HTS)? (4)
2. How is the HTS regulated? (5)

### 2. Your Driving Task

3. How do social, physical, and mental skills work together in your driving task? (6)
4. What are the four steps in the IPDE Process? (6–7)

### 3. Your Driving Responsibilities

5. How will your attitude affect your driving? (8)
6. What are some examples of HTS breakdowns? (9)
7. What are the major causes of collisions? (9)
8. How can drivers help protect our environment? (10)

### 4. Your Driver's License

9. How can a graduated driver licensing program help you drive more safely? (11–12)
10. What are some of the main concepts stressed in a quality driver education program? (13–14)

## Projects

### Individuals

**Investigate** Research to find more information about the National Highway Safety Act. When was this law passed? What are the major features of the law? Write a short report to summarize your findings. Discuss your findings with the class.

**Interview** Interview three drivers. Choose one driver who has been driving for less than two years, one driver who has been driving for between five and ten years, and one who has been driving for more than ten years. Ask these drivers if they feel they have developed any bad driving habits. After the interview, decide what the driver can do to overcome each bad habit mentioned. Discuss your findings with your classmates.

### Groups

**Brainstorm** As a group, list all the possible factors you can think of that may lead to risks in driving. When your list is complete, categorize each risk according to whether or not the driver can control the risk. Then put the risks in order from most to least dangerous. Compare your results with those of the other groups in your class.

**Observe Traffic** As a group, observe the drivers in your school parking lot as they arrive at or leave school for the day. Rate the drivers on a scale of 1 to 5. Drivers rated as 1's show a low-risk, defensive attitude toward driving; 5's show a high-risk, negative attitude. List the reasons, based on the drivers' behaviors, for each score you assign. Discuss your group's findings with your class.

## Reviewing Chapter Objectives

**1.1** You Are Part of the System
See Answers to Review It on page 5.
**1.2** Your Driving Task
See Answers to Review It on page 7.
**1.3** Your Driving Responsibility
See Answers to Review It on page 10.
**1.4** Your Driver's License
See Answers to Review It on page 14.

For additional information refer to the specific page(s) in parentheses after each question.

## Projects

Some of the projects can be assigned at any time while others are more closely tied to the content presented in the student text. The page number where the topic is introduced is indicated.

**Investigate:** p. 5
**Interview:** p. 4
**Brainstorm:** p. 8
**Observe Traffic:** p. 4

The results of student projects will vary.

## Teacher's Resources

### Skills and Applications Workbook
pages 1–4

### Tests and Activities
Chapter 1 Activities 1-1 and 1-2
pages 3–4
Chapter 1 Test A and Test B,
pages 5–8

### TestWorks CD-ROM
Chapter 1 Test

# Review

## Answers to Check Your Knowledge

1. d
2. b
3. b
4. d
5. decide
6. defensively
7. risk
8. highway transportation system (or HTS)

## Answers to Review Vocabulary

9. vehicle code (d)
10. collision (f)
11. Smith System (c)
12. Zone Control System (a)
13. graduated driver licensing program (b)
14. driving task (e)

## Answers to Think Critically

1. Students' answers will vary. Common elements will include responsibility to drive in a safe, low-risk manner; responsibility to focus on the driving task; responsibility to avoid conflict while driving. (pp. 6–7)

2. Answers will vary but should include the fact that inexperience among teen drivers may result in fatal mistakes. (pp. 9–10)

## Chapter Test

### Check Your Knowledge

**Multiple Choice** Copy the number of each sentence below on a sheet of paper. Choose the letter of the answer that best completes the statement or answers the question.

1. Which of the following is part of the highway transportation system (HTS)?
   - (a) vehicles
   - (b) roadways
   - (c) people
   - (d) all of these
2. Safe, low-risk driving is primarily a _____ task.
   - (a) physical
   - (b) mental
   - (c) social
   - (d) none of the above
3. If you drive in a low-risk way, you will
   - (a) get the attention you want.
   - (b) gain others' respect.
   - (c) improve your ability to compete.
   - (d) be able to maneuver easily.
4. Graduated driver licensing programs
   - (a) usually are completed in three licensing stages.
   - (b) are conducted worldwide.
   - (c) have resulted in fewer collisions among young drivers.
   - (d) all of the above

**Completion** Copy the number of each sentence below. After each number, write the word or words that complete the sentence correctly.

5. The four steps of the IPDE Process are identify, predict, _____, and execute.
6. Drive _____ by protecting yourself and others from dangerous and unexpected situations.
7. When applied to driving, the term _____ means the possibility of having a conflict that results in a collision.
8. The _____ is made up of people, vehicles, and roadways.

### Review Vocabulary

Copy the number of each definition in list A. Match the definition in list A with the term it defines in list B.

**List A**
9. federal and state laws that regulate the HTS
10. contact between two or more objects, as when two vehicles hit each other
11. organized method designed to help drivers develop good seeing habits
12. method for managing the space around your vehicle
13. program requiring young drivers to progress through a series of licensing stages
14. all the skills—social, physical, and mental—required to drive

**List B**
a. Zone Control System
b. graduated driver licensing program
c. Smith System
d. vehicle code
e. driving task
f. collision

### Think Critically

Write a paragraph to answer each question.
1. What are your responsibilities as a participant in the highway transportation system (HTS)?
2. Why do you think the death rate for drivers and passengers is higher among teens than other age groups?

## Decision Making

**1.** What part of the HTS is most important in keeping this a low-risk driving situation?

**2.** The IPDE Process is an ongoing process used to avoid conflicts. How can you apply it to this situation?

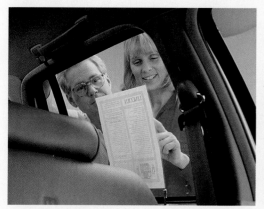

**3.** This car buyer is checking various new car fuel economy ratings. How does this decision help or hurt the environment?

**4.** This driver is receiving supervised instruction from his father. How can this instruction help him become a safer driver?

Chapter 1 You Are The Driver **17**

## Answers to Decision Making

**1.** Roadway users are most important in keeping this a low-risk situation. Drivers must consider the rainy conditions as well as the type of vehicle they are driving as they drive.

**2.** To use the IPDE Process, look well ahead, predict possible points of conflict, and decide how to slow and/or change position at each key spot along the way.

**3.** The decision to consider fuel efficiency in a vehicle buying decision definitely helps the environment. The less fuel that is used, the less air pollution will result.

**4.** All young drivers can benefit from their driving practice experience. They should concentrate on developing safe-driving habits and have as their goal, becoming a low-risk, responsible driver.

# Chapter 2    Planning Guide

**Student Features**

**Teacher's Edition**

| | Student Features | Teacher's Edition |
|---|---|---|
| **Chapter 2**<br>**Signs, Signals, and Roadway Markings** | You Are the Driver! *p. 19* | Projects *p. 18*<br>Special Needs *p. 19* |
| **2.1  Traffic Signs** *pp. 20–26*<br>• State the meaning of the eight shapes and eight colors used for traffic signs.<br>• Describe the actions to take at STOP, YIELD, and speed limit signs.<br>• List five situations where warning signs might be used.<br>• Explain how guide signs and international signs help you when driving. | What Do You Think? *p. 22*<br>Did You Know? *p. 24* | Demonstrate *pp. 21, 22, 23, 25*<br>Activity *pp. 22, 23, 24, 25, 26*<br>Special Needs *p. 26* |
| **2.2  Traffic Signals** *pp. 27–30*<br>• Explain what to do at a green light, a yellow light, and a red light.<br>• Describe the action to take when you approach a flashing red signal or a flashing yellow signal.<br>• Describe the actions to take with pedestrian signals and traffic control officers' signals. | What Do You Think? *p. 9* | Demonstrate *pp. 28, 29*<br>Activity *pp. 28, 29*<br>Special Needs *p. 30* |
| **2.3  Roadway Markings** *pp. 31–34*<br>• Describe the difference between broken yellow lines and broken white lines.<br>• Explain the difference between a shared left-turn lane and a left-turn lane.<br>• List six types of special roadway markings. | Safe Driving Tip *p. 32* | Demonstrate *p. 31*<br>Activity *p. 32*<br>Special Needs *p. 34* |
| **Assessment** | Reviewing Chapter Objectives *p. 35*<br>Projects *p. 35*<br>Chapter Test *p. 36*<br>Decision Making *p. 37* | Answers *pp. 36–37* |

## Teacher's Resource File

## Videos, Overheads, and Software

**Companion** *pp. 10–16*
**Spanish Handbook** *pp. 5–6*

---

**Tests and Activities**
Activity 2-1, *p. 11*

**Demonstration Overhead C**
**Content Overheads 3, 4, 5**

---

**Resource Book**
Teacher's Instructions, *p. 27*

**Demonstration Overhead B**
**Content Overhead 6**

---

**Content Overheads 7, 8**

---

**Skills and Applications**
 **Workbook**, *pp. 5–8*
**Tests and Activities**
Chapter 2 Activities 2-1
 and 2-2, *pp. 11–12*
Chapter 2 Test A and Test B,
 *pp. 13–16*

**TestWorks CD-ROM**
Chapter 2 Test

## Technology Resources

AAA Foundation for Traffic Safety, *Signs, Signals and Markings: Understanding the Language of the Road,* video, 16 minutes

Safety Industries, Inc., *Paint on the Pavement,* video, 10 minutes

Safety Industries, Inc., *Signs and Signals,* video, 10 minutes

3I Company, *Driving Challenge #1: Shapes, Colors, Signals, and Lane Markings,* video

3I Company, *Driving Challenge #2: Signs and Symbols,* video

**Go Online**
PHSchool.com
**For: Chapter 2 online activities**
**Visit: PHSchool.com**
**Web Code: cak-9999**

# Chapter 2

# Signs, Signals, and Roadway Markings

## Chapter Overview

Chapter 2 describes, illustrates, and explains the use of various traffic signs, signals, and roadway markings.

## Chapter Vocabulary

*advisory speed limits, basic speed law, flashing signal, full stop, guide sign, international symbols, lane signal, minimum speed limit, pedestrian signal, regulatory sign, right of way, right-turn-on-red, roadway markings, rumble strips, school zone, shared left-turn lane, traffic signal, warning sign, yield*

## Teacher's Resources

For students to use as they read the chapter:

**Companion**
pages 10–16

**Spanish Handbook**
pages 5–6

## Projects

Review the projects described on page 35. Some of the projects can be assigned at any time while others are more closely tied to the content presented in the student text.

# CHAPTER 2
## Signs, Signals, and Roadway Markings

**2.1**   Traffic Signs

**2.2**   Traffic Signals

**2.3**   Roadway Markings

## You Are the Driver!

Imagine that you are driving on the street shown here. The red traffic light is about to turn green. Are you in the best lane to continue straight? Will you have to stop for other vehicles that plan to turn? How might pedestrians create a problem for you?

Safe, organized driving would be a lot more difficult without signs, signals, and roadway markings. To be a safe and responsible driver, you must know what signs, signals, and roadway markings mean. This chapter discusses these controls and how to respond to them properly.

> **Go Online**
> PHSchool.com
> **For:** Chapter 2 online activities
> **Visit:** PHSchool.com
> **Web Code:** cak-9999

19

## Introducing the Chapter

Discuss how signs, signals, and roadway markings help traffic flow. Discuss what might happen at an intersection if there were no signs, signals, or markings.

## You Are the Driver!

Look at the picture and answer the questions in the text. Make sure students realize that the driver approaching the intersection is not in the correct lane to continue straight ahead. Drivers must stop for any vehicle in the path of travel. Even after the light turns green, drivers should wait until vehicles and pedestrians have passed safely before they can proceed. The white parallel lines are boundaries of the pedestrian crosswalk. A green arrow would allow drivers to turn left while other vehicles are stopped.

## Special Needs

Several games are introduced in this chapter to provide practice that will help the special needs student learn signs, signals, and markings. These games may be modified in future lessons to learn specific terms and concepts. Have students play the games with their partners as assigned for Chapter 1.

Note that the games call for preparation of playing cards with signs, signals, and roadway markings. You might have students make the cards as a way to learn about the traffic controls taught in the chapter. (See pages 26 and 34.)

# Traffic Signs

## 1 Focus

## Summary

This lesson explains the purpose, shape, and color of traffic signs. Regulatory signs, warning signs, guide signs, and international signs are included.

## Vocabulary

*advisory speed limits, basic speed law, full stop, guide sign, international symbols, minimum speed limit, regulatory sign, right of way, school zone, warning sign, yield*

## 2 Teach

## Discuss

Use the illustrations on page 21 or **Content Overheads 3** and **4** to illustrate basic shapes and colors of traffic signs. Ask students to tell the meaning of each shape and color. Discuss why standard shapes and colors are used.

## Objectives

1. State the meaning of the eight shapes and eight colors used for traffic signs.
2. Describe the actions to take at STOP, YIELD, and speed limit signs.
3. List five situations where warning signs might be used.
4. Explain how guide signs and international signs help you when driving.

You will see hundreds of different traffic signs as you drive. While traffic signs serve many purposes, each traffic sign has a specific shape and color.

### Shapes and Colors

Note the eight sign shapes and eight sign colors shown on the opposite page. Each sign shape and color has a special meaning. By knowing the meanings of these shapes and colors, you can get valuable information from a sign—even at a distance.

Each traffic sign has a specific purpose. A **regulatory sign,** such as a STOP sign, controls traffic. A **warning sign,** including a signal ahead sign, alerts you to possible hazards and road conditions. A

**guide sign,** such as an interstate sign, gives directions.

### Regulatory Signs

Regulatory signs tell you about laws that you must obey. The most important signs, STOP and YIELD, have unique shapes. All other regulatory signs are either white squares or rectangles with red or black lettering.

### Stop Sign

A STOP sign is used on a road that crosses a main highway or a through street. The STOP sign is a red octagon with white letters and border.

Always come to a **full stop** at a STOP sign. Once stopped, you must yield the right of way to pedestrians or other vehicles in or approaching

If you were driving the yellow car, the other car should yield the right of way at this 4-way stop. Car colors in all traffic model pictures are as follows:
- Yellow—action car
- White—other cars in motion
- Blue—parked cars

## Teacher's Resources

**Content Overheads**
Overheads 3, 4, and 5

**Demonstration Overheads**
Overhead C

**Tests and Activities**
Activity 2-1, page 11

## Background

**Standard Traffic Controls** Although each state governs its own traffic, the same basic traffic controls are used throughout the nation. Each state uses the *Manual of Uniform Traffic Control Devices* published by the Federal Highway Administration. The manual was first published in 1935 to meet the need for uniform standards. The manual is continually revised and updated by the National Advisory Committee on Uniform Traffic Control Devices, made up of representatives from various organizations involved with highway safety.

the intersection. To **yield** means to allow others to use the intersection before you do. Using the **right of way** means you accept the privilege of immediate use of the roadway. If another driver on a through street must slow or stop after you leave a STOP sign, then you have not yielded the right of way.

The location of a STOP sign or stop line indicates where to make a legal stop. If there is only a STOP sign, stop before entering the intersection. Stop where you can see approaching traffic, but stop before you reach any crosswalk. The yellow car in the picture on the left shows where to stop when a stop line is present.

If your view is blocked as you approach an intersection and you cannot see cross traffic clearly after stopping, move ahead slowly and prepare to stop again. Make sure the way is clear before driving into the intersection.

At some intersections, STOP signs are posted at all four corners. Each STOP sign might include a small sign that says "4-WAY" or "ALL WAYS." Follow these steps at a 4-way stop:

1. The driver who stopped first should be allowed to go first, as the picture shows.
2. When vehicles stop to the right or left of each other at the same time, the driver on the left should yield to the driver on the right.
3. When stopped across the intersection facing oncoming traffic, the driver going straight should be allowed to proceed. A driver turning left should wait.

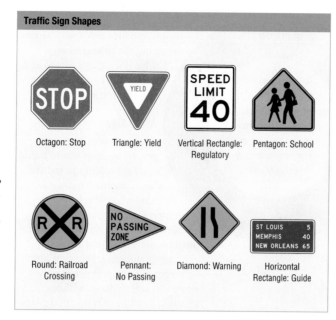

**Traffic Sign Shapes**

Octagon: Stop  
Triangle: Yield  
Vertical Rectangle: Regulatory  
Pentagon: School  
Round: Railroad Crossing  
Pennant: No Passing  
Diamond: Warning  
Horizontal Rectangle: Guide

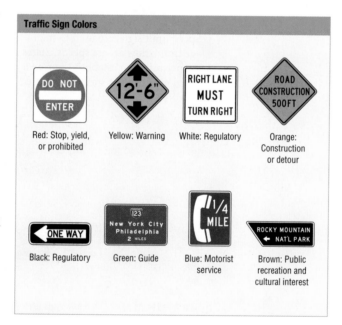

**Traffic Sign Colors**

Red: Stop, yield, or prohibited  
Yellow: Warning  
White: Regulatory  
Orange: Construction or detour  
Black: Regulatory  
Green: Guide  
Blue: Motorist service  
Brown: Public recreation and cultural interest

## Explain

Explain to students that a person does not have to be able to read in order to obtain a driver's license. Note that such drivers must understand the meaning and shape of traffic signs so they can interact on the roadway with other drivers. Stress that this is one reason many traffic signs have pictures, not words, on them.

## Explain

Explain that the law does not allow drivers to take the right of way. Instead, it indicates when they must yield and give the right of way to others.

## Demonstrate

Use videotapes, photographs, or slides to gather examples of roadway signs near your school. Show students examples of shapes, colors, and purposes of various signs.

## Background

**Stop Signs** Making a complete stop at a STOP sign allows the driver enough time to make a good search of the intersection. The driver needs to look for other vehicles and pedestrians and determine who should be granted the right of way. When a STOP sign is used rather than a YIELD sign, it indicates that the design of the intersection, the volume of traffic, or the speed of traffic is such that a STOP sign will give the driver a better opportunity to enter the intersection safely.

## Explain

Explain that if a driver follows speed limits, other drivers and pedestrians can better predict the driver's actions. Explain that drivers should adjust to advisory speed limits early so that others can adjust also.

## Demonstrate

Use **Demonstration Overhead C** and movable cars to illustrate cars approaching an intersection from various directions. Draw STOP signs at each corner with an erasable marker. Ask students which car should be granted the right of way. Also, ask students to indicate where drivers should stop for the STOP sign.

## Discuss

Ask students the *What Do You Think?* question: Do you think the federal government should set national speed limits? What do you see as the advantages and the disadvantages of speed limits?

### What Do You Think?

Do you think the federal government should set national speed limits? What do you see as the advantages and the disadvantages?

4. Show your intention to proceed by moving forward slowly before entering the intersection.

5. Check for traffic ahead and to the sides before entering the intersection.

### Yield Sign

Always slow or stop, and give the right of way to traffic when approaching a red and white triangular YIELD sign. It is found where roadways cross or merge.

Slowing enough ahead of time can often permit you to proceed without completely stopping. However, always be prepared to stop. Proceed only when it is safe to do so, without affecting the flow of traffic in the lane you are entering.

### Speed Limit Signs

Speed limit signs are used to manage traffic flow at safe speeds. States are permitted to establish their own speed limits. What speed limits exist in your state? Check the speed limits of other states before traveling there.

Speed limits are set for ideal driving conditions. When traffic, roadway, or weather conditions are not ideal, you must obey the **basic speed law.** This law states that you may not drive faster than is safe and prudent for existing conditions, regardless of posted speed limits.

A **minimum speed limit** is set on some roadways to keep traffic moving safely, such as primary highways and expressways. This speed limit tells you not to drive slower than the posted minimum speed unless conditions are less than ideal. If conditions are bad, follow the basic speed law and drive slower than the minimum speed limit.

**Advisory speed limits** are set for special conditions such as sharp curves. The signs are often posted below a warning sign. They indicate the maximum suggested speed under

The speed limits posted on these roads tell a safe speed for ideal conditions. When conditions are bad, you must drive slower than posted speeds.

22 Unit 1 The Driving Task

## Activity

**Small Group Activity** This activity will help students understand the shapes and colors of traffic signs. Form the class into groups of three to four students. Give each group a sheet of paper showing outlines of various sign shapes. You can use Activity 2-1 in **Tests and Activities,** page 11. Ask the groups to discuss and record the meaning of each sign's shape and color.

ideal conditions. Speed should be slower when conditions are less than ideal.

In some areas, special speed limits are set for different times of the day. For example, school zones have special speed limits when children are present or during school hours. Night driving speed limits may be lower than daylight limits.

### Other Regulatory Signs

Regulatory signs such as those shown above right are used to
- direct traffic to turn or go straight
- direct one-way traffic
- control parking and passing

Signs with red words on white or white words on red usually tell what *not* to do. Black-lettered words usually tell what you can do. Some signs have a black symbol in a red circle and crossed by a red, diagonal slash. The red circle and slash indicate that a certain action is prohibited.

### Warning Signs

A warning sign can help you avoid surprise situations. Most warning signs are diamond-shaped. Warning signs have black symbols or lettering on a yellow background.

### Diamond-Shaped Warning Signs

Yellow, diamond-shaped signs such as these warn of a danger ahead. Be prepared to slow or stop when you see a warning sign.

**Regulatory Signs**

Turns and Lanes     One Way     Parking and Passing

**Warning Signs**

Road Narrows (from right)     Signal Ahead     Divided Highway Ends

Sharp Right Curve     Side Road (Left)     Left Curve     Two-Way Traffic

Merging Traffic (from right)     Cross Ahead     Divided Highway Begins

Pedestrian Crossing     Hill     Deer Crossing     Low Clearance

## Explain

Drivers can better predict what they will have to do if they recognize the shape of warning signs. Yellow diamond-shaped warning signs warn of upcoming danger that might require the driver to stop or slow down. It is a good idea after seeing a warning sign to check the rearview mirror to be prepared to stop or slow. Also, let the detection of a warning sign serve as a cue to check how your intended path of travel is likely to be altered.

## Demonstrate

Use illustrations on this page or **Content Overhead 5** to explain the meaning of warning signs.

## Activity

**Small Group Activity** This activity will help students understand how traffic signs can become cues for appropriate driving. Divide the class into groups of four. Have the groups use the signs shown on pages 21 and 23 to explain how they as drivers would react to each. Ask the groups to discuss what specific actions they will take after seeing each sign. (For example: seeing a school-crossing sign alerts you to look for children, not only at designated crossings, but in the general area. Seeing a deer-crossing sign alerts you not only to look for deer but also alerts you to check for other vehicles in case braking or swerving is required.)

## Explain

Point out that seeing a school zone sign is a cue that children may be present. If you see a ball rolling toward the roadway, you should anticipate that a child might be running after the ball. Seeing one thing often helps a driver anticipate something else. For example, if you see one bicyclist, expect another; if you see an ice cream vendor, expect children; and if you see a construction sign, expect stopped traffic.

**SCHOOL ZONE SIGNS** A different colored school zone sign was tested around the country in the 1990s. The yellow-green background is made from a new fluorescent material that makes the sign more visible. The fluorescent yellow-green signs are replacing the standard yellow on all school warning signs.

School Zone

School Crossing

No Passing

### School Signs

Two signs are used in school zones. A **school zone** is a portion of a street or highway near a school that is subject to special speed limits. A school zone sign, only showing two children, is posted within a block of a school. A school crossing sign shows children in a crosswalk area. This sign is posted near intersections or crossings used by children. Notice the difference between these two signs.

Be extra alert in a school zone. Children might dart out into the street without looking. They might ride bicycles on the wrong side of the street or take other unexpected actions. Be ready to obey a crossing guard's directions in a school zone.

### No-Passing Sign

A yellow, pennant-shaped sign with black letters, as shown below left, may be posted on the left side of the roadway. The sign appears at the start of a no-passing zone and provides advance warning of where a no-passing zone starts. A no-passing sign is used together with a solid yellow line on the roadway. If you intend to pass, you must safely complete your pass before reaching this sign.

### Construction Signs

An orange sign, in a diamond or rectangular shape, alerts you to construction zones. Orange, triangular warning signs might be used on a construction vehicle to warn that the vehicle is slow-moving. Be alert in a construction zone, as shown in the picture below. Be ready to slow, stop, or drive around workers and equipment. Follow directions from signs and any worker directing traffic. Many states now increase fines for violations in construction zones.

Be alert in a construction zone. What does the orange sign tell you to do?

## Activity

**Class Activity** Use slides or photographs of signs in your community to help students understand the meaning of the various shapes. Ask students to classify each sign by one of three categories: warning, regulatory, or guide. Have students group signs by shape only into three main categories: warning (diamond, pentagon, circular, triangular with point up), regulatory (rectangular—horizontal and vertical, square, X cross buck, octagon, triangular with point down), and guide (square, shield, trapezoid, horizontal rectangle).

## Activity

**Small Group Activity** This activity will help students recognize different types of highways by the route signs. Divide the class into groups of four or five. Ask them to list the four types of route signs used in your state and identify a specific example of each type within your community. (Some states do not have county routes.) Have the groups formulate at least five characteristic features for each type of highway. After the features are listed, have the groups rank them as to whether they make driving on that roadway safe or dangerous.

Railroad Crossing

Crossbuck

The round, yellow sign warns you that a railroad crossing is near. The white crossbuck is at the crossing.

## Railroad Signs

A round, yellow sign with a black "X" and two "Rs" warns of a railroad crossing ahead. This sign is posted about 250 feet before a railroad crossing in an urban area. A railroad crossing sign is posted about 750 feet before a railroad crossing in a rural area. A large "X" might be painted on the roadway as an additional warning. The crossing itself is marked with a white crossbuck sign. It may have the number of tracks posted below the sign. Flashing red lights and/or crossing gates might be added to alert you when a train is coming. A driver must treat the crossbuck sign as a yield sign and flashing lights as a stop sign.

## Guide Signs

A guide sign provides a variety of information. Guide signs mark routes, intersections, service areas, and other points of interest or information.

## Route Signs

Local, state, U.S., and interstate routes are posted with route signs. Notice below that route signs vary according to the type of roadway. State and county route markers will vary from state to state. All the signs below display route numbers.

Interstate route signs are red, white, and blue shields. Notice below that a special numbering system is used for interstate routes.

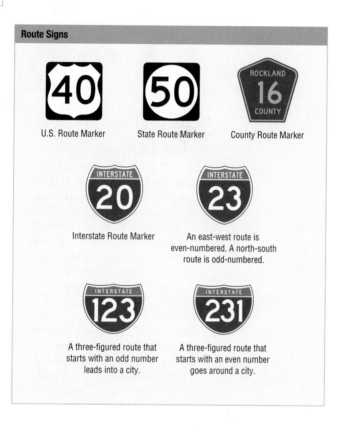

**Route Signs**

U.S. Route Marker

State Route Marker

County Route Marker

Interstate Route Marker

An east-west route is even-numbered. A north-south route is odd-numbered.

A three-figured route that starts with an odd number leads into a city.

A three-figured route that starts with an even number goes around a city.

Chapter 2  Signs, Signals, and Roadway Markings  **25**

## Demonstrate

Explain that a route is not necessarily a single roadway. Use a map to illustrate U.S. Route 66 as it crosses the United States. Give examples of state routes that involve traveling on several types of roadways.

## Apply

List the following headings on the board or an overhead transparency: Interstate Route, U.S. Route, State Route, and Local/County Route. Ask students to give examples of roadways in your community that are marked with each kind of route marker shown at the bottom of page 25.

## Demonstrate

Use slides or photographs to illustrate state and county route markers found in your community. Contact your state's department of transportation for visual aids. Point out that some states do not have county routes.

## Explain

Point out that when driving in an unfamiliar area, the driver might have difficulty keeping track of directions. To avoid this problem, a driver should plan the route in advance. Use guide signs to warn you of any turns. When traveling with a passenger, you can ask the passenger to watch for guide signs.

## Activity

**Class Activity** This activity will give students an opportunity to observe drivers' behaviors at intersections. Identify several intersections close to school and divide the class into groups, with each group assigned to an intersection. Ask each group to observe traffic for a specified amount of time and record their observations. Each group's observation sheet should include the following information: (1) names of the streets that create the intersection (2) type of traffic control (3) time when observation starts and ends (4) number of vehicles going straight

(5) number of vehicles turning (6) number of drivers who do not use turn signals (7) number of drivers making complete stops at red lights and STOP signs (8) number of drivers who stop before making right turns on red (9) number of drivers who do not stop before making right turns on red (10) number of drivers running yellow or red lights. Also have groups record any other observations they make about drivers' behaviors. Have the groups share their observations with each other.

ST LOUIS 5
MEMPHIS 40
NEW ORLEANS 65

Green signs provide information on mileage to other destinations

Blue signs guide you to services near the highway.

ROCKY MOUNTAIN
← NAT'L PARK

Brown signs indicate points of interest.

**International Signs**

Stop

Yield

Road Narrows

No Right Turn

# 3 Assess

## Answers to Review It

**1.** Shapes: octagon—stop; triangle—yield; vertical rectangle—regulatory; pentagon—school; round—railroad crossing; pennant—no passing; diamond—warning; horizontal rectangle—guide.
Colors: red—stop, yield or prohibited; yellow—warning; white—regulatory; orange—construction or detour; black—regulatory; green—guide; blue—motorist services; brown—public recreation and cultural interest (pp. 20–21)

**2.** At a STOP sign, come to a complete stop and yield the right of way to pedestrians and vehicles. At a YIELD sign, slow or stop and give right of way to cross traffic. Speed limit signs indicate the safe maximum or minimum speed. (pp. 20–23)

**3.** Warning signs might be used to indicate a no-passing zone, railroad crossing, school crossing, school zone, or construction zone. (pp. 23–24)

**4.** Guide signs point out routes, intersections, services, and points of interest. International signs use symbols rather than words. (pp. 25–26)

### Other Guide Signs

You will see a wide variety of guide signs in addition to route signs. Note that green signs provide information on destinations ahead and distances to be traveled. Blue signs highlight highway services such as fuel, food, lodging, and nearby hospitals. Brown signs direct you to recreation areas or cultural points of interest.

### International Signs

International signs convey information with symbols rather than words. Drivers who travel from country to country can understand the meaning of these signs without learning several languages. The United States has adopted several **international symbols** for use on highway signs. More and more of these symbols will be used as international travel increases.

### Review It

1. What do the eight shapes and colors of traffic signs mean?
2. What actions should you take at STOP, YIELD, and speed-limit signs?
3. What are some situations where warning signs might be used?
4. What information do guide signs and international signs provide?

26 Unit 1 The Driving Task

## Activity

**Small Group Activity** Divide the class into groups of four or five. The students are to use the observation sheets from the Activity on page 25. Have one member of the group compile the results of all group members' observations. They should discuss what actions are unsafe and why drivers may perform such unsafe behavior, and how that behavior can affect them as drivers. After adequate time, the groups should report their findings to the class.

## Special Needs

Create and play the Signs Fish Card Game. This game helps reinforce the meanings of the colors and shapes of signs. Create a set of cards using various signs with all the colors and shapes. For each sign, you will need four identical cards. Follow the rules for the card game Go Fish.

Traffic lights, arrows, flashing signals, lane signals, and pedestrian signals are used to help traffic flow smoothly. Each of these devices is a **traffic signal.** All traffic signals have specific colors. Red means stop. Yellow means caution: be ready to stop. Green means go: proceed if the way is clear and safe.

### Traffic Lights

Various combinations of traffic lights can be placed at intersections to control traffic. Remember the following types of lights so you will be familiar with them while driving.

**Green Light** The first picture shows a green light. You can proceed only if the intersection is clear. When approaching a green light, check traffic to the left, front, and right before entering the intersection. When approaching a light that has been green for some time, be prepared for the light to turn yellow. The green light will be mounted at the bottom or to the right on the traffic signal.

**Yellow Light** The second picture shows a yellow light. Make every effort to stop safely for a yellow light. Sometimes you might be too close to stop safely when a yellow light appears. You then will have to proceed with caution. The yellow light will appear in the center on the traffic signal.

**Red Light** The third picture shows a red light. You must come to a full

Proceed at a green light only if the intersection is clear.

A yellow light means caution and prepare to stop.

At a red light, come to a complete stop before the entrance to the intersection.

Chapter 2  Signs, Signals, and Roadway Markings  **27**

## Objectives

1. Explain what to do at a green light, a yellow light, and a red light.
2. Describe the action to take when you approach a flashing red signal or a flashing yellow signal.
3. Describe the actions to take with pedestrian signals and traffic control officers' signals.

## Traffic Signals

### 1 Focus

### Summary

This lesson introduces traffic signals including traffic lights, arrows, flashing signals, and pedestrian signals. Officers' signals also are explained.

### Vocabulary

*flashing signal, lane signal, pedestrian signal, right-turn-on-red, traffic signal*

### 2 Teach

### Explain

Explain that a driver should identify traffic and roadway conditions when approaching a green light. By predicting what others might do, the driver can decide on the correct actions and execute them early enough so that others can adjust to the actions.

## Demonstrate

Use **Content Overhead 6** to illustrate the possible types of traffic signals. Point out the locations and types of traffic signals in the photograph on page 18. Explain that some communities have all three types of signals and others have only one or two. Ask students which type of signal is most common in your community and nearby communities. Ask for specific examples.

## Explain

Explain that the driver must assume primary responsibility for yielding when making a right-turn-on-red. All traffic must clear the intersection before the turn is made. All pedestrians must be clear of the intersection before the turn is made. Stress the difficulty of checking at the same time for traffic from left and for pedestrians from the right. The procedure for making a right-turn-on-red is further explained in Chapter 6.

stop at a red light. Stop behind the stop line, crosswalk, or before entering the intersection if no stop lines are used. The red light will be mounted on the top or to the left side on the traffic signal.

**Computerized Traffic Lights**
Computerized traffic light systems are often used to control the flow of traffic. A computer coordinates traffic lights at several intersections. With this system, traffic can flow for several blocks at or near the speed limit without stopping.

Traffic lights also can be set to change when traffic approaches. A sensor in the roadway detects oncoming or stopped traffic. This system can be used where most of the traffic comes from one direction, such as a left-turn lane. They can also be used to regulate traffic entering a limited access highway.

**Right-Turn-on-Red**
All states now allow drivers to make a **right-turn-on-red.** This means turning right when the signal is red. However, some cities restrict such

Before you make a right-turn-on-red, you must yield the way to any vehicle in, or approaching, the intersection.

turns. Procedures for turning right on red are discussed in Chapter 7.

**Left-Turn-on-Red**
Some states permit drivers to make a left turn on a red light when turning from a one-way street into a one-way street. This turn must be made cautiously and only after stopping. A few states permit left-turns on a red light from a left turn lane into a one-way street. Be sure state laws and local ordinances permit such

The flashing red light lets drivers at a distance know that they are approaching a stop.

## Activity

**Class Activity** This is a peer-influence activity to give students an opportunity to evaluate and debate their values regarding motorists running red (signal) lights. Ask students to write on a piece of paper their rating of approval for drivers running red lights. Use a scale of 1 to 10, with 1 equaling that they fully approve of drivers going through red lights, and 10 equaling that they fully disapprove of drivers going through red lights.

See **Resource Book** page 27 for how to form the students into pairs. Have each pair of students express their viewpoints to one another in an attempt to change the other person's value. After adequate time, have the students get back into columns of one to ten, entering a new column if their value changed. Take note of how peers influenced values.

turns. The intersection and cross-walk must be clear of traffic and pedestrians before you turn either left or right on a red light.

### Flashing Signals

A **flashing signal** alerts drivers to dangerous conditions or tells them to stop. These signals are used at intersections and other dangerous locations.

Note the flashing red signal in the bottom picture on the opposite page. Make a full stop when you come to a flashing red signal. A STOP sign and stop line may be used with this signal. After you stop, yield to traffic, and proceed only when the intersection is clear.

When you see a warning sign and a flashing yellow signal, slow down. Be prepared to stop at the traffic light.

### Arrows

Traffic must flow in the direction that a green arrow is pointing. Look at the arrows shown here. These arrows are used together with traffic lights. If you are driving in a lane with a green arrow pointing to the left or right, you must turn in that direction. Remember first to yield to other traffic and pedestrians.

Some cities use left-turn arrows to permit drivers to turn left before oncoming traffic proceeds. Other cities use green left-turn arrows only after oncoming traffic has cleared or has been stopped by a red light. You should be cautious if you are unfamiliar with the left-turn signals you encounter. Always be prepared to yield.

**GO** left only. Be sure that oncoming traffic does not run the red light.

**GO** right only. Yield to pedestrians and vehicles already in the intersection.

**GO** straight ahead only after yielding to vehicles and pedestrians within the intersection.

**WARNING.** The red arrow is about to appear.

**STOP.** You may not go in this direction.

### Explain

Emphasize that a flashing yellow signal is used to give an early warning of a potentially dangerous intersection. The decision to install a signal at a particular location is usually made after a thorough investigation of the traffic, often the result of numerous collisions at the location. Therefore, you should become extra alert for problems when you see a flashing yellow or red light at an intersection.

### Explain

There are several configurations for flashing lights at intersections. In some locations the lights flash red in all directions. In other locations the light flashes yellow in all directions. In still other locations the lights flash red for one roadway and yellow for the crossing roadway.

### Apply

Ask students to identify locations in your community where flashing signals are used to control traffic. Discuss why flashing signals are at these intersections. Have students explain the appropriate response for drivers approaching these locations from each separate direction.

## Activity

**Role Play** This activity will help students form values on why some intersections need traffic signals and others do not. Divide the class into three groups: traffic engineers, citizens, and government officials. The engineers work for a traffic-engineering firm making a proposal to install traffic signals at a hypothetical intersection. The citizens represent drivers who oppose the installation of the traffic signals. The government officials are responsible for deciding whether the traffic signal will be installed. Give the groups 15 minutes to prepare for their roles. The engineers will then have ten minutes to present their proposal along with their rationale. Following the engineer's presentation, the citizens will have ten minutes to explain their objections. After the presentations the government officials will conduct a ten-minute questions and answer session. At the conclusion of the question and answer session, the government officials will vote on the proposal.

## Demonstrate

Explain that some cities use reversible lanes to move the largest volume of traffic into the city in the morning and out of the city in the afternoon. Use **Demonstration Overhead B** to show how the lanes may be used. Use an erasable marker to draw a green arrow pointing down in each of the three right lanes and draw a red X over the far left lane. Explain that three lanes allow traffic to go into the city during morning rush hour. Then erase all green arrows except in the far right lane and put red X's in the two middle lanes. Explain that three lanes move traffic out of the city in the afternoon. Discuss the importance of never entering a travel lane when a red X is over the lane.

## Assess

### Answers to Review It

**1.** At a red light, come to a complete stop behind a stop line, crosswalk, or before an intersection. Make every effort to stop at a yellow light. Go through the intersection at a green light only if it is clear of traffic. (pp. 27–28)

**2.** Come to a complete stop at a flashing red signal. Slow down and prepare to stop at a flashing yellow signal. (p. 29)

**3.** The WALK signal and the green light are for pedestrians and drivers going in the same directions. The DON'T WALK signal usually flashes just before the yellow light appears. A traffic-control officer holds up a hand for stop and waves a hand for go. (p. 30)

When the pedestrian signal says DON'T WALK, predict that your green light will soon change.

### Lane Signals

Sometimes traffic in some lanes needs to go in one direction for a certain period of time and in the opposite direction at another period of time. The direction of these lanes is reversed on some streets and expressways to control morning and evening rush-hour traffic. In these situations, lights hanging overhead show whether or not a lane can be used at that time. Each light is a **lane signal.** These signals are different from the arrows that regulate turns. You will learn more about lane signals on expressways in Chapter 11.

### Pedestrian Signals

A **pedestrian signal** is used at an intersection with heavy traffic. These signals or symbols are mounted near traffic lights as seen in the picture. Pedestrians should only cross at an intersection when they face a WALK signal or symbol. Pedestrians must clear the intersection or wait on a curb when the DON'T WALK signal or symbol flashes or remains lit.

Normally, the WALK signal or symbol and the green traffic light will be on at the same time for pedestrians and drivers going in the same direc-

tion. The DON'T WALK signal or symbol usually begins to flash just before the yellow light appears for drivers. If you approach an intersection and see the DON'T WALK signal flashing, predict that your green light will soon change.

The pedestrian DON'T WALK signal will remain on when a green right- or left-turn signal is permitting a driver's path of travel to cross the crosswalk. Pedestrians must wait until their WALK signal or symbol is lit. When turning on a green left-turn signal, drivers should be alert to pedestrians crossing.

### Officer's Signal

You must obey signals given by a traffic control officer, even if the officer's signals contradict the traffic signal. A hand held up with the palm toward you means stop. A hand waving you on means go. Signals can be given with lighted wands during times of low visibility.

### Review It

1. What should you do when you approach a red light? a yellow light? a green light?
2. What action should you take as you approach a flashing red signal? a flashing yellow signal?
3. How do pedestrian signals and officer's signals help you when driving?

## Special Needs

Many busy intersections have special sound devices to indicate which street has the green or red signal. These devices help persons who are blind or have limited vision to safely cross the street.

**A** roadway marking gives you a warning or direction. These markings are usually lines, words, or arrows painted yellow or white on the roadway. Sometimes special markings are used on curbs and other surfaces.

### Yellow Line Markings

A broken yellow line separates two-way traffic. It also means a driver may pass only when no traffic is coming from the opposite direction.

A solid yellow line on the driver's side of the center line indicates that passing is not allowed. Passing is allowed only when the solid yellow line no longer appears on the driver's

Passing is allowed across a broken yellow line.

No passing is allowed on the side of a road that has a solid yellow line.

side of the highway. Turning left across a solid yellow line into a driveway or alley is allowed after yielding to oncoming traffic.

Two solid yellow lines that divide traffic prohibit passing that involves crossing the solid lines, as shown in the picture on page 32. Some cities permit you to make left turns across these lines after yielding to oncoming traffic.

Many cities use a **shared left-turn lane** to help drivers make safer midblock left turns to and from businesses on a busy street. Solid and broken yellow lines are used with left-turn arrows from both directions to identify a shared left-turn lane.

### White Line Markings

Broken white lines separate lanes of traffic that are moving in the same

Chapter 2 Signs, Signals, and Roadway Markings **31**

## Objectives

1. Describe the difference between broken yellow lines and broken white lines.
2. Explain the differences between a shared left-turn lane and a left-turn lane.
3. List six types of special roadway markings.

---

# Roadway Marking

 **Focus**

## Summary

This lesson presents roadway markings including lines, words, and figures.

## Vocabulary

*roadway markings, rumble strips, shared left-turn lane*

 **Teach**

## Demonstrate

Use the illustrations on this page and page 32 or **Content Overhead 7** to illustrate these three points: Passing is allowed across a broken yellow line. No passing is allowed on the side of a road that has a solid yellow line. No passing is allowed if it involves crossing a double yellow line.

## Demonstrate

Use **Content Overhead 8** to illustrate a shared left-turn lane. Identify the location of a shared left-turn lane in your community, if applicable.

## Explain

Understanding that yellow pavement markings indicate two-way traffic can be helpful when driving in unfamiliar areas.

---

## Teacher's Resources

**Content Overheads**
Overheads 7 and 8

## Background

**British Pavement Markings** In England, yellow pavement markings are used only on the edges of the road and only for no-parking and no-stopping areas. Pedestrian crossing areas have special white zigzag markings on both sides to prevent drivers from parking within 20 feet of a crosswalk. This allows drivers and pedestrians to have a clear view of each other.

## Explain

Point out the white arrows painted on the pavement at the intersection shown in the photograph at the bottom of the page. In some cases drivers cannot see the markings early enough to make lane selection decisions. To remedy this problem, white rectangular signs mounted at curbside or hung above the lane indicate the direction you must go when driving in specific lanes. An overhead sign is shown in the photograph on page 184.

direction. You may cross these broken white lines when changing lanes.

Solid white lane lines keep drivers in their lanes and restrict lane changing. Solid white lines indicate that you should not cross them. These lines identify locations where changing lanes is hazardous. Plan ahead to prevent crossing solid white lane markings.

White arrows are painted in lanes to tell you when and where to turn. If you are in a lane with an arrow and the word ONLY, you *must* continue in the direction of the arrow. You may turn or go straight if there is a curved and straight arrow in your lane.

Solid white lines are used along the side of a roadway to mark the edge of the roadway. These lines help you to see the edge of the roadway at night or under poor visibility driving conditions.

Solid white lines are also used to mark pedestrian crosswalks and stop lines. Some crosswalks have diagonal or perpendicular lines between them or are painted a

No passing is allowed if it involves crossing a double yellow line.

different color to highlight the area. You must yield the right of way to pedestrians in crosswalks. Stop lines across your lane at intersections show where to stop at a STOP sign or a traffic light.

Solid white lines separate traffic lanes and mark pedestrian crosswalks and stop lines. Arrows with the word ONLY indicate the direction you must go when driving in these lanes.

## Activity

**Small Group Activity** This activity will help students identify and understand the meaning of roadway markings. Divide the class into teams of three. Allow ten minutes for the teams to locate examples in the book where pavement markings are illustrated. After the ten minutes identify which group found the most examples. Have the winners give the page numbers for their examples and have the other teams take turns explaining the purpose of the pavement markings found. Cover as many examples from all teams as time permits.

### Rumble Strips and Raised Roadway Markers

**Rumble strips** are short sections of corrugated roadway. These strips alert you through the noise your tires make when you drive over them. Rumble strips warn of hazards such as a major or dangerous intersection, a toll plaza, or an unexpected need to stop or reduce speed. Sometimes a rumble strip is used to warn that you are driving too close to the roadway edge, as the picture shows.

On some highways, drivers might have a difficult time seeing the driving lane at night. Raised or lowered roadway markers are used in such situations. These markers act as small reflectors. They are raised in areas where snow seldom occurs. In snow removal areas, these markers will be lower than the surface of the roadway.

Roadway markers are color coded. White markers are used at the edge of a roadway or between lanes, just as white lines are used. Yellow markers may locate the left edge of an expressway. If you are driving and see red roadway markers, pull off the roadway immediately. These red markers warn that you are driving in the wrong direction. Safely get your car going in the proper direction.

### Other Roadway Markings

A special white marking on the roadway is used to show you where an exit ramp starts. It is dangerous and illegal to make a last minute decision to cross this area.

The railroad markings using an "X" and two "Rs" on each side of the roadway warn you that a railroad crossing is ahead. Do not pass near railroad crossings.

This type of rumble strip will let you know when you have wandered off the roadway.

Roadway markers shine when struck by headlight beams to help drivers see the driving lane at night.

## Explain

Explain that rumble strips and raised roadway markers are especially useful near hazardous areas such as tollbooths. Ask students to describe locations in your community where rumble strips are used.

## Discuss

Discuss with students the value of knowing the general meaning of pavement marking colors. Have them brainstorm to identify as many applications and variations as possible.

## Apply

Gather examples of roadway markings near your school. Use videotape, photographs or slides to present the markings to your students. Have them explain the meaning of each marking.

## Cross Curricular

**Geography** Have students research traffic signs, traffic signals, and roadway markings used in another country. Direct them to library resources related to international travel or travel to a specific country. Travel agencies and automobile clubs are also resources for this activity. Have students work together to create classroom displays related to different countries.

You may not park alongside this yellow curb marking.

These parking spaces are reserved for handicapped drivers or passengers.

## Discuss

Ask: Why is it wrong to park in a Handicapped Parking Only space if you do not have the appropriate permit?

 **Assess**

## Answers to Review It

**1.** Broken yellow lines separate two-way traffic. Broken white lines separate lanes of traffic moving in the same direction. (pp. 31–32)

**2.** Shared left-turn lanes help drivers make safer midblock left turns. These lanes can be used by drivers going in both directions. A left-turn lane is the lane a driver should be in to turn left at an intersection. (pp. 31–32)

**3.** No parking zones, handicapped parking spaces, yellow or white markings for roadway obstructions, railroad crossing markings, white markings that show where an exit ramp begins, and rumble strips to warn you to slow for an upcoming hazard. (pp. 31–34)

Notice the marking for the school crossing below. When you see this white marking, watch for children in the area.

Curbs alongside a road might be painted to indicate warnings or that parking is not permitted. No-Parking zones often are near fire hydrants, curves, and intersections. The curb marking in the top left picture shows a No-Parking zone. The markings may be red, yellow, or white.

The top right picture shows a parking space reserved for vehicles having handicapped drivers or passengers. Check for signs that say HANDICAPPED PARKING ONLY and signs and pavement markings with the handicapped parking symbol. It is illegal to park in this space without proper permit.

### Review It

1. What is the basic difference between broken white lines and broken yellow lines?
2. What are the functions of shared left-turn lanes versus regular left-turn lanes?
3. What are six types of special roadway markings?

Predict that children could be crossing ahead.

**34** Unit 1 The Driving Task

## Special Needs

Create and play in class and at home "Signs, Lines, and Signals" to help students review the signs, traffic signals, and roadway markings taught in this chapter. Create cards with various signs, signals, and roadway markings. Use the cards to have students play Go Fish, Rummy, or War. You could also create Bingo cards.

## Reviewing Chapter Objectives

### 1. Traffic Signs

1. What are the meanings of the eight shapes and eight colors used for traffic signs? (20–21)
2. What actions should you take at STOP, YIELD, and speed limit signs? (20–23)
3. What are five situations where warning signs might be used? (23–25)
4. How can guide signs and international signs help you when driving? (26)

### 2. Traffic Signals

5. What should you do at a green light, a yellow light, and a red light? (27–28)
6. What action should you take when approaching a flashing red signal or a flashing yellow signal? (29)
7. What actions should you take with pedestrian signals and traffic control officers' signals? (30)

### 3. Roadway Markings

8. What is the difference between broken yellow lines and broken white lines? (31–32)
9. What is the difference between a shared left-turn lane and a left-turn lane? (31)
10. What are six types of special roadway markings? (31–34)

## Projects

### Individuals

**Research** Find out about the speed-limit laws in your state. Then find the same information about neighboring states. Notice any similarities or differences in the laws. Write a report comparing the laws.

**Observe Traffic** Observe for fifteen minutes pedestrians and vehicles at an intersection that has a pedestrian signal. Count the number of pedestrians that cross the street. Notice whether the pedestrians and the vehicles are obeying the signals. Compare your results with those of your classmates.

### Groups

**Debate** Divide your group into two and debate the pros and cons of having the federal government set speed limits. Make a list of all the reasons your group mentions. Compare your list with the other groups in your class.

**Practice** Make color flashcards for all the signs shown in this chapter. With a partner from your group, test each other on the meanings of the signs.

---

## Reviewing Chapter Objectives

**2.1** Traffic Signs
See Answers to Review It on page 26.
**2.2** Traffic Signals
See Answers to Review It on page 30.
**2.3** Roadway Markings
See Answers to Review It on page 34.

For additional information refer to the specific page(s) in parentheses after each question.

## Projects

Some of the projects can be assigned at any time while others are more closely tied to the content presented in the student text. The page number where the topic is introduced is indicated.

**Research:** p. 22
**Observe Traffic:** p. 30
**Debate:** p. 22
**Practice:** p. 20

The results of student projects will vary.

---

## Teacher's Resources

**Skills and Applications Workbook**
pages 5–8

**Tests and Activities**
Chapter 2 Activities 2-1 and 2-2
pages 11–12
Chapter 2 Test A and Test B,
pages 13–16

**TestWorks CD-ROM**
Chapter 2 Test

## Answers to Check Your Knowledge

1. b
2. d
3. c
4. a
5. pedestrian
6. symbols
7. shared left-turn lane
8. regulatory

## Answers to Review Vocabulary

9. warning sign (c)
10. flashing signal (a)
11. minimum speed limit (f)
12. lane signal (b)
13. advisory speed limits (d)
14. guide sign (e)

## Answers to Think Critically

Students' answers will vary. For information related to the question refer to the page(s) indicated.

**1.** The basic speed law states that you may not drive faster than is safe for existing conditions, regardless of the posted speed limit. A minimum speed limit tells you not to drive slower than the given speed unless conditions are bad. An advisory speed limit is sometimes set for special conditions such as sharp curves. (p. 22)

**2.** When driving in a foreign country, you will be able to understand the traffic signs if they use international symbols. (p. 26)

### Chapter Test

#### Check Your Knowledge

**Multiple Choice** Copy the number of each sentence below on a sheet of paper. Choose the letter of the answer that best completes the statement or answers the question.

1. What does a round traffic sign mean?
   (a) yield to other traffic   (c) stop
   (b) railroad crossing   (d) pedestrian crossing
2. A construction zone sign is
   (a) yellow.   (c) green.
   (b) blue.   (d) orange.
3. Which of the following is not an example of a traffic signal?
   (a) flashing lights   (c) school zone sign
   (b) arrows   (d) pedestrian signals
4. Two solid yellow center lines on a two-lane highway indicate
   (a) no passing from either way.
   (b) passing both ways.
   (c) passing only with caution.
   (d) passing on the left only.

**Completion** Copy the number of each sentence below. After each number, write the word or words that complete the sentence correctly.

5. A _____ signal is used at heavy traffic intersections to tell people who are walking whether they should proceed or wait.
6. International traffic signs use _____ rather than words.
7. A lane on a busy street that helps drivers make safer mid-block left turns is called a _____.
8. A _____ sign controls traffic.

36   Unit 1  The Driving Task

#### Review Vocabulary

Copy the number of each definition in list A. Match the definition in list A with the term it defines in list B.

**List A**

9. sign that alerts you to possible hazards and road conditions
10. signal that alerts drivers to dangerous conditions or tells them to stop
11. sign set on roadways like primary highways and expressways to keep traffic moving safely
12. signal, usually overhead, that tells whether a lane can or cannot be used at a specific time
13. speed limits set for special conditions such as sharp curves
14. sign that gives directions

**List B**

a. flashing signal
b. lane signal
c. warning sign
d. advisory speed limits
e. guide sign
f. minimum speed limit

#### Think Critically

Write a paragraph to answer each question.

1. What is the difference between a *basic speed law,* a *minimum speed limit,* and an *advisory speed limit*?
2. You are planning to drive in a foreign country that has a different language from yours. What can you do to be sure that you will understand the traffic signs?

## Decision Making

**1.** What is the speed limit in this situation? What speed law might make driving at the posted speed limit illegal?

**2.** You will be making a left turn at the traffic light ahead. Are you in the correct lane to make that turn? Explain your answer.

**3.** The orange sign and arrow ahead are used to warn drivers about what condition? If you were driving the vehicle that the scene is viewed from, what mistake would you have already made?

**4.** You want to pass the slower moving vehicle ahead. Is it safe and legal to pass here? Why or why not?

Chapter 2  Signs, Signals, and Roadway Markings **37**

## Answers to Decision Making

**1.** The speed limit on this roadway is 45 mph. The basic speed law says that you must drive slowly in bad weather conditions. You might be ticketed for driving too fast for conditions if you are driving 45 mph.

**2.** You should be in the lane that is marked with the left-turn arrow to make the left turn, not in the shared left-turn lane. You should be in the left-turn lane as soon as the shared-lane arrows are no longer painted on the roadway.

**3.** The orange signs are used to warn drivers of a construction zone ahead. The driver should already be in the right lane of traffic.

**4.** It is illegal to pass until the solid yellow roadway line changes to a broken yellow line and there is no oncoming traffic. It is unsafe because you cannot see a safe distance ahead in the lane you would use to pass.

| |  Student Features |  Teacher's Edition |
|---|---|---|
| **Chapter 3**<br>**Basic Vehicle Control** | You Are the Driver! *p. 39* | Projects *p. 38*<br>Special Needs *p. 39* |
| **3.1 Instruments, Controls, and Devices** *pp. 40–45*<br>• Identify each gauge and warning light on an instrument panel and explain its function.<br>• Explain the purpose of each control used to operate a vehicle.<br>• Describe the use of the safety, communication, and comfort devices. | Safe Driving Tip *pp. 41, 42*<br>What Do You Think? *p. 44* | Demonstrate *pp. 41, 44*<br>Activity *pp. 42, 44*<br>Special Needs *p. 41* |
| **3.2 Getting Ready to Drive** *pp. 46–47*<br>• List in order the checks you make when preparing to drive.<br>• Describe how to enter a vehicle from the street side.<br>• Describe the correct positioning of the seat and outside rearview mirrors. | | Activity *pp. 46, 47* |
| **3.3 Driving a Vehicle with Automatic Transmission** *pp. 48–52*<br>• Explain the use of each gear.<br>• Describe the procedure for starting an automatic transmission vehicle.<br>• List the steps for putting an automatic transmission vehicle in motion.<br>• Tell the correct procedure to follow when leaving an automatic transmission vehicle from the street side. | | Demonstrate *p. 48*<br>Activity *pp. 49, 50, 51, 52* |
| **3.4 Driving a Vehicle with Manual Transmission** *pp. 53–56*<br>• List the procedures for starting a stickshift vehicle.<br>• Tell the correct procedure for moving a stickshift vehicle in first gear.<br>• Explain the procedure for stopping from higher gears.<br>• Define downshifting and explain its purpose. | Did You Know? *p. 55* | Activity *p. 53*<br>Special Needs *p. 55* |
| **Assessment** | Reviewing Chapter Objectives *p. 57*<br>Projects *p. 57*<br>Chapter Test *p. 58*<br>Decision Making *p. 59* | Answers pp. *58–59* |

**Companion** *pp. 17–24*
**Spanish Handbook** *pp. 7–8*

---

**Resource Book**
Teacher's Instructions, *p. 29*
**Tests and Activities**
Chapter 3 Activities 3-1 *p. 19*

**Demonstration Overhead J**

---

**In-Car Checklists** 1, 2
**Resource Book**
Information, *p. 83*

---

**Resource Book**
Teacher's Instructions,
*pp. 30–32*
**In-Car Checklists** 3, 4, 5

---

**Resource Book**
Teacher's Instructions,
*pp. 33–34*
**In-Car Checklists** 37, 38, 39

---

**Skills and Applications
Workbook**, *pp. 9–12*
**Tests and Activities**
Chapter 3 Activities 3-1
and 3-2, *pp. 19–20*
Chapter 3 Test A and Test B,
*pp. 21–24*

**TestWorks CD-ROM**
Chapter 3 Test

## Technology Resources

Interactive Driving Systems, Inc., *Reference Points,* video, 23 minutes

Interactive Driving Systems, Inc., *Targeting,* video, 15 minutes

Safety Industries, Inc., *Car Tours,* video, 10 minutes

## Kits, Equipment, and Other Resources

Interactive Driving Systems, Inc., *Auto Control Monster*

Interactive Driving Systems, Inc., *Reference Point Demonstration Kit*

**Go Online**
PHSchool.com
**For: Chapter 3 online activities**
**Visit: PHSchool.com**
**Web Code: cak-9999**

# Chapter 3

## Basic Vehicle Control

### Chapter Overview

Chapter 3 explains the purpose and operation of the instruments, devices, and controls in a vehicle. Students will learn the procedures to follow when getting ready to drive. They will also learn the procedures for starting, moving, and stopping both an automatic and manual transmission vehicle.

### Chapter Vocabulary

*alternator warning light, antilock braking system (ABS), backup lights, blind-spot area, clutch pedal, console, cruise control, downshifting, friction point, hazard flasher, head restraints, ignition switch, odometer, riding the clutch, shift indicator, target*

### Teacher's Resources

For students to use as they read the chapter:

**Companion**
pages 17–24

**Spanish Handbook**
pages 7–8

### Projects

Review the projects described on page 57. Some of the projects can be assigned at any time while others are more closely tied to the content presented in the student text.

## You Are the Driver!

For all drivers and especially for new drivers, safety is your primary responsibility. To be a safe driver, you must know the location and function of your vehicle's control devices. Since vehicles differ in so many ways, it is important that you read and understand your owner's manual.

You also must know the procedures to follow when entering, starting, moving, stopping, and leaving your vehicle. What should you check before entering the vehicle? What is the odometer? What should you do before starting the engine? This chapter describes a vehicle's instruments and control devices and how to use them.

Go Online
PHSchool.com
**For:** Chapter 3 online activities
**Visit:** PHSchool.com
**Web Code:** cak-9999

39

## Introducing the Chapter

Discuss with students what the driver should know before beginning to drive.

## You Are the Driver!

Before entering the vehicle and starting the engine, students should identify the type of transmission, odometer, horn, speedometer, fuel gauge, turn-signal lever, and light switch. Emphasize the difference in location of gauges and warning lights among different models of vehicles. Symbols are sometimes used to identify the gauges and devices. Encourage students to read the vehicle owner's manual to familiarize themselves with any vehicle before they drive it.

## Special Needs

Many of the activities and demonstrations in this chapter will help special needs students understand the concepts and learn the basic procedures for driving a vehicle. Use the In-Class Driving Rehearsal activities to help students learn and practice the procedures before instruction in the driver education car. Students might find it helpful to use the **In-Car Checklists**, which list the procedures.

# Instruments, Controls, and Devices

## 1 Focus

### Summary

In this lesson students will be introduced to instruments, controls, and devices that they will use when they begin driving.

### Vocabulary

*alternator warning light, antilock braking system (ABS), blind-spot area, clutch pedal, console, cruise control, hazard flasher, head restraints, ignition switch, odometer*

## 2 Teach

### Apply

Have students take a piece of paper and block from view the text on pages 40 and 41. Ask them to look at the photo and write the names of the instrument represented by each number. After ample time, have the students look at the text to see how many instruments they were able to identify correctly. Review all the instruments and provide feedback to students who are having difficulty.

When you are ready to begin your driving experiences, you must know what the warning lights and gauges on the instrument panel tell you. Read the owner's manual to learn the location and operation of the devices for safety, comfort, and communication.

### Instrument Panel

The instrument panel is the panel directly in front of you as you sit in the driver's seat. The location of the gauges and warning lights varies from one vehicle to another. No matter where these gauges and lights are located, their purposes are the same. You can make sure the warning lights are working if they light when the ignition switch is turned to On.

The picture on the next page shows one example of the location of the gauges and warning lights in a vehicle, though not all vehicles have the same indicators. The numbers correspond to the gauges and lights explained on this and the next page.

**Speedometer (1)** This instrument tells you the speed you are traveling in both miles per hour and kilometers per hour. Some vehicles have a digital speedometer.

**Tachometer (2)** Some vehicles have a tachometer that indicates the engine revolutions per minute. Engine damage may occur if the needle enters the red zone.

**Odometer (3)** The **odometer** indicates the total number of miles the vehicle has been driven. Some vehicles have an additional trip odometer that can be set back to zero when you want to know the number of miles driven during a certain period of time.

**Fuel Gauge (4)** The fuel gauge shows the amount of fuel in the tank. If you let the fuel tank get below one-quarter full, you risk running out of fuel.

Try to keep the fuel tank at least half full in cold weather to help prevent fuel-line freeze. This can occur when moisture condenses and freezes inside the tank and fuel line. Ice particles can then block the flow of fuel.

**Temperature Light or Gauge (5)** This light or gauge warns you when the coolant in the engine is too hot.

**Oil Pressure Warning Light or Gauge (6)** This warning light or gauge warns you when the oil is not circulating at the proper pressure. However, it does not tell you the amount of oil in the engine.

**Alternator Warning Light or Gauge (7)** Your vehicle's electrical system is in trouble if this light comes on or the gauge shows "discharge" while the engine is running. The alternator is not generating enough electricity to run the vehicle. When this happens, the engine must use stored electricity from the battery.

## Teacher's Resources

**Resource Book**
Teacher's Instructions, page 29
**Tests and Activities**
Chapter 3 Activity 3-1, page 19
**Demonstration Overheads**
Overhead J

## Background

**Reading Gauges** It is important to know the normal reading of a gauge. This allows you to recognize when the gauge reading is not normal and indicates that something is wrong.

The next step is to learn what warnings mean and what actions are required. Many drivers see the gauge or warning light but fail to understand the message being given.

### Objectives

1. Identify each gauge and warning light on an instrument panel and explain its function.
2. Explain the purpose of each control used to operate a vehicle.
3. Describe the use of the safety, communication, and comfort devices.

The **alternator warning light** or gauge warns that the battery is being drained. The more electricity used, the sooner the battery will be dead. Turn off as many electrical devices as possible, and have the system checked without delay.

**Brake System Warning Light (8)**
This warning light serves two purposes. First, the light reminds you to release the parking brake before moving the vehicle. Second, if the light comes on while you are pressing the foot brake, or while you are driving, it means that part or all of the braking system is not working properly. If this occurs, brake gradually to a stop, have the vehicle towed, and have the problem corrected.

**Antilock Braking System Light (9)**
This light tells you if the **antilock braking system (ABS)** is functioning properly. ABS keeps the wheels from locking if the driver brakes hard. If this light comes on, it indicates a problem with the system.

**Safety Belt Light (10)** This light reminds you to fasten your safety belt before moving your vehicle. This light comes on when you turn the key. In some vehicles the light stays on for a few seconds after the engine is started.

**Air Bag Warning Light (11)** This light tells you if the air bags are in proper working condition. When the ignition is turned on, the air-bag light comes on for a few seconds and then goes off. If the air bags are not in proper operating condition, the warning light will stay on.

**Turn-Signal Indicators (12)** These indicators tell you the direction you have signaled to turn. Each indicator is usually a small green arrow that flashes when you signal for a turn. The arrow stops flashing after you make the turn or when the turn signal is cancelled.

**High-Beam Indicator (13)** This light glows when the high-beam headlights are on. This indicator usually appears as a small light in some area of the instrument panel.

### Vehicle Controls

The characteristics and locations of vehicle controls vary from one model to another. However, each control performs the same function in each vehicle. The numbers in the pictures on the next four pages match the controls explained.

Your car's instrument panel might look different, but all vehicles have similar devices to provide information.

Chapter 3 Basic Vehicle Control **41**

## Explain

Emphasize that knowing the location of gauges, warning lights, controls, and devices enables the driver to look at or operate them without interfering with driving the vehicle. Point out that trying to learn where they are while driving the vehicle is dangerous. For example, it is important to know where the fuel gauge is and how to read it before you run out of gasoline.

## Demonstrate

Use the owner's manual to show students the instrument panel of the driver education car. You can photocopy the appropriate pages for each student. You can also make an overheard transparency from the photocopy. As an alternative, you can photograph the driver education car's controls.

Have students practice identifying the instruments presented on the pages of this lesson.

## Special Needs

Review the descriptions and functions of the controls and gauges. Help students find them on the driver education car. Ask parents or other adult family members to help special needs students locate and describe the functions of the controls and gauges and to quiz the students. Then have the students draw and label the instrument panel of their families' vehicles.

## Discuss

Discuss that while driving a vehicle with power steering, steering becomes much more difficult when the engine fails. However, one is still able to steer the vehicle by putting an extra amount of force into the steering effort.

## Discuss

Discuss the possible positions of the selector lever and gear-shift lever. Note that they may be located on the steering column or on the console. Refer students to the pictures on page 48.

## Explain

Use the illustration at the bottom of this page to explain the various key positions on the ignition switch. When starting the vehicle, emphasize the importance of releasing twisting pressure as soon as the engine starts, to avoid grinding the starter.

Devices for starting and controlling the movement of a vehicle.

### SAFE DRIVING

Cruise control should *never* be used when road surfaces are wet or slippery or in heavy traffic. You have much less control if a conflict occurs. Using cruise control in areas of steep grades wastes fuel and puts added stress on the engine.

**Steering Wheel (14)**  The steering wheel controls the direction of the front wheels. Turn right to go right; turn left to go left. Use the same steering procedure when backing the vehicle.

**Steering Wheel Adjustment Lever (15)**  Some vehicles have an adjustable steering wheel. The wheel can be tilted up or down for better driving comfort.

**Selector Lever (16)**  Move the selector lever in an automatic transmission vehicle to choose forward or reverse gear. This control is located on the steering column or on the **console.** The console is the compartment mounted between the front seats in a vehicle.

**Gear-Shift Lever (17)**  In a stickshift vehicle, shift gears by moving the shift lever to the desired position. This lever is located on the console.

**Ignition and Starter Switch (18)** Start the engine by putting the key into the **ignition switch.** The picture below shows all of the positions of the key in the starter switch.

**Cruise Control (19)**  This is an optional feature you can have on your vehicle. **Cruise control** is a device that lets you maintain your desired speed without keeping your foot on the accelerator. Tap the footbrake pedal to cancel cruise control.

**Parking Brake (20)**  The parking brake keeps the vehicle in place when it is parked. In many vehicles the parking brake is a pedal located on the far left. Push down on the pedal to set the parking brake. To release the parking brake, push down on the pedal until you hear a click, then lift your foot off the pedal. Some vehicles have a brake-release lever on the left side under the instrument panel. In other vehicles, the parking brake is a lever mounted on the floor or on the

**Lock:** position of key when engine is off. Steering wheel and shift lever are locked in position.

**On:** position of key when engine is running.

**Accessory:** can be used to run accessories (lights radio, etc.) without running engine.

**Start:** position of key to start engine; release when engine starts.

Positions of the key in the starter switch (18)

### Activity

#### In-Class Driving Rehearsal
Have students pretend they are sitting in the driver education car and locate all the basic vehicle controls. Divide the class into groups of three and have students take turns pretending to be the driver. The other two students should offer feedback as the driver locates each control. You can use the checklist for Activity 3-1 in **Activities and Tests,** page 19, or you can make your own checklist of the controls you want the drivers to identify.

All vehicles have a foot-brake pedal and an accelerator pedal. Some vehicles also have a clutch pedal and/or brake pedal.

console to the right of the driver's seat. Push in the button at the tip of the lever and lower the lever to release this type of brake.

**Clutch Pedal (21)** In a stickshift vehicle, the **clutch pedal** is located to the left of the foot-brake pedal. Pushing this pedal down lets you shift gears.

**Foot-Brake Pedal (22)** Pushing down on the foot-brake pedal slows or stops the vehicle. Depressing this pedal also turns on the brake lights in the back of the vehicle.

**Accelerator Pedal (23)** The accelerator pedal is located to the right of the foot-brake pedal. Pushing the accelerator down increases speed; releasing it slows the vehicle.

### Devices for Safety, Communication, and Comfort

Locate and understand the operation of the following devices on any vehicle you drive.

**Safety Belts (24)** Always wear your safety belt when your vehicle is in motion. Safety belts are your best protection against injury in a collision. Fasten your safety belt to a

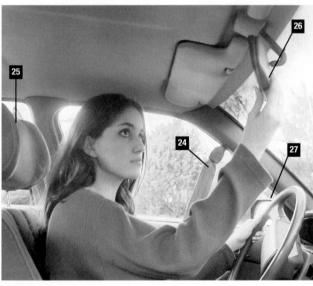

Safety devices help protect you and your passengers.

Chapter 3  Basic Vehicle Control  **43**

## Discuss

Ask: Why is it a good habit always to apply the parking brake? (The parking brake is the primary method of keeping the vehicle secured. In addition to setting the parking brake, you should shift into PARK for a vehicle with automatic transmission and shift into FIRST or REVERSE for a vehicle with manual transmission.)

## Background

**Steering Wheel Tilt** The tilt adjustment of a steering wheel should be positioned to avoid having the air bag directed in an upward force to the face. A lower position adjustment to have the air bag make contact with the driver's chest is best.

## Demonstrate

Use **Demonstration Overhead J** and the yellow transparency car to show the locations of the mirror's blind spots. Use an erasable marker to draw lines to indicate the blind spots, as shown in the picture in the student text. Explain that anything inside these lines will not be seen when that mirror is checked. Move a transparency car from the Demonstration Overheads in various positions to the rear, left-rear, and right-rear of the yellow car. Ask students if they would be able to see the car if they were the driver.

You can also demonstrate blind spots with the driver education car. Have students stand in different positions while a student observes from the driver's seat when they can see students in each mirror. Have students take turns observing. See **Resource Book,** page 29 for more use of this activity.

The dark shading indicates "blind spots"— areas that you cannot see with your mirrors.

## What Do You Think?

Do you think that a federal law should be passed requiring all drivers in the country to have their headlights on whenever they are driving? Why or why not?

snug fit before starting your engine. Most states require drivers and passengers to wear safety belts.

**Head Restraints (25)** Most vehicles have **head restraints,** padded devices on the backs of front seats. Head restraints help reduce whiplash injuries in a collision, especially if your vehicle is struck from the rear.

### Inside and Outside Rearview Mirrors (26–27)

The inside mirror (26) shows the view through the rear window. The left outside mirror (27) shows a view to the left and rear of your vehicle. The right outside mirror shows a view to the right rear. Even when these mirrors are adjusted properly, there are areas they cannot show the driver. These areas, as shown here, are called **blind-spot areas.** For this reason, *never* rely completely on your

rearview mirrors when turning. Always glance over your shoulders to check these areas before changing lanes.

**Horn (28)** The horn usually is located on the steering wheel. Know how to use the horn on each vehicle you drive.

**Hazard Flasher Control (29)** This switch usually is located on the steering column or on the instrument panel. When the **hazard flasher** is on, both front and rear turn-signal lights flash at the same time. These lights warn others that your vehicle is a hazard or that you are in trouble.

**Turn-Signal Lever (30)** This lever is located on the left side of the steering column. Move the lever up to signal a right turn and down to signal a left turn. The turn signal stops flashing when the steering wheel is straightened. You might have to cancel a signal manually if the turn is slight. Hold the signal up or down lightly to signal a lane change. When released, it will cancel.

**Windshield Wipers and Washers (31)** One switch usually operates both the wipers and the washer to clean the outside of the windshield. This control is often mounted on the turn-signal lever. Use a windshield antifreeze solution in winter in the windshield washer container under the hood.

**Light Switch (32)** The light switch is usually a knob or switch located on the left of the instrument panel or on the turn-signal lever. In some vehicles it may be a separate lever

## Activity

**Class Activity** Ask students to check the location of the parking brake in any vehicle in which they regularly ride—family minivan, friend's truck, school bus, etc. In addition to checking the location of the brake, have students observe how the brake is engaged and how it is released. Make this assignment at the end of one week and ask students to share their results at the end of the next week.

These are some of the instruments that control safety and comfort.

attached to the steering column. This device controls headlights, taillights, and side-marker lights, as well as the instrument panel, license plate, and dome light. You can change the headlights from low to high beam by using the dimmer switch, usually located on the turn-signal lever.

**Hood Release Lever (33)** This lever usually is located on the left side under the instrument panel. Pull this lever to release the hood. You will need to operate a second release in the front of the vehicle before the hood will open.

**Heater, Air Conditioner, and Defroster** Heating and air-conditioning systems warm or cool the inside of the vehicle. The defroster keeps the windshield and windows free of moisture. Some vehicles have a separate switch for a rear-window defroster.

**Sun Visor** The sun visors are located above the windshield. Pull the visor down or to the side, to help cut glare from bright sun.

**Seat Adjustment Lever** This lever is usually located at the lower front or left side of the driver's seat. In vehicles with electric seats, the controls are usually on the lower left side of the driver's seat.

## Review It

1. What warnings do the temperature gauge, oil pressure gauge, and brake system lights give you?
2. What is the purpose of the ignition and starter switch?
3. Why must you not rely completely on what your rearview mirrors show you?

---

## Explain

Explain that when adjusting the sun visor you need to make certain that the edge of the visor is not directed at your head. Such a position can cause injuries during a collision. The visors should always be pointing away from the driver and passengers.

## 3 Assess

### Answers to Review It

**1.** The temperature gauge warns you when the coolant in the engine is too hot. The oil pressure gauge warns you when the oil is not circulating at the proper pressure; it does not tell you if there is enough oil in the engine. The brake system warning light serves two purposes. It reminds you to release the parking brake. If it comes on while you are driving, it indicates that a part or all of the brake system is not working properly. (pp. 40–41)

**2.** The ignition and starter switch is used to start the vehicle, run accessories, turn off the engine, and lock the steering wheel. (p. 42)

**3.** Even when mirrors are adjusted properly, there are blind-spot areas. (p. 44)

# Getting Ready to Drive

## 1 Focus

## Summary

This lesson emphasizes the things you need to do before you drive. It focuses on outside checks, getting into the vehicle, and inside checks.

## 2 Teach

## Explain

Explain that the way a driver should approach a vehicle and enter it is different from how a passenger enters the vehicle. Most of us spent at least 16 years as a passenger before becoming a driver. As drivers, we are responsible for the vehicle and its passengers. To gain a driver's perspective requires consciously practicing a set of behaviors until they become habit.

## Discuss

Discuss why it is important for a driver to enter a vehicle by walking around the front and then toward the back. Discuss other safety procedures a driver should follow. See **Resource Book** page 83 for a list of safety tips for driving.

## Objectives

1. List in order the checks you make when preparing to drive.
2. Describe how to enter a vehicle from the street side.
3. Describe the correct positioning of the seat and outside rearview mirrors.

**B**efore you take your place behind the wheel to drive, you should follow certain checks and procedures. People who just get into a vehicle and drive away, with little thought or concern for themselves or others, are demonstrating high-risk driving behaviors.

Inspect your vehicle and the area around it before you get in to drive. An oil stain under the vehicle, for example, indicates there could be a problem.

Be alert for small children playing near your vehicle. Many deaths each year are attributed to driveway back ups. Also look for tools, toys, or any kind of debris that might be near your vehicle. Follow the same steps in the same order each time you get ready to drive to develop safe pre-driving habits.

### Outside Checks

1. Walk around your vehicle with keys in hand and look for objects in the path you intend to take. Also look for water or oil marks under the vehicle.
2. Glance at the tires to see they are inflated properly.
3. Notice the direction the front wheels are pointed. If they are not pointed straight ahead, your vehicle will go to the left or right as soon as you begin to drive.
4. Make sure the windshield, windows, headlights, and taillights

are clear. If windows are covered with snow or ice, clear them completely. Do not clear off just enough for a "peephole."
5. Check the back window ledge for loose objects. Remove any objects before driving.
6. Look inside the vehicle to be sure you do not have unwanted passengers.

If you have been driving for some time on wet roadways, your headlights may be covered with road dirt. Develop the habit of cleaning the headlights often, and clean them every time you get fuel.

Once you have completed all the outside checks, follow these steps in order to safely enter your vehicle.

### Getting into the Vehicle

1. If you enter your vehicle from the street side, have your keys in hand ready to unlock the door. If you use a remote-control device, unlock the vehicle before you walk into the street.
2. Walk around the front of the vehicle toward the back. You then can see oncoming traffic and reduce the risk of being hit. Do not open the door if an oncoming vehicle is near.
3. Get in quickly, close the door, and lock it. Put the key in the ignition.

## Teacher's Resources

**In-Car Checklists**
In-Car Checklists 1, 2

**Resource Book**
Information, page 83

## Activity

**In-Class Driving Rehearsal**
Have students practice appropriate posture for driving. Have the students pretend their chair is the driver's seat of a car. Direct them to lean slightly forward, slide themselves all the way back, and then sit up straight. Ask: Can you feel the support of the chair's back? For contrast, have the students slouch down in their chairs. Ask: Do you feel the lack of support to your back now? Then have them sit up straight again for comparison.

## Inside Checks

1. Lock all doors. Locked doors are less likely to fly open in a collision.
2. Adjust the seat for comfort and best control of foot pedals and steering wheel. Sit with your back firmly against the back of the seat. Sit high enough to see over the steering wheel. Adjust the seat so you are at least 10 inches back from the hub of the wheel to avoid injury in a crash.
3. Your hands should be in a balanced, comfortable position on the steering wheel with your elbows slightly bent. Reach for the accelerator and brake pedal with your right foot to judge a comfortable distance. Your knees should be slightly bent.
4. Adjust the head restraint to the middle of the back of your head.

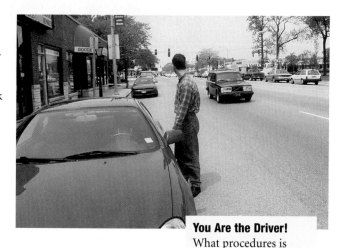

**You Are the Driver!**
What procedures is the driver following to enter the car safely?

5. Adjust the inside rearview mirror so it shows the area behind you through the rear window.
6. Adjust the left and right outside rearview mirrors so they show a slight amount of the sides of the vehicle.
7. Fasten your safety belt and ask all passengers to fasten theirs.

10 inches

Make adjustments so you are comfortable before driving.

### Review It

1. What outside checks should you make before entering the vehicle?
2. Why should you walk around the front of the vehicle when entering from the street side?
3. What is the correct way to position the driver's seat and mirrors of your vehicle?

Chapter 3  Basic Vehicle Control **47**

## Explain

Explain that a console between the two front seats on some vehicles makes it impractical for the driver to enter or leave a vehicle from the curb side.

## 3 Assess

### Answers to Review It

1. Outside checks should include checking for objects in your intended path, looking for water or oil marks under the vehicle, glancing at tires to check inflation, checking which way the front wheels are pointed, making sure all windows and lights are clear, checking back window ledge for loose objects, and checking for unwanted passengers. (p. 46)

2. Walking around the front of the vehicle when entering from the street side allows you to see oncoming traffic. (p. 46)

3. The driver's seat should be adjusted so that you can sit with your back firmly against the back of the seat. If the vehicle has an air bag, the seat should be adjusted so that you are at least 10 inches from the hub of the steering wheel. The inside rearview mirror should show the area behind you through the rear window. The outside rearview mirrors should show just the side of the vehicle and the lane to the rear. (p. 47)

## Activity

**In-Class Driving Rehearsal** In this activity students will practice the procedures for getting ready to drive. Divide the class into groups of three. Have each group use two chairs, side-by-side, to simulate a car. One student in each group should perform the outside checks while the other two observe and provide feedback using the information provided on pages 46–47. The second student in each group should demonstrate the procedure for getting into the vehicle while the other members of the group observe and provide feedback. The last student in the group should perform the inside checks.

As time permits, the activity should be repeated until each student has practiced each of the three procedures at least once.

# Driving a Vehicle with Automatic Transmission

## 1 Focus

### Summary

This lesson introduces basic concepts related to a vehicle with an automatic transmission. The selector-lever positions are described and illustrated. Information about starting the engine, hand positions, and steering is included. Instructions for putting the vehicle in motion, along with stopping, securing, and leaving the vehicle, are provided.

### Vocabulary

*backup lights, shift indicator, target*

## 2 Teach

### Demonstrate

Use the illustrations to demonstrate the possible locations of the selector lever and the gear indicators—on the steering column or on the console to the right of the driver. Point out that various makes and models of vehicles have different gear positions and indicators.

### Objectives

1. Explain the use of each gear.
2. Describe the procedure for starting an automatic transmission vehicle.
3. List the steps for putting an automatic transmission vehicle in motion.
4. Tell the correct procedure to follow when leaving an automatic transmission vehicle from the street side.

Learning the correct steps for starting, moving, and stopping an automatic transmission vehicle is not difficult. You choose the gear you want by moving the gear selector lever. Practice each step in the correct order so that the procedures become a habit.

### Selector-Lever Positions

The **shift indicator** shows the gear positions. This indicator may be located on the steering column, on the instrument panel, or on the console to the right of the driver. The first picture shows the shift indicator on the instrument panel and tells you the vehicle is in PARK. The second picture shows the indicator mounted on the console and tells you the vehicle is in PARK.

**PARK (P)** This gear position locks the transmission. Your vehicle should be in PARK before you start driving. You should also shift to PARK every time you stop driving since the vehicle cannot roll in this gear. Never shift to PARK when the vehicle is moving.

In many vehicles you can remove the key from the ignition only when the lever is in PARK.

**REVERSE (R)** This gear is used for backing. Always come to a complete stop before shifting into REVERSE. Expensive damage to the transmission can result from shifting to REVERSE when the vehicle is moving forward.

When you shift to REVERSE, the **backup lights** come on. These are white lights at the rear and tell others that you are backing.

**NEUTRAL (N)** This position allows the wheels to roll without engine power. If the engine stalls while you are driving, shift to NEUTRAL (not PARK) to restart the engine. Shift to NEUTRAL if you are stopped in traffic for more than a few minutes.

**DRIVE (D)** This position is for moving forward. To keep your vehicle from "jumping" forward, keep firm pressure on the brake pedal every time you shift to DRIVE.

Gear indicators can be on the control panel or on the console.

## Teacher's Resources

**Resource Book**
Teacher's Instructions, pages 30–32

**In-Car Checklists**
In-Car Checklists 3, 4, 5

Many vehicles are equipped with overdrive, shown by a "D." At speeds of 40–45 mph the vehicle automatically shifts into overdrive. Driving in this gear saves fuel and can be used for all normal forward driving.

LOW (**L1 and L2, or 1 and 2**)  These positions allow the engine to send more power to the wheels at lower speeds. Both positions are for slow, hard pulling and for going up and down steep hills. LOW 2 is used when driving in snow. Use LOW 1 when going up or down very steep grades and when pulling heavy loads.

### Starting the Engine

Use this procedure to start the engine of a vehicle with an automatic transmission. The pictures correspond to the steps listed.

1. Make sure the parking brake is set.
2. Make sure the selector lever is in PARK. If you are starting the vehicle after the engine has stalled, place the selector lever in NEUTRAL.
3. Keep your foot off the accelerator.
4. Turn the ignition switch to On. Continue turning the key to start the engine. Release the key as soon as the engine starts.
5. Check the gauges, warning lights, and fuel supply.

Never try to start the engine when it is already running. Expensive damage to the starter can result. Press lightly on the accelerator so you will know whether or not the engine is running. When in doubt, turn the key to "Off" and repeat the starting procedure.

These steps illustrate the basic procedure for starting a vehicle with an automatic transmission.

### Hand Positions for Controlled Steering

Steering is not just a matter of pointing the vehicle in the direction you want it to go. Controlled steering involves a comfortable and balanced hand position on the steering wheel.

Using the proper grip on the steering wheel is just as important as using the proper grip in sports like tennis or golf. With your hands in a comfortable position on the rim of the steering wheel, grip the wheel firmly on each side in a balanced position.

Imagine that the steering wheel is the face of a clock. Many drivers place their hands at the 10 o'clock and 2 o'clock, or the 9 o'clock and 3 o'clock, positions. Other drivers place their hands at the 8 o'clock

## Explain

Describe how to use the selector lever when it is located on the steering column. Explain that there are four possibilities for hand position and direction of hand movement. The shift will be in the palm with the palm facing up, or with the palm facing down. The hand will either move toward the driver's body or away from the driver's body. For example, to shift from PARK to DRIVE the hand goes under the lever with the palm up and the motion is toward the driver's body. To go from DRIVE to NEUTRAL the palm is facing down on top of the lever and the motion is away from the driver's body. Using this method the lever will stop automatically in NEUTRAL. To go from DRIVE to REVERSE or to PARK the palm is facing up and the motion is away from the driver. To go from DRIVE to LOW the palm is facing up and the motion is toward the driver.

## Activity

**In-Class Driving Rehearsal**  In this activity students will simulate moving an automatic selector lever located on the steering column. The objective is to be able to shift the selector lever with the palms of their hands without wrapping their fingers around it. Have students practice by holding a pencil with the thumb and index finger of the left hand to represent an automatic selector lever. They will then shift the pencil with the palm of the right hand while always keeping the fingers extended. Announce a gear and have the students use the proper technique to simulate moving the selector lever to that gear. Continue until all students are making the correct motions consistently.

## Explain

Use the illustration at the top of the page to point out the proper hand positions on the steering wheel. Emphasize the importance of gripping the steering wheel firmly in a balanced position.

## Explain

Explain that when putting a vehicle parked on the left side of a one-way street in motion, the driver should look over the right shoulder to see if any vehicle is approaching from the rear before entering the traffic flow.

and 4 o'clock positions. To avoid injury from an airbag in your vehicle's steering wheel during a collision, keep your hands between the 9 and 3 o'clock position and the 8 and 4 o'clock position.

Always keep your knuckles outside the rim of the steering wheel. Some safety specialists recommend that the thumbs also be outside the rim of the steering wheel to reduce injury in a collision.

### Steering the Vehicle

Once you have selected your comfortable and balanced hand position, you are ready to develop steering-control techniques. Begin your steering practice by picking a **target** far out in the distance. A target is a stationary object that appears in the distance in the center of your path of travel. The target is really the "aiming point" where you want your vehicle to go. Look far ahead to identify clues and hazards that could cause conflicts. In Chapter 4 you will learn different systems of seeing and identifying all the critical areas around your vehicle.

Keeping your vehicle in a straight line requires slight but critical steer-

Don't use the road lines as a guide for where to look when you practice steering.

## Activity

**In-Class Driving Rehearsal**  This activity will help students learn how to aim toward a target while steering. Give all students a simulated steering wheel. Direct the students to stand and hold the steering wheel in a 9 and 3 position. Tell students that you will represent the target. Have all students turn their head to look directly at you and then move the steering wheel until you appear in the center of it.

Move your position to the left or right side of the room. Have students turn their head to look directly at you and then turn the steering wheel to get on target. Walk to the back of the classroom, having students turning their head and steering wheel to keep you in alignment with the center of the steering wheel. Continue doing the activity by walking about the classroom, having the students keeping on target. Give students positive feedback. See **Resource Book,** page 30 for additional information on conducting this activity.

ing corrections. Avoid looking directly in front of your vehicle. Do not use the road lines as guides when you practice steering. Making these mistakes, as the pictures on the bottom of page 50 show, does not allow you to see far in the distance toward the path you want to follow.

Once you learn how to make steering adjustments, you will make them automatically. You then can concentrate on the total driving task.

Most vehicles are now equipped with air bags. Even with an air bag as an added safety device, it is extremely important that you always wear your safety belt when you travel in a vehicle.

### Putting the Vehicle in Motion

After you have started the engine and checked all the gauges, you are ready to put your vehicle in motion. Follow these steps in the same order each time you move your vehicle. The numbered steps correspond to the numbered pictures above.

1. Press firmly on the foot brake.
2. Move the selector lever to DRIVE.
3. Release the parking brake while still pressing the foot-brake pedal.
4. Check for traffic ahead and in rearview mirrors. Look over your left shoulder to see if a vehicle is approaching from the rear.
5. If you are going to move away from the right curb, use the left turn signal to alert other drivers. Check mirrors again.

Putting the vehicle in motion

6. When you know the roadway is clear, release the foot-brake pedal and press gently on the accelerator to increase speed smoothly.
7. Quickly check again over your left shoulder for traffic.
8. Cancel the signal, if necessary.
9. As you reach your desired speed, let up a little on the accelerator. Adjust your speed to traffic.

For best control of the brake pedal and accelerator, rest the heel of your foot on the floor. This position lets you pivot the front part of your foot back and forth between the two pedals as you drive.

In a vehicle with automatic transmission, always come to a full stop before shifting to another gear. This keeps your vehicle from moving before you are ready.

## Explain

Describe how to use the accelerator and brake pedals effectively. (Have students practice by doing the Activity below.) The driver should place the ball of his or her right foot on the brake pedal with the heel resting on the floor directly in alignment with the brake pedal. This allows the leg and foot to be in a straight line while applying the brake, which will give maximum braking control. At the beginning of the braking process, apply as much braking pressure as needed. Then, during the last two seconds before the vehicle stops, release some pressure to change the pitch of the vehicle gradually to eliminate the jerky bouncing of the pitch force.

The heel of the foot stays in place while the foot pivots to make contact with the accelerator. The driver should practice applying pressure to the accelerator in the following manner: Press the accelerator very slightly for the first second then gradually add pressure as speed is to be increased.

## Explain

Point out that for smooth starts and stops you need to squeeze rather than push on the accelerator and foot-brake pedals.

## Activity

**In-Class Driving Rehearsal** In this activity students will practice how to use the accelerator and brake pedals effectively. You will need small oblong balloons and file folders for half of the students. Have students pair off. Give each pair a balloon and a file folder. Have students inflate balloons to nine or ten inches. Insert the balloon inside the file folder. Roll the end of the folder over just enough to cover the balloon with an inch or two of excess folder. Staple the two ends of the excess folder to capture the balloon inside. Cover the seam and staples with masking or duct tape (to be the up side). Draw a 2" X 5" accelerator pedal on the right edge of the up side of the folder. Two inches to the left draw a 5" X 2" brake pedal. Have students take turns as the driver to apply braking or acceleration pressure without breaking the balloon while using correct methods. For more directions on how to construct and conduct this activity, see **Resource Book,** pages 31–32.

## Explain

Emphasize the importance of removing the key from the ignition before leaving the vehicle. Insurance coverage may be canceled if the key is in the ignition when a vehicle is stolen.

## 3 Assess

### Answers to Review It

**1.** PARK (P) locks the transmission. REVERSE (R) is used for backing. NEUTRAL (N) allows the wheels to roll without engine power. DRIVE (D) is used for moving forward. LOW (L1 and L2, or 1 and 2) allows the engine to send more power to the wheels at lower speeds. (pp. 48–49)

**2.** Make sure the parking brake is set and the selector lever is in PARK. Turn the ignition switch to *On* and continue turning the key to start the engine. (p. 49)

**3.** Press firmly on the foot brake and move the selector lever to DRIVE. Release the parking brake while still pressing the foot-brake pedal. Check for traffic and use your turn signal if appropriate. When you know the roadway is clear, release the foot-brake pedal and press gently on the accelerator. (p. 51)

**4.** Check inside and outside mirrors. Make sure you have your keys. Glance over your left shoulder before opening the door. When it is safe, open the door and get out quickly. Lock the vehicle and walk around the rear of the vehicle so you can see approaching traffic. (p. 52)

Stopping the vehicle

Securing the vehicle

### Stopping the Vehicle

The numbered steps correspond to the numbered pictures.

1. Check traffic in both mirrors before slowing down.
2. Let up on the accelerator.
3. Tap the foot brake lightly.
4. Gradually press down on the foot-brake pedal. Ease up on the brake just before stopping. Leave the selector lever in DRIVE if you plan to start moving again immediately. Otherwise, shift to PARK.

### Securing the Vehicle

This procedure applies to both automatic and stickshift vehicles.

1. Once you have stopped, continue pressing the foot brake.
2. Shift to PARK in an automatic or to REVERSE in a stickshift vehicle.
3. Set the parking brake. Turn off all accessories. Close all windows.
4. Turn off the ignition switch. Remove the key. Release the foot brake.
5. Unfasten your safety belt.
6. Lock all doors.

### Leaving the Vehicle

If you leave the vehicle from the street side, follow these steps.

1. Check inside and outside mirrors.
2. Make sure you have your keys.
3. Glance over your left shoulder before opening the door.
4. When it is safe, open the door and get out quickly.
5. Make sure all doors are locked. Walk around the rear of the vehicle to reduce your risk of being hit.

### Review It

1. What is the purpose of each gear in an automatic transmission?
2. How do you start an automatic transmission vehicle?
3. How do you put an automatic transmission vehicle in motion?
4. What procedure do you follow when leaving the vehicle?

## Activity

### In-Class Driving Rehearsal

In this activity students will practice the procedures for putting the vehicle in motion. Divide the class into groups of three. Have each group use two chairs, side-by-side, to simulate a vehicle. One student in each group should perform all nine steps for putting the vehicle in motion while the other two observe and provide feedback using the information provided on this page. The activity should be repeated until each student has practiced each of the procedures at least once.

Learning to drive a vehicle with manual (stickshift) transmission is not difficult, especially if you already know how to drive an automatic transmission vehicle. You must learn how to coordinate using the clutch with the accelerator and gearshift lever. The key to mastering stickshift driving is to engage the clutch smoothly and control the **friction point.** The friction point is where you feel the engine take hold and the vehicle starts to move.

### Selector-Lever Positions

Most stickshift vehicles have either a four-speed or a five-speed shift pattern as the pictures below show. REVERSE is usually in the upper-left corner, or in the lower-left or right corner.

FOURTH gear is used for highway driving, and FIFTH gear is used for speeds over 45 or 50 mph. These gears save fuel because they allow the engine to run slower at any speed.

### Using Stickshift Gears

NEUTRAL (N) This position is the crossbar of the pattern. Use this gear when standing still or when starting the engine.

FIRST (1) Use FIRST gear to start the vehicle moving to a forward speed of 10 to 15 mph. Use FIRST gear also to pull heavy loads and when driving up or down steep hills.

SECOND (2) Use SECOND gear to accelerate to a speed of 15 to 25 mph. Use SECOND gear also for hills or driving on snow or ice.

THIRD (3) Use THIRD gear to accelerate to speeds of 25 to 40 mph.

FOURTH (4) In a four-speed transmission, use FOURTH gear for highway driving. Shift to FOURTH gear at speeds above 35 mph.

FIFTH (5) In a five-speed transmission, use FIFTH gear to drive at speeds over 45 or 50 mph.

REVERSE (R) This gear is used for backing. Never shift into REVERSE while the vehicle is moving forward.

### Using the Clutch

Always press the clutch pedal to the floor before starting the engine, before shifting, or before coming to a stop. Shift smoothly from one gear position to the next. The speeds given here for shifting are only guidelines. Read your owner's manual to know the recommended shifting speeds for your vehicle.

Typical patterns of gear positions for four- and five-speed transmissions. Positions may vary, especially for REVERSE.

### Objectives

1. List the procedures for starting a stickshift vehicle.
2. Tell the correct procedure for moving a stickshift vehicle in FIRST gear.
3. Explain the procedure for stopping from higher gears.
4. Define downshifting and explain its purpose.

---

## Teacher's Resources

**Resource Book**
Teacher's Instructions, pages 33–34

**In-Car Checklists**
In-Car Checklists 37, 38, 39

## Activity

**In-Class Driving Rehearsal** This activity is designed to help students learn to shift with the open-palm method (see Explain on page 54). You will need to make one or more shifting simulators by attaching a piece of dowel to a compression spring and mounting it in a box (see **Resource Book,** pages 33–34).

Have students use the shifting simulator to practice correct application of shifting techniques. Emphasize the importance of being able to shift properly without looking at the selector lever by using the open-palm method.

---

# Driving a Vehicle with Manual Transmission

## 1 Focus

## Summary

This lesson introduces basic concepts related to a vehicle with a manual transmission. The selector-lever positions are described and illustrated. Information about starting the engine and using stickshift gears is included. Instructions for putting the vehicle in motion, along with shifting and stopping, are provided.

## Vocabulary

*downshifting, friction point, riding the clutch*

## 2 Teach

## Explain

A stickshift vehicle requires the driver to coordinate the engine's revolutions to the vehicle's drive wheels by use of the clutch and shift lever. In an automatic transmission this is coordinated without the driver's involvement.

## Explain

Explain to students how to use the open-palm method so that they can easily shift without looking at the shift lever. Students should position the open palm on the shift knob rather than gripping the shift lever. Once they know the location of each gear, they can learn the right feel as they shift gears. Suggest that students practice shifting from low gears to high gears first, and then practice downshifting.

## Apply

Students who have access to a vehicle with manual transmission can practice using stickshift gears without driving the vehicle. Tell students to sit in the vehicle without the engine running and have the parking brake on. Tell them to avoid looking at their hands by focusing vision on some point outside of the vehicle. They can simulate the procedures outlined on these pages. Remind students to get permission from the vehicle's owner and to practice with a responsible adult.

Putting the vehicle in motion

Do not develop the habit of **riding the clutch.** That means resting your foot on the clutch pedal while driving. This practice causes clutch wear and can lead to expensive repairs.

### Starting the Engine

Follow these steps to start a vehicle with manual transmission:

1. Be sure the parking brake is set.
2. Press the clutch pedal to the floor with your left foot.
3. Put the gear-shift lever in NEUTRAL.
4. Turn on ignition switch and check warning lights.
5. Turn the key forward until the engine starts, then release it.

### Putting the Vehicle in Motion

Once the engine is running, follow these steps to put the vehicle in motion. Each numbered step is pictured.

1. Press the clutch pedal to the floor.
2. Move the gear-shift lever to FIRST.
3. Depress the foot brake and release the parking brake.
4. Check traffic ahead and in rear-view mirrors. If you are moving away from the curb, glance over your left shoulder to see if any vehicle is approaching from the rear.
5. Use the turn signal to alert other drivers.
6. If the roadway is clear, accelerate gently and gradually and release the clutch slowly to the friction point. Releasing the clutch suddenly causes the vehicle to jerk forward or stall the engine.
7. Hold the clutch momentarily at the friction point until the vehicle starts to move.
8. Continue gradual acceleration, and let the clutch up all the way.

### Shifting from FIRST to SECOND

At about 10 to 15 mph follow these steps to shift from FIRST to SECOND:

1. Press the clutch down and release the accelerator at the same time.
2. Move the gear-shift lever to SECOND. Pause slightly as you go across NEUTRAL into SECOND. This action helps you shift more smoothly.

54  Unit 1  The Driving Task

---

### Background

**Shifting Gears** The transmission allows the driver to change the amount of power, or torque, that is applied to the tires. Lower gears are designed for pulling power while higher gears are designed to obtain higher speeds.

When the transmission is in FIRST gear there is more leverage, or power, going to the tires to help get the vehicle moving. Pressing on the accelerator pedal feeds fuel to the engine to increase its revolutions. Once the vehicle gets moving, there is less resistance; therefore less power is needed. To change the amount of power going to the tires, you need to shift to another gear.

Before you can shift gears you need to disengage the transmission from the engine. You do this by pressing on the clutch pedal. When you take your foot off the clutch pedal, a plate from the engine comes in contact with a plate from the transmission. These are held together by friction to allow the engine to rotate the gears in the transmission.

Stopping from FIRST, SECOND, or REVERSE

3. Accelerate gently as you slowly release the clutch. Hesitate briefly at the friction point, then release the clutch all the way.

**Stopping from FIRST, SECOND, or REVERSE**

The pictures on this page correspond to these steps:
1. Check traffic in mirrors.
2. Press the clutch pedal down while releasing accelerator.
3. Tap the brake pedal lightly to signal for a stop.
4. Press the foot brake gently to a stop.
5. Shift to NEUTRAL when stopped.

**Shifting to THIRD, FOURTH, and FIFTH**

Once you have accelerated to the higher-speed ranges described for THIRD, FOURTH, and FIFTH gears, follow these step for shifting:

1. Press the clutch down.
2. Release the accelerator.
3. Shift to the desired gear. Do not hurry the shift or you may shift to the wrong gear.
4. Accelerate gradually while releasing the clutch smoothly.

DRIVE RIGHT
**DID YOU KNOW?**

SHIFTING GEARS There is no one correct speed for shifting from one gear to another. Speed for each gear depends on engine power and type of transmission. As you drive different stickshift vehicles, you will develop a feel for proper accelerating and shifting in each one.

## Explain

Explain the importance of pressing the clutch all the way to the floor before moving the gearshift lever.

## Explain

Explain that coordinating the accelerator and the clutch is critical when moving from a stop. Too little acceleration or a sudden release of the clutch can cause the engine to stall.

## Discuss

Ask: While driving a vehicle with a five-speed manual transmission, in which gear should you be before making a turn from a moving position? (You should be in SECOND gear. This allows you to start the turn with your foot on the brake and still have enough power to accelerate after you reach the halfway point of the turn.)

Ask: What should you do in the following situation? You were driving 45 mph in FIFTH gear when you reduced your speed in preparation for a red light. You are traveling 20 mph when the light changes to green. (You will need to downshift from FIFTH to THIRD to regain power and then go through your upshifting sequence to regain speed.)

## Background

**Gear Patterns** There are two popular gear patterns for passenger vehicles: four speed and five speed. Some vehicles have a three-speed gear selection. Regardless of the gear pattern, the skills a student learns for one pattern can be applied to any shift pattern. The shifting pattern is frequently marked on the selector lever.

## Special Needs

Have students practice the shift pattern with the open-palm method over a drawn shift pattern on a paper placed on a desk, or have them do the Activity on page 53. Have them practice coordinating use of the accelerator and clutch by simulating the movements as you call out the steps.

Chapter 3
Basic Vehicle Control | **55**

## 3 Assess

### Answers to Review It

**1.** Be sure the parking brake is set. Press the clutch pedal to the floor and put the gearshift lever in NEUTRAL. Turn on the ignition switch and check warning lights. Turn the key forward until the engine starts. (p. 54)

**2.** Press the clutch pedal to the floor and move the gearshift lever to FIRST. Depress the foot-brake pedal and release the parking brake. Check for traffic and use your turn signal if appropriate. When you know the roadway is clear, accelerate gradually and release the clutch slowly to the friction point. Hold the clutch momentarily at the friction point until the vehicle starts to move. Continue gradual acceleration and let the clutch up all the way. (p. 54)

**3.** Check the mirrors for traffic. Let up on the accelerator and tap the brake to signal a stop. Slow to about 15 or 20 mph and press the clutch pedal down. Brake to a smooth stop. Shift to NEUTRAL when stopped. (p. 56)

**4.** Downshifting means to shift from a higher to a lower gear. You can downshift for added control, for extra power when climbing long or steep hills, and to prevent wear on the brakes when going down long or steep hills. (p. 56)

Stopping from higher gears

### Stopping from Higher Gears

When stopping from THIRD, FOURTH, or FIFTH, slow down before depressing the clutch. The engine helps slow the vehicle. The pictures on this page correspond to these steps:

1. Check the mirrors for traffic.
2. Let up on the accelerator.
3. Tap the brake to signal a stop.
4. Brake to about 15 to 20 mph.
5. Press the clutch pedal down.
6. Brake to a smooth stop.
7. Shift to NEUTRAL when stopped.

### Downshifting

The term **downshifting** means shifting from a higher to a lower gear. The engine has greater pulling power in lower gears than in higher ones. If you have slowed below 30 mph in FOURTH gear, or if you are going uphill, you must downshift to THIRD in order to regain speed. Follow these steps to downshift:

1. Press the clutch pedal down and shift to THIRD. Accelerate gradually while releasing the clutch.

2. Accelerate to over 30 mph. Press the clutch pedal and shift back to FOURTH gear. If you are going uphill, you may have to stay in third gear longer.

You can downshift for added control, as when slowing before a sharp turn. However, be sure to downshift before starting the turn. You need both hands ready to steer.

You can also downshift to gain extra power when climbing long or steep hills. Use a lower gear to go down long or steep hills to prevent wear on the brakes. Let the clutch out smoothly after every downshift.

### Review It

1. What is the procedure for starting a stickshift vehicle?
2. What are the steps for moving a stickshift vehicle in FIRST gear?
3. What steps should you follow when stopping from higher gears?
4. What is meant by downshifting and for what reasons might you downshift?

## Reviewing Chapter Objectives

### 1. Instruments, Controls, and Devices

1. What is the name and function of each gauge on the instrument panel? (40–41)
2. What is the purpose of each control used to operate a vehicle? (42–43)
3. How do you use the safety, communication, and comfort devices on a vehicle? (43–45)

### 2. Getting Ready to Drive

4. What checks should you make when preparing to drive? (46)
5. How should you enter a vehicle from the street side? (46–47)
6. How do you position the seat and outside rearview mirrors of your vehicle? (47)

### 3. Driving a Vehicle with Automatic Transmission

7. What is the use of each gear in an automatic transmission vehicle? (48–49)
8. What is the procedure for starting an automatic transmission vehicle? (49)
9. What are the steps for putting an automatic transmission vehicle in motion? (51)
10. What is the correct procedure to follow when leaving an automatic transmission vehicle from the street side? (52)

### 4. Driving a Vehicle with Manual Transmission

11. How do you start a stickshift vehicle? (53–54)
12. What is the correct procedure for moving a stickshift vehicle in FIRST gear? (54)
13. What is the procedure for stopping a stickshift vehicle from higher gears? (56)
14. What does "downshifting" mean? (56)

## Projects

### Individuals

**Demonstrate** Make a poster that illustrates the instrument panel on your family vehicle. Present the illustration to the class, describing the location, function, and operation of each device on the panel.

**Investigate** Research the antilock braking system (ABS). Who invented this system? How does the system work? When was it first available? What were the first vehicle models to feature the system? Investigate the differences between antilock brakes and brakes that are not antilock. Write a report on your findings.

### Groups

**Use Technology** Each group member should observe the driver of a stickshift vehicle. Record the speed at which the driver shifts out of each gear. Make a group spreadsheet of your findings.

**Demonstrate** Make a video demonstrating the outside checks you should make before getting into and driving a vehicle. Group members should take turns demonstrating the steps. Present the video to your class.

---

## Teacher's Resources

**Skills and Applications Workbook**
pages 9–12

**Tests and Activities**
Chapter 3 Activities 3-1 and 3-2, pages 19–20

Chapter 3 Test A and Test B, pages 21–24

**TestWorks CD-ROM**
Chapter 3 Test

---

## Reviewing Chapter Objectives

**3.1** Instruments, Controls, and Devices
See Answers to Review It on page 45.
**3.2** Getting Ready to Drive
See Answers to Review It on page 47.
**3.3** Driving a Vehicle with Automatic Transmission
See Answers to Review It on page 52.
**3.4** Driving a Vehicle with Manual Transmission
See Answers to Review It on page 56.

For additional information refer to the specific page(s) in parentheses after each question.

## Projects

Some of the projects can be assigned at any time while others are more closely tied to the content presented in the student text. The page number where the topic is introduced is indicated.

**Demonstrate (Individual):** p. 40
**Investigate:** p. 41
**Use Technology:** p. 53
**Demonstrate (Group):** p. 46

The results of student projects will vary.

## Answers to Check Your Knowledge

1. b
2. d
3. c
4. a
5. clutch
6. blind-spot
7. battery

## Answers to Review Vocabulary

8. console (d)
9. odometer (b)
10. target (f)
11. downshifting (a)
12. shift indicator (e)
13. head restraints (c)

## Answers to Think Critically

Students' answers will vary. For information related to the questions refer to the page(s) indicated.

1. Downshifting means to shift from a higher gear to a lower gear. You might downshift to gain more control, to increase power, or to prevent brake wear. (p. 56)

2. Students' answers should include steps listed on page 52.

## Chapter Test

### Check Your Knowledge

**Multiple Choice** Copy the number of each sentence below on a sheet of paper. Choose the letter that best completes the statement or answers the question.

1. Which of the following is *not* found on a vehicle's instrument panel?
   - (a) speedometer
   - (b) horn
   - (c) tachometer
   - (d) fuel gauge
2. When entering a vehicle from the street side, you should
   - (a) be ready to unlock the door.
   - (b) walk around the front of the vehicle toward the back.
   - (c) get in quickly, then close and lock the door.
   - (d) all of the above
3. When starting an automatic transmission vehicle, the selector lever should be in
   - (a) LOW-L1 or L2, or 1 or 2
   - (b) DRIVE-D
   - (c) PARK-P or NEUTRAL-N
   - (d) REVERSE-R
4. The friction point is the point
   - (a) where the vehicle starts to move.
   - (b) where you feel the engine turn off.
   - (c) when you suddenly release the clutch.
   - (d) none of the above

**Completion** Copy the number of each sentence below. After each number, write the word or words that complete the sentence correctly.

5. The _____ pedal in a stickshift vehicle enables a driver to shift gears.
6. A vehicle's rearview mirrors cannot show _____ areas.
7. The alternator warning light warns that the _____ is being drained.

### Review Vocabulary

Copy the number of each definition in List A. Match the definition in List A with the term it defines in List B.

#### List A

8. compartment mounted between the front seats in a vehicle
9. device on the instrument panel indicating the total number of miles the vehicle has been driven
10. stationary object appearing in the distance in the center of your intended path of travel
11. shifting from a higher to a lower gear
12. device that shows the different driving gears and the one being used
13. padded devices on the backs of front seats that help reduce whiplash injuries in a collision

#### List B

a. downshifting
b. odometer
c. head restraints
d. console
e. shift indicator
f. target

### Think Critically

Write a paragraph to answer each question.

1. Explain the term downshifting, and give two reasons for using this action.
2. List and explain the procedure you should follow for securing your vehicle once you have stopped.

## Decision Making

**Fuel**

**Alternator**

**Oil Pressure**

**Temperature**

1. While you are driving, the gauges on the instrument panel could look like the pictures above. What does each gauge tell you? What problems might you have? What should you do?

2. The driver is going to enter the car and drive. Identify the incorrect procedure the driver is following. Explain why the procedure is unsafe. What error should the driver correct? What safety checks should the driver make?

3. What steps did this driver forget when getting ready to drive? Is this a safe steering position? How might the driver achieve more controlled steering? What safety device is missing?

4. You are preparing to turn this very sharp curve. You are driving a four-speed car in FOURTH gear. What should you do before entering the curve? Describe the procedure you would use.

Chapter 3 Basic Vehicle Control 59

## Answers to Decision Making

1. The gauges indicate that the vehicle is low on fuel, there is trouble in the electrical system, the oil pressure is normal, and the coolant in the engine might be too hot. You should stop driving at the earliest, safest place. Then get your vehicle to a service center.

2. If entering a vehicle from the street side, the driver should walk around the front of the vehicle toward the back. This allows the driver to see oncoming traffic. It also reduces the risk of being hit. Once inside, the driver should lock all doors, adjust the seat, adjust hands in a balanced, comfortable steering position, adjust the head restraint, rearview mirrors, and fasten safety belt.

3. The driver forgot to adjust the seat for a comfortable position with elbows slightly bent. The driver forgot to fasten the safety belt and adjust the rearview mirror. More controlled steering can be achieved with hand positions at 9–3, 10–2, or 8–4, with knuckles and thumbs on the outside of the wheel. The head restraint is missing.

4. Before entering the turn, the driver would downshift the car to slow it by first pressing the clutch pedal down and shifting to THIRD. The driver would then accelerate gradually while releasing the clutch.

# Chapter 4   Planning Guide

| |  **Student Features** |  **Teacher's Edition** |
|---|---|---|
| **Chapter 4**<br>**Managing Risk with the IPDE Process** | You Are the Driver! *p. 61* | Projects *p. 60*<br>Special Needs *p. 61* |
| **4.1   The IPDE Process** *pp. 62–64*<br>• Name three major factors that can contribute to the degree of risk you encounter while driving.<br>• Name the four steps of the IPDE Process.<br>• List the five rules of the Smith System.<br>• Explain the structure of the Zone Control System. | What Do You Think? *p. 63*<br>Did You Know? *p. 64* | Activity *pp. 62, 63* |
| **4.2   Identify and Predict** *pp. 65–74*<br>• Describe the location of each of the six zones of the Zone Control System.<br>• Explain what is meant by an open zone and a closed zone.<br>• Describe an orderly visual search pattern.<br>• Explain how knowledge and experience help you make accurate predictions. | Safe Driving Tip *p. 68*<br>Did You Know? *p. 67*<br>What Do You Think? *p. 73* | Demonstrate *pp. 65, 67, 68, 71, 74*<br>Activity *pp. 65, 66, 67, 68, 69, 70, 72, 73, 74*<br>Special Needs *p. 71* |
| **4.3   Decide and Execute** *pp. 75–82*<br>• Name the three decisions you must make when applying the IPDE Process.<br>• Describe the three different lane positions available to you within your lane.<br>• Explain what is meant when you minimize or separate a hazard or compromise space.<br>• List the three most important actions you can take to avoid conflict. | Safe Driving Tip *p. 79*<br>What Do You Think? *p. 80* | Demonstrate *pp. 76, 80, 82*<br>Activity *pp. 75, 77, 78, 81, 82*<br>Special Needs *p. 76* |
| **4.4   Using the IPDE Process** *pp. 83–84*<br>• Explain what is meant by commentary driving.<br>• Describe what is meant by selective use of the IPDE Process.<br>• Explain why the IPDE Process takes time. | | Activity *p. 84* |
| **Assessment** | Reviewing Chapter<br>  Objectives *p. 85*<br>Projects *p. 85*<br>Chapter Test *p. 86*<br>Decision Making *p. 87* | Answers *pp. 86–87* |

## Teacher's Resource File

## Videos, Overheads, and Software

**Companion** *pages 25–33*
**Spanish Handbook** *pp. 9–10*

**Resource Book**
Classroom Activity,
  *pp. 21–22*

**Resource Book**
Roadway Sheet 4, *pp. 4–5*
Teacher's Instructions *p. 35*
**In-Car Checklist** 6

**Demonstration Overheads
  A, B**
**Content Overheads  9, 10, 11**
**Video 1** Segment on the
  IPDE Process

**Resource Book**
Roadway Sheet 2 *pp. 6–7*
Teacher's Instructions, *p. 36*

**Demonstration Overhead  B**
**Content Overhead  12**
**Video 1** Segment on the
  IPDE Process

**Video 1** Segment on the
  IPDE Process

**Skills and Applications
  Workbook**, *pp. 13–16*
**Tests and Activities**
Chapter 4 Activities 4-1
  and 4-2, *pp. 27–28*
Chapter 4 Test A and Test B,
  *pp. 29–32*
Unit 1 Test, *pp. 33–36*

**TestWorks CD-ROM**
  Chapter 4 Test

## Technology Resources

AAA Foundation for Traffic Safety, *Using Your Eyes Effectively*, video, 8 minutes

AAA Foundation for Traffic Safety, *Managing Space and Time for Safe Driving*, video, 8 minutes

AAA Foundation for Traffic Safety, *driver-ZED* CD-ROM

Interactive Driving Systems, Inc., *Habit Development*, video, 38 minutes

Interactive Driving Systems, Inc., *Mottola's Zone Control for Awareness*, video, 38 minutes

Interactive Driving Systems, Inc., *Targeting*, video, 15 minutes

Interactive Driving Systems, Inc., *Zone Control Practice*, video, 18 minutes

Safety Industries, Inc., *Defensive Driving*, video, 10 minutes

Safety Industries, Inc., *The Driving Task*, video, 10 minutes

3I Company, *Drive to Survive: Defensive Driving*, video, 23 minutes

**Go Online**
PHSchool.com
For: Chapter 4 online activities
Visit: PHSchool.com
Web Code: cak-9999

# Managing Risk with the IPDE Process

## Chapter Overview

Chapter 4 describes the IPDE Process (Identify, Predict, Decide, Execute), an organized system for safe driving. Students will be introduced to the Smith System® and Zone Control System and how they are used to enhance the IPDE Process. They will learn how to identify and analyze traffic situations, predict possible outcomes, and make wise decisions for executing safe actions. Students also will learn how to search zones effectively.

## Chapter Vocabulary

*central vision, closed zone, commentary driving, compromise space, decide, execute, field of vision, 4–6 second range, ground viewing, line of sight, minimize a hazard, open zone, orderly visual search pattern, path of travel, peripheral vision, predict, scanning, separate the hazards, space cushion, target area, target area range, traction, 12–15 second range, zone*

60

## Teacher's Resources

For students to use as they read the chapter:

**Companion**
pages 25–33

**Spanish Handbook**
pages 9–10

## Projects

Review the projects described on page 85. Some of the projects can be assigned at any time while others are more closely tied to the content presented in the student text.

# CHAPTER 4
## Managing Risk with the IPDE Process

**4.1** The IPDE Process

**4.2** Identify and Predict

**4.3** Decide and Execute

**4.4** Using the IPDE Process

## You Are the Driver!

Imagine you are approaching the intersection in this picture. You have a green traffic light. What possible hazards can you identify? Should you predict the light will stay green? What action should you take if your intended path of travel becomes closed? If you decide to change speed or direction, how can you communicate with the drivers behind you?

This chapter presents the IPDE Process with its components, the Smith System and the Zone Control System. The IPDE Process will help you reduce risk by making wise decisions and executing safe driving actions.

Go Online
PHSchool.com
**For:** Chapter 4 online activities
**Visit:** PHSchool.com
**Web Code:** cak-9999

61

## Introducing the Chapter

Ask students to study the picture and identify the possible hazards shown. Make a list of the hazards on the board. Let students suggest the actions each vehicle is likely to take.

## You Are the Driver!

Students should imagine that they are driving a car and are looking through the windshield. Review the list students made of possible hazards. Predict what will happen next in regard to each hazard. Discuss actions that should be taken as a result of the predictions.

# The IPDE Process

# 1 Focus

## Summary

This lesson introduces students to three systems that will help them organize their driving skills. When mastered, the IPDE Process—used with the Smith System and the Zone Control System—enables drivers to enjoy low-risk and low-stress driving.

## Vocabulary

**Review:** *IPDE Process, risk, Smith System, Zone Control System.*

# 2 Teach

## Explain

Risk is generated by all three components of the highway transportation system—the driver, the vehicle, and the roadway. A driver is likely to get into trouble when multiple risk factors accumulate at one time. Having a set of good driving habits can help to eliminate or compensate for those unknown risk factors. Developing the habit of using the IPDE Process can give the driver timely information to protect against unknown risk.

## Objectives

1. Name three major factors that can contribute to the degree of risk you encounter while driving.
2. Name the four steps of the IPDE Process.
3. List the five rules of the Smith System.
4. Explain the structure of the Zone Control System.

Nearly every driver uses some kind of system or process to drive. Drivers who do not use some kind of organized system will have more close calls and collisions. Drivers who use an organized system will be better equipped to manage risk and thus reduce the possibility of damage or harm.

### Risk

All activities throughout a person's life involve some degree of risk. Whether playing a sport, working on the job, or driving a vehicle, some degree of risk with the possibility of suffering harm is always present. The risk you take when driving a vehicle is the ever-present possibility of conflict.

Driving a vehicle in today's environment can cause you to be at a very high degree of risk. Risk factors can be contributed by the driver, by the vehicle, and by the roadway and environment. Some examples

**High Risk**

Driver — Vehicle — Roadway

IPDE Process — Zone Control System

Smith System

**Low Risk**

of driver-contributed factors are
- adjusting radio
- being angry
- having blurred vision
- combing hair
- drinking while driving
- using a cellular phone

Driver-contributed risk factors also apply to other drivers on the roadway. These other drivers can increase or decrease your level of risk and chance of conflict.

Some risk factors are contributed by the vehicle. However, most vehicle-related risk factors are really contributed by the vehicle owner. Ownership responsibility requires proper maintenance and repair of your vehicle. Some of these risk factors are
- bald tires
- poorly adjusted brakes
- dirty windshield
- broken headlight
- worn wiper blades

Risk factors contributed by the roadway and the environment may include the following:
- bright sun
- construction
- dark shadows
- snow and ice
- sharp curve

As you drive, be aware that all of these risk factors, and many more, play a major role in the level of risk you face.

Because some degree of risk is always present, try to make sure

## Teacher's Resources

**Resource Book**
Classroom Activity,
pages 21–22

## Activity

**Small Group Activity** This activity will help students evaluate risk factors for driving. Divide the class into groups of three students. Give each member of the group a copy of the Partial Risk Factors sheet from the **Resource Book,** pages 21–22. Ask each group to evaluate the risk factors under one of the three components of the highway transportation system. Have the students classify which risk factors they will be able to eliminate or minimize. After adequate time, have one person from each group report its findings to the class.

nothing about your own condition or the condition of your vehicle raises your level of risk.

Some drivers deliberately take chances. They put not only themselves but others at a high degree of risk. Deliberately taking a chance with a vehicle, with its great capacity for harm and destruction, should be unthinkable. The potential for suffering harm and loss is too great, and the possible penalties are too serious. Drivers who take unnecessary chances demonstrate risk-taking behaviors. A driver who continues to practice these behaviors can develop high-risk habits with the possibility of becoming an unsafe driver.

Good drivers make every effort to manage risk in order to lower the probability of conflict, and thus enjoy more stress-free driving. As you begin your driving experience, make every effort to develop low-risk driving behaviors. Then, through continual practice, these low-risk behaviors will become your safe driving habits.

## The IPDE Process

Good seeing habits and your ability to manage space in the roadway are basic tools for low-risk driving. The IPDE Process, along with the Smith System and Zone Control System, can enable you to enjoy low-risk and low-stress driving.

Safe driving depends upon your ability to see and analyze traffic situations correctly. Good seeing habits are the basic critical factor necessary for staying out of high-risk situations. However, just being able to see well is no guarantee you will identify all critical clues and make correct driving responses in every situation.

The driving task is primarily a thinking task. Your hands and feet do only what your brain tells them to do. Most responsible drivers use a system that deals with all the traffic possibilities they will encounter. These drivers have fewer close calls and collisions than drivers who do not use some kind of system.

The IPDE Process is an organized system of seeing, thinking, and responding. The Smith System and the Zone Control System will help you apply the IPDE Process. The four steps of the IPDE Process are
1. Identify
2. Predict
3. Decide
4. Execute

Some drivers exhibit a high degree of risk. How do such factors as peer pressure, self-image, and ego help cause high-risk behavior?

**IPDE Process**

**1 Identify**

Use visual search pattern to identify
- open and closed zones
- specific clues
- other users
- roadway features and conditions
- traffic controls

**2 Predict**

Use knowledge, judgment, and experience to predict
- actions of other users
- speed
- direction
- control
- points of conflict

**IPDE**

**3 Decide**

Decide to use one or more actions to
- change or maintain speed
- change direction
- communicate

**4 Execute**

Execute your decisions to
- control speed
- steer
- communicate
- combine actions

Chapter 4 Managing Risk with the IPDE Process **63**

## Activity

**Small Group Activity** This activity will help students understand risk factors affecting driving. Divide the class into groups of three. Give each group a piece of blank paper. Have each member take one of the three categories that create risk factors—the driver, the vehicle, or the roadway. Have each member identify five risk factors for the category that are not in the student text. Then have members of the group explain to each other how and why the factors they selected are a risk to drivers.

During the groups' discussions you can walk around the room, helping the groups to focus on the task. After adequate time, one member of each group can report his or her group's findings to the whole class.

## Discuss

Bring in a local newspaper article of a recent vehicle collision. Make copies for distribution to the class. Ask students to read the article and identify all risk factors that are included.

## Explain

Explain how human beings are creatures of habit. If we do something several times on a conscious level, it then becomes habit, taking place seemingly without thought. During this course students will have opportunities to explore and practice many driving behaviors. Some of these behaviors will become habits.

## Discuss

Ask students to explain how habits are formed and how they become established with practice. Have them explain how a habit they have—not related to driving—was developed.

## Discuss

Point out the *What Do You Think?* question. Ask: How do you think peer pressure, self-image, and ego cause an increase in risk factors? What are the solutions to eliminate, or minimize, such risk?

## Apply

Apply the IPDE process to several non-driving situations to show the class how they require a decision-making process.

Use the example of going to see a movie. Apply the IPDE Process by using the following steps. Identify the movie you may want to see. Predict the cost and level of enjoyment you expect. Decide what day and time you will see the movie. Execute your decision by going to see the movie.

Draw examples from the class about how they can use the IPDE Process to make and execute everyday decisions.

 **Assess**

## Answers to Review It

**1.** The three factors contributing to degrees of risk while driving are the driver, the vehicle, and the roadway and environment. (p. 62)

**2.** The four steps of the IPDE Process are Identify, Predict, Decide, and Execute. (p. 63)

**3.** The five keys of the Smith System® are: (1) Aim high in steering.® (2) Get the big picture.® (3) Keep your eyes moving.® (4) Leave yourself an "out."® (5) Make sure they see you.® (p. 64)

**4.** The structure of the Zone Control System includes three steps: (1) See a zone change. (2) Check other zones. (3) Create time and space by getting the best speed control, lane position, and communication. (p. 64)

THE SMITH SYSTEM® Years ago, Harold L. Smith introduced a system for safe driving. The Smith System stresses eye discipline and the idea of a space cushion. Later, the Ford Motor Company asked Mr. Smith to share his system of driving with drivers throughout the United States. This system is still considered basic for safe driving habits.

You begin the IPDE Process by "reading" traffic situations to gather information for your decisions and actions. To process this information properly, you must identify hazards and predict conflict. You then decide how to avoid the conflict by executing the correct action.

The Smith System® is an organized method to help drivers develop good seeing habits by using five keys for driver safety. The five keys of the Smith System are

1. Aim high in steering.®
2. Get the big picture.®
3. Keep your eyes moving.®
4. Leave yourself an "out."®
5. Make sure they see you.®

The Zone Control System is an organized method for managing six zones of space surrounding your vehicle. Zone Control allows you to see and respond to changes in the traffic environment at a time when best control can be achieved.

The structure of the Zone Control System includes the following steps:

1. See a zone change.
2. Check other zones.
3. Create time and space by getting the best speed control, lane position, and communication.

Using the Smith System and Zone Control System with the IPDE Process can put you well on the road toward low-risk driving behaviors.

### Review It

1. What three major factors contribute to your degree of risk while driving?
2. What are the four steps of the IPDE Process?
3. What are the five keys of the Smith System?
4. What is the structure of the Zone Control System?

## Background

**The Zone Control System** In 1972 Zone Control was created by Frederik R. Mottola, a national leader in traffic safety education. This is a systematic method for drivers to acquire good space-management habits. It has been used effectively to reduce motor vehicle collisions for all types of drivers, from police and school bus drivers to fleet and novice drivers.

The Zone Control System is very effective for the development of low-risk driving habits because it gives precise standards for driver performance. These standards are formed into guid-ing principles. As drivers learn these few principles, they may apply them to thousands of different situations. The repeated application of the Zone Control System fosters efficient habit development.

The Identify and Predict steps of the IPDE Process are critical in every driving environment. These two steps begin your thinking process for every situation you encounter. With practice and experience, these steps will seem to occur in your thinking process as happening almost at the same time. As you search in and around your path to identify possible problems, you will be making judgments and predictions about what conflicts may occur.

### Identify

The first step of the IPDE Process is **identify**. This step involves much more than just seeing. When you identify, you give meaning to what you see. You must know when to look, where to look, how to look, and what to look for.

Any aspect of the Highway Transportation System (HTS) can become a hazardous situation. This includes the roadway, your own vehicle, other vehicles or pedestrians, and traffic controls. Clues you identify may cause you to change direction or speed, signal others, or perform any combination of maneuvers. The sooner you identify a possible hazard, the more time you will have to react safely.

### Zones and Searching Ranges

The Zone Control System helps you make quick and accurate use of the IPDE Process by setting a standard of what to identify and what to do when you find it. A **zone** is one of six areas of space around a vehicle that is the width of a lane and extends as far as the driver can see. The picture shows the six zones around your vehicle. Straight ahead is the front zone, to the left is the left-front zone, and to the right is the right-front zone. Behind you is the rear zone, the left-rear zone, and the right-rear zone.

An **open zone** is space where you can drive without a restriction to your **line of sight** or to your intended **path of travel.** Your line of sight is the distance you can see

**Zone Locations**

Front Zone

Left-Front Zone

Right-Front Zone

Left-Rear Zone

Right-Rear Zone

Rear Zone

### Objectives

1. Describe the location of each of the six zones of the Zone Control System.
2. Explain what is meant by an open zone and a closed zone.
3. Describe an orderly visual search pattern.
4. Explain how knowledge and experience help you make accurate predictions.

Chapter 4 Managing Risk with the IPDE Process **65**

# Identify and Predict

 **Focus**

### Summary

Identify and Predict are the IP of the IPDE Process. This lesson focuses on identifying potential hazards and predicting outcomes.

### Vocabulary

*central vision, closed zone, field of vision, 4–6 second range, ground viewing, identify, line of sight, open zone, orderly visual search pattern, path of travel, peripheral vision, predict, scanning, target area, target area range, traction, 12–15 second range, zone.*

 **Teach**

### Demonstrate

Hold a stapler up and ask students to explain how the stapler works. To understand what a stapler can do requires more information than merely seeing it. It requires relying upon stored knowledge that has been built through education and experience. Making accurate and efficient predictions of driving events requires stored knowledge and experience.

---

### Teacher's Resources

**Resource Book**
Roadway Sheet 1, pages 4–5
Teacher's Instructions, page 35

**Demonstration Overheads**
Overheads A, B

**Content Overheads**
Overheads 9, 10, 11

**Video 1**
Segment on the IPDE Process

**In-Car Checklists**
In-Car Checklist 6

### Activity

**Class Activity** This activity will help students understand the importance of knowing where to look and what to look for. Before students arrive, place any two objects on your desk in clear view of the class. Do not call attention to the objects. After five minutes, block the students' view of the objects. Ask students to write the names of the objects that are on the desk. Most likely, only a few students will correctly identify the objects. Reveal the objects to the students and ask why they did not see them earlier.

## Discuss

Call the students' attention to the Zone Locations illustration on page 65, or use **Content Overhead 9.** Ask the following questions: Would you classify a red traffic light in your front zone as an open or a closed zone? (closed) What other zone should you check after seeing the closed front zone? (rear zone) What choice in speed control should you take? (Apply the brake in an attempt to arrive into an open zone.) If there is a parked car in the right-front zone, is your front zone open or closed? (Front zone is open to your path of travel with a closed line-of-sight restriction that prevents you from seeing someone who may enter your path. The right-front zone is closed to your path of travel.)

## Explain

Point out why it is important not to assume you have an open path of travel when there are line-of-sight restrictions.

## Discuss

Ask: While traveling on a two-lane roadway, which zones should you check after seeing a parked car in the right-front zone? Give students time to respond. Use a chalkboard or overhead to list student responses and provide additional information. (Check the rear zone in case you need to slow or stop. Check the left-front zone to see if there is anyone crossing the street to approach the parked car, or to see if there is any oncoming traffic.)

What is your open zone in this situation?

ahead in the direction you are looking. Your intended path of travel is the space your vehicle will occupy. Your path of travel is directed toward the **target area.** The target area is the section of the roadway where the target is located in the center of your intended path, and the area to its right and left.

A **closed zone** is a space not open to you because of a restriction in your line of sight or intended path of travel. A red traffic light is an example of a closed front zone. A parked vehicle to your right represents a closed right-front zone. A closed rear zone might be a vehicle that is following you too closely. The sooner you identify a closed zone, the more time you have to respond. With more time, the better chance you have to achieve control of the situation by lowering the degree of risk.

The driver in the picture on the left has identified the car that is about to enter his or her intended path of travel. The driver will need to treat the front zone as closed, and therefore slow down to open the front zone.

In order to keep alert to the conditions of your zones, there are three searching ranges that need to be evaluated. A searching range is a certain distance ahead of the vehicle where the intended path of travel is systematically evaluated. The picture below shows the three searching ranges. The first searching range is the **target area range,** which is the space from your vehicle to the target area. You search this range to detect early any conditions that might affect your intended path of travel.

Next you will search the **12–15 second range,** which is the space you

Three searching ranges

## Activity

**Model Car Activity** This activity will provide practice in predicting. Divide the class into groups of three students. Give each group Roadway Sheet 1 from **Resource Book,** pages 4–5, two matchbox cars, and a wild card (see pages T18–T19).

Direct students to place one car on the right shoulder of the road and drive the other car to approach the parked car. Ask: What predictions can you make about how this parked car can affect your line of sight?

**Use Demonstration Overhead A** to record

students' predictions. As students give correct information, draw an arrow to show the movement potential of each vehicle.

See **Resource Book,** page 35 for a diagram showing this activity. The predictions are
(1) The car can pull into your travel path.
(2) The driver may open the door into your path.
(3) Someone may come out from in front of it.
(4) Someone may cross the street to approach the car.

Instruct students to use their model cars and wild card to create conditions to close each of the six zones.

will travel in during the next 12–15 seconds. This range is where you need to identify changes in your line of sight or path of travel to make decisions about controlling your intended path. Try to identify the possibility of closed zones by searching to the left and right for anything that might come into your zones.

The **4–6 second range** is the space you will travel in during the next 4–6 seconds. This range is where you need to get the final update of how you are controlling your intended path of travel.

### Orderly Visual Search Pattern

You can use any of several patterns to help develop your own identifying process. An **orderly visual search pattern** is a process of searching critical areas in a regular sequence. To use an orderly visual search pattern, look for clues in and around your intended path of travel in a systematic manner. Below is an example of an orderly visual search pattern for straight-ahead driving.

1. Look ahead to your target area range.
2. Evaluate your left-front, front, and right-front zones in the 12–15 second range. Search driveways and intersections for possible changes in your line of sight and path of travel.
3. Glance in rearview mirror to check your rear zones.
4. Evaluate your 4–6 second range before entering that space.
5. Look ahead again to evaluate another 12–15 second range.
6. Check your 4–6 second range.

**AVOID STARING** Many beginning drivers develop the habit of staring. They fixate for several seconds on the same clue or event. They do not look far into target-area ranges, and often drive with swerves and jerky movements. Do not let yourself become a "stare" driver.

7. Glance in rearview mirror.
8. Check speedometer and gauges.
You will repeat this pattern continually as you move forward. Each look or glance should last only an instant as you evaluate your zones and the areas to the left and right. Be careful not to stare as you search. Practice using your orderly visual search pattern as a passenger—in addition to when you are driving—so it will become a safe driving habit. You will then be able to adjust your search pattern for any maneuver or driving environment.

### Where and How to Look

Different driving environments and traffic situations present a variety of visual search problems. As you gain driving experience, you will learn what kinds of clues and situations are most important to identify in order to keep an open zone in your path of travel.

The area you can see around you, while looking straight ahead, is called your **field of vision**. Many of us can see an area of about 90 degrees to each side, for a total picture of 180

Chapter 4 Managing Risk with the IPDE Process **67**

---

## Activity

**In-Class Driving Rehearsal** This activity will help students practice using targets for steering. Give students a simulated steering wheel. Tell students: Rather than turn the steering wheel, you will pivot your body to keep the steering wheel centered directly in front of you. As I move about the room, I want you to pretend I'm the target. Pivot your body to follow me, keeping the steering wheel directly centered in front of you. As you move, the students will demonstrate their ability to keep the target centered.

## Activity

**Class Activity** This activity will give students an opportunity to practice judging space by estimating distance in seconds. Select a student to walk from the back of the room to a marker in the front of the classroom. Ask the class to call out how many seconds they think it will take the student to reach the marker. When the student begins to walk, count off 1001, 1002, 1003, etc. until the student reaches the marker. Have the class compare their estimates with the actual time. Repeat with different students walking at different paces until estimates are accurate.

## Explain

Use **Content Overhead 10** or the illustration on page 66 to explain how to use the three searching ranges. Show how to use these ranges with the orderly visual search pattern.

## Explain

Tell the students that they are using central vision to see the target. The center of the steering wheel is seen in relation to the target by lower peripheral vision.

## Demonstrate

Use a three or four D-cell adjustable focus flashlight to demonstrate searching ranges. First, demonstrate the 4–6 second range. While standing three feet away from the front wall, turn the flashlight on and completely darken the room. Shine the flashlight on the front wall. Point out that the bright inner circle of light can be compared to the central cone of vision, and the larger outer circle is similar to peripheral vision. To demonstrate the 12–15 second range, move to the back of the classroom. This distance to the wall is like looking to your target area. Shine the beam onto the floor three feet in front of you. The illumination of the room becomes reduced. The lowered beam represents a driver looking only 3–5 seconds ahead of the car. Shining the light to the front wall is like searching to the target area and evaluating your intended path of travel.

## Demonstrate

Demonstrate central and peripheral vision using **Content Overhead 11** or the illustration on this page.

## Explain

Using the IPDE Process with Zone Control, you can peek into your future by looking to your target area and visualizing where your car will be in the next 12–15 seconds. This is a priceless skill that empowers you to have control over your driving future.

## Explain

The "aim high" key from the Smith System® does not mean to look high in the sky. It means to think of your vision as being parallel to the roadway while projecting it as far ahead as possible.

"Aim high" is much the same as "looking to your target area" except the latter is measurable by being able to see a stationary object to define its location. If you use "aim high" effectively, then searching to the "target area" defines where to aim.

## Explain

Explain how selective seeing is effectively increased when a driver identifies a line-of-sight restriction that blocks the view of someone or something. To avoid surprises, assume that another vehicle or a pedestrian may enter your intended path of travel whenever your line of sight is restricted.

## SAFE DRIVING

Even though your peripheral vision is not sharp and clear, it is very important to you while you are driving. When you see some kind of movement or a vehicle or pedestrian in your peripheral vision, you can turn your eyes in that direction to see if there is a potential problem.

degrees. The area you can see clearly and sharply is seen with your **central vision.** This is a narrow cone of only up to 10 degrees. The area you can see to the left and right of central vision is your side vision, or **peripheral vision.** As the distance from central vision increases toward the outer edge of peripheral vision, the less clearly you can identify clues and events.

Three of the Smith System keys can help you learn where and how to look as you develop your visual search pattern.

**Aim High in Steering®** To "aim high" means that you look ahead 12–15 seconds into your target area as you drive. Do not just look at the close area in front of or at the sides of your vehicle. Be a high-aim driver. Looking far ahead with your line of sight will help you identify clues and analyze situations before your zone becomes closed. There are many restrictions to your line of sight that

can cause a closed zone. Some such restrictions are curves, hills, large vehicles, weather conditions, buildings, trees, or even a dirty windshield.

**Keep Your Eyes Moving®** Looking near and far, side to side, and in the mirrors will help you see a zone change before it becomes critical. Keeping your eyes moving does not mean just moving them constantly. You must fixate on an object or an event for an instant in order to identify it. Do not fixate for longer than an instant or you will find yourself staring. Keeping your eyes moving will prevent you from staring at any one object or clue.

Develop the art of **scanning,** glancing continually and quickly with very brief fixations through your orderly visual search pattern. You are looking and seeing as you scan, but not staring at any one event or clue. Staring blocks out side vision, causes lack of attention, and

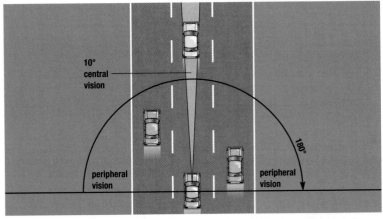

10° central vision

peripheral vision

180°

peripheral vision

You see most clearly in the area of central vision, but peripheral vision is equally important.

## Activity

**Small Group Activity** This activity will help students learn the value of eye pauses for effective searching. Divide the class into groups of four or five students. Each group needs a tester, a driver, and observers. Each student should have a turn as the driver.

Give each tester a set of ten 3-by-5-inch cards, numbered 0–9. Have the tester stand four feet in front of the driver and select two cards without showing them. The tester will hold the two cards side-by-side in one hand to form a two-digit number. Then, instruct the driver to move

his or her head 90 degrees to the left and 90 degrees to the right continually without pausing the eyes. Have the observer stand next to the tester to see if the driver's eyes pause to read the number. Then have the tester hide the numbers and ask the driver to state what number was held. The group will discover that the driver can only identify the numbers correctly when there is a brief pause (fixation) of the eyes.

Then have each student practice correct searching by making brief eye fixations to read numbers the tester holds.

tends to create high-risk driving habits. Keeping your eyes moving helps you stay more alert with your attention at a higher level. You are then more likely to keep up with all the changes in your field of vision.

**Get the Big Picture®** Getting the big picture is the mental process of putting together the critical clues you have selected. It is the result of aiming high and keeping your eyes moving.

### What to Look For

Knowing where and how to look does little good if you do not know what to look for in your target area. Develop the technique of selective seeing in your identifying process. Selective seeing means that you identify and select only those clues and events that restrict your line of sight or can change your intended path of travel.

**Look for Open Zones** Use your visual search pattern to look for specific driving-related clues that might cause an open zone to close.

When searching parked cars on a street, you might identify an important clue, such as front wheels turned toward the street, as the picture shows. You might also identify vapor coming from an exhaust pipe or a driver sitting in a car. These clues indicate that a car might enter your path of travel and cause your front zone to close.

The kinds of clues you search for will change as you drive in different environments. When driving in the city, search for intersections, parked cars, pedestrians, and traffic. On open highways, search areas much farther ahead. Look for crossroads, slow-moving vehicles, and animals. Any of these can suddenly cause an open zone to close, resulting in the need to change your intended path of travel. When you drive on expressways, speeds are higher and scanning all zones becomes even more critical. Regardless of the driving environment, you should always look for other roadway users, roadway features, changing conditions,

**You Are the Driver!**
What procedure would you follow to avoid a possible conflict if your front zone becomes closed?

Front wheels turned toward the street are a clue that the car might pull out and close your zone.

## Activity

**In-Class Driving Rehearsal** This activity will provide practice using the orderly visual search pattern. Print each step of the orderly visual search pattern onto separate 5-by-7-inch cards. Arrange rows of student chairs into a simulated travel lane (see pages T18–T19). Have at least one chair off to the side to represent a right-front zone change caused by a car backing out of a driveway. Have the students walk through the "travel lane" simulating that they are driving a car. Give each student one of the 5-by-7-inch cards and ask them to demonstrate and verbalize

how they are using that step of the orderly visual search pattern. Repeat each step several times by having different students "driving" and explaining the search patterns.

## Explain

Use the photo on this page to explain what you can learn by applying the ground viewing habit. Point out that the front wheels are turned toward your intended path of travel. This is a clue that the right-front zone is of concern to you for controlling your front zone. Tell students that even if the tires were not turned, the parked car is a closure of the right-front zone. Someone could open a door into your travel path. Also, the car is a line-of-sight restriction that can conceal someone entering your path.

## Apply

Ask students to apply target-area searching to the scene in the photograph on this page. Ask: What does the house in the target area tell them? (The street ends or the road turns sharply.) What is the best lane positioning while passing the parked cars if there are no oncoming cars? (left of center) Who has the right of way if there is an oncoming vehicle? (the oncoming vehicle)

## Explain

According to the National Highway Traffic Safety Administration, more than 80 percent of all collisions can be avoided if drivers have one additional second of time. The average driver looks 3–5 seconds ahead of the car. If you look to the 12–15 second range, you will gain 9–12 more seconds than the average driver. Imagine how much less stressful driving would be!

Chapter 4
Managing Risk with the
IPDE Process  **69**

## Discuss

Have students evaluate the photo on this page. Ask them to identify situations that can cause distractions to drivers or pedestrians. Have the students also observe all the vehicles' use of space. Discuss which vehicles are most likely to be victimized by some bad behavior patterns. Furthermore, ask the students to identify which vehicle drivers in the photo have line-of-sight restrictions and which have a closed path of travel. Then ask them to explain what actions each of the drivers should be taking and what their next action should be.

## Discuss

Discuss the following examples of line-of-sight restrictions: a truck stopped in the left-turn lane, a snow bank, a curve with trees to the side, a hillcrest, a parked vehicle, a heavy downpour, a parked ice cream vendor, and a city bus picking up passengers.

## Discuss

Discuss the following examples of path-of-travel restrictions: a red traffic light, a STOP sign, stopped traffic, a car making a left turn, a pedestrian crossing the street, a car entering the roadway, a stopped school bus, and a car changing lanes.

Note that your front zone is open if you are following a moving vehicle with at least 3 seconds of space. (Students will learn about following distance in Chapters 5 and 9.)

and traffic controls that may affect your intended path of travel.

**Look for Other Users** Look for other users who might affect your intended path of travel. Watch for movement of other users, especially in areas that have shadows or shade. Watch for pedestrians and bicyclists. A large truck is easy to identify. However, it creates a restriction in your line of sight and may prevent you from seeing another user. Develop the habit of **ground viewing** as part of your visual search pattern. Ground viewing is making quick glances to the roadway in front of your vehicle. When other vehicles are approaching, use ground viewing to see where they are headed by checking the direction of their front wheels.

Always be on the lookout for problem drivers. Problem drivers usually give clues by their driving behavior. Some fast drivers might be problem drivers. They may try to pass without enough room or in a no-passing zone. They frequently change lanes, trying to get ahead of the normal traffic flow, and can cause a sudden change in your open zone condition.

**Look for Roadway Features and Conditions** The roadway itself is another important area to watch. Identify intersections, hills, and curves early. Be aware ahead of time that the width of your lane might be reduced for road construction or other obstacles. An intersection is a high-risk area where the management of your path of travel needs constant attention. Stopped traffic or entering traffic can cause line-of-sight restrictions or even a closed

Drivers need to look for many different roadway users and roadway conditions that will affect their path of travel.

## Activity

**Small Group Activity** This activity will help students identify possible restrictions to line of sight or path of travel. Divide the class into groups of three or four students. Ask one student in each group to divide a sheet of paper into three columns: Roadway Users, Roadway Features, and Traffic Controls.

Ask each group to list examples of roadway users, roadway features, and traffic controls that can affect their line of sight or path of travel.

After adequate time, have the groups report their findings to the whole class.

zone. A hill is a line-of-sight restriction which could hide a closed zone as you go over the hill. Here are some reasons for changes in roadway features and conditions:

- **Change from multilane to single lane** Multilane roadways often narrow into single-lane roadways. Identify signs warning you of this change early enough to avoid a closed zone in your intended path. When signs indicate roadway repairs ahead, you can expect your front zone will close. Check your left-front, right-front, and rear zones before moving into the through lane. Drivers who wait until the last instant and then try to squeeze into the through lane are demonstrating high-risk behavior with no concern for other drivers.

- **Change in width of lane** Standing water, patches of snow, potholes, or objects in the roadway can cause an open zone to close. Identify the conditions early and then check your rear zone to find out if there will be a problem in case a stop is needed. Check your left-rear zone and left-front zone, as the driver in the picture above is doing, to see if you have space to go around the problem safely.

- **Roadway surface** Identify the roadway surface and condition each time you begin to drive. There will be times when the weather will change while you are driving. Roadway surfaces may be dry when you start out and then

Check your rear zones and left-front zone when an object is in the roadway.

become wet and slippery with rain, snow, or ice as you are driving. Be prepared to adjust your driving for changing weather conditions that might affect the roadway surface. A gravel surface can cause sliding or skidding just like a wet or slippery surface.

- **Roadside hazards** Your identification process should keep you scanning for bicyclists, pedestrians, parked vehicles, and animals. Watch for shopping center entrances and exits, roadside stands, and restaurants. Other drivers can appear from almost any location and cause your open zone to close. Continual scanning of your target areas will help you identify these other drivers in time to avoid sudden actions or conflict.

**Look for Traffic Controls** Learn to look in different places for traffic controls. At major intersections, controls can be overhead, in the center, or on a corner. Identify traffic controls as early as possible so you are ready to make correct responses.

## Demonstrate

Use **Demonstration Overhead B** of a four-lane roadway. Place the yellow car in the lowest part of the right lane. Place a penny or a dime—to serve as a wild card—at the top-most part of the right lane's shoulder. Ask: Which zone is closed? (right-front zone) What could the wild card represent to cause a closed right-front zone? Solicit at least five or six conditions that could create the closed right-front zone. (Answers will vary. Examples: disabled car, hitchhiker, car backing out of a driveway, hot dog vendor, stopped delivery truck, snow bank, construction site, or bicyclist.)

Repeat the activity for each of the zones. You could also move the yellow car into the left lane and repeat the same sequences. This will result in different types of zone conditions.

## Cross Curricular

**Geography** Point out that in some parts of the world, drivers share the roadway with a wide range of users. There are communities where bicycles outnumber automobiles and animal-drawn carts are common.

Ask students to locate a photograph of a busy intersection in another part of the world. Have them identify the various roadway users. Discuss how driving might be different because of these users.

## Special Needs

Help students understand and practice the orderly visual search pattern. Using your hand and forehead to represent the mirrors, position yourself low and in front of a student's desk. Have the student demonstrate orderly visual search patterns for intersections, lane changes, and slowing or stopping. Monitor eye movements critically. This can be done daily while the students are doing some other seated task work.

## Explain

Using the IPDE Process with the Zone Control System, a driver can gain problem-solving experience that can be applied to many unknown situations. For example, seeing the front zone closed by a red signal light requires the driver to check the rear zone and make an attempt to use the least amount of energy to arrive into an open front zone. Each signal light the student approaches can be an experience on how to successfully deal with a closed front zone—if the signal light is seen as a "closed zone" rather than as a "red light."

When the student has developed this habit, the quick closure of the front zone caused by a traffic-stopping collision will result in an automatic response. This automatic response will include an appropriate series of actions that will reduce risk.

### Predict

Once you have identified a hazard, **predict** how this hazard might affect your intended path of travel. When you predict, you interpret the information you have identified. You predict where possible points of conflict can occur. You try to foresee what might happen, how changes in zones may occur, and how you would check other zones for alternate paths. Your predictions will be based upon those conditions that may reduce your line of sight or could change your intended path of travel.

If you had to face just one hazard at a time, you could more easily predict the possible outcome. However, most of the time you will be faced with more than one possible hazard or conflict, so predicting can become more complex.

### How to Predict

Predicting involves what is happening in your zones, what could happen,

What might you predict if this was your oncoming traffic?

and if it does happen, how the change could affect you. To predict, you must evaluate the situation and make a judgment about the possible consequences. The more complex a situation is, the more difficult it is to identify and predict. As you gain driving experience, you will become more selective about which hazards or possible conflicts are critical.

Imagine you are driving the car on the right in the picture below. Your left-front zone is blocked by the bicyclists and oncoming car. You should predict that one or both of the bicyclists might swerve or fall. If so, predict that the oncoming car might enter your front zone, causing it to close.

Using Zone Control, you would check your rear zone in case you need to stop. Check your right-front zone in case you need to move in that direction. You should also check the right-rear zone before moving to the right. Scanning your target areas can help you predict hazards that may affect your path of travel. Your ability to predict and make sound judgments will improve as you gain knowledge and experience.

**Knowledge** One basic part of your driving knowledge comes from the study of traffic laws and driver-education material. Whenever you drive, you also gain knowledge by gathering more information and learning from others.

Think of storing driving knowledge as adding to your safe-driving memory bank. The more you drive, the more you add to your memory bank of knowledge. This knowledge

## Activity

**Model Car Activity** This activity will give students the opportunity to discover and manage left-front zone changes. Organize the class into groups of three students. Give each group Roadway Sheet 1 from **Resource Book**, pages 4–5, two matchbox cars, and a wild card (see pages T18–T19). Have all students rotate into each of the three roles.

Direct students to place the wild card in the oncoming lane and one of the cars behind it. (The situation will be similar to the one shown in the photograph on this page. The wild card replaces the bicyclists.) The other car should be approaching the left-front zone problem created by the oncoming wild card and car. Ask the student with the wild card to explain what type of problem may cause the car in back to swerve around it.

Ask the driver of the car in back of the wild card to describe appropriate behavior to use to avoid being victimized by the wild card. Ask the driver approaching the left-front zone problem to state what other zones will need to be checked for options and what actions should be taken.

will help you identify and predict more quickly and accurately and increase your chances of becoming a low-risk driver.

**Judgment** Making a judgment about a traffic situation involves measuring, comparing, and evaluating. As you drive, you judge speed, time, space, distance, traction, and visibility. You make judgments about your own driving performance as well as the actions and performance of other roadway users. Make every effort to develop the ability to make sound judgments that lead to accurate predictions.

**Experience** In addition to knowledge, experience helps you improve your ability to predict accurately. Exposure to a wide variety of driving experiences provides a solid base for making sound judgments later.

### What to Predict

Nearly all predictions you make as a driver will be related to predicting changes in zones and looking for an "out" or an alternative path of travel. Two major elements in the traffic scene you must make predictions about are

- the actions of other roadway users
- your control of your vehicle and consequences of your actions

**Predicting Actions of Others** Do not assume other roadway users will always take the correct action. Instead watch for clues to what they might do to alter zone conditions.

The most important types of predictions to make concerning the actions of others are

- **Path** Where might the other driver go? What zone might be closed? Will I have an open zone for an "out"? The Smith System rule of leaving yourself an "out" is critical when predicting possible closed zones.
- **Action** What action will other users take? Is more than one action possible? Where will I be then?
- **Space** Will I have an open zone?
- **Point of Conflict** If I have no open zone for escape, where might our paths cross and a conflict occur?

Imagine that you are driving toward the intersection in the picture below. The oncoming driver is signaling for a right turn. Assume the worst and predict that the driver

What might the oncoming driver do? What might the pedestrians do?

## Activity

**Class Activity** This activity will help students discover the benefit of stored knowledge to the decision-making process. Bring into the class a small electric fan with a safety screen on it. Turn the fan on and ask: What would happen if the screen was not on this fan and you were to stick your hand into the whirling blades? After some discussion, point out the following: With stored knowledge, you don't need to touch the fan to know that doing so would be quite painful. You gained your stored knowledge through many different sources without the need

to experience placing your hand into the whirling blade. A small child may see the whirling fan but has no stored knowledge of what will happen when the fan blade is touched. Reading this textbook is one valuable way to gain a treasure of stored knowledge. Using the IPDE Process with Zone Control is like placing the screen around the fan. Even if you don't have the stored knowledge of the danger of the whirling fan, the screen will prevent you from getting hurt.

## Discuss

Ask the class to think of how stored knowledge influences the decisions they make in routine daily situations. Ask the following questions: What happens when you go outside in the rain without an umbrella? What predictions can you make about your hair? Could you make these same predictions if you had never seen rain before?

Ask: What predictions can you make if a china cup is dropped onto a concrete floor? What if the cup is dropped onto a bed?

Reiterate that stored knowledge provides a picture in your mind of what is likely to happen, before it actually happens.

## Explain

Explain that the sooner a traffic element is identified, the more time the mind has to come up with an accurate picture of what to expect. The more stored knowledge you have, the faster and more accurate the predictions become.

## Discuss

Discuss the *What Do You Think?* feature. Help students relate storing up and adding new knowledge to "building a memory bank." Explain the importance of trying to keep knowledge in the bank while adding more to it.

## Explain

Explain that predictions are vital to the smooth flow of traffic. Note that without predictions, drivers could face a series of surprises, sudden moves, and emergencies.

## Discuss

Discuss how a wet, slippery roadway requires good braking habits. Discuss how one's good habits can give protection when something goes wrong.

## Demonstrate

You can use **Video 1** segment on the IPDE Process to demonstrate the Identify and Predict steps now, or you can wait until all four steps have been taught.

## 3 Assess

### Answers to Review It

**1.** The six zone locations are left-front zone, left-rear zone, front zone, rear zone, right-front zone, and right-rear zone. (p. 65)

**2.** An open zone is space where you can drive without restriction to your line of sight or intended path of travel. (pp. 65–66)

**3.** Students' answers will vary. One example of an orderly visual search pattern is the pattern for straight-ahead driving, given on page 67 of the textbook.

**4.** Knowledge and experience improve your ability to make accurate predictions. (pp. 72–73)

**You Are the Driver!**
What effect does the oncoming car have on your IPDE Process?

will turn left into your front zone. Also predict that the pedestrians will step off the curb and close your right front zone. By making these predictions you will be able to slow, swerve, or stop in order to avoid a conflict.

**Predicting Control of Your Vehicle and Possible Consequences** Speed is probably the most important factor in maintaining control of your vehicle. Always be prepared to adjust your speed for different zone conditions and situations. Different traffic, roadway, and weather conditions can change the amount of time and space needed for safe reactions.

The basic requirement for vehicle control is **traction.** Traction is the actual gripping power between the tires and the roadway surface. The more traction there is, the greater the gripping power.

In the picture above, the driver knows the roadway is wet and presumes it is slippery. Visibility is restricted by the weather. The driver predicts that stopping for the STOP sign will take longer than if the roadway were dry. Based on this prediction, the driver checks the rear zone and then slows and brakes earlier.

In many situations you may have a choice of actions to predict. Try to judge and compare the possible consequences before deciding on the best action.

### Review It

1. What is the location of each of the six zones of the Zone Control System?
2. What is an open zone and a closed zone?
3. Give an example of an orderly visual search pattern.
4. What effects do knowledge and experience have on your ability to make accurate predictions?

## Activity

**Class Activity** Ask students to pretend that they are driving the vehicle in the photograph on this page. Ask: Is the front zone open or closed? (closed) What is it that causes the front zone to be closed? (the STOP sign) Where do you make the legal stop? (at the stop line) Before entering the intersection, how will you search for a safe path of travel through the intersection? (check the left, front, and right zones to be certain they are clear) If you are making a left turn, who has the right of way, you or the oncoming vehicle? (the oncoming vehicle)

O nce you have identified a situation and predicted a possible conflict, you then **decide** upon an action. Deciding, like predicting, is also a mental task. There is probably no task more important, though, than making wise decisions and then executing actions to avoid conflict. Drivers must continually identify and predict until they have enough information to make correct decisions.

Once you make a decision, the **execute** step of the IPDE Process will follow. To execute a decision means that you carry out an action that you have decided upon. In order to do this, you will use your vehicle's controls and safety devices.

The driver of the yellow car decided to accelerate to provide space for the passing driver to return to the right lane.

### Decide

As you follow a selected path, your decision might be to maintain speed, change speed, change direction, or communicate your plan to others. Or you might decide to use a combination of these actions. Be prepared to rethink your decisions as zones close and greater hazards are presented. Practice and experience, as well as your judgment and stored knowledge, are the tools you can use to avoid conflict and develop low-risk driving behaviors.

**Decide to Change Speed** Any decision you make will be influenced by the speed of your own vehicle as well as the speed of other vehicles. Many drivers think that slowing down is the only way to avoid a conflict. In many situations, however, you will decide to maintain your speed. Your other choices of actions, rather than maintaining your speed, are to decelerate, brake, or accelerate. Base your decision about speed control on your evaluation of the situation as well as the possible consequences of your actions.

The driver of the yellow car on the two-lane road in the picture decided to accelerate. This decision provided space for the passing driver to return to the right lane. Had the driver of the yellow car decided to brake, there could have been a major collision in that driver's left-front zone.

**Decide to Change Direction** In order to change your position in the

### Objectives

1. Name the three decisions you must make when applying the IPDE Process.
2. Describe the three different lane positions available to you within your lane.
3. Explain what is meant when you minimize or separate a hazard or compromise space.
4. List the three most important actions you can take to avoid conflict.

---

## Teacher's Resources

**Resource Book**
Roadway Sheet 2, pages 6–7
Teacher's Instructions, page 36

**Demonstration Overheads**
Overhead B

**Content Overheads**
Overhead 12

**Video 1**
Segment on the IPDE Process

## Activity

**Model Car Activity** This activity will help students learn ways to select speed control and lane position. Divide the class into groups of three students. Give each group Roadway Sheet 2 from **Resource Book,** pages 6–7, two model cars, and a wild card (see pages T18–T19). Direct students to park one car on the right shoulder of the road and drive the other car forward. Ask: How many choices of speed control and lane positioning can you discover by moving your wild card and your driving car? (See **Resource Book,** page 36, for possible solutions.)

---

# Decide and Execute

## 1 Focus

### Summary

Decide and Execute are the DE of the IPDE Process. This lesson focuses on decision making and execution.

### Vocabulary

*compromise space, decide, execute, minimize a hazard, separate the hazards, space cushion*

## 2 Teach

### Explain

Before making and executing your decisions—for example, regarding a parked car as a closed right-front zone—you want to be certain that you have all information necessary. The first step is to see the parked car as a line-of-sight restriction to your right-front zone. Something could be concealed that could enter your path of travel. This is the IP stage of IPDE. Next check your other zones for conditions and options. Know if you can move into another lane if necessary. This step requires more IP of the IPDE Process. With all the information from the IP steps, you are now ready to Decide and Execute.

## Explain

Use **Content Overhead 12** or the illustration on this page to explain the three lane positions. Explain how effective use of lane positioning provides the driver a "space cushion." Point out that most travel lanes are 12 feet wide and most cars are less than six feet wide. This means it is possible to have enough empty space to either side of the car to provide an escape path for other vehicles. This escape path can help prevent them from colliding with your vehicle.

## Demonstrate

Use **Demonstration Overhead B** of a four-lane roadway. Place the yellow car in the center position of the right lane. Ask the class to shout out which lane position the car is in as you move the car from lane position 1, to 2, to 3, of the right lane. Then repeat the sequence while in the left lane. Then randomly place the car in various positions in either the left or right lane until the students respond correctly in unison.

roadway, you will steer to the right or left. A greater change of direction might even be a lane change.

The Smith System® key to leave yourself an "out" allows you to change direction when necessary. You then can use an escape path into an open zone to avoid conflict. This area of space all around your vehicle is called a **space cushion.**

Three different lane positions are available to you within your lane. You could change to one of these positions in order to avoid a closing zone. Notice the three lane positions in the diagram below.

• **Lane position 1:** The car is centered within the travel lane. This

should be your selected and safest position under normal driving conditions. In this position you have the most space around your vehicle.

• **Lane position 2:** The car is three to six inches away from the left line of your lane. You might decide to use this position when there is a closed right-front zone with an open left-front zone. Just a slight adjustment to the left is necessary.

• **Lane position 3:** The car is three to six inches away from the right line of your lane. Use this position when there is a closed left-front zone with an open right-front zone.

There may be times when the situation requires a greater change in direction than the three lane positions. You may decide that the best position, in some situations, is to straddle a lane line. In these situations, return to lane position 1 as soon as it is safe to do so.

In order to make consistently low-risk decisions, try to detect a changing zone condition at least 15 seconds ahead in your searching area. This gives you ample time to decide on the best action.

**Decide to Communicate** Communicating is the process of sending and receiving messages to and from other users of the roadway. The decision to communicate with others helps reduce the possibility of conflict. The Smith System® key, "Make sure they see you®," tells others where you are and what you plan to do. You can

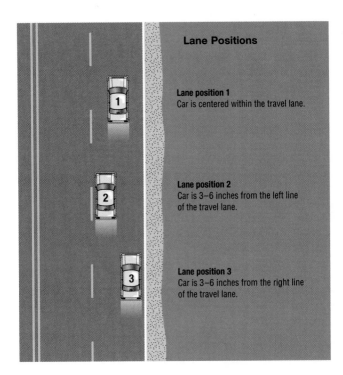

**Lane Positions**

**Lane position 1**
Car is centered within the travel lane.

**Lane position 2**
Car is 3–6 inches from the left line of the travel lane.

**Lane position 3**
Car is 3–6 inches from the right line of the travel lane.

## Facts and Figures

A large percentage of vehicles that end up in a junkyard due to a collision would not be there if the driver had effectively used the full amount of space available in the travel lane.

## Special Needs

For the Demonstrate activity in the teacher's notes on this page, have special needs students work with their partners. Have the partner use sign language (hands and fingers) to indicate the lane positions of the vehicle.

decide to communicate with others by using lights, horn, vehicle position, eye contact, and body movement.

A change in direction or speed can be executed with less risk if you have communicated your intentions to other users. Try to avoid changes in speed or direction without communicating first. Surprises of sudden actions can result in high-risk situations.

You can decide to communicate with others in a variety of ways:

- headlights, taillights, and brake lights
- turn signal lights
- parking lights and hazard flashers
- back-up lights
- horn
- car position
- eye contact and body movement

After deciding the best method of communicating, you will execute that action to inform others of your decision. The driver in the picture below is using body movement by waving the driver on the left through the intersection first.

### Traffic Flow

The IPDE Process, the Smith System, and the Zone Control System will help you make decisions that will enable you to avoid hazards and conflicts in your intended path. The safest position in traffic is the place where the fewest vehicles surround you. Your objective is to keep your vehicle surrounded by space. Continually analyze your left, front, and right zones and make decisions to adjust your speed or direction if one of your zones begins to close. By deciding to adjust your speed or direction, you will avoid unnecessary stops and thus reduce your risk of conflict.

Use body motions to communicate.

## Activity

**In-Class Driving Rehearsal** In this driving rehearsal, students will demonstrate how to communicate on the roadway. Arrange rows of student chairs into a simulated cross-road intersection (see pages T18–T19). Divide the class into four groups and have each group line up in a separate row at the point farthest away from the intersection. Give each student a simulated steering wheel. Have each student make up a driving situation and describe and demonstrate the correct form of communication to use in response to the situation. Have the students move simulated controls as if they were in a car. For example: they might say, "I am making a right turn," as they push upward with their left hand on an imaginary signal lever. Give the students positive feedback when correct behavior is demonstrated. Show them the correct behavior when it is not used.

## Discuss

Discuss with the class how the use of lane positions can minimize the hazardous effects a closed zone can present to your safe path of travel. Use overheads or the chalkboard to illustrate. Show situations when an adjustment of speed can give the best separation when fixed and moving closed zones occur at the same time. Emphasize that when you cannot have at least one zone open to the side, you must compromise by taking lane position 1 and reducing speed. Do some brainstorming with the class to generate various situations in which minimizing, separating, and compromising should be applied.

Use the following techniques to manage time, space, and distance in order to maintain your safe path of travel.

**Minimize a Hazard** You always want to **minimize a hazard,** or reduce the possibility of conflict by deciding to put more distance between yourself and the hazard. As the yellow car in the picture on the right approaches the parked cars on the right, the driver predicts a car door might open. Since there is no oncoming traffic, the driver decides to steer away from the parked cars into lane position 2. After passing the parked cars, the driver will return to lane position 1. The driver has minimized the hazard by using more space.

**Separate Hazards** There will be times when you face more than one

Minimize the hazard of the parked cars by moving to lane position 2.

hazard at a time. When this occurs do not try to handle both or all hazards at once. Instead, decide to adjust your speed so you deal with only one hazard at a time. By following this strategy, you will **separate the hazards.**

The driver of the car in the picture on the left sees the oncoming motor home in the left-front zone and the pedestrians in the right-front zone. The best decision is for the driver to adjust speed by slowing down. The motor home can then pass the pedestrians first. The driver would then meet the motor home with ample space before passing the pedestrians. In this situation, the driver separated the hazards and handled only one at a time.

The driver must separate two hazards—the pedestrians on the right and the approaching vehicle on the left.

**78** Unit 1 The Driving Task

## Background

**Minimizing and Separating Hazards** The structure for managing risk by minimizing and separating hazards and compromising space was created by Gene Carney of Maryland. Carney was one of the original creative thinkers in the Traffic Safety Education field. He developed the principle of creating response time through minimizing one hazard, allowing two hazards to separate, and optimizing position and/or speed when a driver has to compromise between two or more hazards.

## Activity

**Class Activity** Divide the class into groups and have them view the photograph. Ask: Is there a need to communicate to the pedestrians? Why? (No, they appear to be stable in their path on the sidewalk.) Where is the target area? What can you describe about it? (A red truck appears to be in the target area on a straight flat road.) In order to separate the pedestrians from the approaching vehicle, what actions does the driver need to take? (The driver needs to see both at least 12–15 seconds ahead to have an opportunity to change speed to encounter one at a time.)

The driver of the yellow car is compromising space to give more space to the greater hazard—the truck.

**Compromise Space** Sometimes hazards cannot be minimized or separated. When this occurs, you must decide to **compromise space** by giving as much space as possible to the greater hazard.

The truck in the picture on this page might enter the front zone of the yellow car to avoid the parked car leaving the parking space. Although the cars on the right present a hazard, the driver of the yellow car should decide to steer right as far as possible. This decision gives more space to the greater hazard, the approaching truck. In every situation, the action you decide on should be the one involving the least amount of risk.

### Execute

Carrying out your decision in order to avoid conflict is the execute step in the IPDE Process. This step involves the physical skills used in driving. In most cases, you will execute routine actions and maneuvers. Some actions will be using your vehicle's controls such as heater, defroster, wipers, gearshift lever, and others. More important actions, however, involve timing and placement of your vehicle to avoid conflict. The important actions you will execute are

- control speed
- steer
- communicate

**Control Speed** Your decisions to control speed can result in a variety of actions. At times the action you take will be to maintain the speed you are going. Other times your action may be to decelerate. This action can be used successfully as you approach a red light. If you merely release the accelerator far enough before the intersection, you often will arrive at the intersection when the light is green. In this situation, you also may use gentle pressure on the brake if more slowing is needed. Check your rear zone before decelerating.

When greater deceleration is needed, you will execute the action of more firm braking. The amount of braking needed will vary with the situation, the speed of your vehicle, the condition of the roadway, and the condition of your brakes.

Always check your rear zone before decelerating or braking in any

**SAFE DRIVING**

The IPDE Process is a constant interaction of the I, P, and D functions. Don't become a high-risk driver who only *executes*.

## Facts and Figures

According to the National Highway Traffic Safety Administration, 30 percent of all fatal collisions involve speeding.

Speeding includes driving faster than the posted speed limit or driving too fast for conditions. It reduces a driver's ability to steer, safely negotiate curves, or steer around objects in the roadway. It also increases the distance needed to stop a vehicle.

## Discuss

Direct students to the illustration on this page. Ask them what all three drivers could do differently if they were able to relive the last 12 seconds. What could the driver of the car have done to have better separation from the parked cars and the truck? (slowed down) What could the truck driver have done? (slowed down) What actions could the driver of the parked car entering the traffic flow have done better? (waited for the truck to pass) What speed control should each driver now take? (slow to a stop) What happens if the driver of the yellow car is preoccupied by the approaching truck and fails to see a pedestrian step out from between the parked cars that close the right-front zone? (hits pedestrian or swerves into path of truck)

## Explain

Again, ask students to look at the illustration on this page. If you were the driver of the yellow car, you would be in a high-risk situation with both the left-front and the right-front zones closed.

The driver, by having to take a compromised position into a closed zone, would need to reduce speed to a stopped position until the problem of the left-front zone is resolved.

## Discuss

Ask: What are the different ways by which you can achieve speed control? Give some specific examples of each.

## Explain

Explain that parking lights are not to be used when the vehicle is moving. Point out that some states prohibit vehicles from moving when hazard flashers are on.

## Discuss

Ask: When might you need to communicate with a vehicle to your rear? (slow traffic ahead, dangerous road conditions) Point out that you can flash the brake lights by tapping the brake pedal. This is a more dynamic means of communication because it does a better job of getting the driver's attention than a steady brake light.

## Demonstrate

Demonstrate how headlights are effective in daylight when driving in shadows. Bring a powerful flashlight and a piece of black cloth (at least one foot square) to class. Conceal the flashlight by holding the black cloth in front of it. Explain that the flashlight represents a vehicle's headlight and the cloth represents a shadow that the vehicle is driving in. Point out that during the day, the brighter the sun the darker the shadows. Turn the flashlight on and off while covered by the cloth. Ask: As your vehicle travels through a dark shadow, would you like others to perceive your vehicle with the light on or with it off? (on)

manner. Avoid locking the brakes in an emergency stop. Locked brakes make steering impossible because wheels must be turning to provide traction for steering. Some newer vehicles have an antilock braking system. Such a system helps prevent loss of steering control. An antilock braking system, through the use of computers, helps brake your vehicle in an emergency. All you need to do is to apply the brakes hard, continually. No pumping action is needed.

As the driver of the car in the picture below enters the intersection, the white car from the right makes a right turn and enters the driver's path. The driver avoids locking the brakes so as not to lose steering control. Locking the brakes could have caused the car to slide and result in a conflict.

**Steer** When you decide to steer away from a possible conflict, execute just the amount of steering needed. Oversteering can cause you to lose control of your vehicle, especially at higher speeds. Higher speeds also require more space for your maneuver.

Understeering can also present a problem. Try to steer just enough to avoid a conflict without making jerky or sudden movements. Drivers who keep space cushions around their vehicles usually have an escape path to steer into, thus reducing risk.

**Communicate** In many instances your only action will be to communicate. When you do communicate, you must do it early enough so other users know your intentions. Communicate by using the following:

• **Headlights, taillights, and brake lights** Use headlights during

**You Are the Driver!**
What procedures would you follow to avoid conflict? Assume that your vehicle has an antilock braking system.

80  Unit 1  The Driving Task

## Cross Curricular

**Science and Technology** Some daytime running lights are more than headlights that automatically come on during the day. New technology incorporates separate—and more effective—lamps with the headlight. Daytime running lights are already standard equipment on some vehicles.

Have students debate the issue in the *What Do You Think?* feature. Consider how running lights differ from headlights.

periods of reduced visibility. Using headlights during daylight hours, as the driver in this picture is doing, is a safety practice that makes your vehicle more visible to other drivers. Some new vehicles are equipped with daytime running lights—headlights that come on automatically whenever the vehicle is operated. The advantage of these lights is to improve the visibility of the vehicle. Research shows that the use of daytime headlights reduces daytime crashes of all types.

Your vehicle can be seen more easily if your headlights are on, even in daytime.

- **Turn-signal lights** Turn them on three to five seconds before making any change in direction.
- **Parking lights and hazard flashers** When you are parked along the roadway but not in an emergency situation, have your parking lights turned on. If your vehicle is disabled, turn on your hazard flashers. Be prepared to change your path of

travel when you see the blinking or flashing lights of a stopped delivery truck. The driver in the picture below has identified the blocked zone in time to safely pass the truck.

- **Back-up lights** White back-up lights let others know you are backing up. Look for back-up lights on vehicles in parking lots.
- **Horn** A light tap is usually enough for a warning. In an emergency, a loud blast may be necessary.

Be prepared to change your path to go around stopped vehicles.

Chapter 4 Managing Risk with the IPDE Process **81**

## Discuss

Discuss with students what back-up lights can mean to a driver or a pedestrian who is approaching parked vehicles in shopping centers and other parking lots.

## Explain

Explain that communicating by making eye contact should be used very selectively. It is best to use it only in positive situations. For example: You might use eye contact if you are attempting to enter a long line of slow-moving traffic and you want someone to let you in. Establishing eye contact can help to communicate your message: May I enter in front of you?

In some situations another driver may interpret eye contact as confrontational. For example: If another driver cut you off, you would not want to blow your horn and establish eye contact. In this case the message would communicate your anger.

## Activity

**Class Activity** Refer to the photograph at the bottom of this page and ask: What could be concealed in front of the FedEx truck? (pedestrian, small vehicle, bicyclist) Which zones should be checked to successfully manage the closed zone caused by the truck? (left-front and left-rear zones)

What actions would you take to avoid a conflict?

## Explain

Explain the importance of communicating with others using the roadway. Signaling or using other means of communication often eliminates a danger and makes further actions unnecessary.

## Demonstrate

Use **Video 1** segment on the IPDE Process to demonstrate how to apply the four steps of the IPDE Process to a simple driving situation. You can pause at certain points for discussion and replay to reinforce concepts.

## Assess

### Answers to Review It

**1.** Decisions in the Decide part of the IPDE Process include change speed, change direction, and communicate. (pp. 75–76)

**2.** Lane positions available are lane position 1, centered in your lane; lane position 2, 3 to 6 inches away from the left line of your lane; and lane position 3, 3 to 6 inches away from the right line of your lane. (p. 76)

**3.** To maintain a safe path of travel, minimize a hazard, separate hazards, and compromise space. (pp. 78–79)

**4.** Avoid conflict by controlling speed, communicating, and combining actions. (p. 79)

- **Vehicle position** The position of your vehicle in the roadway communicates a message. It indicates to others your intended path of travel. Other drivers may or may not see a light signal, but the position of the vehicle in the lane sends a message.
- **Eye contact and body movement** Try to develop eye contact with other roadway users. You can communicate many messages this way. Body movements such as a wave of the hand may tell a driver to proceed. Other hand movements may ask drivers to wait while you proceed.

### Combine Actions

You often will need to execute a combination of actions. Sometimes you might need to accelerate and steer at the same time. In other situations, you might need to brake, communicate, and steer at the same time.

If you were driving alongside the parked car in the picture above, you would need to combine several

actions. You would first check your rear zone and your left-front zone to see if they are open. Then communicate by signaling as you brake and steer around the open car door. The precision and timing with which you execute these actions will determine whether or not a conflict will occur.

### Review It

1. What are the three basic decisions you make in the Decide part of the IPDE Process?
2. What three different lane positions are available to you within your lane?
3. What are the three techniques you can use to maintain a safe path of travel?
4. What three actions can you execute to avoid conflict?

82 Unit 1 The Driving Task

## Activity

**Class Activity** Refer to the photograph on this page and ask: What actions should the driver have taken if the parked car was seen 12–15 seconds earlier? (Elicit responses that emphasize the value of identifying a zone change while searching the target area.)

Using the IPDE Process, along with the Smith System and the Zone Control System, helps you plan and execute maneuvers to reduce hazards. It is up to every driver to manage space, time, and speed in order to further increase safety within the HTS.

You must continually practice using the IPDE Process so that it will become habit. Once you have developed the habit, you will

- see more
- make accurate predictions and correct decisions
- execute maneuvers more successfully

### IPDE Takes Practice

Practice is necessary for the development and improvement of any skill. As you ride with other drivers, practice the I-P-D steps of the IPDE Process. You can then judge if the actions taken by others were based on correct decisions.

### Commentary Driving

**Commentary driving** is a system of "thinking out loud" as you practice the IPDE Process. When using commentary driving, you verbalize what you identify, predict, and decide.

Imagine you are the driver in the picture on the right practicing commentary driving. Using the IPDE Process, what would you say? Now turn the page to see the picture at the bottom. Did you identify and predict correctly? What action did you decide to execute? Practicing

commentary driving will help make the IPDE Process a basic part of your safe driving behavior.

### Putting IPDE Into Action

Use the four steps of the IPDE Process in order. Once you have learned the techniques for identifying, add the predicting step. You identify the hazards or events, then predict how they might affect your intended path of travel. You then perform the third step, deciding. Finally, you execute your maneuvers based on your decisions.

### Selective Use of IPDE

There will be times when you do not carry out the total IPDE Process. Conditions may change in one or more zones so the process need not be completed. You can use the IPDE Process selectively by beginning a new cycle before completing the previous one.

What warning clues are in this picture? What would you predict? What would you do?

Chapter 4  Managing Risk with the IPDE Process  **83**

### Objectives

1. Explain what is meant by commentary driving.
2. Describe what is meant by selective use of the IPDE Process.
3. Explain why the IPDE Process takes time.

# Using the IPDE Process

 **Focus**

## Summary

This lesson explains how students will put the IPDE Process into action. The lesson also offers reassurance that the process becomes easier and more effective with time and practice.

## Vocabulary

*commentary driving*

## **2** **Teach**

## Discuss

Ask how many students play a musical instrument or participate in a sport. Then ask them how important practice is to developing the skills needed to participate in these activities.

State that driving is much like playing an instrument or playing a sport: While learning to develop habits, actions feel clumsy and uncomfortable. Explain that developing the IPDE Process into a habit takes very precise practice.

## Explain

Commentary driving is one way of bringing practice to a level so that it can be repeated into habit.

## Discuss

Ask students to pretend they are the driver approaching the red light in the photo. Ask: What would you identify? (The pavement is wet and vision is reduced. The front zone is closed by the red light and vehicles in front, and the right-front and left-front zones are closed by traffic. You would need to check the rear zone.) What would you predict? (You will need to slow down, but it might take longer to stop on the wet pavement.) What would you decide and execute? (You would decide to brake slowly. You would execute by flashing your brakes to alert the driver in your rear zone and then by applying the brake.)

## Explain

Emphasize that practice will lead to a memory bank of driving information. Close the class with this thought: As students continue to read this book, they will put good experiences into their memory bank.

## 3 Assess

### Answers to Review It

1. Commentary driving is a system of "thinking out loud" while using the IPDE Process. (p. 83)
2. Use the IPDE Process selectively when conditions change and you need to begin a new cycle before completing one. (p. 83)
3. Complex traffic situations and the feelings and physical condition of the driver can cause the IPDE Process to take more time. (p. 84)

**You Are the Driver!**
How would you use the IPDE Process if you were the driver in this situation?

As you become a more experienced driver, you will learn the more important clues and trouble spots in different areas of the HTS. You will then be able to adjust your selective application of the IPDE Process for those specific areas.

### IPDE Takes Time

Remember that the IPDE Process takes time. You must have time to identify clues and changing zones. You must have time to predict the actions of others and the possibility of closed zones. The more complex the traffic situation and the more risk factors present, the longer it takes to carry out the IPDE Process.

At times your own feelings and physical condition can cause you to take more time to complete the IPDE Process. Do not allow complacency or laziness to creep into your driving habits. By making a conscious effort to continually apply the IPDE Process, you can achieve the reward of low-risk, low-stress driving enjoyment.

Warning clues were the ball in the street and the children in the yard. Did you predict and react correctly?

### Review It

1. What is commentary driving?
2. Explain what is meant by selective use of the IPDE Process.
3. What factors can cause the IPDE Process to take more time?

## Activity

**In-Class Driving Rehearsal** This activity will provide practice using commentary driving. It requires 35 mm slides or videotapes of traffic situations taken from the driver's point of view. Divide the class into teams with two or three students on a team.

Show one slide or a short video segment. Have one student on each team pretend to be the driver and provide a practice commentary. Ask the teammates to comment on the driver's commentary. Select one team to recap the key elements in the commentary. Provide positive feedback and additional information as required.

Show another slide or video segment and repeat the activity with a different member of each team in the role of the driver.

Continue until each student has had several chances to be the driver and each team has provided a recap for one of the situations. For each situation, position yourself to listen to a different student's commentary.

## Review Chapter Objectives

### 1. The IPDE Process

1. What are the three major factors that can contribute to the degree of risk you encounter while driving? (62)
2. What are the four steps in the IPDE Process? (63)
3. What are the five rules of the Smith System? (64)
4. How is the Zone Control System structured? (64)

### 2. Identify and Predict

5. What is the location of each of the six zones of the Zone Control System? (65)
6. What do "open zone" and "closed zone" mean? (65–66)
7. How do you use the identifying process known as an orderly visual search pattern? (67)
8. How can knowledge and experience help you make accurate predictions? (72–73)

### 3. Decide and Execute

9. What three decisions must be made when applying the IPDE Process? (75)
10. What are the three different positions available to you within your lane? (76)
11. How do you minimize a hazard, separate a hazard, and compromise space? (78–79)
12. What are the three most important actions you can take to avoid conflict? (79)

### 4. Using the IPDE Process

13. What does "commentary driving" mean? (83)
14. When is it appropriate to use the IPDE Process selectively? (83)
15. Why does the IPDE Process take time? (84)

## Projects

### Individuals

**Investigate** Visit your library to find more information about Harold Smith, founder of the Smith System. Write a short report about your findings.

**Observe Traffic** As a passenger in a vehicle during heavy traffic, observe the driver's use of the IPDE Process. In your opinion, were the driver's actions based on correct decisions? Discuss your observations with the class.

**Use Technology** Use the Internet to access the State Highway Patrol home page for your state to find information about traffic fatalities. List the risk factors that contributed to the fatalities and present your findings to the class.

**Observe Traffic** Ask students to make observations of the roadways they travel on as passengers to record locations where they are able to find actual examples of line-of-sight restrictions. Also, ask them to try to record five line-of-sight restrictions that were not listed during class. Have them bring their papers back to class for further discussion.

### Groups

**Observe Traffic** Observe for 15 minutes the drivers of the cars that drive past your school. Note risk factors you see. Compile a list of any driver-contributed risk behaviors that you see. Discuss the impact of these behaviors with your class.

**Investigate** Each person in the group should use a different Internet search engine to find more information about the IPDE Process. Discuss your findings with your group and class.

## Teacher's Resources

**Skills and Applications Workbook**
pages 13-16

**Tests and Activities**
Chapter 4 Activities 4-1 and 4-2, pages 27–28
Chapter 4 Test A and Test B, pages 29–32
Unit 1 Test, pages 33–36

**TestWorks CD-ROM**
Chapter 4 Test

## Review Chapter Objectives

**4.1** The IPDE Process
See Answers to Review It on page 64.
**4.2** Identify and Predict
See Answers to Review It on page 74.
**4.3** Decide and Execute
See Answers to Review It on page 82.
**4.4** Using the IPDE Process
See Answers to Review It on page 84.

For additional information, refer to the specific page(s) in parentheses after each question.

## Projects

Some of the projects can be assigned at any time while others are more closely tied to the content presented in the student text. The page number where the topic is introduced is indicated.

**Investigate:** page 64
**Observe Traffic:** page 75
**Use Technology:** page 62
**Observe Traffic:** page 65
**Observe Traffic:** page 62
**Investigate:** page 62

The results of student projects will vary.

## Answers to Check Your Knowledge

1. b
2. c
3. b
4. d
5. line of sight
6. ground viewing
7. prediction

## Answers to Review Vocabulary

8. target area range (e)
9. open zone (a)
10. central vision (f)
11. zone (d)
12. field of vision (g)
13. peripheral vision (b)
14. separate the hazards (c)

## Answers to Think Critically

Students' answers will vary. For information related to the question, refer to the pages indicated.

1. pages 68–69
2. pages 63–65

---

## Chapter Test

### Check Your Knowledge

**Multiple Choice** Copy the number of each sentence below on a sheet of paper. Choose the letter of the answer that best completes the statement or answers the question.

1. Which of the following risk factors is contributed by the roadway and environment?
   - (a) blurred vision
   - (b) bright sun
   - (c) bald tires
   - (d) broken headlight
2. Six areas of space around a vehicle that are the width of a lane and extend as far as the driver can see are called
   - (a) ranges.
   - (b) fields.
   - (c) zones.
   - (d) paths.
3. Peripheral vision refers to the area you can see
   - (a) while looking straight ahead.
   - (b) to the left and right of central vision.
   - (c) clearly and sharply.
   - (d) behind you.
4. Which of the following terms describes glancing continually and quickly through your orderly visual search pattern?
   - (a) ground viewing
   - (b) selective seeing
   - (c) steering
   - (d) scanning

**Completion** Copy the number of each sentence below. After each number, write the word or words that complete the sentence correctly.

5. An open zone is space where you can drive without a restriction to your _____ or to your intended path of travel.
6. Making quick glances to the roadway in front of your vehicle is called _____.
7. Almost every _____ you make as a driver will be related to anticipating zone changes and looking for alternative paths of travel.

### Review Vocabulary

Copy the number of each definition in list A. Match the definition in list A with the term it defines in list B.

**List A**

8. area as far ahead as you can see a target in the center of your intended path, and to its right and left
9. space where you can drive without restriction to your line of sight or intended path of travel
10. cone-shaped area of up to 10 degrees in which you can see clearly while looking straight ahead
11. one of six areas of space around a vehicle that is the width of a lane and extends as far as the driver can see
12. all the area a person can see while looking straight ahead
13. side vision area to the left and right of central vision
14. process of adjusting the speed of a vehicle to handle one hazard at a time when two or more hazards threaten a driver

**List B**

a. open zone
b. peripheral vision
c. separate the hazards
d. zone
e. target area range
f. central vision
g. field of vision

### Think Critically

Write a paragraph to answer each question.

1. Explain what it means to develop the art of scanning. Why is scanning important?
2. What is the relationship between the IPDE Process, the Zone Control System, and the Smith System?

## Decision Making

**1.** You are the driver of the car leaving the football game. Your team has just won. You are driving to a restaurant in town. How might your friends in the car contribute to your level of risk as you drive? What procedures will you follow to maintain a low level of risk?

**2.** How would knowledge and experience help the driver approaching the STOP sign execute a safe stop?

**3.** What do you predict will occur in your front zone? What steps will you take to reduce risk? Which lane position will you use?

**4.** You are the driver meeting the oncoming traffic. What do you predict an oncoming vehicle might do? If a vehicle does enter your lane, how will you complete the IPDE Process?

Chapter 4  Managing Risk with the IPDE Process  **87**

## Answers to Decision Making

**1.** Your attention to the driving task might be distracted by the excited friends in the car. This could cause you to take chances and demonstrate high-risk driving behavior. You should use the IPDE Process with your orderly visual search pattern to maintain a low level of risk.

**2.** Knowledge and experience tell you that traction is poor on wet or slippery roadways and it will take a longer distance to stop. You must check your rearview mirror and slow early and gently.

**3.** I predict that the bicyclist ahead may fall. The pedestrian may cause my front zone to be closed. I will check my rearview mirrors and brake as I move to lane position 2.

**4.** I predict an oncoming vehicle might enter my path of travel. If this occurs, I will check rearview mirrors, brake, and swerve to the right.

# Unit 2

# Controlling
Your
Vehicle

# Controlling
Your Vehicle

## Unit Overview

This unit introduces students to factors involved in controlling the vehicle. Students will discover how natural laws affect car control. They will learn how to perform basic vehicle maneuvers and negotiate various kinds of intersections safely. They will also learn how to interact safely with motorcyclists, bicyclists, pedestrians, and other roadway users.

## About the Photograph

This picture illustrates a scenic road in a coastal environment. As students learn about the basic skills involved in maintaining vehicle control, they will also learn how the surrounding terrain affects driving safety.

# Chapter 5  Planning Guide

**Chapter 5**
**Natural Laws and Car Control**

You Are the Driver! *p. 91*

Projects *p. 90*
Special Needs *p. 91*

---

**5.1  Gravity and Energy of Motion** *pp. 92–93*
- Explain how gravity affects your car.
- Describe the factors that affect energy of motion.

Demonstrate *pp. 92, 93*
Activity *pp. 92, 93*

---

**5.2  Friction and Traction** *pp. 94–97*
- Explain how traction controls your car.
- List three things that can reduce traction.
- Describe how you can check traction while driving.
- List factors that affect your car in a curve.

Demonstrate *p. 95*
Activity *p. 97*

---

**5.3  Stopping Distance** *pp. 98–99*
- Define total stopping distance.
- Explain how to use the four-second rule.
- Name four factors that affect braking distance.

Safe Driving Tip *p. 96*

Demonstrate *p. 99*
Activity *p. 99*

---

**5.4  Controlling Force of Impact** *pp. 100–104*
- List three factors that will change your vehicle's force of impact in a collision.
- Explain the correct way to adjust safety belts.
- Describe how a driver and passengers should position themselves to benefit from air bags.
- Explain how best to position and use child safety seats.

Did You Know? *p. 101*
What Do You Think? *p. 103*

Demonstrate *pp. 101, 102*
Activity *pp. 102, 103, 104*
Special Needs *p. 103*

---

**Assessment**

Reviewing Chapter
  Objectives *p. 105*
Projects *p. 105*
Chapter Test *p. 106*
Decision Making *p. 107*

Answers *pp. 106–107*

---

**Companion** *pp. 34–42*
**Spanish Handbook** *pp. 11–12*

**Video 1** Segment on Energy
of Motion

**Resource Book**
Teacher's Instructions,
*p. 37*

**Content Overhead 13**

**Content Overhead 14**
**Video 1** Segment on
Stopping Distance

**Video 1** Segment on Force
of Impact

**Skills and Applications
Workbook**, *pp. 17–20*
**Tests and Activities**
Chapter 5 Activities 5-1 and
5-2, *pp. 39–40*
Chapter 5 Test A and Test B,
*pp. 41–44*

**TestWorks CD-ROM**
Chapter 5 Test

## Technology Resources

### Audio-Visual and Computer Resources

ABS Education Alliance, *ABS Education Alliance Video*, video,
7 minutes

Coronet/MTI, *The Control Factor; Seatbelt Safety*, video, 30 minutes

Insurance Institute for Highway Safety, *Air Bags Now*, video

Insurance Institute for Highway Safety, *Kids and Airbags*, video,
5 minutes

Insurance Institute for Highway Safety, *Reducing the Risks in the
Crash*, video, 9 minutes

Insurance Institute for Highway Safety, *Understanding Car Crashes:
It's Basic Physics,* video, 22 minutes

Interactive Driving Systems, Inc., *Targeting,* 15 minutes

Meridian Education Corporation, *Staying Alive: A Consumer Reports
Car Safety Special,* video, 28 minutes

Safety Industries, Inc., *Buckle Up*, video, 14 minutes

Safety Industries, Inc., *Driving with Children*, video, 10 minutes

Safety Industries, Inc., *The Physics of Driving*, video, 10 minutes

## Kits, Equipment, and Other Resources

ABS Education Alliance, *ABS Curriculum*

Interactive Driving Systems, Inc., *Auto Control Monster*

Interactive Driving Systems, Inc., *Traction Board Demonstration Kit*

Go Online
PHSchool.com
**For: Chapter 5 online activities**
**Visit: PHSchool.com**
**Web Code: cak-9999**

# Chapter 5

## Natural Laws and Car Control

### Chapter Overview

Chapter 5 presents natural laws that apply to driving. Students learn about gravity, energy of motion, friction, traction, the parts of total stopping distance, and how to estimate stopping distance at different speeds. The force of impact in a collision and the benefits of restraint devices are discussed.

### Chapter Vocabulary

*active restraint device, banked curve, blowout, braking distance, center of gravity, energy of motion, force of impact, friction, gravity, passive restraint device, perception distance, perception time, reaction distance, reaction time, restraint device, total stopping distance, tread*

90

### Teacher's Resources

For students to use as they read the chapter:

**Companion**
pages 34–42

**Spanish Handbook**
pages 11–12

### Projects

Review the projects described on page 105. Some of the projects can be assigned at any time while others are more closely tied to the content presented in the student text.

# CHAPTER 5
## Natural Laws and Car Control

**5.1** Gravity and Energy of Motion

**5.2** Friction and Traction

**5.3** Stopping Distance

**5.4** Controlling Force of Impact

### You Are the Driver!

At the very instant that this picture was taken, tremendous forces were being applied. If you had been the driver and were using your safety belt, the air bag would have helped to prevent serious injury. How will natural laws affect your car control? What are the best hand and seating positions for you and your passengers if air bags inflate?

To be a safe driver, you need to know about natural laws. This chapter will introduce you to these laws and explain why you must respect them.

**Go Online**
PHSchool.com
**For:** Chapter 5 online activities
**Visit:** PHSchool.com
**Web Code:** cak-9999

91

### Introducing the Chapter

Discuss what natural laws take place during a collision. Tell students that as they study natural laws, they will learn about physical forces at play in driving. Ask a volunteer to describe how fast a collision can happen. Discuss how much warning a driver may have before a collision occurs. Emphasize the importance of thinking ahead.

### You Are the Driver!

Pair students to study the picture. Note how important safety belts and air bags are and ask why drivers might not use them. Discuss why safety belts need to be used with air bags. Ask students if they know what hand and seating positions are safe in vehicles with air bags.

### Special Needs

The concepts in this chapter are difficult for most students. Many of the activities and demonstrations in this chapter are crucial for understanding key concepts. Special needs students should work with their partners (as selected in Chapter 1) or assist with group activities. The physical involvement increases their attention, understanding, and retention.

# Gravity and Energy of Motion

 **Focus**

## Summary

This lesson focuses on the natural laws of gravity and energy of motion and how they affect the way vehicles perform. The effects of weight and speed also are presented.

## Vocabulary

*center of gravity, energy of motion, gravity*

 **Teach**

## Discuss

Ask: How does raising a vehicle's center of gravity affect its stability? How does putting oversized tires on a vehicle affect its stability? (It raises the center of gravity, which will make it less stable when a steering action, such as going into a curve, is necessary.)

## Demonstrate

Use **Video 1** Segment on Energy of Motion to demonstrate how speed and weight affect a vehicle's energy of motion.

### Objectives

1. Explain how gravity affects your car.
2. Describe the factors that affect energy of motion.

Gravity and energy of motion are natural laws that will affect the way your vehicle performs. When you operate a light vehicle like a bicycle at low speeds, you can easily maintain control. Control can be tricky, however, when you drive a car or a light truck that weighs almost two tons. In emergency situations, natural laws can create forces that can work for or against you.

### Gravity

**Gravity** is the force that pulls all things to Earth. The lack of gravity in outer space lets astronauts float. However, if you hit a ball, drop a rock, or drive your vehicle over a pothole, gravity pulls each to Earth.

### Driving Up and Down Hills

You can feel the pull of gravity as you drive up and down hills. When you drive uphill, you will lose speed unless you use extra power. To hold the same speed, you must increase the vehicle's power to overcome the pulling force of gravity. On a steep hill in a standard stickshift vehicle,

you will have to use a lower gear to increase power and maintain speed.

Gravity will increase your speed on a downhill road unless you control it. It will take you longer to stop, so you will need to think further ahead. Start braking early and shift to a lower gear on a long downhill stretch of road. This will let the engine—instead of the brakes—slow your vehicle.

How will an uphill or downhill situation affect your intended path of travel? In an uphill situation, your actual braking distance will be shortened a little. On a downhill road, your actual braking distance will be longer. The steeper the incline, the longer your stopping distance will be.

### Center of Gravity

The point around which an object's weight is evenly distributed is called its **center of gravity.** For example, high-wire circus performers use this law by holding long poles to help them maintain balance. As the ends of the pole curve down, the performer's center of gravity is lowered.

**Center of gravity**

**Center of gravity**

**Center of gravity raised**

A vehicle's stability decreases as its center of gravity rises.

## Teacher's Resources

**Video 1**
Segment on Energy of Motion

## Activity

**Class Activity** Have students experience the concept of center of gravity by balancing pencils on their index fingers. Point out that when a pencil is balanced, the heavier eraser end is closer to your finger than the point. Have students place a paper clip on the point end of the pencil. Point out that the center of gravity changes.

This lower center of gravity helps the performers to maintain balance and walk the thin wire without falling.

An automotive engineer tries to make a vehicle's center of gravity low so that it can perform better. Look at the vehicle in the pictures on the left. See how raising the vehicle's center of gravity could make it unstable on a steep hill or sharp turn. How would this vehicle perform in a sudden stop or swerve situation?

### Energy of Motion

When an object moves, it acquires energy. This force is called **energy of motion,** or kinetic energy. The faster your vehicle moves, the more energy of motion it has. Energy of motion is also affected by the weight of the moving object.

The pictures on this page show how a truck's energy of motion increases dramatically as weight and speed increase:

- The truck's energy of motion doubles when its weight is doubled by a load. When the truck weighs twice as much, it needs about twice the distance to stop.
- The truck's energy of motion will change in proportion to the *square* of its change in speed. When the truck's speed doubles, it needs about *four times* the distance to stop. If you triple your speed, you will need *nine times* the distance to stop.

Once you really understand this natural law, you can adjust to traffic

A vehicle's energy of motion increases dramatically with increases in weight and speed.

situations ahead of time. You will see how important it is to slow before an emergency situation develops. Every time you cut your speed in half, you cut your energy of motion by four times.

As a driver, you will feel the laws of gravity and energy of motion affecting your vehicle. Remember these laws when you need to judge how long it will take you to stop your vehicle.

### Review It

1. How does the force of gravity affect your car going downhill?
2. What factors affect energy of motion?

## Activity

**Class Activity** In this activity you will demonstrate the roll force of a vehicle with the center of gravity in different locations. You will need two plastic containers, a ruler, a yardstick, tape, rubber bands, and a 1/24" scale model car.

Tape the ruler to the top of a desk. Place the car on the desk with the left tires resting against the ruler. Tilt the desk until the car rolls over the ruler. Have a student measure and record how far the desk was lifted off the floor.

Secure an empty container to the top of the car with rubber bands and repeat the activity. Secure a water-filled container to the top of the car and repeat the activity.

Ask students to compare measurements and explain the differences. (Measurement for the first activity should be the greatest; second should be less; and third, the least. In the second activity the center of gravity was raised; therefore the vehicle rolled less than when the desk was lifted in the first activity. In the third activity the center of gravity was raised even further.)

### Demonstrate

This demonstration will illustrate how weight affects energy of motion. You will need two balls of similar size, but of different weight—for example, a ping-pong ball and a golf ball. Ask for a volunteer to catch the balls when you drop them from the same height.

Ask: Which had more energy of motion? Which would do more damage if it were to hit a pane of glass? Which represents a compact car and which represents a truck? Repeat the activity with several students to give the class a mental picture of how the energy of motion increases as weight increases.

Then use the heavier ball and drop it from different heights (to represent changes in speed). Compare the results and relate them to collisions at different speeds.

### Explain

Point out that the faster something travels, the more energy there is, and the more distance it will take to eliminate that energy. This is why the faster a vehicle is going, the longer it takes to stop.

 **Assess**

### Answers to Review It

1. The force of gravity will cause your vehicle to speed up when going downhill. (p. 92)
2. Speed and weight affect your energy of motion. (p. 93)

# 5.2

# Friction and Traction

## 1 Focus

### Summary

This lesson focuses on the natural laws of friction and traction and how they affect the way vehicles perform. The effects of improperly inflated tires also are presented.

### Vocabulary

**New:** *banked curve, blowout, friction, tread*

**Review:** *traction*

## 2 Teach

### Explain

Before class, make a footprint of a car tire. Use a jack to lift the car, apply paint to the lower quarter of the tire, lower the car onto a piece of poster board, jack up the car, remove the poster board, and lower the car.

Bring the poster to class and explain that it is a footprint of a car. Point out that four footprints similar to this one are all that is touching the road when you are driving.

### Objectives

1. Explain how traction controls your car.
2. List three things that can reduce traction.
3. Describe how you can check traction while driving.
4. List factors that affect your car in a curve.

Many people believe their steering wheel, brake pedal, and accelerator control their vehicle. Actually, your four tires, and their footprints that touch the road, are the first and one of the most important parts to the control system. Look at the picture below and spot the four footprints created by the car's tires. Each footprint is about as big as a page of this book.

**Friction** is the force that keeps each tire from sliding on the road. You can feel this same force by rubbing your hands together.

The friction created by the tire on the road is called **traction.** Traction makes it possible for your vehicle to grip the road so you can change speed and direction. Press the accelerator, and the drive wheels rotate. The traction of the tires mounted on these wheels makes your vehicle go forward.

Push the brake pedal, and braking friction will slow the four wheels on your vehicle. As the tires on these wheels slow, traction between the tires and the road will slow your

vehicle. This same system will enable your vehicle to turn left or right when the front wheels turn.

### Tires

Tires make a difference in the way your vehicle performs. The simple mistake of driving with low pressure in your tires can mean the difference between avoiding a collision or hitting something.

### Tread and Traction

The grooved surface of a tire that grips the road is called the **tread.** When the road is wet, the tread allows water to flow through the grooves and away from the tire. This action allows the tire tread to cut through the water and grip the road. Thus, the tire will not float on the water and lose traction. This gripping action on wet roads is critically important in preventing skids and hydroplaning (see page 252).

A tire's gripping ability will increase as the amount of tread

The four footprints of your tires on the road are the only contact between your car and the road.

94 Unit 2 Controlling Your Vehicle

## Teacher's Resources

**Resource Book**
Teacher's Instructions, page 37

**Content Overheads**
Overhead 13

## Background

**Friction** The amount of friction between two surfaces depends upon the substance of the material, the roughness of the surfaces, and the amount of force pushing the surfaces together. The softer the material, the more friction; the rougher the surface, the more friction; and the more force, the more friction. The presence of lubricants such as oil, water, or leaves tends to hold the surfaces apart. This results in reduced friction.

touching the road increases. Tire size will also affect the amount of tread and traction on the road. Use care when putting larger tires on a vehicle. Check the owner's manual for your vehicle for the maximum recommended size of tire to use.

A worn, bald tire is dangerous. A bald tire will not grip a wet or icy road. Because it has no tread, the tire may puncture. If this happens, the tire could suffer a **blowout** when all the air escapes at once. Check page 96 to see how to check your vehicle's tire tread depth.

### Inflation and Traction

Each tire is designed to work best between a range of high- and low-inflation air pressures. Check your owner's manual for the best pressure to use. The pictures on this page show how too much or too little pressure can change the amount of tread, or footprint, on the road. The dark gray areas show the best traction areas. The more dark gray area, the better. When your tire pressure is right, you will get your best control. You also will get your best gas mileage and tire wear because tires roll easier at the right pressure.

**Underinflation** When you drive on an underinflated tire (see the middle picture on this page), only the outside edges of the tire provide traction. That means the outside edges will wear out first. When this happens, the life of the tire is shortened. More importantly, in an emergency, the underinflated tire will not perform properly. Finally, an underinflated tire is likely to heat up and

fail more quickly than a properly inflated tire.

**Overinflation** Overinflating a tire should also be avoided. If the tire has too much pressure, only the center of the tire will grip the road properly (see bottom picture on this page). Over time, the overinflated tire will wear out its center tread more quickly than a normal tire.

Outside air temperatures can change the pressure in your tires, too. If the air gets colder, tire pressures will drop. Hot temperatures will increase pressures. Check tire pressures on a regular basis to make sure they have the right amount of air. To assure an accurate reading, check tire pressures when your tires are cold, before you start driving.

### Split Traction

Even under ideal conditions, the amount of traction your tires can produce is limited. The way you use the amount of traction you have is up to you.

In a straight-line braking situation, all traction is used to slow down your vehicle. However, when you are braking and turning, you divide your traction limit. You may use some of your traction to turn and some to slow. Or, you may use some traction to turn and some to speed up. In turning-braking situations, you will have to ease up on your brake pedal to avoid skidding. And remember, always try to drive at a speed where you can hold some traction in reserve.

Many vehicles today are four-wheel, or all-wheel drive. That means they can apply power to all four of

**Proper Inflation for Better Grip on Road**

**Proper Inflation**

**Underinflation**

**Overinflation**

The boxes show the areas of best traction—properly inflated tires grip evenly; underinflated tires grip only by the outer edges; overinflated tires grip only in the center.

## Cross Curricular

✚

**Physical Science** Have students research the terms below and write a brief summary of their findings. Assign one of the terms to each student in the class. The summary should include a definition and an example of how the term relates to driving.

Static friction
Sliding friction
Rolling friction
Internal friction

(Static friction is the holding force between two objects—tires against the road. Sliding friction is

the resistance to motion between two surfaces that are moving across each other—when non-ABS brakes are applied and the tires stop rotating and slide. Rolling friction is the resistance to motion of a rolling object—a rolling tire. Internal friction is the resistance to motion within elastic objects—such as when tires get warm from internal friction as they flex.)

## Demonstrate

Place a rubber band through the center pages and around the spine of an old book. Place the book on a desk and pull on the rubber band to pull the book across the desk. The rubber band stretches, indicating resistance due to friction between the book and the desk. Sprinkle some salt under the book and pull the book by the rubber band. Notice that the band stretches less than before.

Tape several pieces of sandpaper to the desk, sand-side up. Tape a piece of sandpaper to the back of the book. Place the book on the desk sandpaper-to-sandpaper. Pull the rubber band and notice how much greater grip the book has to the desk. Discuss how traction changes with different road surfaces.

See the Background information provided on page 94.

## Discuss

Ask students to think about how footwear and road surface affect traction while walking. Ask: What happens to traction when you walk on ice? (Traction is reduced.) What happens to traction when you run on ice while wearing smooth, leather-soled shoes? (Traction is reduced further.)

## Demonstrate

Use **Content Overhead 13** to illustrate how too much or too little air pressure in tires can reduce traction. Point out that a tire inflated to the correct pressure grips the roadway evenly.

## Explain

Point out that the tread of a tire is designed to work on wet surfaces. A bald tire can work on dry pavement, but will slide on a wet surface. Also, a bald tire is more likely to blow out.

## Explain

Explain that uneven levels of traction (inflation) among tires or uneven braking power can decrease vehicle control. If a vehicle pulls right or left while braking, the driver will only be able to use part of the vehicle's braking power. Remind students to check tire pressure frequently.

## Explain

Point out that if you approach a curve with too much speed, a braking action will be needed. You will have to use some traction for turning and some for braking. Point out that you should always slow down for a curve before you actually reach the curve. By seeing the curve in your target area, you will have plenty of opportunity to get good vehicle control. It is easier to get a proper speed before going into the curve than it is to regain control of the vehicle if speed was too fast in the curve.

Watch for warning signs for curves. As soon as you see the sign, begin slowing. You should reach the speed shown on the advisory speed sign by the time you reach the curve.

their wheels for added pulling power. But again, the basic laws of nature apply. Both two-wheel-drive and four-wheel-drive vehicles can use almost all of their four wheels of traction for stopping or turning. In a split-traction situation, however, you must divide the amount of available traction between stopping or starting and steering.

### Reduced Traction

You need two things to maintain ideal levels of traction. First, your vehicle must be in good condition. Second, the road must be smooth, paved, level, and clean.

### Vehicle Condition

When your vehicle is new, it is easy to control. But as it ages, you need to work hard to make sure it is maintained in top condition so it will perform correctly. If you allow tires, shock absorbers, or steering system parts to wear, traction and control will be reduced.

Good shock absorbers are very important for maintaining traction. Worn shock absorbers will cause your tires to bounce off a rough road and limit your control. Worn shock absorbers must be replaced to regain control.

Worn or improperly inflated tires also will limit your control. In an emergency situation, you will need all the control your tires can provide. Check tire pressure and tread frequently. You can check tire tread with a gauge or a penny. Make sure there is at least one-sixteenth of an inch, as the driver in the picture is doing.

### Road Surface

When you drive on a straight, dry, flat road, traction and control are great. But, if you drive the same vehicle on the same road on a rainy or snowy day, control will be reduced dramatically. When you see the road is about to change, reduce your speed before you reach the reduced-traction area.

Icy weather can be especially dangerous for driving. When ice is covered with water, traction control will be reduced to almost nothing. Be alert that water will freeze in shaded areas and on bridges *before* it does on regular roads.

**Checking Traction** When road conditions are bad, slow down your vehicle. You can use these steps to check how much traction you have:
1. Check your rear zone to make sure no traffic is near.
2. Brake *gently* to see how your vehicle responds.
3. If your vehicle does not slow or if your antilock brakes start to work, reduce speed even further.

If you can see all of Lincoln's head on the penny, switch the tire.

## Background

**Coefficient of Friction** The amount of friction between two surfaces is called coefficient of friction. Coefficient of friction is calculated by dividing the amount of force necessary to pull one surface over another by the amount of force (weight) pressing the two surfaces together.

## Curves

Energy of motion and traction will work on your vehicle as you drive around a curve. The energy of motion in your vehicle will try to make it go straight in a curve. The higher your vehicle's speed, the more it will tend to go straight.

Tire traction is the second force working for you in a curve. But if your speed is too high, you might not have enough traction to make the curve.

### Vehicle Control in Curves

Your vehicle's speed, the sharpness of the curve, the bank of the curve, and your vehicle's load will affect the control you have in a curve.

**Speed** You have no control over how sharp a curve is, but you can adjust your speed. To reduce your chance of skidding, lower your speed before entering a curve. Remember, your energy of motion will change in proportion to the square of your increase or decrease in speed. If you cut your speed in half, the force pushing you off the road will be cut four times.

**Sharpness of Curves** The sharper a curve, the more traction your vehicle needs to grip the road. Use lower speeds for sharp curves.

**Banked Curves** A curve that is higher on the outside than it is on the inside is called a **banked curve.** This type of curve helps to overcome your vehicle's tendency to move to the outside of the curve. This can be very helpful on a road that has a crowned, or higher, center.

This driver slowed ahead of time for this curve.

What should the driver do to adjust for the extra load?

**Load** Your vehicle's load affects your control in a curve. How will adding the load to the vehicle in the right picture affect control? To maintain control, the driver must slow when heavily loaded.

### Vehicle Capabilities

Vehicles of different sizes and power handle differently. Small vehicles like a motorcycle are light and can accelerate quickly. Large trucks and recreational vehicles, on the other hand, take lots of power just to accelerate to highway speeds. Large vehicles can take a long distance to stop. You need to remember these differences when you use the IPDE Process.

### Review It

1. How can traction control your vehicle?
2. What are three things that can reduce your traction?
3. What three steps can you take to check traction while driving?
4. Name three factors that can affect your vehicle in a curve.

# Stopping Distance

## 1 Focus

## Summary

This lesson focuses on stopping distance, reaction time, reaction distance, and braking distance. Students learn how to estimate stopping distance at different speeds. Factors that affect braking distance are discussed.

## Vocabulary

*braking distance, perception distance, perception time, reaction distance, reaction time, total stopping distance*

## 2 Teach

## Explain

In addition to perception, reaction, and braking distances, there is a fourth component that affects total stopping distance—volition. Volition is a conscious or deliberate decision. If a driver chooses not to apply the brake or is indecisive, the stopping distance increases.

For example, three drivers approach an intersection with a STOP sign. One driver never sees the sign and does not stop. The second driver sees the STOP sign but decides not to stop. The third driver sees the STOP sign, decides to stop, applies the brake, and brings the car to a complete stop.

### Objectives

1. Define total stopping distance.
2. Explain how to use the four-second rule.
3. Name four factors that affect braking distance.

When you are driving and have to stop, three things must happen. You must perceive the hazard in your path of travel, react, and brake your car to a stop.

### Total Stopping Distance

The distance your car travels while you make a stop is called your **total stopping distance.** The picture on this page shows how this distance is measured from the point you first see a hazard to the point where your vehicle stops.

### Perception Time and Distance

The length of time you take to identify, predict, and decide to slow for a hazard is called your **perception time.** Perception time will vary greatly depending on visibility, the hazard, and your abilities at the time. The distance your vehicle travels during this time is your **perception distance.**

You cannot consistently estimate your perception distance because your ability to perceive will change. Sometimes it will take longer to perceive a complex driving situation than it will take to brake to a stop. To help compensate for your long perception time, aim high and look 12 seconds or more down the road.

### Reaction Time and Distance

Once you recognize a hazard, the length of time you take to execute your action is your **reaction time.** An average driver's reaction time is

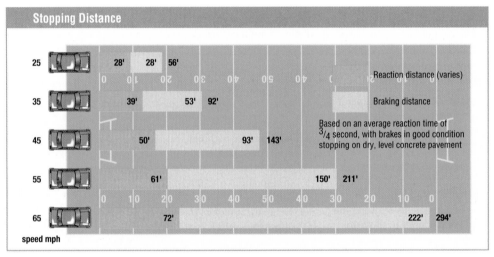

**Stopping Distance**

| speed mph | | | |
|---|---|---|---|
| 25 | 28' | 28' | 56' |
| 35 | 39' | 53' | 92' |
| 45 | 50' | 93' | 143' |
| 55 | 61' | 150' | 211' |
| 65 | 72' | 222' | 294' |

Reaction distance (varies)

Braking distance

Based on an average reaction time of $^3/_4$ second, with brakes in good condition stopping on dry, level concrete pavement

Distances traveled at various speeds once driver perceives hazard and begins to stop

## Teacher's Resources

**Content Overheads**
Overhead 14

 **Video 1**
Segment on Stopping Distance

## Cross Curricular

**Mathematics** Using a formula to estimate braking distance at various speeds (braking distance equals speed squared divided by 20), calculate the *extra* distance needed to stop a car when 5 mph is added to 30 mph and to 60 mph. If following distance were sufficient at 60 mph and not increased when the 5 mph is added, at what speed would you impact the lead car or object? (The extra distance will equal 31 feet—the distance needed to stop a car from 25 mph. This is 5 times more than the speed increase.)

three-fourths of a second. The distance your vehicle travels while you react is called your **reaction distance.**

### Braking Distance

The distance your vehicle travels from the time you apply the brake until you stop is called **braking distance.** A vehicle's energy of motion—and your braking distance—are proportional to the square of the increase in speed. If you accelerate from 20 mph to 40 mph, your braking distance will be about four times longer. If you know you are going to be driving into a high-risk situation, why is it so important to drive at a lower speed?

### Estimating Stopping Distance

The chart on this page shows your reaction distance and braking distance from different speeds.

Use the four-second rule, which enables you to project your approximate stopping distance under ideal conditions at any speed.

1. Pick a fixed checkpoint (a mark or shadow on the road) ahead where you think you could stop.
2. Count off four seconds: "one-thousand-one, one-thousand-two, one-thousand-three, one-thousand-four."
3. Check your vehicle's position. If you have just reached your fixed checkpoint, you can assume the distance you estimated in Step 1 was the approximate distance it would have taken you to stop. Practice estimating your stopping distance from various speeds. Keep

in mind it will take you almost 300 feet, or the length of a football field as shown in the chart, to stop if you are traveling at 65 mph.

### Factors That Affect Braking Distance

These seven factors can affect your total braking distance:
- **Speed** The higher your speed, the longer your braking distance.
- **Vehicle Condition** A vehicle with worn tires, shock absorbers, or brakes needs a longer distance to stop.
- **Roadway Surface** Rain, snow, ice, dirt, wet leaves, and gravel reduce road traction and increase stopping distance.
- **Driver Ability** If you are distracted or impaired, you will take longer to stop your vehicle.
- **Antilock Braking System (ABS)** If your car has an antilock braking system, you can better control your stopping distance while turning.
- **Hills** Your braking distance increases when driving downhill.
- **Loads** Heavy loads increase your braking distance.

Total stopping distance

> ### Review It
> 1. What three parts add up to your total stopping distance?
> 2. How can you estimate your stopping distance?
> 3. What factors can affect your braking distance?

Chapter 5 Natural Laws and Car Control **99**

## Activity

**Small Group Activity** This activity will help students understand reaction distance. You will need several yardsticks—one for every three students. Divide the class into groups of three. For each group, place a piece of masking tape on the wall five feet from the floor. Within each group, have the students choose a role: tester, reactor, or evaluator. Instruct all the testers to hold their yardsticks parallel to the wall with the beginning end even with the masking tape. The reactors are to place one hand 12 inches to the left or right of the yardstick. When the tester

releases the yardstick, the reactor attempts to stop the yardstick from falling. The evaluator measures the distance the yardstick fell before the reactor was able to stop it. Repeat the activity four times with students in the same roles. Switch roles and repeat the activity.

Then for demonstration select three students to do another test. Have one distracted by having a yardstick to either side of his or her hand. Give a false start on one and drop the other. Note the change in reaction time as more factors are added.

# Controlling Force of Impact

## 1 Focus

## Summary

This lesson focuses on the force of impact in a collision. The benefits of restraint devices are discussed.

## Vocabulary

*active restraint device, force of impact, passive restraint device, restraint device*

## 2 Teach

## Explain

Newton's first law states that an object in motion tends to stay in motion unless acted on by an outside force. Explain to students that if an unrestrained driver is traveling 60 mph and the vehicle hits a tree, the driver will continue to travel at 60 mph until acted on by an outside force, such as the windshield or steering wheel.

## Explain

In addition to the original collision, an impact always causes a second collision between the occupants and the inside of the vehicle or their restraint devices. A third collision occurs as occupants' organs impact inside their bodies.

## Objectives

1. List three factors that will change your vehicle's force of impact in a collision.
2. Explain the correct way to adjust safety belts.
3. Describe how a driver and passengers should position themselves to benefit from air bags.
4. Explain how to best position and use child safety seats.

If you have ever seen a severe traffic collision, then you know that collisions happen with blinding speed—usually in less time than it takes to blink your eye—and that these collisions can be violent. The following pages will show you how to protect yourself and your passengers if you are involved in a severe collision.

### Force of Impact

In a violent collision, vehicle occupants need all the protection they can get. If they are not protected, they will be thrown against the vehicle's interior in a second collision or ejected from the vehicle.

The force with which a moving object hits another object is called **force of impact.** Three factors determine how hard something will hit another object—speed, weight, and distance between impact and stopping.

**Speed** Speed is the most important factor in determining how hard a vehicle will hit another object. The force of impact is in proportion to the square of the increase or decrease in the vehicle's speed. Any reduction in speed will greatly reduce the damage inflicted. Always try to reduce speed in an emergency.

**Weight** The heavier a vehicle, the more damage it will cause in a collision. A vehicle weighing twice as much as another vehicle will hit a solid object twice as hard.

**Distance Between Impact and Stopping** The distance a vehicle

covers between the instant it hits an object and the moment it comes to a stop can vary greatly. Imagine hitting barrels filled with sand sitting in front of a light post rather than hitting the post itself. The barrels will slow you as you hit them rather than stopping you like the post would. This is why traffic engineers put cushioning materials in front of solid roadside objects.

### Safety Belts

Three collisions occur when a vehicle hits a solid object. First, the vehicle hits the object and stops. Second, the occupants either hit the inside of the vehicle or their **restraint devices.** Third, occupants may suffer internal collisions as their organs impact inside their bodies.

A restraint device is any part of a vehicle that holds an occupant in a crash. A **passive restraint device,** such as an air bag, is a part that works automatically. A device you have to engage, like a safety belt, is called an **active restraint device.**

### How to Wear Safety Belts

What can you do ahead of time to reduce the possibility of serious injury? Using safety belts is your number one defense. Safety belts will hold you in place during an emergency and prevent you from being thrown from your vehicle. Any time you are in a vehicle, you need to follow these steps for wearing your safety belt:

---

## Teacher's Resources

**Video 1**
Segment on Force of Impact

---

## Cross Curricular

**Mathematics** Have students practice converting miles per hour into feet per second. Ask if anyone knows how many feet are in a mile. (5,280) Explain how to convert one mile per hour to feet per second (5,280 feet ÷ 60 minutes ÷ 60 seconds = 1.467 feet per second). Explain that you can then multiply the number of miles per hour by 1.467 (or 1.5) to get the feet per second. Have students convert these speeds to feet per second: 25 mph (37 feet per second), 40 mph (59 feet per second), and 55 mph (81 feet per second).

1. Adjust your seat to a comfortable upright position. Make sure your safety belt is not twisted.
2. Snap the metal fitting on the end of the safety belt into the buckle. Then adjust the lap part of your safety belt so that it is low and snug across your hips. The bottom edge of the safety belt should just touch your thighs. By making this adjustment, any crash forces will be applied to your pelvic bones.
3. Finally, adjust the shoulder part of your safety belt across your chest. Your shoulder belt should be snug. These adjustments will work for all normal-height individuals, including expectant mothers. For children, see the section on child safety seats later in this chapter. Like the driver shown in the picture, you are responsible for everyone in your vehicle.

### Air Bags

An air bag is a balloon-type device that automatically inflates to protect

Everyone needs to take responsibility for a safe trip.

you. Look at the first page of this chapter to see an inflated air bag. If collisions happen in the blink of an eye, air bags work even more quickly. They deploy at speeds over 200 mph. The following description of a collision between two air-bag-equipped cars will give you some idea of their effectiveness.

The investigation revealed exactly what happened. Driver A had seen

**INVENTOR OF SAFETY BELTS**   Nils Bohlin is the engineer who invented the modern three-point lap and shoulder safety belt while working for the Volvo Automobile Company in Sweden. These belts appear in most vehicles around the world.

According to Mr. Bohlin's design, the belts should fit snugly across the chest. Belts that are too loose will not restrain the chest properly in a crash.

Chapter 5  Natural Laws and Car Control  **101**

## Background

**Safety Belt Advantages**   There are five advantages gained by use of safety belts. (1) The driver stays in the driving compartment, where there is a better chance to steer the vehicle. (2) The driver and occupants stay in the vehicle, reducing the chance of disabling injuries. (3) The body gets slowed down gradually. Without belts the body stops abruptly, which increases brain trauma and internal injuries. (4) Occupants are not thrown into the crash. (5) Occupants with belts on will not crash into the driver, who could then lose vehicle control.

## Facts and Figures

Automobile collisions are the leading cause for an individual to become permanently disabled. Being ejected from a vehicle by not wearing a safety belt increases the risk of becoming disabled.

## Demonstrate

Demonstrate how speed influences force of impact. Use 3 same-size pieces of soft clay. Throw them at the wall or floor at increasing speeds. Compare the increased spread of the clay from the impact.

## Explain

Point out that safety belts allow freedom of movement under normal conditions. In a collision, they lock instantly to protect the wearer.

## Explain

Emphasize the importance of having all occupants properly secured in a vehicle with safety belts or child seats. Removable child seats must be properly secured to the vehicle using safety belts, and children must be properly restrained within the seat. Child seats must be the appropriate size for the child. Do everything possible to emphasize the enormous forces a collision can produce. Point out that it is foolish to think that an adult could hold a child safely during a collision.

## Demonstrate

Use **Video 1** Segment on Force of Impact to demonstrate how force of impact affects vehicles and their occupants during a collision.

## Demonstrate

Use two pieces of chalk and one-half of an egg carton to demonstrate the protection a cushion can provide. Hold one piece of chalk at shoulder height and let it drop to the floor and break. Tape the second piece of chalk inside half an empty egg carton. Drop the carton from the same height and remove the unbroken piece of chalk. Point out that restraint devices in a vehicle use the same principle.

## Explain

Point out the description of a collision that starts on page 101 is a report of an actual collision. The report appeared in the September 1990 *Reader's Digest*.

## Discuss

Ask students to summarize how you can gain the most benefit from air bags. Ask: Why is it important to use safety belts if you have air bags? What can you do to avoid injury from an air bag? What is the best position for a driver in a vehicle with an air bag? How should you position a tilt steering wheel in a vehicle with an air bag? Where should children sit in vehicles with air bags? (Answers to these questions appear in the second column on this page and the first column on page 103.)

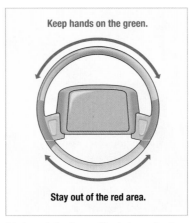

Keep hands on the green.

Stay out of the red area.

A balanced steering position between the 9 and 3 o'clock or the 8 and 4 o'clock position is best to avoid injury from an air bag.

10 inches

You must have 10 inches or more between your chest and the air bag in the steering wheel.

a car heading toward him on his side of the road and had virtually stood on his brakes. Then he was aware that his face was being buried in a balloon-like pillow. Driver B remembers her bag suddenly billowing in front of her nose. "It was a jolt, but not a hard jolt. Like when you were a kid and jumped on a mattress...."

The Insurance Institute for Highway Safety team established that the crash was the equivalent of each of them hitting a stationary object at 68 mph. As the cars slammed together, each driver's head was thrown forward with 1700 pounds of force.... 

By the time the hood of each car began to crumple, both bags were fully inflated and positioned directly in line with the head and torso of each driver. As their heads slammed forward, the folds of the air bag softened the impact, like a big balloon. At maximum inflation, the bags began to vent nitrogen gas to ensure the gentlest impact possible.

Thanks to air bags, both drivers recovered from this collision.

To receive full benefit from air bags, you need to know the following:

• Air bags are designed to work with safety belts. That is why air bags are called a supplemental restraint system. Most air bags protect in frontal collisions only. Safety belts provide front, side, and rollover protection. Some vehicles also have overhead and side-door air bags for extra protection.

• To avoid an air-bag injury, keep your hands on the steering wheel between the 9 and 3 o'clock and the 8 and 4 o'clock position. This balanced steering position will give you your best ready position for steering. Look at the picture above left to see this range. If your hands are too high or too low in an air bag collision, you could suffer a serious hand, arm, head, or eye injury.

## Activity

**Class Activity** This activity will help students understand how safety belts and air bags help protect drivers and passengers. You will need a remote-controlled model car, a small doll, rubber bands, balloons, a sponge, and a video camera.

Place the doll in a sitting position on top of the model car. Have a student drive the car at full speed into a wall. Have another student videotape the collision. Notice how the doll collides into the wall. Use the same starting point and the same speed for all the collisions. Attach the doll to the

car with rubber bands. Drive the car into the wall and videotape it. Inflate and tie a balloon. Attach it on top of the car in front of the doll to simulate an air bag. Repeat the collision and videotape it. Attach the sponge to the wall at the collision site. With doll and balloon attached on top, collide the car into the sponge and videotape the collision. Play back the video segments in slow motion or freeze frame to see the movement of the doll during the crash. Encourage students to discuss the various effects.

- Sit away from an air bag after you are belted. As the driver, your chest should be at least 10 inches away from the steering wheel hub, as shown in the right-hand picture on the opposite page. Use approved pedal extensions if needed to attain this distance. As a front-seat passenger, move your seat as far back as possible.
- If you have a tilt steering wheel, tilt it so your air bag will deploy toward your chest.
- Children in child seats and young people up to the age of twelve must sit in the back seat as shown in the picture. When children, and even short adults, ride in the front seat of an air-bag-equipped vehicle, they can be injured if the air bags deploy.

Always use child seats in the back seat.

### Air Bag Improvements

The air bag has proved to be an effective life-saving device. Engineers are now designing features to make air bags even more effective. The following list highlights some of the features that are being developed:

- **Advanced air bags** Because some people have suffered serious injuries as the bag deploys, some vehicles are now equipped with air bag systems with advanced features. Sensors can measure weight and seat position of passengers and severity of the crash. Then, the air bag deploys in two stages with appropriate speed and intensity.
- **Air bag switches** To give vehicle owners a choice about using an air bag, some owners may ask permission to have a switch installed to turn off the front passenger air bag. This is an enormous compromise. If you are considering this option, check your insurance policy to make sure it will be in full force if you switch off an air bag. Also check your safety belts to see if they are designed to stretch. If you install the switch, you will need to replace those safety belts with belts that do not stretch.

### Other Protection Devices

To reduce risk in collisions, automobile engineers have designed

**What Do You Think?**

Certain people can get permission to have an air bag on/off switch installed. Do you think switches should be available on all vehicles? Why or why not?

## Explain

One reason for turning off the front passenger air bag is to protect children who must sit in the front seat. For example, some sports cars and trucks have no back seat.

## Discuss

Ask students if they or anyone they know has been in a collision where an air bag deployed. Ask about injuries sustained in the collision.

## Discuss

Side-impact air bags are now available on some vehicles. Ask: Do you think that side-impact air bags will become standard equipment?

## Explain

Sitting at least ten inches away from the steering wheel significantly decreases the risk of serious air-bag injury. A small number of individuals may have difficulty reaching the pedals when they sit ten inches away from the steering wheel. An alternative to moving closer to the steering wheel is the use of pedal extenders.

## Activity

**Small Group Activity** This activity will help students understand the importance of seat belts and air bags. Have each student select a newspaper or magazine article related to collisions where drivers and/or passengers were injured. Divide the class into groups of four and have students discuss their articles. Have each group report on the role of safety belts and air bags in the collisions reported in their group's articles.

## Special Needs

Use the Demonstrate activity on page 102. Then demonstrate the same concept by dropping a hard-boiled egg from a height of two feet above the desk onto a towel folded over three or four thicknesses. Point out that very little padding goes a long way.

Ask students to speculate why some drivers do not wear safety belts. Help them list reasons and possible responses.

## Discuss

Ask students to think of devices in vehicles that protect during a collision. Record all contributions on the board. After all responses are made, ask students to evaluate them. Discuss how the device protects you in a collision.

 **Assess**

## Answers to Review It

**1.** Speed, weight, and distance will determine your force of impact. (p. 100)

**2.** When putting on safety belts: (1) Adjust your seat. (2) Adjust the lap part of your belt low and snug across your hips. (3) Adjust the shoulder part of your safety belt so that it is snug across your chest. (p. 101)

**3.** Adjust your seat so that your chest is at least ten inches from the air bag in the steering wheel hub. Use a balanced steering wheel hand position between the positions of 9 and 3 or 8 and 4 o'clock. (p. 102)

**4.** All child seats should be secured in the back seat. (p. 104)

Make sure your lap belt is used with your shoulder belt.

Adjust your head restraint to reach the middle of the back of the head.

additional devices in new vehicles to protect you. These are a few of them:

- **Automatic safety belts** Some vehicles have automatic safety belts for occupant protection. To use these belts, you must make sure your lap belt is buckled low and across your hips. Then when your door is shut, your shoulder belt is drawn into place as shown in the picture.
- **Front and rear crush areas** Vehicles are now designed to have their front or rear end crush on impact. When this happens, the dramatic force of impact is lessened for occupants in the vehicle.
- **Energy-absorbing bumpers** Most vehicles are now equipped with bumpers that are designed to absorb low levels of impact under 5 mph without damage. This will provide protection in many minor collisions.
- **Side door beams** Many vehicles now have steel beams built into the side doors. These beams provide valuable protection in collisions where you are hit on an angle.
- **Reinforced windshield** To avoid flying glass in a collision, vehicles now have laminated windshields. This means the windshield is really two pieces of glass with a thin layer of plastic in the middle.
- **Energy-absorbing steering wheel and column** This type of steering wheel and column is designed to compress when hit.

- **Padded dash** This design feature can reduce injury in all crashes.
- **Child seats** The use of special seats for infants and small children is required in every state. These seats must be used in the back seat of your vehicle, as shown in the picture on page 103. If used in the front seat of a vehicle with air bags, an air bag could seriously injure a child in the event of a crash. Always follow your child seat manufacturer's instructions.
- **Head restraints** Padded head rests on the top of seats are designed to protect you against whiplash injuries. To make sure you get the full benefit of this protection, adjust your head rest as shown in the picture.

### Review It

1. What three factors can affect force of impact?
2. What three steps should you take when putting on safety belts properly?
3. What are the two key steps you should take to protect yourself as the driver of a car with air bags?
4. Where should all child seats be secured in a car?

## Activity

**Class Activity** This activity will help students understand the high risk and low gain of not wearing safety belts. Tell students you have a lottery game where the odds are 100,000 to 1 that a player will win. Ask: How do you like those odds? Explain that each of the 100,000 players writes their name on a piece of paper and places it in a barrel. The barrel is spun, and the person whose name is pulled out pays all the other players one dollar each. You can play this lottery three times a day.

Ask: How many of you would like to play this lottery? What if you were to play it three times a day before you lose? Would it be worth it? (Get the students to tell you that it is foolish to play lottery because the gain of three dollars a day is not worth the potential loss of $100,000.) Then ask: What lottery are people playing when they do not wear safety belts? (Get students to see how easy it is to do something that has a high risk and low gain but nothing happens. They continue to play that low-gain high-risk lottery often enough until they lose.) Is it worth it?

## Reviewing Chapter Objectives

### 1. Gravity and Energy of Motion

1. How does gravity affect your vehicle? (92)
2. What are the factors affecting energy of motion? (93)

### 2. Friction and Traction

3. How does traction control your vehicle? (94)
4. What three things can reduce traction? (95–96)
5. How can you check traction while driving? (96)
6. What are the factors that affect your vehicle in a curve? (97)

### 3. Stopping Distance

7. What is total stopping distance? (98)
8. How do you use the four-second rule? (98–99)
9. What are four factors that affect braking distance? (99)

### 4. Controlling Force of Impact

10. What are three factors that will change your vehicle's force of impact in a collision? (100)
11. What is the correct way to adjust safety belts? (101)
12. How should a driver and passengers position themselves to benefit from air bags? (102)
13. How do you best position and use child safety seats? (103–104)

## Projects

### Individuals

**Investigate** With the owners' permission, examine the tires of at least 10 vehicles. Check for signs of worn tread or bald spots. Write a short report about your findings. In the report, describe the condition of each vehicle's tires. Also give the percentage of vehicles that you checked that have worn tread or bald tires.

**Use Technology** Using a tire-pressure gauge, determine the tire pressure of the vehicles you checked in the Investigate project above. Make a computer spreadsheet for your findings. Your spreadsheet should also include your observations about the conditions of the tire treads.

### Groups

**Research** Observe at least 50 vehicles at a busy intersection. One-third of the group should record the number of drivers wearing safety belts; one-third should record the number of passengers wearing safety belts; one-third should record the number of child seats, and whether the child seat was in the front or back seat of the vehicle. Discuss your results with the class.

**Investigate** Gather advertisements for tires from newspapers or magazines. Make a group list organized by sizes of tires you see in the ads. Also include prices and special features (such as special treads or other safety-related features). Compare your group lists in class.

## Reviewing Chapter Objectives

**5.1** Gravity and Energy of Motion
See Answers to Review It on page 93.
**5.2** Friction and Traction
See Answers to Review It on page 97.
**5.3** Stopping Distance
See Answers to Review It on page 99.
**5.4** Controlling Force of Impact
See Answers to Review It on page 104.

For additional information refer to the specific page(s) in parentheses after each question.

## Projects

Some of the projects can be assigned at any time while others are more closely tied to the content presented in the student text. The page number where the topic is introduced is indicated.

**Investigate (Individuals):** p. 94
**Use Technology:** p. 94
**Research:** p. 100
**Investigate (Groups):** p. 94
The results of student projects will vary.

## Teacher's Resources

### Skills and Applications Workbook
pages 17–20

### Tests and Activities
Chapter 5 Activities 5.1 and 5.2, pages 39–40
Chapter 5 Test A and Test B, pages 41–44

### TestWorks CD-ROM
Chapter 5 Test

## Answers to Check Your Knowledge

1. c
2. d
3. a
4. b
5. gravity
6. square
7. increase
8. higher

## Answers to Review Vocabulary

9. tread (c)
10. center of gravity (e)
11. active device (a)
12. total stopping distance (d)
13. friction (b)

## Answers to Think Critically

Students' answers will vary. For information related to the question refer to the page(s) indicated.

1. See pages 94–95.
2. See page 97.

## Chapter Test

### Check Your Knowledge

**Multiple Choice**  Copy the number of each sentence below on a sheet of paper. Choose the letter of the answer that best completes the statement or answers the question.

1. When an object moves, it acquires
   (a) friction.  (c) energy of motion.
   (b) traction.  (d) speed.
2. The length of time you take to execute an action is called your _____ time.
   (a) total stopping  (c) braking
   (b) perception  (d) reaction
3. Which of the following is an example of a supplemental restraint system?
   (a) air bag  (c) lap and shoulder
   (b) safety belt  belt
   (d) antilock brakes
4. In a _____ situation, you must divide the amount of available traction between stopping or starting and steering.
   (a) reduced traction  (c) sharp curve
   (b) split traction  (d) banked curve

**Completion**  Copy the number of each sentence below. After each number, write the word or words that complete the sentence correctly.

5. The force that pulls all things to earth is called _____.
6. A vehicle's energy of motion will change in proportion to the _____ of its change in speed.
7. The gripping ability of a tire will _____ as the amount of tread touching the road increases.
8. The _____ your speed, the longer your braking distance.

### Review Vocabulary

Copy the number of each definition in List A. Match the definition in List A with the term it defines in List B.

**List A**

9. grooved surface of a tire that grips the road
10. point around which an object's weight is evenly distributed
11. restraint device that you have to engage
12. distance your vehicle travels while you make a stop
13. force that keeps each tire from sliding on the road

**List B**

a. active device
b. friction
c. tread
d. total stopping distance
e. center of gravity

### Think Critically

Write a paragraph to answer each question.

1. Explain the relationship between traction and the amount of air in a vehicle's tires. Use the terms "underinflation" and "overinflation" in your answer.
2. Discuss how speed, sharpness of curve, and your car's load affect how you control your vehicle in a curve. Why are banked curves often beneficial?

## Decision Making

**1.** What two things has this driver done to adjust to the air bag?

**2.** You are driving the yellow car and have locked your standard brakes to avoid a head-on collision. Your wheels are sliding. You want to head for the shoulder to avoid trouble. What should you do?

**3.** You are approaching this curve at 40 mph. To maintain control, when should you adjust your speed?

**4.** The driver ahead is braking to maintain control. What two factors might increase the stopping distance in this situation?

## Answers to Decision Making

**1.** The driver's chest is at least ten inches from the air bag in the steering wheel hub and his hand position is balanced in the 9 and 3 o'clock position.

**2.** Let up on your brake pedal so that your tires will start rolling. Then you will be able to steer to the shoulder.

**3.** Adjust your speed before entering the curve to maintain control.

**4.** The stopping distance could be increased by gravity pulling your vehicle downhill and by the gravel road, which reduces traction.

Chapter 5 Natural Laws and Car Control **107**

**Student Features**

**Teacher's Edition**

## Chapter 6
## Performing Basic Vehicle Maneuvers

You Are the Driver! *p. 109*

Projects *p. 108*
Special Needs *p. 109*

---

### 6.1 Steering, Signaling, and Changing Lanes *pp. 110–112*
- Explain how to steer straight forward and backward.
- Describe the correct use of hand signals and explain when they might be used.
- List the proper steps for changing lanes.

Demonstrate *p. 112*
Activity *p. 112*
Special Needs *p. 111*

---

### 6.2 Making Turns and Turning the Vehicle Around *pp. 113–118*
- Describe hand-over-hand steering.
- List the steps for making right and left turns.
- Describe how to back left and right.
- Describe five turnabouts and tell which is the safest to use.

What Do You Think? *p. 115*

Demonstrate *pp. 114, 115, 116, 117, 118*
Activity *pp. 113, 115, 118*
Special Needs *p. 116*

---

### 6.3 Parking *pp. 119–124*
- Discuss reference points and how to use them as guides when parking your vehicle.
- Describe the procedures for angle, perpendicular, and parallel parking.
- Describe how to park uphill and downhill with and without a curb.
- Explain how to start from an uphill parking space without rolling backwards.

Did You Know? *p. 122*
Safe Driving Tip *p. 124*

Demonstrate *pp. 121, 122*
Activity *pp. 119, 120, 121, 122*

---

### Assessment

Reviewing Chapter Objectives *p. 125*
Projects *p. 125*
Chapter Test *p. 126*
Decision Making *p. 127*

Answers *pp. 126–127*

**Companion** *pp. 43–49*
**Spanish Handbook** *pp. 13–14*

---

**Resource Book**
Roadway Sheet 2, *pp. 6–7*
Information, *pp. 69–74*
**In-Car Checklists** 7, 8

**Demonstration Overheads
B, J**
**Video 1** Segment on
Changing Lanes

---

**Resource Book**
Information, *p. 75*
**In-Car Checklists** 9, 10, 11,
12, 13, 14

**Demonstration Overheads
A, C, D, F**
**Content Overhead 8**

---

**Resource Book**
Roadway Sheet 8 *pp. 18–19*
Teacher's Instructions,
*pp. 39–40*
Information, *p. 77*
**In-Car Checklists** 15, 16,
17, 18, 19, 20, 21, 22

**Demonstration Overhead L**
**Content Overhead 15**

---

**Skills and Applications
Workbook**, *pp. 21–24*
**Tests and Activities**
Chapter 6 Activities 6-1 and
6-2, *pp. 47–48*
Chapter 6 Test A and Test B,
*pp. 49–52*

**TestWorks CD-ROM**
Chapter 6 Test

# Technology Resources

## Audio-Visual and Computer Resources

AAA Foundation for Traffic Safety, *driver-ZED* CD-ROM

Interactive Driving Systems, Inc., *Backing and Parking,* video,
20 minutes

Interactive Driving Systems, Inc., *Precision Turns,* video, 15 minutes

Interactive Driving Systems, Inc., *Reference Points,* video, 23 minutes

National Safety Council, *Parking Safely*, video, 14 minutes

National Safety Council, *Backing Safely*, video, 12 minutes

Safety Industries, Inc., *Basic Car Control*, video, 10 minutes

# Kits, Equipment, and Other Resources

Interactive Driving Systems, Inc., *Auto Control Monster*

Interactive Driving Systems, Inc., *Reference Point Demonstration Kit*

Go Online
PHSchool.com

For: Chapter 6 online activities
Visit: PHSchool.com
Web Code: cak-9999

# Chapter 6

# Performing Basic Vehicle Maneuvers

## Chapter Overview

Chapter 6 presents the basic maneuvers needed for steering, changing lanes, making turns, executing turnabouts, and parking in various situations.

## Chapter Vocabulary

*angle parking, hand-over-hand steering, oversteer, parallel parking, perpendicular parking, personal reference point, push-pull steering, reference point, standard reference point, turnabout, understeer*

108

## Teacher's Resources

For students to use as they read the chapter:

**Companion**
pages 43–49

**Spanish Handbook**
pages 13–14

## Projects

Review the projects described on page 125. Some of the projects can be assigned at any time while others are more closely tied to the content presented in the student text.

# CHAPTER 6
## Performing Basic Vehicle Maneuvers

**6.1** Steering, Signaling, and Changing Lanes

**6.2** Making Turns and Turning the Vehicle Around

**6.3** Parking

## You Are the Driver!

Suppose you are the driver approaching this intersection. What clues tell you that you are traveling on a one-way street? What hazards do the angle-parked vehicles on the left present to you and to their drivers? What conflicts might you anticipate in your right-front zone?

This chapter explains the basic maneuvers of steering, changing lanes, turning, and parking. You will also learn how to turn your vehicle around and how to start and park on hills. Finally, you will learn when and where to perform these maneuvers safely.

**Go Online**
PHSchool.com

**For:** Chapter 6 online activities
**Visit:** PHSchool.com
**Web Code:** cak-9999

109

## Introducing the Chapter

Have students examine the picture. Ask students to suggest maneuvers the driver might make. Discuss the maneuvers to be learned in this chapter. Review the IPDE Process. Explain that all maneuvers a driver will execute must be based on sound judgments and correct decisions.

## You Are the Driver!

Ask students to imagine that they are the driver looking through the windshield at the scene in the picture. Discuss how you know you are driving on a one-way street. Discuss the hazards that can result from the angle-parked vehicle that plans to back up. Then note the potential hazards that a driver backing from an angle parking space must be aware of.

## Special Needs

The classroom activities and demonstrations in this chapter are designed to reduce the teaching time in the car and to allow for more skills practice. Learning the procedures and seeing the visual checkpoints in a nonthreatening classroom environment will speed up the learning process for special needs students as well as for others.

# Steering, Signaling, and Changing Lanes

## 1 Focus

### Summary

This lesson presents the basic skills for steering, signaling, and changing lanes. Proper techniques for steering straight forward and backward are introduced. The proper uses of turn-signal devices and hand signals are presented. Instructions for safely changing lanes are also included.

### Vocabulary

**New:** *oversteer, understeer*

**Review:** *blind-spot areas, friction point*

## 2 Teach

### Explain

Explain that the terms *understeering* and *oversteering* each have two applications. One application refers to what the driver is doing—either not turning the steering wheel fast enough (understeering) or turning it too much (oversteering). The other application refers to how the car is performing—either a loss of traction to the vehicle's front wheels (understeer) or rear wheels (oversteer), which results in the car not responding to the steering actions of the driver.

### Objectives

1. Explain how to steer straight forward and backward.
2. Describe the correct use of hand signals and explain when they might be used.
3. List the proper steps for changing lanes.

Steering control is critical to safe, successful driving. Developing steering control involves acquiring visual habits, such as looking far ahead into your intended path of travel, using space correctly, controlling speed, and continually adjusting the steering wheel.

### Steering Straight Forward

Use a comfortable, balanced hand position, as explained in Chapter 3, as you begin steering control practice. Aim far ahead into your intended path with your visual search. Avoid looking down at your hands or feet.

The steering adjustments you need to make to drive in a straight line are small but critical. Some new drivers tend to turn the steering wheel too much, or **oversteer.** When you oversteer, your vehicle will weave from side to side.

Other new drivers might tend to **understeer.** These drivers do not turn the steering wheel enough to keep the vehicle in the planned path. If you understeer, you continue too far in one direction before you can correct and steer toward your target. Correct understeering by turning the steering wheel only slightly and more often.

Practice will help you think of your vehicle as an extension of yourself. You soon will be able to accurately judge the space your vehicle uses while it is moving and the space you need to make various maneuvers.

### Steering Straight Backward

Backing your vehicle may feel strange at first. Steering when moving backward involves knowing where to look and how to control direction and speed. Before backing, make sure your rear zones are clear, and follow these steps:

1. Hold the brake pedal down and shift to REVERSE.
2. Turn your body to the right, and put your right arm over the back of the passenger seat. Look back through the rear window.
3. Put your left hand at the top

The driver is in the correct position for backing straight.

## Teacher's Resources

**Resource Book**
Roadway Sheet 2, pages 6–7
Information, pages 69–74
**Demonstration Overheads**
Overheads B and J
 **Video 1**
Segment on Changing Lanes
**In-Car Checklists**
In-Car Checklists 7, 8

## Background

**Reference Points** Reference points for use with parking are introduced on page 119. To teach how to use reference points for turns, turnabouts, and basic maneuvers, refer to the **Resource Book,** pages 69–74. The use of reference points teaches drivers how to use central and peripheral vision to judge the vehicle's fender clearance for accuracy.

of the steering wheel at the 12 o'clock position.

4. Release pressure on the brake just enough to allow the vehicle to creep backward slowly.

5. While looking back through the rear window, move the top of the steering wheel toward the direction you want the back of the vehicle to go.

6. Keep your foot over the brake pedal while your vehicle is moving backward. Glance quickly to the front and sides to check traffic. Continue to look back through the rear window as you brake to a stop.

### Backing a Stickshift Vehicle

You can back slowly in a stickshift vehicle by carefully controlling your use of the clutch pedal at the friction point. Follow these steps for backing in a stickshift vehicle:

1. Push the brake and clutch pedals down.

2. Shift to REVERSE.

3. Release the brake, and let the clutch come out slowly to the friction point.

Holding the clutch at the friction point allows you to back the vehicle at a slow, controlled speed. Releasing the clutch suddenly may cause the vehicle to jerk back quickly.

Most stickshift vehicles can move slowly in REVERSE with the clutch at the friction point and with no acceleration. Keep your right foot over the brake pedal, ready for a stop. When stopping, push the clutch pedal down and brake to a smooth stop. Continue to look back until the vehicle is completely stopped.

## Signaling

Develop the habit of signaling every time you plan to turn, change lanes, slow, or stop. Signal well in advance before you begin any maneuver. Doing so gives other drivers time to react.

Even though all vehicles have turn-signal devices, there will be times when you use hand signals for further protection. Hand signals are often easier to see in bright sunlight. If your turn-signal device does not work, use hand signals. Many times a combination of turn lights and hand signals will be more effective.

Notice the hand and arm positions in the pictures. The first picture shows the left arm and hand pointing up for a right turn. The second shows the left arm and hand extended straight out for a left turn. The third picture shows the left arm extended downward, indicating slow or stop.

When using hand signals, use your right hand to maintain steering control. Make all hand and arm signals well in advance of entering a turn. Return your left hand to the steering wheel before you begin to execute the turn.

## Changing Lanes

Drivers must be able to execute the lane-change maneuver smoothly and safely before they learn to pass other vehicles. Changing lanes is a maneuver you will use often on a roadway with two or more lanes of traffic moving in your direction. You also may need to change lanes before making right or left turns.

At times, changing lanes gives you a better position or view when

Right turn

Left turn

Slow or stop

Chapter 6 Performing Basic Vehicle Maneuvers **111**

## Discuss

Discuss the importance of steering backward. Ask students to describe situations where a driver needs to steer backward. (These situations include backing out of a garage, carport, driveway, or parking space. Backing is also part of other maneuvers, such as parallel parking and turnabouts.) Point out that these maneuvers will be addressed later in the chapter.

## Explain

Explain that the type of seat and the size and position of the head restraint can make backing difficult for some drivers. Therefore, it is important to practice the correct position and techniques to overcome the difficulties.

## Discuss

Discuss the importance of signaling and the role it plays in safe driving. Ask: What are some of the consequences of failing to signal or giving the wrong signal? (If you do not signal, you cannot communicate with other drivers. If you use the wrong signal, you might cause confusion.) Why is it important to know hand signals? (You can use hand signals if your turn-signal device or brake lights fail. You can understand signals from bicyclists and other drivers.)

## Apply

Use the photographs to help demonstrate hand signals. Have students practice using hand signals while sitting at their desks.

Oversteering can cause you to take an incorrect path for changing lanes. The picture on the right shows the correct path of travel for a smooth lane change.

## Demonstrate

Use **Demonstration Overheads B** and **J** to demonstrate the steps for making a lane change. Use the yellow car to demonstrate the steps for making a lane change to the left. Repeat the demonstration for a lane change to the right. Also use **Video 1** Segment on Changing Lanes.

## Discuss

Discuss how and why zones should be checked to be sure space will be open while making and completing a lane change. (A driver should make sure that the zone in which the lane change will be completed, and the left or right zone next to it, will not have any line-of-sight restrictions that could cause problems.)

 **Assess**

## Answers to Review It

1. In steering straight forward, look far ahead toward the center of the intended path. Do not oversteer or understeer. See text for the six steps involved in steering straight backward. (pp. 110–111)
2. Point the left arm and hand up for a right turn, straight out for a left turn, and downward for slow or stop. Use hand signals for further protection and when your turn signals do not work. (p. 111)
3. Check traffic, signal, check blind spots, and increase your speed as you steer to the next lane if it is clear. Cancel signal and adjust speed. (p. 112)

driving in traffic. For example, you might change lanes when following a large truck on a multilane highway. By moving to a different lane, you increase your sight distance and get a broader view of the traffic scene.

Steering control is a critical factor as you learn the lane-changing maneuver. Oversteering can cause your vehicle to turn too sharply as you start to enter the adjoining lane. The first picture shows this oversteering error. At higher speeds you could lose steering control.

Change lanes as smoothly as possible. The second picture shows the safe path of travel of a vehicle executing a smooth lane change.

Always follow the same procedure for making a lane change, regardless of your reason for making the lane change. Before changing lanes, check all zones for possible hazards. Make sure you can see far ahead in the lane of your intended path of travel and that there are no obstructions in either lane.

Follow these steps when making a lane change to the left:

1. Check traffic in the front and left-front zones. Check rear zones through the rearview mirrors.
2. Signal and make a blind-spot check over your left shoulder to see if any vehicle is about to pass you.
3. Increase your speed slightly as you steer smoothly into the next lane if it is clear.
4. Cancel your signal and adjust your speed.

Follow the same procedure when making a lane change to the right, with one exception. After checking traffic ahead and through both mirrors, check the blind-spot area over your right shoulder. Take only a glance to make the check. Be careful not to pull the steering wheel to the right as you turn to glance over your right shoulder. Keep steering straight as you check your blind spot. If the lane is clear, complete the lane change to the right the same way you would make a lane change to the left.

### Review It

1. Describe the procedures for steering straight forward and backward.
2. What are the three hand and arm signals for turns and stopping? When might these signals be used?
3. List the steps to follow when changing lanes.

## Activity

**Model Car Activity** This activity will provide an opportunity for students to practice making lane changes. Divide the class into groups of three and assign three roles: driver, instructor, and observer. Give each group one model car and Roadway Sheet 2 from **Resource Book,** pages 6–7. Have the driver position the car in the right lane. Have the instructor read the steps for a lane change to the left and ask the driver to explain and perform each step. The observer provides feedback to the driver and the supervisor. Repeat the activity until each student has played each role.

## Background

**Changing Lanes** Lane changes should be executed so smoothly that if a passenger's eyes were closed the lane change would not be detected. To help make lane changes smoothly, the driver should be in lane position 2 or 3 before making the actual change. For example, when changing lanes to the left, the driver should move to lane position 2 (left side of lane), make final checks, and then enter lane position 3 (right side) of the new lane. When changing lanes to the right, move into lane position 3, and then enter lane position 2 of the new lane.

Making turns properly depends on steering control, speed control, and good visual habits. Look far ahead as you approach the turn. Identify where your vehicle will go, any hazards in your path, and how much to turn.

### Hand-Over-Hand Steering

You use **hand-over-hand steering** by pulling the steering wheel down with one hand while your other hand crosses over to pull the wheel farther down. Follow these steps for a left turn:

1. Begin the turn from a balanced hand position.
2. Start pulling down to the left with your left hand. Your right hand pushes the wheel toward the left about a quarter turn.
3. Release your left hand from the wheel and cross it over your right hand to grasp the wheel near the top. Continue pulling down.

You can complete the turn by continuing to pull down with the left hand as you release the right hand.

Some steering wheels will straighten after a turn if you relax your grip. However, be ready to unwind the wheel hand-over-hand, especially at lower speeds, with front-wheel drive vehicles, and when backing.

### Push-Pull Steering

Some drivers prefer **push-pull steering** for some maneuvers. You push the steering wheel up with one hand and pull it down with the other hand. This method allows you to keep both hands on the wheel at all times.

To use this method, one hand grasps the steering wheel near the 4 or 8 o'clock position. That hand then pushes the wheel up to near the 12 o'clock position. At the same time, the other hand slides up to the 11 or 1 o'clock position and pulls down. As the pulling hand comes down, the pushing hand returns to the original position to continue the process. With this method, you never cross your arms while driving.

### Making Left and Right Turns

Make left and right turns only after checking all traffic. Take

Hand-over-hand steering

Push-pull steering

## Objectives

1. Describe hand-over-hand steering.
2. List the steps for making right and left turns.
3. Describe how to back left and right.
4. Describe five turnabouts and tell which is the safest to use.

# Making Turns and Turning the Vehicle Around

##  1 Focus

### Summary

This lesson focuses on making turns and turning the vehicle around. Hand-over-hand and push-pull steering are explained. Procedures for making right and left turns, including use of the shared left-turn lane are included. Directions are also provided for backing left and right. Directions and precautions for turnabouts are presented.

### Vocabulary

**New:** *hand-over-hand steering, push-pull steering, turnabout*

**Review:** *roadway markings, shared left-turn lane, traffic signal*

## 2 Teach

### Explain

Draw students' attention to the first photograph and the steps for hand-over-hand steering. Point out that the ratio between how much you turn the steering wheel and how far the front wheels turn is different for different vehicles.

## Teacher's Resources

**Resource Book**
Information, page 75
**Demonstration Overheads**
Overheads A, C, D, F
**Content Overheads**
Overhead 8
**In-Car Checklists**
In-Car Checklists 9, 10, 11, 12, 13, 14

## Activity

**In-Class Driving Rehearsal** This activity will give students an opportunity to practice steering techniques in the classroom for in-car preparation. Give each student a simulated steering wheel. Have the students practice the hand-over-hand steering and push-pull steering techniques.

## Explain

Traffic laws in most states require drivers to turn into the nearest lane of traffic going in their direction. Use the illustration at the top of the page to show how the cars are turning into the nearest lane.

## Demonstrate

Use **Demonstration Overheads C, D,** and **F** and movable cars to demonstrate the steps of making left and right turns. Position the cars in various locations and demonstrate the steps for making turns.

## Demonstrate

Use the illustration at the top of the page to illustrate why the steering wheel is turned more when making a right turn than when making a left turn. Also consider using a 1/24-inch scale or larger model car or truck with steerable front wheels to demonstrate the turning radius for making left and right turns.

## Demonstrate

Use **Content Overhead 8** to demonstrate how to move into a shared left turn lane and make a proper left turn.

Steps for making left turns (yellow car) and right turns (white car)

A shared left-turn lane

driveway        driveway

these precautions when executing turns:
- Look for pedestrians and oncoming vehicles. Check rear zones for vehicles about to pass you.
- Plan turns well in advance. Be in the correct lane about a block before your turn.

- Obey all traffic signs, signals, and roadway markings. Remember that you must yield to oncoming traffic when preparing to turn left. When turning in a stickshift vehicle, you might need to downshift before entering a sharp turn. Downshift and release the clutch before the turn so you have both hands free for turning.

**Procedures for Turning**  The numbers in the picture on the left match the following steps for turns:

1. Position your vehicle in the correct lane for the turn. For a right turn, be in lane position 3 if there are no parked vehicles. For a left turn, be in the lane nearest the center line in lane position 2. (On a one-way street, be in the far left lane.) Signal about half a block before the turn.
2. Brake early to reduce speed.
3. Use your visual search pattern to check the front zones for vehicles, pedestrians, and bicyclists.
4. Slow to about 10 mph just before the crosswalk.
5. For a right turn, check to the left again before turning. Then look in the direction of the turn. Begin turning the wheel when your vehicle's front bumper is even with the curbline.
6. For a left turn, check traffic to the left, then right, then left again. Turn the steering wheel just before the front of your vehicle reaches the center of the intersection. Continue looking left into the lane you will enter.
7. As you begin your turn, make a quick blind-spot check through

the right side window. Check front and rear zones. If the intersection is clear, turn into the nearest lane of traffic going in your direction. Accelerate about halfway through the turn as you return the wheel to the straight-ahead position.

### Shared Left-Turn Lane

Some left turns into business areas can be made in midblock from a center lane. This is called a **shared left-turn lane.**

This type of left turn can be hazardous. Before making a turn from a shared left-turn lane, search your front zones. Follow the proper procedure to enter the center lane. Look ahead for oncoming traffic and be prepared to yield to any vehicle whose path you will cross.

### Backing Left and Right

When backing to the left, your visual search will be primarily over your left shoulder through the left side windows. When backing right, you will look over your right shoulder and through the right side windows. Use hand-over-hand steering and follow these steps to make sharp turns when backing.

1. Before backing, check for traffic, pedestrians, parked vehicles, and any stationary objects in front, around, and behind you. Turn your head toward the direction you will be backing.
2. Keep both hands on the wheel, ready for hand-over-hand steering. Pull the wheel to the left to back left. Pull the wheel to the right to back right. The back of

The correct driver positions for backing to the left and to the right, and the space and path of travel the car takes during backing

your vehicle will go in the direction you turn the wheel. Look back toward the direction you want the vehicle to go.

3. Back slowly as you enter the turn. Make quick glances to the front and sides to be sure no one is near. Begin to unwind the steering wheel to finish the turn in a straight position.

When backing left, allow a wide space on the right side. The front wheels will move far to the right of the rear wheels. The front of your vehicle will swing wide to the right. When backing right, allow a wide space on the left side.

**What Do You Think?**

What are the hazards of shared left-turn lanes? Are the hazards too great for safety? Should shared left-turn lanes be prohibited?

### Explain

Point out the potential hazards of making left turns from a shared left-turn lane. (Oncoming traffic uses the same lane.) Identify specific locations in your area where this type of turn can be made.

### Explain

Explain that using a target for backing is similar to using a target while driving forward. The target gives a focus point toward which to position the car. When backing, a driver should not limit his or her search only to the rear. A check of the swing of the front of the car is necessary as the turning takes place.

### Demonstrate

Use a child's wagon or a bicycle to demonstrate the position of the front wheels in relation to the way you want the vehicle to go. Make sure that students understand that when backing, you turn the steering wheel from the top down in the same direction as you want to turn.

### Discuss

If you have not completed the Debate project on page 125, this is an appropriate time to focus on the *What Do You Think?* question on this page. Ask: Are the hazards of shared left-turn lanes too great for safety? Should they be prohibited? (Encourage students to look at all sides of the issue.)

### Activity

**In-Class Driving Rehearsal** This activity will provide practice for backing right and left. Have students select a target that is to the rear and 90 degrees to the right. While using a simulated steering wheel, have students demonstrate backing right with correct steering and visual searching (looking over the correct shoulder and checking the swing of the front of the car). Repeat the activity for backing left.

## Explain

Restrictions related to turnabouts vary from state to state. For example, in some states it is illegal to use a private driveway for a turnabout. Other states do not permit turnabouts at intersections. Provide information about your state's laws regarding U-turns or assign the Investigate Project on page 125. If you live close to a state border, present information about the neighboring state's laws.

## Demonstrate

Use the illustration on the left side of the page or **Demonstration Overhead A** with the movable yellow car to explain the midblock U-turn maneuver. Remind students that some roadways are not wide enough to accommodate this maneuver. Also point out that the size of the vehicle determines the space needed to complete the turn.

## Discuss

Discuss the hazards involved in making a U-turn. Ask: Under what conditions do you think it is safe to make a U-turn? (Students' answers should focus on the width of the street and the lack of traffic. They should also mention any law that applies to U-turns in their state.)

Midblock U-turn

### Turning the Vehicle Around

A **turnabout** is a maneuver for turning your vehicle around to go in the opposite direction. Because turnabouts often require drivers to cross or back into traffic, they should be considered a high-risk maneuver.

Take these precautions when you plan to make a turnabout:

- Be sure local laws permit the turnabout.
- Select a site with at least 500 feet of visibility in each direction.
- Do not make a turnabout near hills or curves or within 200 feet of intersections.
- Never attempt a turnabout in heavy or high-speed traffic.
- Check continually in all zones for traffic and pedestrians.

You must decide which of the five turnabouts described is best for each situation. The steps for each turnabout match the numbered car locations shown in the pictures.

**Midblock U-turn** Make sure local and state laws permit this type of turnabout. You need a wide space to make a U-turn. A U-turn is risky because you must cross several lanes of traffic to execute it.

1. Check traffic ahead and to the rear, and then signal right. Pull to the far right and stop at location 1.
2. Signal left and move toward location 2.
3. Check your front and left-rear zones. Check your left blind spot. Turn sharply left while moving slowly toward location 3. Do not stop if you have enough space to complete the turn.

4. Move slowly toward location 4. Check all zones. Straighten the wheels while you accelerate gently into the proper lane.

### Back into Driveway on Right Side

Choose this turnabout if a clear driveway is on the right and there is no close traffic in your rear zones. This turnabout has the advantage of letting you reenter traffic going forward.

1. Check traffic to the rear. Begin to slow as you proceed beyond the driveway.
2. Stop about three feet from the curb and with your rear bumper just beyond the driveway. Check traffic, and back slowly to the right to location 3. Use hand-over-hand steering. Stop when your vehicle is completely off the street.
3. Signal a left turn. Check traffic.

Back into driveway on right side

---

## Background

**Reference Points** There are three reference points that can be helpful in judging your vehicle's position in relation to the roadway while you are making a turnabout. One reference point helps you judge when your front bumper is even with the curb. Another reference point helps you judge when your back bumper is even with the curb. The third reference point helps you judge when you are able to tell if the curb across the street can be cleared during a turning action. For additional information, see **Resource Book,** page 75.

## Special Needs

Practice making turnabouts and using shared left-turn lanes with model cars or a child's wagon in the classroom. Have the special needs students talk their way through each step. Then practice in the driver education car in a quiet corner of a parking lot before going onto the street.

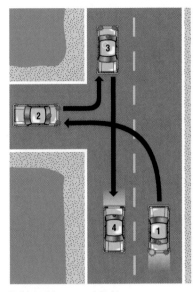

**3.** Accelerate gently, scanning all zones, as you drive forward toward location 4.

### Pull into Driveway on Right Side

This type of turnabout is a high-risk maneuver. To complete it, you must back across two lanes of traffic and into oncoming traffic before moving forward. Avoid this turnabout whenever possible.

1. Check traffic in front and rear zones. Signal a right turn and use the right-turn procedure to move to location 2. Stop when your vehicle is off the street.
2. Check traffic again from both directions. Back slowly across the street, turning left toward location 3. Look to the left, rear, and side when backing. Glance to the front, then continue looking back while

Pull into driveway on left side

**4.** When your path is clear, drive forward to location 4.

### Pull into Driveway on Left Side

You might choose this turnabout if oncoming traffic is light and a driveway on the left is available. The disadvantage is that you must back into traffic before moving forward.

1. Check traffic in front and rear zones. Signal a left turn and use the left-turn procedure to move to location 2. Stay as close to the right side as possible. Stop with your wheels straight when your vehicle is completely off the street.
2. Check traffic again, especially from the right. Back slowly to the right to location 3. Look to the right rear and side while backing. Stop with the wheels straight.

Pull into driveway on right side

Chapter 6 Performing Basic Vehicle Maneuvers **117**

## Background

**Backing** Backing is the highest risk maneuver that drivers routinely perform. A utility company determined that more than 40 percent of collisions involving company vehicles occurred while drivers were backing. Yet their drivers spent less than 1 percent of their driving time backing. When the utility company initiated a driver training program and restricted drivers from backing out of driveways and perpendicular parking spaces, collisions from backing were reduced by 78 percent.

One of the most common backing maneuvers is backing out of a driveway. There are several reasons why this maneuver is dangerous. First, it is difficult for a driver to get a good view of the roadway in order to find a gap. Once a gap is selected, the driver must back out of the driveway, come to a complete stop, shift gears, and start to drive forward. This series of steps requires a gap five times larger than the one needed when driving out of a driveway forward.

### Explain

Explain that the same maneuvers required for a turnabout are used every day by drivers when they pull into their own driveways, park their vehicles, and return later to back out of the driveway.

### Demonstrate

Use the illustrations on pages 116–117 or **Demonstration Overhead F** with the movable yellow car to point out the path of the vehicle in each step of the maneuvers for turning the vehicle around. Point out which gear you are using for each segment of the turn.

### Discuss

Ask: Why is it important to back into the nearest lane when backing from a driveway? (This requires you to cross the fewest lanes of traffic.)

### Discuss

Discuss other ways to turn around. One way is to pull into a parking lot. Ask: What decision would you make for turning around while driving on a four-lane roadway with parking lots on both sides? Would you turn into the parking lot on the right or the one on the left, and why? (The parking lot to the left would be the best choice. To leave the traffic flow, two lanes of traffic—both going in the same direction—will need to be crossed. Coming out of the parking lot, a gap in only one lane will be needed. If the parking lot to the right were selected, you would need a gap in three traffic flows and two directions of traffic.)

## Demonstrate

Use the illustration or **Demonstration Overhead A** with the movable yellow car to show the path of travel involved in a three-point turnabout. Point out which gear you use for each segment of the turn.

## Discuss

Ask: What alternatives do you have with turnabouts? (Answers should include driving around the block and pulling into a parking lot to turn around.)

## ③ Assess

### Answers to Review It

1. Pull the steering wheel down with one hand as the other hand crosses over to pull the wheel farther down. (p. 113)

2. Look for pedestrians and traffic. Obey all traffic signs, signals, and roadway markings. Be in the correct lane, and signal for a turn. Slow by braking, check traffic again, and begin turning into the nearest lane of traffic in your direction. Accelerate halfway through the turn. Return steering wheel to the straight-ahead position. (p. 114)

3. Check for traffic, pedestrians, and stationary objects. Turn your head in the direction you are backing. Turn the wheel in the direction you want to back. Back slowly, and unwind the steering wheel to finish the turn. (p. 115)

4. The safest type of turnabout is usually backing into an alley or driveway on the right. It is safest because you enter traffic forward. (p. 116)

Unit 2
**118** Controlling Your Vehicle

Three-point turnabout

118 Unit 2 Controlling Your Vehicle

stopping with the wheels straight in location 3.
3. Accelerate gently, and drive forward to location 4.

**Three-Point Turnabout** This turnabout is hazardous to perform. You not only cross traffic lanes, but your vehicle is stopped across a traffic lane. Executing this maneuver may put you in a high-risk situation.

1. From location 1 check front and rear zones. Signal right and stop close to the curb as shown in location 2. Check traffic ahead, to the rear, and over your left shoulder. Signal a left turn.
2. Search front and rear zones as you turn sharply left. Move to location 3 with wheels straight. Stop before hitting the curb.
3. Check all traffic again. Turn the wheels sharply right while backing slowly to location 4. Back only as far as necessary to complete the maneuver and before hitting the curb. Stop with wheels straight.
4. Check traffic again and signal left. Move slowly forward while steering left toward location 5.

**Deciding Which Turnabout to Use**
Consider these factors when deciding which turnabout to use:
- legality of the turnabout
- amount of traffic
- types of driveways available
- need to enter traffic lanes forward or backward
- ample space to enter traffic
- number of traffic lanes to cross

Backing into a driveway or alley on

the right side is usually the safest type of turnabout to use because you can enter traffic forward.

Sometimes you might need to make a turnabout in light traffic. If there are driveways on both the left and right sides, choose the left driveway to turn into. This turnabout lets you back into your own lane rather than across both lanes. Select a gap in traffic that gives you ample time to complete the maneuver.

A three-point turnabout should rarely be used. Use this turnabout only when you are on a dead-end street or on a rural roadway with no driveways.

### Review It
1. What is the procedure for hand-over-hand steering?
2. What are the steps for turning left and right?
3. What procedures do you follow to back to the left and to the right?
4. What is the safest type of turnabout to use? Why is that type the safest?

## Activity

**Small Group Activity** This activity will give students the opportunity to evaluate when it is and is not safe to make a turnabout. You will need photographs, slides, or videotapes of various safe and unsafe locations within your community for making turnabouts. Divide the students into small groups and have each group evaluate one or more locations to determine if a turnabout can be executed safely. Have the students determine which kind of turnabout is most appropriate based on what they can see.

Some drivers find parking a vehicle a difficult maneuver to execute, because the size of the parking space often is limited. Parking your vehicle requires speed control, steering control, and accurate judgment.

Parking is easier and safer if you consider these factors:

- Try to find a parking space with ample room for entering and exiting easily. The size of your vehicle is the main factor in determining the space you choose.
- Avoid spaces at the end of parking lanes and near a large vehicle that might block your view. In end spaces your vehicle has a greater chance of being struck by other moving vehicles.
- Avoid spaces with a poorly parked vehicle on either side.
- Use reference points when executing parking maneuvers.

### Reference Points

Many drivers use reference points to serve as guides in determining the position of the vehicle in the roadway. A **reference point** is some part of the outside or inside of the vehicle, as viewed from the driver's seat, that relates to some part of the roadway. Reference points can be developed for the front, side, or rear to help you know where your vehicle is located in the roadway. A **standard reference point** is the point on the vehicle that is typical for most drivers. This could be a sideview mirror, a hood ornament, or the center of the hood. The photograph shows how the center of the hood is used for a standard reference point.

Once you learn standard reference points, you can develop your own **personal reference points.** A personal reference point is an adaptation of a standard reference point for one's own vehicle. You will learn to use different parts of your own vehicle such as wiper blades, door handles, or rearview mirrors as guides.

As you begin to practice parking maneuvers, you will learn which parts of your vehicle to use as personal reference points. You will be able to line up these points with parts of other vehicles to help execute the maneuvers.

To use a standard reference point, the driver's line of sight sees the center of the hood at Arrow A and the curb at Arrow B. This tells the driver that the right tires are close to the curb.

### Objectives

1. Discuss reference points and how to use them as guides when parking your vehicle.
2. Describe the procedures for angle, perpendicular, and parallel parking.
3. Describe how to park uphill and downhill with and without a curb.
4. Explain how to start from an uphill parking space without rolling backwards.

## Parking

 **Focus**

### Summary

This lesson is devoted to all aspects of parking. Reference points are explained as a way to help drivers execute parking maneuvers. Specific instructions for angle, perpendicular, and parallel parking are included. Instructions are given for parking on hills.

### Vocabulary

*angle parking, parallel parking, perpendicular parking, personal reference point, reference point, standard reference point*

**2 Teach**

### Explain

Reference points are the tools necessary for the driver to receive accurate feedback for successful performance. If the maneuver works, then additional attempts will give the same results. If it doesn't work, then a slight adjustment can produce correct results. By going through this process, the driver doesn't just experience parking the car next to a curb, for example. The driver also is able to practice the ability to use the reference point tool, which, once learned, can be used for the structuring of many future driving decisions.

---

## Teacher's Resources

**Resource Book**
Roadway Sheet 8, pages 18–19
Teacher's Instructions, pages 39–40
Information, page 77

**Content Overheads**
Overhead 15

**Demonstration Overheads**
Overhead L

**In-Car Checklists**
In-Car Checklists 15, 16, 17, 18, 19, 20, 21, 22

## Activity

**In-Class Driving Rehearsal** This activity will help students understand personal reference points. Place a table or desk at the front of the room to simulate the hood of a vehicle. Place a chair behind the table to the left to simulate the driver's seat of a vehicle. Place a piece of masking tape on the floor to the right of the table to simulate a curbline. The tape should extend 15 feet beyond the front of the desk. Have students take turns sitting in the driver's seat and explaining their reference points for the curbline in relation to the desk.

## Discuss

Ask: What things do you need to look for when you are leaving an angle or perpendicular parking space in a parking lot. (Students' answers should include traffic, pedestrians, and obstacles such as shopping carts.)

## Explain

Angle parking is intended for head-in parking. The maneuver to angle park your car is simple to perform. But the maneuver to leave the parking space is dangerous. Leaving the parking space requires backing into the traffic flow which can be blocked by a line-of-sight restriction.

## Demonstrate

Use **Demonstration Overhead L** to explain each step involved in angle parking and perpendicular parking. Also demonstrate how to leave an angle and a perpendicular parking space.

Angle parking

The following parking procedures refer to entering a parking space to your right. When parking to your left, adjust your actions and visual checks for the left side. The steps for each procedure match the numbered car locations in the pictures.

### Angle Parking

Use **angle parking** to park your vehicle diagonally to the curb. Angle parking is often used in parking lots and shopping centers.

1. Check for traffic and pedestrians. Position your vehicle at least six feet from the row of parked vehicles. Signal a right turn, check traffic to the rear, and begin braking.
2. Flash your brake lights to warn drivers behind. Check your right blind spot and continue braking.
3. Creep forward until you can see the center of the space without your line of sight cutting across the parking line. This is your reference point to begin turning. Turn the wheels sharply to the right. Slowly enter the stall.
4. Straighten the wheels when you are centered in the space. Determine your forward reference point to place the front of the bumper even with the curb or parking line.

### Perpendicular Parking

Use **perpendicular parking** to park your vehicle at a right angle to the curb.

1. Position your vehicle at least eight feet from the row of parked vehicles, or as far to the left of the lane as possible. Flash your brake lights and signal a right

Perpendicular parking

turn. Check your right blind spot, and begin to brake.
2. Check traffic to the rear, and continue braking.
3. Determine your personal reference point to know when the front bumper of your vehicle passes the left rear taillight of the vehicle to the right of the empty parking space. Turn the wheel sharply right. Slowly enter the stall. Check your right-rear fender for clearance.
4. Straighten the wheels when you are centered in the space. Use a forward reference point, like the driver's side-view mirror, to stop before the wheels strike the curb.

Some drivers prefer backing into a perpendicular parking space. These drivers consider this a safer maneuver because they do not back out into traffic when leaving the space.

## Background

**Parking Skills** Even though all three types of parking are presented in one lesson, it is best for students to experience them one at a time during in-car sessions. This will allow the student to learn and practice one procedure before tackling the next. The progression should be from simple to complex by starting with angle parking, followed by perpendicular, and finally parallel parking. Because some steps are similar, students will build on the skills as they progress from angle to parallel parking.

## Activity

**Class Activity** Have the class walk out to a parking lot. Position a car with the right tires 3 to 6 inches from a line that extends at least 20 feet to the front of the car. Have each student get in the driver's seat and note where the line appears to the driver. See **Resource Book** page 39 for more information about this activity.

## Leaving an Angle or Perpendicular Space

Your view often will be blocked as you begin to back into moving traffic. Back slowly. Look to the rear and to the sides as you search for other roadway users and pedestrians.

1. Creep straight back while you control speed with your foot brake. (Hold the clutch at the friction point in a stickshift vehicle.)
2. When your front bumper is even with the rear bumper of the vehicle on your left, begin to turn right.
3. Back into the nearest lane and stop with the wheels straight. Shift to a forward gear and proceed as you scan your front and rear zones.

## Parallel Parking

Use **parallel parking** to park your vehicle parallel to the curb. Select a space that is five to six feet longer than your vehicle. During the maneuver, the front of your vehicle will swing far to the left. Check over your left shoulder to be sure this needed space is clear.

1. Flash brake lights, and signal a right turn. Stop two to three feet away from the front vehicle with the two rear bumpers even. Shift to REVERSE. Check traffic. Look back over your right shoulder. Back slowly as you turn right. Aim toward the right-rear corner of the space. Control speed with your foot brake (clutch at friction point in a stickshift vehicle).
2. When the back of your seat is even with the rear bumper of the front vehicle, straighten the wheels.

Determine your personal reference point for this position. Slowly back straight. Look over your shoulder, through the rear window.

3. When your front bumper is even with the front vehicle's back bumper, turn your wheels sharply left. Back slowly. Look out the rear window.
4. When your vehicle is parallel to the curb, straighten wheels and stop before you touch the vehicle behind. Develop reference points

Steps for parallel parking

## Demonstrate

Use the illustration on this page or **Content Overhead 15** to explain each step involved in parallel parking. Also, demonstrate how to leave the parking space.

You could also make slides or a videotape to show students how each checkpoint for parallel parking will look to the driver.

## Explain

The key to successful parallel parking is moving the vehicle slowly while turning the steering wheel at the correct time. Point out that a driver's use of reference points are critical for knowing when to execute the maneuvers involved in parallel parking.

## Demonstrate

Demonstrate how reference points are used. See **Resource Book,** page 40 for instructions for constructing and using a reference point demonstrator.

## Activity

**Small Group Activity** This activity will give students the opportunity to compare the three parking procedures. Group students into teams of five. Ask each group to determine the behavioral patterns (steps) that apply from one parking procedure to another. (For example, checking traffic to the rear and signaling for a right turn would be necessary behaviors for all three of the parking procedures.) Also have the students list which behaviors are unique to each procedure. After adequate time, have the groups report their findings to the class.

## Background

**Perpendicular Parking** The main reason for backing into a perpendicular parking space is to make leaving easier and safer. When you back into a space, you leave by driving forward. You do not have to back into the flow of traffic. It is easier and therefore less dangerous to see around other parked cars when you are pulling forward to leave a parking space. See **Resource Book,** page 77 for procedures for backing into a perpendicular parking space effectively.

## Explain

Emphasize the importance of backing up in the parking space as the first step in leaving a parallel parking space.

## Demonstrate

Use a model car with movable front wheels or the photographs on page 123 to illustrate how to park vehicles on hills. Show the direction the wheels should be turned for each situation. (The wheels should be turned out for uphill parking with a curb. The wheels should be turned in for uphill parking without a curb. The wheels should be turned in for downhill parking with a curb. The wheels should be turned in for downhill parking without a curb.)

**DID YOU KNOW?**

PARKING REGULATIONS Parking regulations in most states specify the maximum distance a vehicle may legally be parked from the curb. This distance is usually 6–18 inches. Know the regulations in your state or city.

to know your distance from the curb and from the vehicle behind you. Slowly pull forward to center your vehicle in the space.

### Leaving a Parallel Parking Space

You are responsible for avoiding a collision when leaving a parallel parking space. Yield to all traffic.

1. Back straight slowly until your rear bumper almost touches the vehicle behind. Turn wheels sharply left as you stop.
2. Signal a left turn. Check your left blind spot. Move forward slowly.
3. Check the right-front corner of your vehicle for clearance.
4. Turn your wheels slowly to the right when you are halfway out of the parking space. Scan front zones and accelerate gently as you center your vehicle in the traffic lane.

### Parking on Hills

When parallel parking on a hill, you must be sure your vehicle will not roll down into traffic. Always turn the front wheels and set the parking brake to prevent the vehicle from rolling downhill. Procedures for uphill and

downhill parking apply to parking on the right side of the street or roadway. Adjust your actions and visual checks when parking on the left side.

### Uphill Parking with a Curb

1. Using personal reference points, position your vehicle close to the curb. Just before stopping, turn the steering wheel sharply left as shown in the first picture on the opposite page.
2. Shift to NEUTRAL. Let the vehicle creep back slowly until the back of the right-front tire gently touches the curb.
3. Shift to PARK (FIRST in a stick-shift), and set the parking brake.
4. When leaving the parking space, signal, check traffic, and accelerate gently into the lane of traffic.

### Uphill Parking with No Curb

1. Pull as far off the roadway as possible. Just before you stop, turn the steering wheel sharply right, as in the second picture.
2. Shift to PARK (FIRST in a stick-shift), and set the parking brake.
3. When leaving the parking space, let the vehicle creep backward while straightening the wheels. Signal and check traffic. Shift to DRIVE (FIRST in a stickshift), and accelerate gently into traffic.

### Downhill Parking with a Curb

1. Position your vehicle close to the curb and stop.
2. Let the vehicle creep forward slowly while turning the steering

## Activity

**Model Car Activity** This activity will provide an opportunity for students to practice the parking maneuvers described in this lesson. Divide the class into groups of three and assign three roles: driver, instructor, and observer. Give each group a model car, several wild cards, and Roadway Sheet 8 from **Resource Book,** pages 18–19. Have the instructor read the steps for a parking maneuver, and ask the driver to explain and perform each step. The observer provides feedback to the driver and the instructor.

wheel sharply right, as in the third picture. Let the right-front tire rest gently against the curb.

3. Shift to PARK (REVERSE in a stick-shift), and set the parking brake.

4. When leaving the parking space, check traffic and back a short distance while straightening the wheels. Signal and check traffic again. Shift to DRIVE (FIRST in a stickshift), and accelerate into traffic.

### Downhill Parking with No Curb

Follow the same procedure as down-hill parking with a curb. Turn wheels sharply right as you creep as near to the shoulder as possible. Note this position in the second picture. Use the same steps for parking downhill with a curb to complete the maneuver and to leave the parking space.

When you leave any hilly parking space, make sure you have a big enough gap to enter traffic safely. Traffic coming down the hill may be approaching faster than you think it is.

### Starting on a Hill

At times, you might have to stop while going up a hill. You must then be able to start moving forward again *without rolling back.* Starting on an uphill grade without rolling back involves timing and coordination.

### Using Automatic Transmission

One method for starting on a hill without rolling back involves using

When parking uphill against a curb, turn the front wheels to the left.

When parking uphill or downhill where there is no curb, turn your wheels to the right.

When parking downhill against a curb, turn the front wheels to the right.

Chapter 6 Performing Basic Vehicle Maneuvers **123**

## Explain

Caution students to accelerate gently when leaving an uphill parking space with a curb. Remind students that the front wheel will be turned sharply to the left. The driver needs to be careful that the vehicle does not enter the lane of oncoming traffic before steering is corrected.

## Explain

Point out that when leaving a downhill parking space, the driver should back the vehicle to release pressure on the tire before straightening the wheels. This maneuver avoids damaging the front tire or the steering system.

## Explain

The steepness of a hill often determines the best starting procedure. The parking-brake procedure should be used on very steep hills. The foot-brake procedure should be used on hills that are less steep.

## Background

**Parking Pointers** There are three ways to secure a car while parked: the parking brake, moving the selector lever to PARK or placing the transmission in FIRST or REVERSE on a stickshift vehicle, and curbing the tires. Runaway vehicles are so common in San Francisco that the city has laws requiring a parked vehicle to curb the tires.

## Explain

Refer students to page 53 in Chapter 3 to review the concept of holding the friction point. Explain that this slow speed can be used for backing safely.

## 3 Assess

### Answers to Review It

1. A standard reference point is the point on a vehicle that is typical for most drivers to relate to some part of the roadway. You can use different parts of your vehicle to adapt a standard to a personal reference point. (p. 119)

2. Students should list steps for angle, perpendicular, and parallel parking indicated on pages 120–121.

3. Turn front wheels left when parking uphill with a curb; right when parking uphill with no curb; right when parking downhill with or without a curb. (pp. 122–123)

4. Students should list the steps for using the parking brake to start on a hill without rollback as indicated on page 124.

**SAFE DRIVING**

Starting on a hill in a stickshift can be difficult. Practice first on gentle slopes away from traffic before you need to start moving on a steep hill. Use the method with which you feel most secure and comfortable.

the parking brake. Follow these steps when using this method:

1. While holding the foot brake down, set the parking brake firmly.
2. Move your foot to the accelerator, and accelerate until you feel the engine start to pull.
3. Release the parking brake as you continue to accelerate.

A second method for starting on a hill involves using only the foot brake.

1. Hold the foot brake down with your *left* foot.
2. While still holding the foot brake with your *left* foot, accelerate gradually until the engine starts to pull.
3. Release the foot brake gently as you increase acceleration to move forward.

**Using a Stickshift** One method for starting on a hill in a stickshift vehicle involves the use of the parking brake. Follow these steps in a stickshift vehicle:

1. Be sure the parking brake is set. Shift to FIRST.
2. Use one hand to hold the steering wheel. Hold the parking brake release with the other hand.
3. Accelerate to a fast idle. Let the clutch out to the friction point.
4. Release the parking brake slowly when you feel the engine begin to pull.
5. Increase pressure on the accelerator, and let the clutch all the way up as your vehicle begins to move forward. Completely release the parking brake.

You might be able to coordinate the clutch and accelerator to move

forward without using the parking brake. Follow these steps:

1. Shift to FIRST while stopped.
2. Keep the foot brake down while releasing the clutch slowly, just to the friction point.
3. Move your right foot quickly from the foot brake to the accelerator. Accelerate gently.
4. Release the clutch smoothly, and accelerate gradually.

### Review It

1. What are standard reference points? How can you adapt them to become personal reference points?
2. What are the steps for angle parking? perpendicular parking? parallel parking?
3. Which way should your front wheels be turned when parking uphill with a curb? uphill with no curb? downhill with a curb? downhill with no curb?
4. How do you use the parking brake to start on a hill without rolling backwards?

## Reviewing Chapter Objectives

### 1. Steering, Signaling, and Changing Lanes

1. How do you steer straight forward and backward? (110)
2. How do you use hand signals correctly and when should you use them? (111)
3. What are the proper steps for changing lanes? (112)

### 2. Making Turns and Turning the Vehicle Around

4. What is hand-over-hand steering? (113)
5. What are the steps for making right and left turns? (114)
6. How do you back left and right? (115)
7. How do you execute the five turnabout maneuvers, and which is the safest to use? (116–118)

### 3. Parking

8. What are reference points and how do you use them as guides when parking your vehicle? (119)
9. What are the procedures for angle, perpendicular, and parallel parking? (120–122)
10. How do you park uphill and downhill with and without a curb? (122–123)
11. How do you start from an uphill parking space without rolling backwards? (123–124)

## Projects

### Individuals

**Investigate** Research your state's laws on turnabouts. Which of the turnabouts described in the text are legal in your state, and which are illegal?

**Observe Traffic** Locate a busy street in your area on which vehicles must parallel park. Observe vehicles parallel parking for at least a half hour. Record how many attempts to parallel park each vehicle makes. What are the most common errors the drivers make in attempting to parallel park?

**Practice** Establish personal reference points in your family vehicle that you can use when you park. Compare your personal reference points with those of your classmates. Are the reference points you have in common "standard reference points"? Why or why not?

### Groups

**Debate** Divide the group into two smaller groups to debate the pros and cons of shared left-turn lanes. Make a list of the pros and cons your group discusses. Share the list with your class.

**Demonstrate** Take turns demonstrating the hand and arm signals you use when turning and stopping. Present your group demonstration to the class.

## Reviewing Chapter Objectives

**6.1** Steering, Signaling, and Changing Lanes
See Answers to Review It on page 112.
**6.2** Making Turns and Turning the Vehicle Around
See Answers to Review It on page 118.
**6.3** Parking
See Answers to Review It on page 124.
For additional information refer to the specific page(s) in parentheses after each question.

## Projects

Some of the projects can be assigned at any time while others are more closely tied to the content presented in the student text. The page number where the topic is introduced is indicated.

**Investigate:** p. 116
**Observe Traffic:** p. 121
**Practice:** p. 119
**Debate:** p. 114
**Demonstrate:** p. 111

The results of student projects will vary.

## Teacher's Resources

**Skills and Applications Workbook**
pages 21–24

**Tests and Activities**
Chapter 6 Activities 6-1 and 6-2, pages 47–48
Chapter 6 Test A and Test B, pages 49–52

**TestWorks CD-ROM**
Chapter 6 Test

# Review

## Answers to Check Your Knowledge

1. d
2. a
3. b
4. d
5. rear
6. Hand or Arm
7. oversteering
8. three-point turnabout or U-turn

## Answers to Review Vocabulary

9. reference point (c)
10. understeering (f)
11. angle parking (g)
12. turnabout (a)
13. perpendicular parking (d)
14. push-pull steering (b)
15. oversteering (e)

## Answers to Think Critically

Students' answers will vary. For information related to the question refer to the page(s) indicated.

1. You would make a mid-block U-turn because the tree blocks oncoming traffic and therefore the risks are reduced.

2. Students' answers should include steps listed on pages 122–123.

## Chapter Test

### Check Your Knowledge

**Multiple Choice**   Copy the number of each sentence below on a sheet of paper. Choose the letter of the answer that best completes the statement or answers the question.

1. To steer straight forward, look
   (a) at your hand position on the steering wheel.
   (b) at the center line or lane lines.
   (c) left and right to judge available space.
   (d) far ahead toward the center of your path.
2. To make the correct hand signal for a left turn, your left arm and hand should be
   (a) extended straight.   (c) pointing down.
   (b) pointing up.          (d) waving left.
3. The first step to take before you begin a lane-change maneuver is to
   (a) check the blind spot over your left shoulder.
   (b) check that roadway ahead has no obstructions.
   (c) hand signal a stop.
   (b) steer slightly into the next lane.
4. Backing a stickshift vehicle requires skillful use of the
   (a) brake pedal.        (c) gearshift lever.
   (b) turn signals.        (d) clutch pedal.

**Completion**   Copy the number of each sentence below on a sheet of paper. After the number, write the word or words that complete the sentence correctly.

5. Before backing, make sure your _____ zones are clear.
6. _____ signals are easier to see in bright sunlight.
7. When changing lanes, _____ can cause your vehicle to turn too sharply.
8. Perform a _____ only when there are no driveways to use for another type of turnabout.

### Review Vocabulary

Copy the number of each definition in list A. Match the definition in list A with the term it defines in list B.

**List A**

9. a part of the outside or inside of the vehicle, as viewed from the driver's seat, that relates to some part of the roadway
10. not turning the steering wheel enough
11. parking vehicle diagonally to curb
12. maneuver for turning your vehicle around to go in the opposite direction
13. parking vehicle at right angle to curb
14. pushing the steering wheel up with one hand and down with the other
15. turning the steering wheel too much

**List B**

a. turnabout            e. oversteering
b. push-pull steering   f. understeering
c. reference point      g. angle parking
d. perpendicular parking

### Think Critically

Write a paragraph to answer each question.

1. You are driving down a two-way, two-lane street in a residential area at night during a storm. You notice that a large tree has fallen down across the roadway ahead of you. What type of turnabout should you make and why?
2. When parking on a hill, what can you do to make sure that your vehicle will not roll down into traffic?

## Decision Making

**1.** You are the driver in this picture and need to make a turnabout. What type of turnabout would you choose? Why would you choose this type?

**2.** If you were planning to park in the row of angle-parked vehicles, which parking space would you choose to use? Why is this space the safest?

**3.** What procedure must the driver of the blue car follow when leaving the parallel parking space? If there is a collision, who is at fault? Why?

**4.** Which direction should the front wheels be turned for the vehicles parked uphill? For the vehicles parked downhill? Why is this important?

Chapter 6 Performing Basic Vehicle Maneuvers **127**

## Answers to Decision Making

**1.** Choose to back into the driveway on the right side so you will enter traffic from a forward position.

**2.** You should choose to park in one of the two spaces at the bottom of the picture. The van would restrict your view when backing out, and being in an end space leaves more chance of being struck by moving traffic.

**3.** The driver must signal, check the blind spots, and move slowly into the traffic lane. The driver is at fault if there is a collision because the driver is entering moving traffic.

**4.** Wheels of a vehicle parked uphill with a curb should be turned to the left. If the vehicle is parked downhill, the wheels should be turned to the right. This precaution helps keep a vehicle from rolling downhill if the parking brake is released or if the vehicle is pushed.

# Chapter 7  Planning Guide

## Student Features

## Teacher's Edition

| Chapter 7<br>Negotiating Intersections | Student Features | Teacher's Edition |
|---|---|---|
| | You Are the Driver! *p. 129* | Projects *p. 128*<br>Special Needs *p. 129* |
| **7.1 Searching Intersections** *pp. 130–133*<br>• Explain how to search an intersection after it has been identified.<br>• Tell when you are at the point-of-no-return.<br>• Describe what you should do when you have a closed front zone at an intersection. | | Demonstrate *pp. 130, 132, 133*<br>Activity *pp. 130, 131, 132, 133* |
| **7.2 Controlled Intersections** *pp. 134–138*<br>• Explain how to approach a controlled intersection.<br>• Tell how to move from a STOP sign when your view is blocked.<br>• Describe how to make right turns at controlled intersections. | Safe Driving Tip *p. 137*<br>Did You Know? *p. 138* | Demonstrate *pp. 135, 136, 137, 138*<br>Activity *pp. 135, 137*<br>Special Needs, *p. 136* |
| **7.3 Uncontrolled Intersections** *pp. 139–141*<br>• Tell how to identify an uncontrolled intersection.<br>• Explain the procedures to follow at an uncontrolled intersection.<br>• Describe the proper procedures for crossing uncontrolled railroad tracks. | | Demonstrate *pp. 140, 141*<br>Activity, *pp. 139, 140*<br>Special Needs, *p. 140* |
| **7.4 Determining the Right of Way and Judging Gaps** *pp. 142–144*<br>• Define the right of way.<br>• Describe situations in which you, the driver, must yield the right of way.<br>• Identify how long it takes to cross and join traffic. | | Demonstrate *pp. 143, 144*<br>Activity *pp. 143, 144* |
| **Assessment** | Reviewing Chapter<br>Objectives *p. 145*<br>Projects *p. 145*<br>Chapter Test *p. 146*<br>Decision Making *p. 147* | Answers *pp. 146–147* |

**Companion** *pp. 50–54*
**Spanish Handbook** *pp. 13–14*

**Resource Book**
Roadway Sheet 4, *pp. 10–11*
Teacher's Instructions, *p. 41*
Classroom Activity, *p. 42*
Overhead, *p. 43*
**In-Car Checklist** 23

**Content Overhead 16**
**Video 1** Segment on
Searching Intersections

**Resource Book**
Roadway Sheet 4, *pp. 10–11*
**In-Car Checklist** 23

**Content Overhead 17**
**Demonstration Overhead C**
**Video 1** Segment on
Searching Intersections

**Resource Book**
Roadway Sheets, 3 and 4
*pp. 8–11*
**In-Car Checklist** 23

**Video 1** Segment on
Searching Intersections

**Resource Book**
Roadway Sheets, 3 and 4
*pp. 8–11*

**Content Overhead 18**
**Demonstration Overheads**
**C, E**
**Video 1** Segment on
Judging Size of Gaps

**Skills and Applications**
**Workbook,** *pp. 25–28*
**Tests and Activities**
Chapter 7 Activities 7-1 and
7-2, *pp. 54–55*
Chapter 7 Test A and Test B,
*pp. 56–59*

**TestWorks CD-ROM**
Chapter 7 Test

# Technology Resources

## Audio-Visual and Computer Resources

AAA Foundation for Traffic Safety, *Dangerous Crossings: A Second Thought,* video, 14 minutes

AAA Foundation for Traffic Safety, *driver-ZED* CD-ROM

BFA Educational Media, *Driving Tips to Avoid Accidents,* video, 18 minutes

Interactive Driving Systems, Inc., *Mottola's Zone Control for Awareness,* video, 38 minutes

Interactive Driving Systems, Inc., *Precision Turns,* video, 15 minutes

Interactive Driving Systems, Inc., *Rear Zone Control,* video, 27 minutes

Interactive Driving Systems, Inc., *Searching Intersections,* video, 20 minutes

Interactive Driving Systems, Inc., *Targeting,* video, 20 minutes

Operation Lifesaver, *It's Your Choice: Highway Rail Grade Crossing Safety for Motorists,* video, 10 minutes

Operation Lifesaver, *Staying Alert and Alive,* video, 12 minutes (also available in Spanish)

Safety Industries, Inc., *Right of Way,* video, 10 minutes

**Go Online**
PHSchool.com
For: Chapter 7 online activities
Visit: PHSchool.com
Web Code: cak-9999

# Chapter 7

# Negotiating Intersections

## Chapter Overview

Chapter 7 discusses the knowledge and skills needed to search and negotiate intersections safely. It describes proper searching techniques and judgments involving time, space, and distance related to intersections and railroad crossings. Students also will learn about yielding the right of way and judging gaps.

## Chapter Vocabulary

*controlled intersection, controlled railroad crossing, crossbuck, delayed green light, fresh green light, gap, point-of-no-return, protected left turn, stale green light, traffic circle, uncontrolled intersection, uncontrolled railroad crossing, unprotected left turn*

### Teacher's Resources

For students to use as they read the chapter:

**Companion**
pages 50–54

**Spanish Handbook**
pages 13–14

### Projects

Review the projects described on page 145. Some of the projects can be assigned at any time while others are more closely tied to the content presented in the student text.

# CHAPTER **7**
## Negotiating Intersections

**7.1** Searching Intersections

**7.2** Controlled Intersections

**7.3** Uncontrolled Intersections

**7.4** Determining Right of Way and Judging Gaps

## You Are the Driver!

Imagine you are driving the brown pickup truck waiting for the light to change. You plan to go straight. Are you stopped in the proper location? Where should you search? Your decisions require intensive searching of all zones for accurate assessment of your intended path of travel.

In this chapter, you will learn how to identify and search controlled and uncontrolled intersections for a conflict-free path of travel. You also will learn how to interact safely with other roadway users at intersections.

**Go Online**
PHSchool.com
**For:** Chapter 7 online activities
**Visit:** PHSchool.com
**Web Code:** cak-9999

129

## Introducing the Chapter

Discuss the hazards associated with intersections. Discuss the unpredictable behaviors drivers might see when approaching intersections. Explain how crucial it is to apply the IPDE Process when negotiating intersections.

## You Are the Driver!

Busy intersections such as the one in this photo are easy places for less experienced drivers to become distracted. However, by applying the IPDE process much of the confusion can be minimized and the driver will be better able to negotiate such intersections safely. Before turning left, the driver should look left and right and also look ahead to be sure oncoming traffic has cleared.

## Special Needs

Many difficult concepts in this chapter require the repeated use of videos, slides, photographs of intersections, and walk-through demonstrations. Many of the activities in this chapter are crucial for understanding concepts.

Approaching, going through, and turning at intersections are complex maneuvers that require specific visual and physical procedures to be done quickly. Some students will need to review the activities often to reduce their "thinking" time. Others have physical disabilities that may limit their responses and may need alternative solutions.

# Searching Intersections

##  Focus

### Summary

This lesson focuses on the knowledge and skills needed to negotiate intersections safely. Students will learn how to identify and search intersections. The point-of-no-return is explained.

### Vocabulary

*traffic circle, point-of-no-return*

##  Teach

### Discuss

Call students' attention to the list of clues to identify an intersection located on this page. Write each clue on the chalkboard and ask students to identify where the clue would be detected and what predictions could be made about each. Write the answers on the board. (Examples: A traffic sign can serve as a clue that vehicles may be entering or leaving traffic flow. It can cue you to check your rear zone. Crossing traffic is a clue seen while looking to the target area.)

### Demonstrate

Use the photograph to point out clues that identify the intersection.

### Objectives

1. Explain how to search an intersection after it has been identified.
2. Tell when you are at the point of no return.
3. Describe what you should do when you have a closed front zone at an intersection.

The chances of a collision are greater at intersections than at any other point on a roadway. Intersections are dangerous because many drivers' paths cross there, and many unexpected stops occur there. More than one-third of all collisions and one-fourth of all fatal collisions take place at intersections.

One reason for the large number of collisions at intersections is the driver's failure to identify a safe path of travel through the intersection. In order to identify a safe path of travel you first need to locate the intersection.

Look for these clues to identify an intersection ahead:

- street signs and street lights
- roadway markings
- crossing traffic
- parked vehicles on cross streets
- turning traffic
- rows of fences and mailboxes
- traffic stopping
- power lines

What clues identify this intersection?

130 Unit 2 Controlling Your Vehicle

Intersections can be found in various designs. Most are simply two roadways crossing or a railroad crossing a roadway in a + or an X pattern. Others may form a Y when one roadway divides into two or when two join to form one. Some meet to form a T. A few are formed when several roadways meet at a circle—commonly called a **traffic circle**. A driver needs to know how to identify and be able to safely negotiate each design.

### Approaching an Intersection

After identifying an intersection, you will need to determine if you have an open zone for your intended path of travel into and through the intersection. You will need to search the left-front, front, and right-front zones to be certain that they are open. You also need to look for line-of-sight restrictions that will prevent you from seeing if your intended path of travel is going to be safe. You should search for changes in those zones that could make them closed for your travel as shown in the top picture on the next page.

Remember, line-of-sight restrictions can be caused by the environment or by other highway users. When your line of sight is restricted, your zone checks should become more frequent. You should still primarily be checking your front zone to make sure it is still open for your intended path of travel.

Your search will change when you have identified a closed zone caused

---

 **Teacher's Resources**

**Resource Book**
Roadway Sheet 4, pages 10–11
Teacher's Instructions, page 41
Classroom Activity, page 42
Overhead, page 43

**Content Overheads**
Overhead 16

 **Video 1**
Segment on Searching Intersections

**In-Car Checklists**
In-Car Checklist 23

---

**Activity**

**Small Group Activity** Divide the class into groups of three. Give each member of the group a copy of the intersection drawings from the **Resource Book** on page 42 and read instructions on page 41. Use the overhead from **Resource Book** page 43 to demonstrate the path of a vehicle traveling north crossing the path of a vehicle traveling west. Ask each group to draw the path of travel that vehicles and pedestrians can take in the intersection. See how many points of conflict they are able to illustrate. Have each group report its findings to the class.

Search for changes in your zones to keep your intended path of travel safe.

Ask: Why is it important to look for open zones rather than problems before going through an intersection? (The objective is to get through the intersection. To do that you need clear, open zones. It is often easier to identify problems than it is to identify when the zone will be open. You can easily see vehicles approaching, and this lets you know that you cannot enter the intersection. It is much more helpful to search for open zones so that you can be prepared to enter the gap.)

## Discuss

Ask: What type of line-of-sight restrictions can you expect to find at intersections? (Examples include stopped vehicles making left turns, parked vehicles, buildings, trees, bushes, signs, elevated terrain, snow banks, pedestrians waiting to cross the street.)

Ask: Why are line-of-sight restrictions dangerous to your movement through the intersection? (Line-of-sight restrictions can prevent you from seeing if your intended path of travel is going to be safe.)

## Explain

Tell students that each year in the United States approximately 35 percent of all motor vehicle collisions take place at intersections. Ask: Why do you think there is such a high incidence of collisions at intersections?

by a line-of-sight restriction. That is also true when you make a left turn, make a right turn, or continue through an intersection.

Once you are within 4–6 seconds of the intersection, your searching pattern should widen to include more information from the right and left of your path of travel. If your front zone is clear, you can keep moving. If it is not clear, you will need to prepare to stop or change your path of travel.

When you identify a line-of-sight restriction, you should perform a search of that area. Search for such things as a car stopped on the left, a parked vehicle on the right, or a double-parked delivery truck. Turn your head 45 degrees to the right or left in an attempt to see beyond the line-of-sight restriction as shown in the picture on the right. When searching, you need to briefly pause at each zone to detect objects in that location. Do not move your eyes in a constant scan. If you do not pause at each zone, you could miss objects as large as a car.

### Continue Moving Ahead

You may continue ahead if the traffic light is green, or if the intersec-

tion has no signals or signs, and the front, right-front, and left-front zones are open. At an intersection a driver needs to locate open front zones to move ahead safely. Many times it takes numerous checks of a zone because of a line-of-sight restriction.

If your path of travel is clear, continue searching the left-front, front, and right-front zones for a path-of-travel change or a line-of-sight restriction.

Move your head to see beyond line-of-sight restrictions.

Chapter 7 Negotiating Intersections 131

## Demonstrate

Demonstrate the point-of-no-return in your classroom. Clear space to make a wide aisle. Place a strip of masking tape across the aisle on the floor toward the front of the room.

Have students line up along the sides of the classroom. Select one student and ask him or her to start from the back of the room and run in the open aisle when you say go and to stop when you say stop. When the student is ready, say go. When the student reaches the masking tape, shout stop. Repeat this activity with another student.

Point out how neither student could stop on the line. Ask students to compare the speed of the runners with the speed a vehicle is likely to travel as it approaches an intersection. Discuss why it is important to know what the point-of-no-return is. Emphasize that for a driver to best be prepared for the point-of-no-return it is necessary to know the condition of the rear zone. Most of all, a reduction of speed while covering the brake pedal will allow your point-of-no-return to be closer to the intersection, giving you more time to see and react to a problem.

## Apply

Have a student use an overhead transparency, model vehicles, and a wild card to demonstrate the correct lane position to take for one of the line-of-sight restrictions identified in the Model Car Activity. Repeat this activity for each line-of-sight restriction.

Every intersection has a point of no return.

Change lane position and speed if you have a line-of-sight restriction.

Once you have passed the point-of-no-return, you should continue through the intersection. The **point-of-no-return** is the point beyond which you can no longer stop safely without entering the intersection. Under normal conditions, that point is two seconds from the intersection as shown in the picture on the left.

If you do have a line-of-sight restriction, you may want to change your lane position and reduce your speed. This will give you more time to see what is hidden. If the restriction is on the right and you have an open left-front zone, move to the left side of your lane into lane position 2 and reduce your speed. If the restriction is on the left and you have an open right-front zone, move to lane position 3 and reduce speed. When your left-front and right-front zones are closed, stay in lane position 1 and further reduce speed. By improving your position and reducing your speed, you will have more time to see as well as be seen by others.

When your path of travel is closed and there is a line-of-sight restriction, a lane change may be needed. *Remember, you are not allowed to make lane changes within an intersection.* Therefore, you should select the best path of travel before entering an intersection. You must check your new path of travel before you change your lane position or change lanes.

### Deciding to Stop

You may have to stop at an intersection when you identify or predict a closed zone or a line-of-sight restric-

## Activity

**Model Car Activity** This activity will help students identify line-of-sight restrictions. Divide the class into groups of three. Give each group Roadway Sheet 4 from **Resource Book,** pages 10–11, two model cars and a wild card.

Have students place the cars and wild card in various positions to represent line-of-sight restrictions. Have each group make a list of all conditions they are able to discover which can cause line-of-sight restrictions while approaching two-lane and four-lane roadways. Allow ten min-

utes for this activity. Make a composite list on the chalkboard. (Examples include stopped vehicles making left turns, parked vehicles, buildings, trees, bushes, signs, elevated terrain, snow banks, pedestrians about to cross the street.)

After you have stopped, check your front zone and search 90 degrees to your left and right.

tion ahead. By reducing your speed you can more easily check the zone having a line-of-sight restriction.

A closed front zone is identified by the presence of a yellow or red traffic light, a YIELD sign, or something moving into your intended path of travel. All of these situations would give you less than 10 seconds of an available path of travel and make it a closed zone.

If you have identified a closed zone at an intersection, you will need to prepare to reduce speed or stop. As soon as you identify a closed zone, check your rear zone. If it is open, begin to brake. If the rear zone is closed, tap your brake pedal a few times so that your brake lights communicate to the driver to the rear that you are stopping.

**Moving After a Stop**

After you have stopped and your front zone is clear, search at 90-degree angles to the right and left before you begin moving. Pause briefly at

each target area to get a clear view of possible conflicts.

When turning, your last check should be in the direction of your intended path of travel. You need to know if your intended path of travel is open before you enter an intersection.

If you are stopped behind another vehicle, wait one second after it begins to move before you move. This gives you room to respond to any sudden stop made by the vehicle ahead.

### Review It

1. Which zones should you search when approaching an intersection?
2. Where is your point of no return?
3. What should you do when you identify a closed front zone at the next intersection?

Chapter 7 Negotiating Intersections 133

Ask: Why is it important to make the last intersection check in the direction of your intended path before turning the steering wheel?

Point out that many vehicle-pedestrian and vehicle-bicyclist collisions occur because the driver is looking to the left while turning and moving the vehicle to the right. The only way a driver can be certain that the space the vehicle needs to occupy is vacant is to look at the space before moving into it.

## Demonstrate

Use **Video 1** segment on Searching Intersections to demonstrate the procedures for searching intersections.

 **Assess**

### Answers to Review It

**1.** You will need to search the left-front, front, and right-front zones to be certain that they are open. (p. 130)

**2.** The point-of-no-return is the point beyond which you can no longer stop safely without entering the intersection. Under normal conditions, the point-of-no-return is two seconds from the intersection. (p. 132)

**3.** You will need to prepare to reduce speed or stop. Preparation includes checking your rear zone. (p. 133)

## Activity

**In-Class Driving Rehearsal** Use this exercise to practice searching intersections left, front, and right; making a 45-degree search; making a 90-degree search; and making a legal stop.

You will need three large pieces of cardboard for this activity. Arrange rows of chairs/desks to form a four-way intersection. Put masking tape on the floor to form stop lines.

Select eight students and have them pretend to drive. Have them walk from all four directions. Select three other students and give them each a

piece of cardboard. They represent line-of-sight restrictions likely to be found at intersections. Have students identify themselves as a particular line-of-sight restriction. Instruct the drivers to describe how they are making decisions regarding the line-of-sight restrictions. Give all students the opportunity to be a driver and line-of-sight restriction.

# Controlled Intersections

 **Focus**

## Summary

This lesson discusses the knowledge and skills needed to negotiate controlled intersections safely. It describes judgments involving time, space, and distance related to intersections and railroad crossings. Students also learn about unprotected left turns and turns on red.

## Vocabulary

**New:** *controlled intersection, controlled railroad crossing, delayed green light, fresh green light, protected left turn, stale green light, unprotected left turn*

**Review:** *full stop*

## Teach

### Discuss

Ask: Why do you think traffic controls are necessary at intersections? (Traffic controls allow for an orderly movement of traffic from all directions through an intersection.) What would happen if all intersections were uncontrolled? (The risk of collisions would be extremely high.)

### Objectives

1. Explain how to approach a controlled intersection.
2. Tell how to move from a STOP sign when your view is blocked.
3. Describe how to make right turns and left turns at controlled intersections.

A controlled intersection is one at which traffic signals or signs determine the right of way. Obey all signs and traffic signals when you approach a controlled intersection. Yield the right of way to through traffic.

### Controlled Intersections with Signs

Two kinds of signs control intersections: STOP and YIELD. You must come to a **full stop** for a STOP sign, crosswalk, or stop line. At a YIELD sign, slow and yield the right of way to vehicles on the through street.

#### Blocked View at Stop Sign

Sometimes parked vehicles or other objects cause a line-of-sight restriction. Follow these steps to cross intersections safely and merge with traffic after stopping.

**Crossing Traffic** Follow this procedure when you need to cross traffic through an intersection:

1. Look around and search at a 45-degree angle at location 1 in the picture on the top right. Continue to search left, front, and right as you creep forward. Check your rear zone.
2. Check your path of travel for pedestrians and prepare to make the legal stop before you move beyond location 2. Look for vehicles making turns into your path.
3. Stop with your front bumper even with the curb. Search 90

degrees to the left and right of your target area. When there are parked vehicles, your ideal searching location is when your front bumper is even with the left side of the parked cars, as in location 3.
4. When you have an open front zone and a clear gap of at least seven seconds from the left and right, proceed by accelerating to the proper speed. Once through the intersection, check your rear zone.

**Joining Traffic—Right Turn** Take these steps when turning right to join traffic:

1. At location 1 in the picture in the middle on the right, search your front zones for pedestrians and vehicles turning onto your street. Check your rear zone, and stop.
2. Stop at location 2 where your front bumper is even with the curb. Search 90-degrees to the left and right. Evaluate the target path and your left-front, front, and right-front zones. When clear of any line-of-sight restrictions and with a gap of at least seven seconds, begin your turn. Turn your head toward your target, begin to accelerate, and turn the steering wheel. When you have a line-of-sight restriction to your left that prevents you from clearly seeing at a 90-degree angle, creep forward slightly to improve your view to

---

 **Teacher's Resources**

**Resource Book**
Roadway Sheet 4, pages 10–11

**Demonstration Overheads**
Overhead C

**Content Overheads**
Overhead 17

▶ **Video 1**
Segment on Searching Intersections

**In-Car Checklists**
In-Car Checklist 23

**Background**

**Intersections** Failure to yield the right of way is the most common traffic violation for drivers involved in intersection collisions. Drivers in intersection collisions frequently say, "I didn't see . . ."

Many drivers can be easily distracted at intersections—looking in the wrong place at the wrong time. In addition, many drivers have not learned effective identification and prediction skills for locating closed zones while going into and through an intersection.

the left. Turn your head toward your target path as you accelerate and turn.

3. At location 3, turn so that you end up no farther than three to four feet away from the curb. Accelerate to adjust to traffic and check the rear zone.

**Joining Traffic—Left Turn** Follow these steps when turning left:

1. Before moving beyond location 1 in the picture on the bottom right, your vehicle should be in lane position 2. Search front zones for pedestrians and vehicles turning onto your street. Check your rear zone and stop.

2. Stop when your front bumper is even with the curb. Evaluate your left-front, front, and right-front zones. When you are clear of any line-of-sight restrictions and have a gap of at least seven seconds, begin your turn. Move forward slightly to where your body is even with the curbline. Check your front zones; turn your head toward your target area; accelerate; and turn the steering wheel.

3. At location 3, turn so that you end up in lane position 2. Accelerate to adjust to traffic and check the rear zone.

### Controlled Intersections with Signals

Traffic signals usually have three lights to each cycle—red, yellow, and green. Signals also can have a fourth or fifth light, such as a yellow arrow and a green arrow. Imagine you are

Crossing traffic

Joining Traffic—Right Turn

Joining Traffic—Left Turn

Chapter 7 Negotiating Intersections **135**

---

## Activity

**Model Car Activity** In this activity students will practice the steps for crossing traffic and joining traffic. Divide the class into groups of three. Assign the roles of driver, instructor, and observer. Give each group Roadway Sheet 4 from **Resource Book,** pages 10–11, two cars, and a wild card.

Direct the instructors to refer to page 134 to describe the first step for crossing traffic through an intersection. Have the drivers move their vehicles and demonstrate the step as if actually in the vehicle. The instructors and observers should provide feedback. Have the members of the group switch roles for each of the remaining steps. Repeat the activity for joining traffic—right turn, and for joining traffic—left turn.

---

### Demonstrate

Use **Demonstration Overhead C** Move the car through the intersection, stopping at each of the locations as illustrated on this page. Ask why each step is important.

### Demonstrate

This demonstration will help students learn how to search the right-front, front, and left-front zones effectively. You will need to prepare three sets of 4 by 6 inch index cards. For each set, number the cards 0–9 with three-inch-high numerals.

Select three students and give them each a set of cards. Explain that when you give the signal they should hold up any two cards. Have one student stand in the center of the front wall facing the class. Ask the other two students to move to the sides of the room and stand by the wall.

Direct the remaining students to pretend that they are in a vehicle at an intersection. Ask them to search all three zones and record the numbers from the cards that will be held up. Signal the cardholders to reveal their numbers and then quickly hide them.

Discuss with the class how it is necessary to look 90 degrees to the left and right and to make a brief eye fixation at the front zone to have the ability to clearly read the number.

### Demonstrate

Use the illustrations on this page or **Content Overhead 17** to help students visualize crossing and joining traffic.

Chapter 7 | Negotiating Intersections | **135**

## Discuss

Ask: What prediction can you make after identifying a large number of vehicles stopped at a cross street while you are approaching a green traffic light? (The light for the cross street has been red for a while and your green light is stale.)

## Explain

When stopping and while stopped at an intersection, there is a high risk for being rear-ended. To reduce your risk, continue to search the rear zone for approaching traffic. When you identify a vehicle and predict that the driver might not be aware of your braking or stopped vehicle, flash the brake lights by tapping the brake pedal a few times. Sometimes this is an effective way to communicate with the driver behind you.

## Demonstrate

Put one chair in the front of the classroom and tell students it is a car stopped at an intersection. Take a second chair and bang it into the first chair. Now, position two chairs in back of the first chair to represent cars stopped to the rear (keep two feet of space between each chair). Take another chair and bang it into the last chair in line. Ask: In which chair would you rather have been sitting? In which chair would there have been the greatest force of impact on your body?

The green arrow permits you to make a protected left turn.

stopped at the red light in the picture above. Think of what is about to take place. Proceed with caution when your light turns green.

As you drive toward a signal-controlled intersection, consider if the signal is about to change. Treat each intersection as a separate problem. Searching 12–15 seconds ahead, evaluate the next intersection to see what color that light is. Look for any traffic moving on the cross street. Before you reach the point where you must brake to stop at an intersection, quickly check your front zones. If you predict the light is going to be red, or if cross traffic has closed your front

zone, check your rear zone, reduce speed, and be prepared to stop.

### Signals

Use the IPDE Process to handle traffic signals properly. Identify the color of a signal as soon as you see it. Predict that the color might change as you approach the intersection.

**Stale Green Light** A stale green light is a light that has been green for a long time. If a light remains green after you first identify it, be prepared to slow. Predict that it will turn yellow soon.

**Fresh Green Light** A fresh green light is a light that has just turned green. A fresh green light does not guarantee that you will have a safe path of travel. *Be sure that no driver on the cross street is running the red light.* Check for an open zone before you proceed.

**Yellow Light** When you approach an intersection as the light turns yellow, you must decide whether to stop or proceed. If the light turns yellow before you reach the point of no return, check in the rear zone.

**You Are the Driver!**
What will you do when your signal turns green?

## Facts and Figures

Rear-end collisions account for about 30 percent of all intersection collisions. A vehicle stopped at an intersection is vulnerable to a high-impact rear-end force until there are at least two vehicles stopped to its rear. The more vehicles stopped to the rear, the less the impact force will be.

## Special Needs

Have students stand at various corners with different speed zones. They should practice estimating when a vehicle is 6 or 7 seconds away until they can do so accurately 10 times in a row.

If it is safe to stop, do so. Otherwise, go through the intersection.

Be very careful before making a left turn on a yellow light. Wait for all oncoming traffic to stop before you start your turn.

**Red Light** When the light is red, you must stop. Check your rear zone as you begin to slow.

If you have a vehicle ahead of you, stop at a point where you can see its rear wheels touching the roadway. If you have no vehicles behind you, continue checking your rear zone often.

### Unprotected Left Turns

An **unprotected left turn** is made at a signal-controlled intersection that does not have a special left-turn light. When you turn left, you must yield to oncoming traffic.

### Protected Left Turns

You can make a **protected left turn** when a special left-turn light, green arrow, or delayed green light lets you turn left while oncoming traffic is stopped. Left turns might be prohibited when the protected left-turn signal ends by a sign or a red arrow. If the turn is allowed, respond to it as you would to an unprotected left turn.

**Left-Turn Light** A left-turn light provides a protected left turn. Some left-turn lights are located over the turn lane without using signs.

**Green Arrow** A green arrow can appear with the normal red, yellow, and green signals. In many places the green arrow simply turns off to indicate the protected turn has ended. Others

are followed with a yellow arrow as a warning. Watch for oncoming drivers who might proceed, thinking your green arrow is their green light.

**Delayed Green Light** A delayed green light indicates that one side of an intersection has a green light while the light for the oncoming traffic remains red. This light allows traffic from one side to turn or go straight before the light for oncoming traffic turns green. Obey your signal only. Do not assume that you can proceed when oncoming traffic proceeds.

### Turns on Red

All states and the District of Columbia now permit turns on red. A few local governments may not. Watch for signs posted that prohibit turning on red.

**Right on Red** Before turning right on a red light, come to a full stop as you would at a STOP sign. Move to a position where you can see clearly. Search the front zones for openings. You must yield the right of way to any vehicle or pedestrian in, or approach-

Where should you search for vehicles and pedestrians when turning right on red?

When a light turns yellow as you approach an intersection, prepare to stop. Do not speed up to try to get through the intersection.

## Discuss

Ask: What should you do when approaching an intersection with a signal light that is not operating? (Drivers should assume the light is red. If all lights are out, the intersection becomes an uncontrolled intersection.)

## Demonstrate

For this demonstration you will need a model vehicle with front tires that can be steered. On the chalkboard, draw a crossroads intersection to scale for the vehicle you are using. Demonstrate the importance of keeping the tires straight while waiting to make a left turn at an unprotected intersection. With the tires turned, push the vehicle forward to demonstrate how it will move into the path of oncoming traffic if it is rear-ended. With the tires straight, push the vehicle forward to demonstrate how it will move straight and not into the path of oncoming traffic.

## Discuss

Ask: What are the advantages and disadvantages of permitting a right turn when the traffic light is red? (The main advantage is that drivers do not have to wait for the light to change. Disadvantages include increased risk for bicyclists and pedestrians.) Why are you required to stop before turning right on red? (To allow time to search the intersection.)

## Activity

**Small Group Activity** This activity provides an opportunity for reviewing this lesson while encouraging teamwork and communication. You will need to divide the class into groups of three or four. Let each group select one person as the recorder.

Tell the students that they will be taking a group quiz. Give each member of the group a copy of the quiz. Ask the group to work together to develop a single answer for each question. When the group is satisfied with an answer, the recorder should write it down. When all the ques-

tions have been answered, the recorder will turn in the group's answers for grading. Each member of the group should receive the same grade.

Sample quiz questions include: What is a stale green light? How can you identify a stale green light? What searching actions should you take before entering a fresh red light? How is the point-of-no-return used when the signal light turns yellow? What is an unprotected left turn? What are three different ways that you can make a protected left turn?

## Discuss

Ask: Is a railroad crossing an intersection? (yes) Follow up by asking: What makes it an especially dangerous intersection? (the train's size, weight, speed, and traction on the rails) Point out that a train can take more than a mile to stop. A car-train collision is comparable to a 300-pound football player running at full speed into a small child.

## Demonstrate

Hold a hammer and a peanut. Tell the class the hammer is a train and the peanut is a car. Smash the peanut with the hammer. Cars shatter from the impact of a train like the peanut.

## ③ Assess

### Answers to Review It

**1.** Come to a full stop at a STOP sign, or yield the right of way at a YIELD sign. (p. 134)
**2.** Search constantly as you creep forward. (p. 134)
**3.** Search all zones, search 90 degrees to the left and right, and proceed when there is a clear path and no line-of-sight restrictions. (pp. 134–135)

TRAFFIC SIGNALS  In the early 1920s, Garret Morgan noticed that the traffic signals at a busy intersection did not help traffic move smoothly enough through the streets of Cleveland, Ohio. The signals did not have a caution position to alert drivers that they would soon have to stop. Morgan made a three-position signal. He then sold his idea to a large electric company that developed the red-yellow-green traffic lights still prevalent today.

ing, the intersection. Complete your turn into the nearest right lane.

**Left on Red**  Most states also permit a left turn on red if the turn is from a one-way street onto another one-way street. A few states also permit turning left on red from a left-turn lane on a two-way street onto a one-way street. Follow the same procedure as in a right turn on red, but look for traffic in your front and right-front zones. Then turn into the nearest left lane.

Stop when the gate is down.

138  Unit 2  Controlling Your Vehicle

### Controlled Railroad Crossings

A **controlled railroad crossing** usually has red lights along with crossing gates. Make a complete stop when the lights are flashing and/or the gates are down. Remain stopped until the lights stop flashing and the gates have raised. It is illegal, unsafe, and costly to drive around the gates. When the crossing is clear, proceed cautiously.

### Review It

1. How should you approach a controlled intersection?
2. When your view is blocked at a STOP sign, what should you do?
3. How would you make a right turn or a left turn at a controlled intersection?

## Background

**Car-Train Collisions**  There are nearly 4,000 collisions at railroad crossings each year. More than 50 percent of these collisions occur where active warning devices exist (gates, lights, and/or bells).

There is only one way drivers can be guaranteed that a train will not run into their vehicle, and that is to make a 90 degree search to the left and right to see open zones before crossing the tracks. With proper practice, drivers become aware of line-of-sight restrictions at intersections. This will give the driver the correct behavior to

look way down the track—same as 90 degree searches at intersections—rather than to rely only upon the fact that the red crossing lights are not flashing. Drivers have gotten into car-train collisions because the flashing lights malfunctioned, the flashing lights were ignored, or the sun prevented the driver from seeing the lights. If a driver is able to see open zones in both directions, there will not be a car-train collision.

An **uncontrolled intersection** has no signs or signals to regulate traffic. These intersections usually are found in areas of light traffic, such as residential areas. Although these streets usually are quiet, they can be dangerous because drivers might not be expecting cross traffic or pedestrians.

Sometimes a driver fails to identify an intersection as uncontrolled. The driver assumes the other driver will stop or, on a quiet street, assumes that no one is there. If you do not see a traffic sign or signal, assume that the intersection is uncontrolled. Predict that other traffic will not stop. Reduce speed, search aggressively, and always be prepared to stop.

### Approaching Uncontrolled Intersections

Once an intersection has been identified, check your rear zone for following traffic. Then, you will need to determine if you have an open path of travel into and through the intersection. You will need to search the left-front, front, and right-front zones to be certain that they are open for your use. You need to continue to look for line-of-sight restrictions that could prevent you from seeing if your path of travel is going to be safe.

Be certain that you can clearly see open space in your left-front, front, and right-front zones before entering the intersection. You must search for zone changes that could make them closed.

Your search pattern will change when you have identified a closed zone caused by a line-of-sight restriction. If you identify a closed zone in your path of travel, check your rear zone again. Remove your foot from the accelerator and cover or apply the brake.

If a vehicle is coming from the left or right, the driver on the left must yield to the driver on the right. However, predict the worst in each case. *Never assume that the other driver will yield.* The only safe action is to slow and be prepared to stop.

**You Are the Driver!**
Where are the signs and signals at this intersection?

### Objectives

1. Tell how to identify an uncontrolled intersection.
2. Explain the procedures to follow at an uncontrolled intersection.
3. Describe the proper procedures for crossing uncontrolled railroad tracks.

---

# Uncontrolled Intersections

## 🛡 **1 Focus**

### Summary

This lesson discusses the knowledge and skills needed to negotiate uncontrolled intersections safely. It describes judgments involving time, space, and distance related to intersections and railroad crossings.

### Vocabulary

*crossbuck, uncontrolled intersection, uncontrolled railroad crossing*

## 🛡 **2 Teach**

### Discuss

Ask: How is coming out of the driveway of a house similar to approaching an uncontrolled intersection? (You do not have a STOP sign, YIELD sign, or traffic signal.) Point out that you should treat a driveway as if there is an implied YIELD sign posted in the yard. Driving forward out of a driveway—compared to backing out—gives you a better opportunity to see and enter a gap in traffic. Point out that driveways are a common uncontrolled intersection that many drivers face daily.

---

## 🔧 **Teacher's Resources**

**Resource Book**
Roadway Sheets 3 and 4, pages 8–11

 **Video 1**
Segment on Searching Intersections

**In-Car Checklist**
In-Car Checklist 23

## 🚦 **Activity**

**Small Group Activity** This activity will help students learn the difference between controlled and uncontrolled intersections. For this activity you will need a home video, slides, or photographs of various intersections in your community. Divide the class into groups of three. Show a slide or video segment for one intersection, or give each group a photograph. Direct students to work as a group to classify the intersections as controlled or uncontrolled, and list the clues. Repeat the process for the next slide, video segment, or photograph.

## Discuss

Ask: Who should yield the right of way at uncontrolled intersections? (Drivers must yield the right of way to the driver who first reaches and stops at the intersection.) Point out that pedestrians always have the right of way. Drivers should always yield the right of way to vehicles traveling on the major roadway. Many uncontrolled intersections are at exits from parking lots. Drivers exiting the parking lot should yield the right of way to vehicles that are on the roadway.

## Demonstrate

Use the illustration to demonstrate the three locations near an uncontrolled intersection where you should use the IPDE Process.

## Discuss

Encourage students to identify uncontrolled intersections near your school. Discuss why these intersections do not have signals or signs. Ask students if they think any of the intersections needs a signal or sign.

2 secs.

4–6 secs.

12–15 secs.

You should perform a series of steps at each of these three locations near uncontrolled intersections.

Treat an uncontrolled intersection as you would a YIELD sign and always be prepared to stop.

At a traffic circle you must yield to vehicles already in the circle. Vehicles in the traffic circle will be coming from your left. When you are in the circle, be alert for vehicles entering in your right-front zone.

Always let pedestrians go first— no matter where the pedestrian is crossing. As a driver, you must yield to pedestrians even if they are breaking a traffic law.

### Procedures at Uncontrolled Intersections

When you search your target area and identify an uncontrolled intersection, there are three critical locations at which you must use the IPDE Process. Each location corresponds to a time period measured in seconds. When you approach an uncontrolled intersection, you must perform a series of steps at each of these locations.

### IPDE Process at 12–15 Seconds from Intersection

1. Check roadway conditions as you approach the intersection. Check for closed zones to the left front, front, and right front.
2. Identify whether or not the intersection is controlled.
3. Identify other roadway users in or near the intersection.
4. Search the view to each side. Look for line-of-sight restrictions. Check 45 degrees to each side. When you identify closed zones, solve the problems before you enter those spaces.

5. Locate your point of no return. You cannot stop after passing that point.
6. Check the rearview mirror for following traffic, and slow your vehicle. The more line-of-sight restrictions, the more time you need to use the IPDE Process.

### IPDE Process at 4–6 Seconds from Intersection

1. Recheck your immediate path of travel.
2. Search left front and right front again for an open zone.
3. If a vehicle is coming from the left or right, prepare to stop.
4. Recheck traffic to the rear.

### IPDE Process at 2 Seconds from Intersection

1. Pause your search briefly as you continue evaluating zones for potential conflicts. This is your last chance to stop safely—your point of no return.
2. Brake to a stop if your front zone in the intersection closes.
3. Search again to the left and right.
4. Proceed through the intersection when your path of travel is clear.

### Uncontrolled Railroad Crossings

Trains warn others of their approach, but it is primarily up to the vehicle driver to avoid a collision. Stopping distances of trains will vary. You can be sure that a train's stopping distance will always be longer than that of a car.

An **uncontrolled railroad crossing** does not have flashing red lights or crossing gates. However, nearly

## Activity

**Model Car Activity** Divide the class into groups of three. Assign the roles of driver, instructor and observer. Give each group Roadway Sheets 3 and 4 from **Resource Book,** pages 8–11, two cars, and a wild card.

Direct the instructor to describe each step in the Procedures at Uncontrolled Intersections. As the instructor is describing each step, the driver should demonstrate that step with the model car. The instructor and observer provide feedback to the driver.

## Special Needs

A student observer in behind-the-wheel situations can help provide reinforcement for students. When approaching uncontrolled intersections, the observer can help the driver identify developing problems.

all are marked with a sign as you approach them. In towns and cities, a round, yellow railroad-crossing sign is posted about 250 feet from the actual crossing. In rural areas this warning sign is about 750 feet from the crossing. A **crossbuck,** a large white X-shaped sign, is located beside the crossing. Many times a large white X is painted on the roadway near the crossing.

Treat uncontrolled crossings the same as an intersection with a YIELD sign. Slow and be prepared to stop.

### Crossing Railroad Tracks

Take these actions when you approach an uncontrolled railroad crossing:

1. Slow down. Check tracks to both sides and traffic to the rear as you approach the crossing sign.
2. Turn off the radio, air conditioner, or heater fan to listen for train sounds. Open the window if the area is noisy.
3. Reduce speed to handle a possible rough-road crossing or if there is a line-of-sight restriction. Note the number of track sets.
4. If a train is approaching, stop at a safe distance before the tracks.
5. Wait for the train to clear. Then carefully check the crossing. Be sure another train is not approaching on another set of tracks.
6. If it is safe to cross, increase your speed up to at least 20 mph. Then your vehicle can roll across the tracks should its engine stall.
7. If you have a stickshift vehicle, shift to a lower gear before crossing to prevent stalling on the tracks. Never shift while crossing tracks.

Slow and be prepared to stop at uncontrolled railroad crossings.

8. Drive onto the tracks only after you have enough space and speed to clear the tracks. Make sure any vehicles ahead clear the tracks before you start to cross. Never stop on railroad tracks while waiting for traffic ahead to move.
9. When you follow buses or trucks hauling flammable contents, be prepared to stop. Many states require such vehicles to stop before crossing railroad tracks.

### Review It

1. How can you identify an uncontrolled intersection?
2. What should you do at an uncontrolled intersection?
3. What are the procedures to use when going through an uncontrolled railroad crossing?

## Cross Curricular

**Visual Arts** Have students design a poster with a safety message related to negotiating intersections. Suggest that they use newspaper and magazine photographs that depict collisions at intersections.

### Demonstrate

Use the chalkboard to demonstrate how the line-of-sight restriction caused by a westbound train that just cleared the crossing can easily block a driver's view of an eastbound train.

Ask: How does identifying and responding to line-of-sight restrictions help you safely cross railroad tracks?

### Apply

Have students pretend their desks are cars and that they are approaching railroad tracks. Have students demonstrate and apply each of the nine steps listed under Crossing Railroad Tracks. For each step, select a student and ask: Why is this important?

 **Assess**

### Answers to Review It

**1.** Uncontrolled intersections have no signs or signals to regulate traffic. (p. 139)

**2.** You must use the IPDE Process at three critical locations: 12–15 seconds from the intersection, 4–6 seconds from the intersection, and 2 seconds from the intersection. (p. 140)

**3.** The nine-step procedure appears on page 141.

# Determining Right of Way and Judging Gaps

## ① Focus

### Summary

This lesson continues to focus on the knowledge and skills needed to negotiate intersections safely. Students will learn about yielding the right of way and judging gaps.

### Vocabulary

**New:** *gap*

**Review:** *right of way, yield*

## ② Teach

### Discuss

Ask students to look at the Situations When You Must Yield illustrations on pages 142–143. Read the first statement and ask a student to explain its meaning and apply it to a situation. After some discussion move on to the next statement.

### Objectives

1. Define right of way.
2. Describe situations in which you, the driver, must yield the right of way.
3. Identify how long it takes to cross and join traffic.

A safe driver knows that conflicts often occur at intersections and is prepared to handle these conflicts. To be a safe driver, you need to know when to yield the right of way.

### What Is Right of Way?

The term **right of way** describes the privilege of having immediate use of a certain part of a roadway. You have the right of way only when other drivers give it to you. It is not something you can take.

You will often have to **yield,** by letting others go first, to be safe. Letting others go first is called "yielding the right of way." Sometimes you must yield to prevent a collision. At other times, yielding is an act of courtesy. Most of the time, laws determine who should yield the right of way.

### Situations When You Must Yield

Remember these points in yield situations:

- Your action should not cause those to whom you should yield the right of way to slow, stop, or change their intended path of travel.
- Traffic signs and signals only show who should yield the right of way. They do not stop traffic for you.
- Others can give you the right of way. Do not assume others will always yield to you.
- Many times it is better to yield the right of way even when the law requires the other driver to yield.

- Failure to yield the right of way is one of the most frequent violations in fatal collisions.

You must yield the right of way in many situations. Knowing right-of-way laws will help you make safe decisions. These drawings show the most common situations regarding yielding the right of way. In each situation the yellow car is required to yield.

**Yield at STOP signs to**
- pedestrians in or near the crosswalk
- all traffic on the through street

**Yield at fresh green lights to**
- pedestrians still in the crosswalk
- vehicles still in the intersection

142 Unit 2 Controlling Your Vehicle

## Teacher's Resources

**Resource Book**
Roadway Sheets 3 and 4, pages 8–11

**Content Overheads**
Overhead 18

**Demonstration Overheads**
Overheads C, E

 **Video 1**
Segment on Judging Size of Gaps

**Yield coming from an alley, driveway, or private roadway to**
- pedestrians before reaching the sidewalk
- all vehicles on the street (Make two stops.)

**Yield at all YIELD signs to**
- all pedestrians in or near crosswalks
- all vehicles on the cross street

**Yield to emergency vehicles**
- sounding a siren or using a flashing light (Stop clear of the intersection close to curb. Wait for emergency vehicle to pass.)

**Yield when turning left at any intersection to**
- all pedestrians in your turn path
- all oncoming vehicles that are at all close

**Yield at four-way stops to**
- all pedestrians in or near crosswalks
- vehicles that arrive first
- a vehicle from the right if you arrive at the same time

**Yield at uncontrolled intersections to**
- pedestrians in or near the crosswalk
- any vehicle that has entered the intersection
- a vehicle from the right if you both arrive at the same time

Chapter 7 Negotiating Intersections **143**

## Discuss

Ask students if they agree or disagree with the following statement: Yielding the right of way is an act of courtesy. Ask them to provide examples.

Ask: Which would make you feel better—giving someone twenty dollars or having someone steal it from you? Point out that when you give someone the right of way they cannot steal it from you. That puts you in a win-win situation. Some individuals set themselves up for a lose-lose situation by not giving anyone a break, which often causes high risk and high stress. Being courteous to others is like giving yourself a gift—less stress and more control over the situation.

## Demonstrate

Use **Demonstration Overheads C** and **E** to demonstrate various situations for students to determine which driver should yield the right of way. Name or draw in traffic controls with an erasable marker to demonstrate different situations.

## Activity

**Model Car Activity** Divide the class into groups of three. Give each group Roadway Sheets 3 and 4 from **Resource Book,** pages 8–11, two cars, and three wild cards.

Have students use model cars to recreate the situations on pages 142–143. Have them take one situation at a time. Encourage students to discuss how the rights of way apply and why.

## Explain

Explain the importance of selecting a gap before it is available. Point out that you need to look beyond the intersection in both directions to determine when there will be an acceptable gap. Once a gap is located, the driver must also make sure that nothing from the front zone will interfere with the use of the gap.

## Demonstrate

Use **Video 1** segment on Judging Size of Gaps to demonstrate how to judge gaps. Use the chart on this page or **Content Overhead 18** to reinforce your explanation of gaps needed for different speeds.

## Assess

### Answers to Review It

**1.** Letting others go first is called yielding the right of way. (p. 142)

**2.** Students' answers will vary. Any of the six examples that appears on pages 142–143 is correct.

**3.** You must learn to estimate the speed and distance of the vehicles involved. (p. 144)

| | To Cross Traffic 4–5 Seconds | Turn Right and Join Traffic 6 Seconds | Turn Left and Join Traffic 7 Seconds |
|---|---|---|---|
| 20 mph | more than ½ block away | more than ½ block away | more than ⅔ block away |
| 30 mph | more than ⅔ block away | 1 block away | more than 1 block away |
| 45 mph | more than 1 block away | more than 2 blocks away | more than 2½ blocks away |
| 55 mph | more than 1½ blocks away | more than 3 blocks away | more than 3½ blocks away |

Gap selection for crossing or joining traffic

### Judging the Size of a Gap

You must be able to judge the gaps between vehicles and how long it takes to pass through or enter intersecting traffic lanes.

A **gap** is the distance between vehicles. When you enter a through street after stopping, you must judge the size of the gaps in traffic.

You need different size gaps depending on the maneuver you plan to make and the speed of traffic. From the picture above you see that crossing a two-lane street takes about four to five seconds. Turning right and accelerating to 30 mph takes about six seconds. Turning left and accelerating to 30 mph takes about seven seconds. The same process to judge following distance is adapted to judge gap sizes.

### Crossing and Joining Traffic

You must know how long it takes to turn right, to turn left, and to cross traffic at an intersection. Turning right or left into lanes of other vehicles is called *joining traffic*. Look at the picture to visualize situations that follow.

Crossing an intersection takes four to five seconds from a stop. If traffic on the through street is traveling 30 mph, you need a gap of about two-thirds of a block in each direction.

You need a larger gap to join traffic when turning right than when crossing. You need about six seconds to reach the speed of through-street traffic without interfering with the flow of traffic.

A left turn is more dangerous than a right turn. You cross the paths of traffic from the left before entering traffic from the right. The gap to the left should be greater than when you make a right turn. At 55 mph, you need a gap of more than three and one-half blocks.

### Review It

1. What is meant by "yielding the right of way"?
2. Give six examples of when you should yield the right of way.
3. How many seconds does it take to cross traffic?

## Activity

**In-Class Driving Rehearsal** This exercise will help students learn to judge the size of a gap and how big a gap is needed to join traffic. Arrange the chairs to form a crossroads intersection. Have five students represent westbound traffic, walking with various amounts of distance between each other. Have another five students, arranged with various amounts of distance, represent eastbound traffic. Divide the remaining students into two groups of drivers attempting to enter the intersection. Have one of these groups approach the intersection heading north and the other approach the intersection heading south.

One at a time, ask the northbound and southbound drivers to choose one of three options: cross traffic, turn right, or turn left. Have the driver identify the cars that create an acceptable gap. Instruct the driver to start to count when the first car of the gap clears the intersection and stop counting as the second car of the gap enters the intersection. Have the students use the chart in the illustration to determine if the gap is acceptable.

## Reviewing Chapter Objectives

### 1. Searching Intersections

1. How should you search an intersection once you have identified it? (130–131)
2. How can you tell when you are at the point of no return? (132)
3. What should you do when you have a closed front zone at an intersection? (132–133)

### 2. Controlled Intersections

4. How should you approach a controlled intersection? (134)
5. How should you move from a STOP sign when your view is blocked? (134)
6. How would you make a right turn or a left turn at a controlled intersection? (136–138)

### 3. Uncontrolled Intersections

7. How would you identify an uncontrolled intersection? (139)
8. What procedures should you follow at an uncontrolled intersection? (140)
9. What procedures should you follow at an uncontrolled railroad crossing? (141)

### 4. Determining Right of Way and Judging Gaps

10. What does the term "right of way" mean? (142)
11. In what situations must a driver yield the right of way? (142–143)
12. How would you judge a gap in traffic? (144)
13. How would you cross and join traffic properly? (144)

## Projects

### Individuals

**Observe Traffic** Keep a record for a week of all the railroad tracks you cross as a passenger in a car. Note whether (1) the crossing was controlled or uncontrolled, (2) a train was approaching or proceeding down the track, and (3) the driver took the appropriate actions when approaching the tracks. Discuss your findings with the class.

**Investigate** Clip two articles reporting intersection collisions from your local newspaper. Analyze each report to determine which vehicle should have yielded the right of way. Write a summary of your findings and compare your opinions with classmates who analyzed the same collisions.

### Groups

**Observe Traffic** As a group, observe traffic at an intersection controlled by a STOP sign. Use a stopwatch to measure the gaps between vehicles proceeding through the intersection. Record your measurements, organizing them in a spreadsheet format. Measure gaps for vehicles (1) crossing traffic, (2) joining traffic—right turn, and (3) joining traffic—left turn.

**Use Technology** Make a video of cars progressing through an intersection controlled by traffic signals. In the narration, group members should identify the types of traffic signals and analyze the drivers' responses to the signals.

Chapter 7 Negotiating Intersections **145**

## Review Chapter Objectives

**7.1** Searching Intersections
See Answers to Review It on page 133.
**7.2** Controlled Intersections
See Answers to Review It on page 138.
**7.3** Uncontrolled Intersections
See Answers to Review It on page 141.
**7.4** Determining Right of Way and Judging Gaps
See Answers to Review It on page 144.

For additional information refer to the specific page(s) in parentheses after each question.

## Projects

Some of the projects can be assigned at any time while others are more closely tied to the content presented in the student text. The page number where the topic is introduced is indicated.

**Observe Traffic:** Controlled railroad crossings are introduced on page 138 and uncontrolled railroad crossings are introduced on page 140.
**Investigate:** p. 142
**Observe Traffic:** p. 142
**Use Technology:** p. 134
The results of student projects will vary.

## Teacher's Resources

### Skills and Applications Workbook
pages 25–28

### Tests and Activities
Chapter 7 Activities 7-1 and 7-2, pages 54–55
Chapter 7 Test A and Test B, pages 56–59

### TestWorks CD-ROM
Chapter 7 Test

## Answers to Check Your Knowledge

1. b
2. c
3. d
4. c
5. c
6. intersection
7. intended path of travel
8. yield

## Answers to Review Vocabulary

9. controlled intersection (d)
10. full stop (b)
11. right of way (a)
12. gap (f)
13. uncontrolled intersection (e)
14. stale green light (c)

## Answers to Think Critically

Students' answers will vary. For information related to the question refer to the pages indicated.

1. page 135
2. page 137

## Chapter Test

### Check Your Knowledge

**Multiple** Copy the number of each sentence below on a sheet of paper. Choose the letter that best completes the statement or answers the question.

1. As you approach a yellow or red traffic light, your front zone
   (a) widens.          (c) opens up.
   (b) closes.          (d) narrows.
2. What is the term for a light that has just turned from red?
   (a) yellow light     (c) fresh green light
   (b) stale green light (d) stale red light
3. With which of the following does one side of an intersection have a green light?
   (a) fresh green light  (c) controlled
   (b) stale green light      green light
                          (d) delayed green light
4. Which of the following terms means to allow others to go first?
   (a) stop             (c) yield
   (b) proceed          (d) cycle
5. Which of the following signs identifies an uncontrolled railroad crossing?
   (a) STOP sign        (c) crossbuck
   (b) YIELD sign       (d) red flashing lights

**Completion** Copy the number of each sentence below on a sheet of paper. After each number, write the word or words that completes the sentence correctly.

6. Your chances of collision are greater at a/an _____ than at any other point on a roadway.
7. When turning after a stop, your last check should be in the direction of your _____.
8. As a driver, you must always _____ to pedestrians.

### Review Vocabulary

Copy the number of each definition in List A. Match the definition in List A with the term it defines in List B.

**List A**

9. intersection at which traffic signals or signs determine the right of way
10. complete stop as required at a stop sign or red light
11. privilege of having immediate use of a certain part of a roadway
12. distance between vehicles
13. intersection that has no signs or signals to regulate traffic
14. light that has been green for a long time

**List B**

a. right of way
b. full stop
c. stale green light
d. controlled intersection
e. uncontrolled intersection
f. gap

### Think Critically

Write a paragraph to answer each question.

1. Imagine you are driving a car that is approaching an intersection controlled by a STOP sign. You wish to make a left turn. Describe in detail the steps you would take before, during, and after your turn.
2. What is the difference between a protected left turn and an unprotected left turn? Why do you suppose some left turns are protected at signal-controlled intersections, while others are not?

## Decision Making

**1.** You are driving the yellow car and are approaching an uncontrolled intersection. You and the other car are the same distance from the intersection. What do you predict about the other car? What should you do?

**2.** You have just stopped at a red light. You wish to turn left. Is a left turn at this intersection legal on a red light? Where should you search before turning?

**3.** You are driving the red car. The light turns yellow just after the car in front of you crosses the railroad tracks. Where should you stop? What could happen in this situation?

**4.** You are driving this car that is stopped at the STOP sign. At what speed would you assume the cars on the through roadway would be traveling? How far away would the cars have to be for you to make a safe left turn?

Chapter 7 Negotiating Intersections **147**

## Answers to Decision Making

**1.** The driver on the left is required to yield the right of way to the driver on the right. However, there is no guarantee that the other driver will actually yield. Brake until you are sure the other driver will yield. Otherwise, make a full stop at the intersection.

**2.** Most states permit a left turn on red after a full stop from a one-way street to another one-way street. Check traffic from the right and look for pedestrians crossing the street in your intended path of travel.

**3.** Stop before the tracks. If you pull onto the tracks, a train might come before you have enough space ahead to clear the tracks and a vehicle may be too close behind to allow you to back up.

**4.** Assume the vehicles are traveling at 35 mph—probably the highest speed permitted on the through road. The through traffic would have to be more than 3 blocks away.

| |  **Student Features** |  **Teacher's Edition** |
|---|---|---|
| **Chapter 8**<br>**Sharing the Roadway** | You Are the Driver! *p. 149* | Projects *p. 148*<br>Special Needs *p. 149* |
| **8.1 Sharing the Roadway with Motorcyclists** *pp. 150–154*<br>• Tell why you have the responsibility for protecting motorcyclists.<br>• Explain how to use the IPDE Process to protect motorcyclists.<br>• Describe situations where you should look for motorcyclists. | Safe Driving Tip *p. 152* | Demonstrate *p. 152*<br>Activity *pp. 151, 152, 153* |
| **8.2 Motorcyclist Actions Can Affect You** *pp. 155–158*<br>• Explain the difference in acceleration and braking abilities between motorcycles and other vehicles.<br>• Describe the protective equipment motorcyclists should wear.<br>• Explain motorcyclists' special riding problems. | What Do You Think? *p.156* | Demonstrate *p. 157*<br>Activity *pp. 156, 157* |
| **8.3 Bicycles, Mopeds, and Motor Scooters** *pp. 159–161*<br>• Tell how you can help protect bicyclists from conflict.<br>• List the guidelines that moped and motor scooter drivers should follow when riding. | Did You Know? *p. 160* | Demonstrate *p. 161*<br>Special Needs *p. 161* |
| **8.4 Pedestrians and Special Vehicles** *pp. 162–166*<br>• Explain why you should use extra caution and care to protect pedestrians.<br>• List areas where you can expect to see pedestrians.<br>• Explain procedures to follow to clear the way for emergency vehicles. | Did You Know? *p. 163*<br>Safe Driving Tip *p. 164* | Activity *pp. 163, 164*<br>Special Needs *p. 163* |
| **8.5 Sharing the Road with Trucks** *pp. 167–168*<br>• Define "no-zones" around large trucks.<br>• Explain precautions to take when following large trucks.<br>• List guidelines to follow when passing large trucks. | | Activity *pp. 167, 168* |
| **Assessment** | Reviewing Chapter<br>  Objectives *p. 169*<br>Projects *p. 169*<br>Chapter Test *p. 170*<br>Decision Making *p. 171* | Answers *pp. 170–171* |

## Teacher's Resource File

## Videos, Overheads, and Software

**Companion** *pp. 55–61*
**Spanish Handbook** *pp. 17–18*

**Resource Book**
Roadway Sheets 1–8,
*pp. 4–19*

**Demonstration Overheads
A, B, C, D, J**

**Resource Book**
Teacher's Instructions, *p. 27*

**Content Overhead 19**

**Video 1** Segment on
Sharing the Road

**Skills and Applications
Workbook**, *pp. 29–32*
**Tests and Activities**
Chapter 8 Activities 8-1 and
8-2, *pp. 63–64*
Chapter 8 Test A and Test B,
*pp. 65–68*
Unit 2 Test, *pp. 69–72*

**TestWorks CD-ROM**
Chapter 8 Test

## Technology Resources

### Audio-Visual and Computer Resources

AAA Foundation for Traffic Safety, *The New Children in Traffic*, video, 13 minutes

AAA Foundation for Traffic Safety, *driver-ZED* CD-ROM

AAA Foundation for Traffic Safety, *Semi Conscious—Driving in the Real World*, video, 12 minutes

AAA Foundation for Traffic Safety, *Sharing the Road*, video, 8 minutes

Coronet/MTI, *Bicycle Safety,* 2nd edition, video, 12 minutes

Insurance Institute for Highway Safety, *Helmet Laws: Whose Freedom?,* video, 8 minutes

Interactive Driving Systems, Inc., *Searching Intersections,* video, 20 minutes

Motorcycle Safety Foundation, *Cars, Motorcycles, and a Common Road,* $8\frac{1}{2}$ minutes

Safety Industries, Inc., *Hazard Perception*, video, 15 minutes

Safety Industries, Inc., *Motorcycling*, video, 15 minutes

Go Online
PHSchool.com
**For: Chapter 8 online activities**
**Visit: PHSchool.com**
**Web Code: cak-9999**

# Chapter 8

## Sharing the Roadway

### Chapter Overview

Chapter 8 emphasizes the driver's responsibility for protecting motorcyclists, bicyclists, drivers of other small vehicles, and pedestrians. Students will learn how the actions of cyclists, pedestrians, and large trucks can affect the driver.

### Chapter Vocabulary

*moped, motor scooter, no-zones, protective equipment, recreational vehicle, tractor trailer, tractor-semitrailer*

148

### Teacher's Resources

For students to use as they read the chapter:

**Companion**
pages 55–61

**Spanish Handbook**
pages 17–18

### Projects

Review the projects described on page 169. Some of the projects can be assigned at any time while others are more closely tied to the content presented in the student text.

# CHAPTER 8
## Sharing the Roadway

## You Are the Driver!

As a driver, you will be sharing the roadway with a variety of other vehicles and pedestrians. These other users present their own special problems in every driving environment. Many vehicles are small in size and, like pedestrians, have very little protection if a conflict with a larger vehicle occurs.

What problems might the motorcyclist have in this traffic scene? What should the car driver predict? This chapter explores problems presented by other roadway users and explains your responsibility for protecting other less-protected users.

**Go Online**
PHSchool.com

**For:** Chapter 8 online activities
**Visit:** PHSchool.com
**Web Code:** cak-9999

149

---

## Introducing the Chapter

Ask students to think about the vehicles they see each day on the roadway. Discuss what hazards these vehicles might present.

Discuss the benefits and the hazards of two-wheeled motor vehicles. Emphasize the importance of gaining experience driving a four-wheeled vehicle before learning to ride a motorcycle.

## You Are the Driver

Students should imagine they are approaching the intersection shown in the picture. Have them identify the roadway users that could present problems to the driver (pedestrian, motorcyclist). Ask what they predict might happen when the light turns green. Discuss what actions they would need to take.

## Special Needs

The main problem drivers have with sharing the roadway with smaller vehicles and pedestrians is being aware that they are there. You can teach this concept to special needs students with an example of an optical illusion. Point out that drivers must learn to expect to see motorcyclists and other small vehicles. The same concept applies to pedestrians. The activities in the first section of this chapter are especially helpful in increasing the driver's perception of motorcycles, as well as other small vehicles.

# Sharing the Roadway with Motorcyclists

## 1 Focus

### Summary

This lesson emphasizes the responsibility drivers have for sharing the roadway with motorcyclists. The focus is on what the driver needs to do to protect cyclists.

## 2 Teach

### Explain

Although you can scan through the windows of other vehicles, as illustrated on this page, it is best to treat the car as a line-of-sight restriction. Expect that there could be another vehicle concealed—especially a small vehicle such as a motorcycle.

### Discuss

Discuss the importance of mastering the driving task and gaining experience as a driver of a four-wheeled vehicle before learning to drive a two-wheeled vehicle.

### Explain

Stress that the IPDE Process provides an important means for drivers to protect motorcyclists.

### Objectives

1. Tell why you have the responsibility for protecting motorcyclists.
2. Explain how to use the IPDE Process to protect motorcyclists.
3. Describe situations where you should look for motorcyclists.

Even though many drivers will never ride a motorcycle, they will be safer drivers if they understand problems involved in the cyclist's driving task. Motorcyclists have the same privileges within the HTS as drivers of other vehicles. They also share an equal responsibility for following safe driving practices.

Even though motorcycle registrations make up a very small percentage of all vehicle registrations, about 2,000 cyclist fatalities occur each year. Injuries and deaths from motorcycle crashes result primarily from the exposed position of the rider. Unlike the driver of a larger vehicle, a motorcyclist has little or no protection when conflicts occur.

As a driver of a larger vehicle, you must accept the major share of responsibility for protecting motorcyclists as they interact within the HTS. Show cyclists the same courtesy you show other drivers.

### Using the IPDE Process

Most low-risk drivers tend to be alert for other cars and larger vehicles that might cause conflict. Because motorcycles are smaller and are driven in several different lane positions, they often are not identified in time to prevent conflict. Make a special effort to use the IPDE Process.

The Identify step is crucial for drivers because motorcycles are more difficult to see. Search all the zones so you will not be surprised by the sudden appearance of a motorcycle.

Predict actions of motorcyclists that might enter your path. Base your decisions on the problems that confront the motorcyclist, and execute your actions. Use every technique possible before a closed zone or conflict occurs. The driver in the yellow car in the picture is looking through the approaching car's windows to see the motorcyclist or other roadway users.

### Where to Look for Motorcyclists

Look for motorcyclists in the following situations.

**Vehicle Turning Left in Front of Motorcyclist** When you plan to turn left across one or more lanes of traffic, be sure your planned path of travel is clear. Even though the cyclist in the top picture on the opposite page is signaling for a left turn, the car driver

Scan through the windows of other vehicles to see motorcyclists or other roadway users.

## Teacher's Resources

**Resource Book**
Roadway Sheets 1–8,
pages 4–19
**Demonstration Overheads**
Overheads A, B, C, D, and J

## Facts and Figures

Two percent of all vehicles registered are motorcycles. However, they account for five percent of all traffic fatalities. A major cause of these fatalities is other drivers turning left in front of the motorcyclist. The motorcycle's small size makes it difficult for drivers to predict its speed. It is also difficult for drivers to judge the actual distance between their own vehicle and the motorcycle.

Both the car driver and the motorcyclist want to make left turns. The driver of the car should let the motorcyclist start the turn first.

should predict that the cyclist will continue straight. The car driver should complete the left turn only after scanning front and side zones and after the cyclist has entered his left-turn path.

When you make left turns at night, be especially watchful for oncoming vehicle headlights. The single headlight of a motorcycle can be confused with a larger vehicle that has only one working headlight.

**Vehicle Turning Right at Intersection or Driveway** Drivers of larger vehicles who do not check their rear zones frequently might not be aware of traffic to the rear. Therefore, they may turn right directly in front of a motorcyclist, as the picture below shows.

**Motorcyclist Turning Left** When you are approaching an intersection and there is oncoming traffic, expect

### Discuss

Draw students' attention to the *You Are the Driver!* question. Ask: How could you have avoided a possible conflict with this motorcyclist? (The motorcyclist would have been identified by frequently checking the rear zone. Using your turn indicator would have indicated your intention to turn. Positioning your vehicle within three feet of the curb as a normal habit for right turns will help to prevent a cyclist from even attempting to squeeze by.)

### Explain

Explain that making a wide right turn can send the wrong communication to a following motorcyclist who may think that a left turn is being made. To prevent a motorcyclist from passing you on the right while you are in the process of making a right turn, position your vehicle no more than three feet away from the curb of the street from which you are turning.

### Explain

Explain that a blinking turn indicator on a motorcycle does not always mean the motorcyclist is planning to turn or change lanes. The turn indicator on some vehicles does not automatically cancel the signal after a turn. It is important to be able to identify clues to help predict the motorcyclist's next action—speed, leaning, or lane position.

**You Are the Driver!**
How could you have avoided a possible conflict with this motorcyclist?

Chapter 8 Sharing the Roadway 151

## Activity

**Class Activity** This activity will help students understand how difficult it is to identify a motorcycle in a traffic situation. Hold a black videocassette and a dark colored pencil together with one hand in view of the class for five seconds. Have the pencil along and against the edge of the video. After five seconds put both objects where students cannot see them. Ask students to take out a piece of paper and write down what you just had in your hand. After students have had time to record their response, get feedback from students about what they saw.

Most of the students will have seen the videocassette; very few will have noticed the pencil.

Emphasize that small objects such as motorcycles are difficult to see unless you systematically search for them. Hold up the videocassette and pencil and point out how much easier it is to see the pencil when you are looking for it.

## Demonstrate

Use **Demonstration Overheads A, B, C, D,** and **J** to demonstrate the various conditions under which a motorcyclist can be concealed from the driver's view (vehicle turning left or right, motorcyclist turning left, motorcyclist in blind spot, a tailgating motorcyclist, and motorcyclist passing on the right or left).

## SAFE DRIVING

Motorcyclists should never assume that all other drivers see them. They should make every effort to be as visible as possible in the traffic scene.

smaller vehicles to appear in your path. An approaching motorcyclist who is about to turn left could be blocked from your view. Search your front zones and be aware of any limited sight distance to your left. Be prepared to act to avoid conflict.

**Motorcyclist in Driver's Blind Spot** Because of its relatively small size, a motorcycle is often difficult to see in the blind-spot areas behind your vehicle. The roof-support columns on the back and sides of vehicles add to the problem. Always check the blind spots in your left- and right-rear zones by glancing over your shoulder before turning or changing lanes.

**Tailgating Motorcyclist** The only way to know if you are being tailgated by a motorcyclist is to check your rear zone often. When you see a tailgating cyclist, try to avoid sudden braking. If the driver of the yellow car in the picture brakes suddenly to let the car on the shoulder in, the tailgating motorcyclist could lose control. The motorcyclist does not have enough following distance to stop in time. Check your rearview mirrors often and increase your following distance if a cyclist is following you.

**Motorcyclist Passing Vehicle on Right or Left** Check your rearview mirrors and blind spots frequently as part of your visual search pattern. Anticipate that motorcyclists will pass you. The failure of many drivers to check their rearview mirrors and blind-spot areas can easily lead to conflict with motorcyclists.

Be especially aware of being passed on either the right or left at

Watch for tailgating motorcyclists if you must slow or stop suddenly.

an intersection where there may be more space. Even though motorcyclists should not pass at intersections, always watch for them so you can avoid conflict. When you are being overtaken by a motorcyclist, maintain both your lane position and your speed.

**Motorcyclist Meeting an Oncoming Vehicle** You are more likely to see an oncoming motorcyclist in the daytime if the motorcycle's headlight is on. Many states require that the motorcycle's headlight be on at all times. All motorcycles manufactured today have the headlight come on when the ignition is turned on. Whenever you see an oncoming motorcyclist, stay on your side of the roadway until the motorcyclist has passed. Remember also that having your headlights on at all times makes you more visible to the cyclist.

## Activity

**Model Car Activity** This activity will help students understand the various ways a motorcyclist may be concealed from a driver's view. Divide class into groups of five. Give each group any three roadway sheets from the **Resource Book**, pages 4–19, three model cars, and a wild card. One car represents the driver's viewpoint and the others represent other cars on the roadway. Use the wild card as a motorcyclist. Have each group set up the situation shown on p. 150 and other situations where a motorcyclist might be concealed from the driver's view.

### Passing a Motorcyclist

Never tailgate a cyclist before passing. The appearance of a very close vehicle in the cyclist's rearview mirror could cause an unexpected action and result in conflict. When you plan to overtake and pass a motorcyclist, stay well back until you start to pass.

When the way is clear, execute your passing maneuver. Use the entire left lane for passing, as the car driver in the picture is doing. When you can see the cyclist in your rearview mirror, signal, check your right blind-spot area, and return to the right lane.

### Protecting Motorcyclists

Unlike a driver protected inside a larger vehicle, a motorcyclist is fully exposed to dangers that could cause injury or death. For this reason, you must accept an extra share of responsibility for avoiding conflicts with cyclists. With a larger vehicle under your control, you have the power to cause far more harm than a cyclist. Handle this power with respect.

Develop an attitude of helping others who are less protected. Make it your responsibility to demonstrate habits and behavior that show you care for the safety of your fellow roadway users.

**Motorcyclists Can Lack Experience and Skill** Be alert when approaching a cyclist. Predict judgment and control errors due to inexperience and lack of skill. Some motorcyclists ride rented or borrowed cycles and might not have enough practice to develop sound judgment and good control. Others, who own their own motorcycles, might not have received proper riding instruction.

**Handling Traits of Motorcycles** Help protect motorcyclists by being aware of the handling traits of motorcycles and how they operate.

Use the entire lane when passing a motorcyclist.

Chapter 8 Sharing the Roadway 153

## Explain

Motorcycles are more maneuverable than four-wheel vehicles. Because of this, a motorcyclist might move quickly into a space you are planning to occupy. Once you have identified a motorcycle, you must predict the driver's actions.

## Explain

Emphasize the importance of giving motorcyclists all the space possible when executing a passing maneuver. Point out that approaching too fast or too close could startle the motorcyclist, leading to loss of control.

## Discuss

Ask students to identify problems that motorcyclists might encounter that could create potential hazards for drivers of larger vehicles.

## Activity

**Class Activity** This activity will help students understand the blind spots of a vehicle's mirrors. You will need to use the driver education car and a pair of volunteers for this activity. One volunteer will be the driver and the other will represent a motorcycle.

Have the driver get into the driver's seat and adjust the outside mirrors properly. Have the person representing the motorcycle stand next to the rear bumper on the driver's side and ten feet away from the car's side. Instruct the person representing the motorcycle to walk slowly toward the car and the driver to yell "stop" when he or she is visible in the outside mirror. The motorcycle will be only a few feet away from the car when seen in the mirror.

Tie one end of a piece of string to the mirror and walk to the position of the motorcycle. Explain that anything on the outside of the string would not be seen in the vehicle's mirrors. Have the motorcycle move outside the string. Ask the driver to demonstrate an over-the-shoulder check to detect the motorcycle.

## Explain

Explain that a motorcycle is often tailgated because it is narrow and a driver can easily look beyond it, forgetting that it is there. A motorcyclist also may have stability problems. Therefore, it is especially important to have a following distance of four seconds or more. (Note: Following distance is explained in Chapter 9 on page 178, but you may wish to present some information here.)

 **Assess**

## Answers to Review It

1. Motorcyclists are comparatively unprotected. The instability and handling characteristics of motorcycles add to potential problems. (p. 150)

2. Identify places where motorcyclists can be hidden from view and scan the roadway ahead; predict possible actions of motorcyclists; base decisions on the problems and conditions confronting motorcyclists; and execute actions smoothly, avoiding sudden actions. (p. 150)

3. Areas to look for motorcyclists include rearview mirrors, blind spots when turning, areas where motorcyclists might be turning left, when motorcyclists are passing cars or meeting traffic, and when motorcyclists are tailgating. (pp. 151–152)

Motorcyclists lean when making turns. Watch a motorcyclist's shoulders to anticipate turns.

Notice in the picture that the motorcyclist leans to the side when making a turn. Control of a motorcycle is difficult in a turn or sharp curve. The cyclist can have even more difficulty handling the cycle in a strong wind, or if the roadway is rough or slippery.

### Increase Your Following Distance

A motorcyclist's balance and stability depend on two small areas of tires that grip the roadway. Water, sand, oil, wet leaves, potholes, or loose gravel reduce traction and can make motorcycle control even more uncertain.

Watch for a motorcyclist's balance and stability problems. Predict that the cyclist might swerve or even fall. Give cyclists extra space by increasing your following distance.

### Make the Motorcyclist Aware of You

When following a motorcyclist, do not assume the cyclist is aware of your presence. Traffic and wind noises make it more difficult for the cyclist to hear. Protective helmets worn by cyclists might also muffle some traffic sounds.

The small size of the mirrors on the handlebars and the vibration of the motorcycle can restrict the motorcyclist's view to the rear. Keep extra space in your front zone when you think a cyclist is unaware of your presence.

## Review It

1. Why must drivers of other vehicles accept responsibility for protecting motorcyclists?
2. How can you use the IPDE Process to help protect motorcyclists while driving?
3. Where are five places you should look for motorcyclists while driving?

## Cross Curricular

**Social Studies: Economics** Have groups of students research specific topics related to the impact of motorcycle collisions on society. Allow each group to select their own topic or choose one from the following list: cost of medical attention at collision scene, hospital costs, loss to the work force, property damages, litigation expenses, death benefits, or rehabilitation expenses. Have each group submit a written report and prepare a two-minute oral report on their findings.

Although you share the responsibility for protecting motorcyclists, they have the primary responsibility for avoiding conflict. How motorcyclists ride, how they use protective equipment, and how they handle special problems affect all other roadway users.

### How Motorcyclists Ride

Because motorcyclists share the roadways with others and present special problems, they should develop safe riding skills. All states offer motorcycle safety courses taught by instructors certified by the Motorcycle Safety Foundation. Proper training and widespread helmet use have helped reduce motorcycle fatalities. The student riders in the picture are practicing balance and turns in a motorcycle-riding course taught by a certified instructor.

With proper instruction and training—and an attitude of responsibility and caring—motorcyclists can become cooperative, low-risk users of the HTS.

### Braking and Accelerating

A vehicle driver needs only to step on the foot brake to stop a vehicle. However, a motorcyclist must operate separate brakes for front and rear wheels. A lever on the right handlebar operates the front brake. This brake supplies most of the braking power for stopping. A foot pedal controls the rear brake. A cyclist must coordinate both foot and hand brakes carefully for maximum braking. If either brake is applied too hard it can lock and cause loss of control.

A motorcyclist must coordinate the hand throttle, hand clutch, and foot-gearshift lever to accelerate

Taking a certified training course can help motorcyclists reduce their risks.

### Objectives

1. Explain the difference in acceleration and braking abilities between motorcycles and other vehicles.
2. Describe the protective equipment motorcyclists should wear.
3. Explain motorcyclists' special riding problems.

# Motorcyclist Actions Can Affect You

 **Focus**

## Summary

This lesson will help students understand some of the problems motorcyclists face when sharing the roadway.

## Vocabulary

*protective equipment*

 **Teach**

## Explain

Compared to a car, a motorcycle has larger brakes and tires per vehicle pound. This means that at speeds less than 35 mph, a skilled motorcyclist can stop in less distance than a car driver can. Therefore, a following distance of four or more seconds is essential to avoid rear-ending a motorcyclist.

## Teacher's Resources

**Resource Book**
Teacher's Instructions, page 27
**Content Overhead**
Overhead 19

Many states have passed laws requiring motorcyclists to wear helmets. Should wearing helmets be required by law in all states?

smoothly. Balance problems can occur if these actions are not coordinated.

### Loss of Balance

Unlike four-wheel vehicles, a motorcycle might have difficulty remaining upright while in motion. Be alert and anticipate that the cyclist can lose control, especially if the roadway is wet or covered with oil drippings.

### Following Distance

Motorcyclists should increase their following distance to reduce risk of collisions. Increased following distance also helps prevent cyclists from being hit by pebbles or dirt thrown back by the vehicle ahead. As a driver, check your rearview mirror often. Be aware of following motorcyclists, and avoid making sudden stops.

Identify the protective gear that this motorcyclist is wearing.

156 Unit 2 Controlling Your Vehicle

### Use of Protective Equipment

Because other vehicles can severely injure motorcyclists in a collision, motorcyclists must make every effort to protect themselves. Cyclists can reduce or prevent injuries by using **protective equipment,** as has the rider in the picture.

A motorcyclist's protective equipment includes the following items:
- helmet—the headgear worn to reduce or prevent head injuries
- eye-protection—goggles or a face shield
- heavy shoes or boots
- full-length pants and jacket made of durable material
- full-fingered gloves

Helmets are required by law in most states and are important in saving lives. In a collision, a cyclist who does not wear a helmet is far more likely to suffer fatal neck and head injuries than a rider who does wear a helmet.

### Special Riding Problems

Weather and roadway conditions present greater problems to cyclists than they do to drivers of other vehicles. Allow extra time and space for motorcyclists in all adverse weather conditions. When following motorcyclists who are crossing railroad tracks or carrying passengers, leave extra space.

**Adverse Weather Conditions** A motorcyclist cannot cope with adverse weather conditions as well as a driver in a four-wheel vehicle can. For example, a puddle might hide a pothole that jolts your vehicle.

That same hidden pothole can throw a motorcycle out of control.

Like drivers of other vehicles, the worst time for motorcyclists is immediately after it starts to rain. As rain mixes with dirt and oil on the roadway, traction is greatly reduced. Because balance is important for motorcycle control, reduced traction is far more critical to motorcyclists.

You can turn on your windshield wipers when it rains. When dirt from the roadway splashes up on the windshield, you can use windshield washers. A cyclist has neither device. Therefore, the motorcyclist's vision is greatly reduced and can be distorted under these conditions.

Motorcyclists should use extra caution when riding on or crossing painted lines on a wet roadway. Painted lines can become slippery when wet. Motorcyclists gain extra traction on wet roads by riding in another vehicle's wheel track, as the picture shows.

**Motorcyclist Crossing Railroad Tracks** Railroad tracks are a special problem for motorcyclists. Motorcycle tires can get caught in the grooves of the crossing, causing the motorcyclist to lose balance. A cyclist should cross railroad tracks as close to a right angle as possible, as long as this does not cause the cyclist to enter another lane.

**Motorcyclists Carrying Passengers** A motorcycle carrying two people requires extra caution from other vehicle drivers. Be alert for a difference in acceleration, braking, and turning when a motorcyclist is carry-

Motorcyclists can gain traction on wet roads by riding in another vehicle's wheel track.

ing a passenger. A passenger can create balance and control problems for the cyclist by leaning the wrong way in curves and turns.

### How Motorcyclists Can Help Other Vehicle Drivers

Motorcyclists should use all their skills and techniques to reduce their risks of conflicts. However, nothing the cyclist does should diminish the caution other drivers must practice near motorcyclists. Remember, you must always be ready to yield to cyclists.

Chapter 8 Sharing the Roadway **157**

## Demonstrate

Use **Content Overhead 19** to show the path a motorcyclist should follow when crossing railroad tracks. Emphasize the necessity for being alert for trains as well as maintaining control and avoiding a fall while crossing the tracks. Show how a motorcycle tire could get caught in the railroad track if the approach to the crossing was not properly executed.

## Explain

Adding a passenger on the back of a motorcycle raises the center of gravity. The smaller the cycle, the larger the problem. Be alert for small motorcycles with passengers. Refer to Chapter 5 on natural laws.

## Activity

**Class Activity** Show a video related to sharing the road with motorcycles. Stop the video at various points to discuss interacting situations.

## Explain

At night a motorcyclist might move every few minutes from one edge of the lane to the other so that he or she does not remain in the left taillight area of the vehicle ahead. Riding in the wheel tracks of another vehicle at night makes a motorcycle appear to be part of the other vehicle. This means the motorcycle is less noticeable to other drivers.

## Explain

Motorcyclists can become more visible at night by allowing extra space between them and the vehicle ahead. This will allow oncoming traffic to see the motorcyclists sooner.

 **Assess**

### Answers to Review It

**1.** Motorcyclists use a hand brake and a foot brake; most car drivers use only one foot brake. (Some vehicles are equipped with a hand brake to accommodate a driver's special needs.) Motorcyclists must coordinate use of the throttle with the clutch. (p. 155)

**2.** Protective equipment includes helmet, eye protection, heavy shoes, full length pants, jacket made of durable material, and full-fingered gloves. (p. 156)

**3.** Motorcyclists' control can be affected by adverse weather conditions, crossing railroad tracks, and carrying a passenger. (pp. 156–157)

By riding offset, motorcyclists are more easily seen.

**Riding in Groups** Motorcyclists often travel in groups. When you see one cyclist, be prepared to see others. Cyclists should not ride side by side in traffic. They should be in an offset position, as the picture shows. By riding offset, each cyclist is more easily seen by others and has more space to swerve safely, if necessary.

Like you, motorcyclists should prepare for turns by moving into the correct lane well before the turn. If they are riding in groups, they should be in single file as they approach, enter, and complete the turn.

**Being Visible in Traffic** Motorcyclists should position themselves in traffic so other roadway users can easily see them. Riding in lane position 2 usually makes a motorcyclist

more visible. A rider in the correct position is visible to the driver ahead as well as to oncoming drivers.

Riding in lane position 2 also forces other drivers to use the other full lane to pass. This position adds a degree of safety to the passing maneuver. It also reduces the chance that the cyclist will be forced off the roadway.

Motorcyclists should not ride between lanes of moving vehicles. This practice is dangerous for everyone. In many states it is illegal.

**Riding at Night** It is far more difficult for drivers of other vehicles to judge the speed and position of a motorcycle at night. Because a motorcycle's taillight is relatively small, drivers behind may have difficulty seeing it.

Motorcyclists should take added precautions when riding at night. They can make themselves more visible by putting reflective tape on helmets and clothing and by having reflectors on the motorcycle.

### Review It
1. How do a motorcycle's braking and acceleration differ from those of other vehicles?
2. What protective equipment should a motorcyclist use?
3. What special riding problems can affect a motorcyclist's control?

## Background

**Motorcycle Headlights** You can usually distinguish a car with one headlight from a motorcycle by watching for horizontal and vertical movement of the light. A motorcycle headlight appears to bounce up and down and move side to side, while a car headlight remains constant. Newer motorcycles have oscillating headlights that provide better visibility for the motorcyclist, but eliminate this telltale movement.

Bicycles and low-powered, two-wheel vehicles continue to be popular for transportation, recreation, and business. Bicycles use no gasoline, create no pollution, and provide exercise for the rider. Because of their small sizes, mopeds and motor scooters create very little pollution and provide an economic means of transportation.

Users of smaller two-wheel vehicles have the same privileges and responsibilities as other drivers. Riders of these vehicles should use the IPDE Process and develop a visual search pattern to help themselves be more aware of possible conflicts with other roadway users. However, drivers of larger vehicles, with their greater protection, must accept the major responsibility for avoiding conflict.

Just as you have a major responsibility for protecting motorcyclists, you should be even more cautious and aware of these smaller vehicles because they are so unprotected.

### Bicyclists' Responsibilities

Bicyclists must share the responsibility for avoiding conflicts with other roadway users.

Be a responsible bicyclist by following these safe-riding practices:

- Wear a helmet for protection.
- Know and follow the laws regarding roadway riding, lane position, and sidewalk riding.
- Obey all signs, signals, and laws.

- Wear light-colored clothing and have lights and reflectors on bicycles when riding at night.
- Do not wear earphones while bicycling. Wearing earphones while bicycling or driving a motor vehicle is illegal in many states.
- Keep bicycles in safe operating condition.

When riding at night use a headlight that is visible for at least 500 feet. Reflective tape on the frame and fenders of your bicycle, as well as on your helmet, adds safety for night riding.

### Protecting Bicyclists

As a driver of a larger vehicle, give bicyclists extra space whenever possible. Some bicyclists might not be able to control their bicycles well. When following a bicyclist, be aware of the possible path the bicyclist might take. Vehicle doors opening, railroad tracks, storm drains, potholes, puddles, and other roadway hazards may cause a bicyclist to swerve into your path.

Use the IPDE Process constantly as you encounter bicyclists. Scan wide enough to include the sides of the roadways as well as sidewalks. Try to build into your visual search pattern a special awareness of bicyclists and where they might be. Allow more time and space for bicyclists to change their intended path of travel.

**Preventing Conflicts with Bicyclists**
Passing bicyclists on a two-lane

## Objectives

1. Tell how you can help protect bicyclists from conflict.
2. List the guidelines that moped and motor scooter drivers should follow when riding.

**8.3**

# Bicycles, Mopeds, and Motor Scooters

 **Focus**

## Summary

This lesson covers the other small vehicles that share the roadway with four-wheeled vehicles: bicycles, mopeds, and motor scooters. The lesson discusses the responsibilities that go along with driving smaller vehicles, as well as the responsibilities of four-wheeled vehicles for protecting the smaller-vehicle drivers.

## Vocabulary

*moped, motor scooter*

 **Teach**

## Discuss

Brainstorm with students why it is better for bicyclists to ride in the direction of traffic rather than against traffic. Explain that cyclists riding with the flow of traffic can be better seen, especially by motorists entering a roadway from a side street or driveway. It is also easier to judge travel speed of a cyclist in front of you in order to slow down to pass. Have them discuss what they can do as drivers to be able to detect bicyclists who are riding against the traffic flow. (See Background note on page 160.)

## Explain

Explain why drivers of larger vehicles must give bicyclists more space. Point out that many bicyclists are children. These bicyclists have not learned to use the IPDE Process. Many do not know the rules of the road, and they are often unaware of the vehicle traffic around them.

## Explain

Drivers need to look for bicyclists who run STOP signs and are on the wrong side of the street. This is critical when the driver is turning right at a STOP sign or a red traffic signal and concentrating on traffic from the left. Emphasize how important it is for drivers to turn their head and look in the direction they are planning to move before moving the vehicle. This habit will allow the driver to see the bicyclist traveling the wrong way before putting the vehicle into motion. Also, drivers turning right should look over their right shoulder to make sure no cyclist is coming in the bicycle lane or shoulder.

## Explain

In some states it is legal for bicyclists to use the left-turn lanes. If it is legal in your state, watch for bicyclists to do this. Share information about laws in your state related to bicyclists.

## Discuss

Discuss types of bicycle/vehicle collisions that students know have occurred or are likely to have occurred. Discuss how these collisions could be avoided.

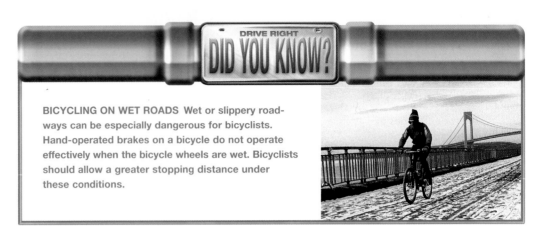

**DID YOU KNOW?**

**BICYCLING ON WET ROADS** Wet or slippery roadways can be especially dangerous for bicyclists. Hand-operated brakes on a bicycle do not operate effectively when the bicycle wheels are wet. Bicyclists should allow a greater stopping distance under these conditions.

roadway presents a problem for both drivers and riders. Consider the position of the cyclist in traffic when you plan to pass.

Start your passing maneuver well behind the bicyclist. You should have at least one-half lane between your vehicle and the bicyclist, as the picture shows. Be even farther away if the traffic lanes are narrow.

Use these techniques to further prevent conflicts with bicyclists:

To pass a bicyclist safely, move to lane position 2.

- Check rear zones and signal early when you plan to slow or stop.
- Help others identify a bicyclist by adjusting your position. At night, use low-beam headlights or a flick of high-beam headlights so that others can see the cyclist.
- Reduce speed and increase space when you are unsure of a bicyclist's control.
- Look for bicyclists before opening the street-side door of your vehicle.

Large tricycles have become popular in many communities, especially in retirement areas. Even though these tricycles are larger than most bicycles and are more readily visible, they can present a hazard. Be alert for and protective of riders of these large tricycles when they are a part of your traffic environment.

### Mopeds and Motor Scooters

A **moped** is a two-wheeled vehicle that can be driven with either a motor or pedal. Its name comes from *mo*tor-driven bicycle and *ped*al-driven

## Background

**Riding with Traffic** A bicyclist should ride in the same direction and on the same side of the road as traffic. When a bicyclist rides with traffic, an approaching driver will have more time to see it. And, the force of impact between the car and bicycle, should a collision occur, will be less damaging. If a bicyclist is traveling 25 mph toward traffic, and traffic is traveling at 30 mph, they close in on each other at the rate of 55 mph. When the bicyclist is traveling with the traffic flow, the car closes in on the bicycle at 5 mph.

bicycle. Like a bicycle, a moped can be pedaled and can be stopped with a hand brake. Like a motorcycle, a moped is powered by an engine and controlled by a hand throttle.

A **motor scooter** is also a low-powered two-wheeled vehicle. It is more powerful than a moped. A motor scooter is similar to a motor-cycle, though most motor scooters require no shifting.

**Moped and Motor Scooter Restrictions** Most states require moped and motor scooter operators to have an operator's license. Mopeds and motor scooters are restricted from certain high-speed roadways. Both the speed and the acceleration of mopeds are limited. Because they do not accelerate to traffic speed as quickly as a motorcycle or other vehicles, they may be unable to keep up with the traffic flow.

**Responsibilities of Moped and Motor Scooter Drivers** Even though these vehicles are smaller than motorcycles, their drivers also can benefit from taking a rider-training course.

In addition to observing laws and local requirements, moped and motor scooter drivers should follow these guidelines:

- Wear protective clothing. At night, wear clothing that has reflective tape on it, as the picture shows.
- Have the headlight on at all times.
- Position the vehicle in the lane so it can be seen by others.
- Keep a space cushion between themselves and other vehicles.
- Use extra care when riding on wet or slippery surfaces.

Reflective tape makes the motor scooter rider more visible to other drivers at night.

- Concentrate on the driving task and use the IPDE Process.

Drivers of other larger vehicles should predict possible sudden actions from drivers of mopeds and motor scooters. Be especially alert when driving near a moped or motor scooter.

> **Review It**
> 1. In what ways can you help protect bicyclists?
> 2. What guidelines should drivers of mopeds and motor scooters follow?

---

**Demonstrate**

Demonstrate in the school parking lot the controls and responses of a bicycle, a moped, and a motor scooter. If you have access to these vehicles and are familiar with them, you can conduct the demonstration yourself. Other-wise, you will need to make arrangements for someone else, possibly a few students, to con-duct the demonstrations. Empha-size the need for drivers of large vehicles to use the IPDE Process and the Zone Control System for the protection of these other road-way users.

 **Assess**

**Answers to Review It**

1. Students should list ways to protect bicyclists as provided on page 160.

2. They should know the laws, wear protective equipment, keep headlights on, position themselves in traffic so they are visible, use the IPDE Process, and set a good example for others. (p. 161)

---

## Special Needs

Demonstrate the invisibility of the different kinds of two-wheeled vehi-cles, including bicycles, motorcycles, mopeds, and motor scooters. Use the school parking lot as a driving range to show the conflicts and the responses of the different kinds of vehicles and drivers.

# 8.4

## Pedestrians and Special Vehicles

## 1 Focus

### Summary

This lesson emphasizes the responsibility drivers have for protecting pedestrians. It also addresses interaction with special vehicles, buses, and emergency vehicles.

### Vocabulary

*recreational vehicle*

## 2 Teach

### Explain

Explain that when exiting alleys, the buildings create a line-of-sight restriction as shown in the photograph. Before crossing the sidewalk, search the intersection at 90 degrees to the left-front and right-front zones to detect pedestrians and bicyclists. Move your vehicle inch by inch until you can see 90 degrees to the left and right.

### Explain

Remind students of the importance of looking for pedestrians in all directions when turning right on red.

### Objectives

1. Explain why you should use extra caution and care to protect pedestrians.
2. List areas where you can expect to see pedestrians.
3. Explain procedures to follow to clear the way for emergency vehicles.

Of all highway users, pedestrians are the most vulnerable. Motorists have a strong moral and legal obligation to protect pedestrians in every situation.

### Pedestrians

Many pedestrians who do not drive are not fully aware of traffic laws and signals. Children and older people are most at risk. Children are less visible to drivers and often lack the judgment to know when it is safe to cross streets. Older people may not hear or see well and may be unaware of possible conflicts.

Other adult pedestrians may just get careless. They are drivers of vehicles and fully understand traffic laws. However, when they are in a hurry or are trying to escape bad weather, they may take chances and forget the risks involved.

Communicate with pedestrians so they will know you are there. A tap on the horn or a wave of your hand can give the message that you are there. Use the IPDE Process continually and always be ready to yield to pedestrians.

Learn where you can expect to see pedestrians and be extra alert when approaching the following areas.

**Alleys and Driveways** Approaching a sidewalk from an alley can be risky if a pedestrian or a bicyclist suddenly appears. The driver in the picture should expect movement from either side when approaching the sidewalk.

Make two stops when driving from an alley. First, stop before the sidewalk and look both ways for pedestrians and bicyclists. Tap your horn as a warning. Second, be pre-

Be especially alert for pedestrians as you drive out of an alley or driveway because buildings can obstruct your view. Be prepared to stop.

162  Unit 2  Controlling Your Vehicle

## Teacher's Resources

No *Drive Right* resources are needed for teaching Section 8.4.

## Background

**Pedestrian Crosswalks**  Some states require drivers to yield the right of way to pedestrians in all crosswalks. In these states, drivers must stop when a pedestrian enters a crosswalk. Discuss with the class what the law is in your state.

pared to stop again as you look for traffic just before you enter the street.

**Business Districts**  Many collisions involving pedestrians occur at intersections and crosswalks in business districts where there is often a high volume of traffic. Many pedestrians assume that drivers will yield the right-of-way to anyone in the crosswalk. Drivers, however, are often looking at traffic signals and other vehicles and may not see the pedestrian in time to avoid a conflict.

Rain and snow often cause pedestrians to be more concerned about protection from weather than protection from traffic. Be extra alert under these conditions. It is often difficult to identify pedestrians at night and during adverse weather conditions.

**Residential Areas**  Many residential streets are used by children as play areas, as the picture shows.

Regardless of the legal aspect of children playing in the street, it is the driver's responsibility and obligation to make the utmost effort to prevent conflict. Search for pedestrians coming from between parked vehicles on residential streets.

**Jogging Areas**  Although joggers are safer using a sidewalk or a jogging path, expect to see them on streets and in traffic lanes. Joggers should yield to moving traffic—but do not expect this to happen. Always be ready to slow, steer around, or stop for joggers.

Watch for children playing on the street.

### The Driver as a Pedestrian

As soon as you step out of your vehicle, you are a pedestrian. You no longer have the protective shield of your vehicle. Because you understand traffic rules and laws, you should be a responsible pedestrian.

Exercise special care at night. Wear something white or carry a light, particularly in rural areas. Try to be where drivers expect to see you. Do not walk into traffic lanes from between parked vehicles.

Regardless of the behaviors practiced by some pedestrians, you should always demonstrate an

**DRIVE RIGHT**
**DID YOU KNOW?**

**STEPPING OFF THE CURB**  Many pedestrians who are struck at intersections are hit just as they step into the street. They often walk into the side of a moving vehicle they do not see.

## Discuss

Discuss the use of the horn by drivers of larger vehicles in cases where pedestrians, children, or joggers might be a potential hazard. Ask: When should you use a tap on the horn? When is a loud blast needed? (Point out that a tap on the horn is usually enough to alert others of your presence. Emphasize that there is rarely a need to give a loud blast of the horn.) Discuss the possible problems that could result from a loud blast.

## Discuss

Ask: What are the advantages and disadvantages of using jogging paths rather than roadways when jogging or running? Encourage students who run and jog to share their experiences.

## Explain

Emphasize the need to make more aggressive searches when line-of-sight restrictions might conceal a pedestrian or a bicyclist. A driver can look in, under, and around parked vehicles for feet, wheels, shadows, and movement. When done at the proper distance, it allows you to see all pedestrians and bicyclists before they create a surprise.

## Activity

**Small Group Activity**  Divide the class into groups of five. Ask each group to list places in the community where vehicles leave alleys or driveways at locations that can be dangerous to pedestrians. For each location, have the group formulate the actions that the driver should take to reduce the risk of hitting a pedestrian. After adequate time have the groups report their findings to the class.

## Special Needs

Take special needs students to the parking lot and practice seeing feet and shadows under vehicles. Have students perform both the role of driver and of the pedestrian.

## Explain

When driving in a parking lot, a driver might have difficulty seeing a person in a wheelchair. You need to be particularly alert when driving in the area of handicapped parking spaces.

## Discuss

Ask: Who is allowed to park in a space designated for handicapped parking only? Why do drivers without disabilities park in these spaces? Point out that not all disabilities are obvious. For example, someone with heart disease may be disabled and entitled to park in these spaces. Share information about state and local laws related to handicapped parking spaces, including information about penalties for illegal use. Also explain how to apply for temporary and permanent permits.

### SAFE DRIVING

Be alert for parking spaces designated for "Handicapped Parking Only." Do not park in these spaces.

attitude of responsibility in your driving. Remember how destructive a large vehicle can be to these less-protected users. Exercise special care whenever pedestrians are around.

### Parking Lots

Parking lots present a high-risk area for drivers, riders, and pedestrians. Like many residential streets, parking lots sometimes are used as recreational areas. Even though drivers are traveling at low speeds, a bicyclist or a skateboarder can cause conflict. Many property damage collisions and injuries occur in parking lots, even at very slow speeds. As a pedestrian in parking lots, you should look for brake lights and backup lights on parked vehicles.

Follow these guidelines to lower your risk when driving in parking lots:

- Obey parking-lot speed limits.
- Follow the routes for traffic flow. Do not drive diagonally across parking-lot lines.
- Be alert for pedestrians, bicyclists, roller-bladers, and skateboarders.

- Avoid tight parking spaces. Try to avoid parking in end spaces.
- Drive far enough into the space so the front or rear of your vehicle will not extend into the path of moving traffic.
- Position your vehicle properly in the parking space.
- Secure the vehicle properly.
- Continually scan in all directions when backing out of a parking space. If vision is blocked by a large vehicle, tap the horn before you back out.
- Watch for others who may back out toward you and may not see your vehicle. The drivers in the picture nearly collided because they were not aware that the other driver was backing out.

### Special-Purpose Vehicles

Besides sharing the roadway with cyclists and pedestrians, you must also share it with an increasing number of special-purpose vehicles. Some special-purpose vehicles can be expected at different times of the

Be alert when leaving a parking space.

### Activity

**Small Group Activity** Divide the class into groups of five. Ask each group to list ways collisions with pedestrians can occur while in a parking lot. Then have the groups identify ways to avoid such problems. (Explain that the driver should back into perpendicular parking spaces to avoid the hazards of backing out of parking spaces. When backing out is necessary, check behind the vehicle before entering it. When backing, the driver should move the vehicle slowly while continuing to check to the rear for any conflicts.)

Allow extra space to increase your sight distance, and use caution when passing.

year. For example, snow plows can be expected in winter months in cold climates. In rural areas large, slow-moving farm machinery should be expected. When mobile homes are being transported, they often are preceded and followed by vehicles that carry a "Wide Load" sign. Use extra caution when meeting or passing such vehicles.

A **recreational vehicle** is a type of vehicle used mainly for pleasure and travel. Some of the more common types of recreational vehicles are vans, motor homes, campers, travel trailers, pickup trucks, and sports utility vehicles. Because of their size, some of these vehicles can decrease your sight distance or completely block your view. Allow these larger vehicles extra space in traffic and increase your following distance.

### Buses

Local buses and school buses are the two most common types of buses you will encounter. Laws governing school buses are more strict than those governing local buses. School buses usually stop for students right in the lane of traffic. Most states require traffic going in both directions on a two-way street to stop when a school bus stops to load or unload passengers. A school bus has flashing red lights and, in some states, a STOP sign that swings out from the side of the bus. Some buses have flashing yellow lights before the flashing red lights begin. Do not proceed until all the lights stop flashing, the STOP sign is withdrawn, and the bus begins to move.

Most states do not require traffic from either direction to stop for local buses. When stopping to discharge or pick up passengers, local buses usually pull in toward the curb out of the lane of traffic. However, just because a stop is not required for local buses, it is your responsibility to keep alert for pedestrians near the bus who might cause a conflict.

## Explain

Most recreational vehicles and rented trucks are not driven by professionals. They may be driven in the wrong lane, or the driver may misjudge the speed or space needed for maneuvers. Give such drivers more room for the errors that can occur.

## Explain

Alert students that during harvesting in a farm area, more farm vehicles will be using the highways. Some harvesting machines are so large that other drivers must use extra care when meeting or passing them.

## Discuss

Ask: When are drivers required to stop for a stopped school bus? Encourage students to share their ideas. After some discussion, share specific information about state laws related to school buses. Include information about laws in neighboring states. Clarify any misinformation that was included in the earlier discussion.

## Explain

Point out that seeing a school bus should alert drivers to look for children who might dart in front of your vehicle. Discuss the importance of using the IPDE Process whenever a stopped school bus is in view. Drivers need to be particularly alert for students who might be running to catch a bus.

## Discuss

Ask: What should drivers do when they hear a siren or see an emergency vehicle with flashing lights? After some discussion, share specific information about state laws related to emergency vehicles. Clarify any misinformation that was included in the earlier discussion.

 **Assess**

## Answers to Review It

**1.** Pedestrians are among the least protected roadway users. Those who do not drive vehicles might not be aware of traffic laws. Children may be impulsive. Some older people do not hear or see well, and some pedestrians are careless. (p. 162)

**2.** Expect pedestrians in crosswalks and intersections, when leaving alleys and driveways, and in jogging areas. (pp. 162–163)

**3.** Look for a place to pull over and stop. Move in the direction other traffic is moving, and leave as much space as possible. Wait until all emergency vehicles have passed. (p. 166)

Yield to emergency vehicles at all times.

Use the following guidelines to protect pedestrians near buses:

- Expect to see school buses more frequently in mornings and afternoons during school opening and closing times.
- Identify school buses by their yellow color, and then be prepared for stops. Expect some local buses to be used as school buses. Although you are not required to stop for local buses, exercise caution when you approach them.
- Expect pedestrians hurrying to catch a bus to be unaware of your presence. Communicate with horn and eye contact.
- Search areas around stopped or parked vehicles that might hide pedestrians.
- Give buses extra space. When passing a stopped bus, be sure no pedestrian who is blocked from view will enter your path.
- Reduce speed and cover the brake, if needed, to give yourself more time to respond.

### Emergency Vehicles

Always yield to emergency vehicles with sirens and flashing lights—regardless of the direction the vehicle is traveling. When you see the lights or hear the siren, pull over to the right as far as possible. Stop if there is space and it is safe to do so. The drivers in the picture have pulled off the roadway and stopped.

If you are in heavy traffic, move in the direction other drivers are moving. Leave as much space for the emergency vehicle as possible.

Some drivers become careless about their response to emergency vehicles. They fail to pull over or stop. Not only are they putting themselves and the emergency vehicle at risk, but they may be harming others who are waiting for the emergency vehicle.

### Review It

1. Why should you use extra caution for pedestrians?
2. In what areas should you expect to see pedestrians?
3. What steps should you follow to clear the way for an emergency vehicle?

Trucks help transport nearly everything we eat, wear, and use in our daily lives. They are an essential part of our national economy.

### Types of Trucks

The three main classifications of trucks are light, medium, and heavy. Most trucks are light or medium and are the types you commonly see as service trucks, pickup trucks, and delivery trucks. Heavy trucks include dump trucks and tractor trailers.

### Tractor Trailers

A truck that has a powerful tractor that pulls a separate trailer is called a **tractor trailer.** The tractor is the front part that includes the engine and the cab. The most common size tractor trailer is the **tractor-semitrailer.** This is a tractor that pulls one trailer and

To avoid conflict, keep out of the open space to the right of a tractor-semitrailer making a right turn.

is commonly called an "eighteen wheeler." Next in size is the double trailer, two trailers pulled by a tractor. The largest trucks, triple trailers, consist of three trailers pulled by a tractor.

Even though most truck drivers practice a high degree of safe-driving behavior, be aware that there are times when drivers suffer from fatigue or loss of sleep. Drivers often face the problem of tight scheduling and drive over long periods of time.

### Large Trucks Making Right Turns

Many drivers following a tractor-semitrailer assume that if the truck moves to the left it is preparing to make a left turn. However, drivers of large trucks usually swing out to the left as the first step in making a *right* turn. If you begin to pass on the right at that time, you could be caught in the "right-turn squeeze," as the picture shows. Always check a truck's turn signals before you start to pass.

### Following Large Trucks

Drivers of large trucks sit high above the road and have an excellent view of the roadway ahead. However, their view to the sides and rear is often restricted by the size of their rig.

Large trucks often create visibility problems for other drivers. When you follow a large truck, the truck causes a line-of-sight restriction.

There are large blind spots in front, to the sides, and to the rear

Chapter 8 Sharing the Roadway **167**

## Objectives

1. Define "no-zones" around large trucks.
2. Explain precautions to take when following large trucks.
3. List guidelines to follow when passing large trucks.

# Sharing the Road with Trucks

 **1 Focus**

## Summary

This lesson focuses on sharing the road with trucks. The procedure for following and passing trucks is emphasized.

## Vocabulary

*no-zones, tractor-semitrailer, tractor trailer.*

**2 Teach**

## Discuss

Ask: Why is it not safe to pass a truck on the right if the driver is signaling for a right turn, even when the truck is not in the right-turn lane? (The driver is probably preparing for a right turn, which needs to begin with a wide turn.)

## Demonstrate

Use Video 1 segment on Sharing the Road to demonstrate the importance of increasing following distance behind trucks and staying out of the truck's no-zones. Also demonstrate how a car's blindspots compare with a truck's no-zones.

## Teacher's Resources

**Video 1**
 Segment on Sharing the Road

## Activity

**Class Activity** Explain to students that some trucking companies require splash reducers known as "hula skirts" to be fastened over the sides of the trailer wheels of their semi-trailers. Have the students observe trucks while riding as a passenger in a vehicle and report on the number of trucks they see with and without this equipment. Discuss whether splash reducers should be required equipment on all tractor-trailers. Encourage students to contact trade organizations and trucking firms to encourage the use of splash reducers.

## Explain

Explain to students that they need to grip the steering wheel firmly when passing or being passed by large trucks. The air turbulence in front of a truck can push your vehicle away from the front of the truck. There also is a vacuum to the rear of the truck that can pull your vehicle in toward the truck. It is necessary to hold the steering wheel firmly in such situations and be prepared to make steering corrections to keep your vehicle heading toward your target area. This is particularly important during heavy rain or a windstorm.

## Assess

### Answers to Review It

**1.** No-zones are large blind spots in front, to the sides, and to the rear of every large truck. (p. 168)

**2.** Increase following distance. Position your vehicle so the truck driver knows you are there. Drive near the left edge of the lane. (p. 168)

**3.** Students should list the guidelines for passing trucks provided on page 168.

Stay out of the No-Zones where truck drivers cannot see you.

of every large truck. These blind-spot areas, called **no-zones,** are where truck drivers cannot see other vehicles and where most collisions occur. The picture at left shows these no-zones.

When drivers travel in a truck's no-zones, they put themselves at a high degree of risk because they cannot be seen by the truck driver. When you are following a large truck, increase your following distance to allow clear sight distance ahead. Stay far enough back so you can see the sideview mirrors of the truck. If you can't see one of the driver's sideview mirrors, then the driver can't see you.

### Passing Large Trucks

Whenever possible, plan to pass a large truck when the driver shifts gears to gain speed. Passing is more easily done when you leave a STOP sign or a traffic light. Do not begin to pass until you are both clear of the intersection.

Use the following guidelines when passing large trucks:

- Check front and rear zones, signal a lane change, and change lanes smoothly.
- Stay in lane position 2 during the passing maneuver, and complete your pass as quickly as possible.
- After you can see both headlights in your rearview mirror, signal, check over your right shoulder, and return to the right lane. CAUTION: *In many trucks, the front no-zone can extend over 20 feet. Be sure you are well beyond that distance before you return to the right lane.*

- Do not slow during or after completing the pass. Maintain your highway speed.

Passing a large truck during rain or snow increases your level of risk. Both traction and visibility are reduced. When passing under such conditions, flash your headlights so the truck driver will know you are passing.

### Meeting Large Trucks

You do not have much room when meeting large trucks on narrow two-lane highways. When you meet a large truck, move to lane position 3. Look well ahead and drive in a straight line. Try to choose a meeting point where the shoulder offers an escape path. Hold the steering wheel firmly because you might encounter a wind gust as you meet the larger vehicle.

### Review It

1. Where are the no-zones?
2. What precautions should you take when following a large truck?
3. How should you pass large trucks?

## Activity

**Guest Speaker** To help students understand the size and location of a truck's blind spots, invite a professional truck driver to bring a large truck to your school for a demonstration. Ask the truck driver to talk about some of the hazards of driving a truck. Set up cones around the truck outlining the areas of no-zones. Station the driver-education vehicle in different no-zones. Have students sit in the truck driver's seat to learn how vehicles in the no-zones can be completely hidden.

## Reviewing Chapter Objectives

### 1. Sharing the Roadway with Motorcyclists

1. Why do drivers have responsibility for protecting motorcyclists? (150)
2. How would you use the IPDE Process to protect motorcyclists while driving? (150)
3. In what situations should you look for motorcyclists while driving? (150–152)

### 2. Motorcyclist Actions Can Affect You

4. What is the difference in acceleration and braking abilities between motorcycles and other vehicles? (155)
5. What protective equipment should motorcyclists wear? (156)
6. What are motorcyclists' riding problems? (156–157)

### 3. Bicycles, Mopeds, and Motor Scooters

7. How can you help protect bicyclists? (160)
8. What guidelines should moped and motor scooter drivers follow when riding? (161)

### 4. Pedestrians and Special Vehicles

9. Why should you use extra caution and care to protect pedestrians? (162)
10. In what areas will you see pedestrians? (162–163)
11. What procedures should you follow to clear the way for emergency vehicles? (166)

### 5. Sharing the Road with Trucks

12. What are the "no-zones" around large trucks? (167–168)
13. What precautions should you take when following large trucks? (167–168)
14. What guidelines should you follow when passing large trucks? (168)

## Projects

### Individuals

**Investigate** Research driving rules or laws in your state as they pertain to motorcyclists. Make a list of rules or laws that motorcyclists must follow that are not required of other drivers.

**Interview** Interview someone you know who drives a truck for a living. Ask the person how driving a truck is different from driving a car. Write a report based on your conversation. (If you don't know anyone who drives a truck, interview a person who drives a motorcycle. Ask how driving a motorcycle is different from driving a car.)

**Observe Traffic** Observe the traffic for fifteen minutes at a busy intersection in your area. Make a record of the different types of vehicles you see (including cars, trucks, bicycles, motorcycles, etc.) Compare your results with those of your classmates.

### Groups

**Debate** Break your group into two and discuss the pros and cons of having two-wheeled vehicles (such as motorcycles, mopeds, and motor scooters) share the roadways with other vehicles.

**Use Technology** Make a group video about bicycle safety. Share the video with your class.

## Teacher's Resources

### Skills and Applications Workbook
pages 29–32

### Tests and Activities
Chapter 8 Activities 8-1 and 8-2, pages 63–64

Chapter 8 Test A and Test B, pages 65–68

### TestWorks CD-ROM
Chapter 8 Test

## Reviewing Chapter Objectives

**8.1** Sharing the Roadway with Motorcyclists
See Answers to Review It on page 154.

**8.2** Motorcyclist Actions Can Affect You
See Answers to Review It on page 158.

**8.3** Bicycles, Mopeds, and Motor Scooters
See Answers to Review It on page 161.

**8.4** Pedestrians and Special Vehicles
See Answers to Review It on page 166.

**8.5** Sharing the Road with Trucks
See Answers to Review It on page 168.

For additional information refer to the specific page(s) in parentheses after each question.

## Projects

Some of the projects can be assigned at any time while others are more closely tied to the content presented in the student text. The page number where the topic is introduced is indicated.

**Investigate:** p. 148
**Interview:** p. 167
**Observe Traffic:** p. 148
**Debate:** p. 159
**Use Technology:** p. 159

The results of student projects will vary.

## Chapter Test

### Check Your Knowledge

**Multiple Choice** Copy the number of each sentence below on a sheet of paper. Choose the letter of the answer that best completes the statement or answers the question.

1. Why do car drivers have responsibility for avoiding collisions with motorcyclists?
   (a) Cars need less stopping distance.
   (b) Motorcycles maneuver more easily.
   (c) Car drivers have more protection.
   (d) Motorcyclists have less experience.

2. Which of the following is NOT a safe practice for bicyclists?
   (a) wearing a helmet
   (b) obeying signs, signals, and traffic laws
   (c) having reflectors on bicycles
   (d) listening to music with headphones while bicycling

3. When meeting a truck on a two-lane road,
   (a) flash your headlights.
   (b) pull off the road and stop.
   (c) move to lane position 3 and drive straight ahead.
   (d) move to lane position 1 and slow down.

**Completion** Copy the number of each sentence below. After each number, write the word or words that complete the sentence correctly.

4. To reduce risk of collision, motorcyclists should increase their _____ .

5. Users of mopeds have limited speed and _____.

6. Many collisions involving pedestrians occur at crosswalks and intersections in _____.

### Review Vocabulary

Copy the number of each definition in list A. Match the definition in list A with the term it defines in list B.

**List A**

7. two-wheeled vehicle that can be driven either with a motor or pedal

8. large blind-spot areas where truck drivers cannot see other vehicles

9. items a motorcyclist wears to protect head, eyes, and body

10. truck that has a powerful tractor that pulls a separate trailer

11. large vehicle used for pleasure and travel

12. type of tractor trailer commonly called an "eighteen wheeler"

**List B**

a. no-zones     d. recreational vehicle
b. tractor trailer     e. protective equipment
c. moped     f. tractor-semitrailer

### Think Critically

Write a paragraph to answer each question.

1. Why is it important for drivers of four-wheel vehicles to use the IPDE Process when encountering two-wheel vehicles?

2. Discuss the different ways in which rain and snow affect pedestrians and motorcyclists.

---

## Answers to Check Your Knowledge

1. c
2. d
3. c
4. following distance
5. acceleration
6. business districts

## Answers to Review Vocabulary

7. moped (c)
8. no-zones (a)
9. protective equipment (e)
10. tractor trailer (b)
11. recreational vehicle (d)
12. tractor-semitrailer (f)

## Answers to Think Critically

Students' answers will vary. For information related to the question refer to the page(s) indicated.

1. Two-wheeled vehicles often are not identified in time to prevent conflict. If the driver of a four-wheeled vehicle uses the Identify and Predict steps of the IPDE Process, conflicts may be eliminated. (p. 150)

2. Rain and snow affect motorcycles because motorcyclists are actually getting wet while driving. This may cause the motorcyclist's vision to be impaired. The wet conditions reduce traction which may cause the motorcyclist to lose balance. Rain and snow may cause pedestrians to be more concerned about protection from weather than protection from traffic. (pp. 156–157, 163)

## Decision Making

1. What is the car driver's responsibility in avoiding a collision? How could the car driver have avoided this possible conflict?

2. What is wrong with the motorcyclists' position in the traffic lane? Why is this position hazardous? What is the correct position for the cyclists in the traffic lane?

3. What should the car driver do to clear the way for the emergency vehicle?

4. If you were the driver of the car following this truck, what error would you be making? What procedure should you follow when driving behind a large truck?

Chapter 8 Sharing the Roadway 171

## Answers to Decision Making

1. The car driver is responsible for avoiding conflict with the motorcyclist. The driver should have checked the rearview mirrors and looked over his or her left shoulder before opening the car door.

2. Motorcyclists should not travel side by side in a traffic lane. This could be hazardous if either lost balance or control. When riding together, motorcyclists should ride in an offset position with the motorcyclist on the left in lane position 2 ahead of the motorcyclist on the right. In this offset position they are more easily seen by other drivers.

3. The car driver should pull over to the right as far as possible and stop if it is safe to do so.

4. The driver of the car is too close to the rear of the truck. Because the car is in the truck driver's rear no-zone, the car cannot be seen by the truck driver. The car driver should create a greater following distance that is far enough back to see one rearview mirror on the truck.

**Unit 3**

# Driving in Different Environments and Situations

# Driving in Different Environments and Situations

## Unit Overview

In this unit students will learn how to drive safely in various environments and conditions. They will learn about the skills needed when driving in urban areas, in rural areas, and on expressways. They will learn how to drive safely under adverse driving conditions, such as poor visibility and poor roadway surfaces. They will also learn what to do in driving emergencies, such as vehicle malfunctions and collisions.

## About the Photograph

This expressway environment resembles limited-access highways throughout the world. Beginning drivers might be reluctant to drive on such high-speed roads. Assure students that as their driving experience increases, they will drive on this type of road many times. New drivers will become confident and skillful in driving on expressways and in urban traffic when they constantly apply the IPDE Process and stay alert for potential hazards.

# Chapter 9 Planning Guide

**Chapter 9
Driving in Urban Traffic**

**9.1 Adjusting to Urban Traffic** *pp. 176–177*
- Name two factors that can make driving difficult in city traffic.
- Describe how to use the IPDE Process for city driving.

**9.2 Following and Meeting Traffic** *pp. 178–181*
- Describe how to use the 3-second following-distance rule.
- Describe how you can safely manage a tailgater.
- List the steps to take to avoid conflict with oncoming traffic.

**9.3 Managing Space in Urban Traffic** *pp. 182–187*
- Describe how far ahead you should look in city traffic.
- Tell how to cover the brake.
- Explain how to select the proper lane for driving.

**9.4 Special Urban Situations** *pp. 188–190*
- Describe the procedure for turning left or right from a one-way street.
- Explain how to warn a driver who is driving the wrong way on a one-way street.

**Assessment**

**Companion** *pp. 62–66*
**Spanish Handbook** *pp. 19–20*

**Resource Book**
Overheads, *pp. 45–46*

**Demonstration Overhead B**
**Video 2** Segment on the IPDE Process in Urban Traffic

**Demonstration Overheads D, J**
**Video 2** Segment on Following Traffic

**Resource Book**
Roadway Sheets 1–8, *pp. 4–19*

**Demonstration Overhead B**
**Content Overhead 20**

**Resource Book**
Roadway Sheets 2, 3, and 4, *pp. 6–11*

**Demonstration Overheads B, D, E**

**Skills and Applications Workbook**, *pp. 33–36*
**Tests and Activities**
Chapter 9 Activities 9-1 and 9-2, *pp. 75–76*
Chapter 9 Test A and Test B, *pp. 77–80*

**TestWorks CD-ROM**
Chapter 9 Test

# Technology Resources

## Audio-Visual and Computer Resources

AAA Foundation for Traffic Safety, *driver-ZED* CD-ROM

AAA Foundation for Traffic Safety, *Managing Space and Time for Safe Driving,* video, 8 minutes

Interactive Driving Systems, Inc., *Approaching Curves,* 28 minutes

Interactive Driving Systems, Inc., *Following Time and Space,* video, 25 minutes

Interactive Driving Systems, Inc., *Habit Development,* video, 16 minutes

Interactive Driving Systems, Inc., *Mottola's Zone Control for Awareness,* video, 38 minutes

Interactive Driving Systems, Inc., *Rear Zone Control,* video, 27 minutes

Interactive Driving Systems, Inc., *Searching Intersections,* video, 20 minutes

Interactive Driving Systems, Inc., *Targeting,* video, 15 minutes

Interactive Driving Systems, Inc., *Zone Control Practice,* video, 18 minutes

Safety Industries, Inc., *Accident Free City Driving,* video, 15 minutes

3I Company, *Driving in Traffic: City Hazards,* video, 20 minutes

# Kits, Equipment, and Other Resources

Interactive Driving Systems, Inc., *Back Seat Decision Maker*

**Go Online**
PHSchool.com
**For: Chapter 9 online activities**
**Visit: PHSchool.com**
**Web Code: cak-9999**

# Chapter 9

## Driving in Urban Traffic

### Chapter Overview

Chapter 9 introduces students to urban driving situations by providing techniques and procedures for safe driving. Students learn how to use a 3-second following distance and how to cover the brake in tight driving situations. Interaction with other road users such as pedestrians and tailgating drivers is addressed.

### Chapter Vocabulary

*cover the brake, overtake, ride the brake, tailgate*

### Teacher's Resources

For students to use as they read the chapter:

**Companion**
pages 62–66

**Spanish Handbook**
pages 19–20

### Projects

Review the projects described on page 191. Some of the projects can be assigned at any time while others are more closely tied to the content presented in the student text.

**9.1** Adjusting to Urban Traffic

**9.2** Following and Meeting Traffic

**9.3** Managing Space in Urban Traffic

**9.4** Special Urban Situations

## You Are the Driver!

Welcome to San Francisco, one of the great international cities of the world. When you drive in this and other cities, you will encounter a wide range of vehicles and numerous pedestrians. In addition, you will have to manage your vehicle in new, unfamiliar, and crowded situations. How will the driver of the red car in this picture have to adjust to zone and line-of-sight changes in this situation?

This chapter will show you how to use the IPDE Process in urban areas. You also will learn how to handle special driving situations so that you can become a low-risk driver in any city.

**Go Online**
PHSchool.com
**For:** Chapter 9 online activities
**Visit:** PHSchool.com
**Web Code:** cak-9999

175

## Introducing the Chapter

Explain that even under the best of conditions, urban drivers can suffer from "information overload." Let students describe difficult urban driving situations they have witnessed. Ask them to analyze these difficulties to find common problems in urban driving.

## You Are the Driver!

Ask students to look at the picture and describe what they see that could cause a driver to be confused as a result of having too many things to respond to. Have them discuss how the driver of the red car in the picture could react to all possible hazards.

## Special Needs

Using slides, photographs, or videos of traffic scenes will be helpful to present examples of lane choice and hazard detection. Include situations with oncoming traffic, parked cars, driveways, pedestrians, and various intersections. Many of the activities and demonstrations in this chapter will help students understand the key concepts and how to apply them.

# Adjusting to Urban Traffic

## 1 Focus

## Summary

This lesson highlights the main factors that make city driving difficult and how to use the IPDE Process in urban traffic.

## Vocabulary

**Review:** *closed zone, decide, execute, identify, line-of-sight restriction, predict*

## 2 Teach

## Discuss

Ask: How often do you expect to drive in an urban setting? (Answers will vary depending on the communities where students live. If your school is in rural area, ask students how often they expect to drive in the closest urban area.)

## Demonstrate

Use **Video 2** Segment on the IPDE Process in Urban Traffic to show how to respond to urban traffic situations.

### Objectives

1. Name two factors that can make driving difficult in city traffic.
2. Describe how to use the IPDE Process for city driving.

O nce you are comfortable making basic maneuvers and using the IPDE Process, you will be ready to start driving in city traffic. City driving will test your best abilities.

### Traffic Complexity

When you drive on a little-used rural road in good weather at a moderate speed, you probably will encounter few critical hazards. However, driving in heavy, fast-moving, city traffic is different and more challenging.

Two main factors make city driving difficult:

- Traffic is more dense in urban areas than it is in rural areas. There are more cars, buses, trucks, and pedestrians per mile.
- City traffic hazards are closer to you than they are in rural areas. Those hazards can quickly block your path.

In rural driving situations, the number of hazards per mile is low; you usually have an adequate "space cushion." You have time to adjust to

the traffic scene. However, in city driving you may have to respond to several close hazards and possible conflicts at the same time.

**Number of Hazards** Mile for mile, city roads have the highest number and variety of hazards. Compare the two pictures of the same location on this page. Which situation is harder to handle. Why?

**Time, Distance, and Speed** As you drive, remember it takes time to use the IPDE Process. You will have to contend with many situations with closed zones and line-of-sight restrictions. If you cannot increase the distance between your vehicle and a hazard, you must change your lane position, slow, or stop to give yourself time to solve the conflict.

### Using the IPDE Process

Heavy urban traffic will test your driving skills. Focus your attention on driving to avoid conflicts and distractions. You might see other

The number of urban hazards can vary dramatically.

**176** Unit 3 Driving in Different Environments and Situations

## Teacher's Resources

**Resource Book**
Overheads, pages 45–46
**Demonstration Overheads**
Overhead B
 **Video 2**
Segment on the IPDE Process in Urban Traffic

## Background

**The IPDE Process and City Driving**
The IPDE Process with the Zone Control System is particularly important in urban situations. In a situation with few hazards, traveling the speed limit probably is safe. The same street with more hazards, such as rush-hour traffic, might demand a lower speed. Lowering the speed gives drivers more time to make identifications and decisions. The IPDE Process provides a standard of acceptable performance during any traffic situation.

You need to slow when your left- and right-front zones are closed.

drivers using cellular phones. You also will see aggressive drivers who needlessly increase the risk in a situation by challenging other drivers. Some extremely angry or thoughtless drivers will actually charge at others as though they are in a rage. In "road rage" situations, be cool and drop back. Give the angry, distracted, or absent-minded driver distance. You can control these situations by avoiding them.

Study the picture above and think about how you would apply the IPDE Process. As you drive, focus on the IPDE Process in these ways:

• **Identify** Be vigorous in using your visual skills. "Aim high" and look well ahead to your target area. Check your searching ranges to make sure your front zone is open and you have time to spot things like a line-of-sight restriction.

• **Predict** Predict possible points of conflict quickly and gain valuable time to respond.
• **Decide** Always be ready to communicate or adjust your vehicle position by changing speed and/or using distance effectively.
• **Execute** Be ready to use your vehicle's controls to make smooth low-risk maneuvers in traffic.

### Review It

1. What two factors can make city driving difficult?
2. How can you best use the IPDE Process in city driving?

### SAFE DRIVING

Studies have shown that using a cellular phone while driving can increase the risk of collision. Drivers should not split their attention between driving and other attention-intensive activities.

Chapter 9 Driving in Urban Traffic **177**

## Activity

**Class Activity** The first part of this activity will help students understand that there is a limit to how much information can be processed at one time. The second part will help students understand the need to limit what they are looking for. You will need an overhead projector and can make an overhead from the master in **Resource Book,** page 45.

For each number on the transparency give students one second to look and then ten seconds to write down what they can remember. Start with the smallest number and progress to

the greatest. Read off the numbers and see how many students recalled them correctly. Point out that most people's ability to recall the number decreases as the number of digits increases. Just as you can be overloaded with numbers, you can be overloaded with information in urban traffic.

Tell students that you will show them the four numbers again, but this time they are to write down how many times the numeral 4 appears in each number. Provide the correct answers and point out that the second activity was easier because the search was limited.

# Following and Meeting Traffic

## Focus

### Summary

This lesson focuses on maintaining a space cushion between your vehicle and possible hazards.

### Vocabulary

*tailgate*

## Teach

### Explain

Explain to students that it will take practice to make the 3-second technique a habit. To learn how to judge space in seconds, students should first take a guess. Then they should count off to see how accurate the guess was. The feedback received by counting off the space lets them know if they were successful. They also should count out loud to make sure they count slowly enough, and check the accuracy of their counting with a stopwatch. With practice, they will be able to judge the space in seconds accurately and consistently.

### Deomonstrate

Use **Video 2** Segment on Following Traffic to show how to maintain a safe following distance.

## Objectives

1. Describe how to use the 3-second following-distance rule.
2. Describe how you can safely manage a tailgater.
3. List the steps to take to avoid conflicts with oncoming traffic.

You need to maintain an ample space cushion between your vehicle and possible hazards in all driving environments. Managing the space cushion, or distance, between your vehicle and the vehicle ahead is the first step.

### Following Others

An adequate following distance has these advantages:
- You can see further ahead to get the "big picture."
- Others can see you better.
- You have more time to use the IPDE Process.
- You are in a better position to avoid the car ahead if it stops suddenly.

### 3-Second Following Distance

A 3-second following distance provides a safe space cushion from the vehicle ahead in most normal driving situations. Use these steps to measure your 3-second following distance.

1. Pick a fixed checkpoint on the road ahead. Road marks or shadows make good fixed checkpoints.
2. When the vehicle ahead of you passes your checkpoint, count: "one-thousand-one, one-thousand-two, one-thousand-three," for your 3-second count.
3. Now, check to see that your vehicle is still short of your fixed checkpoint. If not, slow and add more distance.

Check your following distance frequently. Imagine you are driving the car in the picture below. Do you have a 3-second following distance?

This 3-second technique works well at all speeds for measuring a normal following distance. As your speed increases, so does the distance your vehicle travels during your 3-second count. Thus, when you count off 3 seconds, your following distance will increase at higher speeds.

This 3-second distance is not the total stopping distance you need to avoid hitting a stationary object. A 3-second following distance only protects you from colliding with the vehicle you are following.

Increase your following distance to more than 3 seconds under adverse conditions, or if you need more time to complete the IPDE Process. Maintain extra distance in these situations:

To determine a 3-second following distance, start counting as the rear of the car ahead passes your fixed checkpoint (bridge shadow).

## Teacher's Resources

**Demonstration Overheads**
Overheads D, J

**Video 2**
Segment on Following Traffic

## Background

**3-Second Following Distance** With less than a 3-second following distance you will not have adequate opportunity to respond when approaching a slower moving vehicle. The rate at which a driver approaches a slower moving vehicle is called the closure rate. The slower the front vehicle is going the greater the rate of closure will be. The greater the following distance you have, the sooner you become aware of closing space. You need three seconds or more to have enough time to use the IPDE Process.

**HIGH-MOUNT BRAKE LIGHTS** Since September 1, 1985, all new vehicles in the United States have been required to have at least one high-mount brake light. These lights are designed to give following drivers an added warning that you intend to slow or stop. They are effective for alerting the driver to your immediate rear and those further back. Vehicles with high-mount brake lights experience up to 7% fewer rear-end collisions.

- You are just learning to drive. Your ability to use the IPDE Process is not yet fully developed.
- A tailgating driver has closed your rear zone.
- You are approaching a line-of-sight restriction.
- Traction is low.
- You are carrying a heavy load or pulling a trailer.
- The driver ahead seems unsure.
- You are following a motorcycle.

### Looking Beyond the Vehicle Ahead

The 3-second rule is only one technique to use when following other vehicles. Also look over, through, and around the vehicle you are following. You can even see the reflection of brake lights on wet pavement by looking under the vehicle ahead. Be alert for brake lights, including high-mount brake lights, as shown in the picture on this page. Always try to anticipate what the driver ahead is likely to do in response to a changing zone condition.

### Areas for Sudden Stops

Be alert in areas where sudden stops can occur. Three high-risk areas where closed zones and sudden stops can happen are

- intersections where drivers may have to stop for traffic or pedestrians
- lanes next to parked vehicles
- business driveways with high-volume traffic

### When to Look Away

Imagine driving in an unfamiliar area while also looking for an address. If you are looking away from the road and the driver ahead stops suddenly, you may collide. Take these steps to prevent making this mistake:

- Make sure the zone ahead is stable and open. If you are following another vehicle, increase your following

## Demonstrate

Use **Demonstration Overhead J** to demonstrate that a following vehicle should not go faster than the vehicle being followed. You will need to tape two transparency cars together about three inches apart. Identify a marker that the front car is about to pass. Time your movement of the cars so that it will take at least three seconds for the second car to pass the marker. Ask: Was the second car going any faster than the first car? (No.) If the second car were closer to the first car, would it be traveling any faster? (No.)

## Discuss

Point out that the 3-second distance is recommended as the minimum for safe driving in normal driving conditions and that there are many circumstances that require additional distance between you and the vehicle you are following. Ask: What situations might require you to maintain extra distance? (Students' answers will vary. Refer to the bulleted list in the first column.)

## Activity

**In-Class Driving Rehearsal** In this activity students will learn how to judge a 3-second following distance and see how it relates to the distance between vehicles and speeds. Put a piece of masking tape on the floor in the front of the classroom. Ask five students to line up behind the tape and start to walk around the classroom maintaining a 1-second following distance between students. Have a student in the class count the seconds out loud. Make sure that everyone is maintaining the 1-second distance when they cross the tape. Point out that the distance between all students is the same. Ask the students to increase to a 2-second following distance. Point out that the space between students has increased. Ask a different group of students to walk around the classroom while maintaining a 3-second following distance. After one trip around the classroom, have the students jog while maintaining a 3-second following distance. Point out that the space between the students has increased as speed has increased. Discuss the advantages of a following distance of three seconds or more.

## Discuss

Point out that looking for things like a street address or a business requires you to take your eyes away from your travel path. Ask: What can you do to make this situation safer? One of the best controls you can have is to be aware of the traffic in your rear zone and have an accurate accounting of your path of travel for the next 4–5 seconds. If you have traffic to the rear, then you must make certain drivers are aware of what you will be doing. If there are traffic conditions that can affect your path of travel, you must solve them before devoting your attention elsewhere.

## Explain

Remind students that they cannot change another driver's behavior. In the case of a tailgater, they can only control their own behavior. This includes taking steps to lower the risk of a collision.

## Explain

Explain the three types of tailgaters described in the Background at right. Tell students that the more you use the rearview mirror to see what an approaching driver has done to other vehicles in back of you, the more it will help you learn the tailgater's type. Knowing the type of tailgater can help you better solve the rear-zone problems.

distance to more than three seconds.
- Lower your speed even further when you have line-of-sight restrictions.
- Keep your eyes moving; take split-second glances rather than one long look.
- If you have a passenger, ask that person to look for an address.

### Being Followed

You are in a high-risk closed rear zone situation when someone **tailgates,** or follows too closely. You can take several steps to lower the risk in this type of situation.

### Tailgaters Are Hazards

A tailgater is a hazard because if you have to stop fast, the tailgating driver can hit you from the rear. Tailgating drivers often think they can save time or make other drivers go faster. Neither is true.

**Managing Tailgaters** If you are being tailgated, take these actions to avoid being hit from the rear:
- Increase your following distance to at least four seconds. Imagine you

The driver ahead has moved slightly to the right to allow the tailgater to see traffic farther ahead.

**180** Unit 3 Driving in Different Environments and Situations

The yellow car driver has added tailgater protection by using a following distance longer than three seconds.

are driving the yellow car in the picture above. You have identified the tailgating driver and determined your rear zone is closed. By using a following distance of at least four seconds, you have increased your space cushion from the vehicle ahead. If you must slow or stop, you can do it more slowly and give the tailgater more time to respond.
- Move slightly to the right. Look at both pictures on this page. How have the drivers being tailgated helped the tailgating driver to see better?
- Signal early for turns, stops, and lane changes. Flash your brake lights ahead of time to warn a tailgater that you plan to slow or stop. Slow sooner to make a gradual stop.

## Background

**Tailgaters** Every tailgating situation is not the same, but they are all dangerous. Most tailgaters can be grouped into three broad categories: chargers, one-pace tailgaters, and habitual tailgaters.

The charger approaches you with excessive speed and wants to pass. The charger may try to force an opportunity to pass and might have the potential for road rage if unable to pass. The one-pace tailgater likes to travel at a set pace—often above the speed limit. This kind of tailgater will gradually approach your vehicle, shortening the

distance between the two vehicles. This driver might not pass at the first opportunity—passing requires a change of pace. Perhaps the most dangerous type is the habitual tailgater. This is a driver who consistently tailgates and probably does not realize he or she is tailgating. The habitual tailgater will stay with you when your speed increases, but often does not slow down when your speed decreases. The habitual tailgater is frequently a distracted driver—talking to passengers or using a cellular phone. Trying to pass is not always important to the habitual tailgater.

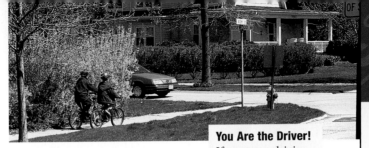

- In extreme situations, change lanes, or pull out of traffic to avoid the tailgater. To reduce stress and risk, your best defense is to avoid tailgaters.

### Responding to Oncoming Traffic

If a driver closes your front zone by crossing the center line, you must react instantly. Knowing how to predict and respond to this type of situation ahead of time may give you enough time to avoid a collision.

### Reasons for Crossing the Center Line

A driver might cross into your path of travel for these reasons:

- **Driver impairment** A driver might be drowsy, distracted, confused, intoxicated, or ill.
- **Poor judgment** A driver might misjudge speed, distance, or position.
- **Poor visibility** Direct sunlight, blinding headlights, or bad weather can reduce a driver's ability to see.
- **Reduced space** A snowbank, narrow bridge, or an object in or near the road might force a driver across the center line.
- **Sudden moves by others** Children, bicycles, pedestrians, animals, or a vehicle door opening can force a driver to make a last-second move.
- **Vehicle failure** A driver might lose control of a vehicle due to mechanical failure.
- **Turning buses and trucks** Long vehicles need extra room just to make normal turns. Vehicles

pulling trailers can create the same situation.

- **Double-Parked Vehicles** Drivers or delivery drivers may park carelessly and close your front zone.

### Avoiding Conflicts

If a vehicle comes at you, take these actions to avoid a collision:

- Slow until the other driver can return to the normal lane. You can also slow so that you meet the other driver at a point where there is room to pass.
- Turn on or flash your headlights and blow your horn.
- If your right-front zone is open, move to the right to give the oncoming driver more room. Swerve sharply to an open space on the right if needed.

**You Are the Driver!**
If you were driving a car approaching this intersection, what would you predict the driver of the blue car might do?

### Review It

1. How many seconds should you use for a normal following distance?
2. What can you do to manage a tailgater safely?
3. How can you avoid a conflict with an oncoming vehicle in your lane?

Chapter 9 Driving in Urban Traffic **181**

## Discuss

Draw students' attention to the photograph and ask: How can the driver of the blue car use lane positioning to minimize any risks at the intersection? (The driver identifies the bushes as a line-of-sight restriction. The driver then checks the left-front zone and, if it is open, uses lane position 2—left side of lane. Using lane position 2 allows greater lateral separation from what might be concealed by the bushes. This gives extra time and space to avoid any potential risk caused by the bicyclists.)

 **Assess**

### Answers to Review It

1. Use 3 seconds to determine a normal following distance. (p. 178)
2. Increase following distance to at least 4 seconds. Move slightly right to give the tailgater a better view. Signal early for turns, stops, or lane changes. Flash brake lights early before slowing or stopping. In extreme situations, pull out of traffic to avoid the tailgater. (p. 180)
3. Slow, flash your headlights, blow your horn, and move right. (p. 181)

## Activity

**Class Activity** Use **Demonstration Overhead D,** a four-way intersection, to show how lane positioning gives the driver more time and space to see and avoid conflicts.

Place a two-inch square object at the southeast corner of the intersection to represent a building. One car length east of the intersection, place a white car heading west.

For the first part of the activity, place the yellow car three car lengths south of the intersection heading north. Begin with the car in the right-hand lane in lane position 3—the far right side. Place

the eraser end of a pencil where the driver would be seated and pivot the pointed end to demonstrate looking to the right. Move the yellow car and pencil forward until the driver is able to see the car approaching from the east without being blocked by the building. Point out how close the yellow car is to the intersection before the driver can see beyond the line-of-sight restriction.

Repeat the activity with the yellow car in the left lane and place it in lane position 2—the far left side. Point out how much sooner the driver can see beyond the line-of-sight restriction.

# Managing Space in Urban Traffic

## Focus

### Summary

This lesson focuses on managing space in urban traffic. Appropriate procedures for approaching traffic signals are included. Strategies for adjusting speed are addressed. Techniques for selecting a lane and procedures for changing lanes and passing are described.

### Vocabulary

**New:** *cover the brake, overtake, ride the brake*

**Review:** *stale green light, point-of-no-return*

## Teach

### Discuss

Ask: How is your view of a movie screen affected if someone sits directly in front of you? How would your view be affected if that person was over six feet tall and weighed 300 pounds? What difference would it make if the same person sat five rows ahead of you? Point out that the further away the obstruction, the better you are able to see the movie screen. Similarly, the greater the distance between you and the vehicle ahead of you, the better you are able to see the scene ahead.

## Objectives

1. Describe how far ahead you should look in city traffic.
2. Tell how to cover the brake.
3. Explain how to select the proper lane for driving.

When driving in urban traffic, you must respond to a wide variety of situations. Unfamiliar streets, line-of-sight restrictions, small zones created by narrow lanes, and high-density traffic all make your driving task difficult. To manage these situations, you will need to use your best skills combined with a positive, heads-up, alert attitude.

### Looking Ahead While Staying Back

How far ahead should you look to make sure you are aiming high enough while driving in the city? In addition to looking around your vehicle, look a block or more ahead. By looking far ahead to your target area to protect your path of travel, you will be able to spot zone problems in time to adjust your speed and/or position as needed.

Imagine you are the driver following the truck in these pictures. Maintain a safe following distance of three seconds or more to have a good view of the road ahead. By doing so, you can identify and predict possible points of conflict. You also will be able to better manage the distance between your vehicle and the truck ahead.

### Approaching Traffic Signals

Look at your target area to detect traffic signals. By doing so, you will have more time to respond.

If the light is red, slow and be ready to stop. If the signals on your street are synchronized to work together, you should be able to drive at or near the speed limit for several blocks as lights turn green.

If the light is green when you first see it, predict it will change

The truck creates a line-of-sight restriction ahead because you are tailgating.

View of road ahead with 3 or more seconds of following distance.

182 Unit 3 Driving in Different Environments and Situations

## Teacher's Resources

**Resource Book**
Roadway Sheets 1–8, pages 4–19
**Demonstration Overheads**
Overhead B
**Content Overheads**
Overhead 20

The flashing DON'T WALK signal is a warning that your green signal is about to turn yellow.

soon. A traffic light that has been green and will soon turn yellow is called a stale green light. Watch for a DON'T WALK pedestrian signal that has started to flash like the one in the top picture on this page. This signal warns you that the light is about to turn yellow. If the signal is flashing, you must decide if you have time to drive through the intersection safely before the light turns yellow. Your decision will depend on your distance to the intersection and your speed.

*Never speed up to get through a green light before it changes.* At any speed, you will reach a point-of-no-return, or a point where you must start braking if you are going to stop before the intersection. If you were the driver in the bottom picture, could you stop before the light turns red? How might a tailgater force you into a collision?

### Covering the Brake

You can maintain a normal speed if you are driving into a stable, hazard-free traffic situation. But, if you are driving into a scene like the one shown on the top of page 184, you might have to stop quickly. To get

In this changing zone situation, you need to check your speed, distance, and other traffic when deciding whether to stop.

## Background

**Red-Light Cameras** Drivers who run red lights have caused so many collisions in some cities that red-light cameras are beginning to be used for enforcement. With this red-light camera system, a photograph would be taken as the vehicle runs a red light and captures an image of its license plate. The owner of that vehicle would then be issued a traffic ticket for this moving violation.

## Demonstrate

Ask three students to help you demonstrate how the greater the distance between you and the vehicle ahead of you, the better you are able to read the traffic scene ahead. Assign the role of front car to the tallest student and the roles of driver and front-zone problem to other students.

Have the student representing the front-zone problem write on a 4-by-6-inch index card a two-inch letter to represent a front-zone problem (e.g., R for red light, S for stopped traffic). Have this student stand with his or her back to the side wall of the classroom. Have the driver sit in a chair against the opposite wall and the person representing the front car stand directly in front of the driver. Ask the student representing a front-zone problem to hold up the card. Have the front car walk across the room, and ask the driver to let you know when the letter is visible. Point out how much distance is needed between the front car and the driver before the letter is visible. Then have the driver guess what front-zone problem the letter represents.

Repeat this demonstration with different students and different front-zone problems.

## Demonstrate

Ask two students to help you demonstrate the benefit of using the ready position of covering the brake. You will need a tennis ball for this demonstration.

Have the two students stand next to each other facing the side of the classroom. Position yourself facing the two students about three feet away from them. Hold the tennis ball in your hand and raise your arm to shoulder height. Move your arm back and forth in front of the two students. Instruct the students to keep their arms at their sides until you drop the ball in front of one of them. Tell each student to try to catch the ball when you drop it in front of him or her. Drop the ball in front of each student several times. Point out that if they keep their arms at their sides until you drop the ball, they cannot catch it.

Instruct the students to hold their arms out with the palms of their hands turned up ready to catch the ball. Hold the tennis ball in your hand and raise your arm to shoulder height. Move your arm back and forth in front of the two students. Tell them to try to catch the ball when you drop it in front of them. Drop the ball in front of each student several times. Ask the students to tell the class how much easier it was to catch the ball when they were in a ready position. Point out that this is the principle behind covering the brake.

Be ready for doors to open at the last second.

ready to stop, you need to **cover the brake.** Take your foot off the accelerator, and hold it over the brake pedal. You can use this technique whenever you sense a possible conflict. This could cut your reaction time and help you avoid a collision.

When you cover your brake, make sure not to rest your foot on the brake pedal, or **ride the brake.** When you do so, your brakes heat up and wear faster. In addition, your brake lights stay on, confusing drivers behind you. Only flash your brake lights to warn drivers behind you when you know you are going to slow or stop.

Take these actions to identify and respond to the risk of parked vehicles:

- Cover your brake and move left in your lane to lane position 2.
- Look for drivers through the windows of parked vehicles.
- Be alert for the parked vehicles' brake lights, exhaust, or wheels turned out.
- Lightly tap your horn if needed.
- Be ready to stop or swerve. Swerve only if your left-front zone is open.

While driving past parked vehicles, watch for doors that might

Adjust your speed early as you enter a town after driving on a highway.

**184** Unit 3 Driving in Different Environments and Situations

## Activity

**Class Activity** Have students look at the top photo. Ask: What are the advantages of having the car in lane position 2 before the parked car's door is flung open? (There will be room for the door to open without interfering with the driver's path of travel.)

Have students look at the bottom photo. Ask: What actions should a driver take to be ready for the light to change? (The foot should be covering the brake. The driver should turn his or her head to a 45-degree angle to the right to see if there is anything approaching from a line-of-sight-restriction.)

## Cross Curricular

**Mathematics** Apply the information presented in the graph on page 185 about the amount of time saved by increasing speed. Imagine that on your route to school there is a 10-mile stretch of roadway where the speed limit is 40 mph. When you drive at the speed limit, how long does it take you to drive the 10 miles? (15 minutes) If you drive 45 mph, how long does it take you? (13 minutes and 20 seconds). If you drive 50 mph, how long does it take you? (12 minutes). Ask students: Is it worth the risk to use excess speed to save two or three minutes?

**Minutes Saved/10 miles by Driving 5 mph Faster**

Look at the graph to see how much time you save by driving 5 mph faster for 10 miles. Is driving faster worth it?

open unexpectedly, as shown in the top picture on left page. Try to drive at least one car door's width away from parked vehicles. Otherwise, reduce speed.

### Adjusting Speed

Imagine that you have been driving for an hour on a highway. You are just entering the town shown in the bottom picture on left page. The speed limit is 25 mph. However, traffic conditions should tell you to adjust your speed, and drive even slower.

Blending into traffic is one of the most common city driving skills you will need. Use these techniques to select your best driving speed:
- Drive with the traffic flow.
- Stay within the speed limit.
- Adjust speed and position ahead of time for other drivers who might block your way.

Look at the graph and driver pictured on this page. If you are as hurried as this driver, remember this: You only save a few seconds by driving even 5 mph faster. And, the time savings are less and less at higher speeds.

### Selecting the Best Lane

When driving in multilane traffic, you will use different lanes at different times. Select the lane or zone with the fewest number of hazards.

The left lane is usually for faster traffic. But at times, traffic can be held up by drivers waiting to turn left. These left-turning drivers can be a problem when only two lanes are going in your direction.

If your street has multiple lanes going your way, choose the lane where the traffic flow is smoothest. Imagine driving the yellow car in the picture on the next page. Why is the center lane the best for drivers going straight?

## Explain

Call students' attention to the chart or use **Content Overhead 20.** Point to the first bar on the graph and explain that it takes 24 minutes to travel 10 miles at 25 mph. If you traveled the same distance at 30 mph it would only take 20 minutes—you would save four minutes. Now point to the last bar on the chart and explain that it takes six minutes to travel 10 miles at 60 mph. If you traveled the same distance at 65 mph it would take about five minutes and 15 seconds—you save less than a minute. Point out how the minutes saved decrease as you move across the chart. This indicates that the amount of time you save decreases dramatically as speed increases.

## Discuss

Ask: Can you think of a non-driving situation in which you were rushing to do something and you made a mistake? Have students describe a few situations.

## Activity

**Small Group Activity** This activity will give students an opportunity to express their knowledge and attitudes about speeding. Divide the class into small discussion groups. Ask each group to discuss the following questions: Why do drivers speed? What are the legal consequences of speeding? When does speeding have a high collision potential? What good habits can drivers develop to avoid speeding? After adequate time, have each group report their findings to the class. Encourage students to come to a consensus.

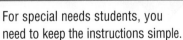

## Special Needs

For special needs students, you need to keep the instructions simple. Teach these students four simple rules to help them remember what to do when choosing a lane:
1. Best vision
2. Widest lane
3. Avoid double yellow lines
4. Avoid parked cars

## Discuss

Ask: Why is it unsafe to pass in intersections and at railroad crossings?

## Demonstrate

Use the illustration on this page to explain why through traffic should use the center lane.

## Demonstrate

Use **Demonstration Overhead B** to demonstrate the various problems associated with driving in the left and right lanes of an urban area. Place the yellow car in a lane and ask what problems a driver in this lane might expect. Create the common problems outlined in the Background information below. Ask students to choose the best lane position for each situation.

MASS TRANSIT Before pollution and global warming were serious concerns, London was forced to come to grips with crippling traffic jams. In the late 1800s, Londoners designed and built a subway system. Today in London and many other European cities, subways are the best means of transportation. In the United States, subways and light-rail systems are expanding. Thousands of people who might drive or ride at street level now travel by these rail systems in New York, Chicago, Los Angeles, Atlanta, Boston, San Francisco, and Washington, D.C.

**Lane Positioning**  Use these techniques to position your vehicle in multilane city traffic:
- Increase your following distance to more than three seconds in heavy traffic.

Through traffic should use the center lane to avoid slowdowns or stops.

- Adjust your speed and lane position as needed to stay out of other drivers' blind-spot areas.
- Move to another lane if your front zone closes.

### Changing Lanes

Once you start driving in a lane, try to stay in that lane. If you must change lanes, follow these steps:
1. Use your mirrors to check traffic in your rear zones.
2. Signal your lane change early.
3. Quickly check your blind-spot area.
4. Change lanes without slowing.
5. Cancel your signal.
Repeat this procedure if you need to change more than one lane.

### Overtaking and Passing

At times, you might decide to **overtake,** or pass, a vehicle ahead. To overtake another vehicle, use the lane-changing procedure and drive

186  Unit 3  Driving in Different Environments and Situations

## Background

### Right- and Left-Lane Zone Changes

Many streets in urban areas have two lanes of traffic traveling in the same direction. There are some common zone changes associated with each lane. The zone changes you will most likely encounter when driving in the right lane are front- and right-front zone changes. Front-zone changes include double-parked vehicles and vehicles entering from parking spaces and side streets. Right-front-zone changes include parked cars, entering traffic, and pedestrians preparing to cross the street. Lane position 2 (to the left side

of the lane) is generally the best lane position when driving in the right lane. Lane position 2 provides increased distance between you and right-front problems.

When driving in the left lane, common zone changes include front-zone changes caused by vehicles stopped to make a left turn and oncoming traffic turning left in front of you, or swerving over the center line. Generally, lane position 3 (to the right side of the lane) is the best lane position when traveling in the left lane.

Carpooling saves time and fuel. It also reduces traffic and parking problems.

past the slower moving vehicle. Signal briefly and return to your lane when both headlights of the vehicle you have passed appear in your inside rearview mirror. You will learn more about the procedures for passing in Chapter 10.

Passing in a city can be dangerous. You must be alert for pedestrians, cross traffic, signals, and an endless number of line-of-sight restrictions.

If you must overtake another moving vehicle on a two-lane two-way street, make sure you can do so safely and legally. It is illegal to pass at intersections or over double-yellow center lines.

### Special Traffic Lanes

To help move rush-hour travel, many cities now have special lanes for bus and/or carpool drivers.

Drivers who travel alone must use the regular, more crowded, slower lanes. By using these special lanes, people, as shown in the picture above, ride together to save time and fuel, and to reduce pollution and parking problems.

### Review It

1. How far ahead should you look in city traffic?
2. How do you cover your brake?
3. How do you select the best lane on a multilane street?

## Activity

**Model Car Activity** Divide the class into groups of three. Give each group two cars, three wild cards, and each a different set of roadway sheets from **Resource Book,** pages 4–19. Have them formulate three problems that could affect their path of travel or their line of sight while traveling on urban roadways. Have each group demonstrate how to use lane positioning, speed control, and communication to minimize each zone change.

## Discuss

Have students evaluate the photograph on this page. Ask: What are you able to observe about following distance of cars on the highway? (There is a cluster of cars all grouped together in the forward-moving traffic lanes. The last vehicle in the second lane from the left is tailgating with less than one car length. The car in front of the car being tailgated is making a lane change into less than one second of space. But there is plenty of space behind the cluster.) Point out that these cars are mismanaging space within that cluster. If a driver sets the goal to get the best space available, he or she usually can. There is plenty of empty space between the cluster of cars.

##  Assess

### Answers to Review It

1. You need to look ahead one block or more. (p. 182)
2. Take your foot off the accelerator, and hold it over the brake pedal to be ready to brake quickly. (p. 184)
3. Decide which lane best suits your needs. For example, if you proceed straight, use the center lane when three lanes are going your way. (p. 185)

# 9.4

# Special Urban Situations

## 1 Focus

## Summary

This lesson teaches students how to identify one-way streets and how to enter and exit one-way streets.

## Vocabulary

**Review:** *uncontrolled intersection*

## 2 Teach

## Discuss

Ask students to identify local urban streets where a driver might encounter line-of-sight restrictions and frequent changes to the path of travel. Have students describe the problems they have seen.

## Demonstrate

Use the illustrations on page 189 to explain how to identify one-way streets. Also demonstrate correct lanes to use when making left and right turns.

## Discuss

Direct students' attention to the *You Are the Driver!* photograph. Ask students: What clues identify this as a one-way street? (ONE-WAY sign, parked cars point in one direction)

### Objectives

1. Describe the procedure for turning left or right from a one-way street.
2. Explain how to warn a driver who is driving the wrong way on a street.

You will encounter a wide range of situations in city driving. By using the IPDE Process, you will be ready to adjust to each situation ahead of time.

### Driving on Two-Way Streets

Most city roadways are two-way streets with one lane going in each direction. Other streets have two or more lanes going in the same direction.

Many city intersections do not have traffic controls. You cannot be sure what other drivers will do as you approach an uncontrolled or blind intersection.

Some intersections have special left-turn lanes. If you turn left at an uncontrolled intersection, you must yield to oncoming traffic.

### Driving on One-Way Streets

One-way streets can move a greater volume of traffic with fewer conflicts than two-way streets. Generally, one-way streets are less congested than two-way streets, so fewer conflicts occur.

### Identifying One-Way Streets

When you come to an unfamiliar street, first determine if it is a one-way street. These clues can help you identify a one-way street:

- ONE WAY signs are posted on most one-way streets.
- All moving traffic and parked vehicles point in the same direction.
- Broken white lines are used to separate lanes.
- Most traffic signs will be facing the same direction. If you are driving on a street and the signs are facing the other way, you probably are going the wrong way on a one-way street.

### Entering One-Way Streets

Imagine you are driving the yellow car in the top picture on the opposite page. To enter the one-way street, turn from the right lane to the nearest right lane.

To make a left turn onto a one-way street, position your vehicle in the nearest left lane. Make a sharp

**You Are the Driver!**
Imagine you are approaching this intersection. What clues identify this as a one-way street?

188

## Teacher's Resources

**Resource Book**
Roadway Sheets 2, 3, and 4, pages 6–11
**Demonstration Overheads**
Overheads B, D, and E

left turn into the nearest lane going left. Signs are used to alert you when your street is about to become a one-way street.

### Lane Choice on One-Way Streets

If you plan to drive on a one-way street for a distance, try to avoid a lane that is next to parked vehicles. A parked vehicle could pull out and close your front zone. Each parked vehicle creates a line-of-sight restriction. If a center lane is available, use it to reduce possible conflicts.

When you plan to turn, position your vehicle ahead of time. Move into the right or left lane at least one block before your turn.

### Leaving One-Way Streets

Imagine you are driving the yellow car in the picture on the right. To turn left from your one-way street, position your vehicle in the far left lane ahead of time. To turn right, position your vehicle in the far right lane ahead of time. Complete your turn by entering the nearest lane going your way.

On some one-way streets, the outside lane may be for turns only. On other one-way streets, you can turn into a multilane street from more than one lane. Road markings or overhead signs will direct you.

You will need to adjust when a one-way street turns into a two-way street. Your left lane might end. Signs or lights will warn you when a one-way street is about to change to a two-way street.

To turn right onto a one-way street, turn from the far right lane into the first available right lane.

To turn left from a one-way street, turn from the far left lane to the first available lane going left.

## Activity

**Model Car Activity** Divide the class into groups of three. Give each group two cars, three wild cards, and Roadway Sheets 2, 3, and 4 from **Resource Book,** pages 6–11. Use roadway sheets as either two-way or one-way streets. Have them use one roadway sheet, the cars, and the wild cards to create problems that affect their path of travel and/or their line of sight while traveling on a two-way street. Then, have them use the same roadway sheet as if it were a one-way street to discover how the problems are different from two-way streets. After adequate

discovery time with one roadway sheet, have them repeat the process with the other two sheets. Have the groups report their findings to the class. Students can use **Demonstration Overheads B, D,** and **E** to illustrate their discoveries to the class.

### What Do You Think?

High-speed city traffic and residential neighborhoods don't mix—especially when small children are involved. How can traffic be controlled in these settings?

### Signaling Wrong-Way Drivers

If you encounter a vehicle headed the wrong way on a one-way street, slow, steer right, and sound your horn. If you have time, flash your headlights to warn the other driver.

### Unexpected Situations on Crowded Streets

Imagine you are driving in the situation pictured below on the left. A vehicle suddenly emerges from an alley and is about to enter your path of travel. The street is so narrow that you have little room to maneuver.

Slow and cover your brake to maintain a safe path of travel. If necessary, let traffic clear before you move ahead.

When driving on city streets, you should maintain a continuous orderly visual search pattern. Even though drivers may have a green

You might not be able to see a pedestrian in front of a vehicle that is stopped at a green light.

light, they are required to stop for a pedestrian as this driver in the right picture has done.

Angle or parallel parking is allowed on most streets. If you must drive close to parked vehicles, be alert for possible conflicts. At the first hint of movement from a vehicle or pedestrian, slow, stop, or move to another lane.

### Review It

1. What lanes should you use when making a right or left turn from a one-way street?
2. What can you do if another driver approaches you from the wrong direction on a one-way street?

If you cannot move left, be prepared to stop.

**190** Unit 3 Driving in Different Environments and Situations

## Reviewing Chapter Objectives

### 1. Adjusting to Urban Traffic

1. What are the two main factors that make driving difficult in the city? (176)
2. How do you use the IPDE Process for city driving? (177)

### 2. Following and Meeting Traffic

3. How do you use the 3-second following-distance rule? (178)
4. How can you safely manage a tailgater? (180)
5. What steps should you take to avoid conflicts with oncoming traffic? (181)

### 3. Managing Space in Urban Traffic

6. How far ahead should you look when driving in city traffic? (182)
7. What should you avoid doing when covering the brake? (184)
8. How do you select the proper lane for driving on a multilane street? (186)

### 4. Special Urban Situations

9. What is the procedure for turning left or right from a one-way street? (188–189)
10. How can you warn a driver who is driving the wrong way on a one-way street? (189–190)

## Projects

### Individuals

**Investigate** Research local newspapers to find articles about accidents that have been caused by drivers running red lights. Are some intersections mentioned more often than others? Compare your results with those of your classmates.

**Observe Traffic** As a passenger in a vehicle, look for signs of "road rage" in drivers of other vehicles. Also look for signs of distracted or absent-minded drivers. Make a list of the actions you observe. Discuss your findings with your class.

### Groups

**Investigate** Research alternate transportation systems found in large cities. Each group member should research a different city and make a list of all the transportation systems available in that city. Note similarities and differences among the transportation systems listed. Prepare a group report that contains each group member's findings.

**Use Technology** Use the Internet to find street maps of large cities in the United States. Each group member should research a different city and observe whether there are more one-way streets or two-way streets in that city. Compare your findings with those of others in your group.

## Reviewing Chapter Objectives

**9.1** Adjusting to Urban Traffic
See Answers to Review It on page 177.
**9.2** Following and Meeting Traffic
See Answers to Review It on page 181.
**9.3** Managing Space in Urban Traffic
See Answers to Review It on page 187.
**9.4** Special Urban Situations
See Answers to Review It on page 190.

For additional information refer to the specific page(s) in parentheses after each question.

## Projects

Some of the projects can be assigned at any time while others are more closely tied to the content presented in the student text. The page number where the topic is introduced is indicated.

**Investigate (Individual):** p. 177
**Observe Traffic:** p. 181
**Investigate (Group):** p. 182
**Use Technology:** p. 188
The results of student projects will vary.

## Teacher's Resources

### Skills and Applications Workbook
pages 33–36

### Tests and Activities
Chapter 9 Activities 9-1 and 9-2, pages 75–76

Chapter 9 Test A and B, pages 77–80

### TestWorks CD-ROM
Chapter 9 Test

## Answers to Check Your Knowledge

**1.** c
**2.** b
**3.** a
**4.** b
**5.** decrease
**6.** hazards

## Answers to Review Vocabulary

**7.** cover the brake (d)
**8.** ride the brake (b)
**9.** overtake (a)
**10.** tailgate (c)

## Answers to Think Critically

Students' answers will vary. For information related to the question refer to the page(s) indicated.

**1.** In urban traffic, there are more hazards per mile and you have to deal with them more frequently. Multilane streets might involve drivers who change lanes often. Both one-way and two-way streets may be present. (pp. 176–177)

**2.** When clear, move the vehicle into the far-left lane. Make the turn, entering the left-hand lane of the street. (p. 189)

**3.** One-way streets can move a greater volume of traffic than two-way streets. There may be fewer conflicts. Head-on collisions are less likely. Special turn lanes may be available. Both moving traffic and parked cars are pointed in the same direction. (p. 188)

### Chapter Test

#### Check Your Knowledge

**Multiple Choice** Copy the number of each sentence below on a sheet of paper. Choose the letter that best completes the statement or answers the question.

1. While driving in urban situations,
   (a) keep your vehicle close to others.
   (b) cover the brake pedal.
   (c) be ready to reduce speed and change vehicle position.
   (d) maintain the posted speed.
2. The 3-second following distance technique
   (a) should be decreased in adverse conditions.
   (b) is safe for most conditions.
   (c) is the same as total stopping distance.
   (d) is not safe at speeds over 40 mph.
3. You can avoid being hit by a tailgater if you
   (a) increase your following distance to four seconds or more.
   (b) move to the left side of your lane.
   (c) look in the rearview mirror and warn the tailgater.
   (d) keep steady pressure on the brake.
4. It is illegal to pass another vehicle
   (a) over a broken lane marker.
   (b) at an intersection.
   (c) on a multilane street.
   (d) on a one-way street.

**Completion** Copy the number of each sentence below. After each number, write the word or words that complete the sentence correctly.

5. To give yourself adequate time to react to a hazard, you should _____ your speed.
6. Urban streets and roads have the highest number of _____ per mile.

192   Unit 3  Driving in Different Environments and Situations

#### Review Vocabulary

Copy the number of each definition in List A. Match the definition in List A with the item it defines in List B.

**List A**

7. take your foot off the accelerator and hold it over the brake pedal to be ready to brake quickly
8. rest your foot on the brake
9. pass the car ahead
10. follow another vehicle too closely

**List B**

a. overtake
b. ride the brake
c. tailgate
d. cover the brake

#### Think Critically

Write a paragraph to answer each question.

1. Driving in urban traffic can be a challenge. What characteristics of urban traffic make driving more difficult than in other environments?
2. You are driving in the right-hand lane of a one-way street. You discover that you need to make a left-hand turn at the next light. What should you do?
3. What are some advantages of driving on one-way streets?

**1.** How long should it take this car to pass by the speed limit sign?

**2.** You are following this truck. How can you improve your line-of-sight view ahead?

**3.** What clue do you have to indicate this is not a stale green light?

**4.** What can you do to alert this oncoming driver and avoid trouble?

## Answers to Decision Making

**1.** It should take 3 seconds before the car's front wheels move by the speed limit sign.

**2.** By using an increased following distance, you can improve the view ahead.

**3.** The white WALK sign tells the driver that this light will stay green for a little bit longer.

**4.** To avoid a conflict in this situation, you should slow down, steer right, sound your horn, and flash your headlights.

Chapter 9 Driving in Urban Traffic **193**

# Chapter 10   Planning Guide

 **Student Features**

 **Teacher's Edition**

**Companion** *pp. 67–71*
**Spanish Handbook** *pp. 21–22*

**Resource Book**
Roadway Sheets 1, 5, and 6,
*pp. 4–5, 12–15*
**In-Car Checklist** 24

**Demonstration Overheads G, H**
**Video 2** Segment on the IPDE Process in Rural Areas

**In-Car Checklist** 25

**Content Overheads**
Overhead 7
**Demonstration Overheads A, G, H**
**Video 2** Segment on Passing

**Resource Book**
Roadway Sheets 1, 5,
*pp. 4–5, 12–13*
Teacher's Instructions, *p. 47*

**TestWorks CD-ROM**
Chapter 10 Test

**Skills and Applications Workbook**, *pp. 37–40*
**Tests and Activities**
Chapter 10 Activities 10-1
and 10-2, *pp. 83–84*
Chapter 10 Test A and
Test B, *pp. 85–88*

# Technology Resources

## Audio-Visual and Computer Resources

AAA Foundation for Traffic Safety, *driver-ZED* CD-ROM

Interactive Driving Systems, Inc., *Approaching Curves,* 28 minutes

Interactive Driving Systems, Inc., *Following Time and Space,* video, 25 minutes

Interactive Driving Systems, Inc., *Habit Development,* video, 16 minutes

Interactive Driving Systems, Inc., *Mottola's Zone Control for Awareness,* video, 38 minutes

Interactive Driving Systems, Inc., *Rear Zone Control,* video, 27 minutes

Interactive Driving Systems, Inc., *Searching Intersections,* video, 20 minutes

Interactive Driving Systems, Inc., *Targeting,* video, 15 minutes

Interactive Driving Systems, Inc., *Zone Control Practice,* video, 18 minutes

Safety Industries, Inc., *Rural Driving*, video, 10 minutes

Safety Industries, Inc., *Mountain Driving*, video, 15 minutes

3I Company, *Driving in Traffic: Rural Highway Hazards*, video, 22 minutes

# Kits, Equipment, and Other Resources

Interactive Driving Systems, Inc., *Back Seat Decision Maker*

**Go Online**
PHSchool.com
**For:** Chapter 10 online activities
**Visit:** PHSchool.com
**Web Code:** cak-9999

# Chapter 10

## Driving in Rural Areas

### Chapter Overview

Chapter 10 explains driving on two-lane and multilane rural roads. It also describes characteristics of rural traffic, basic skills used in rural areas, passing and being passed, situations peculiar to rural roadways, and special driving environments.

### Chapter Vocabulary

*advisory speed sign, median, pull-out area, runaway vehicle ramp, slow-moving vehicle, switchback*

194

## Teacher's Resources

For students to use as they read the chapter:

**Companion**
pages 67–71

**Spanish Handbook**
pages 21–22

## Projects

Review the projects described on page 217. Some of the projects can be assigned at any time while others are more closely tied to the content presented in the student text.

## You Are the Driver!

About 82 percent of all miles of roadways in the United States are rural roads. Rural roads can be two-lane or multilane. What problems might occur along this rural road? How does it differ from a city street? Will this vehicle most likely be traveling faster or slower than the posted speed limit? What action should you take as you approach this vehicle?

Even if you live in an urban area, you will likely drive in rural areas. This chapter discusses characteristics and problems you might encounter in rural and other environments. It explains how you can apply the IPDE Process to deal with various hazards.

Go **O**nline

PHSchool.com

**For:** Chapter 10 online activities
**Visit:** PHSchool.com
**Web Code:** cak-9999

195

## Introducing the Chapter

Pair students to study the picture. Ask them to describe how what they see in the picture is different from what a picture of a city street would show. Ask them how driving in rural areas would be different from driving in urban areas.

## You Are the Driver!

Encourage students to describe problems they would encounter if they were driving the vehicle and looking through the windshield at the scene in the picture. Have them discuss the questions in the *You Are the Driver!* text about line of sight and lane position. Students should recognize that the number of hazards in rural driving is not necessarily determined by the number of vehicles present. Many one-vehicle collisions occur on rural roads, often because the time available to use the IPDE Process is shorter.

## Special Needs

Many of the activities and demonstrations in this chapter are crucial for understanding key concepts. It would be helpful for special needs students to work with their partners (as selected for Chapter 1) for many of these activities.

The Demonstrate activity on page 199 is especially good for special needs students. Because they process information slowly, these students might need to drive more slowly. Driving more slowly may create problems with tailgating and passing.

Students with overly aggressive personalities might benefit from learning about methods of practicing patience. Discuss ways to cope with angry feelings, especially when following a slow-moving vehicle, choosing a safe speed for conditions, or being tailgated or cut off by another vehicle during highway driving.

# Characteristics of Rural Traffic

 **Focus**

## Summary

This lesson focuses on the characteristics of rural traffic including roadways, speed, traffic controls, and roadway hazards.

## Vocabulary

**Review:** *line of sight, path of travel*

 **Teach**

## Explain

Explain that some drivers tend to regard a rural road as being equally safe everywhere. Lane width, roadway surface, and shoulder conditions can change drastically within short distances. In addition to the actual road conditions, rural roads have many line-of-sight restrictions close to the driver's intended path of travel. These restrictions can create a sudden closing of the front zone. It is especially important that a driver identify line-of-sight restrictions with ample time to make adjustments in speed or positioning to best manage driving space.

## Discuss

Have students debate the issue of a national speed limit presented in *What Do You Think?*

## Objectives

1. Describe rural roadways.
2. Describe factors to consider when selecting a safe speed.
3. Identify traffic controls and how they help inform, warn, and regulate drivers on rural roads.

Wide open spaces and less traffic are common in rural areas. After driving for long periods of time, you might mistakenly assume that conflicts will not occur. However, collisions in rural areas account for nearly twice as many highway deaths as collisions in urban areas.

### Roadways

Rural roads are constructed of many different types of materials. Some are paved and others not. Shoulders can be wide or narrow, paved or gravel. Road surfaces may be smooth or in very poor condition.

At night, the lack of adequate lighting causes difficulty in seeing. Be alert to potential changes that could arise. Conditions in rural areas can change suddenly with little warning.

### Speed

Determining a safe speed is critical for safe rural driving. Speed affects
- your line of sight
- your stopping distance
- your vehicle control
- the amount of damage and injury in the event of a collision

Many rural roads have a speed limit of 55 mph. Some states allow speeds greater than 55 mph. Where conditions require, lower speeds are posted.

There is a difference between safe speeds and posted speeds. Posted speeds are the maximum speeds allowed under ideal conditions. When conditions are not ideal, safe speeds should be used. These are slower speeds. Factors that affect safe speed selection include other highway users, inclement weather, hills, curves, intersections and very nar-

**You Are the Driver!**
How many traffic hazards can you identify in this picture?

196 Unit 3 Driving in Different Environments and Situations

## Teacher's Resources

No *Drive Right* resources are needed for teaching Section 10.1.

## Facts and Figures

According to the Insurance Institute for Highway Safety, vehicles leaving the roadway and hitting fixed objects such as trees and utility poles account for about one third of all motor vehicle deaths. Most of these collisions involve a single vehicle. These roadside hazards are mostly a problem at curves and downhill sections of rural roads. Each year approximately 42 percent of deaths in roadside collisions occur on curves. About one third of all roadside collisions involve a vehicle that rolls over, and about one third involve occupant ejection.

Be prepared to stop as you near the crest of the hill.

row roads or lanes. *Always use your common sense and never drive faster than conditions permit.*

## Traffic Controls

Traffic controls—signs, signals, and markings—direct, regulate, inform, and warn drivers. Traffic controls provide advance information and warning of

- hazards that you cannot yet identify
- major intersections ahead
- unusual or hazardous conditions (curves, animal crossings)
- traffic channeled into reduced space

Many warning signs use graphics to warn of a hazardous condition ahead. Note the sign shown above. The hill blocks your line of sight and view of the hazard.

Traffic controls can be complex, especially at intersections where rural highways cross. Identify them early and know their meanings so you can avoid conflicts.

### Roadside Hazards

Consider the existing conditions in selecting a safe speed. Rural roads, especially older, narrow, and less traveled ones, present hazards.

Shoulders may be uneven with the edge of the roadway, soft, or narrow. Danger may be only a few feet away. Bridges, guardrails, bushes or trees may be near the road's edge. Sign posts may only be a few feet away from the actual roadway. A steep slope might run from the shoulder down to a drainage ditch.

Entrances to businesses, homes, or fields are always points of possible conflict. Be alert for these areas. Drivers ahead of you could decide at the last moment to turn right or left.

Trees, shrubs, or piles of plowed or drifted snow create line-of-sight restrictions. Drivers trying to enter the roadway may not be able to adequately see traffic. They may turn out into, or across, your path of travel.

## What Do You Think?

Federal law no longer mandates a maximum speed limit. Do you think there should be a maximum national speed limit? Why or why not?

### Review It

1. What roadway conditions are common to rural driving?
2. What factors need to be considered in selecting a safe speed?
3. What advance information do traffic controls provide?

## Activity

**Small Group Activity** This activity will help students to define the characteristics of rural roadways. List on the chalkboard the road features to the right. Divide the class into groups of five. Ask each group to identify an example of each of the listed situations on local roads. After the groups have compiled their lists, have them answer the following questions for each item on their lists. Which locations involve line-of-sight restrictions? What causes the restriction? Which locations require reduced speed and why? After adequate time, have the groups report their findings to the class.

bridges
bushes close to the road
crowned roads
gravel roads
guardrails
narrow lanes
newly paved roads
objects close to roadside
paved roads in need of repaving
roads with no shoulders
roads with potholes
sharp curves

## Explain

Point out how traffic controls provide drivers with a cue that something could affect their path of travel or line of sight. Discuss that when a traffic sign indicates a road entering from the right, it is actually alerting the driver to the possibility that a vehicle may enter the path of travel.

## Discuss

Draw students' attention to the photograph. Ask: Assuming the photo was taken from your view as the driver, how would you describe your target? (The target is at the horizon in the center of the right lane.) What do you see in the target area? (a hillcrest) What do you see to tell you that there will be a closed front zone? (Hillcrest will create a line-of-sight restriction to your front zone. The warning sign tells you that there will be a STOP sign causing a closed front zone.)

## 3 Assess

### Answers to Review It

1. Wide open spaces and less traffic are common in rural areas. (p. 196)
2. Factors that affect safe speed selection include other highway users, inclement weather, hills, curves, intersections, and very narrow roads or lanes. (p. 196)
3. Traffic controls provide information and warning of hazards you cannot yet identify, major intersections ahead, or traffic channeled into reduced space. (p. 197)

# Using Basic Skills in Rural Areas

## 1 Focus

### Summary

This lesson focuses on how the IPDE Process should be used in rural driving, safe vehicle handling in a curve, the rural situations that require increased following distance, and how to enter a multi-lane rural highway.

### Vocabulary

**New:** *advisory speed sign, median*

**Review:** *line-of-sight restriction, orderly visual search pattern, risk, tailgate, 12–15 second range, warning sign, zone*

## 2 Teach

### Discuss

Draw students' attention to the photograph at the bottom of the page. Ask: If you were the driver behind the red truck, what conflicts might occur in your path of travel? (The right-front zone is closed by a car that may pull into your path of travel. The black truck ahead of you is attempting to make a left turn. With oncoming traffic in the left lane, the driver may not make the left turn before you get there. The construction sign warns of changes to your path of travel.)

A seemingly quiet rural traffic scene can change quickly with little or no warning. Risk is present whenever and wherever you drive, but you can manage the level of risk by applying the IPDE Process.

### Applying the IPDE Process

Rural driving typically involves driving at higher speeds. The faster you drive, the greater your chance of having a severe collision. You have less time to identify and respond to a situation or hazard. You may be forced to make an emergency response. Sudden responses at higher speeds increase the risk of losing control of your vehicle.

While traveling on rural roads, there are many ways your zones can become closed. To best apply the IPDE Process, you must manage your speed control. The slower your speed, the more time you have to solve problems. One or two additional seconds can make a great difference in your ability to successfully apply the IPDE Process and manage space. Apply the IPDE Process whenever you drive.

Maintaining vehicle control at higher speeds is more difficult than at lower speeds. It takes longer to stop. Excessive braking or steering can result in a skid and loss of vehicle control.

Drive at a speed where you know you will be able to brake and steer your vehicle without losing control. Assess road conditions and the amount of traction available. Adjust your speed to conditions. Always

Where on this road might conflicts occur?

198 Unit 3 Driving in Different Environments and Situations

## Teacher's Resources

**Resource Book**
Roadway Sheets 1, 5, and 6, pages 4–5, 12–15

**Demonstration Overheads**
Overheads G and H

 **Video 2**
Segment on the IPDE Process in Rural Areas

**In-Car Checklists**
In-Car Checklist 24

What do the signs indicate about the curve ahead?

drive at a speed that allows you to stop or swerve to avoid a collision.

## Visual Search Pattern

Remember the orderly visual search pattern described in Chapter 4? Apply those same techniques in rural areas. In your 12–15 second search range look for clues of hazards that have the potential of closing your front zone. Higher rural speeds extend the actual distance covered by your 12–15 second search area compared to lower speeds.

Strive to maintain a 12–15 second visual lead. This is the distance your vehicle will travel in the next 12 to 15 seconds. The higher the speed, the greater that distance will be. Maintaining a 12–15 second visual lead will help you to identify hazards early. It also gives you time to predict and execute an appropriate response.

## Driving on Two-Lane Roads

Knowing about some common, but important, characteristics of rural roads will help you handle them safely. Some of these characteristics include curves, warning and advisory signs, hills, and intersections.

**Curves** Rural roads typically have many curves. Collisions occur at curves because speed on the approach is too great. Before approaching a curve, you likely will notice a yellow warning sign that warns of a potential hazard (a curve) ahead. Warning signs are usually placed anywhere from 250 to 700 feet before the actual hazard. A warning sign for a curve has a curved black arrow on it. The sharper the curve of the arrow, the sharper the roadway curve ahead.

Curve warning signs often have **advisory speed signs** posted below

## SAFE DRIVING

Driving and using a cellular phone or reading a map can be dangerous. Get out of traffic, stop, and then make the call or read the map.

## Demonstrate

Demonstrate how speed affects the ability to gather information for effective processing. Place 30 or more ordinary objects on a tray and cover it to hide the objects from the students. Examples of items you could use include a book, a candy bar, a rubber band, a soda can, and a tennis ball. Tell students that they will have five seconds to look at the contents of the tray and one minute to write down what they saw. Uncover the tray and let students look at the contents for five seconds and then cover the tray. Instruct students to write down what they saw.

After one minute have students put their pens and pencils down. Ask students if they had adequate time to gather information from the tray. Repeat the activity allowing students to look at the tray for fifteen seconds. Ask how many students felt they performed better the second time than the first. Ask: How does time relate to solving traffic problems when traveling fast as compared to traveling slower? Make the point that in order to use the IPDE Process, there must be time to gather all the information.

## Discuss

Draw students' attention to the photograph at the top of the page. Ask: What is in your target area? (a closed front zone caused by a very sharp curve to the right) As you get closer to the curve, where do you want to direct your searching? (Turn your head to the right at a 45-degree angle before steering into the curve.)

## Activity

**Model Car Activity** This activity will give students an opportunity to practice a visual search pattern for rural roadways. Divide the class into groups of three and assign three roles: driver, instructor, and observer. Give each group one model car and Roadway Sheets 1 and 5 from **Resource Book,** pages 4–5 and 12–13 to represent rural roadways. Have the driver position the car on an approach to a curve. Have the instructor read the steps for approaching a curve from page 67 of Chapter 4 and ask the driver to explain and perform each step. The observer provides feedback to the driver and the instructor. Repeat the activity until each student has played each role. After adequate time you can use overhead transparencies to give the class feedback for each step of the orderly visual search pattern.

## Demonstrate

Demonstrate how speed can cause a vehicle to go out of control at a curve in the road. You will need a ten-inch plastic plate and a golf ball for this demonstration. Tell students to observe the demonstration and to be prepared to discuss how it applies to a vehicle entering a curve. Hold the plate in the palm of one hand so that the eating surface is parallel to the floor and place the golf ball in the channel on the outer perimeter of the upside-down plate. Move your arm in a circular motion in order to make the ball move around the plate in the channel. Have the ball move slowly while staying within the channel. Then increase the rotational force until the ball flies out of the channel.

Ask: What effects did you notice that speed had upon the control of the ball? (As the ball moved at a slow speed, it was able to stay in the channel. This represents staying in the driving lane while approaching a curve in the road. When the ball traveled faster, it eventually was not able to stay in the channel. This represents skidding off the roadway.)

What type of restriction do the shrubs create? Are there any other hazards?

them on the sign post. These indicate suggested travel speeds when conditions are ideal. Follow the recommended speeds, and when conditions are not ideal, use a slower speed. Natural forces work to push you to the outside of the curve when you travel at higher speeds.

When you approach a curve, follow these steps:

1. See the curve in your target area.
2. Check your rear zone.
3. Check your left-front zone for oncoming traffic.
4. Check your right-front zone to determine if it is open or closed to your line of sight and path of travel.
5. Stay in lane position 1.
6. If the curve is sharp, lightly apply your brakes before you turn the steering wheel.
7. As you get closer to the curve, look in the direction the road curves. See if your path of travel is going to be open.

8. Once you are beyond the mid-point of the curve, begin to accelerate gently if conditions permit.
9. Evaluate your new target area and search for zone changes.

**Hills** Unless they have very steep slopes, hills are usually not marked. Hills restrict your line of sight. Slow as you approach the crest of the hill. Take lane position 1 as you crest the hill. Look for oncoming traffic and an escape path to the right.

**Intersections** In Chapter 7 you learned about how to handle intersections. Follow the same procedures for rural intersections.

Rural intersections can vary a great deal. Some intersections may have traffic lights; others may just have STOP signs. Early identification of traffic controls will help you predict potential conflicts.

A typical rural intersection is one where a side road crosses a main road. The side road will usually have the STOP sign. Tall crops, trees, or shrubs create line-of-sight restrictions that can block the vision of drivers at the edge of, or across from, an intersection.

Treat driveways like intersections. Look well in advance for clues of driveways, such as:

• loose gravel projecting into the main road
• electrical, phone, and other utility lines crossing the road
• reflectors marking a driveway
• mailboxes, typically located at the edge of, or across from, a driveway

200 Unit 3 Driving in Different Environments and Situations

## Activity

**Model Car Activity** This activity will give students an opportunity to practice the steps used to approach a curve as listed on this page. Divide the class into groups of three and assign three roles: driver, instructor, and observer. Give each group one model car and Roadway Sheets 5 and 6 from **Resource Book,** pages 12–15. Have the instructor read each step and ask the driver to explain and demonstrate how it is performed. The observer provides feedback to the driver and the supervisor. Repeat the activity until each student has played each role.

## Special Needs

Review reasons why drivers speed. Brainstorm why drivers may enter a curve too fast. List ways to prevent speeding into a curve. Patience and quick information processing may be a problem for these students. They must be aware of the early warning signs for curves or danger areas.

When discussing following distance with these students, emphasize that they need three or more seconds to have more thinking time to respond to hazards.

## Following Traffic

Establishing and maintaining at least a 3-second following distance is very important in rural areas. At high speeds, a hazard can quickly develop into a conflict. A 3-second following distance provides you space and time to prevent conflicts under normal conditions.

In special situations, you should increase your following distance to four seconds or more. A longer following distance gives you more control when you are

- being tailgated
- driving on a steep downhill slope
- following a motorcycle
- following a snowplow
- pulling a loaded trailer
- following a large vehicle (truck, motorhome, or bus)
- driving on wet or icy roads

Keeping at least three seconds gives you an open front zone. This helps to give you control over the actions of other drivers. When other drivers do dangerous things, it is less likely to affect you if you are following at a distance of three seconds or more.

### Driving on Multilane Roads

Many rural roads have four or more lanes of traffic. Posted speed limits usually are higher on two-lane rural roads. Unlike interstate highways, multilane roads may have intersections rather than exit and entrance ramps. Some intersections may have a two-lane road crossing a large four-lane road; others may involve two major multilane roads that cross.

**Multilane Roadways with Center Lines** Some multilane roadways may only have a yellow line (dashed or solid) separating high-speed traffic moving in opposite directions. Drivers should never cross a solid yellow line or double yellow lines except to make a left turn or clear an obstacle blocking their lane. Whenever you cross a yellow line, you are responsible to do so safely.

**You Are the Driver!**
You are driving behind this car. Is your following distance adequate?

Chapter 10  Driving in Rural Areas  **201**

## Explain

Point out that a good time to practice measuring following distance is when you are a passenger in a vehicle. Remind students how to measure the following distance. Explain that when the vehicle they are riding in is following another vehicle, they should take a guess at how many seconds of following space the vehicle has. Then use a marker to count off the actual space. Suggest that they count by saying, "1001, 1002, 1003" and so on to count off the seconds until they reach the marker.

## Discuss

Draw students' attention to the *You Are the Driver!* photograph on this page. Ask: Is your following distance adequate? (no, not for the speed on a rural highway).

## Activity

**Class Activity** Use the photograph on this page to ask these questions: What do you see in the target area? (There is a hillcrest.) What zone changes do you identify within your 12–15 second range? (There is an intersection with a STOP sign and a line-of-sight restriction to the right-front zone caused by the barn.) Are you able to identify a dip in the road located after the intersection? (Notice how you can see a change in the roadway's elevation shortly after the intersection.) What problem is a driver likely to have if the vehicle drifts onto the shoulder of the highway? (There is a drop-off from the paved surface of the highway to the dirt-grass area of the shoulder. There also is an outward slope to the shoulder. If the vehicle drifts onto this shoulder, a braking action could cause the car to skid.)

## Demonstrate

Use **Demonstration Overheads G** and **H** to help students identify line-of-sight restrictions on curves and hills and to discuss how to deal with them. Place a small object (such as the cap from a tube of toothpaste or a small bottle) on the transparency as a wild card. Ask the class what it could represent. For example: Use **Demonstration Overhead H** and place the wild card on the yellow center line directly at the hill's crest. It would represent an oncoming vehicle. Place the wild card to the right side of the road at the crest, and it could represent a disabled vehicle on the other side of the hillcrest. For each problem, generate discussion as to what would be the best lane position and speed selection.

**Divided Roadways** Divided roads always have lanes of traffic moving in opposite directions separated in some way. The division may be simply a guardrail or a **median.** A median is an area of ground separating traffic that moves in opposite directions. A median can be a few inches to several feet wide, as seen here.

If you need to cross a multilane highway, cross each half of the multilane road as though it were a one-way street. If a large enough crossover area exists, move into it after you cross the first lanes of traffic. Stop, look for a large enough gap. You will be turning into the fastest lane of traffic, so you may need to look for a gap of six seconds or greater.

**Lane Choice** Whenever possible, drive in the right lane on a multilane highway, unless signs indicate otherwise. The left lane is usually for passing or preparing to turn left.

**Turning at an Intersection** When leaving a multilane roadway, turn right from the right lane. When

making a left turn, turn from the lane nearest the center line or median strip.

Some intersections may have special turn lanes for right and left turns. To turn, check your rearview mirrors for any possible conflicts in your rear zone. Signal your intention to turn at least five seconds before the actual turn because speeds are much higher on rural multilane roads.

Signaling well in advance gives traffic behind a chance to adjust speed and position to avoid any conflicts. If turning left, keep your wheels straight until you start your turn. If you are hit from behind, you will not be pushed into oncoming traffic.

If you see a vehicle approaching at a high speed from behind, forget your turn, accelerate quickly, and proceed straight ahead across the intersection to avoid being hit from behind. To do this safely, you must be aware of the conditions in the intersection.

**Entering a Multilane Road** Follow these procedures if you are on a side

A median strip safely separates high-speed traffic that moves in opposite directions.

## Activity

**Class Activity** Draw students' attention to the photograph on page 203. Ask: Where do you think the truck in the median came from? (the side street) From all the gaps in the left lane of the northbound traffic that you are able to see, which would be a suitable gap for the truck to enter? (the gap between the third and fourth cars from the bottom of the photo) What is the difference between a southbound and northbound vehicle wanting to make a left turn? (There is no left turn lane for southbound traffic; therefore, it would most likely be prohibited.)

To make a left turn from a side road onto a multilane highway, a median strip provides a safe place to wait for a gap.

road and wish to enter a multilane roadway:

- To turn right, check to the left and right of where your target area is located. Make sure the left, front and right zones will be open. Enter the nearest right lane as you turn. Steer toward your target and accelerate quickly to the prevailing speed. Change lanes only after you clear the intersection and reach the prevailing speed.
- Left turns require larger gaps than right turns. First, cross the lanes on your side of the roadway. Choose a time when no traffic is approaching in the lane just across from the center line. Then turn into the nearest lane. Accelerate more quickly to the prevailing speed than you would for a right turn.

Entering the roadway from a driveway presents problems similar to entering from a side road. Oncoming drivers may not see you due to a line-of-sight restriction. Though drivers on multilane roadways may have advance warning signs of intersections ahead, there rarely are such signs for driveways.

### Review It

1. How should you apply the IPDE Process when driving on rural roads?
2. What steps should you take to safely handle a curve?
3. List five situations that require more than a 3-second following distance.
4. What is the procedure for entering a multilane rural highway?

## Demonstrate

Use **Video 2** Segment on The IPDE Process in Rural Areas to demonstrate various strategies for rural driving.

## 3 Assess

### Answers to Review It

**1.** Manage your speed control and use your orderly visual search pattern. (p. 198)

**2.** Students' answers should include the nine steps on page 200.

**3.** Students' answers should include any five of the following situations: being tailgated, driving on a steep downhill slope, following a motorcycle, following a snowplow, pulling a loaded trailer, following a large vehicle, and driving on wet or icy roads. (p. 201)

**4.** To turn right, check your target area and front zones, enter the right lane as you turn, and accelerate to prevailing speed. To turn left, watch for a safe gap and cross the lanes on your side of the road. When it is safe, turn into the nearest lane and accelerate. (p. 203)

## Background

### Left Turns on Divided Highways

When drivers are making left turns from multilane divided highways, the use of a turn opening in the median strip, as the photo on this page shows, can be very helpful. However, drivers sometimes get confused as to which side of the median's opening should be used. Do they drive to the right or to the left? The *Manual on Uniform Traffic Control Devices* recommends drivers keep to the left to allow traffic from both directions to execute left turns without crossing each other's paths.

When there is a yellow line separating the two holding lanes, the driver should move to the right of the median opening. This may occur when a left turn is made only from one direction and entry into the median is possible from a side street. Also, a STOP sign and a stop line are on one side of the median and control where the car should be positioned. If a STOP sign and line are on the right side, the vehicle should be on right side. A driver should always look into the turn to gather all information before making and executing the decision.

# 10.3

# Passing and Being Passed on Rural Roads

## 1 Focus

### Summary

This lesson focuses on the procedure for passing on rural roads including two-lane and multilane roads and no-passing situations. Driver responsibilities when being passed also are addressed.

### Vocabulary

**Review:** *zone*

## 2 Teach

### Demonstrate

Use **Demonstration Overhead A** to demonstrate passing on a two-lane roadway. Use two transparency cars—one yellow and one white. Place the white car in position to be passed and the yellow car to do the passing. Ask questions of the class to develop the meaning of all of the steps for preparing to pass on page 204 and for executing a pass on page 205.

### Demonstrate

Use **Content Overhead 7** to review roadway markings for passing. See pages 31–32 for more information.

### Objectives

1. List the checks to make before passing another vehicle.
2. List the steps for passing on a two-lane rural road.
3. List situations where passing should never be attempted.

### SAFE DRIVING

Although some states allow passing drivers to exceed the speed limit, it is safer to pass within the posted speed limit.

---

Main body right side

Passing on a two-lane road carries a higher level of risk than passing on a multilane road. When you pass on a two-lane rural road, you will be in the same lane as oncoming traffic for a short period of time. Use parts of the IPDE Process to help lower your risk when passing.

### Passing

Passing another vehicle is really a three-stage procedure. You decide to pass, prepare to pass, and execute the maneuver.

#### Deciding to Pass

Before you pass a vehicle, assess your situation. Ask yourself these questions:

- Is it worth it to pass?
- Is it legal to pass?
- Is it safe to pass?

Consider passing only if you can answer "yes" to all of these questions. The major responsibility for passing safely belongs to the driver who is passing.

#### Preparing to Pass

Take these actions when preparing to pass:

- When you find your front zone closing to less than three seconds, identify the reasons. Is the vehicle ahead going slower than the posted speed limit? Is it likely to be making a turn? If so, hold back and eliminate passing. If conditions indicate you should

pass, continue the steps in preparing to pass.

- Check roadway markings and signs ahead. Make certain that passing is legal.
- Look ahead to your target area. Is your line of sight adequate? You may have to move to lane position 2 to get the best view ahead. Is it safe to pass?
- Check the roadway conditions. If traction is limited, you probably should not pass. If you must pass under poor conditions, you will need to accelerate gently and gradually while passing.
- Check the roadway shoulders and sides ahead that might cause the vehicle you are passing to swerve to the left.
- Check your rearview mirrors for any potential conflicts to your rear zone. If a vehicle is rapidly closing in behind you, delay your pass.
- Glance quickly over your left shoulder. Make sure there are no vehicles in your blind spot.
- Check the oncoming traffic lane again. Make sure no vehicles are approaching and there is enough space for you to pass safely. Any approaching vehicles must be at least 20–30 seconds away. You will need 10–15 seconds to complete the pass. *If in doubt, do not pass.*
- Check ahead for driveways and side roads. Make sure no traffic will be entering the roadway.

---

## Teacher's Resources

**Content Overheads**
Overhead 7
**Demonstration Overheads**
Overheads A, G, H
 **Video 2**
Segment on Passing
**In-Car Checklists**
In-Car Checklist 25

---

## Activity

**Small Group Activity** Divide the class into groups of four. Tell students to pretend they are on a two-lane roadway following a slow-moving truck. Ask them to discuss how they will handle the situation. How are they likely to feel? How closely will they follow the truck? What will determine if they will have an opportunity to pass? What if they are not able to pass—what will it cost them in terms of time and stress? After adequate discussion, have the groups report their findings to the class.

After you have determined that your left-front zone (the path to be taken) is clear, you are ready to pass. If you identify a problem, slow down and establish at least a 3-second following distance. Repeat the steps to prepare to pass again. In time these steps will become part of your normal driving behavior.

### Executing a Pass on Two-Lane Roads

Follow these steps when passing on a two-lane road:

1. Get in your ready position by keeping at least 3 seconds of following distance.
2. When it is safe to pass, signal for a left-lane change and glance over your left shoulder to check your blindspot.
3. Change lanes smoothly.
4. Accelerate at least 10 mph faster than the vehicle you are passing. *All passing should be done within the speed limit.*
5. Make your final evaluations. If you notice a problem that is within 20–30 seconds ahead, you can still change your mind—provided you have not gone beyond the vehicle you are trying to pass. If it is clear, continue to accelerate to the proper speed.
6. Maintain your speed. Remain in the left lane until you can see two headlights of the vehicle you are passing in your inside rearview mirror.
7. Signal for a right-lane change.
8. Return smoothly to the right lane. Do not slow down.

Chapter 10 Driving in Rural Areas **205**

## Activity

**In-Class Driving Rehearsal** Form the classroom desks into a two-lane roadway. Have the students form into two opposing columns. One column of students collectively will represent a driver preparing for and passing. The other column will represent zone changes and things that can go wrong while passing. (The students will each represent a different problem for the passing driver. For example: One student could say he or she is a car that makes a left turn into the passing lane from a driveway.) Each of the passing students will take turns demonstrating how to do one step of preparing to pass and executing a pass on two-lane roads. With textbook turned to pages 204 and 205 in hand, ask the first student in the passing column to explain the meaning and demonstrate "when you find your front zone closing . . . ." The first student in the problem column is to state a problem that could take place during that step. The second student in line takes the next step, etc. After going through all the steps one time, have the groups switch roles, and begin with the end of the column.

## Discuss

Discuss that sometimes when driving on multilane highways, passing on the right may be necessary. Point out that the driver should signal for the lane change and should check the inside and outside rearview mirrors and blind spots. If traffic is clear, the driver should change lanes smoothly and cancel the turn signal.

## Demonstrate

Use **Demonstration Overhead H** to depict the situation shown in the top illustration on this page. Use **Demonstration Overhead G** to depict the situation shown in the bottom illustration on page 207.

The solid yellow line means that drivers in the right lane must not pass. They would be unable to see vehicles coming over the hill.

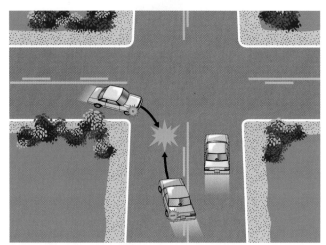

Passing at or near an intersection is dangerous. A driver turning from the crossroad might enter your lane.

9. Cancel the signal. Adjust your speed and vehicle's lane position. If you are passing a large truck, you will need more time and space. It is a good idea to make sure that you have at least 30 seconds of clear space when passing a large truck.

### No-Passing Situations

No-passing situations are marked by solid yellow lines, as shown in the pictures. Signs can also mark no passing zones. Rectangular white signs on the right side of the road will indicate DO NOT PASS; yellow pennant-shaped signs are on the left side of the road and indicate NO PASSING ZONE. Passing is illegal and unsafe when

- your line of sight is restricted
- space is narrow, and your front zones are closed
- cross-traffic is present, even if no warning signs or lines are present

How do these conditions apply to the following situations?

**No Passing on Roads Going Uphill** Passing is not allowed within 700 to 1,000 feet before the top of a hill. Notice that the driver of the yellow car in the top picture has too great a restricted line of sight to pass safely.

**No Passing at Intersections** Passing is illegal within 100 feet of an intersection. Slow down when approaching an intersection.

**Other No-Passing Situations** There are other situations where passing is prohibited or should not be attempted. Examples include:

- Within 100 feet before a railroad crossing.

## Activity

**Small Group Activity** This activity will help students develop judgment about when to pass or not pass. Divide the class into groups of five. Ask each group to evaluate the situations shown in the photographs on pages 194, 198, 199, and 201. For each photograph the students should determine if it is or is not safe to pass and explain their decisions. After adequate time, have the groups share their findings with the class.

- On a two-lane bridge or underpass.
- On curves, where your line of sight is so restricted you can not see around the curve.
- When the vehicle ahead is traveling at or near the speed limit. Remember, *most passing should not require a driver to exceed the posted speed limit.*
- When your line of sight is limited by fog, snow, or rain.
- When several vehicles are ahead of you, pass only one vehicle at a time.
- When you cannot complete a pass before the start of a no passing zone
- Any time oncoming traffic is too close.
- When you will be stopping or turning soon.

### Passing on Multilane Roads

You need to be cautious on a multilane highway with only a center line to separate traffic. Check all lanes going in your direction before you pass on a multilane roadway. Make sure that no one will move into your front zones taking away your path of travel. The vehicle you intend to pass should be going several miles per hour slower than you.

Generally, all passing should be done in the left lane. Passing on the right is often illegal. Sometimes, it becomes necessary to use the right lane to pass a vehicle. Remember the procedures for passing and follow them every time you pass.

Do not pass on bridges and near underpasses, since they might not have shoulders to provide escape areas.

Passing is illegal in both lanes around this curve.

Chapter 10 Driving in Rural Areas **207**

## Explain

The act of passing has the potential to be the most dangerous action a driver can take. The decision to pass should be very deliberate and well calculated. Before deciding to pass, a driver should ask: What will I gain by passing? Often drivers pass without evaluating the potential gain and, more importantly, the potential loss. When there are many vehicles on a two-lane roadway, a successful pass will not be beneficial to the driver because the next vehicle ahead is traveling at the same speed as the vehicle that was just passed. Each pass is a high-risk maneuver. Each successful pass only presents the driver with another vehicle to pass and another risk.

## Explain

Being in a hurry is a common cause of driver error. Leaving earlier for destinations will eliminate the rushed or pressured feeling and should reduce the desire to pass or reduce the number of bad passing decisions. High levels of risk become acceptable based upon the perceived, rather than the actual, need.

## Explain

Point out that while another driver is passing you, there is risk for you as well as for the driver doing the passing. If the vehicle that is trying to pass you is involved in a head-on collision situation, your vehicle also is likely to be involved. While the vehicle is passing you, it creates a closed zone taking away an escape path in that direction. You can help the driver of the passing vehicle by reducing your speed.

 **Assess**

## Answers to Review It

**1.** Check the following: That passing is legal, roadway markings and signs, line of sight, roadway conditions, roadway shoulders, mirrors for approaching traffic, left blind spot, oncoming lane, and driveways and intersections ahead. (p. 204)

**2.** Students should list the steps provided on page 205.

**3.** You should not pass when a solid yellow line is in your lane, when line of sight is restricted, when space is narrow and front zones closed, when cross-traffic is a hazard, when approaching the crest of a hill, at an intersection, when approaching a bridge or underpass, and when on a curve. (pp. 206–207)

Glance regularly into your mirror to see if a car is about to pass you.

### Being Passed

If you are the passing driver, you have the majority of the responsibility for passing safely. However, you also have responsibilities when being passed.

You must be aware that another vehicle is passing, even when the driver of the vehicle fails to properly warn you. Check your mirrors often to identify vehicles approaching from the rear.

When another vehicle passes, it may help to move to lane position 3. By doing so, you provide an extra space cushion and provide the passing driver with a better view ahead.

If the passing driver is having a difficult time trying to pass, slow down to help that driver. *Intentionally speeding up while being passed is illegal.* Only speed up when the driver has decided not to pass and drops back. This will quickly open a space behind you.

### Review It
1. What are the checks you should make when preparing to pass?
2. What are the steps for passing on a two-lane rural road?
3. In what situations should you never pass?

## Background

**Tailgaters and Passing** Refer to the Background note in Chapter 9 on page 180. Knowing the three types of tailgaters will help a driver determine where and when a driver is likely to pass you. If a charger is behind you, look ahead to see where the pass may occur. Reducing speed and moving into lane position 3 will be an invitation for the pass to occur. If a habitual tailgater is behind you, concentrate more on the front zone to make sure no sudden stops occur.

In rural areas you may encounter vehicles, animals, and situations that you do not encounter on city streets. Apply the same driving techniques in rural areas as you would in urban areas. For example, in a rural area you would respond to a tractor pulling a plow the same way you would a large truck or bus in the city. Applying the IPDE Process whenever you drive will maximize your ability to more easily recognize conflicts and solve problems.

### Slow-Moving Vehicles

A **slow-moving vehicle** is one that is unable to travel at highway speed. Most tractors and other large farm machinery can only travel at lower speeds. They are not designed, nor intended, as means for personal transportation.

Identify slow-moving vehicles as early as possible. The sooner you do, the more time you have to respond. Apply the IPDE Process. Most slow-moving vehicles have an orange and red triangular sign like the one in the picture.

When driving at a higher speed, you will rapidly close in on a slow-moving vehicle. If you find yourself closing to less than three seconds, be aware that you may have a problem. Slow down and prepare to pass when it is safe to do so. Stay far enough behind and in a lane position that gives you the ability to check for oncoming traffic.

### Animals

Animals can be a problem on rural roads. They can easily become frightened and dart out into your path. Each year millions of dollars in property damage occur when animals and motor vehicles collide.

Hitting a large animal can result in damage to your vehicle, and serious injury or death to you, your passengers, and the animal. In areas where large wild animals are common, reduce your speed and search

The vehicle has closed your front zone. Is it safe to pass in this situation?

## Objectives

1. Explain how to pass a slow-moving vehicle.
2. Explain the steps to take to deal with animals on or along the roadway.
3. Explain how you can allow hazards to separate when meeting traffic.

# Rural Situations You Might Encounter

 **Focus**

### Summary

This lesson focuses on situations you might encounter while driving in rural settings. Slow-moving vehicles and animals are addressed. Information is provided about meeting oncoming traffic and railroad crossings.

### Vocabulary

**New:** *slow-moving vehicle*

**Review:** *line-of-sight restriction, zone*

 **Teach**

### Discuss

Direct students' attention to the photograph. Point out that the slow-moving vehicle has closed your front zone. Ask: Is it safe to pass in this situation? (No, there is an oncoming vehicle.)

### Explain

When you see a slow-moving vehicle approaching from the opposite direction, you should be alert to the possibility of another vehicle trying to pass the slow-moving vehicle. This could mean an oncoming vehicle in your lane.

## Teacher's Resources

**Resource Book**
Roadway Sheets 1 and 5, pages 4–5, 12–13
Teacher's Instructions, page 47

## Explain

Explain that seeing an animal warning sign should have very specific appropriate behavior associated with it. When the warning sign is seen, it should cue the driver to prepare for the best space management if an animal should suddenly leap into his or her path. Without mental preparation, a driver is most likely to be surprised and react to, rather than prepare for, the animal's appearance. A driver has the ability to anticipate that an animal may dart into the vehicle's path of travel. The driver can have a mindset that prepares him or her for the best action to take when an animal appears.

a much wider area than usual. If you see one animal, anticipate the presence of more.

You may see warning signs where large animals are common. If you see an animal warning sign, let it serve as a clue, and do the following:

- Evaluate your left- and right-front zones for line-of-sight restrictions from which animals could enter.
- Check your rear zone to determine if you will be able to slow or stop quickly.
- Check your left-front zone to see if it will be open for an escape path.

If you happen to observe one or more animals crossing the road, stop well in advance. Be patient and wait until it is clear to proceed. Do not get out and attempt to hurry any stragglers across the road. You are much safer in your vehicle.

When a smaller animal suddenly appears in your front zone, you may be tempted to brake hard or swerve. Follow the same procedures

as above. Be careful not to risk a more serious collision by trying to avoid the animal.

**Meeting Oncoming Traffic**
Meeting traffic on two-way roads can be dangerous. Very little space separates you from oncoming traffic. With traffic moving at higher speeds, a head-on collision can cause serious damage, injury, or death.

If you identify an oncoming vehicle, check your right-front zone for an alternate path of travel and for line-of-sight restrictions. Try to adjust your timing to have the oncoming vehicle approach you when you have the least problem in your right-front zone.

Use these guidelines for selecting a place to meet oncoming traffic.

- Separate the hazards in or next to your path of travel. Adjust your speed to deal with only one hazard at a time. In most situations slowing down is your best action. Imagine the hazard is a narrow bridge as in the picture. You judge that you might meet the

210   Unit 3  Driving in Different Environments and Situations

## Background

**Deer-Vehicle Collisions** According to the *Road Management & Engineering Journal,* 90 percent of deer-vehicle collisions occur between dusk and dawn. This is a time when many animals are active and when motorists have the most difficulty detecting them. In some areas, signs are posted to warn motorists. There also are efforts to limit animal populations in some areas.

Other countermeasures have been tried. Some drivers mount whistles on their bumpers that are only audible to deer in an effort to frighten the deer away from the roadway. Some states have

built expensive underpasses that allow deer to cross beneath highways, and some have set up diversionary feeding areas away from highways. Such practices are expensive with limited effectiveness. Some highway departments have installed roadside reflectors that reflect light from approaching vehicles and bounce it off the right side of the roadway into the woods. The reflection is a low-intensity red beam not seen by drivers. Studies on the effectiveness of the reflectors have had mixed results.

approaching vehicle just about the time you approach the hazard. By slowing down and letting the approaching vehicle clear the hazard first, you separate the hazards.

- Meet where the most space is available. When you must meet oncoming traffic, try to select a location where you have an open right-front zone to move into if you need to swerve to avoid conflict.
- If you are meeting a line of vehicles, slow down and move into lane position 3 to provide a little more space between you and the approaching vehicles.

Oncoming drivers may cross into your lane on rural roads for several reasons. Examples include:

- a blowout, hitting or swerving to avoid a pothole or other debris on the road
- an unexpected loss of traction due to ice, snow, rain, or mud
- a distraction

**ANIMAL COLLISIONS** More than 4 percent of all collisions reported in the United States involve animals, and that percentage is rising. Most of these collisions occur with deer—about 500,000 a year. Collisions with animals are more likely to occur at dawn or dusk. Most of these collisions occur in October and November during the deer mating season.

- an impairment due to alcohol, other drugs, or medications
- an impairment due to illness or fatigue
- a vehicle failure

**Meeting Slow-Moving Vehicles**

When you see a slow-moving vehicle or stopped vehicle in your left-front zone, check to the rear of the vehicle for a passing vehicle. The passing

**Discuss**

Discuss how slow-moving vehicles can be a problem when they are traveling in the same lane or in an oncoming lane. When a slow-moving vehicle is in the same lane, you have a fast closure rate. When a slow-moving vehicle is in an oncoming lane, other vehicles may pull around to pass, thereby creating potential for a head-on collision.

Adjust your speed and position to allow the hazards to separate.

Chapter 10 Driving in Rural Areas **211**

**Activity**

**Model Car Activity** This activity will give students an opportunity to practice using the guidelines for selecting a place to meet oncoming traffic on rural roadways. Divide the class into groups of three. Give each group two model cars, a wild card, and Roadway Sheets 1 and 5 from **Resource Book,** pages 4–5 and 12–13 to represent rural roadways. Have them demonstrate those behaviors listed on page 211 and see how many additional situations each group is able to think of that could cause a head-on collision.

## Demonstrate

Demonstrate the recovery time eyes need after being over-stimulated by headlights. See **Resource Book,** page 47 for construction of the test box and the other supplies you will need. Have a student look into the box through the viewer's opening. Hold one of the number cards against the display end to make the number visible to the student. Ask another student to record how many seconds it takes the student to read the correct number. With the student still looking into the box opening, shine a flashlight into the student's eyes for three seconds. Then hold another number card in the display opening. Have the recorder keep track of how many seconds lapse before the student is able to read the numbers. (It could be 10–20 seconds.) Repeat the demonstration with different students. Then have students do the Cross Curricular activity below to see how far a driver can travel without being able to see details in the path of travel.

 **Assess**

### Answers to Review It

**1.** Identify slow-moving vehicles as early as possible. Slow down and prepare to pass when it is safe. (p. 209)

**2.** Students should list the steps provided on page 210.

**3.** Students should include examples listed on pages 210–211.

Not all railroad crossings have lights and gates.

driver may not see you. If you are applying the IPDE Process, you will check your right-front zone and move into lane position 3, or onto the road shoulder if necessary. Always know where you have an open zone into which you can move. If you do not have an open zone, brake enough to create space for yourself or the passing driver.

### Meeting at Night

Be alert when driving at night. You need to be aware of vehicles in the distance. Keep your windshield clean.

At night, headlights shining over the crest of a hill can warn you of an approaching vehicle. If you have your high beams on, switch them to low beam anytime you are within 500 feet of an approaching vehicle. Do not look directly into the headlights of the approaching vehicle; you could be temporarily blinded, especially if their headlights are on high beam. Glance instead to the right edge of the road. There is often a white line to help you maintain position in your lane.

### Railroad Crossings

Many railroad crossings do not have complete controls (flashing lights and gates). In rural areas, trains travel at high speeds. Be alert for railroad-crossing warning signs. Slow and check left and right before crossing. Never cross a railroad crossing until you know it is absolutely safe to do so. Remember, when a vehicle and a train collide, the *train always wins.*

### Review It

1. Identify the steps in safely passing a slow-moving vehicle.
2. List the steps to take to deal with animals on or along the roadway.
3. Explain two examples of how you can allow hazards to separate when meeting traffic.

## Cross Curricular

**Mathematics** Have students calculate how far they would travel before their eyes could recover after being over-stimulated by headlights. Tell the class that a car travels at the rate of approximately 1.5 feet per second per mile. If a car is traveling at 50 mph how many feet per second is the car moving? (75 feet). If it takes 10 seconds before a driver can see details, how far would the car have traveled? (750 feet) Point out that this is the distance a driver would travel without being able to see details, such as a child running into the roadway.

## Facts and Figures

According to Operation Lifesaver, more than 50 percent of collisions at railroad crossings occur where active warning devices (gates, lights, bells) exist. Most of the remaining collisions at railroad crossings without active warning devices take place on rural roadways. Drivers cannot take lightly the danger of a railroad crossing because it has only a warning sign to control it.

Driving through mountains and deserts can challenge your patience, energy, and skills. Make certain your vehicle is in good working condition. Adhere to the speed limits and warning signs. Particularly be aware of your vehicle's gauges while driving.

### Mountain Driving

Mountain driving presents more problems and special situations than driving in flatter areas. The effects of gravity are constantly at work. Gravity will make your vehicle go faster when going downhill, and slow your vehicle when going uphill.

Mountain roads often zigzag across a mountain with a series of sharp turns called **switchbacks.** A switchback bends sharply in the opposite direction. In the picture, the sign warns that a switchback is ahead.

### Driving Up a Mountain

Accelerate steadily when driving uphill to maintain speed because gravity is pulling your vehicle downhill. If the slope is steep, you might need to downshift to a lower gear. An automatic transmission vehicle will downshift by itself. On extremely steep inclines, when extra power is needed, you may need to manually shift an automatic transmission vehicle into a lower gear (LOW 1 or LOW 2).

When you can't see around a curve, reduce your speed, move into lane position 1, and tap your horn. Evaluate your path of travel through the curve. An oncoming vehicle could cross into your lane because it has built up too much downhill speed before the curve. Driving too fast is a leading cause of collisions in the mountains.

At the switchback this road reverses direction.

## Teacher's Resources

No *Drive Right* resources are needed for teaching Section 10.5.

# Special Driving Environments

 **Focus**

## Summary

This lesson focuses on the safety precautions drivers should take for mountain and desert driving.

## Vocabulary

**New:** *pull-out area, runaway vehicle ramp, switchback*

**Review:** *downshifting*

 **Teach**

## Explain

Explain that if the uphill grade is steep enough to keep the automatic transmission shifting back and forth, the driver should downshift manually. The overdrive in an automatic transmission is not the best gear for mountain driving, whether going uphill or downhill. The engine and transmission will operate more efficiently when the driver manually controls the gear setting for the driving conditions. Generally, the second gear—one gear higher than the lowest gear—is the best gear to use in mountain driving.

### Objectives

1. Describe special safety precautions for mountain driving.
2. Describe special safety precautions for desert driving.

## Demonstrate

Demonstrate the need for controlling speed when entering a curve while on a downgrade. For this demonstration you will need: a model car, a plastic plate, and a cardboard tube from a roll of paper towels. Cut the cardboard tube in half lengthwise to form a "chute." Cut one end at 45 degree angles to either side to form a point. Place the plate right-side up on a level table. Place the point of the cardboard chute inside the plate toward the outer perimeter (the outer perimeter acts like a banked road). Hold the tube at a 30–40 degree angle to create a downward tilt. Insert the car into the top of the chute and allow it to roll down into the perimeter of the plate. It should be able to roll around the perimeter, which represents a curve on a level road. Then tilt the plate toward the chute to represent driving into a curve with an upgrade. Insert another car. Notice it doesn't travel very far around the plate's perimeter; in fact, it will roll backward toward the chute. Now, tilt the plate away from the chute to represent a curve with a downgrade. Place the car into the chute. It will not stay in the perimeter of the plate. This represents the car skidding off the roadway. The steeper the downgrade, the slower the speed into the curve must be in order to maintain control of the vehicle.

Loaded trucks, recreational vehicles (RVs), and vehicles pulling trailers move more slowly up mountain roads. Follow these vehicles at their speeds and maintain at least a 4-second following distance. Some mountain roads have locations called **pull-out areas** where an additional right lane is provided for slower-moving vehicles. When slower-moving vehicles move into such areas, it allows faster-moving vehicles an opportunity to safely pass and proceed.

### Driving Down a Mountain

When driving down a mountain road, downshift *before* you start traveling downhill. Never coast downhill because the vehicle will speed up and you might lose control.

Some mountain roads have areas along the side of the road for cars to safely pull over and stop.

Adjust your speed with an occasional use of the brakes. Do not ride your brakes, because doing so can overheat them and make them fade. If you are braking often, shift to a lower gear; your transmission can help slow you down and can reduce the need to brake as much. Finally, keep your speed low enough to maintain control and stay in your lane.

Large vehicles can experience serious brake problems going downhill, especially on long steep downgrades. Some mountain roadways have **runaway vehicle ramps,** as the picture on the next page shows. Runaway ramps provide a place for vehicles, especially large trucks, to safely get out of traffic and stop when their brakes are no longer effective.

### Weather in the Mountains

Fog, snow, and ice can make mountain driving even more difficult. Some mountain roads become blocked with excessive snow. Weather conditions can suddenly change in the mountains. If weather conditions are poor, call the highway department or state police hotline. Tune your radio to frequencies that update travelers on weather and road conditions. These frequencies are often identified on blue driver-service signs along the side of the road.

### Effects of Altitude on Drivers

High altitudes can affect the driver, causing shortness of breath, faster heartbeat, and headache. Lower amounts of oxygen at higher altitudes can reduce concentration and

## Cross Curricular

**Geography** Have students report on the driving environments they might encounter while driving from their home to a specific destination in another state. Have students highlight their route on a map and describe the various environments they expect to encounter. As an alternative, have students select a city anywhere in the world and then locate another city approximately 200 miles away. Have them highlight their route and describe the driving environments they might encounter on a trip between the two cities.

cause drowsiness. Effects can be worse for tired drivers. Do not drive if you feel these effects or are tired.

### Effects of Altitude on Vehicles

The thin mountain air can affect your vehicle's engine. Climbing power is reduced. Acceleration can become sluggish. The temperature of the water in your radiator may increase significantly and could cause overheating. If your air conditioner is on, turn it off.

Check your gauges and warning lights often. If the temperature light comes on, safely pull over and stop to let the engine cool. Turning on your heater may help remove some of the heat built up in the engine.

Engines can get extremely hot when driving in mountains. When you shut off your engine, vapor lock occurs. The engine will not start because the fuel cannot be pumped in a gaseous state. Allow the engine to cool. Then try restarting it.

If you do a lot of mountain driving, have your vehicle serviced regularly for maximum performance.

### Desert Driving

Deserts are often hotter and larger that most drivers realize. Desert driving is hard on the driver, the car, and the roadway. Always prepare yourself and your vehicle in advance.

### Effects of Heat on Drivers

Intense daytime heat can cause great stress on you when driving long distances. The sameness of the scenery can lull you into a false sense of

**You Are the Driver!**
How would this ramp help a runaway vehicle?

security. The glare from the intense sun can reduce your vision.

To help reduce the effects of hot desert driving, you should
- wear good quality sunglasses to help reduce the effects of sun glare
- plan more frequent stops and change drivers often
- carry an ample supply of water

### Effects of Heat on Vehicles

Extensive desert driving requires more frequent vehicle service. Battery fluids should be checked daily if the battery is not self-contained. Radiator fluids should be checked at every fuel stop.

CAUTION: *Never remove a radiator cap from a hot radiator.* The steam and hot fluid could burn you. Check the fluid level in your radiator recovery tank. If you must check the level in the radiator, wait until your engine cools.

Check tire pressure regularly. Tire pressure will increase as you drive. Do not reduce the tire pres-

## Discuss

Draw students' attention to the *You Are the Driver!* photograph. Ask: How would this ramp help a runaway vehicle? (The ramp would provide a place for a runaway vehicle to safely get out of traffic and stop when its brakes are no longer effective on a downhill grade.)

## Special Needs

Have students create bulletin board displays of special driving situations with tips on how to drive in each situation. Preparing the display and discussing the driving techniques will help them understand the reasoning behind the techniques and remember them.

Visibility can be very limited in a sand storm.

### SAFE DRIVING

Do not drive over water-covered roads or streams in the desert. The water may be deeper and running more swiftly than you think.

sure below the lowest recommended pressure. A tire with low air pressure will run hotter, which could result in tire failure.

### The Desert Roadway

Well-designed highways with gentle curves invite higher speeds. Be careful of the sandy roadside shoulders, because your wheels could sink quickly into the sand if it is not firm and compacted. If you need to pull over, make sure the location you select is firm and out of traffic.

### Sandstorms and Dust Storms

Windy conditions in deserts often create visibility problems. Avoid driving in sandstorms or dust storms. If you encounter such a storm, slow immediately and find a safe place to pull over. Turn off your headlights and turn on your hazard flashers. Wait in your vehicle until the storm passes.

If you must drive, go slowly. Use your low-beam headlights to help see and be seen. As soon as possible after the storm, have your oil, and

oil and air filters changed. Dirt particles from the storm that remain in your fuel injection system and engine oil can cause excessive engine wear and damage.

### Flash Floods

A flash flood is a sudden unexpected rush of water from heavy rain. A flash flood can develop quickly and unexpectedly. This condition is especially dangerous in the desert because the ground washes away easily. If you encounter a flash flood, seek higher ground immediately and wait for the water to recede. Stay away from creeks or natural drainage areas.

### Review It

1. What safety precautions should you take for driving in mountains?
2. What safety precautions should you take for desert driving?

216 Unit 3 Driving in Different Environments and Situations

## Reviewing Chapter Objectives

### 1. Characteristics of Rural Traffic

1. What are rural roadways like? (196)
2. What factors should you consider when selecting a safe speed? (196)
3. How do traffic controls inform, warn, and regulate drivers on rural roads? (196–197)

### 2. Using Basic Skills in Rural Areas

4. How should you use the IPDE Process in rural driving? (198)
5. What steps should you take to safely handle a curve? (200)
6. What are some rural situations that require increased following distance? (201)
7. How do you enter a multilane rural highway? (203)

### 3. Passing and Being Passed on Rural Roads

8. What checks do you make before passing another vehicle? (204)
9. What steps should you take when passing on a two-lane rural road? (205–206)
10. In what situations should you never attempt passing? (206–207)

### 4. Rural Situations You Might Encounter

11. How do you pass a slow-moving vehicle? (209)
12. What steps should you take to deal with animals on or along the roadway? (209–210)
13. How can you allow hazards to separate when meeting traffic? (210)

### 5. Special Driving Environments

14. What special safety precautions should you take for mountain driving? (213–214)
15. What special safety precautions should you take for desert driving? (215–216)

## Projects

### Individuals

**Investigate**  Research to find out which states have a 55 mph speed limit and which do not. Also examine the number of traffic fatalities that occur each year in each state. Is there a correlation between speed limit and number of fatalities?

**Use Technology**  Use the Internet to find out current conditions on mountain roads (either in your state or another state). Discuss with the class what precautions you would take if you were driving in those conditions.

### Groups

**Debate**  Divide your group into two and debate the issue of mandatory speed limits. One side should argue for keeping a 55 mph speed limit; the other side should argue for allowing speeds greater than 55 mph.

**Demonstrate**  Make a group poster that illustrates the hazards or other situations you might encounter while driving on a rural road. Present the poster to your class. Group members should take turns explaining what each illustration means and what to do if the hazard or situation is encountered while driving.

## Teacher's Resources

**Skills and Applications Workbook**
page 37–40

**Tests and Activities**
Chapter 10 Activities 10-1 and 10-2, pages 83–84
Chapter 10 Test A and Test B, pages 85–88

**TestWorks CD-ROM**
Chapter 10 Test

## Reviewing Chapter Objectives

**10.1** Characteristics of Rural Traffic
See Answers to Review It on page 197.
**10.2** Using Basic Skills in Rural Areas
See Answers to Review It on page 203.
**10.3** Passing and Being Passed on Rural Roads
See Answers to Review It on page 208.
**10.4** Rural Situations You Might Encounter
See Answers to Review It on page 212.
**10.5** Special Driving Environments
See Answers to Review It on page 216.
    For additional information refer to the specific page(s) in parentheses after each question.

## Projects

Some of the projects can be assigned at any time while others are more closely tied to the content presented in the student text. The page number where the topic is introduced is indicated.
    **Investigate:** p. 196
    **Use Technology:** p. 214
    **Debate:** p. 196
    **Demonstrate:** p. 196
The results of student projects will vary.

# Review

## Answers to Check Your Knowledge

1. c
2. d
3. b
4. a
5. Divided
6. gravity
7. flash flood

## Answers to Review Vocabulary

8. pull-out area (a)
9. advisory speed signs (c)
10. runaway vehicle ramp (e)
11. median (f)
12. slow-moving vehicle (b)
13. switchbacks (d)

## Answers to Think Critically

Students' answers will vary. For information related to the question refer to the page(s) indicated.

1. Most roadway miles (about 82 percent) in the United States are rural. Many rural roads present hazards such as uneven shoulders; bridges, guardrails, and bushes or trees near the road edge; and slow-moving vehicles and animals. Rural driving involves driving at higher speeds, which results in the greater chance of a severe collision. (p. 198)

2. Student's answers will vary, but should mention that a driver must continuously check left- and right-front zones for line-of-sight restrictions and should be prepared for an animal to dart into his or her path of travel. (pp. 209–210)

## Chapter Test

### Check Your Knowledge

**Multiple Choice** Copy the number of each sentence below on a sheet of paper. Choose the letter that best completes the sentence or answers the question.

1. Posted speed signs indicate
   (a) the safest speeds possible in any conditions.
   (b) minimum speeds under ideal conditions.
   (c) maximum speeds under ideal conditions.
   (d) suggested speeds that legally may be exceeded.
2. Which of the following provides advance information and warning about approaching driving situations?
   (a) roadways    (b) road shoulder conditions
   (c) posted speeds  (d) traffic controls
3. What effect does increased speed have on the time available to complete the IPDE Process?
   (a) increases time available
   (b) decreases time available
   (c) varies with number of hazards present
   (d) no effect
4. Solid yellow lines indicate
   (a) no passing situations.
   (b) conditions are favorable for passing.
   (c) you must pass with caution.
   (d) hazards in the roadway.

**Completion** Copy the number of each sentence below. After each number, write the word or words that complete the sentence correctly.

5. _____ roadways have separated lanes of traffic moving in opposite directions.
6. The force that makes your vehicle go slower when driving uphill is called _____.
7. A _____ is a sudden unexpected rush of water from heavy rain.

### Review Vocabulary

Copy the number of each definition in List A. Match the definition in List A with the term it defines in List B.

**List A**

8. place on mountain roads for vehicles to safely get out of traffic when their brakes are not effective
9. sign posts on a curve with suggested speeds for ideal conditions
10. additional right lane on mountain roads for slower moving vehicles
11. area of ground separating traffic moving in opposite directions
12. vehicle unable to travel at highway speed
13. turns that bend sharply in the opposite direction

**List B**

a. pull-out area
b. slow-moving vehicle
c. advisory speed signs
d. switchbacks
e. runaway vehicle ramp
f. median

### Think Critically

Write a paragraph to answer each question.

1. Why do you think that rural collisions account for a majority of highway deaths?
2. What types of animals might you expect to see in areas with animal-warning signs? What should you do if you pass an animal-warning sign while you are driving?

**1.** What hazards do you see? Which zones are open? How would you respond to avoid the hazards?

**2.** You are driving the yellow car, and a car is attempting to pass you. What should you do to help the passing driver?

**3.** You are approaching a curve. What do you identify and predict? What actions should you take to safely handle the situation ahead?

**4.** You are driving the yellow car. What possible conflicts do you identify? What should you do?

Chapter 10 Driving in Rural Areas **219**

## Answers to Decision Making

**1.** The hazards are: a bicycle; an oncoming vehicle that might turn left or cross the center line in an attempt to pass the bicycle; a vehicle from a side road that might pull into your lane; and a curve. Currently your front zone is still open, however that could change due to action of the oncoming vehicle or the vehicle on the side road, should it pull out into your lane. You should respond by releasing the accelerator, covering the brake, and being prepared to move to the right portion of your lane.

**2.** If the driver continues to speed up, brake and drop back. If the driver drops back, accelerate.

**3.** You identify a curve ahead and predict an oncoming vehicle might come into your lane. Slow down well before the curve. Keep checking the farthest point you can see ahead through the curve, in case an oncoming driver might occupy part of your lane. Stay to the right; this will give you a little extra safety cushion in case an oncoming vehicle appears in the curve.

**4.** You identify that you are approaching a situation of limited space. The oncoming large truck is straddling the center lane line, and the guardrail has closed your right-front zone. You should adjust your speed so that you and the truck do not meet on the narrow bridge. Let the truck cross first, and move into lane position 3.

**Student Features**

**Teacher's Edition**

| | Student Features | Teacher's Edition |
|---|---|---|
| **Chapter 11**<br>**Driving in Rural Areas** | You Are the Driver! *p. 221* | Projects *p. 220*<br>Special Needs *p. 221* |
| **11.1 Characteristics of Expressway Driving** *pp. 222–224*<br>• List five reasons why expressways have lower collision rates than other highways.<br>• Describe four different types of expressway interchanges.<br>• List strategies for low-risk driving on expressways. | Safe Driving Tip *p. 224* | Demonstrate *p. 224*<br>Activity *pp. 223, 224* |
| **11.2 Entering an Expressway** *pp. 225–228*<br>• Explain how to enter an expressway properly.<br>• Describe four possible entrance problems.<br>• Explain why entering an expressway from the left is more hazardous than entering from the right. | Safe Driving Tip *p. 228* | Demonstrate *p. 228*<br>Activity *pp. 225, 226, 227, 228*<br>Special Needs *p. 227* |
| **11.3 Strategies for Driving on Expressways** *pp. 229–234*<br>• Explain how to use the IPDE Process to achieve a safe path of travel.<br>• Describe when following distances should be increased for expressway driving.<br>• Tell what actions to take when you are being tailgated.<br>• Describe three actions that should be automatic when you are changing lanes on an expressway. | What Do You Think? *p. 230* | Demonstrate *pp. 230, 231, 233, 234*<br>Activity *pp. 232, 233, 234*<br>Special Needs *p. 230* |
| **11.4 Exiting Expressways** *pp. 235–237*<br>• Explain how to apply the IPDE Process to exit an expressway.<br>• List the steps for exiting an expressway.<br>• Describe three possible exiting problems. | | Demonstrate *p. 236*<br>Activity *p. 236* |
| **11.5 Special Expressway Problems** *pp. 238–240*<br>• Describe the cause of highway hypnosis and tell what actions to take to stay alert.<br>• Explain what to do if your vehicle becomes disabled.<br>• List three key factors that contribute to safe driving on expressways. | Did You Know? *p. 238*<br>Safe Driving Tip *p. 239* | Activity *pp. 239, 240* |
| **Assessment** | Reviewing Chapter Objectives *p. 241*<br>Projects *p. 241*<br>Chapter Test *p. 242*<br>Decision Making *p. 243* | Answers *pp. 242–243* |

**Companion** *pp. 72–75*
**Spanish Handbook** *pp. 23–24*

**Resource Book**
Roadway Sheets 6 and 7,
*pp. 14–17*
Classroom Activity, *p. 49*

**Resource Book**
Roadway Sheets 6 and 7,
*pp. 14–17*
**In-Car Checklist** 26

**Demonstration Overhead I**
**Video 2** Segment on
Entering an Expressway

**Resource Book**
Roadway Sheet 2, *pp. 6–7*
**In-Car Checklist** 27

**Demonstration Overheads
I, J**
**Content Overhead 21**
**Video 2** Segment on Driving
on Expressways

**In-Car Checklist** 28

**Demonstration Overhead K**
**Content Overhead 22**

**Resource Book**
Roadway Sheet 2, *pp. 6–7*
Teacher's Instructions, *p. 50*

**Skills and Applications
Workbook,** *pp. 41–44*
**Tests and Activities**
Chapter 11 Activities 11-1
and 11-2, *pp. 91–92*
Chapter 11 Test A and
Test B, *pp. 93–96*

**TestWorks CD-ROM**
Chapter 11 Test

# Technology Resources

## Audio-Visual and Computer Resources

AAA Foundation for Traffic Safety, *Freeway Driving,* video, 8 minutes

AAA Foundation for Traffic Safety, *driver-ZED* CD-ROM

Interactive Driving Systems, Inc., *Approaching Curves,* video, 28 minutes

Interactive Driving Systems, Inc., *Following Time and Space,* video, 25 minutes

Interactive Driving Systems, Inc., *Habit Development,* video, 16 minutes

Interactive Driving Systems, Inc., *Mottola's Zone Control for Awareness,* video, 38 minutes

Interactive Driving Systems, Inc., *Rear Zone Control,* video, 27 minutes

Interactive Driving Systems, Inc., *Searching Intersections,* video, 20 minutes

Interactive Driving Systems, Inc., *Targeting,* video, 15 minutes

Interactive Driving Systems, Inc., *Zone Control Practice,* video, 18 minutes

Safety Industries, Inc., *Freeway Driving*, video, 11 minutes

3I Company, *Driving in Traffic: Expressway Hazards,* video, 22 minutes

## Kits, Equipment, and Other Resources

Interactive Driving Systems, Inc., *Back Seat Decision Maker*

Go Online
PHSchool.com
**For: Chapter 11 online activities**
**Visit: PHSchool.com**
**Web Code: cak-9999**

# Chapter 11

## Driving on Expressways

### Chapter Overview

Chapter 11 discusses steps for entering, driving on, and exiting expressways. Students will also learn about special problems encountered on expressways.

### Chapter Vocabulary

*acceleration lane, common speed, controlled-access highway, deceleration lane, entrance ramp, exit ramp, highway hypnosis, merging area, velocitation, wolf pack*

220

### Teacher's Resources

For students to use as they read the chapter:

**Companion**
pages 72–75

**Spanish Handbook**
pages 23–24

### Projects

Review the projects described on page 241. Some of the projects can be assigned at any time while others are more closely tied to the content presented in the student text.

# CHAPTER 11
## Driving on Expressways

### You Are the Driver!

Imagine you are driving the sport utility vehicle on the entrance ramp to this expressway. The traffic on the expressway is heavy and is moving fast. The driver of the vehicle behind you may be in a hurry and is following you too closely. How can you communicate with that driver? What action should you take as you enter the acceleration lane?

In this chapter you will learn the necessary skills for entering, driving on, and exiting expressways. You will also learn strategies for low-risk expressway driving.

**Go Online**
PHSchool.com

**For:** Chapter 11 online activities
**Visit:** PHSchool.com
**Web Code:** cak-9999

221

## Introducing the Chapter

Discuss how expressways are different from other highways. Discuss possible hazards that the vehicles entering and exiting an expressway must avoid.

## You Are the Driver!

Students should imagine that they are driving the sport utility vehicle on the entrance ramp. Ask: How should you react to the car that is following you too closely? Discuss the importance of using the IPDE Process during all phases of expressway driving. Emphasize that planning ahead and predicting the actions of others are even more critical at the higher speeds allowed on expressways and interchanges.

## Special Needs

Expressways are different from other roadways. Special needs students often are more nervous on expressways than most new drivers. Calm their fears by using many of the visual skills taught in the *Drive Right* program. Give them more entry experiences during in-car instruction, and encourage parents to provide more practice on expressways. Students need to feel confident. Use the Demonstrate strategies and Model Car Activities suggested in the teacher notes.

# Characteristics of Expressway Driving

## Focus

### Summary

In this lesson students will be introduced to the characteristics of expressway driving. The advantages of expressways as well as the physical characteristics of expressway interchanges are introduced. Strategies for safe driving on expressways are included.

### Vocabulary

*controlled-access highway*

## 2 Teach

### Explain

Explain that the cloverleaf interchange is composed of two design features. One part is a diamond interchange and the other part is a cloverleaf. The cloverleaf design allows drivers to make left turns without interfering with the crossing traffic flow. This is accomplished through grade separation by driving over or under the crossing traffic. The diamond component of the interchange allows drivers to make right turns.

### Objectives

1. List five reasons why expressways have lower collision rates than other highways.
2. Describe four different types of expressway interchanges.
3. List strategies for low-risk driving on expressways.

An expressway is a limited-access or **controlled-access highway.** Vehicles can enter and leave expressways only at interchanges. Expressways include interstate highways, freeways, turnpikes, toll roads, parkways, and some beltways. Most of these terms are used interchangeably and designate any type of controlled-access highway.

### Advantages of Expressways

Expressways are designed for low-risk higher-speed travel. Despite the high speeds and heavy traffic, you are safer on expressways than on other highways.

Expressways have fewer collisions for five main reasons:
- Cross traffic is eliminated.
- Expressways have a median or barrier between opposing lanes of traffic.

Cloverleaf interchange

**222** Unit 3 Driving in Different Environments and Situations

- Pedestrians, nonmotorized vehicles, and slow-moving vehicles are not permitted on most expressways.
- Wide shoulders and extra-wide underpasses provide good escape paths.
- Expressway signs are designed to help drivers anticipate conditions well ahead.

### Expressway Interchanges

These pictures show the most common types of expressway interchanges. Interchanges are places where drivers can cross over or under as well as enter or leave the expressway.

#### Cloverleaf Interchange

A cloverleaf interchange has a series of entrance and exit ramps that resemble the outline of a four-leaf clover. This type of interchange enables drivers to proceed in either direction on either highway.

#### Diamond Interchange

A diamond interchange is used when a road that has little traffic crosses a busy expressway. A complete cloverleaf is not needed because left turns by exiting traffic can be made easily on the less-busy road.

#### Trumpet Interchange

A trumpet interchange is used where a side road forms a T intersection with an expressway.

## Teacher's Resources

**Resource Book**
Classroom Activity,
   page 49
Roadway Sheets 6 and 7,
   pages 14–17

## Cross Curricular

**History** Have students research the history of the interstate highway system and prepare a short report. Consider having students work in pairs or small groups. Ask students to answer some or all of these questions in their reports: When was the system conceived and when did construction begin? What was the initial cost projection for the system? What, if any, military considerations were incorporated? How were the numbers assigned?

### All-Directional Interchange

An all-directional interchange is used in complicated intersections with high-volume traffic. From this interchange, traffic is channeled in many different directions.

### Safe Driving Strategies

Although expressways have advantages compared to other types of roadways, collisions on expressways are often more serious. Higher speeds often place greater demands on both drivers and vehicles.

When driving on expressways, you should travel at about the same speed as other vehicles. Driving faster than other traffic may cause you to be constantly passing other vehicles. If you drive too slowly, you can block the smooth flow of traffic and become a hazard. Conform to posted minimum and maximum speed limits. Have your headlights on at all times so you are more visible to other drivers.

Use the following strategies to help you become a safe expressway driver.

### Prepare Yourself and Your Vehicle

Preparation for driving on any expressway should include a travel plan, regardless of the length of the trip. For short trips, know the name, route, or number for both the entrance and exit you will use.

For long-distance trips, plan stops for food, fuel, and rest. Make every effort to stay alert, use the IPDE Process constantly, and be aware of traffic conditions in all your zones at all times.

Mechanical failure can occur even on a short trip. Keep your vehicle in

Diamond interchange

Trumpet interchange

All-directional interchange

Chapter 11  Driving on Expressways  **223**

## Discuss

Have the students evaluate the trumpet interchange and compare it to the cloverleaf and the diamond design. State that the trumpet design is used when there are only two directional choices rather than three from each direction of travel. Ask: When making a change in direction to the left with a trumpet interchange, will it be necessary to cross the other highway? When making a directional change to the right, will it be the same as using a diamond interchange?

## Activity

**Small Group Activity** This activity will help students understand the function of the cloverleaf and diamond interchanges. Make copies of the Expressway Interchange sheet from **Resource Book,** page 49 and distribute to students. Divide the class into groups of three. Ask the group to plot out directional changes at the interchange. Ask them to record their discovery about making directional changes at a cloverleaf interchange. (Vehicles making a directional change to their right—northbound changing to eastbound—will exit before going over or under the crossing highway by using the diamond part of the interchange. Vehicles making a directional change to the left—northbound changing to westbound—will exit after going over the crossing highway by using the cloverleaf part of the interchange.)

## Demonstrate

Demonstrate the patterns of traffic flow on an expressway. Show a video or slides that illustrate expressway driving, including various types of interchanges and components of the entrances and exits. Show a slide or a short video segment, and then ask students to explain what they are seeing. You can use an existing video or make your own video or slides for this demonstration.

## ③ Assess

## Answers to Review It

**1.** Five reasons why expressways have fewer collisions are (1) cross traffic is eliminated because there are no intersections; (2) expressways have a median strip or barrier between opposing lanes of traffic; (3) pedestrians, nonmotorized vehicles, and slow-moving vehicles are not permitted on most expressways; (4) wide shoulders and extra-wide underpasses provide good escape paths; and (5) expressways are designed to help drivers anticipate conditions ahead. (p. 222)

**2.** Four types of expressway interchanges are cloverleaf, diamond, trumpet, and all-directional. (pp. 222–223)

**3.** Prepare yourself and your vehicle, build experience gradually, concentrate on driving, and cooperate with others. (pp. 223–224)

Until you gain experience, avoid driving in heavy rush-hour traffic.

**SAFE DRIVING**

Traveling at the same speed as other traffic on the expressway does not mean that you should keep up with drivers who are exceeding the speed limit or driving too fast for conditions.

top condition to guard against mechanical failure when driving on expressways.

**Build Experience Gradually** When you first drive alone on an expressway, choose a time when traffic is light. Avoid driving in the heavy rush-hour traffic like this photograph shows. Practice entering and exiting several times before driving in heavier traffic. When you are driving in very light traffic, practice lane changes even when there are no vehicles to pass. Once you develop self-confidence, you will be better prepared to drive in heavier traffic.

**Concentrate on the Driving Task** Traffic conflicts can develop more rapidly at higher speeds, especially on multilane expressways. Give full attention to the driving task and do not allow yourself to become complacent. Never lose sight of the fact that high-speed expressway driving can present a high degree of risk.

224  Unit 3  Driving in Different Environments and Situations

**Cooperate with Other Drivers** You must cooperate with others when driving on expressways. Resist the urge to challenge other drivers for any reason. Road rage, an extreme act of aggression, can be a serious factor leading to a major conflict in high-speed expressway traffic. React cautiously if someone cuts you off or moves into your front zone too soon.

## Review It
1. What are five reasons why fewer collisions occur on expressways than on other types of roadways?
2. What are four different types of expressway interchanges?
3. Explain what strategies you can use to become a low-risk driver on expressways.

## Activity

**Model Car Activity** This activity will help prepare students for using a cloverleaf interchange. Give students Roadway Sheets 6 and 7 from **Resource Book**, pages 14–17 to demonstrate a cloverleaf interchange. Have them demonstrate how to move the car into all 12 possible directional changes. Have them record when the diamond part of the interchange and when the cloverleaf part is used. Have them record when they will make a directional change before the underpass or overpass and when the change will be made after it.

**B**efore you enter an expressway, make sure you are using the correct entrance ramp. Guide signs mark most entrances and give the route number, direction, and name of a major city located in that direction. Many drivers have mistakenly tried to enter an expressway by using an exit ramp. To help prevent this error, most states post signs saying WRONG WAY or DO NOT ENTER.

The parts of an expressway entrance

If you start to enter at an entrance you do not want, go ahead and get on the expressway. You can then safely exit at the first opportunity.

### Expressway Entrances

Most expressway entrances have three parts:

- The **entrance ramp** gives you time to evaluate zone conditions and determine the best speed as you prepare to enter the expressway.
- The **acceleration lane** is usually long enough for you to search for a gap in which to merge and accelerate to the speed of traffic on the expressway. However, accelerating to expressway speeds in the acceleration lane is determined by the volume of traffic both on the expressway and in the acceleration lane.
- The **merging area** is the third part of an expressway entrance where vehicles blend into the expressway traffic. Evaluate how much time and space you have in your open front zones for merging into the flow of traffic. Try to merge at about the same speed as the vehicles in the nearest lane.

### Steps for Entering

Follow these steps to enter an expressway smoothly and safely:

1. Make sure the entrance is the one you want. Look for a red and white WRONG WAY or DO NOT ENTER sign.

Chapter 11 Driving on Expressways **225**

### Objectives

1. Explain how to enter an expressway properly.
2. Describe four possible entrance problems.
3. Explain why entering an expressway from the left is more hazardous than entering from the right.

---

# Entering an Expressway

 **Focus**

## Summary

This lesson focuses on entering expressways. It also addresses possible entrance problems.

## Vocabulary

*acceleration lane, entrance ramp, merging area*

 **Teach**

## Explain

When entering an expressway, driving at the correct speed on the entrance ramp gives you an opportunity to select a safe gap to enter. In general, entrance-ramp speeds should not exceed 40 mph. The slower the entrance ramp speed, the more time you will have to select a gap. A common mistake is accelerating to highway speed while on the entrance ramp before selecting a gap. This can cut in half the opportunity to enter a gap. For example, if an entrance ramp is 300 feet long and a vehicle is going 40 mph, the driver will have approximately five seconds to search for a gap. However, if the driver is going 60 mph on the same ramp, the driver will have only three seconds to search for a gap.

---

## Teacher's Resources

**Resource Book**
Roadway Sheets 6 and 7, pages 14–17
**Demonstration Overheads**
Overhead I
 **Video 2**
Segment on Entering an Expressway
**In-Car Checklists**
In-Car Checklist 26

## Activity

**Class Activity** This activity will help students understand the three parts of an expressway entrance area. Use **Demonstration Overhead I** and a transparency car to illustrate the three parts of the expressway entrance. Place the car at the beginning of the entrance ramp and ask students what they should attempt to accomplish at this point. After discussion, move the car to the acceleration lane and ask what would you try to accomplish here. Then, move the car to the merge area and ask what is to be achieved here.

## Explain

There are two kinds of gaps drivers should look for when trying to merge into expressway traffic—the gap between cars and the gap between two wolf packs of cars (see the illustration on page 231). The gap between the wolf packs is sometimes referred to as a break in traffic, a hole in traffic, or a gap between the packs. When attempting to merge onto a highway, the driver should first look for a break in traffic. This type of gap provides the best low-stress opportunity for entering the highway. When there is no obvious break in traffic, look for a gap between two vehicles. This gap needs to be at least four seconds.

## Demonstrate

Use Video 2 segment on Entering an Expressway to demonstrate how to select a gap and enter an expressway safely.

Make sure the entrance is the one you want. Check front and rear zones. Find a gap.

When in the acceleration lane, decide where to enter the gap.

Merge smoothly into traffic.

226 Unit 3 Driving in Different Environments and Situations

2. Once on the entrance ramp, check your front and rear zones. Signal and take quick glances through your left outside rearview mirror and over your left shoulder to find a gap in traffic where you can safely merge. Look for an entrance ramp signal light and be prepared to stop if it is red.

3. Once you are in the acceleration lane, gradually increase your speed. Continue to quickly glance over your left shoulder and through your outside rearview mirror. Decide when it is a safe time and place to merge into the gap in traffic.

4. Before entering the merging area, decide which vehicle to follow in the flow of the expressway traffic. As you enter the merging area, adjust your speed to match the traffic flow. Position your vehicle at a safe interval behind the vehicle you plan to follow. Merge smoothly.

5. Once on the expressway, cancel your signal and adjust to the speed of traffic. Keep a space cushion around your vehicle.

### Possible Entrance Problems

Entrance driver errors cause many conflicts and collisions on expressways. Many drivers feel insecure when they have to merge into fast-moving traffic. Short entrance ramps, short acceleration lanes, and high dividing walls also can cause entrance problems.

Using the IPDE Process at all expressway entrances is critical.

## Activity

**Class Activity** Ask students to observe traffic and detect gaps in various traffic environments while riding as a passenger during the next week. Announce the date when the results of this activity will be discussed in class. This could take place while riding on a school bus or while in another vehicle. Instruct students to study traffic patterns of the oncoming traffic in various traffic environments in order to detect gaps. Have them record what type of road it was and the time of day. They should record how many vehicles were grouped together in the cluster, how many seconds of time there were between the clusters, and how many vehicles were operating within the gap between clusters. Each student should record information of at least 10 different gaps. On the day the assignment is due, divide the class into groups of four and have students compare information and discuss what they observed.

- Make your visual checks and zone evaluations quickly. Identify possible problems on each part of the expressway entrance.
- Predict actions of other drivers.
- Decide on your entrance gap and speed.
- Execute your merge into traffic smoothly and safely.

**Entrance Ramp Problems** If you make an error and enter the wrong entrance ramp, continue onto the expressway. Drive to the next exit. *Never back up on an entrance ramp or on an expressway.*

If other vehicles are on the entrance ramp, adjust your speed to avoid conflict. Some ramps, particularly ramps with sharp curves, have yellow advisory signs posting a speed limit. Stay within the speed limit.

Begin looking immediately for a gap in traffic if the entrance ramp is short or there is no acceleration lane. If you have a closed front zone, reduce your speed to give the vehicle in front more time to find a gap. Check your rear zone and avoid a sudden slow or stop.

Some entrance ramps have high walls that divide expressway traffic and entering traffic. These walls restrict your line of sight to expressway traffic. On some ramps, you will be very close to the merge area before you can see the expressway traffic. Reduce your speed until you have a clear line of sight.

**Entrance Ramp Signal Lights** Some entrance ramps have signal lights to help space traffic entering the expressway. The lights are usually red

When the signal light on an entrance ramp is red, wait for the green light before proceeding onto the expressway.

and green. The timing of the signal lights is determined electronically by the volume of traffic at any given time. You must wait for the green light before entering the expressway, as the picture shows.

**Acceleration Lane Problems** During rush hours, the large number of vehicles entering and on the expressway can make it almost impossible to accelerate to expressway speeds. Under these conditions, try to match the speed of traffic around you.

Some entrances have very short acceleration lanes. In such cases, you usually do not have the space to accelerate to the speed of expressway traffic. You need a longer gap to enter traffic and accelerate to the traffic speed.

Make every effort to enter an expressway without stopping. A driver behind you might be looking for a gap and not realize that you are stopped. If you must stop, take these precautions:

1. Flash your brake lights to warn drivers behind you.

**Explain**

Entering and merging below the speed of traffic invites tailgating and encourages road rage. Learn how to predict the location of the gap in the traffic pattern and enter there.

## Activity

**Model Car Activity** Divide the class into groups of three. Give each group Roadway Sheets 6 and 7 from **Resource Book,** pages 14–17 and two model cars. Have one student driving the car entering the highway, another driving a car on the highway, and the third student evaluating how the two drivers perform. The two drivers should move their cars and explain their actions. Repeat the activity three times so that each student has an opportunity to play each role.

## Special Needs

Obtain slides or videos showing the driver's viewpoint. Give the students opportunities to see the various components of getting on an expressway to supplement text information. Have students practice getting on an expressway using Roadway Sheet 7 from **Resource Book,** pages 16–17. Make sure students follow the procedures explained in the text-book.

## Demonstrate

Use **Demonstration Overhead I** to illustrate the procedure for entering an expressway from the left. You will need to flip the overhead in order to position the entrance ramp on the left.

 **Assess**

## Answers to Review It

**1.** Students should list the steps identified on pages 225–226.

**2.** Possible problems are heavy expressway traffic; short entrance ramps and acceleration lanes; no acceleration lane; a vehicle ahead stopping, and high dividing walls. (p. 227)

**3.** When entering from the left, you merge into the lane used for higher speed traffic. Checking traffic over your right shoulder can be more difficult than over the left. (p. 228)

### SAFE DRIVING

If you have to stop before merging onto an expressway, you will need to accelerate more from a stopped position. Consider this as you determine the speed needed for your entry.

Entering an expressway from the left can be more difficult than entering from the right.

**2.** Pull onto the shoulder at the end of the acceleration lane or merge area.

**3.** You are now in an emergency situation. Wait for a large, safe gap. Signal and accelerate quickly as you join the traffic flow.

**Merging Area Problems** Adjusting your speed is critical to timing a smooth entrance into traffic. A closed front zone may cause you to reduce your speed and even to select a new gap. Once you are on the expressway, accelerate as you establish your safe following distance.

**Entrance Ramp on Left** Some expressway entrance ramps are located on the left of the expressway, as the picture shows. The acceleration lane merges into the far-left lane of expressway traffic. Since this lane is usually used for high-speed traffic, the potential for conflict is greater than when you enter from the right.

Checking fast-moving traffic over your right shoulder can be more difficult than checking to your left. Some vehicle roof supports and head restraints can obstruct your view of the oncoming expressway traffic. You might have difficulty seeing a motorcyclist or a very small car. Signal early as you look for a gap. When you see a gap, accelerate and merge into the traffic lane.

### Review It

**1.** What are the proper steps for entering an expressway?

**2.** What problems could make entering an expressway difficult?

**3.** Why is the chance for conflict greater when entering an expressway from the left than from the right?

## Activity

**Small Group Activity** Form class into groups of three or four. Have the groups read and discuss the possible entrance problems as listed in the text.

Once you are on the expressway, stay alert as you adjust to the constantly changing traffic scene. Use your IPDE Process continually. Use the process to predict any conflict and decide accurately how to respond.

### Applying the IPDE Process

Expressway driving can make using the IPDE Process more difficult than when driving on two-lane roads. Higher speeds, multiple lanes, and a heavier volume of traffic can make the Identify and Predict steps more difficult.

**Identify** Expressways are designed to give drivers a long sight distance. However, higher speeds and multiple lanes reduce the amount of visual information you can gather. You need to identify the volume of traffic around you, as well as signs, signals, and roadway markings. You also need to identify closed front zones early. Never allow yourself to become trapped between two large vehicles, as the driver in the picture has done.

Be aware of drivers who do not seem to have their full attention on the driving task. These may be drivers talking on cellular phones or reading a map. Increase your space cushion when you are around these distracted drivers.

**Predict** A predictable traffic flow is a safety feature of expressways. However, you must search ahead to your target area to watch for sudden slowing traffic or drivers changing lanes. Anticipate closed zones and points of conflict before they occur. Predict that a parked vehicle on the shoulder might suddenly pull onto the expressway or even back up. At a distance, a vehicle backing up may still look like it is moving forward.

**Decide** Speeds seem to magnify a driver's indecision. Yet faster driving speeds demand that you make quicker decisions. Last-second decisions and driving adjustments can change your safe path of travel into a closed zone or point of conflict. Interchanges can be high-collision areas since so many driver decisions are made there. Open zones can very quickly become closed zones.

**Execute** Execute your decisions smoothly. Avoid sudden moves.

The driver of this vehicle has become trapped with closed left-front and front zones and a line-of-sight restriction.

## Objectives

1. Explain how to use the IPDE Process to achieve a safe path of travel.
2. Describe when following distances should be increased for expressway driving.
3. Tell what actions to take when you are being tailgated.
4. Describe three actions that should be automatic when you are changing lanes on an expressway.

 **Focus**

## Summary

This lesson focuses on strategies for driving on expressways. Use of the IPDE Process is emphasized.

## Vocabulary

**New:** *common speed, wolf pack*

**Review:** *basic speed law, minimum speed limit*

 **Teach**

## Explain

Explain that you need to use an orderly visual search pattern to maximize the time to detect a zone change that can affect your path of travel. Search to your target area to see any problem at the earliest moment.

 **Teacher's Resources**

**Resource Book**
Roadway Sheet 2,
    pages 6–7
**Demonstration Overheads**
Overheads I and J

**Content Overheads**
Overhead 21

**Video 2**
Segment on Driving on Expressways

**In-Car Checklists**
In-Car Checklist 27

## Demonstrate

Demonstrate use of the lane-change position on the signal lever to avoid leaving it blinking after the lane change. Explain how to use only the tips of the fingers and not to let go of the steering wheel while the signal lever is softly touched. To demonstrate the proper technique in class, have the students hold a pencil in the right hand to simulate the signal lever. After they demonstrate correct behavior in the classroom, have them practice in the driver-education car with the ignition key turned only to the accessory position.

## Discuss

Discuss the *What Do You Think?* question. Ask: Should all states be required to post maximum speed limits on expressways?

## Discuss

Draw students' attention to the *You Are the Driver!* photograph. Ask: What should you do if you suddenly realize this is the exit that you want to take?

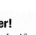

**What Do You Think?**

Some states do not have a maximum speed limit. Should all states be required to post maximum speed limits on expressways?

Signal early for every maneuver and maintain a safe following distance.

### Lane Choice

On the expressway, decide the best lane in which to drive. Generally, it is safer to drive in the right lane and pass on the left. Reserve the center and left lanes for drivers who are passing and for faster traffic.

When traffic is heavy in the right lane, especially at entrance ramps during rush-hour traffic, use the center or left lane to avoid conflicts in the far right lane. Drivers entering, as well as drivers on the expressway, share responsibility for protecting each other from conflict.

Large trucks and vehicles towing trailers are required to travel in the right lane on many expressways. Although you may sometimes share the right lane with them, let the traffic dictate the lane you will use. Avoid driving between two large vehicles. Do not straddle lane lines because this prevents the other drivers from maintaining their proper lane positions.

### Signs, Signals, and Roadway Markings

Part of your decision of lane choice is based on information from expressway signs, signals, and roadway markings. You are better able to maintain a safe path of travel and avoid making sudden last-second decisions if you

- know your destination
- read signs and roadway markings
- always think ahead

On some expressways, several overhead signs are posted at the same place. Scan the signs quickly to get the information you need to continue in a safe path. In many states, an overhead sign with a yellow panel indicates the exit lane, as shown in the picture. All traffic in this lane must exit.

Some overhead signs tell you if lanes are open or closed to traffic. A green arrow means that the lane is open for traffic. A yellow **X** over your

**You Are the Driver!**
What should you do if you suddenly realize this is the exit that you want to take?

230 Unit 3 Driving in Different Environments and Situations

## Background

**Lane Selection** Each lane of the expressway presents a certain amount of stress for drivers. Driving in the far-left lane is the most stressful of all lanes. This is where aggressive, competitive tailgaters are most likely to be found. Driving in the right lane has the least amount of stress from rear traffic, but the most stress from vehicles exiting and entering the highway. Because restrictions prevent trucks from driving in the left lane of certain roadways, the middle lane becomes their passing lane.

## Special Needs

Special needs students often need more direction to learn lane-change signal usage. Those with poor motor skills may not be able to learn it easily. Remind students that they will need to remember to check that the signal is off after a lane change. Have students practice using the method described above in Demonstrate. It is also important to provide supervised practice in a simulator or the driver-education car.

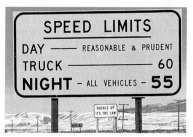
Some signs show special speed limits for different times of day and types of vehicles.

lane warns you that the lane will be closed ahead. In this case you must prepare to move into another lane. A red **X** farther ahead indicates that the lane already is closed.

Many expressways into and out of cities often have express lanes. In most cases, these lanes have very few entrances and exits. If you are not sure where your exit is, do not enter the express lanes. Otherwise, you may be forced to drive beyond your intended exit.

### Speed Limits

Most states post maximum speed limits on expressways. Some states have no maximum speed limit, and others post lower speed limits for trucks and larger vehicles.

When you drive in areas with no posted speed limit, follow the basic speed law. Drive at the speed that is safe and prudent for the weather and roadway conditions.

**Minimum Speed Limit** Driving too slowly could be very dangerous in fast-moving traffic and could cause rear-end collisions. A minimum speed limit is posted on many

expressways to keep traffic from moving too slowly. This speed limit is the lowest legal speed you can drive under ideal conditions. During adverse conditions such as rain, fog, snow, or slippery roadways, driving under the minimum speed limit is both legal and wise. Use the far right lane when you are driving at or under the minimum speed limit.

**Common Speed** If you drive at the **common speed,** the speed used by most drivers, you can better blend with expressway traffic. Sometimes the common speed is above the maximum speed limit. Resist the temptation to increase your speed to keep up with the faster vehicles. Drivers who exceed the common speed are likely to weave in and out of traffic to pass other vehicles. This practice is dangerous not only to the driver exceeding the speed limit, but also to other drivers on the expressway.

**Wolf Packs** A responsible driver tries to avoid bunches of vehicles known as **wolf packs.** Reduce your chances of being involved in a conflict by being a "loner" on the expressway. This may be difficult to do in today's high-volume expressway traffic. However, when you travel in the middle of a pack, all zones may be closed. Adjust your speed to avoid wolf packs. The picture shows two wolf packs. The driver of the yellow car in the center lane has wisely chosen to be a "loner" by driving between the packs.

### Following

The high speeds of expressway traffic demand that you maintain at least

Adjust your speed to avoid being in a wolf pack.

## Facts and Figures

**Common Speed** Vehicles get grouped together into clusters by chance during expressway driving. A study has shown that 75–80 percent of drivers travel at a common speed. About 15 percent travel above the common speed, and some 10 percent travel below the common speed. The driver traveling faster than common speed is likely to be an aggressive driver who weaves in and out of lanes to fight his or her way to the front of the pack. After making it to the front of one pack, the driver speeds through the space between packs to catch up to the next pack. When the driver catches up to the next pack, he or she weaves through that pack and repeats the process again and again. For the average trip of 30 miles, the aggressive driver might save only two minutes while subjecting himself or herself to 30 minutes of very stressful driving.

## Discuss

Discuss the importance of making a blind-spot check before changing lanes to be sure that another vehicle is not moving into the same space. Discuss procedures for moving both left and right.

## Discuss

Draw students' attention to the photograph. Ask: Which of these drivers has created a closed front zone by following too closely? What can the driver of the first car do when being followed too closely?

Which of these drivers is following too closely?

a 3-second following distance. A shorter following distance reduces your sight distance and leaves little time and space to react to a closed front zone.

Applying the 3-second following distance rule on the expressway is a safe plan under ideal conditions. The blue car in the left lane of the picture has a good space cushion and a safe following distance. However, the black vehicle behind the blue car is following too closely and does not have enough space in the front zone. Keeping an ample space cushion around your vehicle gives you both time and space for an "out."

Continually scan the traffic scene around you to be aware of any situation that may affect your safe path of travel. If a driver cuts into your space ahead, keep cool. Do not react in a manner that could cause another driver to exhibit road rage. Slow and reestablish a safe following distance.

Increase your following distance to at least 4 seconds when conditions are less than ideal. Increasing your

following distance is especially important when you are
- following a large vehicle that is blocking your vision
- following a motorcyclist
- driving in bad weather or road-way conditions
- driving in heavy traffic
- being tailgated
- driving a heavy vehicle or pulling a trailer
- operating a motorcycle
- entering or exiting an expressway

**Blind Spots** Remember that you have blind spots in both your left-rear and right-rear zones. Check these zones often and be alert for other drivers who may pass you. When you are behind a vehicle in the next lane, keep far enough back so you are not in that driver's blind spot. Reduce your speed or accelerate and pass in order to stay out of another driver's blind spot.

### Being Followed

Vehicles following you too closely, or tailgating, can put you in a danger-ous situation. Many drivers tend to think that they have no control over the space in their rear zones. Encourage tailgaters to pass you by reducing your speed gradually. However, do not reduce your speed if heavy traffic prevents tailgaters from passing. If a driver continues to tailgate, change lanes when it is safe to do so. Frequently check your rear zones to stay aware of any tailgaters.

### Lane Changing

Avoid changing lanes too often. Unnecessary weaving from one lane

## Activity

**Class Activity** This activity will help students understand blind spots. Take the class to the driver education car and ask one student to sit in the driver's seat. Have the outside mirrors properly adjusted. Walk from the rear bumper toward the car. Ask the student in the driver's seat to say "stop" when he or she is able to see you in the mirror. Take note of the mirror's range of detection and, more important-ly, call students' attention to the areas to the vehicle's rear that are not seen in the mirrors. Repeat this activity with other students.

to another can lead to a collision. Take these steps to change lanes on the expressway:

1. Change lanes one lane at a time. Signal *every* lane change, whether or not other vehicles are present.
2. Check traffic in the outside and inside rearview mirrors. Check the blind-spot area in the direction you want to move.
3. If your path is clear, accelerate gently and move to the next lane.
4. Cancel your signal after you have changed lanes.

Once you have made a lane change, establish your position in that lane before moving to another. Drive at the speed of traffic in that lane if it is within the speed limit.

Changing lanes on an expressway is more complicated when three or more lanes of traffic are moving in the same direction. Many times a potential conflict is created when two drivers head for the same space at the same time, as the top picture shows. A quick glance over the shoulder lets you check the lane to see if it is open.

Sometimes you will change lanes so traffic entering the expressway can merge safely. Remember that some expressways have entrance ramps on the left as well as on the right. If you are driving in the left lane and see a driver entering from the left, predict a closed front zone. Signal right, check your right zones, and change lanes as the yellow car in the picture is doing.

Lanes are often closed for construction and road repair. When a lane is closed, drive only in the lanes open for traffic. It is both illegal and hazardous to use the shoulder or

A conflict can occur when two drivers head for the same space at the same time.

The driver of the yellow car predicted a closed front zone and decided to change lanes.

Chapter 11 Driving on Expressways **233**

## Explain

Emphasize the importance of changing only one lane at a time. In some states, changing more than one lane at a time is illegal. Time the lane change to blend smoothly with other moving traffic. Avoid changing lanes into a closed left-front or closed right-front zone.

## Discuss

Discuss reasons for not driving on the shoulder when lanes are closed. Emphasize that this is illegal and could result in loss of life if emergency vehicles do not have a clear path of travel.

## Explain

Never change lanes if you are parallel to a vehicle and only one lane is open between you. Change speed, and then change lanes.

## Demonstrate

Use **Demonstration Overhead J** to illustrate how a conflict can occur when two drivers head for the same space. Use the illustration at the top of the page for reference.

## Demonstrate

Use **Demonstration Overhead I** to illustrate how a driver entering an expressway can predict a closed front zone and avoid the hazard by changing lanes. Use the illustration at the bottom of the page for reference. You will need to flip the overhead to illustrate the entrance ramp on the left. Demonstrate a similar problem when entering on the right.

## Activity

**Model Car Activity** This activity will help students evaluate the procedure and risk of making a lane change. Divide the class into groups of three. Give each group two model cars and Roadway Sheet 2 from **Resource Book,** pages 6–7. Each group is to create a list of valid reasons for changing lanes. Have the first student identify a valid reason for making a lane change. If all three members of the group agree that this is a valid reason for a lane change, the student should put it on the list. The student then demonstrates and explains each step necessary for making the lane change.

The second student identifies a valid reason for a lane change, adds it to the list after the others agree, and demonstrates the lane change. The third member of the group identifies another reason to change lanes, gets consensus, and demonstrates the change.

Each student in the group should take another turn. The groups should continue the activity until it is time to discuss their findings with the class.

## Demonstrate

Use **Demonstration Overhead J** to demonstrate lane changing and passing procedures. Place the transparency car on the roadway and ask students to explain what actions should be taken for various conditions. Use a wild card (see pages T18–T19) to have students recognize situations when lane change or passing should not take place.

 **Assess**

## Answers to Review It

**1.** Students should list the ways discussed on pages 229–230.

**2.** Students should list the situations described on page 232.

**3.** Reduce speed or change lanes to avoid tailgaters. (p. 232)

**4.** When passing on an expressway, you should always evaluate the zone you are entering, signal your lane change, and check your blind-spot area. (p. 234)

Use signals and constantly check traffic when passing on an expressway.

median as a driving lane when traffic is backed up. Drivers who drive illegally on the shoulder are also preventing emergency vehicles from having an open path of travel.

### Passing and Being Passed

Passing other vehicles on an expressway usually is safer than passing on a two-lane highway. Because a median separates you from oncoming traffic on an expressway, a head-on collision is not a threat. However, expressway speeds and a high volume of traffic demand caution and concentration, along with the constant use of the IPDE Process, when passing. Always make sure conditions are safe for passing before you begin your maneuver.

Passing on the left is common on expressways. However, passing on the right is permitted if a slower driver is in the left lane.

When passing another vehicle, follow the procedure for making a lane change to the left. The yellow car in the picture is following the correct lane-change procedure to pass vehicles in the two right lanes.

After passing, return to your original lane by making a safe lane change.

Make these actions automatic when you pass:

- Evaluate the zone you are entering.
- Signal your lane change.
- Check blind-spot area by glancing over your shoulder to the left or right, as necessary.

When you are being passed, be aware of the position of the vehicle passing you. If you do not have enough space cushion to the side,

move to lane position 2 or 3. Continue to check the vehicle that is passing you. Keep your speed steady and do not accelerate.

If you are continually being passed on the right, move to the lane on your right when it is safe to do so. When you are frequently being passed on both sides, you are in a potentially dangerous situation. You have reduced the space in your left and right zones and have greatly increased your degree of risk. Blending into the flow of traffic is just as important during passing as it is when entering or exiting an expressway.

### Review It

1. How can using the IPDE Process help you maintain a safe path of travel on expressways?
2. When should following distances be increased for expressway driving?
3. What actions could you take when you are being tailgated?
4. What three actions should be automatic when changing lanes to pass on an expressway?

234   Unit 3   Driving in Different Environments and Situations

## Activity

**In-Class Driving Rehearsal** This activity will give students the opportunity to practice passing maneuvers in the classroom in preparation for in-car performance. Students will simulate various passing situations as they walk in traffic lanes created by placing masking tape on the classroom floor.

Have students line up in the traffic lane. Have one student move several feet to the front of the group to simulate a car that will be passed. Have the next student in line explain the first step to be considered in preparation for passing the student

"car" ahead. Then the next student in line takes over as the passing car and explains the next step. Continue going through all passing steps. Repeat the procedure from the start until all students have correctly identified the step for which they are responsible.

Leaving an expressway safely requires planning and skill. Plan for your exit as early as possible. Scan signs to know which exit to take. When you see the sign for your exit, move into the lane designated by the sign. Most expressway exits provide a **deceleration lane,** an added lane in which to slow your

The parts of an expressway exit.

vehicle without blocking the vehicles behind. Try not to decelerate until you are off the expressway and in the deceleration lane.

The deceleration lane leads into the **exit ramp,** the ramp leading off the expressway. Identify the sign that shows the exit-ramp speed. If you do not slow your vehicle enough in the deceleration lane, you might enter the exit ramp at too high a speed.

Many exit ramps lead into a sharp curve. The posted ramp speed limit indicates the top speed possible for negotiating the exit safely. Remember, if you miss the exit you want, go on to the next exit. *Never stop or back up if you go past your exit.*

### Applying the IPDE Process

Use the IPDE Process to plan your exit well in advance:

1. Identify the green expressway guide signs showing the distance to your exit.
2. Predict actions of other drivers who might be using the same exit.
3. Decide on the safe speed for exiting.
4. Execute your maneuver smoothly and blend with slower traffic.

### Steps for Exiting

Follow these steps to exit an expressway:

1. At least one-half mile before the exit, check front and rear zones for traffic. Signal and move into lane position 3 in the lane that

### Teacher's Resources

**Demonstration Overheads**
Overhead K

**Content Overheads**
Overhead 22

**In-Car Checklists**
In-Car Checklist 28

# Exiting Expressways

## Objectives

1. Explain how to apply the IPDE Process to exit an expressway.
2. List the steps for exiting an expressway.
3. Describe three possible exiting problems.

 **Focus**

### Summary

This lesson focuses on exiting expressways properly. It also addresses possible exit problems.

### Vocabulary

*deceleration lane, exit ramp*

 **Teach**

### Explain

Explain that some drivers fail to use the full length of the deceleration lane. These drivers are apt to cut you off as they attempt to get to the exit. When approaching an exit, even before reaching the deceleration lane, you need to check your left-rear zone for drivers who might attempt to exit. You may need to adjust your speed and position to avoid conflict and to help them to exit safely.

## Demonstrate

Use **Demonstration Overhead K** and a transparency car to illustrate the four steps for exiting an expressway.

## Explain

Applying your brake when you get into the deceleration lane is a good habit to acquire. This allows you to test the traction of the tires to the roadway and to detect brake failure early.

## Explain

Use the illustration on page 237 or **Content Overhead 22** to illustrate how drivers' paths can cross while entering or exiting an expressway.

Be in lane position 3 before you get to the deceleration lane.

Move into the deceleration lane.

Slow to the posted speed limit.

**236** Unit 3 Driving in Different Environments and Situations

leads into the deceleration lane. This is shown in the first picture. Change only one lane at a time. Avoid last-second decisions and sudden moves. Do not reduce your speed until you are in the deceleration lane.

2. Move into the deceleration lane. Cancel your signal.

3. Flash your brake lights to warn drivers behind that you are slowing. Check your rear zones so you will know the speed of following traffic. Slow gradually and keep a safe space cushion ahead and behind you.

4. Identify the exit-ramp speed sign, as shown in the bottom picture. Check your own speed, and adjust to the posted speed limit. Predict a STOP or YIELD sign at the end of the exit ramp.

Be alert when entering traffic on a local highway or street after leaving the expressway. Expect two-way traffic, pedestrians, intersections, and the need for lower speeds. Check your speedometer frequently and be alert for the typical hazards of two-way streets and roads.

### Possible Exiting Problems

Even though leaving an expressway should be a smooth operation, problems can occur. Be alert and ready to adjust to problem situations.

**Crossing Paths** On some expressways, like the one shown in the first picture on the next page, the same lane is used as both an entrance and an exit. Exiting traffic should merge behind entering traffic since entering traffic is accelerating.

**Ramp Overflow** Traffic can back up from an exit ramp onto the expressway, as the second picture shows. Rather than joining the overflow and risking a rear-end collision, go past the exit and use the next exit. Some drivers pull off on the shoulder out of the lane of traffic. This is both unsafe and illegal.

Start slowing early if you must use a backed-up exit. If you see vehicles backed up near the exit ramp, check your rear zone, flash your brake lights, and begin to slow. Check your rear zone again to make sure traffic is slowing. If traffic is not slowing, try to pass the exit area smoothly, and drive on to the next exit.

**Short Deceleration Lane** Slow more quickly if the deceleration lane is short. Evaluate your rear zones. This is critical in such situations. As you enter the deceleration lane
- judge the lane's length
- identify the exit-ramp speed
- check speed while braking
- check traffic in rear zones

## Review It

1. How should you use the IPDE Process when planning an exit from an expressway?
2. What steps should you follow when exiting an expressway?
3. What are three possible exiting problems?

Driver's paths might cross when the same lane is used for entering and exiting.

What should drivers do when traffic is backed up near an exit ramp?

Chapter 11 Driving on Expressways **237**

# Special Expressway Problems

## 1 Focus

## Summary

This lesson focuses on problems one might encounter on expressways, including highway hypnosis and vehicle breakdowns. It also discusses factors that affect safe driving on expressways.

## Vocabulary

**New:** *highway hypnosis, velocitation*

**Review:** *rumble strip*

## 2 Teach

## Discuss

To help students recognize symptoms of a drowsy condition, discuss with the class situations other than driving—such as watching television—when individuals are likely to get drowsy. What symptoms do they display just moments before falling asleep? (head nodding, eyelids lowering, etc.)

## Discuss

Ask students what they can do to combat drowsiness when driving. List the student suggestions on the board and discuss each option.

## Objectives

1. Describe the cause of highway hypnosis and tell what actions to take to stay alert.
2. Explain what to do if your vehicle becomes disabled.
3. List three key factors that contribute to safe driving on expressways.

Expressways can provide the safest type of driving. Even so, problems can arise that present hazards and possible conflicts.

### Driver Condition

Driving for long periods of time can affect drivers. Be alert for problems that can affect you and the other drivers on the road.

### Highway Hypnosis

Staying alert can be a problem when you travel long distances on expressways. You may drive mile after mile at steady speeds with few hills, curves, or interchanges. You can be lulled into an inattentive, drowsy state known as **highway hypnosis.**

When you first notice that you are becoming drowsy or your attention is less focused, sit up straighter and open a window. Stop at the next exit and stretch or exercise. If you need more rest, stop at a safe place and take a brief nap.

### Fall-Asleep Collisions

More than 100,000 collisions in the United States each year are caused by sleepiness. Fall-asleep collisions are twice as likely to involve fatalities as other types of collisions.

Sleepiness is a preventable cause of vehicle collisions. Drivers who fail to recognize their own fatigue and sleepiness, or even ignore it, pose a high-risk threat to themselves and to others on the roadway. All drivers are at risk for fall-asleep collisions.

### Velocitation

Hours of driving can fool you into thinking your vehicle is traveling slower than it really is. You might then unconsciously drive too fast. This condition, called **velocitation,**

**DID YOU KNOW?**

**LEAVING EXPRESSWAYS** Many drivers have difficulty adjusting to lower speeds after leaving an expressway. Some drivers fail to slow down to the posted speed limit and find themselves stopped by police officers. These drivers usually will be issued tickets for speed-limit violations.

238 Unit 3 Driving in Different Environments and Situations

## Teacher's Resources

**Resource Book**
Roadway Sheet 2,
   pages 6–7
Teacher's Instructions,
   page 50

## Background

**Driving While Drowsy** Drivers do not suddenly go from alertness to falling asleep. There are stages. Drivers' attention to traffic ahead becomes shortened. When drivers have the habit of looking 30 seconds ahead, they will find themselves looking a shorter distance when drowsy. Their eyes will not move as easily to search the left-front and right-front and rear zones. Therefore, when it becomes a struggle to check mirrors, that could serve as a sign that they are a step closer to becoming influenced by drowsiness.

can be especially hazardous when you exit an expressway.

The roadways you drive on after exiting usually have a lower speed limit than the expressway. If you are "velocitized," you might continue to drive at expressway speeds after making your exit. To prevent exceeding the local speed limit, check your speed often after exiting the expressway.

## Roadway Conditions

Be aware of the characteristics of certain expressways in order to drive safely on them. Even under the safest conditions, roadway problems can still arise.

## Expressways Through Cities

City expressways have more exit and entrance ramps than rural expressways. More ramps increase merging traffic conflicts and give indecisive drivers more opportunities for dangerous last-second decisions.

Remember the following points when driving on an expressway through a city, especially during rush hour:

- In most cases, drive in the center or left lane to avoid merging vehicles.
- Know well in advance where you want to exit. Get in the correct lane early. Fast-moving traffic can make lane changing difficult and dangerous.
- Search constantly for signs, signals, and roadway markings.
- Predict that other drivers are less alert and less aware than you are.

## Disabled Vehicle

Take these steps with the first sign of trouble with your vehicle:

1. Check rear zones and signal. Pull as far as possible onto the shoulder or the median.
2. Turn on your hazard flashers. If the vehicle is not very far off the road, get everyone out and away from traffic.
3. When it is safe to do so, raise the hood and tie a white cloth to the antenna or door handle. If you have a cellular phone, call for help.
4. If you have emergency flares or reflectors, set them out at least 500 feet behind your vehicle when it is safe to do so.
5. Get back into your vehicle and lock all doors. Ask anyone who stops to assist you to go to a phone and call for help. Never get into a stranger's vehicle.
6. Do not stand in the expressway to direct traffic.

## Roadway Repair

Be alert for roadway repair zones. Watch for orange construction signs and be prepared to slow as soon as you identify the first one. Early-warning construction signs with blinking lights indicate the construction-zone speed limit. Reduce your speed and follow the directions of the construction workers.

## Rural Interstate Highways

Driving long distances on rural interstate highways can become monotonous. Check your speed frequently, and look as far ahead as possible into your target area.

If your vehicle becomes disabled, pull as far as possible onto the shoulder or median.

**SAFE DRIVING**

Fines are often doubled for speeding violations in construction zone areas.

## Explain

A disabled vehicle stopped in the breakdown lane of an expressway seems to have a "magnetic effect" on some drivers. This effect is most dangerous when the disabled vehicle is within one mile of an exit. When the driver approaches the disabled vehicle, he or she erroneously identifies the disabled vehicle as moving rather than stopped. In addition, the driver assumes the disabled vehicle is in the traffic lane and unknowingly aims for the back of the disabled vehicle. By the time the approaching driver is close enough to the disabled vehicle to realize that it is not moving and not in the traffic lane, there may not be enough time or space to avoid colliding into it.

## Activity

**Model Car Activity** Divide the class into groups of three. Give each group a model car and Roadway Sheet 2 from **Resource Book,** pages 6–7. Have students simulate situations involving a disabled vehicle on an expressway. Have the students drive the vehicle to the breakdown lane while explaining the actions necessary to take. Each group should explain what happened to their vehicle and answer the following questions: What will they do? How will they get out of the travel lane? How will they position safety reflectors or flares? (See **Resource Book,** page 50 for more information and diagrams for class use.) What safety equipment will they have in the car to call for help? (Cellular phone or a portable CB radio will be helpful.) Where will they wait for help to arrive? What are the advantages and disadvantages of waiting inside the car or outside the car? (Waiting inside the car with doors locked, safety belts on, head up against the head restraint usually is desirable. If the car is stopped in a location at risk for a rear impact, it is safer to wait outside the car away from traffic.)

## Discuss

Explain to the class that approaching and stopping at a toll booth contains many risks. Get students to brainstorm about the risks and what actions can they take to minimize the risk. (Rear zone is extremely dangerous. There are many collisions, some with multiple fatalities, as drivers to the rear fail to realize that traffic is stopped for the toll booth. Some drivers are drowsy and/or under the influence of alcohol or drugs. Other drivers are distracted as they reach into pockets and handbags for toll money. Drivers often change lanes both as they approach and leave the toll plaza. Approaching the toll booths, drivers make sudden lane changes in order to reach the shortest line. After paying the toll, drivers change lanes as they merge into the traffic lanes.

 **Assess**

## Answers to Review It

**1.** Driving mile after mile at steady speeds with few hills, curves, or interchanges causes highway hypnosis. Sitting up straight, opening the window, and stopping to stretch or exercise may help you stay alert. (p. 238)

**2.** Students should list the steps identified on page 239.

**3.** Key factors to driving safely on the expressway are cooperation among drivers, concentration on the driving task, and use of the IPDE Process. (p. 240)

Unit 3
Driving in Different
**240** Environments and Situations

Select your lane well in advance. Stay in that lane and have your money ready.

Try not to let larger vehicles tailgate you. Remember that they cannot stop as quickly as you can. Pass larger, slower-moving vehicles only when it is safe to do so.

### Tollbooths

Tollbooth plazas are located along many expressways. You stop at a tollbooth and pay a fee, or toll, for driving on that expressway.

Rough sections of roadway, called *rumble strips,* are built into the approach lanes of some toll plazas. These strips warn you of the tollbooths ahead and remind you to check your speed.

When approaching a tollbooth plaza, look for a green light above a tollbooth. The green light indicates that the lane is open for traffic.

Many toll plazas have signs overhead in different colors, as the picture shows. These colors indicate the lanes for the tollbooths that are electronic, require exact change, or are attendant operated.

Toll plazas have at least three types of tollbooths. One type is automatic; the driver deposits coins into

a machine. The second type is operated by an attendant for drivers without exact change and drivers of larger vehicles.

Another type of tollbooth is operated electronically. An electronic device is placed inside the driver's vehicle on the windshield or on the dashboard. As the driver approaches the designated toll lane, the device communicates electronically with a computer in the lane. The toll is then subtracted from a previously prepaid account.

### Using Expressways Safely

Three key factors contribute to safe driving on expressways:
- cooperation among drivers
- concentration on the driving task
- use of the IPDE Process

Keeping these factors in mind as you gain expressway experience will enable you to contribute to low-risk expressway driving.

### Review It

1. What are causes of highway hypnosis? What actions can you take to stay alert?
2. What should you do if your vehicle becomes disabled?
3. What are three key factors that can help you drive safely on expressways?

**240** Unit 3 Driving in Different Environments and Situations

## Activity

**Small Group Activity** This activity will help students learn to identify early symptoms of drowsiness, ways to prevent drowsiness, ways to combat drowsiness, and myths related to drowsiness. Divide the class into three groups and ask each group to create a poster or display related to drowsiness and driving. Assign one of the following topics to each of the three groups: early symptoms of drowsiness, ways to prevent and combat drowsiness, and myths related to drowsiness.

## Background

**Calling for Help** Some states have an emergency phone system along the expressways. Some interstate highways now have coded mile markers to help cellular phone users identify their location when calling for help.

## Reviewing Chapter Objectives

### 1. Characteristics of Expressway Driving

1. What are five reasons expressways have lower collision rates than other highways? (222)
2. What are four different types of expressway interchanges? (222–223)
3. What strategies can you follow for low-risk driving on expressways? (223–224)

### 2. Entering an Expressway

4. How do you properly enter an expressway? (225–226)
5. What are four possible problems you may have when entering an expressway? (227)
6. Why is entering an expressway from the left more hazardous than entering from the right? (228)

### 3. Strategies for Driving on Expressways

7. How can you use the IPDE Process to achieve a safe path of travel? (229–230)
8. When should following distances be increased for expressway driving? (232)

### 4. Exiting Expressways

9. How can you apply the IPDE Process to exit an expressway? (235)
10. What steps should you take when exiting an expressway? (235–236)
11. What are three possible exiting problems? (236–237)

### 5. Special Expressway Problems

12. How is highway hypnosis caused and what actions can you take to stay alert? (238)
13. What should you do if your vehicle becomes disabled on an expressway? (239)
14. What three key factors contribute to safe driving on expressways? (240)

## Projects

### Individuals

**Observe Traffic** As a passenger in a vehicle, observe vehicles that pass both the vehicle you are in and other vehicles. Record the number of vehicles you see passing in a five-minute period. Note the number of vehicles passing on the right and the number passing on the left. Also note whether the vehicles seem to be exceeding the speed limit. Discuss your observations in class.

**Investigate** Locate the interchanges on a map of your area and nearest city. Identify each as cloverleaf, diamond, trumpet, or all-directional. Discuss your findings in class.

### Groups

**Use Technology** Use the Internet or other sources to research the use of tollbooth plazas in your state and neighboring states. Find out how many tollbooth plazas are being used. Find out whether the tollbooths operate with toll attendants, automatically, or electronically. Also find out how much money the booths collect annually and how the money is used. Write a group report based on your findings.

**Demonstrate** As a group, make an expressway model and label the various components. Present your model to the class. Group members should take turns explaining the purpose and potential problems related to each expressway component.

## Reviewing Chapter Objectives

**11.1** Characteristics of Expressway Driving
See Answers to Review It on page 224.
**11.2** Entering an Expressway
See Answers to Review It on page 228.
**11.3** Strategies for Driving on Expressways
See Answers to Review It on page 234.
**11.4** Exiting Expressways
See Answers to Review It on page 237.
**11.5** Special Expressway Problems
See Answers to Review It on page 240.

For additional information refer to the specific page(s) in parentheses after each question.

## Projects

Some of the projects can be assigned at any time while others are more closely tied to the content presented in the student text. The page number where the topic is introduced is indicated.

**Observe Traffic:** p. 234
**Investigate:** p. 222
**Use Technology:** p. 240
**Demonstrate:** p. 222

The results of student projects will vary.

## Teacher's Resources

### Skills and Applications Workbook
pages 41–44

### Tests and Activities
Chapter 11 Activities 11-1 and 11-2, pages 91–92

Chapter 11 Test A and Test B, pages 93–96

### TestWorks CD-ROM
Chapter 11 Test

## Chapter Test

### Check Your Knowledge

**Multiple Choice** Copy the number of each sentence below on a sheet of paper. Choose the letter of the answer that best completes the statement or answers the question.

1. Expressways are safer than other types of roads because
   (a) there is less traffic.
   (b) there are no intersections or cross traffic.
   (c) average speeds are higher.
   (d) there is no barrier between opposing traffic lanes.
2. If traffic is backed up on the exit ramp you want to use, you should
   (a) pass the ramp and use the next exit.
   (b) stop on the expressway until the ramp is clear.
   (c) pull onto the shoulder and wait.
   (d) none of the above
3. Expressway collisions tend to be more serious than those on other types of roads, because expressways
   (a) have median strips.
   (b) have so many conflicts.
   (c) have higher-speed travel.
   (d) have more hazards.

**Completion** Copy the number of each sentence below. After each number, write the word or words that complete the sentence correctly.
4. You slow your vehicle without blocking those behind you when you are in the _____ lane.
5. A _____ interchange is used when a side road forms a T intersection with an expressway.
6. The right edge of the expressway should be marked with a _____ line.

### Review Vocabulary

Copy the number of each definition in list A. Match the definition in list A with the term it defines in list B.

**List A**
7. group or formation of vehicles traveling on an expressway
8. speed used by most drivers on an expressway
9. condition of unconsciously driving too fast as a result of driving for long periods at high speeds
10. lane that permits drivers entering an expressway to accelerate to the speed of expressway traffic
11. stretch of roadway at the end of an acceleration lane where vehicles join the flow of traffic

**List B**
a. acceleration lane
b. velocitation
c. wolf pack
d. common speed
e. merging area

### Think Critically

Write a paragraph to answer each question.
1. What are the pros and cons of higher-speed driving on an expressway?
2. How do you think wolf packs form on expressways?

---

## Answers to Check Your Knowledge

1. b
2. a
3. c
4. deceleration
5. trumpet
6. white

## Answers to Review Vocabulary

7. wolf pack (c)
8. common speed (d)
9. velocitation (b)
10. acceleration lane (a)
11. merging area (e)

## Answers to Think Critically

Students' answers will vary. For information related to the question refer to the page(s) indicated.

1. Traveling at higher speeds is safer on expressways than on other highways (see reasons listed on p. 222). However, higher speeds may also result in more serious collisions. Higher expressway speeds also pose more danger for those traveling at lower speeds and thus could result in rear-end collisions. (p. 223)

2. Accept all reasonable answers. One possible answer: Wolf packs may form when drivers driving at a common speed stay together. The entire pack will pass the slower-moving vehicles to maintain their common speed. (p. 231)

## Decision Making

**1.** The yellow car is about to enter the merge area. What should car 1 do? How can car 2 help? What should car 3 predict? What action should the driver of the yellow car be executing?

**2.** What unsafe practice is the driver of the yellow car following? What options does this driver have to improve the situation? How might the tailgater affect the yellow car driver's decision?

**3.** The driver of the yellow car plans to exit the expressway. The same lane is used for exiting and entering. What should the driver of the yellow car do? Why is this a wise decision?

**4.** What is the driver of the car required to do when driving through the construction zone?

Chapter 11 Driving on Expressways **243**

## Answers to Decision Making

**1.** Car 1 should change lanes to the left. Car 2 can help by accelerating. Car 3 should predict that car 1 will change lanes. The driver of the yellow car should be accelerating.

**2.** The driver of the yellow car is driving in the truck driver's blind spot. This driver can either accelerate or slow down to get out of the blind spot. The tailgater might present a problem if the driver of the yellow car decides to slow down.

**3.** The driver of the yellow car should allow the first merging car to go first, and then enter the deceleration lane ahead of the entering car behind. The merging car is accelerating. The driver of the yellow car is slowing.

**4.** The driver is required to drive no faster than the indicated speed limit.

# Chapter 12    Planning Guide

**Student Features**

**Teacher's Edition**

| | | |
|---|---|---|
| **Chapter 12** **Driving in Adverse Conditions** | You Are the Driver! *p. 245* | Projects *p. 244* Special Needs *p. 245* |
| **12.1 Reduced Visibility** *pp. 246–251* <br>• Tell how to use the IPDE Process to manage risks in bad weather. <br>• Explain what you can do to help others see you at dawn and dusk. <br>• Describe the special techniques you can use for night driving. <br>• Explain the procedure to use at night when an oncoming driver fails to use low-beam headlights. | Safe Driving Tip *p. 248* | Demonstrate *p. 247* Activity *pp. 246, 247, 248, 250, 251* Special Needs *p. 250* |
| **12.2 Reduced Traction** *pp. 252–259* <br>• Describe what happens to traction during rain and snow. <br>• List the steps you can take to avoid hydroplaning. <br>• Describe how to correct a rear-wheel skid. <br>• Tell how to use the controlled-braking technique. | Did You Know? *p. 254* | Demonstrate *pp. 253, 256, 257, 259* Activity *pp. 253 254, 255, 256, 257, 258, 259* |
| **12.3 Other Adverse Weather Conditions** *pp. 260–262* <br>• Explain how to control your vehicle in windy conditions. <br>• List precautions for driving in extremely hot or cold weather. <br>• Describe what to do to maintain vehicle control during winter driving. | | Demonstrate *p. 260* Activity *p. 260* |
| **Assessment** | Reviewing Chapter Objectives *p. 263* Projects *p. 263* Chapter Test *p. 264* Decision Making *p. 265* | Answers *pp. 264–265* |

## Teacher's Resource File

## Videos, Overheads, and Software

**Companion** *pp. 76–80*
**Spanish Handbook** *pp. 25–26*

---

**Resource Book**
Overheads, *pp. 51–52*

**Demonstration Overhead G**

---

**Resource Book**
Teacher's Instructions,
  *pp. 53–56*
Classroom Activity, *pp. 57–58*
Information, *pp. 78–80*
**In-Car Checklists 29, 30**

**Demonstration Overheads C, H**
**Content Overheads 23, 24**

---

**Skills and Applications**
  **Workbook**, *pp. 45–48*
**Tests and Activities**
Chapter 12 Activities 12-1
  and 12-2, *pp. 99–100*
Chapter 12 Test A and
  Test B, *pp. 101–104*

**TestWorks CD-ROM**
Chapter 12 Test

---

## Technology Resources

### Audio-Visual and Computer Resources

AAA Foundation for Traffic Safety, *Driving in Bad Weather*, video, 8 minutes

AAA Foundation for Traffic Safety, *Night Driving*, video, 8 minutes

AAA Foundation for Traffic Safety, *Ready, Set, Winter*, video, 17 minutes

American Automobile Association, *Get a Grip*, video, 19 minutes

National Safety Council, *Low Visibility and Driving*, video, 10 minutes

Safety Industries, Inc., *Driving Under Adverse Conditions*, video, 15 minutes

Safety Industries, Inc., *Night Vision*, video

3I Company, *Drive to Survive: Adverse Conditions,* video, 24 minutes

## Kits, Equipment, and Other Resources

Interactive Driving Systems, Inc., *Auto Control Monster*

**Go Online**
PHSchool.com

**For: Chapter 12 online activities**
**Visit: PHSchool.com**
**Web Code: cak-9999**

# Driving in Adverse Conditions

## Chapter Overview

Chapter 12 presents techniques and suggestions for driving in a wide variety of adverse conditions. Students will find out about problems related to bad weather. They will learn steps to use when driving at night and under other conditions of reduced visibility. They will learn how to deal with reduced traction and how to take steps to correct various types of skids. Other exceptional weather conditions, especially winter driving conditions, are described.

## Chapter Vocabulary

*controlled braking, fishtail, hydroplaning, overdriving headlights, rocking a vehicle, skid*

244

## Teacher's Resources

For students to use as they read the chapter:

**Companion**
pages 76–80

**Spanish Handbook**
pages 25–26

## Projects

Review the projects described on page 263. Some of the projects can be assigned at any time while others are more closely tied to the content presented in the student text.

# CHAPTER 12
## Driving in Adverse Conditions

**12.1** Reduced Visibility

**12.2** Reduced Traction

**12.3** Other Adverse Weather Conditions

### You Are the Driver!

Driving in traffic during good weather is difficult enough—but imagine driving in these snowy conditions! The unpredictable nature of other drivers makes this a high-risk situation. What will you predict others might do? How can you control your vehicle? Can you prepare for this ahead of time?

Extreme situations will raise many questions on how to drive safely. This chapter will help you answer those questions and show you how to better manage risk in these situations.

**Go Online**
PHSchool.com
**For:** Chapter 12 online activities
**Visit:** PHSchool.com
**Web Code:** cak-9999

245

### Introducing the Chapter

Explain what an experienced driver should do in adverse conditions. Suggest that for an inexperienced driver, the best thing to do might be not to drive at all.

### You Are the Driver!

← This picture shows how abnormal conditions can turn a driving situation into a real test. Have students list the adverse conditions shown. Ask students how they would respond to such conditions, including how they would control a minor skid and what the consequences could be if they failed.

### Special Needs

In adverse conditions, all drivers have special needs. Use the various teaching suggestions, demonstrations, and activities in this chapter with the special needs students as well as other students. If weather and conditions permit, try to include dawn, dusk, night, and rain as part of the school's in-car driving experience. Advise parents and guardians to provide supervised driving in low-light situations and various adverse conditions.

# Reduced Visibility

 **Focus**

## Summary

This lesson focuses on how adverse conditions reduce visibility and what drivers can do to compensate. The importance of keeping vehicle windows clean is stressed. The lesson includes information about driving at different times including dawn, dusk, and night. Weather conditions such as fog, rain, and snow also are addressed.

## Vocabulary

*overdriving headlights*

## ② **Teach**

## Explain

Caution students that icy or snow-covered windows should always be cleared before driving. Emphasize that all windows should be cleared, not just the windshield. It is also important to clear snow and ice from headlights and taillights.

## Discuss

Ask: How does using headlights in the daytime affect driving in adverse conditions? (Daytime headlights help other drivers see your vehicle during adverse daytime conditions.)

## Objectives

1. Tell how to use the IPDE Process to manage risks in bad weather.
2. Explain what you can do to help others see you at dawn and dusk.
3. Describe the special techniques you can use for night driving.
4. Explain the procedure to use at night when an oncoming driver fails to use low-beam headlights.

Whenever visibility is reduced drivers need more time to use the IPDE Process. You can maintain a safe intended path of travel by

- slowing down to give yourself more time
- scanning in and around your path of travel to the target area to identify hazards early
- predicting others will make maneuvers into your intended path of travel
- deciding to position your vehicle ahead of time with an extra space cushion around it
- executing driving actions gently to maintain control so others know what you are doing

### Your Vehicle Windows

The most important rule for your vehicle's glass is "keep it clean!" If dirty windows become a line-of-sight restriction, you will have a much harder time using the IPDE Process effectively.

A simple thing like moisture forming on the inside of your windshield can make the difference between safe, low-risk driving and colliding with another vehicle. Take these steps when the slightest amount of moisture builds up:

- Turn on your front-window defroster.
- Switch on your rear defogger.
- Use air conditioning and/or heater if it will help.
- Open windows as needed.

Clean all windows and lights ahead of time in bad weather. Keep a close check on any ice, snow, or dirt buildup, especially on headlights and taillights. Stop to clear them by hand.

Imagine what important things you don't see in the night.

246 Unit 3 Driving in Different Environments and Situations

 **Teacher's Resources**

**Resource Book**
Overhead, pages 51–52
**Demonstration Overheads**
Overhead G

## Activity

**Small Group Activity** After the students have been given this chapter as a reading assignment, form the class into groups of four or five. With textbooks closed, have them list all the ways that reduced visibility can occur while driving. Then, for each way listed, have them state how a driver can avoid or minimize the reduced visibility condition. After adequate time, have each group use the textbook as a reference. Have groups report to the class the reduced visibility conditions they discussed that were not listed in the book.

Even in good weather, clean windows can be a problem. The plastics used in many vehicle interiors can give off vapors that coat the inside of windows over time. Cigarette smoke also can create a dirty-window problem. By keeping windows clear, you improve your ability to identify, especially at night.

### Sun Glare

At times the sun can create severe and blinding glare conditions. Sun glasses and a sun visor can help, but try to avoid looking toward the sun.

By driving with low-beam headlights on all the time, you help other drivers see you. The brightest day will create the darkest shadows. With severe-glare situations and the sun behind you, be prepared for other drivers to miss seeing your signal or even seeing your vehicle.

### Dawn and Dusk

Dawn and dusk driving situations can be very dangerous. The low visual contrast between moving vehicles and the driving scene can be deceiving. Again, by always driving with your headlights on low beam, you can help others to see you. How would you defend yourself if the oncoming driver in the top picture did not have headlights on?

### Night

Low levels of light at night severely limit your ability to use the IPDE Process. Look at the picture on the left. Even with street lights, how do these nighttime conditions make driving more difficult? Would day-

Dawn driving without headlights on can set many traps.

light make it easier? What things might you see during day-time driving that you would miss while driving at night?

**Headlights** Keep these points in mind when driving with your headlights on at night:

- Use high-beam headlights to see further down the road. Also, look beyond your headlights for important information. Only use your high-beam headlights when vehicles are more than one-half mile in front of you. Switch to low-beam headlights the instant you see the headlights of an oncoming vehicle, the taillights of a vehicle you are approaching, or the taillights of a vehicle that has just passed you. This prevents you from

Chapter 12 Driving in Adverse Conditions **247**

## Demonstrate

Use **Demonstration Overhead G** and four transparency screens to illustrate how visibility can be restricted by many factors. See **Resource Book,** pages 51–52 for information on preparing the transparency screens. Place the yellow transparency car at the bottom of the transparency driving toward the bushes and place the transparency motorcycle coming over the center line in the area by the bushes. Point out that the driver of the yellow car can clearly see the motorcycle. One at a time, add the four transparency screens and explain that each represents a different factor that can affect the windshield: dirt on the outside, smoke film on the inside, plastic vapor film on the inside, and moisture fogging up the inside. Point out that with each addition visibility is reduced.

## Discuss

Discuss why night driving is difficult. Point out that drivers face a combination of factors, such as low visibility, oncoming drivers' headlights, and the presence of other drivers who might be tired or who might have been drinking.

## Discuss

Ask: Should you keep your high-beam headlights on to force an oncoming driver to use low-beam headlights? Have students explain their answers. (The appropriate response is to flick your high-beam headlights to remind the oncoming driver to use low-beam headlights. Keeping your high-beam headlights on when approaching another vehicle serves no purpose.)

## Explain

Explain the importance of having as much time as possible to use the IPDE Process at night. Note that, when possible, drivers should use high-beam headlights and look beyond the headlights for clues to possible conflicts in the path of travel.

## Discuss

Have the students brainstorm about the information a driver is able to receive by looking beyond the range of the headlights. Make a list during the brainstorming session. Then, after a list is developed, have students explain the value of each item on the list.

Be ready to adjust to a new situation beyond the headlights.

**SAFE DRIVING**

**To give yourself more time for the IPDE Process at night, look beyond the range of your headlights.**

blinding the other driver with your headlights.

• Use low-beam lights in bad weather. In snow, heavy rain, or fog, high-beam headlights will reflect more light back into your eyes; as a result, you will see less.

**Meeting Other Vehicles** Take these actions if an oncoming driver fails to use low-beam headlights after you switch to low-beam headlights:

1. Is the oncoming driver far enough away to respond to you? Briefly flick your headlights from low to high to low to remind the oncoming driver to switch to low-beam headlights. Most new vehicles make this easy by having a flash-to-pass position on their high-beam control switch.

2. Is the oncoming driver still using high-beam headlights? Slow, move to lane position 3, and glance at the right edge of the road as shown here.

3. Could you be blinded by bright oncoming headlights? Look ahead with frequent quick glances to check oncoming traffic. *Do not stare directly into oncoming high-beam headlights.*

4. Is it possible you will encounter a hazard to the right after the oncoming vehicle? Be ready to adjust to a new situation beyond the oncoming headlights.

**Overdriving Headlights** The term **overdriving headlights** means driving at a speed that makes your stopping distance longer than the distance lighted by your headlights. Make sure you do not overdrive your headlights, especially in bad weather or on a slick road.

In normal driving conditions, use this 4-second stopping distance rule to see if you are driving within the range of your headlights.

1. Pick a fixed-checkpoint ahead the instant the checkpoint

## Activity

**Class Activity** This activity is designed to help students understand how high-beam headlights from an approaching vehicle reduce your visibility. You will need two flashlights for this activity. Ask for two volunteers: one to represent the driver and one to represent an oncoming vehicle. Have the volunteers stand ten feet apart facing each other and give them each a flashlight. Darken the room (the room must be totally dark for this activity to be effective) and stand behind the student representing the oncoming vehicle. Instruct the student in

front of you to shine the flashlight directly at the other student—the driver. Hold up three fingers and ask the driver to tell you how many fingers you are holding up. When the driver cannot tell you how many fingers you are holding up, instruct him or her to shine the flashlight at the oncoming vehicle. Ask again how many fingers you are holding up. The driver's ability to see will not be improved by shining the flashlight directly at the oncoming vehicle. Repeat this activity with different students.

appears in the area lit by your headlights as shown here.

2. Count off four seconds: "one-thousand-one, one-thousand-two, one-thousand-three, one-thousand-four."

3. Check your vehicle's position. When you have just reached your fixed checkpoint, you can assume your stopping distance on dry pavement is within the range of your headlights.

### Fog

When your headlights shine into fog, light is reflected back by water particles in the fog. This makes it harder for you to see. If you use high-beam headlights, your ability to see is reduced even further. Always use low-beam headlights in fog as shown below.

Fog also can reduce your ability to judge distances. Oncoming vehicles may be closer than you think. Avoid trouble by slowing and increasing the space cushion around your vehicle.

The stop sign is five seconds away. Are you overdriving your headlights?

Thick fog, and in some situations heavy industrial smoke, can be very dangerous. Before entering fog, be prepared to slow or even park safely off the side of the road. Better yet, park in a rest area or parking lot.

## Explain

Explain the difference between overdriving your headlights and seeing beyond your headlights. Point out that headlights are intended merely to illuminate the road surface within the stopping distance of the vehicle. A driver who develops proper searching techniques for routine driving situations during daytime conditions (such as learning how to see to the target area and how to evaluate the intended path of travel) is also learning the skills necessary for seeing effectively beyond the headlights.

Explain that it is extremely important that a driver learns how to see beyond the headlights. Students should not think that seeing within the range of the headlights is adequate.

In fog, oncoming traffic may be closer than the driver perceives.

Chapter 12  Driving in Adverse Conditions **249**

## Cross Curricular

**Science** Have students write short reports on weather conditions that affect driving in different parts of the country at different times of the year. Let students pick areas of the country based on their own interest.

## Background

**Following Distance** A driver who makes a habit of using at least a 3-second following distance has more time to become aware of a rapid closure rate than a driver who uses a following distance of less than three seconds. Most of the time a driver is able to differentiate between stopped and moving traffic. When stopped traffic is incorrectly perceived as moving, following distance is crucial. The problem is magnified during conditions of reduced visibility. A greater following distance allows for more time to realize that the traffic is stopped.

## Explain

The habits one acquires for looking 12–15 seconds ahead will provide a feedback system to alert a driver to a condition of low visibility.

## Apply

Share information from newspaper and magazine articles about collisions where reduced visibility was a contributing factor. Focus on articles related to conditions students are likely to face in your community as well as other parts of the country.

## Discuss

Ask: What kinds of weather conditions can you expect when driving close to home? (Answers will vary depending on the climate in your community.) Ask: Why is it important to know about driving in all kinds of weather? (Most drivers will likely drive in other climates at some time in their lives.)

## Explain

A key to safe winter driving is allowing adequate time to properly remove snow and ice from a vehicle before driving it.

If you stop at the side of the roadway, use your hazard lights to warn others that you are stopped.

### Rain

Heavy rain reduces your ability to see and be seen. Keep your windshield clear by using your wipers and defroster on high. Make sure your low-beam headlights are already on as shown in the picture. Many states require low-beam headlights to be on when wipers are on. Reduce your speed. As with fog, if the rain is so heavy that you cannot see well, be prepared to pull off the road and sit out the storm in a safe location. Don't forget to use your hazard flashers.

### Snow

Wind-driven snow can reduce your vision, cover roadway markings, and make steering more difficult. Be prepared to slow and steer carefully. Heavy snow can block your rear window, reducing visibility. Slush or ice also can build up on your windshield wipers. If snow, slush, or ice builds up, pull off the roadway and clean it off. Also clear your headlights, taillights, and other parts of your vehicle that need it.

By using headlights all the time, you won't have to remember to turn them on in the rain.

## Activity

**Small Group Activity** Divide students into groups of four or five. Assign a recorder for each group. Explain the following scenario. During a winter trip to a northern state, you wake up to find that overnight snow has resulted in eight inches of accumulation. What steps should you take to prepare this vehicle for travel?

After adequate time, ask each group to contribute as you create a master list. Encourage discussion.

## Special Needs

Some students have difficulty understanding the effects of driving conditions that they have not experienced. Find videos or videotape television weather reports to show students examples of adverse weather driving conditions. Have students note how rain and snow hide pavement markings and cause low aim. Note how foggy windows and mirrors reduce vision behind as well as ahead. Point out deep water indicators and the tire tracks on wet pavement from the vehicle ahead.

**You Are the Driver!**
What special actions should you be prepared to take in this heavy snow situation?

In blizzard conditions, the last thing you want is to be stranded in the middle of nowhere. If the weather is that bad, try to delay travel until roads and weather improve.

Use low-beam headlights when it snows, day or night. Reduce your speed to maintain control and to give others time to respond to you. If snow covers the road, closing your right-front zone, do not crowd the center of the road by moving to lane position 2. This action has the effect of narrowing the road and could lead to a head-on collision.

## Review It

1. What actions should you take when using the IPDE Process in limited-visibility situations?
2. What steps can you take to help others see you at dawn and dusk?
3. When should you use low-beam headlights at night?
4. What steps should you take when an oncoming driver fails to use low-beam headlights?

## Activity

**Class Activity** Give the class a problem to solve: You are driving at night after several inches of snow have fallen and the roads have been plowed and sanded. You run out of windshield washer fluid, and you still have four miles to travel. There are no stores available. You are now having a very hard time seeing through your grimy, streaked windshield. What should you do? (Pull off the road in a secure area and use clean snow to wash the windshield and the headlights.)

## Discuss

Draw your students' attention to the *You Are the Driver!* question. Ask: What special actions should you be prepared to take in this heavy snow situation? (Be prepared to slow and steer carefully. Keep windows, headlights, and taillights free of snow and slush. Consider delaying travel until roads and weather conditions improve.)

## Explain

Warn students that in situations where visibility is low, a driver might have difficulty seeing and judging distance. This combination causes many chain-reaction collisions.

 **Assess**

## Answers to Review It

1. To use the IPDE Process, slow down, search aggressively, predict others will enter your path of travel, and use an extra space cushion. (p. 246)
2. Turn on low-beam headlights. (p. 247)
3. Switch to low-beam headlights when another driver is approaching, when following another driver, or when another driver passes you. (p. 247)
4. Briefly flick your headlights from low to high to low to signal the oncoming driver. If the oncoming driver does not switch to low-beam headlights, move to lane position 3 and glance at the right edge of the roadway. Look ahead with frequent quick glances. (p. 248–249)

# Reduced Traction

 **Focus**

## Summary

This lesson focuses on how rain, snow, ice, and sand reduce traction and what drivers can do to compensate. Types of skids and skid recovery are explained.

## Vocabulary

**New:** *controlled braking, fishtail, hydroplaning, rocking a vehicle, skid*

**Review:** *antilock braking system (ABS), traction*

 **Teach**

## Explain

Some drivers do not realize that the road surface is slippery when it is raining. Many drivers fail to reduce speed to cope with rain-slicked roadways. Therefore, when a quick braking action or steering action is taken, there is inadequate traction and the vehicle goes into a skid.

## Discuss

Direct students' attention to the *You Are the Driver!* question. Ask: What action should be taken to avoid hydroplaning before driving through the water? (Reduce speed and use tires with good tread.)

## Objectives

1. Describe what happens to traction during rain and snow.
2. List the steps you can take to avoid hydroplaning.
3. Describe how to correct a rear-wheel skid.
4. Tell how to use the controlled-braking technique.

As discussed in Chapter 5, traction allows your tires to grip the road so that you can control your vehicle. Rain, snow, ice, sand, and other materials can limit your traction. Reduced traction can create high-risk driving situations.

### Wet Roadways

Rain-slick roads can create a problem for any driver. You can avoid trouble by knowing the right actions to take ahead of time.

**When Rain Starts**  When rain starts to fall, it mixes with dust and oil on the road. This mix can make the road very slippery, until more rain washes it away.

Reduce speed to make better use of your limited traction on wet roads. You can get a little better traction by following the tire tracks left by the driver ahead.

**Hydroplaning**  When a tire loses road contact by rising up on top of water and no longer has contact with the road, **hydroplaning** occurs. Hydroplaning is caused by a combination of standing water, speed, and tire condition. The deep tread of new, properly inflated tires will cut through the water and grip the road. But even with good tires, hydroplaning can occur at speeds of 35 mph, in water as little as 1/12-inch deep. Tires that are bald or underinflated can start to lose their grip and hydroplane at less than 35 mph. Slushy snow in standing water also increases the risk of hydroplaning.

If you must drive through standing water, take these steps to avoid hydroplaning:

- Reduce speed—especially if the water is deep enough to have raindrops "splash" on the water's surface.

**You Are the Driver!**
What action should be taken to avoid hydroplaning before driving through the water?

## Teacher's Resources

**Resource Book**
Teacher's Instructions, pages 53–56
Classroom Activity, pages 57–58
Information, pages 78–80

**Demonstration Overheads**
Overheads C, H

**Content Overheads**
Overheads 23 and 24

**In-Car Checklists**
In-Car Checklists 29, 30

Deep water can be dangerous.

**Moving water exerts force on a car — the deeper the water, the stronger the force.**

**Bouyancy can make a car seem half its weight.**

**Water about 2 feet deep can carry away an average car.**

- Use properly inflated tires with good tread.

**Deep Water** When you don't know how deep the water ahead is, do not drive through it. Floods cause more deaths than any other weather condition, and 60 percent are vehicle related. If you must drive through deep water, use the following steps:

1. Estimate water depth by watching other vehicles and looking at objects such as fire hydrants, fence posts, and parked vehicles. *If there is even a possibility of the water coming up to the bottom of your vehicle—do not enter the water.*

2. If the water is just over the rims of your tires, drive slowly in low gear. Avoid driving on a soft shoulder. Try to drive on the higher, center of the road.

3. When driving at a low speed through water, apply a light brake pressure with your left foot to build friction and create heat on your brake pads. This heat will help dry your brakes and keep them working.

4. After leaving the water, squeeze your brake pedal lightly to see if your brakes are working normally. If your vehicle pulls to one side or does not slow, drive for a short distance while applying a light brake-pedal pressure with your left foot to help dry your brakes.

**Snow**

Different types of snow can produce different levels of traction. When fresh snow falls at low temperatures, traction can be fairly good. When traffic packs the snow at places like intersections, traction can be reduced. In subzero weather, even the moisture from vehicle exhaust can freeze into dangerous ice on the pavement.

Chapter 12 Driving in Adverse Conditions **253**

## Demonstrate

Demonstrate how road grime, including oil, becomes slippery as rain starts to fall. For this demonstration you will need to bring the following items to class: a cut section of a tire, a sheet of coarse sandpaper, a shallow tray, a small container of water, and a small container of oil.

Take the section of tire and rub it against the sandpaper to accumulate the tire grindings. Dump the grindings into the tray. Explain that these grindings are what gets onto the road surface when the brakes are applied, or when the vehicle starts into motion from a stopped position. Point out that skid marks are mostly the residue from the tires grinding against the road surface.

Add some oil to the grindings and mix while explaining that vehicles leak oil onto the road surface. Point out that stopping, starting, and oil leaks all take place near intersections.

Add some water to the mixture and point out how the oil and tire grindings float to the surface. Ask the class what is likely to happen if there was a need for a fast braking action and this mixture was on the road surface.

## Activity

**Class Activity** Ask each student to locate a magazine or newspaper article related to a motor vehicle collision that occurred during rainy conditions. Have students bring their articles to class and be prepared to discuss them.

## Explain

Explain that a thermometer that measures temperatures outside the vehicle is a safety feature to have in a vehicle. Being able to see when the outside temperature is approaching the freezing mark can help alert a driver to the potential for dangerous road conditions.

Use gentle control actions to rock your vehicle.

Temperatures at or just below the freezing point (32°F or 0°C) can create dangerous traction situations. The combination of snow, slushy water, and ice can make for extremely slippery surfaces.

**Driving Techniques for Snow**
Gentle acceleration, steering, and braking are the keys to vehicle control in snow. Put your vehicle in motion by gently squeezing the accelerator.

If your drive wheels slip, release your accelerator and start again.

To improve traction on snow, use all-season tires. To improve traction even more, many states allow the use of tire chains at certain times. Chains are placed over the tread on the tires to increase traction.

**Rocking a Vehicle** Often you can move your vehicle out of deep snow, mud, or sand by driving forward a little and then back a little. By repeating this sequence, you can work your way out. This technique is called **rocking a vehicle.** Check your owner's manual to make sure this procedure will not hurt your transmission. If it is okay, follow these steps:

1. Straighten front wheels as the driver in the picture above has done.
2. Gently accelerate forward. *Do not spin your wheels.*
3. Let up on your accelerator. Pause just long enough to let the engine slow. Shift to REVERSE and gently move backwards. Let up on your

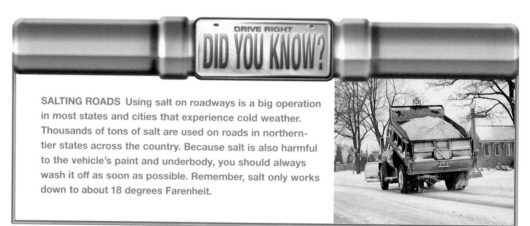

DRIVE RIGHT
**DID YOU KNOW?**

**SALTING ROADS** Using salt on roadways is a big operation in most states and cities that experience cold weather. Thousands of tons of salt are used on roads in northern-tier states across the country. Because salt is also harmful to the vehicle's paint and underbody, you should always wash it off as soon as possible. Remember, salt only works down to about 18 degrees Farenheit.

## Activity

**Class Activity** This activity will help students understand how road conditions can become slippery when ice and snow are near the freezing point (32 degrees Farenheit, 0 degrees Celsius). If you have easy access to a freezer, you can do this activity in your classroom. Otherwise you will need to have students do this at home and report their findings. Take ice cubes out of the freezer and have students hold them between two fingers for a few seconds. Point out that the cubes are sticky. Have students place the cubes in a dish at room temperature for a few

minutes. Have students pick up the ice cubes with two fingers. Point out that the cubes are now slippery.

Ask students to explain the difference and how this relates to road conditions. (When exposed to the warmer than freezing temperature of the room, the melting ice cube becomes coated with a layer of water. When temperatures get above freezing, the ice warms up and begins to melt, placing a layer of water on top of the road surface.)

Cold air circulating over and under bridges causes water to freeze.

Warm ground keeps water from freezing on the pavement.

Ice forms on bridges first.

accelerator and shift to DRIVE to move forward.

4. Continue this backward-and-forward movement until your vehicle has cleared tracks that are long enough to drive out.

### Ice

Be especially alert if temperatures drop below freezing and it is raining. These conditions are just right for snow, ice, and sleet. Predict the worst when ice begins to form.

Temperatures will change the amount of traction you will have on ice. If the temperature of ice warms from 0 degrees to 32 degrees Farenheit, your traction will be cut in half.

Squeeze your brakes lightly to check your traction in icy areas. Only do this at low speeds away from traffic. Slow gradually if your vehicle starts to slide.

Windows and windshield wipers can also ice up in severe weather. If your defroster cannot keep your windshield clear, pull out of traffic and clear it manually. It might be best not to drive at all.

If you must drive, be extra alert for these icy situations:

• **Ice on Bridges** Bridge roadways tend to freeze before other roadway surfaces. Cold air circulates above and below the roadway on bridges and overpasses as shown in the picture.

• **Black Ice** Be alert for "black ice" that forms in thin sheets. This can be extremely hard to see. Be extra careful for this type of ice in winter mountain situations.

Chapter 12 Driving in Adverse Conditions **255**

## Explain

Temperature changes should be closely monitored during potentially freezing weather. Sometimes daytime temperatures melt snow and ice and water runs on to road surfaces. As the sun sets and the temperatures drop, the thin layer of water on the road can freeze and create black ice.

## Explain

Point out that gravel, wet leaves, sand, and other loose materials on the roadway can reduce traction just as snow and ice do. Many drivers encounter these reduced traction situations more frequently than they drive on ice or snow.

## Activity

**Class Activity** Have students respond to decision-making situations during icy roadway conditions. Use **Demonstration Overhead H** and a movable yellow car. Place the yellow car halfway up the hill and explain that the road surface is slippery. Ask: What action should the driver take at this point? (Reduce speed, and downshift before entering the hillcrest.) For the next situation, place the yellow car at the hillcrest and coming down the hill. Explain that the roadway is very slippery and the driver cannot get traction to reduce speed. Ask: What should the driver do? (Steer the car to get the right tires off the road surface and onto the shoulder. The shoulder will have a more abrasive surface with better traction than the slick road surface.)

Chapter 12
Driving in Adverse Conditions | **255**

## Demonstrate

Demonstrate the effects of traction on steering using a 1/24-inch-scale model car with steerable front wheels. You will also need a piece of plywood (or heavy cardboard) two feet wide and four feet long to simulate the road surface. Place one end of the plywood on your desk and elevate the other end one foot to create an incline. Turn the tires of the model car to the right, and place the car at the top of the incline. Let go of the car and let it roll down and to the right. (Have a student be ready to catch it before it goes off the board.)

Ask: What would happen to the car if traction to the front wheels is lost and the tires are not able to grip the road? After hearing answers from the class, demonstrate loss of traction. Turn the wheels to the right and stick a piece of masking tape to the sidewall of both front wheels to prevent them from rotating. Place the car at the top of the incline and let it go. Ask students to explain what happened. (The car slid straight down the incline because the traction to the front wheels was lost.)

Ask: What would happen if traction is lost to the rear wheels? After hearing answers from the class, demonstrate loss of traction to the rear wheels. Tape both rear wheels so that they cannot rotate. Place the car at the top of the incline and let it slide down the board. Ask students to explain what happened. (The rear of the car will rotate 180 degrees into a rear-wheel skid.) See **Resource Book,** pages 53–54 for more activities.

Gravel on the road will affect your control.

- **Ice in Tire Tracks** Snow can pack down into ice in the normal driving tracks. Avoid these slippery tracks by moving a little to the right in lane position 3 to use the unpacked, less-slick portion of your lane.

### Other Reduced-Traction Situations

Braking distance will always increase in low-traction situations. Slow early and then be ready to slow even more.

**Gravel Roads** Loose gravel on roads can act like marbles under your tires and cause skids. Well-packed wheel paths usually form on heavily traveled gravel roads. Drive in these paths for better traction and control. If you need to move out of the wheel paths, slow and hold your steering wheel firmly.

**Leaves** Wet leaves on the road can decrease traction and reduce your stopping and steering control. Slow ahead of time if you see wet leaves on the pavement.

**Construction Areas** Construction trucks and other equipment can leave mud, dirt, or sand on the road. Slow, steer gently, and obey workers' directions. Be especially careful for workers and construction drivers who do not see you. Use an extra space cushion to protect them. In many states, traffic fines double in construction zones.

### Skidding

In Chapter 5 you learned how traction allows your vehicle to grip the road. You also learned what factors can reduce traction. In extreme reduced-traction situations, your tires may lose all or part of their grip on the road and **skid.** Skidding can happen on any surface while you are braking, accelerating, or steering.

In addition to slowing ahead of time, early detection is one of your best defenses to control skidding. What is the best way to detect a skid? Aim high to see your target

Respect the dangers around a construction site by lowering your speed and being ready to stop.

---

## Activity

**Small Group Activity** Divide students into groups of three to discuss the effects of reduced traction. Have students discuss the following: conditions that can cause reduced traction, procedures for preventing and detecting skid situations, differences between loss of traction to front and rear wheels, and actions required to correct each type of skid. After adequate time, each group should report its findings to the class.

This set of photos shows two examples of a car skidding off target (the yellow circle). If your vehicle skids off target to the right, steer back toward your target area by turning the wheel to the left.

If your vehicle skids off target to the left, steer back toward your target area by turning the wheel to the right.

well down the road. The instant you see your vehicle is not traveling in your intended path of travel toward your target, you need to start correcting the skid. If you wait until you feel your vehicle skidding, you may not be able to correct the skid in time to avoid trouble.

These pages will show you how to correct most skidding situations.

In all these situations, remember:
1. A locked or spinning wheel provides no steering control.
2. Never give up trying to correct a skid.

**Over-Power Skid** If you apply too much power to your drive wheels, they may spin, thus causing a skid. To correct this, simply let off your accelerator.

Chapter 12 Driving in Adverse Conditions **257**

Tell students to use the photographs on this page with the explanation of a rear-wheel skid on the next page. Use **Content Overhead 23** to explain what to do if fishtailing occurs.

## Demonstrate

Demonstrate how to detect a rear-wheel skid (explained on page 258) and how to use targeting skills to determine the direction, extent, and speed of steering actions. You will need a chair that is capable of swiveling. Have one student sit in the chair with a simulated steering wheel and pretend he or she is driving a vehicle. Explain that in this simulation the intended path of travel is toward the target of the classroom door. Tell the student that he or she is to keep the vehicle on target, and that as soon as the vehicle gets off target, he or she is to turn the steering wheel to get the front of the vehicle back on target. Remind the driver that if the vehicle moves slightly off target, a slight steering action is needed; if the vehicle begins to move quickly off target, a very rapid and full turning of the wheel would be necessary to get the tires back on target.

Stand to the rear of the chair, and swing the chair slightly off target in one direction or the other. Observe how the student responds with steering and head movement toward the target. Swing the chair again, changing the direction and the quickness. Have other students provide feedback to the student about head position and the direction, speed, and extent of steering wheel turns.

## Activity

**In-Class Driving Rehearsal** After performing the Demonstration on this page, have other students practice the same situations. If available, use additional swivel chairs. Divide the class into groups based on the number of chairs. Have one student pretend to drive while another student moves the chair. Have other members of the group provide feedback. Rotate roles until all students have a chance to be the driver.

Chapter 12
Driving in Adverse Conditions **257**

## Explain

Explain that when the rear skidding action is stopped, but the front of the vehicle is not pointing toward the target area, there is a high risk for a secondary skid to occur. The front tires are pointing toward the target because of the steering action. During this pause, all four wheels are sliding and therefore the vehicle is sliding. The driver at this moment relaxes, thinking the vehicle is under control. The driver should let the vehicle slide. This will reduce the vehicle's speed until traction is regained and the tires are able to grip the road. This is when a secondary skid can occur. As soon as the driver sees that the front of the vehicle is moving toward the target, he or she should straighten the steering wheel. By keeping your head and eyes pointing toward the target area, you are most easily able to see when the front of the vehicle begins to move toward the target, which gives you time to straighten the tires quickly.

Correcting a fishtailing skid

**Over-Braking Skid** If your vehicle does not have an antilock braking system (ABS) and you over-brake, the wheels may stop while you are still moving. To correct this, release your brake pedal enough to get your wheels rolling. See the controlled braking section on the next page for more details.

**Front-Wheel Skid** You are in a front-wheel skid if you turn the steering wheel and your vehicle wants to slide straight ahead. Your vehicle responds less than you want it to. To correct this skid, you need to regain traction for steering. To do this, you need to

1. Release accelerator or brake pedal pressure.
2. Quickly apply and release the brake pedal to slow if your vehicle does not have ABS.
3. Continue to look and steer at the path of travel you want to follow.

**Rear-Wheel Skid** If you are steering straight and your vehicle starts to move off target to the left or right, you probably are just starting a rear wheel skid. This skid can be caused by using too much power or braking on slick surfaces. The instant this skid starts, do the following:

1. Release your accelerator or brake. With manual transmission, depress your clutch pedal.
2. Steer quickly and precisely in the direction your vehicle needs to go, as shown on page 257. On a straight road, steer for your target and intended path of travel. Be careful not to overcorrect for the skid by steering too much.

3. The rear end of your vehicle probably will continue to slide a little from side to side, or **fishtail,** after you have corrected the initial skid. Steer and countersteer in the direction your vehicle needs to go. As your speed drops, your control will increase. Look at the illustration to the left to see how you can provide precise, smooth, continuous steering actions to correct a fishtail skid sequence.

**Skidding in a Curve** Slow ahead of time to avoid skidding in a curve. If you do skid in a curve, you probably are going to go off the road. If so, use the steps to correct a front-wheel or rear-wheel skid and steer for an off-road path of travel that is as safe as possible.

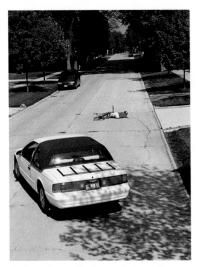

ABS enables you to steer and stop at the same time.

258  Unit 3  Driving in Different Environments and Situations

## Activity

**In-Class Driving Rehearsal** This activity will give students an opportunity to make decisions to control a vehicle in various reduced-traction situations. Use **Demonstration Overhead C** and the yellow transparency car to simulate reduced-traction situations. Explain that you will create a situation on the overhead and that they are to react as if they were driving the yellow car. Have them hold their simulated steering wheels and place their foot on an imaginary accelerator and brake pedal.

For the first situation, tell students to place their foot on the accelerator and pretend that they are traveling at 40 mph. Place the yellow car on the roadway below the intersection. Move the front of the car 10 degrees off target to the left. (The students should move their steering wheel to the right to get the car back on target; no braking, foot off accelerator.) Provide feedback.

For the second situation, move the yellow car to the right quickly. (Students should turn the wheel to the right with a faster movement.)

See **Resource Book,** pages 55–56 for more situations to use with this activity.

## Controlled Braking

A panic stop can lock your wheels, causing a skid and loss of steering control.

Use **controlled braking** to reduce your speed as quickly as possible while maintaining steering control of your vehicle. Controlled braking is a technique of applying your brakes to slow or stop quickly without locking your wheels. Follow these steps to use controlled braking:

1. With the heel of your foot on the floor, let the ball of your foot press your brake pedal. You must press hard enough to slow your vehicle rapidly without locking your wheels.

2. If your wheels lock and your vehicle skids, ease up on your brake pedal just enough to let your wheels start rolling.

3. Keep using this squeeze-relax a little-squeeze process until you stop.

Using just the right amount of pressure is the hardest part in controlled braking situations. To overcome this problem, most new vehicles are equipped with an anti-lock braking system (ABS).

An ABS-equipped vehicle uses a computer to prevent its wheels from locking—even in an emergency stop. If your vehicle has an ABS, just press the brake pedal as hard as you can in an emergency. You may feel little pulses through the brake pedal or hear the ABS at work. Don't let up on the brake pedal; maintain firm pressure until you stop. Also remember, ABS vehicles will allow you

to steer and brake at the same time as shown in the picture on the left. *They will not enable you to stop in a shorter distance.*

The chart shows how long it takes to stop from 20 mph. Notice the difference that different tires and road surfaces can make.

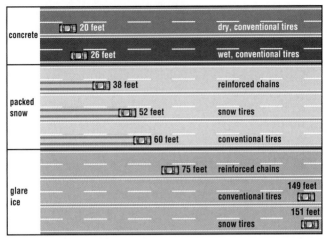

| | | |
|---|---|---|
| concrete | 20 feet | dry, conventional tires |
| | 26 feet | wet, conventional tires |
| packed snow | 38 feet | reinforced chains |
| | 52 feet | snow tires |
| | 60 feet | conventional tires |
| glare ice | 75 feet | reinforced chains |
| | 149 feet | conventional tires |
| | 151 feet | snow tires |

Braking Distances at 20 mph

### Review It

1. What happens to traction during rain and snow?
2. What happens when a vehicle hydroplanes?
3. What are the steps you need to take to correct a rear-wheel skid?
4. What does controlled braking enable you to do?

## Explain

Explain the importance of knowing if the vehicle you are driving has an antilock braking system (ABS). Remind student that if they have ABS, they should press the brake as hard as possible during an emergency. Do not pump the brake. See **Resource Book,** pages 78–80 for more information.

## Demonstrate

Use **Content Overhead 24** to illustrate how braking distances vary with type of tires and adverse roadway conditions.

## ③ Assess

### Answers to Review It

1. Traction is reduced in rain and snow. (p. 252)
2. The tires of a vehicle ride up on water and lose control when it hydroplanes. (p. 252)
3. Let up on your accelerator or brake, steer precisely in the direction your vehicle needs to go, correct any fishtail skids that follow. (p. 258)
4. Controlled braking enables you to slow and steer at the same time. (p. 258)

## Activity

**In-Class Driving Rehearsal** This activity will give students an opportunity to demonstrate correct actions to take during reduced-traction situations. Divide students into groups of three and assign three roles: driver, instructor, and observer. Give each group a set of cue cards that list problems and correct driver responses to be taken (see **Resource Book,** pages 57–58). While the driver pretends to be in a vehicle, the instructor reads one of the problems from the cue card and asks the driver to describe and perform the correct actions. The observer and instructor provide feedback. Repeat the activity until each student has played each role.

# Other Adverse Weather Conditions

 **Focus**

## Summary

This lesson focuses on three adverse weather conditions: wind, hot weather, and cold weather. Tips for smooth winter driving are also included.

## ② **Teach**

## Demonstrate

This demonstration will show that there is turbulent air to the front and rear of a passing truck. You will need a small block of wood and a shallow tray with an inch of sand in it. Move the block of wood through the sand and call attention to how the sand is accumulating to the front and sides of the block of wood, while leaving a void of sand to the rear. When a truck is approaching and getting ready to pass, there is the same type of movement of the air. The accumulation of air to the front of the truck can push a vehicle out of a travel lane away from the side of the truck. To the rear of the truck the void of air creates a vacuum that can draw a vehicle into the direction of the truck. The effects from the truck's air turbulence will be most dominant when a vehicle is in a reduced traction situation.

### Objectives

1. Explain how to control your vehicle in windy conditions.
2. List precautions for driving in extremely hot or cold weather.
3. Describe what to do to maintain vehicle control during winter driving.

Extreme weather conditions can make routine driving very difficult. Other adverse conditions such as wind, extreme temperatures, and winter weather may also affect the control you have while driving.

## Wind

Strong winds can reduce your vehicle control. Imagine the truck pictured here is passing you on the left. A strong wind is blowing from the left. What should you expect? How can you maintain control?

Anticipate a strong blast of wind from the left after the truck passes. To maintain control, be ready to slow a little, move to lane position 3, and apply extra steering to the left just to keep moving in your intended path of travel.

You may experience this type of situation when driving out from under a bridge or from a tunnel. Just remember to keep a balanced grip on the steering wheel and be ready to make steering corrections for cross winds.

In the unlikely event you are in an area where tornadoes are spotted, be ready to act. The last place you want to be in a tornado is in a car. If you see a tornado and there is no place to take cover, stop, get out of your vehicle, and lay down in a ditch or under a bridge.

Expect the combination of a high cross wind and truck traffic to make driving tough.

## Teacher's Resources

No *Drive Right* resources are needed for teaching Section 12.3.

## Activity

 **Class Activity** Ask students to do this activity the next time they are passengers in vehicles driving on a highway. Ask students to listen to the sound of the air flow change as trucks approach and pass. Tell them to sit in the rear seat on the driver's side. Have them open the side window about one inch and listen as trucks pass on the left. Ask them to notice the difference between the sound before the truck passes, while it is passing, and just after it passes.

In deep snow, make sure exhaust can get away from your vehicle.

## Hot Weather

Your vehicle is designed to operate in a wide range of temperatures. It has a cooling system to help it warm up in winter and stay cool in the summer. But in extreme conditions, problems can develop.

Your temperature light or gauge indicates when your engine is too hot. When this happens, turn off your air conditioner. You may be uncomfortable, but you might also be able to cool your engine enough by turning on your heater. If the engine temperature warning light stays on, stop and park in a safe place to let the engine cool. Once cool, check your coolant level in your cooling-system surge tank. Never remove the radiator cap on a hot engine because the hot liquid inside can scald you. If needed, refill and repair your cooling system.

## Cold Weather

Very cold weather creates problems. Be prepared by taking the following steps:

- **Be Alert for Exhaust Leaks**
  Carbon monoxide gas is created when your engine runs. This gas is colorless, odorless, and deadly. Even a small exhaust leak can be trouble. When driving, always have a source of fresh air coming into your vehicle—even if you have to open a window a little. If you are stuck in snow with your engine running, make sure your exhaust pipe is not blocked as this driver is doing.
- **Do Not Race a Cold Engine**
  Racing a cold engine will increase wear on it. Do not run a cold engine at high speeds.
- **Do Not Set Your Parking Brake**
  Ice or slush stuck to the underside of your vehicle can freeze your parking brake when you park your vehicle. In these conditions, use your automatic transmission park gear or reverse with a standard transmission.

## Tips for Smooth Winter Driving

Winter driving will test the best of your IPDE driving skills. The extra

Chapter 12  Driving in Adverse Conditions  **261**

## Background

**Fuel Tanks and Cold Weather**

During cold weather there are advantages to keeping the fuel tank nearly full. It will reduce the amount of moisture formed by air condensing in the fuel tank. Condensation could freeze and block the fuel line. Also, by keeping the tank in a near-full condition, you will have more weight over your rear tires, which can help give you better traction.

## Discuss

Tell students to imagine they are driving a vehicle during hot weather in stop-and-go traffic. Ask: How can you detect that your vehicle is beginning to overheat? (The temperature gauge begins to move from a normal position or the temperature light comes on.) Ask: What should you do next? (Turn off the air conditioner and turn on your heater; monitor the temperature gauge or light.) What should you do if the vehicle continues to get hot? (Locate a safe place to park, preferably in the shade. Turn off the engine and wait for it to cool.)

## Explain

If your vehicle overheats, you need to wait about an hour before restarting the engine. It is a good idea to open the hood during this time.

## Explain

When your vehicle first appears to be overheating you can try several things. Turn off the air conditioner and turn on the heater. You can also stop the vehicle, shift to NEUTRAL, and race the engine slightly. If the temperature gauge does not return to the normal position or the temperature light stays on, you need to stop.

## Explain

Explain that snow should be brushed off the roof, hood, and trunk. Snow could slide down from the roof to cover the windshield or rear window when the vehicle is in motion. Also, snow that blows off the vehicle is a distraction to drivers following and may blow against their windshield, blocking their vision.

 **Assess**

### Answers to Review It

**1.** Slow and be ready to steer slightly into the wind. (p. 260)

**2.** Turn off your air conditioner and turn on your heater if needed. If the temperature light stays on, park your vehicle, let it cool, and check for cooling system leaks. (p. 261)

**3.** You vehicle's energy of motion will carry it through many snowy situations. (p. 262)

Clear snow off your roof, hood, and trunk so it will not blow off and block your vision.

effort you make to maintain an adequate line of sight and open zones is worth it. You can help smooth the way by following these tips:

- **Look and Listen for Traffic Reports** Be alert to television and radio reports about accidents, road repairs, and bad weather. You also can take advantage of Internet information sources.
- **Keep Windows Clear** Remove snow and ice before driving as this driver is doing. Don't forget your headlights and taillights. You want to see and be seen.
- **Respect Lower Speeds** Travel with the flow of traffic, but always maintain control of your vehicle.

- **Keep a Safe Following Distance** Allow six, seven, or more seconds of following distance just to make sure you have room.
- **Try to Keep Moving in Snow** If you must be out in a blizzard, be alert for drivers who are stalled, disabled, or moving extremely slowly. Try to avoid getting stuck behind them. Slow down and maneuver to avoid others and to keep moving. The energy of motion created by your moving vehicle can help carry you through snowy situations.
- **Use a Lower Gear on Slippery Roads** Use a lower gear to maintain control on ice or snow. Remember, keep moving to avoid getting stuck.
- **Avoid Cruise Control** Do not use cruise control on slippery roads. The system could cause you to lose control.

### Review It

1. What actions must you take to maintain vehicle control in strong winds?
2. What can you do to cool an overheated engine?
3. Why should you try to keep moving at low speeds in heavy snow?

262 Unit 3 Driving in Different Environments and Situations

## Reviewing Chapter Objectives

### 1. Reduced Visibility

1. How do you use the IPDE Process to manage risks in bad weather? (246)
2. What can you do to help others see you at dawn and dusk? (247)
3. What special techniques can you use for night driving? (247–249)

### 2. Reduced Traction

4. What happens to traction during rain and snow? (252)
5. What steps can you take to avoid hydro-planing? (252)
6. How do you correct a rear-wheel skid? (257)
7. How do you use the controlled-braking technique? (257–258)

### 3. Other Adverse Weather Conditions

8. How can you control your vehicle in windy conditions? (260)
9. What precautions can you take for driving in extremely hot or cold weather? (261)
10. What should you do to maintain vehicle control during winter driving? (262)

## Projects

### Individuals

**Investigate** Make a list of all the sources available to you to check on traffic conditions. Your list should include sources for local conditions as well as sources for conditions across the country.

**Use Technology** Use the Internet to check weather conditions throughout the United States. Identify places with weather conditions that could affect travel. Compare your findings with those of your classmates.

### Groups

**Demonstrate** Using model vehicles, demonstrate to the class the various types of skids discussed in the text. Explain how the skids occur and how to correct for them.

**Practice** With the owners' permission, practice cleaning the outside windows of the vehicles parked in your school parking lot.

## Reviewing Chapter Objectives

**12.1** Reduced Visibility
See Answers to Review It on page 251.
**12.2** Reduced Traction
See Answers to Review It on page 259.
**12.3** Other Adverse Weather Conditions
See Answers to Review It on page 262.
    For additional information refer to the specific page(s) in parentheses after each question.

## Projects

Some of the projects can be assigned at any time while others are more closely tied to the content presented in the student text. The page number where the topic is introduced is indicated.
    **Investigate:** p. 262
    **Use Technology:** p. 250
    **Demonstrate (Group)** p. 256
    **Practice:** p. 246
The results of student projects will vary.

## Teacher's Resources

**Skills and Applications Workbook**
pages 45–48

**Tests and Activities**
Activities 12-1 and 12-2
pages 99–100
Chapter 12 Test A and Test B,
pages 101–104

**TestWorks CD-ROM**
Chapter 12 Test

## Answers to Check Your Knowledge

1. c
2. b
3. d
4. a
5. glare
6. low-beam
7. Antilock

## Answers to Review Vocabulary

8. skid (d)
9. rocking a vehicle (c)
10. controlled braking (a)
11. overdriving headlights (e)
12. hydroplaning (b)

## Answers to Think Critically

Students' answers will vary. For information related to the question refer to the page(s) indicated.

1. Refer to the first paragraph and bulleted list on page 246.

2. Use low-beam headlights when driving at night during adverse weather conditions. Heavy rain, falling snow, and fog cause more light to be reflected back to your eyes, making seeing more difficult and limiting your sight distance. (p. 248)

## Chapter Test

### Check Your Knowledge

**Multiple Choice** Copy the number of each sentence below on a sheet of paper. Choose the letter of the answer that best completes the sentence or answers the question.

1. When visibility is reduced, the first action to take is to
   (a) maintain a steady speed.  (b) stop.
   (c) slow down.
   (d) move closer to the windshield.
2. If traction conditions are hazardous, you should
   (a) drive slowly.          (b) not drive at all.
   (c) drive close to other vehicles.
   (d) use emergency flashers.
3. Traction on wet roads can be improved by driving
   (a) toward the right edge of the roadway.
   (b) at or near the posted speed limit.
   (c) with reduced tire air pressure.
   (d) in the tire tracks of the vehicle ahead.
4. When your temperature gauge indicates that your engine is too hot, you should
   (a) turn on your heater.
   (b) remove the radiator cap.
   (c) turn on your air conditioner.
   (d) none of the above

**Completion** Copy the number of each sentence below. After each number, write the word or words that complete the sentence correctly.

5. Wearing sun glasses and a sun visor helps you deal with blinding _____ conditions.
6. If it is snowing during the day or at night, you should always use _____ headlights.
7. _____ brakes allow you to steer and stop at the same time.

### Review Vocabulary

Copy the number of each definition in List A. Match the definition in List A with the term it defines in List B.

**List A**

8. vehicle loses part or all of its grip on the road
9. repeating the sequence of driving forward a little and then back a little to move your vehicle out of deep snow, mud, or sand
10. reducing speed as quickly as possible while maintaining steering control of your vehicle
11. driving at a speed that makes your stopping distance longer than the distance lighted by your headlights
12. occurs when a tire loses road contact by rising up on top of water

**List B**

a. controlled braking     d. skid
b. hydroplaning           e. overdriving headlights
c. rocking a vehicle

### Think Critically

Write a paragraph to answer each question.

1. Using the IPDE Process as your guide, explain how you can maintain a safe intended path of travel when visibility is reduced.
2. Which headlights (low-beam or high-beam) should you use when driving at night in adverse weather conditions? Explain your answer.

## Decision Making

1. What actions should you take in this skidding situation?

2. In this winter situation, what precautions should you take when approaching the bridge?

3. As you approach this situation and see that the blue van has stopped, how would you use controlled braking?

4. What visual habit should you use to avoid being blinded by these oncoming high-beam headlights?

Chapter 12 Driving in Adverse Conditions **265**

## Answers to Decision Making

1. Let up on your accelerator; do not brake. Steer to the right (toward your target). Straighten your wheels when your vehicle comes out of the skid. (p. 258)

2. The road over the bridge is wet and might be icy. You should reduce speed when approaching this bridge. (p. 255)

3. Apply your brakes hard enough to slow to a stop. (pp. 258–259)

4. Look down and use the right edge of the roadway as a guide. Glance forward frequently to check the position of oncoming traffic. Do not look directly into the headlights. (p. 248)

| | Student Features | Teacher's Edition |
|---|---|---|
| **Chapter 13**<br>**Handling Emergencies** | You Are the Driver! *p. 267* | Projects *p. 266*<br>Special Needs *p. 267* |
| **13.1 Vehicle Malfunctions** *pp. 268–275*<br>• List actions to take if a tire blows out.<br>• List the proper steps to follow if the brakes fail.<br>• Explain what to do if your accelerator sticks.<br>• Describe what to do in case of steering failure. | Safe Driving Tip *p. 270* | Demonstrate *pp. 269, 271, 273, 274*<br>Activity *pp. 268, 269, 270, 271, 272*<br>Special Needs *p. 275* |
| **13.2 Driver Errors** *pp. 276–278*<br>• Describe how to return to the roadway if your vehicle runs off the roadway.<br>• Explain when to use an emergency swerve. | What Do You Think?<br>*p. 277* | Demonstrate *p. 277*<br>Activity *p. 277* |
| **13.3 Roadway Hazards** *pp. 279–280*<br>• Describe how to minimize vehicle damage caused by potholes.<br>• Explain what to do if you enter a curve too fast.<br>• Tell how to escape from a vehicle that is sinking in water. | | Activity *p. 279* |
| **13.4 Collisions** *pp. 281–284*<br>• Explain how to avoid or minimize head-on, side-impact, and rear-end collisions.<br>• List the immediate steps to take if a collision occurs.<br>• Describe other follow-up steps needed after a collision. | Safe Driving Tip *p. 282*<br>Did You Know? *p. 283* | Demonstrate *pp. 281, 282*<br>Activity *pp. 281, 283, 284* |
| **Assessment** | Reviewing Chapter<br>  Objectives *p. 285*<br>Projects *p. 285*<br>Chapter Test *p. 286*<br>Decision Making *p. 287* | Answers *pp. 286–287* |

## Teacher's Resource File

## Videos, Overheads, and Software

**Companion** *pp. 81–86*
**Spanish Handbook** *pp. 27–28*

---

**Resource Book**
Roadway Sheets 1–8,
  *pp. 4–19*
**In-Car Checklists** 31, 32

---

**In-Car Checklists** 33, 34

**Content Overheads 25, 26**

---

**Resource Book**
Roadway Sheets 1–8,
  *pp. 4–19*
**In-Car Checklists** 35, 36

**Demonstration Overheads
F, H**

---

**Skills and Applications
  Workbook,** *pp. 49–52*
**Tests and Activities**
Chapter 13 Activities 13-1
  and 13-2, *pp. 107–108*
Chapter 13 Test A and
  Test B, *pp. 109–112*
Unit 3 Test, *pp. 113–116*

**TestWorks CD-ROM**
  Chapter 13 Test

## Technology Resources

### Audio-Visual and Computer Resources

AAA Foundation for Traffic Safety, *On the Scene: A Guide to Bystander Care at a Roadside Emergency,* video, 15 minutes

BFA Educational Media, *Auto Accident: What to Do Afterward,* video, 10 minutes

Safety Industries, Inc., *Emergency Situations,* video, 10 minutes

**Go Online**
PHSchool.com
**For:** Chapter 13 online activities
**Visit:** PHSchool.com
**Web Code:** cak-9999

# Chapter 13

## Handling Emergencies

### Chapter Overview

Chapter 13 discusses driving emergencies caused by vehicle malfunction and driver error. Students learn how to handle emergencies and what actions to take after a collision.

### Chapter Vocabulary

*blowout, brake fade, counter-steer, jack, lug nuts*

## Teacher's Resources

For students to use as they read the chapter:

**Companion**
pages 81–86

**Spanish Handbook**
pages 27–28

## Projects

Review the projects described on page 285. Some of the projects can be assigned at any time while others are more closely tied to the content presented in the student text.

# CHAPTER 13
## Handling Emergencies

## You Are the Driver!

Imagine that you are driving the blue car in this situation. The red car on your right pulls out in front of you. What should you do? What should you do if a collision occurs?

Vehicle malfunctions, driver errors, and roadway hazards can cause emergencies. In all cases, you must be prepared to act quickly to avoid or minimize a collision.

In this chapter you will learn how to handle many kinds of emergencies, and what steps to take if you are involved in a collision.

**Go Online**
PHSchool.com

**For:** Chapter 13 online activities
**Visit:** PHSchool.com
**Web Code:** cak-9999

267

## Introducing the Chapter

Ask students what emergencies they might encounter as a driver. Discuss how these emergencies can be avoided.

## You Are the Driver!

Students should imagine they are driving the car indicated. Ask them how they would respond to the emergency shown. Discuss when to brake and when to swerve. Indicate the importance of reacting quickly and accurately in such a situation. Discuss what procedures to follow if a collision occurs.

## Special Needs

The activities and demonstrations in this chapter are exactly what special needs students need to develop their knowledge and skills. Be sure these students are included in small groups or work with their partners. Try to provide practice in the driver education car for emergency procedures. Students might find it helpful to use the **In-Car Checklists,** pages 31–36.

# Vehicle Malfunctions

 **Focus**

## Summary

This lesson is devoted to common vehicle malfunctions including tire failure, brake failure, accelerator malfunction, engine failure, and steering failure. These malfunctions are identified and appropriate reactions are described. Loss of forward vision, vehicle fires, and stalling on railroad crossings are also addressed.

## Vocabulary

*blowout, brake fade, jack, lug nuts*

 **Teach**

## Discuss

Ask: Which is more dangerous, coping with a tire blowout or changing a tire? Point out that more people are killed while attending to a disabled vehicle than during a blowout. Stress that selecting a safe location is more important than changing the tire. Ask: How far can you drive with a flat tire? Many drivers erroneously stop at the location where the blowout occurs. A vehicle should be capable of traveling at least a few miles, at very slow speeds, to get to a safe location.

## Objectives

1. List actions to take if a tire blows out.
2. List the proper steps to follow if the brakes fail.
3. Explain what to do if your accelerator sticks.
4. Describe what to do in case of steering failure.

Proper maintenance can prevent most vehicle malfunctions. When your vehicle gives you any warning signs, promptly make the necessary repairs.

Vehicle equipment sometimes will malfunction with no warning. A sudden malfunction can create an emergency. If prepared for an emergency, you will reduce your risk of serious trouble in traffic.

### Tire Failure

Tires wear more quickly under unfavorable driving and poor maintenance conditions. Abrupt braking and sharp steering shorten tire life. Bumps, potholes, and poor roadway surfaces add to tire stress and can cause sudden damage to tires. Unbalanced wheels and poor alignment can cause tires to wear unevenly. Underinflation and overinflation are other causes of tire wear.

### Blowout

A **blowout** occurs when a tire loses air pressure suddenly. A blowout might occur if the tire hits an object on the roadway or a pothole. Older, badly worn, or underinflated tires are more likely to blow out.

When a front tire blows out, the vehicle quickly pulls in the direction of the deflated tire. You must steer firmly against the pull of the vehicle. A left-front tire blowout is especially dangerous, since the vehicle will pull toward the lane of oncoming traffic.

When a rear tire blows out, the back of the vehicle can fishtail. When fishtailing occurs, the rear of the vehicle swerves back and forth. Handle a rear blowout like a skid.

Take the following actions when a tire blows out:
1. Grip the steering wheel firmly.
2. Ease up on the accelerator to slow the vehicle. *Do not brake.* Braking can cause the vehicle to swerve.
3. Check the traffic situation as you gain control of the vehicle.
4. Drive off the roadway slowly, braking gently.
5. Turn on hazard flashers. Drive slowly until you find a safe location to stop.

### Changing a Tire

Even if you are an auto club member, you should know how to change a tire. Tire-changing instructions are included in the owner's manual for your vehicle. Practice changing a tire in a safe place.

To change a tire, you will need a **jack**, a hand-operated device used to lift and hold one corner or side of the vehicle. An elevated vehicle might slip off a jack. Never put yourself in a position where the vehicle could fall on you.

Follow these steps to change a tire:
1. Park on a level area away from traffic. Turn on the hazard flashers. Put the selector lever in PARK; use REVERSE in a stick-shift vehicle.

 **Teacher's Resources**

**Resource Book**
Roadway Sheets 1–8, pages 4–9
**In-Car Checklists**
In-Car Checklists 31, 32

 **Activity**

**Model Car Activity** Organize the class into groups of three with roles of driver, teacher, and supervisor. Give each group a model car, the complete set of roadway sheets from **Resource Book,** pages 4–19, and a few wild cards. Have the driver move a disabled car out of traffic flow. Have the supervisor create unsafe conditions with the wild cards for the driver to respond to. Have the teacher give feedback. Students should take turns in each role, with each using a different roadway. Have them discover the safest place to stand in each situation.

2. Set the parking brake.
3. Block the wheel that is diagonally opposite the flat tire. Carry two blocks of wood or two bricks in your trunk for this purpose. Place one block in front of the wheel and another block firmly behind the wheel. Blocking helps keep the vehicle from rolling once it is raised up by the jack.
4. Ask your passengers to get out of the vehicle and move to a safe place away from the roadway.
5. Take out the spare tire, jack, and lug wrench.
6. Assemble the jack. Position it under the vehicle.
7. Jack up the vehicle partway. The flat tire should touch the ground so that the wheel cannot turn.
8. Remove the wheel cover. Loosen the **lug nuts,** the devices that hold the wheel to the vehicle.
9. Jack up the vehicle until the tire completely clears the ground.
10. Use the lug wrench to remove the lug nuts. Place them in a safe place, such as your pocket.

If a left-front tire blows out, the vehicle might pull toward oncoming traffic.

11. Remove the wheel with the flat tire. Place the wheel to the side.
12. Mount the wheel with the spare tire. Rock it gently into position.
13. Replace and tighten the lug nuts.
14. Lower the vehicle slowly and remove the jack.
15. Use the lug wrench to tighten all the lug nuts again.
16. Leave the wheel cover off as a reminder to fix the flat. Put the wheel cover, flat tire, and tire changing equipment into the trunk. Remove the blocks. Replace or repair the flat tire as soon as possible. If your spare tire is

Rock the spare tire into position as you mount it.

## Demonstrate

Use the driver education car to demonstrate the proper technique for changing a tire. Ask a volunteer to change a tire while other members of the class provide instructions. Ask: What is the first step after the car is stopped in a safe location? (Turn on hazard flashers and put the selector lever in PARK.) Ask students to provide step-by-step instructions to the volunteer. Use the instructions provided by the manufacturer for assembling the jack and other steps that are specific to the vehicle. After students correctly explain each step, have the volunteer complete the step on the driver education car. Continue until all steps have been completed. Ask for another volunteer and repeat the demonstration to replace the original tire.

## Explain

Remind students of the importance of not braking hard when experiencing steering problems caused by a flat tire. Also point out that correct hand position on the steering wheel can be important in a vehicle malfunction.

## Explain

Explain that even though emergency services are available, every driver should be able to change a flat tire.

## Activity

**Class Activity** This activity will help students understand the roles of friction and heat in tire failure. Give each student a two-inch jumbo paper clip. Instruct students to undo the bends to create a six-inch wire. The original bends will still be discernable. Tell them to put their forefingers and thumbs close to one of the bends near the center of the wire and rapidly flex the wire back and forth. Point out that the wire will heat up as they flex it. After a few seconds of flexing, tell them to touch the wire to feel the heat.

Have them continue to flex the wire until it breaks. This is an example of internal friction.

Explain that tire damage occurs when a tire is underinflated because the tire is flexing back and forth. This flexing is similar to what happened to the paper clips. The heat generated by an underinflated tire is so great that it causes the tire's reinforcement cords to break away from its rubber encasement and eventually results in tire failure.

## Discuss

Ask: How does your braking style affect your ability to react to brake failure? (Drivers who have the habit of seeing a closed front zone and making early braking applications will have more opportunities and more time to solve problems. One such problem is brake failure.)

## Explain

Point out that when a great amount of steering is needed, turning off the engine is not recommended as a solution for handling a stuck accelerator. Remind students how steering is affected by the key position in the ignition. When the key is in the *On* position, you can steer, and if the vehicle has power steering, the power steering functions. When the key is in the *Off* position, you can steer, but you lose the power steering. This means you will need to put more muscle into the steering effort. When the key is in the locked position, the steering wheel locks, and you cannot steer. However, the key can only be placed into the locked position when the car is stopped. Therefore, this cannot happen while moving.

A quick look around your vehicle before driving may help you identify a worn tire, burned out light, or other problem—before a vehicle failure occurs.

a temporary or compact spare, drive on it only as necessary under the manufacturer's conditions of its use.

### Brake Failure

Vehicles are required to have a two-part braking system. If one part fails, the other part still brakes two wheels. The brake warning light signals a brake failure. If both braking parts fail at the same time, your foot brake will have no braking power at all.

### Total Brake Failure

Total brake failure rarely happens. When it does occur, the driver is usually braking hard for a stop.

Follow these steps immediately if your brakes fail:

1. Pump the brake pedal. Pumping might temporarily restore enough brake-fluid pressure to slow or stop your vehicle. You will know after three or four pumps if your brakes are going to hold.
2. Downshift to a lower gear. This uses the braking power of the engine to slow.

If your brakes fail, apply the parking brake, but hold the button at "Off" or hold the release lever out.

270   Unit 3  Driving in Different Environments and Situations

3. Pull and hold the parking-brake release lever out or hold the parking-brake button at "Off." Apply the parking brake. You can quickly release the parking brake for a moment if the vehicle begins to skid.
4. Search for an open zone. You can still steer. As a last resort, rub the wheels against a curb to reduce speed. If a collision is unavoidable, steer for a sideswipe rather than colliding head-on into something solid.

**Power Brake Failure**  Brake "failure" with power or power-assisted brakes is usually the loss of power that helps you brake. The power stops if the engine stops, but the brakes have not failed. You must push the brake pedal harder.

### Other Brake Failures

When brakes overheat, they can lose effectiveness. This condition, called **brake fade,** occurs after continuous hard braking. To regain full braking ability, stop the vehicle and let the brakes cool. Overheating can warp the rotors on disc brakes. As a result, braking becomes uneven, and the vehicle might surge forward as you brake. To restore smooth braking, you might need to have the rotors repaired.

Driving through water also can cause temporary brake failure. Gently brake after you leave the water. Friction can help generate heat to dry the brakes. Test them again to be sure they work properly.

## Activity

**In-Class Driving Rehearsal**  This activity will provide practice in dealing with brake failure. Divide the class into pairs. There will be a driver and an observer in each pair. Tell students that as you describe a scenario, the drivers are to react as if they were actually driving a vehicle, and the observers are to watch their partners' reactions. Instruct the drivers to hold their hands on an imaginary steering wheel and put their foot on an imaginary acceleration pedal. Describe the following scenario: You are driving at 40 mph while approaching a left curve

in the road. You look through the curve 12 seconds ahead and see traffic stopped for construction. You have the good habit of early braking. When you put your foot on the brake pedal, it goes all the way to the floor and does not slow your vehicle. Take the appropriate action right now. Remind the observers to watch their partners. Have the observers state what they observed that was appropriate for the situation and what they observed that was not.

Have the pairs switch roles for the In-Class Driving Rehearsal on the next page.

## Accelerator Malfunctions

You can lose control of your engine's speed when the accelerator malfunctions. Some problems can cause your vehicle to accelerate more than you intend, and other problems can keep your vehicle from accelerating.

### Broken Spring

A broken accelerator spring is a serious problem. The accelerator pedal might be flat on the floor. You can no longer control engine speed with the accelerator.

If you have this problem, shift to NEUTRAL. Put on your hazard flashers, check traffic, and brake safely to the side of the road. Do not drive the vehicle until the spring is repaired.

### Stuck Accelerator

The accelerator is stuck if the engine does not return to idling speed when you release the accelerator. One cause of a stuck accelerator is a wadded floor mat around the pedal.

A stuck accelerator is a critical emergency. While driving at a steady speed, you have no warning that the accelerator is stuck. You discover that there is a problem when you need to turn or stop.

Take these actions if your accelerator sticks:

1. Kick the side of the accelerator once to try to jar it free.
2. Apply the brakes.
3. Choose an escape path that leads to an open zone off the roadway. Continue braking.
4. If you are steering into a sharp curve or turn, shift to NEUTRAL. Depress the clutch in a stickshift

While stopped or driving in light traffic, you can try to free a stuck accelerator by putting your toe under it and lifting.

vehicle. The engine will race, but power is removed from the wheels. You might damage the engine or transmission in an automatic transmission, but you might also avoid a collision.
5. Follow your escape path off the roadway.
6. Turn off the ignition once you are off the roadway.

If you are in a light-traffic area, you might try to free a stuck accelerator while driving. Put your toe under the accelerator pedal and lift. *Never reach down with your hand to lift the pedal while driving*. You cannot see or drive safely from this position.

After stopping, take these actions:
• Remove any obstructions around, under, or over the accelerator.
• Tap the accelerator repeatedly.
• Put your toe or hand under the accelerator and lift.

After freeing the accelerator, test it before you drive. If a broken spring is the problem, do not drive until it is repaired.

Chapter 13 Handling Emergencies **271**

## Demonstrate

Demonstrate how the steering wheel is likely to be unintentionally moved when the driver bends to pick something off the floorboard or to lift a stuck accelerator. You will need a pencil, a golf ball, a golf tee, a tennis ball, tape, and a sheet of paper. Tape the golf tee to the eraser end of the pencil. Make a small dot in the center of the sheet of paper. Place the paper on a student's desktop. Ask the student to use his or her left hand to hold the pencil perpendicular to the paper with the pencil point on the dot. Place the golf ball on the tee that is taped to the pencil and instruct the student to keep the ball on the tee. Place the tennis ball on the floor touching the front of the student's right shoe. Direct the student to pick up the tennis ball. Point out the movement of the pencil and the golf ball. Re-set the pencil and golf ball and place the tennis ball further away from the student's shoe. Again, direct the student to pick up the tennis ball. Roll the ball from left to right under the chair and have the student stop the ball. Repeat this demonstration with several other students.

Explain that the movement of the pencil, along with the golf ball falling off the tee, represents unintentional movement of the steering wheel. Point out that at 60 mph, each inch of pencil movement would represent one lane change per second. If the pencil moves three inches, the vehicle is three lanes over in one second!

## Activity

**In-Class Driving Rehearsal** This activity will provide practice in dealing with a stuck accelerator. Divide the class into pairs. There will be a driver and an observer in each pair. (Use the same pairs from the In-Class Driving Rehearsal on the previous page and switch roles.) Tell students that as you describe a scenario, the drivers are to react as if they were actually driving a vehicle, and the observers are to watch their partners' reactions. Instruct the drivers to hold their hands on an imaginary steering wheel and put their foot on an imaginary accelera-

tion pedal. Describe the following scenario: You are driving at 40 mph while approaching a red traffic light 12 seconds ahead. You have the good habit of early braking for a closed front zone. When you take your foot off the accelerator, you realize it is stuck. Take the appropriate action right now. Remind the observers to watch their partners. Have the observers state what they observed that was appropriate for the situation and what they observed that was not.

## Discuss

Discuss the importance of having time to take the correct action when vehicle malfunctions occur. This means extra time for braking, steering, and/or acceleration. Ask students to provide examples of when extra time is needed and what habits will provide the best opportunity to cope with the problems.

## Explain

The most common cause of engine failure is an empty fuel tank. Ask: What can you do to make sure you do not run out of gas? (Get into the habit of checking the fuel gauge every time you start the engine, and add fuel when the gauge indicates the tank is 1/4 full.)

## Explain

Power-brake systems have a reserve that allows the power assist to continue to work when the engine fails. However, the reserve is limited. Therefore, a driver should avoid pumping the brake pedal to conserve the power assistance. With a stalled engine, three or four pumps on the brake pedal will deplete it. After the reserve is depleted, the brakes will function, but without power assist. You will need to exert more force to push the brake pedal down.

### Engine Failure

Usually you have very little warning that your engine is going to sputter or stop. With a stalled engine, you can still steer your vehicle. If you have power steering, you will have to steer harder.

Follow these steps if your engine stops suddenly:

1. Shift to NEUTRAL when the engine first sputters or stops.
2. Begin moving out of traffic to the nearest shoulder. Turn on the hazard flashers. Do not brake.
3. Try to restart the engine while you are moving. If the engine starts, shift into a forward gear and proceed. If it does not start, move onto the shoulder or to the curb, if possible. Steering will be harder when power is lost by engine failure. Try again to start the engine.
4. If the engine still fails to start, raise the hood and leave the hazard flashers on. Go for help. If you have a cellular phone, use it to secure assistance.

If your vehicle becomes disabled in risky locations, set flares or other

If your engine fails, turn on the hazard flashers, move safely off the roadway, and raise the hood to signal you need help.

warning devices to alert other roadway users.

### Flooded Engine

When too much fuel and not enough air reach the engine, it becomes flooded. You can flood the engine if you pump the accelerator when trying to start the vehicle.

Follow these steps to start a flooded engine:

1. Hold the accelerator pedal to the floor to let air in and to clear excess fuel from engine.
2. While holding the accelerator down, turn the ignition switch on steadily for five seconds. If the engine does not start, wait several minutes, and try again.
3. When the engine starts, release the accelerator gradually to help clear excess fuel from the engine.

### Overheated Engine

Sometimes even a well maintained engine overheats in hot weather or in stop-and-go traffic. Driving up long hills with the air conditioner on also can cause overheating. The temperature light or gauge warns you if the engine overheats.

Take these steps if your engine overheats:

1. Turn off the air conditioner.
2. Turn on the heater to draw heat from the engine. You might be uncomfortable, but this will lower engine temperature.
3. During stops, shift to NEUTRAL. Press the accelerator gently to speed up the engine slightly.
4. If the temperature light stays on or if the gauge points to *hot,*

## Activity

**In-Class Driving Rehearsal** This activity will give students the opportunity to practice skills needed to cope with vehicle malfunctions. Divide the class into groups of three. There will be a driver and two observers in each group. Instruct the drivers to describe the appropriate reaction to engine failure. The observers are to listen and provide feedback using the textbook as a reference. Have students rotate roles and repeat the activity for each of the following problems: flooded engine, overheated engine, steering failure, power-steering failure, and headlight failure.

move to a safe place. Stop, turn off the engine, raise the hood, and let the engine cool. Do not add water to the radiator until the engine has cooled.

### Steering Failure

Complete steering-system failure seldom occurs but is extremely serious.

### Total Steering Failure

Take these actions if your steering fails completely:

1. Use your horn and hazard flashers to communicate your emergency.
2. Stop as quickly and safely as possible. Lift your foot from the accelerator. *Do not brake.* Braking could cause the vehicle to skid. Use the parking brake. Hold the parking brake release "Off" and use a quick on-off action.
3. Shift to a lower gear.

### Power-Steering Failure

Power-steering failure occurs when the engine dies, when the power-steering fluid level is low, or when a drive belt slips or breaks. The steering mechanism still works, but you must exert more effort to steer.

### Loss of Forward Vision

If you have lost forward vision, you must act promptly to regain your driving view. Slow and continue to drive in your path of travel.

### The Hood Flies Up

This rare emergency usually occurs because the hood is not securely latched. Stop your vehicle if the

If your hood flies up, look through the space below the open hood and steer to a safe place.

hood is vibrating. Release the hood and secure it.

Take these actions if the hood flies up while you are driving:

1. Slouch down in your seat to look through the crack below the open hood. Check the rear zone.
2. If you cannot see under the hood, roll down your window. Look in the direction that you are driving.
3. Turn on the hazard flashers. Pump the brakes gently to warn other drivers of your emergency.
4. Slow down, and drive out of the traffic flow to a safe location.

### Headlights Fail

If you are driving at night and your headlights flicker, move quickly off the roadway to a safe place.

Follow these steps if your headlights fail entirely:

1. Turn on your right turn signal to light up an escape path to the right.
2. Immediately slow down and bring your vehicle to a safe stop.
3. Try the dimmer switch, parking lights, and hazard flashers. Some circuits might still work. If so, use

## Demonstrate

Demonstrate the value of looking ahead to your target area at a time when your headlights fail. You will need a flashlight and a waste paper basket for this demonstration. Place the waste paper basket in the middle aisle halfway between the front and back walls. Take the flashlight and stand at the back of the middle aisle facing the front of the room. Ask one of the students to turn off the lights. Shine the flashlight to the front wall. Point out that the beam of the flashlight illuminates the waste paper basket. Then shine the flashlight on the floor about three feet ahead of where you are standing. Point out that the waste paper basket is not illuminated.

Explain that if you have the habit of looking ahead to your target area, you will know about an obstacle even if your headlights fail. This will give you time to stop your vehicle before you hit an obstacle. If you only look a few feet ahead of your vehicle, you will not know what is in your path of travel.

## Discuss

Many emergencies are not extreme or life threatening unless they happen in moderate to heavy traffic. Have a class discussion concerning what times of the day, days of the week, and months of the year each emergency would tend most to happen. What clues from traffic, weather, roadway, radio, clock, or calendar might you need to know? Prevention is always better than surprise.

## Cross Curricular

**Language Arts** Have each student prepare a two-minute presentation related to one of these topics: blowouts, flat tires, brake failure, accelerator malfunctions, engine failure, steering failure, vehicle fires, or a stalled vehicle at a railroad crossing. Announce when presentations will be made to classmates. Be sure to allow enough time for students to research, plan, and practice their presentations.

## Discuss

Ask: Why shouldn't you head for a service station if your engine catches on fire? (Service stations are home to gasoline and other highly flammable chemicals.)

## Demonstrate

Demonstrate the proper use of an A-B-C-type fire extinguisher. Follow the manufacturer's instructions. Consult your local fire department for tips on doing a demonstration or to arrange for a firefighter to visit your class. Explain the meaning of A, B, and C types of fires and why an A-B-C fire extinguisher should be carried in a vehicle.

parking or hazard lights to help you drive off the roadway to a safe location.

4. Use the light from street lights, signs, buildings, or other vehicles to help you see. Move off the roadway to a safe location when the vehicle has slowed. Use a flashlight to check fuses or fuse clips. If necessary, replace or reseat the fuse before proceeding.

### Splashed Windshield

Your windshield might be splashed with snow, slush, or mud. Immediately turn on your windshield wipers. Slow, and try to maintain your path of travel until you regain visibility. If you anticipate that your windshield will be splashed, turn on wipers before you lose vision.

### Vehicle on Fire

A vehicle fire can be dangerous. The fire can involve fuel, oil, grease, ordinary combustibles, electrical

Do not open the hood if smoke is coming from under it.

274 Unit 3 Driving in Different Environments and Situations

equipment, or a combination of sources. Carry an A-B-C-type fire extinguisher that is designed to control such fires. Notify the fire department of any vehicle fires.

### Engine Compartment Fire

Most vehicle fires start in the engine compartment. Take these actions in case of fire:

1. Quickly steer the vehicle off the roadway to a safe, open area. Stay away from buildings and service stations. Turn off the ignition.
2. Have passengers move at least 100 feet away from the vehicle.
3. Estimate how serious the fire is. You might see flames and smoke around the hood. Do not try to put out the fire. Leave the hood closed. Move away from the vehicle while you wait for the fire department. The fuel tank could explode.

If you think that the fire is small enough to control and you have an A-B-C-type fire extinguisher, you should take these steps:

1. Use gloves or a rag to protect your hands. Turn your face away to protect yourself from the heat and flames. Carefully open the hood. Once the hood is up, the fire will burn freely.
2. Direct the extinguisher on the fire. Water will not put out oil and fuel fires and can spread the fire.
3. Never try to disconnect the battery or work with your hands under the hood while it is still hot.

Fire is possible in any collision where the engine compartment is smashed. Turn off the ignition, and

## Background

**Vehicle Fires** Each year drivers are surprised to see their vehicle go up in smoke shortly after the vehicle is parked. The catalytic converter, located underneath the vehicle, produces a great deal of heat as it decreases exhaust emissions. Heat from the catalytic converter, which can reach 1,200 degrees, can ignite combustible substances—such as leaves or dry grass. Once a fire starts underneath a vehicle, it does not take long for the vehicle to catch fire.

get passengers out and away from the vehicle.

### Passenger Compartment Fire

A passenger compartment fire usually is caused by a carelessly handled match or burning tobacco product. Pull off the roadway. Use water or a fire extinguisher, and make sure the fire is completely out. Upholstery fires often restart.

### Vehicle Stalls on Railroad Tracks

Weather, driver, or roadway conditions may cause a vehicle's engine to stall while crossing railroad tracks. Take these actions if your vehicle stalls on the tracks:

1. Check carefully to be sure no train is coming. Try to restart the vehicle. If the engine floods, hold the accelerator to the floor as you restart the engine.
2. If you cannot restart the engine, have passengers leave the vehicle. Have one passenger watch for trains, and ask others to help you.
3. Shift to NEUTRAL and push the vehicle off the tracks.
4. If a train is coming, abandon your vehicle. Move away from the tracks in the direction the train is approaching. This helps you avoid injury from flying fragments.

### Review It

1. What actions should you take if a tire blows out?
2. What should you do if the brakes fail?
3. What actions should you take if the accelerator sticks?
4. What actions should you take if your steering fails?

## Special Needs

Since most emergencies are a surprise, there is little time to "think your way through the steps." The response needs to be almost instinctive. The only way to ensure this is to actually practice each response with each student. Use the In-Class Driving Rehearsal activities on pages 270 and 271, and adapt for other vehicle malfunctions. You can also practice in the driver education car. Choose very controlled situations and low speeds to begin with. Correct execution must be attained before speeds are increased.

## Discuss

Direct students' attention to the *You Are the Driver!* photograph. Ask: What direction should you run when you abandon the car? (It is always best to run in the direction from which the train is approaching to avoid being hit by debris from the car. For the situation shown in the photograph, you should run to the front of the car—away from the tracks—and then toward the train in case another train is approaching.)

 **Assess**

## Answers to Review It

**1.** When a tire blows out, you need to gain control of your vehicle without braking. You need to drive off the roadway slowly, turn on hazard flashers, and find a safe location to stop. (p. 268)

**2.** When your brakes fail, you need to pump the brake three or four times, downshift to a lower gear, apply the parking brake, and search for an open zone. (p. 270)

**3.** When the accelerator sticks, you should kick the side of the accelerator in an attempt to jar it free. Then you should apply the brakes and choose an escape path that leads to an open zone. Turn off the engine once you are off the roadway. (p. 271)

**4.** When your steering fails, you should use your horn and hazard flashers to communicate your emergency. Stop as quickly and safely as possible without braking. (p. 273)

## Driver Errors

### 1 Focus

#### Summary

This lesson focuses on what to do if your vehicle runs off the roadway and how to use emergency swerving.

#### Vocabulary

*countersteer*

### 2 Teach

#### Explain

A fatal one-vehicle collision can occur if a driver turns the steering wheel too fast and too soon to return to the roadway, or does not countersteer after returning to the roadway. As a result, the vehicle can roll over, cross the roadway, and slide off the left side of the roadway.

#### Objectives

1. Describe how to return to the roadway if your vehicle runs off the roadway.
2. Explain when to use an emergency swerve.

Driver errors cause many more emergencies than do vehicle malfunctions. Errors due to inexperience, lack of attention, or poor decisions often create driving emergencies. Any driver can be put in an emergency situation by the unpredictable act of another driver.

Developing automatic responses to emergencies is a critical part of the total driving task. Identifying an emergency, predicting its consequences, making correct decisions, and executing decisions quickly will help you avoid a collision.

#### Driving Off the Road

When a front wheel leaves the edge of the roadway, returning to the roadway can be easy if the shoulder is paved and in good condition. However, the shoulder is often not paved.

Many fatal one-vehicle collisions result when drivers brake and return suddenly to the roadway. In such a situation, the vehicle often rolls over. Other collisions can occur when drivers quickly return to the roadway and abruptly cross into other traffic.

#### Off-Road Recovery

Each different type of off-road situation requires a specific recovery technique. For example, if the drop-off is moderate and the shoulder of the road is not steeply sloped, follow these steps for a safe off-road recovery:

1. Hold the steering wheel firmly with both hands. The greater the drop-off between roadway and shoulder, the greater amount of steering control you need. Keep your vehicle heading straight toward your target.

**IF YOU VEER OFF THE ROAD, DON'T TURN SHARPLY**
If you veer off the road, turning the wheel sharply to try to get back onto the road can cause a roll-over crash. If you do veer off the road, you should brake gradually and steer straight. Try to come to a complete stop. Then, after confirming the road is clear of traffic, proceed at a very slow speed and steer the car slightly to get back onto the road.

276   Unit 3  Driving in Different Environments and Situations

### Teacher's Resources

**Content Overheads**
Overheads 25, 26

**In-Car Checklists**
In-Car Checklists 33, 34

### Background

**Off-Road Recoveries** Many drivers make dangerous off-road recoveries because of improper steering techniques. When the shoulder drop-off is steep and there is inadequate space to reduce speed, the driver either turns the wheel too much or too little. For effective steering the driver needs to use targeting. When the driver is focused on the target, it is obvious where the vehicle should go and how much steering is necessary. If necessary, the driver can countersteer to get the vehicle heading toward the target area.

2. Let up on the accelerator and brake gently to 5 or 10 mph. Avoid hard braking.

3. Position your vehicle so it straddles the roadway edge.

4. Select a place to return to the roadway where the shoulder is nearest the level of the roadway.

5. Check for traffic. Signal, check your blind spot, and return to the roadway.

6. Steer 1/8 to 1/4 of a turn toward the roadway to return. If the drop off is severe, you might need to slow more and turn very sharply to get back onto the pavement.

7. Countersteer sharply the instant the front tire touches the roadway. You **countersteer** when you steer in the opposite direction.

8. Center the vehicle in lane position 1 and reestablish your target. Cancel your signal. Accelerate to match the flow of traffic.

If traffic is heavy when you go off the roadway, drive entirely off the roadway. Stop and wait for a large gap in traffic before you reenter.

Sometimes an obstruction, such as a bridge or guardrail, might be on the shoulder ahead. In this case, you must make a quick recovery. Grip the steering wheel firmly. Countersteer *immediately* when the front wheel touches the roadway.

### Emergency Swerving

Swerving is a last-second emergency means of avoiding a collision. Swerve only when you believe that braking will not prevent a collision. At speeds over 30 mph, you can usually swerve to a new path in less distance than the distance you needed to stop safely.

### The Stop-Swerve Decision

The picture below shows a dangerous situation. The driver of the yellow vehicle might hit the brakes to stop. In some situations, this action will be the only choice. However, if the driver hits and locks the brakes, the vehicle might slide into the vehicle ahead. When moving at 30 mph or more, the traction created by the vehicle's tires can turn the vehicle sideways faster than braking traction can stop it.

When deciding whether to swerve around an object, be sure that no other vehicle is in the lane that you will enter.

**What Do You Think?**

Do you think it would be a good idea to practice an emergency swerve in your family vehicle? If you do practice, what precautions should you take?

Should the driver of the yellow car stop or swerve?

Chapter 13 Handling Emergencies **277**

### Discuss

Ask: When is it better to swerve around an object than to stop? Ask for examples. Point out that the decision is not an easy one to make. Emphasize that if a driver is effectively using the IPDE Process, emergency swerves and harsh braking actions are usually unnecessary. Point out that most emergency swerves are performed as a physical reaction to compensate for a mental error.

### Demonstrate

Use the illustration on this page or **Content Overhead 25** to illustrate hazardous situations such as the stop-swerve decision.

### Explain

Use the illustration on page 278 or **Content Overhead 26** to explain how sharply to swerve when executing an emergency swerve. Point out that the amount of time available to swerve determines how sharply you must swerve. Remind students that distance and speed determine how much time you have to swerve. Illustrate the steps to use when executing an emergency swerve.

### Discuss

Draw students' attention to the *What Do You Think?* question. Discuss the reasons for and against practicing an emergency swerve. Discuss what precautions would need to be taken.

## Activity

**In-Class Driving Rehearsal** This activity will help students understand the importance of targeting while trying to perform an off-road recovery. Place tape on the floor to simulate the edge of the road. Use about ten feet of tape. Have students use a simulated steering wheel and form a line along the left side of the tape. Instruct the students to pretend that they are vehicles and their feet are the vehicles' tires. The tape is the edge of the road where their tire (right foot) is going off the roadway. Stand at the front of the line and face the students as if you are in the center of the travel lane with the tape slightly to your left. Instruct each student to walk and steer through the critical steps of an off-road recovery. Tell the students to use you as the target area. Observe all the students' actions, including head and eye movement, and provide feedback.

1. You must swerve sharply around a close object. 2. When the object is farther away, swerve less sharply. 3. The swerve is less sharp at a greater distance.

## Explain

The need for an emergency swerve is almost always the result of the driver being surprised. Eliminating the surprise will go a long way toward eliminating the need for an emergency swerve. Two things that help drivers eliminate surprises are identifying a clear path of travel and identifying a line-of-sight restriction that prevents you from seeing something that can come into your path. A closed front zone requires a reduction in speed. By reducing speed you give yourself more time to make slight prevention actions rather than executing an emergency swerve.

 **Assess**

### Answers to Review It

**1.** Hold the steering wheel firmly and steer straight toward your target. Remove foot from accelerator and brake gently to 5–10 mph. Straddle the roadway where the shoulder is nearest the level of the roadway. Check traffic and signal to indicate you are reentering traffic. Steer sharply left until the right front wheel comes back on the roadway edge. Immediately countersteer and center your vehicle in the lane. Cancel the signal and adjust speed to traffic flow. (p. 276)

**2.** Swerve in an emergency only when you cannot prevent a collision by stepping down hard on the brakes. (p. 277)

The stop-swerve decision is not an easy one to make. Any sudden action should be used only as a last resort. If a pedestrian steps in front of you, you might be forced to make a stop-swerve decision.

Use the IPDE Process and Zone Control System to protect yourself in stop-swerve situations. In addition, allow at least three seconds between yourself and the vehicle ahead.

**Executing an Emergency Swerve**
Follow these steps if you decide to swerve:

1. Identify the escape path.
2. Grip the steering wheel firmly and turn the wheel sharply in the direction of the swerve.
3. In the same rhythmic motion, countersteer to stabilize your vehicle. Straighten the wheel, and continue to steer in your path.

**How Sharply to Swerve?**
The amount of time available to swerve determines how sharply you must swerve. Consider two factors—distance and speed—when determining how much time is available. When the stopped vehicle is farther away, as shown above, the swerve will be less severe and easier to execute.

As speed increases, the less time you have to swerve. For example, you have about 2 seconds to swerve at 40 mph. You have just 1 second at 60 mph.

### Review It

1. How should you return safely to the roadway if your vehicle runs off the roadway?
2. Under what conditions should you make an emergency swerve?

## Background

**Avoiding Emergency Swerves** A driver can develop three behaviors into habits that will serve as an insurance policy against driving into situations requiring an emergency swerve. First, keep at least three seconds of following distance. This will eliminate the swerves caused by vehicles in front stopping abruptly. Second, use lane positioning and speed reductions in response to identifying closed zones and line-of-sight restrictions. Third, never put the vehicle into a space unless you can see that the space is empty.

Unusual and unexpected roadway hazards can cause you to lose control of your vehicle. Driving into deep water, sharp curves, and objects on the roadway can result in emergency situations.

### Potholes in the Roadway

Potholes can develop as water collects in cracks in the roadway. The water can freeze and thaw, causing the cracks to expand. As vehicles drive over these water-filled cracks, they break up the roadway even more.

Potholes often have sharp edges which can severely damage tires. You can lose control of your vehicle—and severely damage it—if you hit a pothole at a fast speed.

Watch for potholes and avoid hitting them whenever possible. Drive carefully around or straddle a pothole. Stay in your own lane and check front zones as you try to avoid potholes in the roadway.

Drive slowly through potholes to prevent tire damage.

If you must drive through a pothole, slow down to prevent tire damage. By driving slowly, you can better keep control of your vehicle.

### Sharp Curve

Driving around a curve fast is dangerous. Poor road conditions or crossing the center line might lead to a collision. The standard warning sign may not indicate exactly how sharp the curve is. Also, the warning sign might not have an advisory speed sign.

Take these actions if you enter a curve too fast:

1. Brake gently as soon as you realize your problem. If you are not yet in the curve, brake more firmly. If you are already in the curve, brake, but do not lock the wheels.
2. About halfway through the curve, look to your target and accelerate gently to help stabilize your vehicle.

### Object on the Roadway

An object on the roadway creates a hazard, whether it is an object, leaves, an animal, or a person. A cardboard box in the street might not appear to be dangerous. Neither does a pile of leaves raked from a yard. However, avoid these and other objects on the roadway. You might not be able to identify the contents of the box. You cannot see a rake or other object in the leaf pile.

### Objectives

1. Describe how to minimize vehicle damage caused by potholes.
2. Explain what to do if you enter a curve too fast.
3. Tell how to escape from a vehicle that is sinking in water.

Chapter 13 Handling Emergencies **279**

# Roadway Hazards

##  Focus

### Summary

This lesson identifies roadway hazards, including potholes and objects in the roadway, and how to avoid them. Instructions for dealing with sharp curves are also included. The lesson also focuses on what to do if a vehicle goes into deep water.

## ② Teach

### Discuss

Ask: What kind of roadway emergencies have you observed as passengers? Based on the emergencies described, ask students to suggest ways that these emergencies might have been prevented.

---

## Teacher's Resources

No *Drive Right* resources are needed for teaching Section 13.3.

## Activity

**Class Activity** Have students survey the community for roadway hazards such as potholes, deep water near the roadway, sharp curves, and objects on the roadway. Suggest that they observe and report to the class how drivers respond to the hazards. Discuss whether the responses were correct ones.

## ③ Assess

### Answers to Review It

**1.** Drive carefully around the pothole. Stay in your own lane. When it is unavoidable, drive slowly through the pothole. (p. 279)

**2.** Brake firmly if you are not yet in the curve. Brake gently if you have already entered the curve. Accelerate gently about halfway through the curve. (p. 279)

**3.** Unfasten safety belts. Open the window that is the most out of the water. Exit promptly through the open window. (p. 280)

**You Are the Driver!**
Should you steer around, brake, straddle, or drive over the object?

First check traffic, and then decide whether to steer around, brake, straddle, or drive over the object. Choose to straddle the object only if your vehicle can clear it and you cannot safely steer around it. Avoid swerving left across the center line because you could encounter other traffic. *Drive over an object only as a last resort.*

### Vehicle in Deep Water

Do not attempt to drive through deep water on the roadway. Turn around or take another route.

Take these actions if your vehicle goes into deep water:

1. Open the window that is the most out of the water. Power windows might short circuit in water so open these windows immediately.
2. Unfasten your safety belt. Check your passengers, and have them unfasten their safety belts.
3. Exit promptly through the open window.

If the windows will not open, attempt to exit through a door. Do not panic if the door is slow to open. Pressure will equalize as water enters your vehicle. You then can open the door.

If your vehicle is totally submerged underwater, some air will be trapped for a brief time toward the highest point of the vehicle. Try to get a full breath or two of air while locating a window or door that is facing up. Open the window or door and leave your vehicle.

If you become trapped in your vehicle underwater, turn on your headlights. This can help rescuers find your vehicle more quickly.

### Review It

1. What should you do if you see a pothole in your path of travel?
2. What actions should you take if you enter a curve too fast?
3. How should you escape a vehicle that is sinking in deep water?

280   Unit 3  Driving in Different Environments and Situations

---

### Background

**Safety Belts and Deep Water**  Some drivers do not wear safety belts because they are afraid of being trapped in their vehicle in deep water. This is not a valid reason for not wearing safety belts because less than one percent of all collisions involve deep water.

Most drivers are involved in a collision at some time during their lives. If you know in advance how to react, you can lessen the effects of a collision.

### Minimizing Effects of a Collision

Suddenly, a vehicle emerges from a driveway and enters your path of travel. You know that you cannot avoid a collision. What should you do? If a collision is about to occur, act as follows:

- Above all, *do not give up*. Keep control of your vehicle. Any change of speed or direction that lessens the impact will help.
- Steer for something "soft" if you leave the roadway. Look for bushes or an open field.
- Avoid objects, such as trees and parked vehicles.
- Get yourself and passengers out and away from your vehicle if there is a chance of another vehicle colliding with yours.

### Threat of a Head-on Collision

Because a head-on collision produces the greatest force of impact of any collision, serious injuries and/or death are more likely to occur. Take these steps if you are threatened with a head-on collision:

1. Maintain vehicle control. Brake hard, but do not lock the wheels. Slowing lessens the force of impact and gives the other driver space and time to recover control.
2. Blow the horn and flash the headlights. These actions might alert an impaired driver. Continue braking and move to the right if the driver does not heed your warning.
3. Steer right toward the shoulder. *Do not steer left.* The other driver likely will try to steer back into the proper lane. Prepare to drive entirely off the roadway to the right, if necessary.

### Threat of a Side-Impact Collision

Take these steps to avoid or lessen the effect of a side-impact collision:

1. Brake or accelerate quickly. Do whichever seems more likely to lessen the collision impact.

Steer to the right if a head-on collision seems about to occur.

## Objectives

1. Explain how to avoid or minimize head-on, side-impact, and rear-end collisions.
2. List the immediate steps to take if a collision occurs.
3. Describe other follow-up steps needed after a collision.

# Collisions

 **Focus**

## Summary

This lesson focuses on how to avoid collisions and what to do if a collision occurs. It also presents follow-up steps needed after a collision.

 **Teach**

## Discuss

Read a newspaper article about a collision aloud. Ask: What do you think the driver(s) could have done to avoid this collision?

## Explain

Explain that when a driver realizes he or she is driving in the wrong lane, the response is to return to the appropriate lane. For this reason, a driver trying to avoid a head-on collision should usually steer to the right.

## Demonstrate

Use **Demonstration Overhead H** to illustrate the threat of a head-on collision and what steps to take.

## Teacher's Resources

**Resource Book**
Roadway Sheets 1–8, pages 4–19

**Demonstration Overheads**
Overheads F, H

**In-Car Checklists**
In-Car Checklists 35–36,

## Activity

**Model Car Activity** Divide the class into groups of three. Give each group a model car, a wild card, and three roadway sheets from **Resource Book,** pages 4–19 (different sheets for each group). Instruct the students to create as many realistic collision situations as possible in 20 minutes. Have each group make a list of their situations. Have the groups take turns describing situations to other class members. Ask the class to offer suggestions on how these collisions could be avoided.

## Explain

All drivers involved in a potential collision situation can play a role in avoiding or reducing damage. One driver is often responsible for the initial action that sets up a situation that can lead to a collision. However, other drivers who are using the IPDE Process can help to prevent the collision from occurring or limit the damage.

## Explain

Drivers should always be aware of the danger to the rear. Anytime a vehicle is stopped in a traffic flow, the driver should monitor the rear zone and know the options available if another vehicle approaches too fast. Point out that you should not relax until there are at least two vehicles behind you. These stopped vehicles will act like barriers absorbing the force of a rear-end collision.

## Demonstrate

Use **Demonstration Overhead F** to illustrate a collision that might result from driver error at a driveway. Discuss strategies for possible side-impact collisions and for stop-swerve decisions.

What can the driver of the white car do to minimize the effects of a second collision on the passengers?

2. Blow the horn to alert the other driver.
3. Change lanes or swerve away from the impact. Be aware of the constantly changing traffic situation around you.

The driver of the white car crossing the road in the picture above might find it difficult to avoid being hit from the side. However, by accelerating, the driver might avoid having the passenger compartment crushed. An impact to the passenger compartment often causes a second

What would you do if you saw this car approaching from the rear?

collision between passengers and the inside of the vehicle.

### Threat of a Rear-End Collision

You are nearly defenseless against a rear-end collision when your vehicle is stopped. If your vehicle is in motion, you might not realize that a vehicle approaching from the rear is coming too fast and might not be able to avoid hitting your vehicle.

Take these actions if you are threatened with a rear-end collision:

1. Flash your brake lights early to alert the driver behind you.
2. As the vehicle nears, check your front zones for open space and move forward, if possible. This precaution gives the driver approaching from the rear more time and space to stop safely.
3. If the intersection is clear, accelerate to give the other driver more space to stop. If your path is not clear, turn right.
4. If a collision is unavoidable, release your brakes just before the collision occurs. This helps

## Facts and Figures

Thirty percent of all intersection crashes are the result of vehicles being rear-ended. Therefore, it is especially important for drivers to acquire the habit of checking the rear zone before, during, and after any braking action. Only when drivers have the habit of checking the rear zone do they have maximum options to protect against a rear-end collision.

What procedures should you follow in a collision, even before help arrives?

soften the impact. Brake immediately after the collision to avoid sliding into another traffic lane.

Maintaining a 3-second following distance and stopping so that you see the tires of the vehicle ahead are good habits. These actions often can help you avoid being hit from behind.

### If You Have a Collision

If you collide with another vehicle, a pedestrian, or someone's property, you are legally required to follow specific procedures.

### Your First Steps

Each state has specific procedures that you must follow immediately when involved in a collision. All states require you to take these five steps.

**1. Stop Immediately.** Failure to stop is a serious offense. Move your vehicle to the side of the road. Do not leave your vehicle where it can block traffic unless it is so damaged it cannot be moved. Turn off ignition.

If you damage a parked vehicle even slightly, try to find the owner. If

you cannot, write your name, address, and phone number on a note. Leave the note under a windshield wiper. Notify the police.

**2. Aid the Injured.** *Never move an injured person unless there is danger of fire or another collision.* Send for paramedics if anyone is seriously injured. Administer basic first aid for injuries such as severe bleeding, shock, and breathing stoppage only if you have completed a certified first-aid course.

DRIVE RIGHT
# DID YOU KNOW?

**DIALING 911** Dialing 911 to report emergencies is a relatively new system. As late as the mid-1980s, you had to call the full number for the service you wanted. As recent as the late 1960s, you may have called the local funeral home for ambulance service. Dialing 911 gets you fast, appropriate service when it is needed.

Chapter 13  Handling Emergencies  **283**

## Apply

Provide students with a copy of the legal requirements in your state for drivers involved in collisions. The Department of Motor Vehicles, the State Highway Patrol, and insurance companies are good resources for this information. Have students take turns reading portions of the requirements aloud.

## Explain

Share information about your state's "Good Samaritan Law" to clarify the protection for those administering first aid to others.

## Apply

Bring to class sample forms for reporting a collision. Have students practice filling out these forms. You could supply descriptions of collisions or have students find them in the newspaper.

# 3 Assess

## Answers to Review It

**1.** Head-on collision: Maintain driving control. Slow without locking the wheels. Blow the horn and flash the headlights to warn the oncoming driver. Steer toward the right shoulder. Look for a soft impact if you do not have a clear escape path. Side-impact collision: Brake or accelerate, whichever seems more likely to prevent or lessen a collision directly into the passenger compartment. Blow the horn. Change lanes or swerve away from the impact. Rear-end collision: Flash the brake lights. Move forward if the path is clear. Release the brakes just before impact. (pp. 281–282)

**2.** Stop, aid the injured, prevent further damage to vehicles, call the police, and exchange pertinent information. (p. 283)

**3.** Record information about witnesses to the collision, give accurate facts to the police, see a doctor if you are injured, and file necessary reports. (p. 284)

Exchange information with all drivers involved in a collision.

**3. Prevent Further Damage.** Warn oncoming traffic with flares or reflectors placed at least 100 feet ahead of and behind the collision site (500 feet away in high-speed traffic). If you do not have such devices, another person might stand in advance of the site and direct vehicles around the collision. Do not put yourself or others in danger while directing traffic.

**4. Send for Police.** You must call the police if anyone is injured or killed. Some states require you to call the police for any collision, even if no personal injuries are evident.

**5. Exchange Information.** Get and provide this following information from other drivers involved in the collision: names, addresses, driver's license numbers, license plate numbers, and insurance company names and addresses.

Note the names and addresses of passengers, the positions in which they were sitting, and the extent of their injuries. Getting and giving this information is your responsibility.

### Additional Steps

Take these additional steps after a collision:

**Record Witnesses' Names and Addresses** Note the names and addresses of any witnesses to the collision. Make a sketch of the collision scene or take a photo. Record such facts as time, date, location, weather, and driving conditions. Note the name of the hospital to which any injured persons were taken. Note the name and badge number of the police officer at the collision scene.

**Give Police the Facts** Provide honest, accurate facts. Never argue about who was to blame, and never admit blame. Stay at the scene until all information has been recorded. Take your vehicle to a repair shop for any necessary repairs. You generally need two repair estimates for insurance purposes. Keep all bills.

**File Necessary Reports** Each state requires drivers involved in a collision to file a written report if someone was killed or injured, or if property damage exceeds a set amount. Some states require that a report be filed within 24 hours of the collision.

You must also produce proof of financial responsibility by showing a card that lists your current insurance coverage, or a bond card. Finally, notify your insurance agent promptly. If you fail to do this within the time specified in your policy, the company might refuse to pay your claim.

### Review It

1. How can you minimize the impact of a head-on collision? a side-impact collision? a rear-end collision?
2. What steps should you take immediately if you are involved in a collision?
3. What additional steps should you take following a collision?

# Activity

**Model Car Activity** Divide the class into groups of four. Give each group two model cars and a roadway sheet—different roadway sheets for each group—from **Resource Book,** pages 4–19. Have each group develop a collision scenario involving two cars, two drivers and two passengers. Instruct the students to simulate the collision and act out their roles as drivers and passengers. Each group should record the actions and words of the collision victims. When the group is finished with this part of the activity, instruct them to compare what happened in their collision scenario with the steps outlined on pages 283–284. Ask the groups to analyze what actions each driver could have taken to avoid the collision.

## Reviewing Chapter Objectives

### 1. Vehicle Malfunctions

1. What actions should you take if a tire blows out? (268–269)
2. What are the proper steps to follow if the brakes fail? (270)
3. What should you do if your accelerator sticks? (271)
4. What should you do in case of steering failure? (273)

### 2. Driver Errors

5. If your vehicle runs off the roadway, how should you return it to the roadway? (276–277)
6. When should you use an emergency swerve? (277–278)

### 3. Roadway Hazards

7. How could you minimize vehicle damage caused by potholes? (279)
8. What should you do if you enter a curve too fast? (279)
9. How would you escape a vehicle that is sinking in water? (280)

### 4. Collisions

10. How do you avoid or minimize head-on, side-impact, and rear-end collisions? (281–282)
11. What are the immediate steps you should take if a collision occurs? (283–284)
12. What are the follow-up steps you should take after a collision? (284)

## Projects

### Individuals

**Investigate** Research the specific procedures you must follow when involved in a collision in your state. Write a report of your findings.

**Observe** As a passenger in a vehicle, look for hazards in the roadway for a week. Make a list of the hazards you see. Discuss the hazards with your class.

**Interview** Visit a local vehicle repair shop. Obtain the manager's permission to interview a mechanic. Ask the mechanic to explain the most common causes of engine failure. Report your results to the class.

### Groups

**Practice** As a group, practice changing a tire on a vehicle provided by your instructor for this purpose. Group members should take turns performing the various steps.

**Demonstrate** List the possible vehicle malfunctions described in this chapter on separate pieces of paper. Each group member should draw one piece of paper, then explain to the group what should be done if faced with that malfunction.

Chapter 13 Handling Emergencies **285**

## Reviewing Chapter Objectives

**13.1** Vehicle Malfunctions
See Answers to Review It on page 275.
**13.2** Driver Errors
See Answers to Review It on page 278.
**13.3** Roadway Hazards
See Answers to Review It on page 280.
**13.4** Collisions
See Answers to Review It on page 284.

For additional information refer to the specific page(s) in parentheses after each question.

## Projects

Some of the projects can be assigned at any time while others are more closely tied to the content presented in the student text. The page number where the topic is introduced is indicated.

**Investigate:** p. 283
**Observe:** p. 279
**Interview:** p. 272
**Practice:** p. 268
**Demonstrate:** p. 268

The results of student projects will vary.

## Teacher's Resources

**Skills and Applications Workbook**
pages 49–52

**Tests and Activities**
Chapter 13 Activities 13-1 and 13-2, pages 107–108

Chapter 13 Test A and Test B, pages 109–112

**TestWorks CD-ROM**
Chapter 13 Test

## Answers to Check Your Knowledge

**1.** c
**2.** d
**3.** b
**4.** floods
**5.** engine compartment
**6.** potholes
**7.** head-on

## Answers to Review Vocabulary

**8.** lug nuts (c)
**9.** countersteer (e)
**10.** blowout (f)
**11.** jack (a)
**12.** brake fade (d)
**13.** fishtailing (b)

## Answers to Think Critically

Students' answers will vary. For information related to the question refer to the page(s) indicated.

**1.** Students' answers should include steps outlined on page 270.

**2.** Students' answers should include steps outlined on pages 283–284.

### Chapter Test

#### Check Your Knowledge

**Multiple Choice**  Copy the number of each sentence below on a sheet of paper. Choose the letter that best completes the statement or answers the question.

1. If you have a blowout, which action should you avoid?
   (a) ease up on accelerator
   (b) pull off onto the shoulder slowly
   (c) brake hard
   (d) turn on hazard lights
2. Which action should you take first if the accelerator sticks while you are driving?
   (a) shift into a lower gear
   (b) turn off the ignition
   (c) apply the parking brake
   (d) kick the side of the accelerator
3. To avoid a side-impact collision, you should
   (a) lock your brakes.      (b) brake or accelerate quickly.
   (c) steer to the left.      (d) steer to the right.

**Completion**  Copy the number of each sentence below. After each number, write the word or words that complete the sentence correctly.

4. An engine _____ when it has too much fuel and not enough air.
5. Vehicle fires generally start in the _____.
6. When water collects in roadway cracks, _____ can develop.
7. A _____ collision produces the greatest force of impact of any collision.

#### Review Vocabulary

Copy the number of each definition in List A. Match the definition in List A with the term it defines in List B.

**List A**

8. devices that hold the wheel to the vehicle
9. steer in the opposite direction
10. sudden loss of tire air pressure while driving
11. hand-operated device used to lift and hold one corner or side of the vehicle
12. loss of braking effectiveness caused by over-heating of the brakes after long, continuous, hard braking
13. back and forth swerving of the rear of a vehicle

**List B**

a. jack
b. fishtailing
c. lug nuts

d. brake fade
e. countersteer
f. blowout

#### Think Critically

Write a paragraph to answer each question.

1. You are driving in a residential area and identify a vehicle in your right-front zone backing out of a driveway. You hit your brakes hard, but your vehicle does not slow or stop. What steps should you take?
2. You are involved in a collision on the freeway in a neighboring state. You are not hurt but are not sure about the driver of the other vehicle. What should you do?

## Decision Making

**1.** This car just had a right-front tire blowout. What steps should the driver take to handle this emergency safely?

**2.** You are traveling at 30 mph. You brake for the stop ahead, but then realize that your brakes do not work. What should you do to stop the vehicle?

**3.** The driver cannot possibly stop in time to avoid hitting the bicyclist. What should the driver do?

**4.** You are driving the gray car. Both you and the driver in the white car are traveling 30 mph. The other driver is not aware of your car. What can you do to prevent a collision or keep the collision from being too serious?

Chapter 13 Handling Emergencies **287**

## Answers to Decision Making

**1.** Grip the steering wheel firmly, decelerate, and steer the vehicle left in the lane. Check traffic, turn on the hazard flashers, and drive to a safe, level place to stop.

**2.** Pump the brake pedal fast and hard. Downshift to a lower gear. Pull and hold the parking-brake release lever out or hold the parking-brake button at *Off.* Apply the parking brake. If necessary, steer into the bushes.

**3.** Hold the steering wheel firmly and swerve around the bicyclist. Countersteer to return to the roadway. Stop on the shoulder when the car is under control. Help the bicyclist.

**4.** Brake to stop. If you cannot stop in time, steer to avoid colliding into the passenger compartment of the other vehicle.

# Being a Responsible Driver

## Unit 4

# Being a Responsible Driver

# Being a Responsible Driver

## Unit Overview

In this unit students will learn that not only their skills, but also their physical and emotional conditions can affect how well and how safely they drive. They will find out how alcohol and other drugs affect a person's ability to drive. Students will also learn about the responsibilities of a vehicle owner in buying, insuring, and maintaining a vehicle. Finally, the unit suggests ways to plan and safely execute short- and long-distance trips.

## About the Photograph

Driving through a dry, mountainous region presents challenges to vehicles and to drivers. Drivers should always be in good emotional and physical condition to handle different types of driving environments. New drivers will enjoy scenic routes such as this one as they learn to plan their trips carefully and maintain their vehicles in peak operating condition.

# Chapter 14    Planning Guide

**Student Features**

**Teacher's Edition**

| | Student Features | Teacher's Edition |
|---|---|---|
| **Chapter 14**<br>**Effects of Driver Condition** | You Are the Driver! *p. 291* | Projects *p. 290*<br>Special Needs *p. 291* |
| **14.1 Emotions and Driving** *pp. 292–297*<br>• Tell how anger can affect your ability to drive.<br>• Explain how passengers can help a driver.<br>• Tell how you can manage your emotions while driving.<br>• Describe the influence emotions have on your willingness to accept risk. | What Do You Think?<br>*p. 293*<br>Safe Driving Tip *p. 294*<br>Did You Know? *p. 297* | Activity *pp. 292, 294, 295, 296, 297*<br>Special Needs *p. 293* |
| **14.2 Physical Senses and Driving** *pp. 298–303*<br>• Define the parts of your field of vision.<br>• Describe what you can do to compensate for poor depth perception.<br>• Explain how your senses help you drive. | | Demonstrate *pp. 299, 300, 303*<br>Activity *pp. 299, 300, 301, 302*<br>Special Needs *p. 302* |
| **14.3 Physical Disabilities** *pp. 304–308*<br>• Tell what you can do to combat fatigue.<br>• Explain what to do to avoid carbon monoxide exposure and how to deal with its effects.<br>• Describe what drivers who have permanent disabilities can do to compensate. | Did You Know? *p. 305*<br>Safe Driving Tip *p. 308* | Demonstrate *p. 305*<br>Activity *p. 307* |
| **Assessment** | Reviewing Chapter<br>Objectives *p. 309*<br>Projects *p. 309*<br>Chapter Test *p. 310*<br>Decision Making *p. 311* | Answers *pp. 310–311* |

**Companion** *pp. 87–91*
**Spanish Handbook** *pp. 29–30*

**Resource Book**
Classroom Activity,
  *pp. 59–60*

**Resource Book**
Teacher's Instructions,
  *pp. 47, 61*

**Demonstration Overhead D**
**Content Overhead 3**

**Skills and Applications**
  **Workbook,** *pp. 53–56*
**Tests and Activities**
Chapter 14 Activities 14-1
  and 14-2, *pp. 119–120*
Chapter 14 Test A and
  Test B, *pp. 121–124*

**TestWorks CD-ROM**
  Chapter 14 Test

## Technology Resources

### Audio-Visual and Computer Resources

AAA Foundation for Traffic Safety, *Breaking the Accident Chain of Events,* video, 8 minutes

AAA Foundation for Traffic Safety, *Night Driving,* video, 8 minutes

AAA Foundation for Traffic Safety, *Preventing Road Rage,* video

National Safety Council, *Road Rage: How You Can Protect Yourself,* video, 10 minutes

Safety Industries, Inc., *Physical and Mental Conditions,* video, 10 minutes

**Go Online**
PHSchool.com

**For: Chapter 14 online activities**
**Visit: PHSchool.com**
**Web Code: cak-9999**

# Effects of Driver Condition

## Chapter Overview

Chapter 14 focuses on how emotions affect driving. It also focuses on the physical abilities needed for safe driving and how physical limitations can affect driving. Driving requires students to focus all their mental and physical abilities in order to manage the risks involved. Students must make special efforts to control the effects their emotions have on their driving abilities.

## Chapter Vocabulary

*carbon monoxide, color-blindness, depth perception, emotion, glare recovery time, glare resistance, night blindness, speed smear, tunnel vision, visual acuity*

290

## Teacher's Resources

For students to use as they read the chapter:

**Companion**
pages 87–91

**Spanish Handbook**
pages 29–30

## Projects

Review the projects described on page 309. Some of the projects can be assigned at any time while others are more closely tied to the content presented in the student text.

# CHAPTER 14
## Effects of Driver Condition

**14.1** Emotions and Driving

**14.2** Physical Senses and Driving

**14.3** Physical Disabilities

## You Are the Driver!

Imagine you have just been bicycle riding like these people. Every activity you do—including driving—involves some risk. You can keep your driving risks low if you are mentally alert, emotionally fit, and physically healthy. You must rely on your senses to help you stay on a safe, conflict-free path of travel.

This chapter discusses both your emotional and physical abilities as they relate to your driving. You will learn how your senses can help lower the risks involved in driving. You also will discover how a driver can compensate for physical disabilities that affect driving.

**Go Online**
PHSchool.com

**For:** Chapter 14 online activities
**Visit:** PHSchool.com
**Web Code:** cak-9999

291

## Introducing the Chapter

Compare the kinds of risks that are involved in riding a bicycle with the kinds of risks involved in driving a vehicle. Explain how physical senses are important in driving. Vision is the most helpful sense. Explain ways to control emotions, especially anger. Describe possible temporary physical disabilities. Note the importance of avoiding situations in which carbon monoxide might enter the vehicle.

## You Are the Driver

Have students examine the picture. Ask them to list the risks the bicyclists face. Initiate a discussion about how controlling emotions can lower the risks for all roadway users.

# Emotions and Driving

## Focus

### Summary

This lesson focuses on how emotions affect driving and ways to control emotions. The concept of road rage is integrated throughout the lesson.

### Vocabulary

*emotion*

## Teach

### Explain

Explain that a person can never be in control of other drivers' actions. You can, however, develop a driving style that will give you control and reduce the effects of other drivers' actions. If you expect other drivers to do things correctly, you may be surprised and stressed by wrongful actions of others. Being prepared for the errant behavior of others eliminates surprises and reduces stress.

### Discuss

Draw students' attention to the *You Are the Driver!* photograph. Ask: How would you feel if this driver cut into your lane? (Answers will vary.) How would you respond? What might the driver behind you think of your response? (Answers will vary.)

---

### Objectives

1. Tell how anger can affect your ability to drive.
2. Explain how passengers can help a driver.
3. Tell how you can manage your emotions while driving.
4. Describe the influence emotions have on your willingness to accept risk.

The word **emotion** is used to name a strong feeling. Anger, fear, and joy are examples of emotions. Emotions add a special flavor to life.

#### How Emotions Affect Driving

Emotions influence the way you think and act. When emotions affect your thoughts and actions, they can change the way you normally assess risk and make driving decisions. They can lead you to accept more or less risk than normal for the gain you receive. Emotions can be infectious; they can affect others in your vehicle and in vehicles around you.

A driver can minimize the effects of emotions by using courteous driving strategies. Using courtesy to influence the effects of emotions on others empowers you. In effect it can help keep you in control of yourself and others.

#### Mental Effects of Emotions

Strong emotions can interfere with your ability to think, reason, and make wise decisions. They can increase your chances of making a mistake. Emotions can affect the way you make judgments in a driving situation.

In some situations, a strong emotion can cause you to focus your attention on one event. You might miss other important events in a driving scene. In the picture, the driver in front has just cut over to the right lane and started to slow. This action could startle following drivers. It may cause them to become upset or angry. However, instead of becoming upset, they should increase the space between themselves and the vehicle ahead. Drivers need to reduce their own risk, rather than seek revenge or get even.

**You Are the Driver!**
How would you feel if this driver cut into your lane? What might the driver behind you think of your response?

---

### Teacher's Resources

**Resource Book**
Classroom Activity, pages 59–60

### Activity

**Class Activity** Ask students to write three of their pet peeves regarding other drivers' actions that make them angry. Then have them write what they could do in each situation. After adequate time, have the students form into groups of five. Have members in the groups report their situations to each other. Then have the group select two of the situations to report to the whole class for discussion.

## Physical Effects of Emotions

Strong emotions also can cause changes in your bodily functions. Your body prepares itself for the stressful event. Your heartbeat increases, your breathing quickens, your digestion slows, and your muscles tighten.

Some emotional stress is needed to sustain life. However, continued emotional stress can exhaust you and contribute to adverse effects on the body such as heart disease and digestive disorders. The more tasks to be handled, the more complex and stressful the situation. Rush hour traffic can cause stress and fatigue in all drivers. Bumper-to-bumper driving situations in the city can also cause stress.

### Anger While Driving

You usually rely upon a set of assumptions or expectations when driving. You assume that others will drive and act in a safe, responsible manner. You might be tempted to react angrily when you must change your expectations.

In normal driving situations, other drivers might interfere with your intended speed or path of travel. They might slow or change lanes improperly. They might not yield, may fail to signal, or may not move quickly enough when a traffic light changes. Sometimes you might think that other drivers are trying to irritate you. As a result, you might become angry.

Anger occurs more often to drivers than any other emotion. It can range from mild irritation to furious rage and can result in aggressive actions or even violent acts of "road rage."

In this picture, the driver is angry at the people who are talking and blocking his way. The driver is angry because he might be late for an appointment. If he cannot maintain emotional control, he might remain angry and react aggressively.

Anger can impair all of your driving skills. You might take risks

Some people believe that "road rage" is as dangerous as drunk driving. Do you agree? What makes you think that way?

The driver might remain angry long after the people have cleared his path.

## Apply

Have students find two newspaper or magazine articles that describe events that took place because of an individual's anger. Give them a week, including the weekend, to complete this assignment. When the articles are brought to class, divide the class into groups of four. Each group should review all the articles brought in by group members. After reviewing the articles, group members should discuss how the negative consequences of the situation could have been prevented.

## Discuss

Discuss the *What Do You Think?* question. Ask: Some people believe that road rage is as dangerous as drunk driving. Do you agree? What makes you think that way? Continue the discussion by asking: What do you think you can do to prevent being the target of road rage? List students' answers on the board. (Examples: Always signal when changing lanes, ignore obscene gestures by other drivers, limit use of the horn, and do not tailgate.)

## Background

**Road Violence** Road violence is on the rise. Between 1990 and 1995, it increased 51 percent, according to a study by the American Automobile Association Foundation for Traffic Safety. The report was based on thousands of police reports and newspaper articles. But the report might not tell the whole story. There are many acts of road rage that are not reported to police or reported by the media.

## Special Needs

Some students have more difficulty controlling their emotions than others. In addition, some students' emotional responses last longer than others'. Because emotions tend to affect everyone's ability to think clearly, it is important to help students recognize when they need to pull over and cool down rather than continue to drive while agitated or in fear. Work with special needs students to develop good driving habits that will help them avoid or handle emotionally tense situations.

## Discuss

Initiate a discussion about high-stress driving situations and how these situations can cause strong emotions, such as anxiety, to surface. Have students identify high-stress driving situations. (High-stress situations include heavy traffic, tailgating, and cutting in front of another driver.) Discuss the techniques for coping with various situations.

## Explain

Explain that a driver needs time to complete each step of the IPDE Process. Stress that emotions can increase the amount of time a driver needs to use the IPDE Process.

## Explain

Explain that a person who is angry before beginning to drive tends to become angry more quickly at any traffic frustration. Note that advance trip planning can help relieve driving-related anxiety.

### SAFE DRIVING

Avoid situations that could evoke anger. Do not make emotional, last-second decisions when driving in heavy traffic.

you would not take if you were calm. You also might not see everything you should see and miss an important clue. You might force other drivers to stop or swerve abruptly. These last-second actions can cause conflicts and added stress not only for you, but for other drivers as well. Good drivers never surprise others.

What might you do when you become angry while driving—or confront other drivers who are? Think positively. Leave punishment to the police. Your acts of punishment may just aggravate the other drivers even more. Model good behavior. Consider that other drivers may have good reasons for their actions. Can you recall times when you have made similar decisions?

### Other Emotions and Driving

Sorrow, depression, and anxiety are among other emotions that can adversely affect driving. These emotions can also slow body processes and reduce mental alertness.

Anxiety differs from anger. You might be anxious when driving in an unfamiliar, difficult situation. You might have trouble identifying hazards when you are confused. You might even feel panic-stricken. As a responsible driver, work to recognize difficult situations, and try your best to cope. It may mean delaying driving, but your risks will be reduced.

Excitement and happiness also can prevent you from fully concentrating on your driving task. A happy, excited driver can be just as impaired as an angry driver. After an intense event, such as a sports event, be sure that strong emotions do not impair your driving ability.

### Emotions and the IPDE Process

The successful use of the IPDE Process requires total concentration on the driving task. You need time to use the IPDE Process. In a tight, high-stress situation, you need even more time to use the IPDE Process to keep from making wrong or late decisions.

You would need to have your emotions under control if you were driving into this situation.

## Activity

**Class Activity** This activity will help students understand how being in a hurry is less productive and results in more errors and stress. Divide the class into two groups—left and right side of the room. Give the students on the right side sheet A and students on the left side sheet B (see **Resource Book,** pages 59–60). Tell students on the right side that they have three minutes to add all the columns of numbers. They must finish adding all columns to receive credit. Tell students on the left side that they are to add as many columns of numbers as

time permits. After the three minutes, have the groups switch papers to be corrected (students need not put their name on the papers). Compare the results. The group without the pressure to complete all columns will probably have more correct answers. Ask the class how many students felt stress. Lead a discussion on why stress was felt and how stress affects behavior.

Spirits might be high after winning a game, but drivers must remain in control.

Your emotional condition can drastically affect your driving ability.

Think how emotions could affect your driving if you were beside the truck pictured on the opposite page. The car ahead has been slowing and forcing you to slow. The truck driver has just decided to pass the car. You are not sure what the driver ahead is going to do. Another truck is behind the passing truck. As a result, the driver ahead and the truck drivers could cause you to make quick, irresponsible errors.

## Passengers and Emotions

Peer pressure can be a very strong force, depending upon the situation. In a baseball game, team spirit can help win the game. In a vehicle, your passengers can strongly influence the way you drive.

In most group situations, one or more people need to assume responsibility and lead the group. When you are driving, you must be the leader and take control. You are responsible for the safety of your passengers.

In this picture, a championship soccer match has just ended. Everyone is going to celebrate. Emotions will be running high. The driver will be under special pressures to concentrate on the driving task. However, to make sure that nothing goes wrong, the driver must be the leader and maintain control of the situation.

Passengers can help the driver maintain control while driving. Here are actions you, as a passenger, can take to assist a driver:

- Avoid saying or doing anything that might distract or upset the driver. Refrain from heated discussions. Talk about positive events.
- Discourage the driver from taking reckless actions. Be prepared to intervene if the driver endangers others by reckless driving. Encourage the driver to let someone else drive, or refuse to ride in the same vehicle. Do what you must to protect yourself and others.

Chapter 14 Effects of Driver Condition **295**

## Discuss

Ask: Which would make you feel better—to give someone a gift, or to have someone steal from you? Make a comparison that being courteous to others is like giving them a gift. When you try to prevent others from cutting in front of you, and they do, it may seem like they took something away from you. You are the one who can set the rules of the game being played. You can create a win-win situation when you help others and receive a good feeling by doing so. Or you can create a win-lose situation where others win and you lose because they took something away from you.

## Discuss

Initiate a discussion about the effect of peer pressure on young drivers. Ask: How can peer pressure affect your driving? Why is it important that the driver be in control? What can passengers do to help the driver maintain control?

## Activity

**Small Group Activity** This activity will help students evaluate how good driving habits can help to eliminate road rage situations. Divide the class into groups of four. Have students write all driving behavior that, when formed into habits, will help drivers to avoid road rage situations. (Discuss habits such as maintaining a minimum 3-second following distance, making blind-spot checks, searching intersections effectively, etc.) For each driving behavior, the groups should state how the behavior will help to eliminate road rage.

## Discuss

Good driving habits can empower you while bad habits will victimize you. Having good habits will give you control over conditions that you may not be able to avoid.

## Explain

Explain that maturity is a state of mind—not a condition of age. Some teen drivers are more mature than some adult or elderly drivers. How a person handles a situation determines whether they have taken a mature, responsible action.

- Do not hesitate to compliment the driver for doing a good job of driving in a difficult situation. You might need the same support when you are the driver.

### Effects on Risk Taking

Your emotions have a big influence on the amount of risk you are willing to take. You probably will be more likely to take risks if you are angry than if you are happy. When a driver cuts you off after passing, you might want to get even by taking chances that you would not normally take.

Mature, responsible drivers do not let their emotions make them take unnecessary risks. Taking a chance while driving can be deadly. You must be mature enough to adjust your behavior so that you do not drive into or create high-risk situations. You also must be mature enough to refuse to take part when other people suggest activities that could endanger you, your passengers, or other drivers.

Your emotions might cause you to take chances at different times on the same roadway. For example, if you were driving an injured friend to the hospital, your concern might cause

you to drive fast, increasing the risks. An hour later, you probably would not drive home in the same manner. You then would drive more cautiously and courteously.

On the other hand, sometimes you might be so uninterested in your trip that you don't give your complete attention to the driving task. Driving the same route over and over may cause you to pay less attention to the driving task.

### Controlling Emotions

During some performances, you are asked to hold your applause until a certain point. You must manage your emotions until the proper time. In driving, you must develop this same type of emotional discipline. You must strive to keep emotions from affecting your driving ability.

**Coping with Emotions** High-stress driving situations can cause emotions to surface. These techniques can help you manage your emotions while driving:

- Use the IPDE Process to drive in an organized manner. Learn and use correct driving procedures until they become habits. You then will be more likely to execute the proper action, even when under emotional stress.
- Anticipate emotion-producing situations, and adjust your expectations. Say to yourself, "I know there will be delays during rush hour, so I will allow more time to get home. I will not let the actions of others bother me."

Even if you drive on the same street every day, always be aware of potential risks.

## Activity

**Class Activity** This activity will help students understand how anger makes situations worse rather than better. Have students write a description of one non-driving situation in which they got angry and did something or said something that they later regretted. Tell students that you will not collect the papers. Then have them write what actions they could have taken before getting angry that would have resulted in a better solution. Ask: Is it easier to prevent yourself from getting angry or to control your behavior once you are angry?

## Activity

**Class Activity** Use a collision-avoidance simulation film clip or a heavy-traffic video clip to show all of the options available before the collision trap is sprung and how few options exist when the driver does not plan ahead. If using a high-energy collision avoidance film, shout orders and confusing comments to heighten the emotional stress and confusion. Discuss the impact of the passenger distractions.

**AGGRESSIVE DRIVING** Citizens Against Speeding and Aggressive Driving (CASAD) is a fairly new grassroots organization dedicated to making safer roads. CASAD members feel aggressive driving has become an epidemic. They believe it is socially unacceptable to speed and drive aggressively on any road under any circumstance.

- If you encounter an aggressive driver, do not challenge the driver. Avoid eye contact, ignore gestures, and remain calm. Adopt a "yield" attitude.
- Try to adjust your route to avoid irritating traffic situations.
- If you are tired, make a special effort to manage your emotions. A tired person can become upset more easily.
- Analyze your mistakes. Learn from them so that you are less likely to repeat the same mistakes.
- Keep courtesy as one of your personal rules of the road.

### Goal of Emotional Control

Emotions are complicated and powerful forces. Learning about emotions and how to manage them is something most individuals work at all their lives. Maintaining an attitude of "I will always work to manage my emotions when driving" is a big step toward actually mastering your emotions. If you can manage your emotions and maintain your driving ability, those skills will help keep the risks of driving low as well as your stress level.

### Review It

1. How can anger affect your ability to drive?
2. How can you help a driver when you are a passenger?
3. What can you do to manage your emotions while driving?
4. How can your emotions affect the risks of driving?

You can earn the respect of others if your emotions do not interfere with your driving ability.

Chapter 14 Effects of Driver Condition **297**

# Physical Senses and Driving

## 1 Focus

### Summary

This lesson focuses on the senses involved in driving: sight, hearing, smell, and sense of motion. Visual acuity, color vision, field of vision, depth perception, night vision, and glare are addressed.

### Vocabulary

**New:** *color-blindness, depth perception, glare recovery time, glare resistance, night blindness, speed smear, tunnel vision, visual acuity*

**Review:** *central vision, field of vision, peripheral vision*

## 2 Teach

### Explain

Explain that at highway speeds, 20/40 vision gives you only half as much time to read information on signs. This could be critical when searching for a freeway exit in heavy traffic. Corrected vision makes driving less stressful.

## Objectives

1. Define the parts of your field of vision.
2. Describe what you can do to compensate for poor depth perception.
3. Explain how your senses help you drive.

Your senses play a vital role in using the IPDE Process. You use your abilities to see, hear, smell, and detect motion to know what is occurring in and around your vehicle.

Driving, like other activities such as sports and mowing the lawn, exposes you to risks. As you drive, your senses help you stay alert and be aware of changing situations. If you know your physical abilities, you have a better chance of maintaining control over your vehicle and minimizing your driving risks.

### Seeing

More than 90 percent of the information you gather while driving is received through your eyes. You must be able to clearly and quickly identify closing zones in your intended path of travel.

Your brain directs your eyes to focus on objects in and around your path of travel. Information is sent to your brain and combined with stored information. As a result, you can identify hazards, predict conflicts, decide to maintain or adjust your speed and position, and execute your decisions.

### Visual Acuity

When driving you need the ability to see things clearly both near and far away. For example, you may need to read the gauges on your instrument panel in one instant, then identify

# IPDE

You have 20/20 vision in each eye if you can read these letters with each eye from 20 feet away.

oncoming traffic in the next. The ability to see things clearly is called **visual acuity.**

A person with normal visual acuity—called 20/20 vision—can read 11/32-inch letters on an eye chart from 20 feet away. If you have 20/20 vision, you should be able to read the term IPDE in the block on this page from 20 feet away.

You must pass a visual acuity test in order to obtain a learner's permit, and possibly again to get a driver's license. Most states require a minimum corrected visual acuity of 20/40 to drive. A person with 20/40 vision must be twice as close to an object to see it as clearly as a person with 20/20 vision must be. With 20/200, the person would have to be 10 times closer. If you must wear glasses or contact lenses to pass the vision test, then you must wear them whenever you drive.

### Color Vision

Color vision is the ability to distinguish one color from another. Not being able to distinguish colors is called **color blindness.** Being able to see the colors red, green, and yellow is particularly important since these colors give the messages stop, go, and slow or caution. The most common type of color blindness is the difficulty to distinguish red and green.

A color-blind driver can compensate by

## Teacher's Resources

**Resource Book**
Teacher's Instructions, pages 47, 61

**Demonstration Overheads**
Overhead D

**Content Overhead**
Overhead 3

- remembering the order of the lights in a traffic signal. If the lights are vertical, the red light is at the top. If horizontal, the red light is on the left.
- knowing the meanings of traffic signs by their shapes
- reading all signs that appear with traffic signals
- checking all zones and 90 degrees to left and right before proceeding at traffic signals
- taking cues from other drivers

## Field of Vision

Your field of vision is all the area that you can see around you while looking straight ahead. From this position, most people can see about 90 degrees to each side, or about a half circle. However, you can only see clearly in your area of central vision as shown in the pictures. This straight-ahead part of your field of vision is a small, 10-degree, cone-shaped area. As you drive, direct your central vision to your target

You see most clearly in the area of central vision, but the fringe vision is also important.

area and 12–15 seconds ahead to identify zone changes.

Surrounding your central vision is peripheral vision. The farther from the central vision, the less clear the view. The part of your peripheral vision closest to your central vision

Use your central vision to check your target area and front zones. Use your fringe vision to check reference points and detect changes in your rearview mirror.

## Explain

Use **Content Overhead 3** to explain field of vision, central vision, fringe vision, and peripheral vision. Point out why drivers with tunnel vision must compensate by using more frequent head and eye movements.

## Demonstrate

Demonstrate fringe vision with the help of two student volunteers—a driver and a tester. Have the driver and the tester face the same way and have the tester stand four feet behind the driver. Instruct the driver not to move his or her head. Instruct the tester to wave one arm up and down a few times. Ask the driver which arm the tester moved. (The driver will not be able to see the movement.) Repeat the exercise with one exception. This time, allow the driver to move his or her head. (The driver will be able to see the movement.) Repeat the demonstration with two other students. Point out that using head movement along with fringe vision allows a driver a wide range of view.

## Activity

**In-Class Driving Rehearsal** This activity will help students understand fringe vision. You will need colored index cards and a piece of cardboard 2′ wide and 6′ long. Make a mark, about the size of a penny, in the center of the top edge of the long side of the cardboard. Attach two blue index cards along the top edge of the cardboard one foot on either side of the mark. See **Resource Book,** page 61 for additional directions.

Divide the class into groups of four—a driver, two testers, and a monitor. Have the testers hold the cardboard by the short sides and position

it perpendicular to the floor. The driver will stand one foot away and facing the mark. The monitor will face the driver to monitor his or her eye movement. Instruct the driver to stare at the mark. Instruct the testers to move yellow index cards from the end of the cardboard toward the blue cards. Ask the driver to announce when the yellow cards are even with the blue cards. Repeat the activity after moving the blue cards six inches away from the center mark. Continue to repeat until the driver is no longer able to identify when the yellow cards are even with the blue cards.

## Explain

Explain that darkness complicates depth perception. When it is dark, you cannot clearly see items that you normally use as references for judging distance. Your ability to judge distance is also affected by the level of darkness. Some nights are darker than others because of the phases of the moon and cloud cover. Difficulty in judging distances can be a contributory factor when drivers make poor judgments in nighttime passing situations.

## Demonstrate

Demonstrate how depth perception can be temporarily affected by an eye injury. Try to place a finger on the tip of a pencil with one eye closed. Use various distances from the person from one to three feet. Have several students try it. Under such conditions, the driver must not expect to make the same depth perception judgments. The driver should increase the following distance to compensate for the loss of depth perception.

## Explain

Explain that a driver can improve depth perception by using seconds to judge acceptable gaps in traffic. Tell students that as a passenger in a vehicle, they can get practice judging the size of a gap. They can take a guess at how many seconds away an approaching vehicle is. Then count off the seconds to measure how many seconds it took the vehicle to arrive. By repeating the trials, one can soon increase the ability to make accurate judgments.

is called fringe vision. Side fringe vision is used to monitor a zone condition after it has been identified in central vision. The upper fringe vision is used to detect changes in the rear mirror. The lower fringe vision is used to monitor reference points for vehicle position.

Some people see less than a total of 180 degrees. A narrow field of vision—140 degrees or less—is called **tunnel vision.** A driver who has tunnel vision must compensate with more frequent head and eye movements.

### Depth Perception

The ability to judge distance between yourself and other objects is **depth perception.** When driving you must judge the distance between your vehicle and other vehicles and other objects. Accurate judgment is more difficult when the other vehicle is moving.

A driver can compensate for poor depth perception by

- using a following distance greater than three seconds

You can see nearby objects and distant ones clearly in daylight.

- allowing for additional clear distance ahead before passing
- allowing greater distances at night than at daytime. (Darkness hides many guides you use in the daytime.)

### Night Vision

The ability to see at night varies from person to person. Some people who see clearly in the daytime have poor night vision. Not being able to see well at night is called **night blindness.**

All people see less at night than in daylight. Colors are harder to identify. Details of objects do not appear as sharp as in daylight.

Your night vision is limited to the area lit by headlights, streetlights, and other lights. In rural areas, you might be in total darkness except for the area lit by your headlights.

At night you might not be able to see anything to the sides. You might be less able to read signs and roadway markings. Compare the two pictures that show the same situation.

Your ability to see objects and judge distance is limited at night.

## Activity

**Class Activity** This activity will help students understand how depth perception is altered when another vehicle is moving. You will need two matchbox cars, a file folder, and some string. Cut a 4″ square window in the front flap of the file folder. The bottom edge of the window should be at the fold and the window should be in the middle of the folder. Tape the back of the folder to a table or desk. Lift up the front of the folder and place a soda can on the back of the folder to make the front stay up. Attach a 6′ piece of string to the front of one of the cars. Attach a 3′ piece to the back of the same car. Place the car with the string on the file folder, one foot behind the window, and facing away from you. Run the front string forward, under the table and back to your side of the table. You will use the strings to move the car forward and backward. Place the other car next to the window. Have a student look through the file folder window. Have the student tell you when the two cars are aligned. Move the car toward the window and past the stationary car. Ask the student to close one eye and repeat the activity. Ask students what effect this has on the results.

**You Are the Driver!**
Some vehicles reflect sunlight into your eyes. How can you compensate?

The only difference is that one picture was taken during the day and the other one was taken at night. Notice that you cannot see as much at night. Your ability to judge distances accurately also decreases.

### Glare

Glare occurs in the daytime when bright sunlight is reflected off shiny surfaces. Sunroofs and convertibles let in additional sunlight that can produce glare. At night, glare occurs when bright lights reflect off shiny surfaces. The term **glare resistance** describes the ability to continue seeing when looking at bright lights. Glare resistance varies from person to person. Some people are more sensitive to light than others.

Sudden glare can blind a person temporarily, especially at night. Headlights turn toward you at intersections. Bright lights appear from over hills and around curves. A vehicle using high-beam headlights approaches from behind. Your pupils open wide at night to let in all available light. When your eyes are suddenly exposed to bright lights, your pupils contract. You might be temporarily blinded before your pupils can adjust to the bright lights.

The term **glare recovery time** describes the time your eyes need to regain clear vision after being affected by glare. Your pupils can take 5–10 seconds to readjust. At 40 mph, you can travel more than the length of a football field while partially blinded.

Take these steps to avoid or recover from glare:

- Avoid looking directly at bright lights. Use the right edge of the roadway as a guide.
- Anticipate glare situations and glance away or squint.
- Use side fringe vision rather than central vision to check your lane position and the location of oncoming vehicles.
- If you are impaired by glare, slow until your vision clears.
- Wear sunglasses and use your vehicle's sun visor in bright sunlight.
- Adjust your rearview mirror for night use.

## Discuss

Ask students how night driving is likely to be combined with fatigue and the presence of other drivers who are alcohol-impaired. Discuss how this difficult mix can increase the level of driving-related risk.

## Explain

Point out that when you are driving at night it is easy to stare only at the area illuminated by your headlights. This causes eye fatigue and reduced peripheral vision, especially on curves.

## Discuss

Draw students' attention to the *You Are the Driver!* photograph. Ask: Some vehicles reflect sunlight into your eyes. How can you compensate? (Wear sunglasses or use your vehicle's sun visor, glance away or squint, and use your fringe vision as much as possible.)

## Activity

**In-Class Driving Rehearsal** This activity will help students experience the recovery time eyes need in order to be able to see after being over-stimulated by headlights. See **Resource Book,** page 47 for construction of test box. Have a student driver look into the box through the viewer's opening. Hold a 4″ X 6″ index card with a five-digit number printed in the center of it against the display end to make the number visible to the driver. Record how many seconds it took the driver to read the correct number. Repeat with two other numbers. Then, with the driver still looking into the box opening, shine the flashlight in the display end to be directed into the driver's eyes. Have the driver stare at the flashlight for three seconds. Then hold another set of numbers in the display opening. Have another student keep track of how many seconds lapse before the driver is able to read the numbers.

## Explain

Explain that the need to focus farther ahead at higher speeds tends to cause tunnel vision. The only solution is to force yourself to look to the sides more often. Continual use of the side mirrors is a good way to keep track of other drivers. Reading as many road signs as possible is another way to keep the field of vision as wide as possible.

## Discuss

Ask: What sounds should you listen for when you are driving? (vehicle horns; police and train whistles; sirens; engine and brake noises from other vehicles; unusual noise from your own vehicle) What might prevent you from hearing important audio driving clues? (closed windows; radio, cassettes, or CDs; conversation with passengers or on a cellular phone; heater or air conditioning fans blowing) How can you compensate for what you cannot hear? (Vision becomes even more important when driving under these conditions.)

### Vehicle Speed and Vision

As your vehicle's speed increases, your need for accurate vision also increases. Yet, at higher speeds, you have less time to see clearly. Your field of vision also is narrowed. At 55 mph, your clear side-vision area is less than half as wide as at 20 mph.

Objects off to your sides become blurred and distorted as your speed increases. This blur, or **speed smear,** as shown in the picture, has an effect much like tunnel vision. Your eyes tend to focus far ahead to where the roadway appears to come to a point. You see less and less of what is happening on the sides. Increase the frequency of your side glances when driving at highway speeds.

### Other Senses and Driving

Sometimes you need to depend on other senses to identify threats to your path of travel. In complex driving situations, you may have to use more than one sense at a time.

### Hearing

Your sense of hearing can alert you to the sounds of vehicle horns, train whistles, emergency-vehicle sirens, and engines and brakes of trucks and buses. You can also get early warning of mechanical problems by listening for unusual noises from your vehicle.

Drivers who have sounds blocked from them can be dangerous to themselves and to others. Driving with closed windows and with stereo or headsets on may make a driver unaware of critical traffic sounds. Using a cellular phone while driving creates a similar problem.

Drivers who are deaf know that they must compensate for what they cannot hear. They use their eyes more than drivers who have normal hearing.

### Smell

Your sense of smell can identify an overheated engine or overheated brakes. Smelling exhaust fumes inside your vehicle can give you an

When you drive at higher speeds, your side vision is less clear.

## Activity

**Class Activity** This activity will provide the opportunity to practice reading road signs when traveling at higher speeds. You will need a slide projector and slides of road signs. Place groups of five slides in a carousel leaving three empty slots between each group. Hold the advance button to move through one group as fast as possible. Stop at one of the empty slots. Have students write down the message on all five signs. Repeat for each group of slides. Identifying the message on four signs out of every group of five is a realistic goal.

## Special Needs

Record 15-second segments of sounds such as sirens, horns, tires, brake wear, etc. The school auto shop or a local auto repair business may be helpful in getting a clear recording of some sounds. Play each segment individually and ask students to identify the sound. For each segment, ask students to explain why it is important to be able to recognize the sound.

For students with hearing loss, discuss clues other than sirens or horns that can indicate the presence of emergency vehicles.

early warning to the presence of deadly gases.

### Sense of Motion

Certain sensations can give you clues to the movement of your vehicle. Your sense of balance tells you that you are veering right or left, changing speed, or going around a curve. A sudden vibration of the vehicle or jerk of the steering wheel might warn you of a mechanical problem, a flat tire, or a change in the roadway surface.

### Risk Management

You increase or decrease your risk of becoming involved in a collision by changing the level of control you have over your vehicle. Impairment or inadequate use of senses of vision, hearing, smell, and motion will affect your ability to manage risks. Also, anything that distracts you from using your senses and concentrating on the driving task will increase your risk of a collision.

### Distractions

A driver needs to focus on the driving task at all times. The driving scene can change quickly, and you need to be alert to changes so that you make decisions and act quickly.

An audio system in your vehicle can cause distractions, although it can be helpful if used safely. You need to keep the volume at a level that allows you to hear important traffic sounds such as sirens and horns. Also, do not wear headphones while driving. Headphones will block traffic sounds, and it is illegal in many states to wear them while driving. Avoid changing

radio stations, tapes, and CDs while driving. You increase your risk of a collision any time you take your eyes off the road and a hand off the steering wheel.

Cellular phones can be helpful in a vehicle in emergencies, but they are dangerous to use while driving. Research studies have found that drivers talking on a cell phone were four times more likely to be involved in a collision. You should turn off your cell phone while driving. If you need to use the phone, pull off the road and stop the car.

Other distractions can come from people or pets in the vehicle. The driver is responsible for keeping passengers under control. Pets need to be placed in carriers or secured with special harnesses. The more distractions you can eliminate, the better you will be able to manage risks to avoid collisions while driving.

## Review It

1. What is your field of vision? What part of your field of vision provides you with your clearest vision?
2. What can you do to compensate for poor depth perception?
3. How do your senses of seeing, hearing, smelling, and motion help you assess driving situations?

Chapter 14 Effects of Driver Condition **303**

## Background

**Sense of Motion** A driver can acquire a sensitivity to changes in a vehicle's motion. In addition to providing a comfortable ride, smooth acceleration and braking actions can help a driver identify unusual situations. For example, when routine braking consistently results in a smooth action, a jerky braking response would let the driver know that something is wrong.

## Cross Curricular

**Science/Health** This activity will help students understand how senses help to identify driving-related problems. Divide the class into groups of five. Assign a sense to each group and ask them to make a list of driving-related problems that might be detected by the assigned sense. Make sure students understand that their lists should include examples not mentioned in the textbook. After adequate time, have the groups report their findings to the class.

## Discuss

Discuss why using cellular phones while driving is risky. Tell students that a Canadian study found that drivers talking on a cellular phone were four times more likely to be involved in a collision. The study also found that the risk was the same for outgoing and incoming calls, and hands-free cellular phones did not reduce the risk of a collision by much. Ask: What does this study show to be the main source of risk? (driver distraction) Why might talking on a cellular phone be more distracting than talking with passengers?

 **Assess**

## Answers to Review It

**1.** Your field of vision is all the area you can see when looking straight ahead. Your clearest sight is in your area of central vision. (p. 299)

**2.** To compensate for poor depth perception, use greater following distance, allow for extra clearance before passing, use known distances to judge distance, and allow for greater distances at night. (p. 300)

**3.** You can see other vehicles through vision, listen for horns and sirens with hearing, sense burning or exhaust fumes with smell, and tell when your vehicle is slowing or turning by sense of motion. (pp. 302–303)

# Physical Disabilities

## 1 Focus

### Summary

This lesson focuses on recognizing and compensating for disabilities that affect driving abilities.

### Vocabulary

*carbon monoxide*

## 2 Teach

### Explain

Explain that there are certain times of the day when a person is at greater risk of being drowsy. A high-risk period occurs at the halfway point of the hours that a person is awake. If you normally get up at 6:00 A.M. and go to bed at 11:00 P.M., you are awake for 17 hours. Somewhere around 2:30 P.M. you are biologically susceptible to fatigue. There is greater risk during the afternoon commuter hour traffic than there is during the morning commute, in part due to afternoon drowsiness. (See Background on page 305 for information on adolescent sleep needs.)

### Objectives

1. Tell what you can do to combat fatigue.
2. Explain what to do to avoid carbon monoxide exposure and how to deal with its effects.
3. Describe what drivers who have permanent disabilities can do to compensate.

Experienced drivers have learned to respond to temporary and permanent disabilities. Generally, driving is possible for people who have moderate to severe disabilities. However, a disability needs to be recognized before it can be overcome, whether temporary or permanent.

### Temporary Disabilities

Sometimes you must drive even though you are not at your physical best. While you can compensate for some temporary disabilities, with others you should not drive until they no longer exist.

### Fatigue

Mental or physical work, emotional stress, or loss of sleep can cause fatigue. Fatigue lessens your fitness to perform tasks, including driving. It dulls your senses and slows both mental and physical processes. If you are fatigued, you will need more time to use the IPDE Process.

Fatigue can also cause drowsiness. Drowsy driving is estimated to cause at least 100,000 collisions a year.

There are several danger signs of drowsiness:

- trouble keeping your head up
- drifting between lane positions
- wandering, disconnected thoughts
- inability to stop yawning
- eyes closing or going out of focus
- inability to concentrate on driving task

When are you about to fall asleep? That is hard to predict. Most people biologically prefer to sleep between 12:00 A.M. and 6:00 A.M., and again around 2:00 P.M. You may experience drowsiness during these times. Be cautious.

Drowsiness can interfere with a person's driving abilities.

## Teacher's Resources

No *Drive Right* resources are needed for teaching Section 14.3.

Rest is the only safe remedy for fatigue. However, people often need to drive even when they are tired. If you are tired after work or school, take a break for a few minutes before you drive. You might also choose a quieter, less congested route home.

Take these actions to deal with fatigue on long drives:

- Rest before you start.
- Change drivers often.
- Stop every two hours. Walk, stretch, get a beverage or snack, or take a nap on long trips.
- Wear sunglasses in bright sunlight and to shield against snow glare.
- Use your orderly visual search pattern to keep your eyes moving.
- Be active—listen to the radio, sing, or talk with your passengers.
- Stop in a safe, well-lighted place if you feel drowsy. Lock the vehicle and take a nap.

If you feel tired often, check with your doctor. You may have a chronic illness or sleep disorder.

### Temporary Illness or Injury

Any illness, even a cold, can impair driving to some extent. A temporary physical injury, such as a broken bone or a sprained ankle, also can

impair your driving. These and other temporary conditions can cause discomfort and pain, limit physical movement, lessen endurance and strength, or dull your senses.

### Effects of Medicines

Many medicines have side effects that can interfere with your driving ability and risks. For example, medicine that reduces headache pain or relieves hay fever, might also cause drowsiness, dizziness, or reduced alertness.

If you take medicine, consider these points before you drive:

- Read the label to learn the possible side effects, as shown in the picture. Ask your physician or pharmacist about side effects.

Many commonly used medicines can affect your driving ability.

## Background

**Adolescent Sleep Needs** Research studies show that adolescents' biological sleep patterns are delayed. Adolescents tend to fall asleep later and wake up later than people in other age groups. The typical adolescent falls asleep at 11:00 P.M. or later. Adolescents require 8.5 to 9.25 hours of sleep a night. Studies of the sleep behavior of adolescents indicate that they typically do not get enough sleep and their sleep patterns are irregular (especially variations between weekdays and weekends). These behaviors contribute to problems falling asleep and

awakening and poor quality sleep. Poor sleep can affect school performance and the ability to control emotions, as well as greatly increase the risk of falling asleep at the wheel. A research study in North Carolina found that 55 percent of fall-asleep collisions were caused by drivers age 25 and younger.

## Explain

Everyone has experienced nodding off in the middle of class. Sometimes you feel it coming on and other times you don't realize it until your head nods and you wake yourself up. Unfortunately, one of these unplanned catnaps while you are behind the wheel can be life threatening. If you drift off for 5 seconds while driving 55 mph, you will travel more than 100 yards. That is more than enough time to cause a collision with serious, or fatal, consequences.

## Demonstrate

Create a display using labels and instruction sheets from over-the-counter medications that have driving-related warnings. Discuss the importance of avoiding these medicines before driving.

## Explain

Explain that a feeling of dizziness can be the warning of an eye, inner ear, or other problem. Encourage students to consult a physician if they experience such a condition.

## Explain

Point out that driving is performed best by drivers who are physically fit and mentally alert. Conditions that affect vision, dull thinking, or slow actions lessen driving competence.

## Explain

Explain that backing into a snow bank and leaving the engine running can force exhaust fumes containing carbon monoxide inside the vehicle. Point out that any opening near the tailpipe can allow carbon monoxide to enter the passenger compartment.

If you are carrying a large load that requires you to drive with the trunk, tailgate, hatchback, or back window open, be sure to have front vents and side windows open to keep fresh air moving through the vehicle.

In heavy traffic, your intakes might draw in carbon monoxide from the exhaust of the car ahead.

- A medicine can affect you differently at different times.
- If possible, drive to your destination before taking the medicine.
- If you must drive after taking medicine, try to choose a quiet, less-congested route.

**Effects of Carbon Monoxide** Your vehicle's exhaust fumes contain **carbon monoxide,** a colorless, odorless, and tasteless gas. Carbon monoxide is present in all engine exhaust gases.

You can sometimes detect carbon monoxide in a vehicle because it is mixed with other exhaust fumes that do have an odor. However, you cannot tell how concentrated the carbon monoxide is by the odor of the exhaust fumes. If there is no odor, you cannot be sure there is no carbon monoxide.

Small amounts of carbon monoxide can cause drowsiness, headaches, muscular weakness, mental dullness, and nausea. Too much carbon monoxide can cause death.

Be alert for the danger of carbon monoxide in heavy traffic and in such enclosed areas as tunnels and underground parking facilities. Your heater or air conditioner vents might draw in exhaust fumes from the car ahead, as shown here. Leaving a rear window open might create a slight vacuum that pulls in exhaust fumes.

Take these actions to prevent carbon monoxide exposure and combat its effect:

- If your vehicle is parked in a garage at home, open the garage door before starting the engine.
- Avoid running the engine inside a garage. Move your vehicle outside after starting the engine.
- In stop-and-go traffic, keep a three-second following distance. Stop where you can see the tires of the vehicle ahead touching the pavement.
- In traffic jams, especially in enclosed areas, turn off the engine when possible.
- Check your exhaust system regularly.
- Do not drive with the rear windows open.

- Move a person who is overcome by carbon monoxide into fresh air. Seek medical help immediately.

**Smoking** Be aware that smoking while driving is dangerous. Smoking raises the carbon monoxide level in a person's blood. Smoke residue accumulates on windows and affects vision.

Discourage your passengers from smoking. Carbon monoxide from tobacco smoke can affect even non-smokers in an enclosed area such as a vehicle. If someone does smoke in your vehicle, open a window to provide fresh air.

### Effects on Risk Taking

Temporary illness, such as a cold, can affect a driver's risk-taking decisions. Because they are temporary, many drivers do not recognize the illness's influence on their driving skills. They might be more willing to, and often do, take chances they would not take if they were well. Being tired or under the influence of medicines can increase your chances of being in a collision. Be aware of the side effects of medicines by reading the labels. Compensate for side effects of medicines and for illness by using an extra space cushion and taking even fewer chances.

### Permanent and Physical Disabilities

Special vehicle equipment and controls can make it possible for many people with permanent disabilities to drive, as shown in the picture. Still others can control their disabilities with medication.

**Older Drivers** As a nation, we are healthier and living longer. As a result, more older drivers are using the roadways. One in six drivers is over age 65. Eighty percent of drivers over age 75

Vehicles are often adapted to help physically challenged people maintain independence.

### Answers to Review It

**1.** To compensate for the effects of fatigue, rest before driving, change drivers, stop regularly for rest, wear sunglasses when needed, use good eye habits, and be active. (p. 305)

**2.** To avoid and combat carbon monoxide exposure, open the garage door before starting the engine, do not run the engine inside the garage, increase distance between vehicles in heavy traffic, check the exhaust system, and move a person who is overcome into fresh air and get medical help. (pp. 306–307)

**3.** Permanent disabilities can affect driving in a variety of ways. Medications taken by people with chronic illnesses may cause drowsiness, slowed reflexes, dulled vision, and weak or inflexible muscles. (pp. 307–308)

Special parking areas and license plates help disabled drivers reach their destinations safely.

### SAFE DRIVING

It is illegal to park in handicapped-designated parking spaces unless you have special identification.

take prescribed medicines. Aging slows reflexes, dulls vision and concentration, can make muscles weaker and inflexible, and reduces depth perception and field of vision. Failure to yield the right of way is the main factor in collisions involving older drivers. However, drivers over 65 are still involved in fewer collisions per mile driven than those under 30.

**Chronic Illnesses** A chronic illness is an ailment that lasts over a period of years. Some chronic illnesses have little effect on driving. Other illnesses, such as heart disease, could seriously impair a person's ability to drive.

Some chronic illnesses require regular medications that can cause side effects that interfere with driving. Some people have diseases that cause sudden loss of consciousness or muscular control. Before these individuals can receive a driver's license, they must provide medical proof that their chronic illness is under control.

#### Effects on Risk Taking

Most drivers with permanent disabilities do not take unnecessary chances with driving decisions influenced by their disabilities. These drivers often understand that the disability itself may put them at a higher level of risk. The solution is knowing that you have the disability, admitting you have it, and compensating for it.

Whatever the illness or disability, everyone who can perform the driving tasks safely and successfully earns the privilege of being licensed to drive when all other requirements are met. Sometimes they are required to take more frequent testing to maintain that privilege.

Some drivers with permanent disabilities have special license plates or window cards with the handicapped symbol. The symbol also appears on license plates or window cards of drivers who often transport handicapped people. Vehicles with these license plates can park in specially marked areas in parking lots and on streets.

### Review It

1. How can you compensate for the effects of fatigue?
2. How can you avoid and combat exposure to carbon monoxide?
3. How can a permanent disability affect your driving?

**308** Unit 4 Being a Responsible Driver

### Background

**Handicapped Parking** Federal, state, and local laws provide special parking for persons with disabilities. The spaces are clearly marked with signs to indicate that they are reserved for persons with disabilities. While the signs usually show a symbol depicting a wheelchair, the spaces are reserved for persons who have a wide range of disabilities including heart disease, breathing disorders, and physical limitations that do not require the use of a wheelchair.

In recent years it has become common to see these parking spaces in parking lots, but they are also located on city streets. Some urban communities designate on-street parking spaces near the homes of persons with disabilities.

In most situations, a permit is needed to park in a handicapped parking space. To get a permit, a driver usually must submit proof of a disability, including a physician's signature.

It might be tempting to park in a handicapped space because of the convenient location, but it is wrong. In many communities it is also illegal, and parking tickets carry high fines.

## Reviewing Chapter Objectives

### 1. Emotions and Driving

1. How can anger affect your ability to drive? (293–294)
2. How can you help a driver when you are a passenger? (295–296)
3. What can you do to manage your emotions while driving? (296–297)
4. How do emotions influence your willingness to accept risk? (296)

### 2. Physical Senses and Driving

5. What are the parts of your field of vision? (299–300)
6. What can you do to compensate for poor depth perception? (300)
7. How do your senses help you drive? (298–303)

### 3. Physical Disabilities

8. What can you do to combat fatigue? (304–305)
9. What can you do to avoid carbon monoxide exposure and deal with its effects? (306–307)
10. What can drivers who have permanent disabilities do to compensate? (307–308)

## Projects

### Individuals

**Investigate** Research newspaper articles about traffic collisions involving drivers who were fatigued. Write a report about a collision involving a driver who fell asleep at the wheel.

**Observe Traffic** Keep track of the sounds you hear for a week as a passenger in a vehicle. Make a list of each sound you hear, and count the number of times you hear that particular sound. (Focus on vehicle-related sounds and sounds coming from outside the vehicle. Do not include sounds made by the driver or passengers.) At the end of the week, compare your results with those of your classmates.

### Groups

**Demonstrate** Prepare a short skit that takes place in a vehicle. Six students have just attended a football game at another school. They are on their way to a victory party. Demonstrate examples of good as well as unacceptable behaviors in the vehicle. Present the skit to your class.

**Use Technology** Prepare a spreadsheet that contains each group member's visual acuity score. (If you do not know your visual acuity score, you need to take a visual acuity test to find out.) List the different ratios in descending order.

## Reviewing Chapter Objectives

**14.1** Emotions and Driving
See Answers to Review It on page 297.
**14.2** Physical Senses and Driving
See Answers to Review It on page 304.
**14.3** Physical Disabilities
See Answers to Review It on page 308.

For additional information refer to the specific page(s) in parentheses after each question.

## Projects

Some of the projects can be assigned at any time while others are more closely tied to the content presented in the student text. The page number where the topic is introduced is indicated.

**Investigate:** p. 305
**Observe Traffic:** p. 298
**Demonstrate:** p. 292
**Use Technology:** p. 298
The results of student projects will vary.

---

## Teacher's Resources

**Skills and Applications Workbook**
pages 53–56

**Tests and Activities**
Chapter 14 Activities 14-1 and 14-2, pages 119–120
Chapter 14 Test A and Test B, pages 121–124

**TestWorks CD-ROM**
Chapter 14 Test

## Answers to Check Your Knowledge

1. d
2. b
3. a
4. d
5. anger
6. depth perception
7. exhaust fumes
8. yield the right of way

## Answers to Review Vocabulary

9. glare resistance (f)
10. speed smear (b)
11. visual acuity (d)
12. glare recovery time (c)
13. depth perception (g)
14. color blindness (a)
15. night blindness (e)
16. tunnel vision (h)

## Answers to Think Critically

Students' answers will vary. For information related to the question refer to the page(s) indicated.

**1.** Show courtesy to other drivers; think positively, do not try to "punish" other drivers, pull off the road until you have your emotions under control. (pp. 292, 294)

**2.** Use the following steps to avoid carbon monoxide exposure. 1. Avoid running the vehicle engine. 2. Keep vehicle well ventilated. 3. In stop-and-go traffic, keep a half-vehicle length or more between your vehicle and the vehicle ahead of you. 4. In traffic jams, turn off the engine when possible. 5. Check your exhaust system regularly. (p. 306)

### Chapter Test

#### Check Your Knowledge

**Multiple Choice** Copy the number of each sentence below on a sheet of paper. Choose the letter of the answer that best completes the statement or answers the question.

1. Emotions influence driving because they
   (a) cause you to drive fast.
   (b) change the way you assess risk.
   (c) change the way you make driving decisions.
   (d) both b and c
2. A person who must be twice as close to an object to see it as clearly as a person with normal visual acuity has
   (a) 20/20 vision.　　(c) 20/60 vision.
   (b) 20/40 vision.　　(d) 20/200 vision.
3. The part of your peripheral vision closest to your central vision is called
   (a) fringe vision.　　(c) depth perception.
   (b) tunnel vision.　　(d) side perception.
4. The best way to prevent fatigue on long drives is to
   (a) increase speed to shorten trip time.
   (b) wear sunglasses.
   (c) turn on the air conditioner.
   (d) rest before you start.

**Completion** Copy the number of each sentence below. After each number, write the word or words that complete the sentence correctly.

5. While driving, drivers experience the emotion of _____ more often than any other.
6. Your _____ allows you to judge the distance between yourself and other objects.
7. Carbon monoxide gas is present in the _____ of a vehicle.
8. Most collisions involving older drivers are caused by failure to _____.

#### Review Vocabulary

Copy the number of each definition in list A. Match the definition in list A with the term it defines in list B.

**List A**

9. ability to continue seeing when looking at bright lights
10. occurs when objects off to your sides become blurred and distorted as your speed increases
11. ability to see things clearly both near and far away
12. time your eyes need to regain clear vision after being affected by glare
13. ability to judge distance between yourself and other objects
14. not being able to distinguish colors
15. not being able to see well at night
16. narrow field of vision of 140 degrees or less

**List B**

a. color blindness　　e. night blindness
b. speed smear　　　f. glare resistance
c. glare recovery time　g. depth perception
d. visual acuity　　　h. tunnel vision

#### Think Critically

Write a paragraph to answer each question.

1. List and discuss the techniques you can use to control your emotions while driving.
2. Explain how you would prevent exposure to carbon monoxide poisoning in the vehicle you drive.

## Decision Making

**1.** Where should you direct your clear central vision in the next few seconds of driving?

**2.** What is causing this driver to be impaired for a few seconds? What actions could the driver have taken to prevent this impairment? What can the driver do now to minimize the danger?

**3.** These people are having an argument. How could the argument affect the driver's ability to drive?

**4.** How are these passengers affecting the driver? What should they be doing to help?

Chapter 14 Effects of Driver Condition **311**

## Answers to Decision Making

**1.** Direct your central vision to your target area about 12–15 seconds ahead to identify zone changes.

**2.** Glare from the bright sun ahead is causing the driver to be impaired. Wearing sunglasses, using the sun visor, and looking away from the high-intensity glare area could prevent the impairment. To minimize the damage, the driver could slow until vision clears and use side fringe vision to check vehicle's lane position and the location of others.

**3.** If this driver becomes angry, he might not be able to steer, brake, or accelerate smoothly. In addition, he might not see other driving hazards and take last-second actions that might surprise other drivers.

**4.** The passengers are distracting the driver. They should be helping the driver concentrate on the driving task by not creating needless distractions.

| |  **Student Features** |  **Teacher's Edition** |
|---|---|---|
| **Chapter 15**<br>**Alcohol, Other Drugs, and Driving** | You Are the Driver! *p. 313* | Projects *p. 312*<br>Special Needs *p. 313* |
| **15.1 Effects of Alcohol on Driving Safely** *pp. 314–320*<br>• Explain how alcohol affects mental and physical abilities needed for driving.<br>• Define blood-alcohol concentration.<br>• Explain factors that affect blood-alcohol concentration.<br>• List five myths and truths about the use of alcohol. | What Do You Think? *p. 315*<br>Safe Driving Tip *p. 318* | Demonstrate *pp. 315, 316, 318, 319*<br>Activity *pp. 314, 315, 316, 317, 320* |
| **15.2 Other Drugs and Driving** *pp. 321–322*<br>• Explain the difference between the purchase of over-the-counter medicine and the purchase of prescription medicine.<br>• Explain how depressants, stimulants, and hallucinogenic drugs can affect a driver.<br>• Describe the effects of combining alcohol with other drugs. | Did You Know? *p. 322* | Activity *p. 321* |
| **15.3 Traffic Laws Governing the Use of Alcohol** *pp. 323–325*<br>• Explain what is meant by the implied-consent law.<br>• Describe zero-tolerance levels of intoxication, and tell how these levels can be measured.<br>• Explain what a driver should do when stopped by a police officer. | Did You Know? *p. 330* | Demonstrate *p. 324*<br>Activity *pp. 324, 325* |
| **15.4 Coping with Peer Pressure** *pp. 326–330*<br>• Tell how peer pressure might affect one's decision about drinking and driving.<br>• List five steps involved in making a responsible decision.<br>• Explain what is meant by peer education.<br>• Explain why everyone should share the responsibility of preventing friends from drinking and driving. | | Demonstrate *p. 327*<br>Activity *pp. 326, 327, 328, 329* |
| **Assessment** | Reviewing Chapter<br>  Objectives *p. 331*<br>Projects *p. 331*<br>Chapter Test *p. 332*<br>Decision Making *p. 333* | Answers *pp. 332–333* |

**Companion** *pp. 92–96*
**Spanish Handbook** *pp. 31–32*

**Content Overheads 27, 28, 29**

# Technology Resources

## Audio-Visual and Computer Resources

AAA Foundation for Traffic Safety, *Just Another Saturday Night,* video, 13 minutes

AIMS Media, *Drinking and Driving: A Deadly Combination,* video, 22 minutes

AIMS Media, *Saying NO to Drinking Drivers,* video, 23 minutes

AIMS Media, *The Designated Driver...Be a Friend for Life,* video, 21 minutes

Drunk Busters of America, *Jane: A film,* video

Insurance Institute for Highway Safety, *Sober Thoughts on Drinking and Driving,* video, 14 minutes

National Commission Against Drunk Driving, *Drunk Driving: Your Choice?* video, 20 minutes

National Safety Council, *Drunk Driving: Real People, Real Tragedies,* video, 18 minutes

Safety Industries, Inc., *Drunk Driving: The Party's Over,* video, 23 minutes

## Kits, Equipment, and Other Resources

Drunk Busters of America: *Drunk Busters Impairment Goggles*

Innocorp, Ltd.: *Fatal Vision Goggles*

**Go Online**
PHSchool.com
**For: Chapter 15 online activities**
**Visit: PHSchool.com**
**Web Code: cak-9999**

**Skills and Applications
  Workbook,** *pp. 57–60*
**Tests and Activities**
Chapter 15 Activities 15-1
  and 15-2, *pp. 127–128*
Chapter 15 Test A and
  Test B, *pp. 129–132*

**TestWorks CD-ROM**
Chapter 15 Test

# Chapter 15

## Alcohol, Other Drugs, and Driving

### Chapter Overview

Chapter 15 explains effects of alcohol and other drugs on driver performance. Laws governing the use of alcohol are described. Students also learn about how peer pressure might affect their decisions about drinking and driving.

### Chapter Vocabulary

*blood-alcohol concentration (BAC), depressant, designated driver, driving under the influence (DUI), driving while intoxicated (DWI), euphoria, field sobriety test, implied-consent law, inhibitions, intoxilyzer, nystagmus, over-the-counter medicine, peer education, peer pressure, prescription medicine, stimulant, zero-tolerance law*

312

### Teacher's Resources

For students to use as they read the chapter:

**Companion**
pages 92–96

**Spanish Handbook**
pages 31–32

### Projects

Review the projects described on page 331. Some of the projects can be assigned at any time while others are more closely tied to the content presented in the student text.

# CHAPTER 15
## Alcohol, Other Drugs, and Driving

**15.1** Effects of Alcohol on Driving Safely

**15.2** Other Drugs and Driving

**15.3** Traffic Laws Governing the Use of Alcohol

**15.4** Coping with Peer Pressure

### You Are the Driver!

These people are attending a music concert. They have been at the concert for several hours. Some of the adults drank a few alcoholic beverages. What driving abilities might be impaired when a person uses alcohol? What tests might drivers have to take if the police stop them? What can you do if you believe a person who had several drinks thinks it is safe to drive? This chapter discusses the effects of alcohol and other drugs. It will help you understand why you should never drink and drive.

**Go Online**
PHSchool.com

**For:** Chapter 15 online activities
**Visit:** PHSchool.com
**Web Code:** cak-9999

313

### Introducing the Chapter

Review what students know about the effects of alcohol and other drugs on driving ability. Discuss how these effects can affect safety. Discuss occasions where people might drink and drive. Discuss what can happen when people drive after drinking. Ask students to suggest ways to avoid such situations.

### You Are the Driver!

⬅ Direct students to look at the picture. Ask: What would you do if you were supposed to ride in the car with a driver who had been drinking at the party? Discuss the questions in the *You Are the Driver!* text.

### Special Needs

Since alcohol is the number one factor in fatal collisions for young people, this chapter is important for *all* students. Be sure to involve special needs students in the discussions and activities in this chapter, many of which help students explore values in relation to behavior. Some of these students might be especially influenced by peer pressure because of a need for acceptance and self-worth. Therefore, role-play activities such as the one on page 329 should be used with these students.

# Effects of Alcohol on Driving Safely

## 1 Focus

### Summary

This lesson focuses on the effects of alcohol on driving safely. Facts about alcohol are presented along with information about how alcohol affects behavior. Myths and truths about alcohol are included.

### Vocabulary

*blood-alcohol concentration (BAC), designated driver, euphoria, inhibitions*

## 2 Teach

### Discuss

Ask students to list possible reasons why a high percentage of alcohol-related deaths involve young people. Note the young driver's inexperience in both driving and the way they might drink (such as large amounts in short periods of time). Ask: What are some reasons that young people under the legal drinking age choose to drink?

### Objectives

1. Explain how alcohol affects mental and physical abilities needed for driving.
2. Define blood-alcohol concentration.
3. Explain factors that affect blood-alcohol concentration.
4. List five myths and truths about the use of alcohol.

**A**lcohol is the most commonly used drug in our society today. It is by far the most frequently found drug in fatally injured drivers.

Young people in their teens are among those in our society who use and abuse alcohol. Even though it is illegal for teens to drink, a significant percentage of them do drink. This segment of young people who drink alcohol presents a major problem for highway safety when they mix drinking with driving.

All states now enforce a minimum drinking age of 21. Laws against underage drinking and driving are more strictly and more vigorously enforced now than ever. Alcohol-related educational programs within schools, homes, and communities have increased. Nevertheless, alcohol-related collisions are still a major safety problem.

### Alcohol Facts

Some people are not aware that alcohol is a drug. After all, it can be purchased legally. And commercial advertising depicts alcoholic beverage consumption as harmless fun.

The word *alcohol* is the commonly used term for the chemical substance ethanol, grain alcohol, or ethyl alcohol. Alcohol is the product of the fermentation of fruits, grains, or other plants. Alcohol is classified as a drug because of its effects on the body's central nervous system.

The effects of alcohol vary from person to person. However, everyone who uses alcohol is affected by it to some degree. One of the most serious problems of alcohol is the problem of the drinking driver. Drivers cannot afford to increase the risks of driving by having their abilities diminished by alcohol.

Alcohol is the most commonly found drug in fatally injured drivers.

## Teacher's Resources

**Content Overheads**
Overheads 27, 28, and 29

## Activity

**Small Group Activity** This activity will give students an opportunity to express their values regarding alcohol use. Divide the class into groups of five. Ask the groups to discuss the following questions: Why do people drink alcoholic beverages? Why do people drive while under the influence? How is driving under the influence similar to pointing a loaded gun at someone? During the discussion, walk among the groups, taking note of what you hear. After adequate time, ask the class to comment on the various values you noted.

Consider these facts about alcohol and driving:

- Young drinking drivers are involved in fatal crashes at twice the rate of drivers aged 21 and older.
- Drivers aged 16 through 20 are more likely to be alcohol-impaired than any other age group.
- Nearly half of those killed in alcohol-related collisions had not been drinking but were victims of drunk drivers.
- More than half of all fatalities during holidays are alcohol related.

## How Alcohol Affects Behavior

As soon as alcohol from a drink reaches the brain, it affects the way people think and behave. Just one drink can affect a person's behavior, both mentally and physically, regardless of the type of alcoholic drink. The same amount of alcohol does not affect all people the same way. Alcohol does not even affect the same person in the same way in all situations. The best way to avoid changes in behavior is to abstain from drinking.

## Mental Abilities and Alcohol

Alcohol acts on the central nervous system like an anesthetic, slowing the activity of the brain. Alcohol is not digested. It is absorbed directly and quickly into the bloodstream through the walls and linings of the entire digestive tract.

Once alcohol enters the bloodstream, it quickly flows to the brain. Alcohol has the greatest effect on the parts of the brain that control judgment and reasoning—the two

| Effects of Alcohol on Behavior | | |
|---|---|---|
| Number of drinks in one hour | BAC | Effects |
| 1 serving | .02–.03% | Inhibitions are lessened. Judgment and reasoning begin to be affected. |
| 3 servings | .05–.09% | Unable to think clearly. Judgment and reasoning are not reliable. Muscular coordination is impaired. |
| 4 servings | .10–.12% | After four drinks, hearing, speech, vision, and balance are affected. Most behaviors are affected. |

most critical mental skills needed by drivers. Physical abilities become impaired soon afterward.

**Judgment and Reasoning** A driver affected by alcohol has a decreased ability to reason clearly and make sound judgments. At the same time, the driver actually feels as though thinking and judging abilities are sharper, quicker, and more accurate than usual. In a way, alcohol puts sound judgment on hold.

A person in this condition can develop a false feeling of well-being. This feeling is known as **euphoria.** People in a euphoric state of mind may take chances they normally would not take. This behavior can be deadly when behind the wheel of a vehicle.

**What Do You Think?**

All states require a person to be 21 years old to purchase or consume alcoholic beverages. Should the minimum drinking age be lower than 21 years?

Chapter 15  Alcohol, Other Drugs, and Driving **315**

## Discuss

Ask: What is meant by maturity? Discuss what each of the following are and when or how alcohol affects each: emotional maturity, physical maturity, and mental maturity.

## Demonstrate

Use the illustration on this page or **Content Overhead 27** to illustrate the effects of alcohol on behavior. Make sure that students understand that driving ability is affected with even one drink.

## Discuss

Ask students the *What Do You Think?* question: All states require a person to be 21 years old to purchase or consume alcoholic beverages. Should the minimum drinking age be lower than 21 years? After some discussion, ask: What problems might result from a neighboring state having a lower drinking age than your state?

## Activity

**Small Group Activity** This activity will help students identify behavior associated with alcohol consumption. Divide the class into groups of four. Have students list different types of behavior and actions by people in a euphoric state. After adequate time, have groups share their lists with the class.

## Demonstrate

This demonstration will illustrate how the changing of a physiological condition affects skill performance. Have a student volunteer sit in a swivel office chair. With three foam balls (tennis-ball size) in hand, stand about six feet away from the student. Explain that each ball represents a risk factor: a left curve in the road, the car going 15 mph over the speed limit, and a tired driver. Throw one ball at a time in rapid succession. If the student catches all three, continue with the next phase of the demonstration. If not, continue throwing all three balls until the student is able to catch them.

Then, with the student's feet off the floor, have another student spin the chair for about a minute to simulate disorientation that can occur from alcohol. While the chair is spinning, throw all three balls at the student in the chair. The student will most likely catch only one ball and may not catch any. Make the point that having alcohol in your system will prevent you from being able to focus effectively on dealing with many factors at the same time.

You can repeat the demonstration with other students. Increase the spinning time to represent increased quantities of alcohol.

The IPDE Process is affected when judgment and reasoning abilities are reduced. An alcohol-impaired driver is less able to correctly interpret what he or she sees. Target areas may become unclear and scanning of zones may become erratic.

Because alcohol distorts vision, it reduces the effectiveness of the driver's orderly visual search pattern. A drinking driver's eyes are more likely to fixate in a stare, thus reducing the scanning and searching process. The driver is likely to look straight ahead or at any object that attracts attention. Staring usually results in the driver being unaware of vehicles to the sides as well as to the rear.

**Inhibitions** Alcohol weakens a person's **inhibitions,** the inner forces of personality that restrain or hold back one's impulsive behavior. As alcohol content in the body increases, a driver's inhibitions weaken. The person

A driver who has been drinking would have difficulty seeing this pedestrian and reacting soon enough to stop.

might drive too fast, take needless risks, or even drive into emergency situations without knowing or caring.

### Physical Abilities and Alcohol

As alcohol enters the bloodstream, the area of the brain that controls muscular movements, reflexes, and balance begins to slow down. The driver may recognize a dangerous situation, but the brain takes longer to process the information and react to the danger.

**Reaction Time and Coordination**
Alcohol slows reflexes and reaction time. Muscular coordination becomes slow and clumsy. A driver might oversteer, brake late, or accelerate suddenly. Alcohol especially affects the reflexes and reactions of beginning drivers.

**Seeing and Speaking Abilities** One of the most dangerous effects of alcohol is impaired vision. Impairment occurs in visual acuity, peripheral vision, night vision, color vision, and depth perception. Impaired vision combined with diminished judgment and slow reaction time can cause a driver who has been drinking to be in a conflict. For example, the driver in the picture might not identify the pedestrian in time to stop safely.

After only a few alcoholic drinks, the driver's visual acuity can become impaired. A person's ability to focus becomes fuzzy and unclear.

Alcohol also affects the reflex action of the eyes. At night, this impairment can be critical. As headlights of oncoming vehicles come

## Activity

**Class Activity** Obtain a pair of goggles that simulate alcohol impairment. (See page 312b for information about SAAS Eyewear from Vision in Space, Fatal Vision™ goggles from Oliver & Company, and Drunk Busters Impairment Goggles from Drunk Busters of America.) Do the Demonstrate activity described on this page, and compare the results of a student with the goggles and a student without them.

closer, the pupils of the eyes normally become smaller to shut out excess light. This reflex keeps you from being blinded by the glare of the headlights. When the lights have passed, the pupils enlarge again to let in all available light. The ability of your eyes to make this change is extremely important.

After only a few drinks, this reflex action is impaired. The pupils do not become small rapidly as the bright lights approach, and they are slow to open after the bright lights pass. As a result, the driver can be blinded temporarily and may continue to have blurred vision for some time after meeting each vehicle.

After excessive drinking, a person might see multiple images. Each eye normally picks up a separate image of an object. These two images are coordinated by the brain so that the person sees only one image. After several drinks, however, coordination of the images becomes impaired. When driving, the person might see numerous images of a roadway center line, or of traffic signs, as the picture shows.

Alcohol also impairs depth perception. The drinking driver may misjudge the distance of oncoming or cross-traffic vehicles. A vehicle is perceived as being farther away than it actually is. In addition, drinking drivers cannot accurately determine the speed or distance of approaching vehicles. These drivers even lose the ability to judge their own speed or the distance they need for stopping.

Peripheral vision also is impaired by alcohol. When peripheral vision is

After several drinks, a driver may see multiple images of roadway signs.

narrowed, the driver must turn and look to the sides for potential problems. However, these drivers are usually not aware of this impairment so they do not make the effort to turn and look to the sides for potential conflicts. They often become a hazard themselves.

Alcohol also can affect a person's speech. The speech pattern may become slurred and fuzzy, and spoken sentences may fail to convey meaning. With the lack of inhibitions, and with the feelings of euphoria, the drinking person often becomes more and more talkative with language that becomes less and less meaningful.

### Other Physical Problems

As a person continues to drink, the center of the brain that controls breathing and heartbeat can become impaired. Death can occur if a large amount of alcohol is consumed over a short period of time. Usually, a person becomes unconscious and stops drinking before this point.

Chapter 15 Alcohol, Other Drugs, and Driving **317**

---

## Activity

**Class Activity** This activity will help students understand the impact of alcohol abuse on society. Have students look through newspapers and magazines for articles dealing with situations where alcohol was involved. The articles should not be limited to driving. They should cover all types of situations, including domestic disputes, injuries, and murders. Ask each student to share one article with classmates. Encourage discussion about each article.

## Discuss

Discuss the term *inhibitions* and ask students to name different inhibitions. Emphasize how these personal characteristics can be changed and weakened through the use of alcohol. Ask students why weakened inhibitions might affect their behavior.

## Explain

Explain the driving hazards that can result from seeing blurred or multiple images. Emphasize the added hazards that result from drinking and driving after dark.

## Discuss

Discuss the reasons some people give for abusing alcohol and other drugs. Discuss the devastating effects of this behavior. Include the hazards of alcoholism resulting from early drinking habits.

## Amount of Alcohol in Standard Drinks

| | Drink volume | | Percentage of alcohol | | Amount of alcohol |
|---|---|---|---|---|---|
| | 12 ounces beer | × | 5% | = | .60 ounces |
| | 5 ounces wine | × | 12% | = | .60 ounces |
| | 1½ ounces whiskey (80 proof) | × | 40% | = | .60 ounces |

## Explain

Review the definition of blood-alcohol concentration and remind students that BAC measures only the amount of alcohol in the bloodstream. It does not indicate how a particular person reacts to alcohol.

## Explain

Emphasize that the kind and amount of food in the stomach has little effect on the absorption of alcohol.

## Demonstrate

To illustrate how small an amount of alcohol constitutes 0.10 percent, use a medicine dropper to add 2 milliliters of rubbing alcohol to a 2-liter soda bottle filled with water.

## Demonstrate

Use the illustrations on page 318 or **Content Overhead 28** to illustrate the amount of alcohol in standard drinks. Explain why drinking a glass of wine or a beer is the same as drinking hard liquor. Some people think that because beer has a lower percentage of alcohol by volume, it is not as dangerous as drinking whiskey. Point out that 12 ounces of beer, 5 ounces of wine, and 1½ ounces of whiskey have exactly the same amount of alcohol, and they all affect you the same way.

**SAFE DRIVING**

The seriousness as well as the number of collisions increases as the BAC increases.

**Long-Term Effects** Long-term use of alcohol can lead to alcoholism, an addiction to alcohol. Alcoholism is a major problem in our society today. It has far-reaching effects, not only for the problem drinker, but for families and communities as well.

### Alcohol in the Body

The percentage of alcohol in a person's bloodstream can be determined by chemical tests. The amount of alcohol in the blood is called **blood-alcohol concentration (BAC).**

The level of intoxication is determined by the percent of alcohol in the bloodstream. Each drink adds about 0.02 to 0.03 percent to the person's BAC. The greater the BAC, the more dangerous driving becomes.

### Amount of Alcohol in a Drink

Beer, wine, and liquor can all be thought of as "drinks." In standard sizes, drinks all have about the same amount of alcohol, as the chart shows.

The term "proof" describes the strength of liquor. Divide a liquor's

proof number by two to determine its approximate percentage of alcohol. The chart shows that 80-proof whiskey is about 40 percent alcohol. A 100-proof liquor is about 50 percent alcohol.

**Factors Affecting BAC** The percentage of alcohol in the bloodstream depends on the following factors:

• **Amount of alcohol consumed** The more a person drinks, the higher the BAC.
• **Amount of time over which a given amount of alcohol is consumed** A person's BAC rises more rapidly if only short periods of time elapse between drinks.
• **Person's body weight** If other factors are equal, a heavier person may be affected less by the same amount of alcohol than a lighter person would be.

To a lesser degree, some types of food in the stomach may make a difference in the rate the alcohol is absorbed. However, even with food in the stomach, the absorption rate of alcohol into the bloodstream is

## Background

### Alcohol and Carbonated Beverages

The absorption rate is faster when alcohol is mixed with carbonated beverages. These beverages usually cause the pyloric valve to open more quickly than usual. The pyloric valve is between the stomach and the small intestine. When this valve is open, alcohol passes quickly into the small intestine, where it is rapidly absorbed into the bloodstream.

| The Time It Takes for the Body to Rid Itself of Alcohol* | | |
|---|---|---|
| Number of Drinks | BAC Range | Approximate Time to Eliminate Alcohol |
| | .02 – .03 | 1½ hours |
| | .04 – .06 | 3 hours |
| | .06 – .09 | 4 to 5 hours |
| | .08 – .12 | 5 to 7 hours |

*The number will vary depending on the alcohol content of the drinks and rate of consumption.

rapid. When alcohol is mixed with carbonated beverages, the rate of absorption is even faster.

The safest decision a person can make about alcoholic beverages is the decision to abstain from drinking. At a social gathering, a person can choose a soft drink, set down an alcoholic drink and walk away from it, or say *no.*

Some people may decide they want to drink. Responsible friends can encourage them to limit their drinking by taking the following actions:

- Get them involved in other activities.
- Encourage them to decide on a limit of drinks in advance and stick to it.
- Ask them to avoid drinks with a high concentration of alcohol.
- Encourage them to sip a drink slowly. Suggest that they not drink more than one alcoholic beverage in an hour.

- Make them aware of their mental and physical behavior.

**Controlling Impairment** Alcohol is absorbed into the brain and the rest of the body very quickly, but it is very slow to leave. Alcohol continues to circulate throughout the body until it is oxidized and removed by the liver. The body rids itself of alcohol at a rate of about three-fourths of a standard drink an hour.

A person who has one drink needs about one and a half hours to rid the body of the alcohol in that drink. After consuming three drinks in an hour, a person needs more than four hours to oxidize and eliminate most of the alcohol. A person should not drive during those time periods. *Only time can reduce the body's BAC and that person's degree of impairment.* The chart shows the time needed for the body to rid itself of alcohol at the rate of about three-fourths of a drink in an hour.

Chapter 15 Alcohol, Other Drugs, and Driving **319**

## Discuss

Draw students' attention to the *You Are the Driver!* photograph. Point out that the man in the picture has been to a party where he had several drinks. Ask: Which activity pictured would lower his BAC so that he could drive home? (None of these activities will lower his BAC. Only time will allow the body to rid itself of alcohol.)

## Discuss

Ask: What are some of the mistaken ideas that people have about alcohol? How might these ideas affect a person's decision to drive? (Make sure the myths listed in the textbook are included in the discussion.)

 **Assess**

### Answers to Review It

**1.** Judgment and reason are affected. Alcohol reduces the ability to use an effective visual search pattern and causes the driver to stare. It can distort depth perception and cause a driver to make errors in judging distance, speed, space, and shape. (pp. 315–317)

**2.** Blood-alcohol concentration (BAC) is the percent of alcohol in a person's bloodstream. (p. 318)

**3.** Students should list factors indicated on page 318.

**4.** Students should list the myths indicated on page 320 and the truth given about each myth.

**You Are the Driver!**
This man has had several drinks at a party. Which activity would lower his BAC so that he could drive home?

### Myths and Truths About Alcohol

The following ideas about alcohol are *not* true. They are only myths.

- **I can sober up by drinking black coffee, taking a cold shower, or doing exercises.** The truth is that these activities do not reduce the BAC. The person may seem more alert, but the BAC is not reduced.
- **One little drink won't hurt me.** The truth is that taking one drink can make it easier to take the second and third drinks.
- **I will not be affected because I am only drinking beer.** The truth is that a 12-ounce can of beer contains as much alcohol as an average cocktail.
- **I can drive better after a few drinks.** The truth is that your driving abilities are diminished, not improved.
- **A young person cannot become a problem drinker.** The truth is that some young people become problem drinkers even as teens.

### Reducing Driving Risk

As a responsible driver, you can help reduce the risk of drinking and driving. Always refuse to ride with drivers who have been drinking. Make every effort to keep others from driving when they have been drinking.

One way to reduce the risk involved with drinking and driving is to appoint a person to be the **designated driver.** That person decides ahead of time not to drink.

### Review It

1. How does alcohol affect mental and physical abilities needed for driving?
2. What is meant by blood-alcohol concentration?
3. Describe factors that affect blood-alcohol concentration.
4. What are three myths about alcohol, and what is the truth about each myth?

### Activity

**Class Activity** This activity will have students learn about organizations that help people with drinking problems or help their friends or family. Divide the class into three groups. Have each group find out about one of these organizations: Alcoholics Anonymous, Alanon, and Alateen. Have them find out the purpose of the organization both locally and nationally.

**B**esides alcohol, there are many other types of drugs that are both legal and illegal. When used properly, most legal drugs have a positive effect. However, even medicines designed for good can cause hazardous driving situations.

### Types of Drugs

Most drugs are classified according to the effects they have on the central nervous system and bodily functions. Some drugs depress, or slow down, the central nervous system. Others stimulate it, or speed it up.

When legal drugs are taken in the prescribed amounts and for the right reasons, they are relatively safe.

Learn about the side effects of a medicine by checking with the pharmacist.

However, any drug can become dangerous if it is taken in excess, combined with other drugs, or otherwise misused or abused.

### Over-the-Counter Medicines

Drugs that can be obtained legally without a doctor's prescription are called **over-the-counter medicines,** or OTCs. Many over-the-counter medicines have side effects that can include drowsiness, dizziness, slowed reaction time, and poor judgment.

When buying any medicine, check the label for warnings of how it might affect driving performance. Check with the pharmacist, as the person in the picture is doing, if you are not sure of the labeling or of the possible side effects.

### Prescription Medicines

A drug that can be purchased legally only when ordered by a doctor is called a **prescription medicine.** The law requires a prescription because the drug used can have very strong effects on the body.

### Depressants

A **depressant** is a drug that can slow down, or depress, the central nervous system. Depressants such as barbiturates, sleeping pills, and tranquilizers are used to relieve tension, calm nerves, and treat high blood pressure.

A driver using depressants can become very relaxed, lose inhibitions, and have difficulty identifying,

### Objectives

1. Explain the difference between the purchase of over-the-counter medicine and the purchase of prescription medicine.
2. Explain how depressants, stimulants, and hallucinogenic drugs can affect a driver.
3. Describe the effects of combining alcohol with other drugs.

---

## Teacher's Resources

No *Drive Right* resources are needed for teaching Section 15.2.

## Activity

**Guest Speaker** Invite a pharmacist to speak to your class about the use and misuse of drugs. Ask the speaker to provide information about how medicines and illegal drugs can affect driving ability. Have the speaker talk about drugs that are beneficial when used properly but can cause damage when used improperly by drivers. Request that the topic of drug interactions be addressed. Consider developing a handout of patient instructions regarding the use of a certain medicine and its possible effects on the driving task.

---

# Other Drugs and Driving

 **Focus**

## Summary

This lesson focuses on how drugs, including over-the-counter medicines, prescription drugs, and hallucinogens, can affect driving. The effects of combining drugs also are addressed.

## Vocabulary

*depressant, over-the-counter medicine, prescription medicine, stimulant*

 **Teach**

## Explain

Develop and distribute to students a list of legal drugs. Discuss how many can be used to save lives when administered properly, but can destroy lives when used improperly.

## Explain

Personal reactions to medications can differ from day to day. Reactions vary due to fatigue, nutritional needs, and daily changes in body chemistry. Drivers need to monitor their reactions before deciding to drive any time they take medication—even over-the-counter medicines.

## Explain

Review different categories of drugs, including depressants, stimulants, and hallucinogens. Emphasize that the effects of drugs can be unpredictable. Point out that the chemicals in marijuana can remain in the body for weeks.

## Discuss

Ask: What are the risks associated with taking depressants, stimulants, and hallucinogens? Is it ever worth the risk? (Remind students that legally prescribed medication, when taken as directed by a physician, offers many benefits to individuals for whom they are prescribed.)

## 3 Assess

### Answers to Review It

**1.** You can purchase over-the-counter medicines without a doctor's prescription. Prescription drugs can be purchased legally only when ordered by a doctor. (p. 321)

**2.** Depressants can cause a driver to become very relaxed, lose inhibitions, and have difficulty identifying, predicting, deciding, and executing. Stimulants can cause a driver to become very tired very quickly. Hallucinogens can impair judgment, memory, depth perception, and coordination. (pp. 321–322)

**3.** Combining alcohol with another drug multiplies the effects of both. (p. 322)

MARIJUANA Chemicals in marijuana can remain in the body for weeks. Drivers can be given a test for drugs and can be issued a violation ticket if any trace of marijuana is found in the body. Traces of marijuana can be detected in the bloodstream even weeks after the person uses the drug.

predicting, deciding, and executing. Alcohol also is a depressant.

### Stimulants

A **stimulant** is a drug that can speed up, or stimulate, the central nervous system. Amphetamines are a type of stimulant. When first taken, the user gets a feeling of high energy and alertness. Some people misuse these drugs to try to stay awake while driving long distances. However, the feeling of alertness soon wears off and the person becomes very tired very quickly, thus increasing driver-related risk.

### Hallucinogens

Hallucinogens are unpredictable mind-altering drugs that can alter personality and cause panic or terror as they distort a person's sense of direction, distance, and time.

**Marijuana** Marijuana is a powerful mind-altering drug that affects the brain and other parts of the central nervous system. Marijuana can impair judgment, memory, depth perception, and coordination.

322 Unit 4 Being a Responsible Driver

A marijuana user might feel that the effects have worn off, and it is safe to drive after a few hours. In reality, driving abilities remain impaired for a very long time.

### Combining Drugs

You should not take more than one over-the-counter or prescription medicine without first consulting your doctor or a pharmacist.

Using alcohol while taking medicine is especially dangerous. If a person uses alcohol while taking an antihistamine for a cold, the nervous system can be slowed down much more than by using either drug alone. When other drugs are combined with alcohol, the effects of both drugs can be multiplied, rather than just added together. This is known as a synergistic effect.

Drug-alcohol combinations increase driving risks. Driving a vehicle after taking certain medications and drinking alcohol is neither wise nor legal.

### Review It

1. How does the purchase of over-the-counter medicine differ from the purchase of prescription medicine?
2. How do depressants, stimulants, and hallucinogenic drugs affect a driver?
3. What is the effect of combining alcohol with other drugs?

## Background

**Drugs and Development** Development of the human body begins before birth and continues throughout the teen years. For many young men, the process continues into the early twenties. All kinds of drugs, including alcohol, prescription medications, over-the-counter medicine, and illegal drugs, can have harmful affects on human development. They can affect growth, brain development, and sexual development. A teenager's liver is usually smaller than the liver of the average adult. This means that drugs generally stay in a teenager's body longer than they stay in an adult's body. This means there is more opportunity for the drugs to cause harm. Research indicates that drug addiction happens more quickly in teenagers than adults.

**15.3**

**A**ll 50 states have become uniform in requiring a person to be 21 years of age to purchase or consume alcoholic beverages.

Alcohol-related vehicle collisions among teenagers dropped after states raised the drinking age to 21. Young drivers are less likely than adults to drive after drinking. However, the risk of collision is substantially higher when teenagers do drive after drinking.

### Implied-Consent Law

Every state has an **implied-consent law** for drivers. Implied consent means that anyone who receives a driver's license automatically consents to be tested for BAC and other drugs if stopped for suspicion of drug use while driving.

If the driver does not cooperate with the officer and refuses to be tested for BAC, that driver's license can be suspended.

### Levels of Intoxication

Because there is no "safe" amount of alcohol for drivers, all states have set a BAC level at which drivers could be charged with **driving while intoxicated (DWI)**. In the past, that level was set at 0.10 percent or higher. However, research shows that the vast majority of drinking drivers are significantly impaired at 0.08 percent. The impairment primarily affects judgment and such critical driving tasks as braking, steering, and changing lanes.

In an effort to further reduce alcohol-related collisions, all states have set 0.08 BAC limits. For drivers over 21, if you drive with a BAC over 0.08, you are guilty of DWI.

In many states, a charge of **driving under the influence (DUI)** can be made if the driver's BAC is 0.05 or more. Other states make no distinction between DWI and DUI.

### Penalties for Conviction

The penalties for conviction of driving while intoxicated and driving under the influence involve one or more of the following:

- suspension or revocation of driver's license
- payment of a fine
- serving a prison term

The most common penalty is suspension of the driver's license for a specified period of time.

Some states post the BAC level for intoxication on highways.

### Objectives

1. Explain what is meant by the implied-consent law.
2. Describe zero-tolerance levels of intoxication, and tell how these levels can be measured.
3. Explain what a driver should do when stopped by a police officer.

# Traffic Laws Governing the Use of Alcohol

 **Focus**

## Summary

This lesson introduces students to the traffic laws governing the use of alcohol. Topics include implied-consent law, levels of intoxication, and penalties for conviction. Zero-tolerance laws are discussed. Tests for intoxication, including chemical and field sobriety tests, are presented.

## Vocabulary

*driving under the influence (DUI), driving while intoxicated (DWI), field sobriety test, implied-consent law, intoxilyzer, nystagmus, zero-tolerance law*

 **Teach**

## Discuss

Ask: Why do you think the risk of collisions is higher when teenagers drive after drinking? Point out that alcohol affects young people differently than adults. Most teenagers weigh less than adults and have smaller livers. This means that a teen's BAC can rise more quickly and he or she can become intoxicated after consuming less alcohol.

---

## Teacher's Resources

No *Drive Right* resources are needed for teaching Section 15.3.

## Background

**Federal Law on 0.08** Congress passed a federal law in October 2000 requiring all states to adopt 0.08 BAC as the minimum standard for the legal level for DWI by 2004. Any state that did not adopt the 0.08 BAC minimum standard would have lost millions of dollars in federal highway funds.

## Discuss

Discuss the possible consequences of driving after drinking. Consider injuries, fatalities, economic loss, and loss of license. Discuss the impact of the implied-consent law on drivers who have been drinking.

## Demonstrate

Invite a police officer to speak to the class regarding chemical testing and field sobriety testing in your community. Ask the officer to bring an intoxilyzer to demonstrate the breath test. Also have the officer demonstrate some field sobriety tests, including the nystagmus test *[where the officer watches the suspect's eyes as the suspect follows an object that the officer moves from side to side in front of the suspect]*.

## Explain

Explain the DUI and DWI laws in your state and adjacent states. Provide details about the penalties for DUI and DWI, including penalties if a collision results in injury or death.

## Discuss

Ask: Do you think the penalties for DUI and DWI in our state are appropriate? Should they be more severe or less severe?

Penalties are more severe if an intoxicated driver is involved in a collision. If a fatality results from the collision, the driver could be found guilty of manslaughter or even murder.

Drivers who are convicted of a second DWI or DUI offense usually receive much harsher penalties than for the first conviction. Licenses can be revoked for as long as three years. Prison terms can be longer and fines more costly.

**Zero-Tolerance Law** A **zero-tolerance law** makes it illegal for persons under the age of 21 to drive with any measurable amount of alcohol in the blood. All states have implemented zero-tolerance BAC levels for drivers under the age of 21. Most states have set the zero-tolerance BAC at 0.00 to 0.01 percent. Some states use a 0.01 or 0.02 BAC to define zero tolerance to allow for variations in alcohol testing instruments.

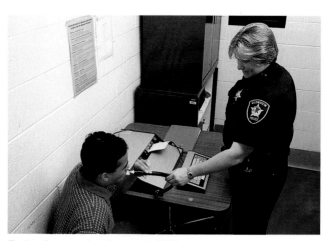

The intoxilyzer can show the person's BAC level.

If you are a driver under 21 and you have a BAC greater than 0.00–0.02 (depending on your state laws), you are guilty of DWI. Some states have also adopted a policy of "Zero tolerance means zero chances." In other words, drivers under the age of 21 receive harsh penalties for even their first offense.

### Tests for Intoxication

Law enforcement agencies place a high priority on enforcing DUI and DWI laws. Several tests can be used to evaluate a person suspected of DUI or DWI. Tests can be given in the police station or on the roadside.

### Chemical Testing

Chemical analysis of blood, urine, or breath can accurately determine BAC. The breath test is a widely used and simple analysis.

The breath-test machine most commonly used for determining BAC is an **intoxilyzer.** The person breathes into the intoxilyzer tube, as the man in the picture is doing. The intoxilyzer determines the BAC, which is then indicated on both the intoxilyzer screen and on a paper printout.

### Field Sobriety Testing

Law officers in many states can give a **field sobriety test** when they suspect a driver of DUI or DWI. Field sobriety testing includes a series of on-the-spot, roadside tests that help an officer detect driver impairment. A variety of coordination tests and eye checks might be used.

## Activity

**Class Activity** Divide the class into two groups: those who favor the zero-tolerance law and those who oppose it. Give the groups time to formulate arguments for their viewpoint in an attempt to persuade the other side to support their contentions. After adequate time have one member of either group state one reason for their point of view. Have the other group respond. Continue until all points by both groups have been discussed.

## Background

**Ignition Locking Devices** Most drivers face a breath test only after a stop for suspicion of DUI. In 30 states, some repeat DUI offenders face a breath test every time they start their vehicle. Ignition locking devices prevent someone with an elevated BAC from starting the vehicle. To prevent a driver from drinking after the vehicle is started, the devices require breath analysis at regular intervals. If the BAC becomes elevated or the driver does not retake the test while driving, the horn sounds continuously until the vehicle is turned off.

One such test is the horizontal-gaze nystagmus test. The term **nystagmus** refers to the involuntary jerking of the eyes as the person gazes to the side. Most people show some nystagmus as their eyes track from straight ahead to the side. This test determines the point where the jerking begins. As the BAC increases, the jerking begins at an earlier point. Trained officers can estimate a person's BAC that will be accurate to within 0.02 percent of chemical test readings.

Other roadside tests demonstrate both physical and mental impairment. Balance, coordination, the ability to follow simple instructions, and the ability to perform two tasks at once may be tested. The inability to perform two tasks at once is called *divided-attention impairment.*

A simple divided-attention test might require the driver to walk heel to toe a certain number of steps, while at the same time giving an oral count of the number of steps taken. This procedure not only tests the person's ability to follow a set of instructions, but also tests both balance and counting abilities.

### If You Are Stopped by a Police Officer

When a driver sees the flashing lights of a police vehicle in the rearview mirrors, it is usually a signal to pull over and stop. If you see such a signal, slow your vehicle until you are sure the officer is signaling for you. Pull over to the right and stop in a safe place, as the driver in the picture is doing. You might need to pull into a parking lot or a side street to be

**You Are the Driver!**
What tests might you be required to take if the police officer suspects alcohol or drug impairment?

out of the way of moving traffic. Keep your hands visible as the officer approaches.

Stay in your vehicle and follow the instructions the officer gives you. You will be required to show your driver's license, and in states with mandatory insurance laws, you will need to show your certificate of insurance.

### Review It

1. What is the implied-consent law for drivers?
2. What are zero-tolerance levels for intoxication, and how can they be measured?
3. What must a driver do when stopped by a police officer?

## Explain

Emphasize the importance of field sobriety tests, especially the divided attention test. Point out that the divided attention test assesses the person's balance along with the ability to count and follow directions. There is a direct correlation between being able to balance, count, and follow directions—and the person's ability to control a vehicle.

## Discuss

Draw students' attention to the *You Are the Driver!* photograph. Ask: What tests might you be required to take if the police officer suspects alcohol or drug impairment?

## 3 Assess

## Answers to Review It

1. When a person receives a driver's license, he or she automatically gives consent to be tested for BAC if arrested on suspicion of driving under the influence of alcohol. (p. 323)
2. Most states have set the zero-tolerance BAC at 0.00 to 0.01 percent. The BAC can be determined by analysis of blood, urine, or breath. (p. 324)
3. If stopped by a police officer, slow down, pull to the right, and stop as soon as it is safe to do so. Keep your hands visible as the officer approaches. Stay in your vehicle and follow the instructions the officer gives you. (p. 325)

## Activity

**In-Class Driving Rehearsal** This activity will allow students to role-play being stopped by a police officer and its consequences. Divide the class into teams of three. Have one student be the teen driver, one the police officer, and one the teen's parent. Have them demonstrate the procedure to follow when being questioned by the police officer. Then, have the police officer call the parent to come to the police station. Have the teen explain the situation to the parent. The parent should react according to students' expectations of their parent's behavior.

## Activity

**Class Activity** This activity will help students understand the consequences of a DUI conviction. Have students simulate a jury deliberation for a DUI conviction. Provide details about the evidence, including information about injuries, damage, BAC, criminal record, and driving history. Instruct the jury members first to determine whether to rehabilitate, punish, or make an example to deter others. Then have them actually determine the various parts of the sentence such as fines, jail time, license sanctions, parole, community service, etc.

# Coping with Peer Pressure

## 1 Focus

## Summary

This lesson addresses peer pressure, both positive and negative. The emphasis is on understanding peer pressure and learning to make responsible decisions.

## Vocabulary

*peer education, peer pressure*

## 2 Teach

## Discuss

Ask students to discuss possible results of peer pressure. Emphasize the importance of personal values. Discuss what it means to be your own best friend.

## Discuss

To demonstrate peer influence, show students photographs or parts of a video that feature hair and clothing styles from 20 years ago. Then, show a video or photographs that feature current styles. Ask: What similarities did you see among the people in the two groups? Discuss why each group wore the clothes and hairstyles they did. Remind students that we experience peer pressure our whole lives, and as we get older, we learn to handle it better.

## Objectives

1. Tell how peer pressure might affect one's decision about drinking and driving.
2. List five steps involved in making a responsible decision.
3. Explain what is meant by peer education.
4. Explain why everyone should share the responsibility of preventing friends from drinking and driving.

Many factors and influences have an impact on young people's decisions about how they want to live their lives. Pressure from other individuals and groups can cause conflicts or unsure feelings about decisions they will need to make.

### Understanding Peer Pressure

The influence of others of a similar age is called **peer pressure.** Peers greatly influence each other because people naturally tend to want to belong to a group. Some of the strongest influences in a person's life are the attitudes and actions of friends and peers. Peer relationships are very powerful forces in shaping a person's future. Many decisions are made based on positive peer pressure or negative peer pressure.

### Positive Peer Pressure

When peers exert a pressure on you in a positive way, they want to be helpful and encouraging. The students in the picture are demonstrating positive peer pressure as they cheer for their team to win the track meet.

Talking a friend out of drinking alcoholic beverages at a party or refusing to ride with someone who has been drinking are other examples of positive peer pressure. Exerting positive peer pressure on friends also can help strengthen positive decisions in young people, as they search for their own identity and struggle to fit in.

### Negative Peer Pressure

Negative peer pressure occurs when others encourage you to do something that you believe is wrong or danger-

Cheering for friends to win a race is an example of positive peer pressure.

## Teacher's Resources

No *Drive Right* resources are needed for teaching Section 15.4.

## Activity

**Class Activity** This activity will help students understand peer pressure. Divide the class into two groups. Have each group develop a situation involving drinking and peer pressure. Have the groups exchange situations. Instruct each group to react to the situation presented by the other group. Their reaction should include information about what effect peer influence is likely to have on their decision making, how they would handle the situation, and what level of risk they believe would be involved.

| Steps for Making Responsible Decisions |
| --- |
| 1. Know when a decision is needed. |
| 2. Consider the choices. |
| 3. Consider the consequences and ask yourself these questions:<br>■ Is it legal?<br>■ Is it safe?<br>■ What would my parents and other family members think?<br>■ Does it show respect for myself and others? |
| 4. Decide which choice is best. |
| 5. Evaluate your decision to know if it was a responsible decision. |

ous. When peers exert negative pressure, they do not have your best interests in mind. Because some people worry a great deal about what others think of them, negative pressure might result in them doing things that are against their beliefs and values. People who tell others that they can drive safely after drinking are exerting negative peer pressure.

Some people might also submit to indirect peer pressure. This type of pressure often occurs when a person *feels* pressure to use alcohol or other drugs just to fit in with the group.

Refusing to do things that you believe to be wrong and being able to say no without fear of losing friends indicates responsible behavior. Mature, independent thinking is especially important if you face peer pressure to use alcohol or other drugs when you will be driving.

### Making Responsible Decisions

Learning how to make responsible decisions can help you be more in control of your life. Following the five steps listed in the decision-making chart will help you make responsible decisions.

**Deciding About Drinking** Each person must make his or her own decision whether or not to drink. The best decision a person can make is not to drink. Individuals who decide not to drink alcoholic beverages never need to worry about alcohol impairing their driving performance. However, nondrinkers must share general concern and care about people who do drink and then drive.

### Peer Education

Underage drinking is a national problem with many causes and no simple solutions. Many schools have organized student programs for **peer education.** Peer education is a process in which young people help other young people make decisions and determine goals. Peer programs may be known by many other names, including peer counseling, peer men-

## Demonstrate

Use the chart on this page to explain the steps for making responsible decisions. Show students how they can use the list to evaluate different kinds of situations related to drugs, alcohol, and other risky behavior. Use multiple examples including underage drinking, drinking and driving, riding in a vehicle when you know the driver has been drinking, not wearing a seat belt, and speeding.

## Discuss

Discuss the rewards of being able to say no without fear of losing friends. Ask students to suggest different ways of saying no. Suggest that students think about how they make decisions when confronted with peer pressure.

## Activity

**Small Group Activity** This activity will help students understand how the media promotes alcoholic beverages. Bring in six magazines that are generally considered appropriate for teenagers. Divide the class into six groups and give each group a magazine to review. Have them find articles and/or advertisements that they feel promote alcoholic beverages. Have the groups present their findings to the class. Ask students to give other examples of media promotion of alcoholic beverages. Discuss how the media influences them.

## Explain

Share information about various designated-driver programs in your community. Emphasize the value of these programs.

## Discuss

Discuss how peer education programs can help young people. Have students who have been involved in such programs share their experiences. If there are no peer education programs in your school, discuss how programs could be established.

Peer leaders direct activities such as the "trust fall" to help others to develop trust.

toring, or peer helpers. Regardless of the name, the purposes and goals of such programs are the same.

Peer education programs help young people influence one another in a positive way. Many young people are more sensitive to the thoughts and opinions of their peers than to the thoughts and opinions of adults. Peer groups have properly trained peer leaders who can be more than a friend or a considerate listener. Peer leaders learn specific skills for helping others deal effectively with problems through activities that develop cooperation, trust, support, and confidence. The students in the picture are participating in such an activity.

Teachers, counselors, and other professionals supervise training of peer leaders. Peer leaders learn communication skills, referral skills, and problem-solving skills.

### Actions You Can Take

The following activities can help peer groups get involved in school and community programs to help combat the underage drinking problem:

- Investigate the facts through local health departments, law enforcement officials, community recreation directors, doctors, and other youth.
- Get the word out. Work with your school to create and distribute flyers and newsletters about your program. Contact other community leaders and solicit their cooperation.
- Communicate your support of zero-tolerance laws to your governor, state legislature, and community officials.
- Work with local park district and summer recreation officials to expand summer recreation programs.

## Activity

**Class Activity** This activity will help students learn about school and community programs designed to combat underage drinking. Divide the class into groups of three. Have each group research a program or organization such as SADD and PJYE. Have each group present their findings to the class, including the organization's name, mission, and activities. Be sure to facilitate any interest in developing such programs at your school, or getting students to join if your school has a program.

Many schools have developed programs, through the assistance of other organizations, to help influence people about the harmful effects of alcohol, as well as the problem of drinking and driving. Some of these organizations include Mothers Against Drunk Drivers (MADD), Alliance Against Intoxicated Motorists (AAIM), and Students Against Dangerous Decisions (SADD). Another program, sponsored by the National Highway Traffic Safety Administration, is a court program—Peer Justice and Youth Empowerment (PJYE). Teen drinking prevention plans can be implemented with the help of The United States Department of Health and Human Services.

**FRIENDS DON'T LET FRIENDS DRIVE DRUNK**

### Responsibility to Others

When people are in situations where alcoholic drinks are served, their first responsibility is for their own actions. However, a person's responsibility increases when the situation involves drinking and driving.

To what extent should a person take responsibility for the actions of others? Some people hesitate to interfere in other people's lives. However, most people wisely realize that they are being caring friends when they prevent friends from driving after drinking. Just as the sign says, *Friends Don't Let Friends Drive Drunk.*

The drinker has the responsibility of not driving after drinking. However, everyone should accept the responsibility of trying to keep a drinker from driving. In some states, a person who serves alcohol is legally responsible if someone is injured or killed as a result of the actions of the

drinking driver. A responsible host plans a party where no alcoholic beverages are served.

You must be able to recognize the signs of too much drinking in order to share the responsibility of friends who drink. If friends are drinking, look for these signs of impairment:

- walking unsteadily or stumbling
- demonstrating poor judgment in behavior
- slurred, unclear speech
- talking loudly
- losing track of time or day of week

Remember that peer pressure is a forceful reason for people to drink or not to drink. Some people will think that drinking helps them to be accepted by a certain group.

Problems can come into being when a person drinks as a part of a group. Group drinking can become competitive and one may be urged to drink to keep up.

Don't forget that only one drink can cause a person's BAC to reach 0.03 percent. Driving abilities can be impaired even at that BAC. The risk of collision increases greatly as drinking increases.

Chapter 15 Alcohol, Other Drugs, and Driving **329**

### Discuss

Focus students' attention on the sign with the phrase "friends don't let friends drive drunk." Ask: What does this phrase mean? Brainstorm ways to keep a friend from driving after drinking alcohol.

### Discuss

Ask: What makes a successful party? Review the non-drinker's responsibility for friends who might drink and drive. Have students brainstorm ways to avoid use of alcohol at parties.

## Activity

**Small Group Activity** This activity will allow students to role-play situations where alcohol is involved. Divide the class into groups of five. Give each group a scenario and ask them to react. Some sample scenarios include: (1) You are in a home with a group of friends while the parents are not home. One person opens a liquor cabinet and tries to persuade the group to drink some liquor. What will you do? What will the expectations of your friends be? (2) You are with a friend who has been drinking and is planning to drive home. What will you do?

What is her or his reaction likely to be? (3) You are at a party and your good friend has passed out from drinking. What will you do? What are the medical consequences? What are the parental consequences? What are the legal consequences? (4) Your parents are out of town and some of your friends find out and decide to throw a party at your house. They arrive, uninvited, with alcohol. What will you do? How would your parents react if they found out?

## Discuss

Ask: How can society better control the problem of drinking and driving? Make sure the discussion addresses community involvement and pressure on advertisers.

## ③ Assess

### Answers to Review It

**1.** Negative peer pressure might affect a young person's decision to drink because of the feeling of wanting to belong. (pp. 326–327)

**2.** Students should list steps provided on page 327.

**3.** Peer education is a process in which young people help other young people make decisions and determine goals. (pp. 327–328)

**4.** Everyone should share the responsibility of preventing friends from drinking and driving because of the possibility that someone, including friends, could be injured or killed. (p. 329)

**PLAN AHEAD** Two-thirds of drivers involved in alcohol-related traffic fatalities have a BAC of 0.14 or higher. Help reduce this fatal injury rate by taking responsible actions toward friends who may drink at a party where alcoholic beverages are served. When you plan to ride with a friend to a party, make alternate plans ahead of time to ensure a safe trip home.

**What You and Others Can Do**

A nondrinker has decisions to make about keeping drinking friends from driving. A friend will help get a drinking friend home safely.

A nondrinker might also have to decide whether or not to ride with a drinking driver. There is only one safe decision. Find other transportation to get home safely. Stay overnight where you are, if necessary.

When friends plan parties, encourage them to refrain from serving alcoholic beverages. Also encourage them to invite nondrinkers. If you know that some people will bring alcoholic drinks, consider not attending the party.

The effects of alcohol can be very harmful, if not deadly, especially when operating a motor vehicle. Keeping unsafe drivers off the road is everyone's responsibility. Every driver has the additional responsibility of driving safely. Even though heavy drinkers are a major cause of alcohol-related injuries and fatalities, social drinkers share a great responsibility

for alcohol-related collisions. Responsible drivers decide not to become a part of the drinking problem. Instead, they contribute to its solution.

### Review It

1. How might peer pressure affect one's decision about drinking and driving?
2. What five steps are involved in making a responsible decision?
3. What is meant by peer education?
4. Why should everyone share the responsibility of preventing friends from drinking and driving?

## Reviewing Chapter Objectives

### 1. Effects of Alcohol on Driving Safely

1. How does alcohol affect mental and physical abilities needed for driving? (315–317)
2. What is blood-alcohol concentration? (318)
3. What factors affect blood-alcohol concentration and how do they work? (318)
4. What are five myths about the use of alcohol and what is the truth about each myth? (320)

### 2. Other Drugs and Driving

5. How do purchasing over-the-counter medicine and prescription medicine differ? (321)
6. How do depressants, stimulants, and hallu-cinogenic drugs affect a driver? (321–322)
7. What is the effect of combining alcohol with other drugs? (322)

### 3. Traffic Laws Governing the Use of Alcohol

8. What is the implied-consent law? (323)
9. What are zero-tolerance levels of intoxication and how can these levels be measured? (324)
10. What should a driver do when stopped by a police officer? (325)

### 4. Coping with Peer Pressure

11. How might peer pressure affect one's decision about drinking and driving? (326–327)
12. What are the five steps involved in making a responsible decision? (327)
13. What is peer education? (327–328)
14. Why should everyone share the responsibility of preventing friends from drinking and driving? (329–330)

## Projects

### Individuals

**Investigate** Find out as much information as you can about collisions that occurred in your state last year involving underage drivers who were drinking. Use this information to write a persuasive argument about why teenagers should not drink and drive.

**Use Technology** Research the technology used in your state to determine blood-alcohol concentration. Find out how this technology works. Also find out the levels at which adults can be charged with *driving while intoxicated* or *driving under the influence* in your state. Share your results with the class.

### Groups

**Lobby** Write letters to state and community officials communicating your support of zero-tolerance laws. Each student should address the letter to a different official. Share the letters with your class.

**Debate** Divide the class into two groups and debate the pros and cons of setting the drinking age at 21. Make a list of all reasons cited. Have one member from each group summarize the reasons and report them to the class.

## Reviewing Chapter Objectives

**15.1** Effects of Alcohol on Driving Safely
See Answers to Review It on page 320.
**15.2** Other Drugs and Driving
See Answers to Review It on page 322.
**15.3** Traffic Laws Governing the Use of Alcohol
See Answers to Review It on page 325.
**15.4** Coping with Peer Pressure
See Answers to Review It on page 330.

For additional information refer to the specific page(s) in parentheses after each question.

## Projects

Some of the projects can be assigned at any time while others are more closely tied to the content presented in the student text. The page number where the topic is introduced is indicated.

> **Investigate:** p. 314
> **Use Technology:** p. 323
> **Lobby:** p. 324
> **Debate:** p. 315

The results of student projects will vary.

## Teacher's Resources

### Skills and Applications Workbook
pages 57–60

### Tests and Activities
Chapter 15 Activity 15-1 and 15-2
pages 127–128
Chapter 15 Test A and Test B,
pages 129–132

### TestWorks CD-ROM
Chapter 15 Test

## Answers to Check Your Knowledge

**1.** d
**2.** c
**3.** a
**4.** b
**5.** zero-tolerance
**6.** peer education
**7.** designated driver

## Answers to Review Vocabulary

**8.** depressant (d)
**9.** stimulant (c)
**10.** blood-alcohol concentration (f)
**11.** over-the-counter medicine (a)
**12.** inhibitions (b)
**13.** nystagmus (e)

## Answers to Think Critically

Students' answers will vary. For information related to the question refer to the page(s) indicated.

**1.** Alcohol consumption impairs all four steps of the IPDE Process. The Identify and Predict steps are affected because the driver is less able to interpret what is seen. The Decide and Execute steps are affected because the driver's judgment is impaired; the driver will likely be more aggressive or take needless risks. (p. 316)

**2.** Students' answers will vary but may include the idea of preparing what they will say in advance to peers who exert pressure about drinking and driving. They may also include the idea that becoming a responsible adult involves making mature, independent decisions. (p. 327)

## Chapter Test

### Check Your Knowledge

**Multiple Choice** Copy the number of each sentence below on a sheet of paper. Choose the letter of the answer that best completes the statement or answers the question.

1. All states enforce a minimum drinking age of
   (a) 18.   (b) 19.   (c) 20.   (d) 21.
2. Which of the following type of drugs slows down the central nervous system?
   (a) stimulant        (c) depressant
   (b) hallucinogen   (d) none of the above
3. The most common penalty for a first-time conviction of a DUI or DWI is
   (a) driver's license suspension.
   (b) prison term.
   (c) payment of a fine.
   (d) vehicle impoundment.
4. What advice should you give a social drinker planning to drive?
   (a) Don't drink on an empty stomach.
   (b) Appoint a designated driver.
   (c) Be extra careful if you drink and drive.
   (d) Wait one hour after drinking before driving.

**Completion** Copy the number of each sentence below. After each number, write the word or words that complete the sentence correctly.

5. The _____ law makes it illegal for persons under the age of 21 to drive with any measurable amount of alcohol in the blood.
6. In the process of _____, young people help other young people make decisions.
7. A person who decides ahead of time not to drink and is appointed to drive others who do drink is known as a _____.

### Review Vocabulary

Copy the number of each definition in list A. Match the definition in list A with the term it defines in list B.

**List A**
8. drug that can slow down the central nervous system
9. drug that speeds up the central nervous system
10. amount of alcohol in the blood expressed as a percentage of alcohol in the bloodstream
11. drugs that can be obtained legally without a doctor's prescription
12. inner forces of personality that restrain or hold back one's impulsive behavior
13. involuntary jerking of the eyes as a person gazes to the side

**List B**
a. over-the-counter medicines
b. inhibitions
c. stimulant
d. depressant
e. nystagmus
f. blood-alcohol concentration

### Think Critically

Write a paragraph to answer each question.
1. Using the framework of the IPDE Process, describe how alcohol impairs your ability to drive.
2. What strategies can you use to overcome negative peer pressure as it relates to drinking and driving?

## Decision Making

1. This driver stopped for an hour on his way home from work. During that time he drank three beers. What effects might the beer have on the driver's abilities to drive safely?

2. This girl is about to purchase over-the-counter medicine to treat her cold. Why is it important that she read the label on the medicine bottle?

3. This driver has been stopped by police for suspicion of driving while intoxicated. What types of tests might he be requested to take? What can the tests detect and measure? What could happen if the driver refuses to take the tests?

4. Students can solicit support from community officials in an effort to combat the problem of underage drinking in their community. What type of activities might students and community leaders pursue in their endeavor?

Chapter 15 Alcohol, Other Drugs, and Driving **333**

## Answers to Decision Making

**1.** The driver might be unable to think clearly. His judgment might not be reliable. Muscle coordination might be impaired. His use of the IPDE Process might be reduced. He may not measure speed or distance correctly and may see multiple images of road signs or roadway users.

**2.** Many over-the-counter medicines have side effects including drowsiness, poor judgment, and slowed reaction time. She needs to read the warning label to determine how this particular medicine might affect her driving behavior and whether she should drive at all when using the medicine.

**3.** The officer can request this driver to take a field sobriety test or a chemical test on an intoxilyzer. These tests can detect impairment and also measure BAC. If the driver refuses to take the test, his license can be suspended.

**4.** Students and community leaders might investigate the underage drinking problem by gathering alcohol-related traffic violation and conviction facts. They can distribute information to the community explaining their goals and plans. They can become involved with organizations that help influence people about the harmful effects of alcohol abuse.

# Chapter 16    Planning Guide

## Student Features

## Teacher's Edition

| | Student Features | Teacher's Edition |
|---|---|---|
| **Chapter 16**<br>**Buying and Owning a Vehicle** | You Are the Driver! *p. 335* | Projects *p. 334*<br>Special Needs *p. 335* |
| **16.1 Buying a Vehicle** *pp. 336–341*<br>• List the responsibilities of owning or leasing a vehicle.<br>• List the various costs associated with owning and operating a vehicle.<br>• Explain how to select a used vehicle.<br>• Describe the options and steps in buying a vehicle. | What Do You Think? *p. 338*<br>Did You Know? *p. 339* | Demonstrate *pp. 337, 340*<br>Activity *pp. 337, 338, 339, 340, 341*<br>Special Needs *p. 338* |
| **16.2 Insuring a Vehicle** *pp. 342–346*<br>• Explain what financial responsibility laws require.<br>• Explain how auto insurance works.<br>• Explain what different kinds of auto insurance cover.<br>• List factors that affect the cost of insurance. | Consumer Tip *p. 344*<br>Did You Know? *p. 345*<br>What Do You Think? *p. 346* | Demonstrate *p. 345*<br>Activity *pp. 343, 344, 345*<br>Special Needs *p. 345* |
| **16.3 Environmental Concerns** *pp. 347–350*<br>• Describe how vehicle use adversely affects the environment.<br>• Identify ways individuals can reduce the effects of vehicles on the environment. | | Activity *pp. 348, 349* |
| **Assessment** | Reviewing Chapter Objectives *p. 351*<br>Projects *p. 351*<br>Chapter Test *p. 352*<br>Decision Making *p. 353* | Answers *pp. 352–353* |

**Companion** *pp. 97–100*
**Spanish Handbook** *pp. 33–34*

---

**Resource Book**
Classroom Activity, *p. 63*
Information, *pp. 81–82*

**Content Overhead 30**

---

**Content Overhead 31**

---

**Skills and Applications**
  **Workbook**, *pp. 61–64*
**Tests and Activities**
Chapter 16 Activities 16-1
  and 16-2, *pp. 135–136*
Chapter 16 Test A and
  Test B, *pp. 137–140*

**TestWorks CD-ROM**
  Chapter 16 Test

## Technology Resources

### Audio-Visual and Computer Resources

Safety Industries, Inc., *Buying and Insuring a Car*, video, 10 minutes

**Go Online**
PHSchool.com

**For: Chapter 16 online activities**
**Visit: PHSchool.com**
**Web Code: cak-9999**

# Chapter 16

## Buying and Owning a Vehicle

### Chapter Overview

Chapter 16 presents financial and legal responsibilities of vehicle ownership. Students study factors to consider when buying a vehicle and learn how to check out a used vehicle. The chapter describes how insurance works, types of insurance, and factors that affect the cost of insurance. Environmental effects of vehicle use also are included.

### Chapter Vocabulary

*assigned-risk insurance, blue-book price, bodily-injury insurance, car pooling, collision insurance, comprehensive insurance, deductible, depreciation, financial responsibility law, leasing, liability insurance, mass transportation, no-fault insurance, premium, property damage insurance, solar-powered vehicle, underinsured motorist insurance, uninsured motorist insurance, van pooling, warranty*

334

## Teacher's Resources

For students to use as they read the chapter:

**Companion**
pages 97–100

**Spanish Handbook**
pages 33–34

## Projects

Review the projects described on page 351. Some of the projects can be assigned at any time while others are more closely tied to the content presented in the student text.

# CHAPTER 16
## Buying and Owning a Vehicle

## You Are the Driver!

There are many responsibilities that go along with vehicle ownership. What type of vehicle will best meet your needs? What features and options should you select? What can you afford? Should you buy or lease? What are the vehicle's operating costs? What is a fair price? What kinds and amounts of insurance will you need? What will the insurance cost? The choices can be overwhelming.

This chapter discusses various aspects of owning and operating a vehicle. It also covers vehicle insurance, environmental concerns, and personal responsibilities of owning and operating a vehicle.

**Go Online**
PHSchool.com
**For:** Chapter 16 online activities
**Visit:** PHSchool.com
**Web Code:** cak-9999

335

## Introducing the Chapter

List the costs of owning and driving a vehicle. Discuss how the costs would vary among vehicles. Expenses can be much higher than students expect.

## You Are the Driver

Imagine the excitement and apprehension the car buyer probably feels. Emphasize the variety of vehicles available. Discuss how to determine what features and options to select. Discuss how to evaluate what is a fair price and whether to buy or lease.

## Special Needs

How to purchase and insure a vehicle is best learned by doing, but you can have special needs students and their partners role play simple transactions. The special needs student can participate in the role-playing activities for small groups explained on pages 340 and 341, or the activities can be simplified to partnering activities.

# Buying a Vehicle

##  Focus

### Summary

This lesson presents financial and legal responsibilities of vehicle ownership. Students study factors to consider when buying a vehicle and how to evaluate a used vehicle.

### Vocabulary

*blue-book price, depreciation, leasing, warranty*

##  Teach

### Explain

Explain that purchasing a vehicle is a major event in a person's life. The possibility of making a bad financial decision is very real. A buyer needs to become knowledgeable about the vehicle in order to make an informed decision. All 50 states have passed "lemon laws." These laws protect consumers from buying malfunctioning, problem-ridden vehicles.

### Explain

Explain that it is sometimes a good idea to obtain pre-approval for a loan. This lets you know how much the lending institution is willing to lend you and what your payment options are.

### Objectives

1. List the responsibilities of owning or leasing a vehicle.
2. List the various costs associated with owning and operating a vehicle.
3. Explain how to select a used vehicle.
4. Describe the options and steps in buying a vehicle.

Having your own vehicle gives you a lot of freedom and mobility. *It also carries a lot of responsibilities.* You will need to be able to afford the vehicle and to maintain it. If you are under the age of 18, you will likely share the responsibilities with your parents. You also will likely share the additional expenses for maintenance, repairs, insurance, and fuel.

### Do You Need a Vehicle?

Are your driving needs great enough to justify owning a vehicle? Are there alternatives to buying a vehicle? The answers to these questions will help you decide whether your needs justify the expense of owning a vehicle.

### Can You Afford to Own a Vehicle?

The cost of owning a vehicle can be more than you expect. Some of the major expenses of vehicle ownership are described below:

- **Purchase Price** The purchase price is the amount a person is charged and willing to pay for the vehicle. Consider what you can afford before selecting a specific type of vehicle. Shop around and compare prices of different makes and models. Newspaper ads and the Internet are good ways to compare prices.
- **Depreciation** A vehicle's value drops steadily over time, whether you use the vehicle a lot or very little. This decrease is called **depreciation.**

- **Financing** If you are able to purchase a vehicle by paying cash, you eliminate having to pay interest on a loan. Most people, however, obtain a loan when they purchase a vehicle. Make sure you shop around for the best loan rates available. Banks, credit unions, savings and loan associations, and car dealerships are often good sources.
- **Other Costs** Operating costs include fuel, oil, tires, repairs, and replacement parts. Licensing, registration, insurance, taxes, and loan interest also are costs to be considered. Costs also may include parking and toll fees. Vehicle expenses can increase from year to year. Your annual operating costs will depend on how much you drive, where you drive, and your fuel economy. The more you drive, the greater the costs.

### What Kind of Vehicle Should You Buy?

If you decide you absolutely need and can afford a vehicle, what type will you get? Examine your needs, wants, and budget. Ask yourself these questions:
- What will I use the vehicle for?
- Do I need certain passenger and cargo capacities? Will I need to tow anything?
- How many miles will I drive each year?
- Will I use the vehicle more for short trips or long trips?
- How long will I expect to keep the vehicle?

## Teacher's Resources

**Resource Book**
Classroom Activity, page 63
Information, pages 81–82

**Content Overheads**
Overhead 30

## Background

**Miles per Gallon** The mpg figures you see when shopping for a vehicle are estimates only. Your actual fuel economy depends on how you drive, speed traveled, and the condition of the engine and other equipment.

You need to consider many factors when determining what type of vehicle to buy. Consider all factors carefully before you go out and look at any vehicles.

## Vehicle Size

Size is an important factor in buying a vehicle. What size vehicle will serve your needs? Consider these points:

- A smaller, lighter vehicle usually gets better gas mileage but does not offer as much protection in a collision as a larger, heavier vehicle.
- Smaller vehicles are easier to maneuver than larger vehicles, especially when parking.
- A larger vehicle provides a more comfortable ride but is usually more costly to operate than a smaller vehicle.
- A larger vehicle has a greater capacity for passengers and parcels than a smaller vehicle.

## Engine Size and Types

Smaller engines usually are more fuel efficient than larger engines. However, a larger engine may be more feasible in a fully-equipped vehicle. Vehicles with larger engines typically cost more to maintain and repair.

## Transmission

Most vehicles today are equipped with automatic transmissions that include automatic overdrive. This makes the vehicles nearly as fuel efficient as stickshift vehicles. Although the costs of repairs for an automatic transmission are usually higher, stickshifts may require repairs more often.

## Optional Equipment

Decide what optional equipment you want, but be aware that options add to the cost of the vehicle. Technological advancements have resulted in "smarter" vehicles with options

Fuel efficient . . .

or sporty but expensive.

More room for passengers . . .

and more cargo capacity.

Chapter 16 Buying and Owning a Vehicle **337**

## Demonstrate

Use **Content Overhead 30** to illustrate how the amount of the loan and the interest rate affect loan payments.

## Explain

When you apply for a vehicle loan, you must provide a significant amount of personal information. In most cases you will be asked about your personal assets, your credit history, and your income. Questions about your driving record and any criminal record also are common. To minimize their risk, financial lenders will check on some or all of the information that you provide on your application. It is illegal to sign a loan application that contains false information. Depending on where you live, you might have to be 18 years old before you can apply for a vehicle loan.

## Discuss

Ask: Do you think that owning a vehicle requires significant time and money? What impact does owning and maintaining a vehicle have on academics, athletics, and social activities?

## Activity

**Class Activity** This activity will give students the opportunity to practice making sound decisions about purchasing a vehicle. Have students write down answers to questions you will pose to them. Ask: Do you need a vehicle? (Continue to ask students the other questions listed under this heading on page 336.) Can you afford to own a vehicle? (Have them list purchase price, depreciation, financing, and other costs.) What kind of vehicle should you buy? (Ask the questions listed under this heading on page 336 but change "I" to "you.") What size vehicle will serve your needs?

After giving students an opportunity to write their responses, ask: Are there any questions asked that you need more information about? (Discuss their concerns, or direct students to sources for additional information.) Are there any additional questions that you may have? Conduct discussion on responses the students recorded.

## Explain

Explain to students that the IPDE Process also applies to buying a vehicle. They should identify several vehicles that may be considered for purchase. Then make predictions about each vehicle: Is the vehicle going to meet their needs? Is the cost going to be within their budget? Is the vehicle of good value to them? Is the vehicle mechanically sound? Then after making several predictions about each vehicle identified, a decision will need to be made. Which one will you buy? After a decision is made there must be an execution of the decision. You will need to go to the vehicle seller, exchange financial consideration for the vehicle, and obtain the legal documentation.

## Discuss

Ask students the *What Do You Think?* question: Why might leasing be more desirable than purchasing a vehicle? (Leasing often lets you drive a more expensive vehicle with lower monthly payments than if you were purchasing the same vehicle. The down payment for a lease is often less than for a purchase.) Point out that while leasing is a good option for some drivers, at the end of a lease contract, you have no vehicle to sell or to use as a down payment for another vehicle.

## Explain

Though leasing is most often associated with new vehicles, some dealers also lease used vehicles.

### What Do You Think?

Some people prefer to lease a vehicle for a certain number of years. Why might leasing be more desirable than purchasing a vehicle?

designed for safety, comfort, and information.

Consider the potential for voice-activated controls for controlling the temperature inside the vehicle. Or, imagine a radar-like blind-spot warning device that helps you avoid backing into objects you can't see.

Know what safety options are included. Comfort options may make you feel good, but safety options can save lives, reduce injuries, and save you money. Ask your insurance agent about safety options that can save you money on insurance premiums.

### Leasing a Vehicle

An alternative to purchasing a vehicle is **leasing.** In some ways, leasing is similar to owning a vehicle. You are responsible for monthly payments, fuel, and all the other types of operating costs you would incur if purchasing a vehicle.

The main difference is that after your lease contract expires, you do not own the vehicle. At the end of your lease, you must choose one of the following three options:

1. Return the vehicle and lease another vehicle.
2. Purchase the vehicle at a cost determined at the start of your lease.
3. Return the vehicle with no obligations to either lease another vehicle or purchase the vehicle you returned.

Lease payments are based on the difference of the value of the vehicle at the start of the lease, and the value at the end of the lease, plus interest. In contrast, when you take out a loan to purchase a vehicle, your monthly payments cover the entire cost of the vehicle over the term of the loan, plus loan interest.

Leasing is not for everyone. Most lease agreements limit how many miles you can put on the vehicle. Extra miles are likely to cost you an

## Purchase New Car for $16,283

**LEASE FOR**
**$129** per month
For 36 months*

**PURCHASE**
with loan for
**$444** per month
For 36 months**

**\*LEASE**
$2,995 down
$45 document fee
12,000 miles/year - fee of 15¢ per mile over
Payment = $129 per month

**\*\*PURCHASE**
$1,399 down
$45 document fee
4.5% APR financing
Payment = $444 per month

Compare the costs of leasing a vehicle to purchasing using a loan.

## Activity

**Small Group Activity** Divide the class into groups of five. Have the groups make checklists that students will be able to carry with them to compare vehicles. After all groups have finished the checklists, pass them around to the other groups. The groups will rate each checklist according to a scale of 1 (to represent very little value) to 10 (to represent extremely valuable). After all groups have given a value rating to each checklist, total the points and tell the students you will make copies of the "winning" checklist for all students to have.

## Special Needs

Create a "buyers guide" sheet and have the student fill in the items needed. If special equipment is needed for disabilities, contact local agencies for prices and for suggestions for styles of vehicles best suited. Have the students take the sheet home to discuss with their parents. If students have physical disabilities, parents can help locate resources and make certain all needs are met.

additional charge. Normal wear is considered, but any wear considered excessive will result in an extra charge. Make sure you understand all the terms of the contract before you sign a lease agreement.

### Buying a Used Vehicle

You may decide to purchase a used vehicle if you cannot afford a new vehicle. Used vehicles can be purchased from a used-car dealer, a new-car dealer, or a private owner.

Buying a vehicle from a private owner may cost less. However, you need to consider the following:

- A private owner will seldom repair the vehicle or provide you with a **warranty.** A warranty is a written guarantee that the seller will make certain repairs for a stated period of time.
- In nearly all cases, a private sale is final.
- Used-car dealers usually have a large selection of vehicles available. Many used vehicles purchased from car dealerships carry a warranty.

Be aware that warranties do not cover everything. *Read the warranty carefully and know what is covered before you buy.*

### How Much Should You Pay?

Publications like the *NADA Guide* (National Auto Dealers Association Guide) provide what are referred to as suggested **blue-book prices** for used vehicles. A blue-book price is the average market value for that model and age of vehicle. The value of a vehicle depends a great deal on the vehicle's

**SHOPPING ON THE INTERNET** More people use the Internet or special CD-ROM software each year when shopping for vehicles. This technology helps you review and compare vehicles and prices, apply for loans, and even purchase vehicles. Prices are often not negotiable and can be hundreds to thousands of dollars less than you would pay at a dealership.

condition. You can also use the Internet to compare prices of different makes and models of vehicles.

### Choosing a Used Vehicle

Selecting a good used vehicle takes time. When you find a vehicle you like, check it out.

- Besides looking good, make sure the vehicle is in good mechanical condition.
- Determine whether it was ever involved in a collision, or needs repairs.
- When possible, talk to the previous owner about the condition of the vehicle and previous maintenance service that was done on the vehicle.

### Outside and Inside Checks

Walk around the vehicle to inspect it. Be sure to check
- doors and locks
- vehicle appearance
- fluid leaks
- evidence of collision damage

Chapter 16  Buying and Owning a Vehicle  **339**

## Discuss

Ask: What options would you like to have on a vehicle? Make a list of the responses and ask students to indicate which, if any, of the options they identified relate to safety.

## Explain

Explain different types of warranties offered. Examples could include: 30 or 90 days parts and labor; 1 year parts only; 1 year parts and labor; 5 years or 50,000 miles; and so forth.

## Explain

Explain that artificial lighting does not reveal the true condition of the paint or of the body panels. Therefore, buyers should inspect a vehicle in daylight. Adverse weather and other conditions might also impede close scrutiny of the vehicle.

## Activity

**Guest Speaker** Invite a consumer advocate to speak to your class about lemon laws and other consumer protection laws that apply to the purchase of new and used vehicles. Resources for finding appropriate speakers include the Better Business Bureau, your state's consumer protection agency or Attorney General's office, and consumer reporters from local television stations and newspapers.

## Explain

Explain that variations in vehicle performance can be compared if a buyer establishes a particular test route ahead of time and uses it to test drive each vehicle considered for purchase.

Point out that the test drive is an opportunity for family members to share in the decision to buy a certain vehicle. It's a good idea to have other family members or friends test drive the vehicle or be present during the test drive.

## Demonstrate

Demonstrate how to use Vehicle Inspection Checklist (**Resource Book,** pages 81–82). If possible, take the class to the school parking lot to evaluate a vehicle that you have arranged to be available for inspection.

Enter the vehicle to check
- seats for comfort and condition
- lights and accessories
- mileage (odometer)
- pedals and steering wheel

Check the trunk to find
- evidence of damage
- spare tire
- tire jack

Open the hood to check
- signs of collision damage
- hoses and radiator for leaks
- condition of belts
- coolant level
- battery and cables

**Test Drive** Always take a vehicle you intend to purchase for a test drive. If the owner refuses to let you test drive the vehicle, look for another vehicle.

When you take a test drive, drive in areas and on roads with which you are familiar. Keep the following questions in mind as you test drive a vehicle:
- What do you hear and feel?
- Are the brakes in good condition?
- Is the steering firm?

- How is the suspension?
- Does the vehicle hesitate when you quickly accelerate?
- Is the vehicle comfortable?

Make these checks during the test drive:
- Turn the ignition switch on and check to see that all warning lights, signals, and headlights work.
- Start the engine. It should start easily. Warning lights should go out in a few seconds.
- Drive at low speeds and test the brakes several times. The vehicle should stop smoothly and straight.
- Make a number of right and left turns. There should not be any play in the wheel, and it should steer easily.
- Accelerate moderately. The vehicle should accelerate smoothly from 0–40 mph without hesitation.
- Test the brakes at various speeds. They should not grab or pull to one side. If equipped with antilock brakes, brake hard to ensure that the system works.

Carefully inspect the vehicle inside and out. Then have it inspected by a professional mechanic or technician.

## Activity

**Role-Play: Introduction** This activity allows students to act out various roles involved in the purchase of a vehicle. The roles include buyer, buyer's friend, buyer's parent, car dealer, insurance agent, and loan officer. You or your students will need to gather information ahead of time for some of the roles, as described on page 341. Make copies of the Sample Buyer Profiles from the **Resource Book,** page 63, to hand out to students.

Divide the class into groups of six and assign roles. Instruct the buyer to visit the car dealer and choose an appropriate vehicle. Before making a purchase the buyer must visit the loan officer and the insurance agent to obtain information about financing and insurance coverage. The parent and friend can help the buyer with these activities. The buyer returns to the car dealer to make a purchase or to continue shopping, depending on the results of the meetings about financing and insurance.

Have the buyer from each group describe the process and outcome of his or her experience to the class. Discuss each buyer's decision.

Check under the hood when the engine is cool and running.

- Drive on a rough road at 25 mph, and turn off the radio. The vehicle should not rattle or feel unstable.
- Check oil pressure gauges and warning lights for low pressure, overheating, or any other malfunctions indicated by warning lights.

**Have the Vehicle Inspected** You have inspected the vehicle yourself—both inside and outside. Before you commit to buying it, you should have a trained technician also inspect it. It's an investment of time and money that may save you a lot in the long run.

Talk with the technician about possible needed maintenance or repairs. Obtain estimates on related costs for the repairs or maintenance. Problems with the transmission, brakes, gears, clutch, radiator, and exhaust system can be costly.

**Before You Close the Deal**
If the seller is going to make repairs, have the repairs written into the sales

agreement. Make sure the vehicle includes an owner's manual and receipts of service repairs.

After you purchase the vehicle, read the owner's manual. The owner's manual is a valuable resource for learning about features of your new vehicle and the proper care and maintenance needs of the vehicle.

---

### Review It

1. What are the responsibilities of owning or leasing a vehicle?
2. What are some of the costs of owning and operating a vehicle?
3. What procedures should you use to select a used vehicle?
4. What options and steps should you consider when buying a vehicle?

---

Explain that vehicle buyers tend to underestimate the cost of repairs. They also might overestimate their ability to detect serious mechanical problems. Point out that many serious vehicle problems can be masked, and that only a competent mechanic has the equipment and experience to detect them.

 **Assess**

## Answers to Review It

1. The owner must be able to afford the vehicle and maintain it. (p. 336)
2. Major costs include the purchase price of the vehicle, the insurance premiums, operating expenses, and repairs. (pp. 336–337)
3. Make outside and inside checks, make checks under the hood, and test drive the vehicle. Have a mechanic check the vehicle. Consider the cost of repairs. Arrange for financing. (pp. 339–341)
4. Consider your budget, needs, and wants. Consider what the vehicle will be used for, how much it will be driven, the size and type, type of transmission, and fuel economy. Consider the costs of insurance and vehicle maintenance. (pp. 336–338)

---

## Activity

**Role-Play: Preparation** Gather information for these roles for the activities described on page 340.

**Insurance Agent:** Contact a local insurance agent to help you develop this role. You will need a sample insurance application and a sample premium schedule based on the buyer profiles you are using.

**Loan Officer:** Contact a loan officer to help you develop this role. You will need a sample loan application and a table showing monthly payments for a three-year loan at current interest

rates for several different amounts—$2,000, $5,000, $10,000, and $15,000.

**Car Dealer:** Obtain 15 vehicle advertisements for each group. Select new and used vehicles that range in price from $2,000 to $16,000.

## Insuring a Vehicle

**16.2**
**Insuring a Vehicle**

### 1 Focus

## Summary

This lesson provides an overview of financial responsibility laws. It also describes how insurance works, types of insurance, and factors that affect the cost of insurance.

## Vocabulary

*assigned-risk insurance, bodily-injury insurance, collision insurance, comprehensive insurance, deductible, financial responsibility law, liability insurance, no-fault insurance, premium, property damage insurance, underinsured motorist insurance, uninsured motorist insurance*

### 2 Teach

## Discuss

Discuss that the basic principle of insurance is spreading the risk. All people who are insured are helping to pay for each other's losses.

## Objectives

1. Explain what financial responsibility laws require.
2. Explain how auto insurance works.
3. Explain what different kinds of auto insurance cover.
4. List factors that affect the cost of insurance.

If you are involved in a collision, you may find that the largest expense of owning a vehicle is paying for damages you cause. Every state has a **financial responsibility law.** This law requires you to prove that you can pay for damages you cause that result in death, injury, or property damage.

What does your state say about financial responsibility? What type of penalties can be invoked for not complying with the financial responsibility laws in your state?

### What Is Vehicle Insurance?

Insuring your vehicle is financial responsibility. You buy insurance from a company by paying a **premium,** a specified amount of money for coverage over a specified period of time, to the company. A policy is a written contract between you—the insured—and the insurance company. A policy includes the terms and conditions of insurance coverage.

### Kinds of Insurance

There are many different types of insurance. Refer to the chart for a summary of various types of insurance and what each type covers.

### Liability Insurance

Every state requires individuals to carry **liability insurance.** It is the most important insurance to have. Liability insurance protects the driver who caused the collision. It provides compensation for a harm or wrong to a third party for which the insured is legally obligated to pay. Liability insurance covers others when you are at fault.

**Bodily-Injury Insurance** One type of liability insurance, **bodily-injury insurance,** covers the driver who is at fault against claims. (*Claims* are formal requests for payments related to injuries to other people.) Most states require drivers to hold a specified minimum level of liability insurance.

**Property-Damage Insurance** Another type of liability insurance, **property-damage insurance,** protects the driver who is at fault against claims for damages to another person's property, up to specified limits. Make sure your level of coverage is adequate.

### Medical Payment Insurance

This insurance pays medical and funeral expenses for bodily injuries sustained by occupants in an insured vehicle. It pays expenses up to stated amounts. This coverage does not depend on who was at fault in the accident.

### No-Fault Insurance

Because of the backlog and long delays in litigation cases coming to a trial, some states have **no-fault insurance.** In such states, people involved in collisions recover losses and expenses associated with the

## Teacher's Resources

**Content Overheads**
Overhead 31

## Background

**History of Insurance** Insurance has been around for many years. Babylonian laws from the 18th century B.C. included a form of credit insurance, and records from ancient Greece and Rome include references to disability insurance.

As early as the 14th century in Europe, ships' cargos were protected by marine insurance. The oldest known policy written in English covered the voyage of a ship called the *Santa Crux* around 1555.

| Kind of Insurance | Coverage | Claim Includes | Minimum Amount | Notes |
|---|---|---|---|---|
| **Bodily-injury liability** | Pays claim against owner if someone is killed or injured and owner is at fault. | Hospital and doctor bills<br>Legal fees<br>Court costs<br>Loss of wages | States normally specify minimum: $10,000–$30,000 for one person; $20,000–$100,000 for several persons. | Required in many states. Needed by all car owners. Minimum coverage required is generally too low. |
| **Property-damage liability** | Pays claim against owner if property of others is damaged and owner is at fault. | Other car and possessions in car. Damage to house, telephone pole, and traffic light. | States normally specify minimum: $5,000–$25,000 | Required in many states. Needed by all car owners. |
| **Uninsured-motorist\* and underinsured-motorist** | Pays for injuries to you and your passengers in case of hit-and-run collision, uninsured or underinsured motorist. | Hospital and doctor bills<br>Legal fees<br>Court costs<br>Loss of wages<br>(Does not cover property damage.) | Usually same as bodily-injury liability. | Required in many states. Needed by all car owners. |
| **Collision** | Pays cost of repairing or replacing owner's car when owner is at fault or when owner cannot collect from person at fault. | Repair or replacement of any car driven by owner or with owner's permission. | Insures for depreciated value of car. Owner decides on $100 to $500 (or more) deductible to reduce cost of premium. | Important for new or expensive car. Drop after 7–10 years of ownership or when value of car no longer justifies cost of coverages. |
| **Comprehensive** | Pays cost of repairing or replacing owner's car. | Fire   Earthquake<br>Theft   Storm<br>Flood   Riots<br>Wind   Vandalism | Insures for depreciated value of car, usually with $100 to $500 (or more) deductible to reduce cost of premium. | Important for new or expensive car. Drop after 7 to 10 years of ownership. |
| **Medical-payments** | Pays medical costs for you and your passengers injured in any collision, regardless of fault. | Pays all immediate medical costs (generally in addition to other medical insurance). | Insures for $500 to $5,000 per person. | This insurance does not require a legal process to determine fault, while bodily-injury coverage usually does. |
| **Towing** | Pays cost of towing or minor repair to disabled car. | Dead battery<br>Out of gas<br>Flat tire<br>Accident (regardless of cause or fault). | Usually pays amount validated by towing company. | Good to have. Not needed if owner belongs to automobile club with towing service. |

\*Note that uninsured-motorist insurance covers collision-related injuries only, not property damage.
Some states now allow insurance companies to offer uninsured-motorist property damage insurance.

## Activity

**Class Activity** This activity will help students understand the various types of insurance coverage. Read the scenarios described below. Ask a volunteer to identify the kind of insurance that is most likely to cover each situation.

- Your windshield shatters while you are driving. (comprehensive)
- Your vehicle will not start after a game. (towing)
- You kill your friend's purebred show dog while backing out of the friend's driveway. (property-damage liability)
- You knock down a neighbor's mailbox when your vehicle slides off the road during an ice storm. (property-damage liability)
- You injure a pedestrian in a crosswalk; there is no damage to your vehicle. (medical-payments and/or bodily-injury liability)
- Your vehicle is damaged by hail. (comprehensive)
- Vandals knock outside rearview mirrors off of all the vehicles parked on your street, including yours. (comprehensive)
- You lock your keys in your vehicle. (towing)

## Explain

Some states place limits on how much a person or family can collect for certain types of property damage and personal injuries, or even deaths. Have students find out the policy in your state.

## Discuss

Ask: What happens if you are driving someone else's vehicle and are involved in a collision where you are at fault? Whose insurance would be primarily responsible? (Allow students to offer their ideas, but be sure to point out that they need to check with their insurance agent to determine how their policy would apply to this situation.)

## Discuss

Ask: When you rent a vehicle, does you insurance policy cover you and your passengers? Does it cover the rental vehicle? Do you need to buy added insurance from the rental company? (Allow students to offer their ideas, but be sure to point out that they need to check with their insurance agent to determine how their policy applies to rented vehicles. You can also point out that most companies that rent vehicles impose strict age restrictions on who can rent and drive their vehicles.)

## Explain

Some states allow drivers to post bonds or deposit a certain amount of cash with the state, rather than requiring them to have auto insurance. Have students find out the policy in your state.

## Explain

Explain that as the deductible amount increases, the premium usually decreases. A policy with a $100 deductible has a higher premium than a policy with a $500 deductible amount. Some insurance companies may require a $500 deductible amount, based on the age of the vehicle. Discuss the advantages and disadvantages for having a higher deductible amount.

## Explain

After a vehicle is several years old, it may have depreciated so much that it is no longer worth continuing comprehensive and collision coverage on that vehicle. You can save money by removing comprehensive coverage on older vehicles.

### CONSUMER TIP

You should carry higher than minimum levels of bodily-injury liability insurance. The amounts of today's court settlements can be quite high.

collision directly from their own insurance company—regardless of who is at fault. However, coverage is limited as specified in the insurance policy. Details in how no-fault insurance is handled differs significantly from one state to another.

### Collision Insurance

**Collision insurance** covers you if you are at fault in a collision, or not able to collect from the person who is at fault. Your collision insurance provides coverage to pay the costs of repair or replacement of your vehicle, less the **deductible** you have selected. A deductible is the amount you agree to pay towards the repair or replacement of the vehicle. Your insurance company agrees to cover the balance up to specified maximum limits. Know what the limit is with the company you choose.

You can select your deductible level. The higher the deductible you select, the greater the amount you are required to pay out of your pocket. However, the higher deductible you select, the lower your premium will be.

### Comprehensive Insurance

What if your vehicle is damaged for some reason other than a collision? Your policy's **comprehensive insurance** can pay for replacement or repair of your vehicle. You also can select a deductible amount for comprehensive insurance. As with a collision deductible, the higher deductible you select, the more you agree to pay, and the lower your premium will be. Most insurance companies will only

pay up to the estimated current value of the vehicle.

Damage caused by severe wind, hail, vandalism, or similar situations are typically included under comprehensive insurance. Most companies have restrictions on what causes qualify for comprehensive coverage. Check your policy to see what restrictions apply.

### Uninsured and Underinsured Motorist Insurance

**Uninsured motorist insurance** protects you if you are struck by another vehicle whose driver has no insurance. Your company covers the costs of injuries to you and your passengers, up to a specified amount. Most states require insurance companies to provide this type of insurance.

If you have **underinsured motorist insurance** your insurance company will pay any costs that exceed what the other person's insurance company will pay as a result of a collision. Most states now require that companies offer this type of insurance to their customers.

### Insurance Rates

A number of factors determine what you pay for insurance. Data on different factors are reviewed and statistics developed. Rates are then established based on the statistics. Factors upon which statistics are based and rates determined include:

- **Driving Record** Drivers with a certain number of convictions for moving violations and collisions pay higher premiums.

## Activity

**Small Group Activity** This activity will help students understand what information an insurance agent needs from a potential client. Divide the class into groups of three and assign a number to each group. Using the textbook as a guide, have each group develop a checklist containing questions an insurance agent might ask a potential client.

After all groups have compiled a checklist, have each group critique the checklist of another group. Have the first group critique the second group's checklist, have the second group critique

the third group's checklist, etc.

Return the checklists for revisions to the groups that developed them. Have each member of the group complete the revised checklist and share the results with other members of their group.

Insurance companies consider them greater risks to insure.

- **Age** Younger drivers have a proportionally higher number of collisions; thus, they have higher premiums. Older, more experienced drivers have fewer moving violations and are involved in comparatively fewer collisions. A principal driver is a person who will drive a certain vehicle most often. A person under the age of 25 listed as the principal driver of a vehicle could pay as much as four times more than an older driver.
- **Miles Driven** The more miles a vehicle is driven on a regular basis (usually annual), the greater the premium. This is because the vehicle is more exposed to the possibility of a collision.
- **Driver Gender** Male drivers tend to pay higher premiums. Historically, statistics have shown they drive more, have more

INSURANCE Even though financial responsibility laws exist, a significant number of drivers do not have insurance. Without insurance people risk losing their life savings and can be forced to liquidate assets to cover required payments. Always comply with your state's financial responsibility laws.

collisions, and their crashes tend to be more severe than those involving young female drivers. However, the gap based on gender has narrowed.
- **Marital Status** Married drivers statistically have fewer collisions than unmarried drivers.
- **Type of Vehicle** Sports cars, some vans, and sport utility vehicles are very popular. They

## Demonstrate

Use **Content Overhead 31** to illustrate how insurance rates vary based on age, gender, and marital status.

## Explain

Point out that many insurance agents work hard to find all the discounts for which a client is eligible, but that the consumer should also take responsibility for learning about various discounts. Consumers are also responsible for letting insurance agents know about changes that might have an impact on insurance premiums.

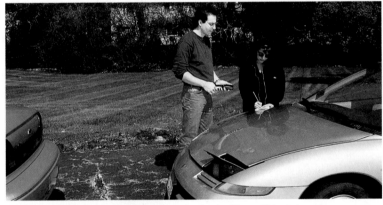

Part of the procedure you should follow if you are involved in a collision is to exchange insurance information with the other drivers.

Chapter 16  Buying and Owning a Vehicle  **345**

## Activity

**Guest Speaker** Invite one or more local insurance agents to speak to your class and answer students' questions about vehicle insurance. Ask the speakers to be prepared to address the following topics: minimum insurance coverage in your state, no-fault insurance, uninsured motorist coverage, average rates for young drivers, and rewards for low-risk drivers.

## Special Needs

Help students role-play the purchase of insurance. Guide them to list questions and determine needs before deciding on amount and types of insurance coverage.

## Discuss

Ask students the *What Do You Think?* question: The difference in the amount of insurance premiums paid by young males and females is narrowing. Why do you suppose this is true?

## 3 Assess

### Answers to Review It

**1.** Such laws require drivers to be able to prove that they have the ability to pay for damages they cause in a traffic collision that results in death, injury, or property damage. Financial responsibility laws typically have minimum levels of liability coverage people must be able to meet. (p. 342)

**2.** To protect drivers from financial loss when they are at fault in a traffic collision and cause damage, harm, injury, or death to others or their property. Insurance is the most common form of showing financial responsibility. (p. 342)

**3.** Examples: Liability (bodily injury and property damage liability); medical; no-fault; comprehensive; collision; and underinsured and uninsured motorist insurance. (pp. 342–344)

**4.** Factors include where you live and drive; the number of miles you drive each year; the type of vehicle you drive and its value (cost to repair if damaged); your age, gender, and driving record. (pp. 344–346)

**What Do You Think?**

The difference in the amount of insurance premiums paid by young males and females is narrowing. Why do you suppose this is true?

also tend to be stolen or vandalized more often and cost more to repair. Many larger vans, trucks, and sport utility vehicles tend to cause greater damage to vehicles they strike. Some insurance companies may charge higher rates to people who drive such vehicles.

- **Where the Driver Lives and Drives** Traffic density in urban areas increases the potential for collisions. Therefore, drivers who live in rural areas tend to pay less for insurance than those who live in larger metropolitan areas.
- **Driver's Claim Record** Higher and more frequent claims, especially for comprehensive and collision coverage, usually result in higher premiums.

### Reduced Premiums

Most insurance companies reward low-risk drivers with reduced premiums. Premiums are often reduced for drivers who have

- maintained good grades in school, and in some cases, have successfully completed an approved driver education program
- had no claims or convictions for three years
- multiple vehicles insured under the same policy
- vehicles with certain safety features like airbags and anti-theft devices

### Assigned-Risk Insurance

Some companies cancel an insurance policy if the driver or other insured drivers on the policy have been convicted of a drug- or alcohol-related violation. A driver who has several collisions or traffic convictions can be the cause for a company canceling a family's policy.

Drivers who have had their insurance canceled due to a poor driving record may not be eligible to obtain coverage at standard rates. Often times the only coverage these drivers can obtain is **assigned-risk insurance.** Assigned-risk insurance provides bodily injury and property damage liability coverage to high-risk drivers for a much higher premium. Assigned-risk drivers must drive violation-free several years before they can qualify for standard insurance.

### Review It

1. What do financial responsibility laws require?
2. What is the purpose of auto insurance?
3. What are the different types of auto insurance?
4. What factors determine the premiums for auto insurance?

Owning and driving a vehicle places many responsibilities on you. One is being aware of how vehicles affect our environment. Drivers must act responsibly to minimize the harm they may cause to the environment.

### How Do Vehicles Affect the Environment?

All vehicle owners have a responsibility for ensuring that they do not harm the environment. This includes using more environmentally friendly products, and properly disposing vehicle parts, fluids, and components.

Almost every motor vehicle that uses gasoline or diesel fuel creates engine exhaust. Some exhaust gases contribute to air pollution.

### Exhaust Gases

Over the years, improvements in the engineering of vehicles have resulted in smaller amounts of harmful exhaust emissions. Today's vehicles also get better gas mileage. However, each year drivers in the United States drive more vehicles more miles.

**Carbon Dioxide** Carbon dioxide ($CO_2$) is one of several gases in vehicle exhaust. Large amounts of this gas produce a "greenhouse effect," which warms the earth. Some scientists fear that too much warming will change the earth's climate.

Regularly maintaining your vehicle can help reduce the number of pollutants your vehicle emits. The less fuel your vehicle burns,

the lower the levels of pollutants in its exhaust.

A number of states have implemented auto emissions inspection programs. These programs require owners to have their vehicle's emission levels periodically inspected. A vehicle must pass the inspection before its license can be renewed.

**CFCs** Until quite recently, most air conditioners contained freon gas, a chlorinated fluorocarbon (abbreviated CFC). Though effective in cooling air, when freon is released into the atmosphere, it breaks down the atmosphere's ozone layer.

The ozone layer shields the earth from the sun's ultraviolet rays, a known cause of skin cancer. If the earth's ozone layer continues to be reduced, it is likely rates of skin cancer will rise.

Does your state require vehicle testing at an auto emissions inspection center?

## Objectives

1. Describe how vehicle use adversely affects the environment.
2. Identify ways individuals can reduce the effects of vehicles on the environment.

# Environmental Concerns

 **Focus**

## Summary

This lesson focuses on the environmental effects of vehicle use. It also provides information on how drivers can help the environment.

## Vocabulary

*car pooling, mass transportation, solar-powered vehicle, van pooling*

 **Teach**

## Discuss

Draw students' attention to the photograph and ask: Does your state or any nearby state require vehicle testing at an auto emissions inspection center? (Answers will vary. Provide specific information about the requirements for your state and nearby states.)

## Discuss

Discuss the impact of various kinds of vehicles on the environment. You might ask students to locate and read a recent newspaper or magazine article on the subject. Ask students to bring the article to class and be prepared to discuss it.

## Teacher's Resources

No *Drive Right* resources are needed for teaching Section 16.3.

## Background

**Vehicles and the Environment** Air pollution is often the focus of environmental concerns related to driving, but it is not the only driving-related environmental concern. Discarded vehicles and tires fill limited landfill space and create a visual blot on the countryside. In some cases, the decomposing parts contaminate groundwater. Mass transportation may provide solutions for environmental problems as well as the problems of traffic gridlock, fuel usage, and high costs of transportation.

## Explain

Provide information about regulations in your community for disposing of vehicle parts and fluids, including batteries, filters, tires, and vehicle fluids. Also include information on recycling for tires, pipes, glass, and other solid materials.

## Explain

Explain that some communities have banned the use of an old tire as the backyard sandbox because tires have been found to attract snakes and insects. Have students find out if a local ordinance prohibits this use of tires. Have students investigate the options in the local community for disposing of used tires.

Refrigerant recovery systems are used on older vehicles to keep CFCs from escaping into the atmosphere.

All new vehicles use an alternative refrigerant in their air conditioning systems. Auto repair shops that service older vehicles whose air conditioners require freon are required to utilize refrigerant recovery systems. These systems capture any freon that escapes while the shop recharges a vehicle's air conditioning system.

### Disposal of Vehicle Parts and Fluids

Vehicle batteries, oil filters, and fluids —oil, gasoline, transmission fluid, brake fluid, and antifreeze—contain hazardous substances. Never dump or dispose of these items in the garbage or down a drain. Collect these items and take them to the nearest hazardous waste collection center, or other appropriate collection location. Contact your local health department. They will probably know of appropriate drop-off locations for your hazardous wastes.

Other solid materials like tires, exhaust pipes, and mufflers also need to be disposed of properly. Piles of older tires placed out in the open are not only eyesores, they can become breeding grounds for insects and rodents that carry dangerous diseases.

Many vehicle parts can be recycled. Old tires now are being used to make floor mats and other rubber products. Glass and tires can be recycled into road-paving materials. Various plastics are being used to make other commonly used plastic products.

### How Can Drivers Help the Environment?

Each person can utilize transportation and still help the environment. As technology increases, more and more alternatives are available.

## Activity

**Guest Speaker** Invite a representative of a government agency that deals with the environment or environmental health to speak to your class. Describe your course content to the speaker and ask him or her to address an environmental concern related to motor vehicle transportation.

## Cross Curricular

**Science** Have students research one environmental concern related to motor vehicle transportation and prepare a two-minute presentation on the topic. Spend some time in class discussing appropriate topics and resources. Encourage students to illustrate their presentations with charts, graphs, or handouts. Consider having students work in pairs.

## Mass Transportation

Several forms of **mass transportation** (also called mass transit) are available throughout the United States. Mass transportation involves moving large numbers of people together from place to place.

Mass transportation is safe, efficient, and environmentally responsible. It includes small buses, city and suburban buses, and rail trams. It also includes urban mass transit systems common to some of our larger cities. Some rapid transit systems are already in place. Others are being developed. Using mass transit reduces the cost per passenger mile and decreases exhaust emissions.

## Car and Van Pools

Other environmentally responsible systems include **car pooling** or **van pooling.** These are systems where several individuals share transportation to one or more destinations. As an incentive to car or van pooling, some highways have special lanes for use only by vehicles containing a certain number of passengers.

Many companies and government agencies provide vans and vehicles for use in a car or van pool. These systems help reduce the number of vehicles on the road, save fuel consumption, reduce overall amounts of exhaust, and decrease the amount of space needed for parking.

## Alternative-Fueled Vehicles

Although many alternative-fueled vehicles are still in early stages of development, this is another option drivers have in reducing the harmful effects of driving on the environment. Many government agencies

Car or van pooling reduces the number of vehicles on the road, exhaust, and conserves the amount of gasoline consumed.

## Activity

**Small Group Activity** Have students explore options to alleviate a traffic situation that contributes to air pollution. Divide the class into groups of five. Ask each group to identify a congested traffic situation in your community or a nearby community that often creates a bottleneck. (Common situations include an intersection, a bridge, a tunnel, or a roadway during commuter traffic.) Once the situation has been identified, the group should discuss options for improving the situation. Each group should end the discussion by developing an action plan. After adequate time the groups will report their findings to the class. Encourage the class to discuss the plans and ask questions. Ask the class to determine if any of the action plans should be passed on to a government agency as a suggested solution. Help students follow through with contacting the appropriate agency.

### Discuss

Ask: What can you do as a driver to help the environment? (Answers will vary. Guide the discussion so that mass transportation, car and van pooling, and alternative-fueled vehicles are all addressed.)

### Explain

Depending on the size and location of your community, students may or may not be familiar with mass transportation and organized car pooling. Provide examples of nearby communities that have mass transportation systems.

### Discuss

Ask: What kinds of mass transportation have you used? (Answers will vary. Encourage students to talk about their experiences in other communities—including other countries.)

### Explain

To help increase fuel conservation, most states allow drivers to turn right on red unless a restriction is posted. Allowing right turns on red reduces the length of time vehicles have to stop and idle. This results in less fuel being burned. Coordinated traffic signals are also fuel savers. These signals are timed so that drivers traveling the speed limit will encounter mostly green lights. This means less idling and less fuel burned.

## Explain

A hybrid vehicle combines two or more sources of power. One style of hybrid automobile combines gasoline and electric energy sources. Some gas-electric hybrids use a high efficiency gasoline engine combined with one or more electric motors. A computer orchestrates how this engine combination operates. For example, during city driving, the computer could shut off the gasoline engine and engage the electric motor(s). When a vehicle is moving without the gasoline engine running, the amount of gasoline and harmful emissions decrease.

Where does the electricity come from to power the electric motor(s)? Some hybrids employ electric generators in the wheels or axles of the auto. As the brakes are applied, the electric generators are engaged. This action assists the normal vehicle brakes in slowing the vehicle and at the same time generates electricity, which is stored in one or more batteries.

 **Assess**

## Answers to Review It

**1.** Vehicles adversely affect the environment by polluting the air, causing a greenhouse effect, and breaking down the ozone layer. Students might also identify ground and water pollution. (pp. 347–348).

**2.** Use environmentally friendly products. Properly dispose of vehicle parts, fluids, and components. Maintain your vehicle properly. (p. 347)

Hybrid vehicles use a combination of a gasoline-powered engine and electric motors, which reduces the amount of fuel used and harmful emissions.

have fleet vehicles that use cleaner burning fuels.

The worldwide supply of fossil fuels, including gasoline, continues to decrease. In an effort to reduce the dependence on gasoline, several alternative-fuel technologies are being explored. **Solar-powered vehicles** capture light energy from the sun and transform it into electricity. Other alternative-fuel technologies are hydrogen fuel cells and ethanol-burning engines. However, engineers have not completely addressed some

of the problems associated with these technologies.

Another alternative technology is hybrid vehicles. Hybrid vehicles have both a gasoline-powered engine and one or more electric motors. Usually, the electricity that powers the electric motor is generated by the motion of the vehicle itself.

Most of these new alternative-energy technologies have two benefits. They use less gasoline while also reducing the emissions that harm our environment.

Hydrogen fuel cells provide energy by converting hydrogen into electricity.

### Review It

1. What are some ways vehicles adversely affect the environment?
2. Name three ways individuals can reduce the harmful effects vehicles have on the environment.

## Cross Curricular

**Mathematics** Ask students to calculate the gas mileage of a vehicle belonging to a friend or family member. Explain how to calculate gas mileage: 1. Fill the gasoline tank and write down the current odometer reading. 2. Immediately before refueling, write down the current odometer reading. 3. Fill the gasoline tank and write down the amount of gasoline it takes to fill the tank. 4. Subtract the first odometer reading from the second to calculate miles traveled. 5. Divide miles traveled by the number of gallons it took to fill the tank in step 3. For example, if you drove 275

miles between fill ups and it took 11 gallons to fill the tank, your vehicle used one gallon of gasoline for every 25 miles traveled ($275 \div 11 = 25$).

Have students calculate the yearly cost of gasoline based on driving 15,000 miles per year and the current price of gasoline in your area. For example, a vehicle that gets 25 miles to a gallon consumes 600 gallons per year ($15,000 \div 25 = 600$). If the current price of gasoline is \$2.80 per gallon, the yearly cost would be \$1,680 ($600 \times \$2.80 = \$1,680$). Have students share their results.

## Reviewing Chapter Objectives

### 1. Buying a Vehicle
1. What are the responsibilities of owning or leasing a vehicle? (336)
2. What are the various costs associated with owning and operating a vehicle? (336–337)
3. How would you select a used vehicle? (339–341)
4. What are the options you have and the steps you take when buying a vehicle? (337–341)

### 2. Insuring a Vehicle
5. What do financial responsibility laws require? (342)
6. How does auto insurance work? (342)
7. What do different kinds of auto insurance cover? (342–344)
8. What factors affect the cost of insurance? (344–346)

### 3. Environmental Concerns
9. How does vehicle use adversely affect the environment? (347–348)
10. In what ways can individuals reduce the effects of vehicles on the environment? (348–350)

## Projects

### Individuals
**Use Technology** Search the Internet for Web sites that deal with automobile sales. Choose one vehicle model. Compare options and prices for this model on several sites. Print out the pages that show these prices and bring them to class.

**Investigate** Go to the library (or search the Internet) to obtain a copy of the NADA Guide (or blue book). Look up the blue-book prices for the vehicles your family owns. Find out the original prices of the vehicles. Calculate how much each vehicle has depreciated.

### Groups
**Debate** Form two teams. Debate the pros and cons of owning a large versus a small vehicle. Make a list of the reasons each team mentions. Compare your list with those of the other teams in your class.

**Demonstrate** Divide into groups of four or five. Each group member should obtain permission to inspect a vehicle in the school parking lot. Demonstrate to the group the steps you would take in inspecting the vehicle if you were considering buying it. Each group member should take notes on the others' inspections. Discuss whether you would buy the vehicles inspected.

## Reviewing Chapter Objectives

**16.1** Buying a Vehicle
See Answers to Review It on page 342.
**16.2** Insuring a Vehicle
See Answers to Review It on page 346.
**16.3** Environmental Concerns
See Answers to Review It on page 350.

For additional information refer to the specific page(s) in parentheses after each question.

## Projects

Some of the projects can be assigned at any time while others are more closely tied to the content presented in the student text. The page number where the topic is introduced is indicated.

**Use Technology:** p. 336
**Investigate:** p. 336
**Debate:** p. 337
**Demonstrate:** p. 339
The results of student projects will vary.

Chapter 16 Buying and Owning a Vehicle **351**

## Teacher's Resources

### Skills and Applications Workbook
pages 61–64

### Tests and Activities
Chapter 16 Activity 16-1 and 16-2, pages 135–136
Chapter 16 Test A and Test B, pages 137–140

### TestWorks CD-ROM
Chapter 16 Test

# Review

## Chapter Test

### Check Your Knowledge

**Multiple Choice** Copy the number of each sentence below on a sheet of paper. Choose the letter of the answer that best completes the statement or answers the question.

1. The value of a vehicle drops steadily over time due to
   (a) loan interest.
   (c) operating costs.
   (b) depreciation.
   (d) insurance premiums.

2. If the used vehicle you are considering passes your tests, you should
   (a) have a mechanic make a final check.
   (b) buy it immediately.
   (c) have a friend test drive the vehicle.
   (d) buy it only if a warranty is offered.

3. Vehicle insurance that pays for damage caused by something other than a collision is called
   (a) liability insurance.
   (b) collision insurance.
   (c) comprehensive insurance.
   (d) uninsured motorist insurance.

4. Which of the following does nothing to help protect the environment?
   (a) using mass transportation.
   (b) driving alone in a vehicle.
   (c) van pooling.
   (d) using an alternative-fueled vehicle.

**Completion** Copy the number of each sentence below. After each number, write the word or words that complete the sentence correctly.

5. A driver whose insurance is canceled due to a poor driving record needs to obtain _____ insurance.

6. Large amounts of $CO_2$ in the atmosphere produce a _____, which warms the earth.

### Review Vocabulary

Copy the number of each definition in list A. Match the definition in list A with the term it defines in list B.

**List A**

7. covers an insured's losses and expenses associated with a collision regardless of who is at fault

8. requires you to prove that you can pay for damages you cause that result in death, injury, or property damage

9. amount you agree to pay toward the repair or replacement of the vehicle

10. provides bodily injury and property damage liability coverage to high-risk drivers for a much higher premium

11. specified amount of money paid over a specified period of time paid for insurance coverage

12. covers the driver who is at fault against claims

**List B**

a. deductible
b. premium
c. no-fault insurance
d. bodily-injury insurance
e. assigned-risk insurance
f. financial responsibility law

### Think Critically

Write a paragraph to answer each question.

1. List and discuss the advantages and disadvantages of leasing a vehicle.

2. How might you reduce premium rates for vehicle insurance?

---

## Answers to Check Your Knowledge

1. b
2. a
3. c
4. b
5. assigned-risk insurance
6. greenhouse effect

## Answers to Review Vocabulary

7. no-fault insurance (c)
8. financial responsibility law (f)
9. deductible (a)
10. assigned-risk insurance (e)
11. premium (b)
12. bodily-injury insurance (d)

## Answers to Think Critically

Students' answers will vary. For information related to the question refer to the page(s) indicated.

1. Advantages are not specifically addressed in the text, but they include: person who leases is not responsible for the costs of maintaining the vehicle; lease payments may be lower than loan payment would be. Disadvantages are that you do not own the vehicle once the lease contract expires; driving extra miles may cost extra. (pp. 338–339)

2. To reduce premium rates: carry a high deductible; maintain a violation-free driving record; minimize miles driven; drive vehicle models that are not expensive to insure; if a student, maintain good grades in school and complete an approved driver education program. (pp. 344–346)

## Decision Making

**1.** You have a part-time job. What are the arguments for and against buying a vehicle?

**2.** You know the type of vehicle you want. You have found vehicles at a private seller, a used-car dealer, and a new-car dealer. How would you decide which vehicle to buy?

**3.** How should this person properly dispose of the used oil?

**4.** Your vehicle has been vandalized. What should you do? What type of insurance will cover the repairs?

Chapter 16 Buying and Owning a Vehicle **353**

## Answers to Decision Making

**1.** A vehicle provides convenient personal transportation and a sense of independence. You might need more time to earn the money for the vehicle's upkeep, and thus have less time for study and social activities. Grades may drop.

**2.** You might buy a used vehicle from a private owner to get a better price. In some cases, used-car dealers have a variety of vehicles for sale, but may not offer a warranty. You might buy from a new-car dealer to get a good used vehicle that was traded in for a new one. The price will probably be higher, but you will usually get a warranty.

**3.** Take the oil to a hazardous waste collection center in the community.

**4.** Comprehensive insurance will pay for damage from vandalism.

# Chapter 17  Planning Guide

**Student Features**

**Teacher's Edition**

| | Student Features | Teacher's Edition |
|---|---|---|
| **Chapter 17**<br>**Maintaining Your Vehicle** | You Are the Driver!  *p. 355* | Projects  *p. 354*<br>Special Needs  *p. 355* |
| **17.1 Maintaining the Power Systems**  *pp. 356–362*<br>• Identify the warning signs for needed repairs for the power and drive systems, ignition and electrical systems, lubrication and cooling systems, and fuel and exhaust systems.<br>• Describe the steps to follow to start a vehicle that has a dead battery. | Did You Know?  *p. 358*<br>Consumer Tip  *p. 361* | Demonstrate  *pp. 357, 358, 360*<br>Activity  *pp. 360, 362* |
| **17.2 Maintaining the Control Systems**  *pp. 363–367*<br>• Identify the warning signs that might indicate the need for repair of the steering, brake, or suspension systems.<br>• Identify ways to maintain tires for longer wear. | | Demonstrate  *pp. 365, 366*<br>Activity  *pp. 363, 367*<br>Special Needs  *p. 364* |
| **17.3 Preventive Maintenance**  *pp. 368–369*<br>• List preventive maintenance checks to make before and after starting the vehicle, while driving, and when fueling or servicing the vehicle.<br>• Explain how to find a qualified mechanic or technician. | Consumer Tip  *p. 368* | |
| **17.4 Fuel-Saving and Recycling Strategies**  *pp. 370–372*<br>• Identify ways you can improve a vehicle's fuel efficiency.<br>• Explain how to calculate miles per gallon of fuel consumption.<br>• Identify strategies for recycling automotive-related materials. | What Do You Think?  *p. 372* | Activity  *pp. 371, 372* |
| **Assessment** | Reviewing Chapter<br>  Objectives  *p. 373*<br>Projects  *p. 373*<br>Chapter Test  *p. 374*<br>Decision Making  *p. 375* | Answers  *pp. 374–375* |

**Companion** *pp. 101–103*
**Spanish Handbook** *pp. 35–36*

**Content Overheads 32, 33, 34**

## Technology Resources

### Audio-Visual and Computer Resources

BFA Educational Media, *Auto Maintenance: Play It Safe*, video, 18 minutes

Safety Industries, Inc., *How Your Car Runs*, video, 15 minutes

Safety Industries, Inc., *Taking Care of Your Car*, video, 12 minutes

Go Online
PHSchool.com

For: Chapter 17 online activities
Visit: PHSchool.com
Web Code: cak-9999

**Skills and Applications Workbook**, *pp. 65–68*
**Tests and Activities**
Chapter 17 Activities 17-1 and 17-2, *pp. 143–144*
Chapter 17 Test A and Test B, *pp. 145–148*

**TestWorks CD-ROM**
Chapter 17 Test

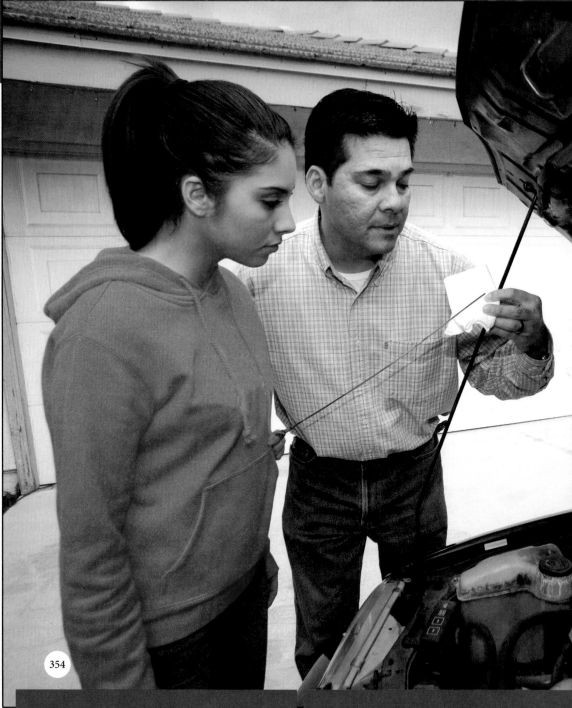

# Chapter 17

## Maintaining Your Vehicle

### Chapter Overview

Chapter 17 explains proper maintenance of a vehicle for safety, efficiency, and economy of operation. Students will learn how various systems operate and how to maintain them. Preventive maintenance is addressed, including day-to-day care and routine servicing. The lesson on fuel-saving and recycling strategies includes facts about fuel efficiency and vehicle design.

### Chapter Vocabulary

*alternator, belted tire, carburetor, catalytic converter, differential, drive shaft, engine management system, fuel-injection system, master cylinder, muffler, oil pump, powerplant, power steering, preventive maintenance, radial tire, radiator, thermostat, transaxle, transmission, water pump*

354

## Teacher's Resources

For students to use as they read the chapter:

**Companion**
pages 101–103

**Spanish Handbook**
pages 35–36

## Projects

Review the projects described on page 373. Some of the projects can be assigned at any time while others are more closely tied to the content presented in the student text.

# CHAPTER 17
## Maintaining Your Vehicle

## You Are the Driver!

Imagine you own your own vehicle. Do you know how to check the oil level? Do you know what the tire pressure should be? What vehicle maintenance can you do? What maintenance should a mechanic or automotive technician do? Have you read the owner's manual for your vehicle?

The vehicles you drive are complex machines made up of many systems and parts. All vehicles need preventive maintenance and periodic repairs to help reduce operating costs. This chapter will familiarize you with the different systems of your vehicle and explain how to maintain your vehicle.

Go Online
PHSchool.com
**For:** Chapter 17 online activities
**Visit:** PHSchool.com
**Web Code:** cak-9999

355

## Introducing the Chapter

Pair students to discuss what they already know about how a vehicle operates and how often various kinds of services should be performed.

## You Are the Driver

 Ask students to look at the picture and suggest what kinds of vehicle maintenance can be performed by the owner. Ask volunteers to describe how these maintenance operations are performed. Discuss which services and repairs should be performed by mechanics.

## Special Needs

Many special needs students are mechanically inclined. Don't miss an opportunity to let them be the "expert." Call upon students who are knowledgeable of automotive mechanics to help with demonstrations or explanations in class or with the driver education car.

The terminology in this chapter may be difficult for some students. Help them learn the most important terms in relation to vehicle maintenance rather than all of the parts of each system.

# Maintaining the Power Systems

## ① Focus

### Summary

This lesson introduces vehicle power systems, explains their functions, and describes the procedures for maintaining them. The power systems addressed are power and drive systems, ignition and electrical systems, lubrication and cooling systems, and fuel and emission systems.

### Vocabulary

*alternator, carburetor, catalytic converter, differential, drive shaft, fuel-injection system, muffler, oil pump, powerplant, radiator, thermostat, transaxle, transmission, water pump*

## ② Teach

### Discuss

Discuss how understanding the way vehicle systems work is an important part of being an informed consumer. Ask: What maintenance can the owner do? Which services must a qualified mechanic perform? Tell students to consider these questions as they study this chapter.

### Objectives

1. Identify the warning signs for needed repairs for the power and drive systems, ignition and electrical systems, lubrication and cooling systems, and fuel and exhaust systems.
2. Describe the steps to follow to start a vehicle that has a dead battery.

Your vehicle consists of many systems. Knowing about the different systems and the care they need can help you recognize and handle problems if they occur. Your owner's manual provides valuable information about how to maintain your vehicle and its various systems.

### Power and Drive Systems

A vehicle's engine needs fuel to burn to create the power to move. The power generated from the **powerplant,** also known as the vehicle's engine or motor, is transmitted to a drive system that operates the front wheels, rear wheels, or all wheels in some vehicles. The powerplant is the source of energy that maintains a vehicle's movement.

New vehicles are powered by different types of internal combustion engines and a variety of electric motors or engine combinations. Selection of powerplant for a particular vehicle is based on its weight, usage, and government regulations.

Different drive-train systems are used for different vehicles. Some vehicles are rear-wheel drive, some front-wheel drive, and others all-wheel drive. The picture shows a front-wheel drive system.

Depending on the type of vehicle, the drive train has different components including

- powerplant (engine or motor)
- transmission
- clutch (in a stickshift)
- drive shaft or half shafts
- differential
- transaxle
- drive axles
- universal, or constant velocity joints

A vehicle's **transmission** houses different gears. The gears of the transmission enable the engine to deliver power to the drive wheels. Lower gears are for power and let the engine turn faster. Higher gears are for greater speed and let the engine turn more slowly and efficiently.

The **drive shaft** is a long metal tube in rear-wheel drive vehicles. The drive shaft carries power from the transmission to the **differential** in the rear of the vehicle. The differential has gears that allow one wheel to turn more slowly than the other when turning a corner.

In front-wheel drive vehicles, power is carried to the front wheels by two half shafts. A **transaxle** is

Transmitting power in a front-wheel drive vehicle

## Teacher's Resources

### Content Overheads
Overheads 32, 33, and 34

## Background

**Engine Valves** Most engines have two valves for every cylinder. Some engines have more than two valves for every cylinder. A 16-valve engine has four cylinders with four valves for each cylinder. Additional valves increase the efficiency of the engine. They increase power, and in some cases, fuel efficiency. Though maintenance costs do not increase with multiple valves, repair costs do increase because of the additional parts. Future engines will very likely have more valves, as these engines are more fuel-efficient.

located between the two half shafts and replaces the transmission and differential.

Check your automatic transmission or transaxle fluid once a month. Jerky shifting, slipping in and out of gears while driving, or pauses before the vehicle starts to move are signs of a low transmission fluid level. Your owner's manual explains how to check the fluid level.

### Ignition and Electrical Systems

The ignition system sets off combustion in your engine's cylinders. The electrical system is involved in the ignition process and also provides the electrical power needed to operate your vehicle's lights, controls, and accessories.

### Alternator

When you turn your key in the ignition, an electrical current sent from the battery to the electric starter turns the engine. Once the engine is running, the **alternator** generates an electrical current that recharges the battery. A belt drives the alternator. Current from the battery continues to power the ignition system. This system delivers energy to each spark plug at the proper time to ignite the air–fuel mixture in each cylinder.

If the alternator light comes on while you are driving, or the battery gauge displays a strong discharge, the alternator is not working properly. It is not generating electricity. The problem could be as simple as a broken or loose belt, or as complicated as an internal electrical problem.

### Battery

A vehicle's starter, lights, computer-assisted controls, and other electrical accessories depend on the electrical power stored in the battery.

Extreme cold or hot weather makes starting your vehicle difficult. A battery has less power when it is cold or overheated. Keep your battery charged to avoid failure. If the engine turns over very slowly when you try to start your vehicle, have the battery charged or replaced.

Keep battery cables tight and free of corrosion, especially where the terminals connect to the battery. Most batteries in today's vehicles are sealed and do not need to have their fluid levels checked. Read your owner's manual for maintenance information.

Always wear eye protection and gloves when working with, or around, a battery. A battery releases hydrogen gas, which is very explosive. Never expose a battery to an open flame or electrical spark. Never let

Ignition and electrical system

---

## Demonstrate

Use **Content Overhead 32** to illustrate the power and drive systems of vehicles with rear-wheel drive and front-wheel drive.

## Explain

Warn students that the voltage delivered to spark plugs is dangerously high and can cause injury.

## Explain

Although an engine tune up is expensive, you can look at it as an investment. A tune up could last 100,000 miles. If you spread the cost of a tune up over the miles driven, the cost is relatively low.

## Explain

Sealed batteries have indicators that warn you when the battery needs to be serviced or replaced. For vehicles with older batteries that have vent caps, you need to check the fluid levels in the battery cells monthly. If fluid is needed, use distilled water.

---

## Background

**Battery Acid** Battery acid can cause burns to skin and eyes, and can ruin clothing and paint. When checking the condition of the battery, look for a build-up of acid at the battery's terminals. The acid build-up will have a bluish-white cotton-like appearance. To clean the acid build-up from a terminal, pour a small amount of baking soda on it and then rinse with clear water. Products are available to protect the terminal connectors to help prevent further acid build-up.

## Demonstrate

Use **Content Overhead 33** to demonstrate the proper connections for the jumper cables when jump-starting a vehicle. Refer to steps 4–6.

## Discuss

It may be helpful to comment on jumper cable connections and how to remember which battery gets connected first. The positive cable is connected first from the good battery's positive terminal to the bad battery's positive terminal. Then clamp one end of the negative cable to the negative terminal of the good battery or good car's engine ground. The last connection goes to the negative ground on the bad battery's engine. Keep the jumper cables away from moving engine parts, such as the fans or belts. When done, reverse the order to disconnect.

battery fluid touch your eyes, skin, or clothing. The fluid is a strong acid that can cause severe injury.

### Starting a Vehicle That Has a Dead Battery

If you turn the ignition key while in PARK or NEUTRAL and the starter makes no sound, it usually indicates a dead battery or bad battery connection. You may be able to jump-start your vehicle by using a jumper cable connected to another vehicle that has a good battery. Check both owner's manuals before you attempt to jump a dead battery. Follow the recommended procedures for your vehicle. *Note:* Both batteries must be the same voltage.

Remove any battery vent caps on your battery (if not a self-contained battery). *Do not jump a dead battery that has frozen cells; the battery might explode.* If the battery is frozen, remove the battery and place it in a warm area for several hours, away from direct heat, before trying to jump-start it.

Follow these steps when making a jumper cable connection:

1. Bring the two vehicles close together, but not touching. The jumper cables need to be able to reach both batteries and engines.
2. Turn off the engine of the vehicle with the good battery and all accessories on both vehicles. Shift the gears of each vehicle into NEUTRAL or PARK. Set the parking brakes.
3. Each battery has two terminals or posts. Each post should be marked with a plus (+) or minus (−) sign, or POS or NEG.
4. Securely clamp one end of the positive jumper cable (marked + or red) to the positive terminal of the good battery. Clamp the other end of the same cable to the positive terminal of the dead battery.
5. Clamp one end of the negative cable (marked − or black) to the negative terminal on the vehicle with the good battery. Note: Some owner's manuals may require the connection be to a negative ground somewhere on the engine away from moving parts.
6. Clamp the other end of the negative cable to a negative ground on the vehicle with the dead battery. A negative ground could be a large unpainted piece of metal away from moving engine parts and the battery. *Do not clamp the negative cable to the bad battery's negative post.*
7. Start the vehicle that has the good battery first. Let the vehicle idle for a few minutes. Then start the

## Background

**The Right Connections** When jump-starting a vehicle, connecting the negative cable of the vehicle with the good battery to the engine ground of the vehicle with the bad battery reduces the chance of a spark that might cause an explosion or damage the vehicle.

Newer vehicles have electrical computer systems that can be damaged by static electricity and electrical surges. Therefore, some auto technicians suggest that both negative cable connections be attached to engine grounds.

Engine Block or Frame

Negative Clamps

Negative Terminals

Dead Battery

Good Battery

Positive Terminals

Positive Clamps

Jumper cable connections for jump-starting a vehicle

vehicle with the dead battery. Keep the vehicle with the dead battery running, but only at idle, until the jumper cables are removed.

8. Remove the cables in the opposite order from which they were attached. Store them in the trunk for future use.

9. Replace any vent caps. Throw away any cloth used to wipe the battery parts because the cloth may have acid on it.

### Lights

Your lights not only help you see, but also help others see you. Defective lights and bulbs need to be replaced immediately. Check your headlights, taillights, backup lights, and turn signals often.

If a turn signal indicator on your instrument panel does not flash, but remains on, it is likely that the turn signal light is burnt out. Determine which signal light is out and replace it. Check your owner's manual for specific types of bulbs and lights for your vehicle.

### Lubrication and Cooling Systems

*Lubrication* is the use of oil, grease, or other substances to reduce damage to moving parts from heat caused by friction. *Cooling* is a process of reducing heat that builds up in a vehicle's engine or transmission. Excessive heat can destroy the engine and other moving parts of the vehicle. Proper lubrication and cooling keeps the systems operating efficiently.

### Lubrication System

Lubricants, such as oil, help the engine operate efficiently by reducing friction, carrying away engine heat, and cleansing engine parts.

The **oil pump** forces oil from the oil pan at the bottom of the

Chapter 17 Maintaining Your Vehicle **359**

### Explain

Keep your headlights aimed properly. Headlights aimed too high can temporarily blind other drivers. Headlights aimed too low can reduce your sight distance at night or in low-visibility conditions.

### Explain

Cold temperatures thicken oil. Thick oil does not flow well. Check your owner's manual for types of oils that can be used in your vehicle, based on your local climate. It is suggested that you use the lowest-weight oil your owner's manual identifies for the climate conditions in which you drive.

### Background

**Approved Oil** Always look for a starburst symbol on a motor oil container. This symbol indicates that the product meets the oil industry's requirements for protection against wear, corrosion, oxidation, and deposits. Using unauthorized oils and oil additives may void the warranty on your vehicle's engine. Check your owner's manual carefully.

### Background

**Oil Changes** Engines with turbo chargers require frequent oil changes to protect the moving parts of the turbo charger. The owner's manual for the vehicle provides information on the recommended frequency for oil changes. Although there is expense involved with each oil change, the money spent on oil changes will reduce the need for costly repairs.

## Demonstrate

Use **Content Overhead 34** or the illustration on this page to demonstrate how oil travels through the engine.

## Explain

Explain that coolant is a mixture of water and antifreeze fluid. The concentration of antifreeze fluid in the mixture determines the mixture's ability to resist freezing and boiling over at specified temperatures. A chart on the antifreeze container tells how to mix the solution correctly.

## Explain

Point out that you can use the temperature gauge as an early-warning device to cooling system problems. Overheating one time can rob you of years worth of trouble-free engine wear.

## Explain

If the temperature gauge or warning light indicates overheating, you may need to add coolant. In many vehicles you add coolant to a surge tank, but in some you add it directly to the radiator. If you need to add coolant directly to the radiator, you must first turn off your engine and let it cool. It is dangerous to remove the radiator cap from a hot radiator. Once the radiator is cooled, carefully remove the radiator cap. Then restart your engine and slowly add coolant to the radiator. Replace the radiator cap before closing the hood of your vehicle. Have a mechanic check your vehicle to determine why it is overheating.

Lubrication system

engine through the oil filter. From the filter, the oil flows through oil lines to the engine's moving parts. Oil is returned to the oil pan, and the cycle is repeated.

All vehicles need to have the oil changed, either after a specific number of miles or months. Oil filters are typically replaced at the same time. If you make a lot of short trips, you may need to have your oil and filter changed more often than recommended.

If the oil-pressure warning light comes on while you are driving, it indicates oil is not going through your engine quickly enough to lubricate it. Pull over to the side of the road when it is safe to do so. Turn off your engine and wait a while before checking the oil level. If your oil level is not the problem, your vehicle needs service right away. Low oil pressure can damage an engine very quickly.

Your vehicle also needs to be greased periodically. Grease is com-

monly used to lubricate such things as the axles, suspension parts, and steering components. Check your owner's manual for the recommended schedule for all of your vehicle's lubrication needs.

### Cooling System

Although lubricating oil removes some engine heat, the engine requires additional cooling. The cooling system provides additional cooling. It also provides a source of heat for your vehicle's interior in cold weather.

The cooling system includes a fan, fan belt or electric motor, radiator, water pump, coolant recovery (or surge) tank, thermostat, and hoses that connect the radiator to the engine. The **radiator** holds and cools the coolant, a mixture of water and antifreeze. The owner's manual indicates the correct mixture to use in your vehicle.

The **water pump** draws coolant from the radiator and forces it through the engine's cooling passages. The fan draws air through the radiator and helps cool the coolant.

The **thermostat** opens and shuts to control the flow of coolant to the radiator. When the temperature in the system rises to the correct level, the thermostat opens to let coolant flow to the radiator and maintain a stable temperature.

Overheating can damage your engine as a result of a low coolant level, blocked radiator airflow, frozen coolant in the system, or a faulty thermostat. Check your coolant level at least once a month. Check the

## Activity

**Class Activity** This activity demonstrates how lubricants reduce friction. You will need towels and a spray bottle filled with water. Have all students forcefully rub their hands together as fast as possible. After 15 seconds ask: What do you feel? (heat) What causes the heat? (friction)

Ask a volunteer to come to the front of the room and rub his or her hands together—this time for 30 seconds. Ask the volunteer to make a mental note of how the heat feels. Now, spray the volunteer's hands with the water and ask him or

her to rub hands in the same manner. Continue to spray water as the rubbing continues. After 30 seconds, ask the volunteer to describe how much heat was felt. (None will be felt.)

Point out that engine parts move thousands of times faster and generate far more heat than the hands in this demonstration. Also point out that just having the water nearby would not have reduced the heat generated by the rubbing hands—the water needed to be on the hands. In the case of an engine, the oil pressure is needed to get oil into the many moving parts.

coolant surge tank before you start the engine. If the coolant level is low, pour a 50/50 mixture of water and coolant into the surge tank to the prescribed level.

Check your radiator hoses every time you change your oil. Look for cracks and squeeze the hoses to feel for spongy spots. Replace hoses that are cracked, leaking, or have a spongy feel to them.

Many vehicle manufacturers suggest the cooling system be flushed and replenished with fresh coolant at least once every two years. Check your owner's manual for recommended service intervals for your vehicle.

### Fuel and Emission Systems

The purpose of the fuel system is to provide fuel needed for the creation of power to move a vehicle. The fuel system includes a fuel tank, fuel line, fuel pump, air cleaner, fuel filter, and carburetor or fuel-injection system.

The emission (or exhaust) system takes the exhaust created by the burning of fuel, and forces it through the exhaust system to the outside of the vehicle. The system includes the positive crankcase ventilation system (PCV), the exhaust gas recirculation system (EGR), the heat control valve, the catalytic converter, exhaust pipe, muffler, and tailpipe.

### Fuel System

The fuel pump draws fuel from the fuel tank through the fuel line. Fuel is then pumped to the **carburetor** or **fuel-injection system.** Air is drawn through the air filter and mixes with the fuel. The fuel–air mixture

radiator cap · fan · coolant circulates through engine · coolant recovery tank · radiator · hoses · water pump · fan belt

Cooling system

becomes a fine mist for combustion in the cylinders of the engine.

Most new vehicles have electronic fuel-injection systems rather than carburetor systems. Fuel-injection systems deliver the exact amount of fuel to each of the engine's cylinders at the proper time to give maximum power and fuel efficiency. Fuel-injection systems also reduce the amount of pollution-causing gases.

If your vehicle hesitates or sputters while accelerating, or if the "service engine" light comes on, you may need to have your fuel system inspected.

### Emission System

The combustion process creates exhaust. The emission system takes the exhaust and recirculates unburned fuel back into the combustion process for greater efficiency. The **catalytic converter** then converts harmful gases into less harmful gases and water. It also cuts down levels of nitrogen oxides, which the sun heats into smog.

**CONSUMER**

Never add water alone to your cooling system. It will boil much faster causing the vehicle to overheat. Use an appropriate water–antifreeze mixture.

Chapter 17 Maintaining Your Vehicle **361**

## Explain

The PCV (positive crankcase ventilation) system recycles leaking gases to be reburned. The EGR (exhaust gas recirculation) system reduces the amount of nitrogen oxides. Nitrogen oxides are turned into smog by the sun's heat. The heat control valve helps make the engine run more efficiently and reduces emissions. It helps keep the temperature up in the combustion chamber to burn fuel more efficiently. The catalytic converter turns harmful gases (carbon monoxide and unburned gasoline) into water. Many newer converters also are designed to help break down nitrogen oxides.

## Background

**Vehicle Fires** Each year drivers are surprised to see their vehicle go up in smoke shortly after parking it. The catalytic converter located underneath the vehicle produces a great deal of heat as it decreases exhaust emissions. Heat from the catalytic converter (which can reach 1,200 degrees) can ignite combustible substances—such as leaves or dry grass.

## Answers to Review It

**1.** For each of the eight systems listed, students should name at least one of the warning signs that indicates needed repairs: power (p. 356), drive (p. 356), ignition (pp. 357–358), electrical (pp. 357–358), lubrication (pp. 359–360), cooling (p. 360), fuel (p. 361), and exhaust, (p. 361).

**2.** Students should list the nine-step sequence indicated on pages 358–359.

positive crankcase ventilation system

muffler

carburetor or fuel-injection system

exhaust gas recirculation system

catalytic converter

tailpipe

Vehicle emission system

The **muffler** reduces the noise from combustion sounds in the engine. Over time, holes develop in mufflers due to rust. If you notice that your vehicle's engine sounds louder and louder over time, it is likely you have a hole in your muffler.

After passing through the muffler, the exhaust leaves the exhaust system through the tailpipe at the rear of the vehicle.

Have your emission system checked periodically to ensure there are no leaks in the system. By doing this, you reduce your risk of carbon monoxide poisoning while driving.

### Review It

1. Name at least one warning sign that indicates needed repairs for each of these systems: power, drive, ignition, electrical, lubrication, cooling, fuel, and exhaust.
2. What are the proper steps for starting a vehicle that has a dead battery?

## Activity

**Class Activity** This activity will help students learn and remember the names and locations of the major components and systems in the engine compartment. You will need to use the driver education vehicle for this activity.

Open the hood of the driver education vehicle and give students an opportunity to look around. Point to different components and ask students to identify them and explain their purposes. Consider repeating this activity and having someone video-tape it. Make the tape available as a study aid.

Vital to the safe control of your vehicle are several different, but interrelated, systems and components. The steering, brake, and suspension systems are all part of your vehicle's traction-control system. Your tires are also components of your vehicle's traction-control system. All of these contribute to a vehicle's control, stability, and riding comfort.

### Steering System

The steering system includes the steering wheel, steering column, steering gear, and the connections to the front wheels. The steering column transmits your steering input to move the front wheels of your vehicle in the direction you choose.

Most vehicles today have **power steering,** a system that uses a hydraulic pump and fluid to make steering easier for you. Avoid turning the steering wheel when the vehicle is not moving. This causes wear on the steering system.

Steering problems often develop gradually rather than suddenly. This may make them difficult to recognize. Any steering problem is serious and should be repaired immediately. Common indications of problems include

- "play" or excess movement in the steering wheel
- steering difficulty, even though the tires are properly inflated
- shimmying or wobbling, or shaking or pulling to one side under normal driving conditions

- squealing sounds when you make turns

### Brake System

Good brakes are essential for the safe operation of a vehicle. The life expectancy and performance of your brakes depend on how you use and maintain them. A vehicle's brake system is composed of four individual brakes (one on each wheel), brake lines, brake fluid, wheel cylinders, and a master cylinder.

The brake system's **master cylinder** contains two parts. Each part controls two wheels. When a driver applies pressure on the brake pedal, brake fluid is forced from the master cylinder through the brake lines to each wheel's brake cylinder. The cylinder at each wheel forces the brake shoes or brake pads against a brake drum or disk. The pressure causes friction, which slows or stops the wheel.

master cylinder · rear drum brakes · brake pedal · brake lines · front disk brake

Brake system

Chapter 17 Maintaining Your Vehicle **363**

### Objectives

1. Identify the warning signs that might indicate the need for repair of the steering, brake, or suspension systems.
2. Identify ways to maintain tires for longer wear.

---

# Maintaining the Control Systems

 **Focus**

## Summary

This lesson introduces the vehicle's control systems, explains their functions, and describes the procedures for maintaining them. The control systems addressed are steering, brake, suspension, and traction control.

## Vocabulary

*belted tire, master cylinder, power steering, radial tire*

 **Teach**

## Explain

Some newer vehicles have limited power-assist steering. These systems provide more power for easier steering at slower speeds, and less power at higher speeds when less assistance is needed.

---

## Teacher's Resources

No *Drive Right* resources are needed for teaching Section 17.2.

## Activity

**Small Group Activity** Divide the class into groups of four. Ask the students to discuss common indications that their vehicle may have a steering or braking system problem. Let them attempt to describe what sounds and feelings they will experience from each problem. After adequate time, have the students refer to pages 363 and 364 to see if their group included the problems stated on these pages.

## Explain

Explain that many new vehicles are equipped with an antilock braking system (ABS). A computer, through sensors at each wheel, detects when a wheel is about to lock up. Adjustments are made 15–20 times a second to free the wheel from any lock up. The major benefit of antilock brakes is that they provide the driver with steering ability while maintaining maximum braking capability. Never pump antilock brakes. Hold your foot firmly down and let the antilock braking system do its job.

## Explain

When you start a vehicle with ABS, a light indicates that the system is working. If the antilock brake light stays on longer than normal or comes on while you are driving, stop your vehicle, wait a few minutes, and restart the vehicle. This will allow the computer system controlling your ABS to reset itself. If the light stays on, have the vehicle serviced.

**DISK BRAKES AND DRUM BRAKES** Many vehicles have a disk brake on each front wheel and a drum brake on each rear wheel. Some vehicles have disk brakes on all four wheels. A disk brake works as fluid pressure presses the pads against the sides of the rotating disk inside the wheel. A drum brake works as fluid pressure forces the brake shoes against the hollow cylinder drum inside the wheel. Each type of brake causes friction that slows or stops the turning wheels.

Most vehicles' brake systems are designed with fail-safe systems. If a leak develops in the brake system, the brake warning light on the instrument panel will likely come on. Because of the dual master cylinder, however, fluid under pressure should still reach one pair of the wheels. Stopping distance will increase and handling may be erratic. The braking system must be checked and repaired immediately. *Never drive a vehicle with a faulty brake system, regardless of the distance.*

A vehicle's disk and drum brakes self-adjust when braking in reverse. If you notice that the brake pedal goes closer than two inches to the floor when you press the brake pedal hard, adjust the brakes. To adjust the brakes, stop, back up, and brake firmly. Repeat this procedure several times. If the problem persists, have your brake system inspected.

If the brake or antilock brake warning light stays on after starting your vehicle or comes on while driving, these are indicators of possible brake problems. Some other indications of potential problems include
- "spongy" feel in the brake pedal
- pulling to one side when stopping with dry brakes
- grabbing or uneven brake action
- squealing or chattering noises in the brakes
- a need to push the brake harder than usual to stop the vehicle

The parking brake is a separate brake system. A steel cable connects the parking brake pedal or lever to a separate brake assembly on the rear wheels only. When properly adjusted and engaged, the parking brake should hold a vehicle on a hill. If the parking brake doesn't hold, have it repaired.

Keep the brake fluid in the master cylinder at the proper level. Use the brake fluid specified for your vehicle. Have your brakes checked on an annual basis, or as soon as you notice potential problems. Proper maintenance of your vehicle's brakes may not only save you money, but could save your life.

## Special Needs

Arrange to take your students to the automotive class in your school to help them understand the automotive systems taught in this chapter. Have the students identify all major components on a display engine and on vehicles there to be repaired. If any of the students are in an automotive class, have them explain how the systems work and how to maintain them.

## Suspension System

The suspension system includes a series of rods, bars, springs, and other components. This system keeps the wheels and tires pointed in the direction you are steering. The springs in the suspension system support the vehicle to allow a gentle up-and-down motion while driving. A shock absorber or strut assembly unit is located at each wheel to control hard bouncing and to keep the tires on the roadway.

If you notice your vehicle bouncing more than usual, or you find uneven tire wear, there may be a problem with its suspension. Check your owner's manual for the recommended intervals for servicing or replacing your vehicle's shocks, struts, and joints.

### Tires: A Traction Control System

Your tires are your vehicle's lifelines to the roadway. It is important to understand your vehicle's tires and to ensure that your vehicle is equipped with tires that best meet your driving needs.

### Tire Construction

A tire is made of rubber reinforced with layers of material under the tread. Each layer, called a *ply*, strengthens the tire and gives it shape.

A **belted tire** has special layers added to a bias-ply tire for improved strength, performance, and mileage. A **radial tire** has plies that run straight across under the tread, and strengthening belts of steel or other materials that circle the tire. Radial tires give improved tread mileage,

belted      radial

Tire construction

traction, and fuel economy, compared to other tires.

Information about the tire's construction, size, recommended inflation levels, and carrying capacity is clearly marked on the sidewall of the tire. New tires usually have a paper label attached with additional information.

### Inflation and Tread

Maintain the manufacturer's recommended air pressure in the tires at all times. Keep a reliable tire gauge in your vehicle and use it regularly. Maintaining the proper air pressure

brand name

MANUFACTURER'S NAME or identifying code

pressure/
load maximums

size

"DOT"
(certifies compliance)

construction
(plies, cord material;
how many and how much)

tire code number
(who made it, where and when)

Information on the sidewall

## Explain

Explain that heavy-duty suspension components, such as springs and shock absorbers, should be used on any vehicle that will pull a trailer or carry heavy loads. Such components are available as an option when a new vehicle is ordered from the factory. Installing these items after the vehicle has been purchased is usually much more expensive.

## Demonstrate

Contact a local tire dealer to help you create a display to illustrate various tire wear patterns. Use sections of tires to show each of the following wear patterns: (1) out of balance, (2) overinflation, (3) underinflation, (4) turning the steering wheel while the vehicle is not moving, (5) out of alignment, (6) worn shock absorbers, and (7) speeding on curves. Be sure to identify each wear pattern on your display.

Consider making a second display without identification cards. This could be used as a study aid or to assess students' knowledge.

## Explain

Low inflation causes tires to wear quickly. It can cause tire failure in two ways: (1) from excessive heat build-up, or (2) from the tire being compressed too much when it comes in contact with a pothole or object on the road. A puncture or faulty valve stem can cause a slow leak and deflate a tire, causing your vehicle to act as if it had a blowout.

## Explain

The owner's manual is the best source for the recommended tire rotation pattern for any particular vehicle. If your vehicle has a full-size spare, include it in the rotation pattern. This ensures that all five tires wear at the same rate. Rotating all five tires also means that you or a service mechanic handles each tire regularly. This reduces the risk that your spare will be flat when you need to use it.

## Demonstrate

Use the photograph at the bottom of the page to illustrate tread wear bars. Most wear bars appear when only 1/16 inch of tread remains. A new tire typically has anywhere from 9/16 inch to 11/16 inch of tread. If you see one wear bar, it may be time to replace the tire. If you see three, there is no doubt that a replacement is needed.

in the tire will yield maximum fuel efficiency and tire mileage. Too little air in one of your tires can make handling the vehicle more difficult.

Air pressure in a tire rises in warmer weather and falls in cooler weather. Air pressure increases whenever the vehicle is driven, regardless of the distance of the trip. Don't let air out of a warm tire in an attempt to reduce the air pressure to the recommended level. The tire will be underinflated when it cools. Overall, cool tires will provide the most accurate and stable readings.

### Rotation and Alignment

Rotate your tires regularly to promote longer tire life. Different rotation patterns are recommended for different vehicles and tires. See your owner's manual for the recommended pattern and schedule you should follow for your vehicle. The illustration shows different rotation patterns for different vehicles and tires.

In addition to rotating your tires, have them balanced periodically to promote even wear. Whenever

you have your tires balanced, it is also a good idea to have your wheels aligned. Alignment is especially important on front-wheel drive vehicles. Proper wheel alignment also increases the life of the tires and reduces excessive and uneven wear.

### Replacing Tires

Most tires have wear bars built into them. A smooth bar will appear across your tire when the tread has worn down. A worn tire has poor traction on wet roads and is more likely to fail. When you can see one or more wear bars on any tire, it is time to replace that tire.

Replacement tires should be the same size and type as the tires they are replacing. Never use radial tires with any other type of tire on the vehicle. Radial tires do not react the same as belted tires.

### Tire Quality and Grading

All tires sold in the United States are rated on the Uniform Tire Quality Grading System, as seen in the chart.

Tire rotation patterns

Notice the wear bar!

## Background

**Special Tires** Low-inflation tires, also called run-flat tires, allow a driver to continue to drive for up to 50 miles at speeds greater than 50 mph, even though the tire has lost its pressure. Another innovation is a tire that seals itself when punctured by things like nails.

**Grades of Tires**

| Tire Grading | Traction | Temperature | Treadwear |
|---|---|---|---|
| Highest | A | A | 200 |
| | | | 190 |
| | | | 180 |
| | | | 170 |
| | | | 160 |
| | B | B | 150 |
| | | | 140 |
| | | | 130 |
| | | | 120 |
| | | | 110 |
| | | | 100 |
| Lowest | C | C | 90 |
| | | | 80 |
| | | | 70 |
| | | | 60 |
| | | | 50 |

- A tire's traction is measured by its ability to stop a car in straight-ahead motion on a wet surface. An A-graded tire has the best traction performance.
- Temperature resistance indicates a tire's ability to withstand heat. A tire graded A is the most heat-resistant, and is the least likely to suffer a blowout under the same conditions as tires with grades of B or C.
- The higher the treadwear rating, the greater the mileage. A tire with a treadwear rating of 150 is expected to last 50 percent longer than one graded at 100.

A tire's performance is measured under ideal controlled conditions on specific test surfaces and over a special test route. They are rated by traction, temperature, and treadwear performance.

Keep safety in mind when you are in need of new tires. Compare and decide which type of tire offers the best value for the kind of driving you do. Check your owner's manual for recommendations on tires for your vehicle.

## Review It

1. Identify at least one repair warning sign for the steering, brake, and suspension systems.
2. How can you maintain tires for longer wear?

## Explain

Most tires have a rubber life as well as a tread life. Check tires periodically for cracks and dryness. This is particularly important for low-mileage vehicles.

## Explain

A vehicle with oversize tires may not display or record accurate speed or mile readings on the speedometer or odometer.

 ## Assess

## Answers to Review It

**1.** For each of the three systems listed, students should name at least one of the warning signs that indicates needed repairs: steering (p. 363), brake (pp. 363–364), and suspension (p. 365).

**2.** To maintain tires for longer wear, you need to maintain proper air pressure, rotate and balance tires, and have wheels aligned (p. 366).

## Activity

**Guest Speaker** Invite a tire retailer to speak to your class about various types of tires and how to determine which tires will best meet different driving needs. If possible, ask the retailer to include information about tires for cars, vans, sport utility vehicles, and trucks, and for different driving conditions. Brochures, videotapes, and display boards might be used as visual aids.

# Preventive Maintenance

## 1 Focus

## Summary

This lesson introduces preventive maintenance, including routine checks and scheduled service. Suggestions for selecting a qualified technician are included.

## Vocabulary

*preventive maintenance*

## 2 Teach

## Explain

Explain to students that in order to gain benefits from the vehicle's warning lights, one needs to first know which lights should come on after the key is turned on, before starting the engine.

## Discuss

Ask students how they would select a qualified mechanic. Discuss how some people compare the selection of a good technician or mechanic to looking for a family physician. You want someone who is well-trained, experienced, professional, and trustworthy. Proper maintenance and repairs will help preserve your vehicle, one of your largest investments.

## Objectives

1. List preventive maintenance checks to make before and after starting the vehicle, while driving, and when fueling or servicing the vehicle.
2. Explain how to find a qualified mechanic or technician.

### CONSUMER TIP

How to find leaks: At night, take light-colored paper and place it underneath your vehicle. In the morning, check the paper for fluid spots and their locations. Have any leaks repaired.

The routine care and attention you give your vehicle to avoid trouble later on is called **preventive maintenance.** This attention includes not only the day-to-day care, but also the periodic servicing recommended in your owner's manual.

The schedule of service for maintenance jobs is important. The manufacturer or dealer warranty may not stay in effect if maintenance schedules are not followed.

### Routine Checks

You should make it a habit to pay attention to your vehicle's condition. Notice changes in its condition before driving and while you drive.

### Before Starting the Engine

Before you enter the vehicle and start the engine, make a few quick inspections to avoid trouble while driving. Here are some examples:

- Look for signs of fluid leaks on the pavement under the vehicle. The color and location of the fluid can help you determine the type and source of the leak. The colors in the picture indicate the different types of fluids.
- Make sure your lights and horn work. When you turn the ignition on (without starting the engine) see that your warning lights come on. If one does not come on, check your fuses first. If the fuses are not the problem, then have the vehicle checked by a technician.

Power steering fluid Check system

Water Usually normal condensation

Motor oil Check the engine.

Coolant Check the water pump, radiator, or hose.

Transmission fluid Check the transmission seals.

Colors indicate the type of fluid leaking out.

### After Starting the Engine

After you start your engine, follow the steps and checks as described in Chapter 3. If you have any concerns, see your owner's manual.

### While Driving

Follow the steps and procedures you learned in earlier chapters to measure your vehicle's performance. Notice any unusual instrument panel readings. Observe any out-of-the-ordinary sounds, odors, or vibrations of the vehicle.

### Teacher's Resources

No *Drive Right* resources are needed for teaching Section 17.3.

### Background

**Alert Lights** An alert light tells you a system is on or functioning or reminds you to perform a function. For example, when you start your vehicle, the parking-brake light tells you the parking brake is on; the ABS light tells you that the antilock braking system is functioning; and the safety-belt light reminds you to fasten your safety belt. A warning light tells you of impending problems or dangerous activity. For example, the low-fuel light tells you that you are low on fuel, while the oil-pressure light indicates a more serious problem.

### At a Fuel Stop

Most drivers fill their own vehicle's fuel tanks at self-service stations. Turn off your engine before you begin refueling. Follow posted instructions for refueling. Smoking is *always prohibited* near fuel pumps.

Almost every gas station offers a selection of types and grades of fuel. Check your owner's manual for your vehicle's recommended octane rating.

Alternative fuels are becoming more common. One type of alternative fuel is gasohol. Gasohol is a blend of gasoline and either methyl or ethyl alcohol.

Whenever you stop for fuel, it's a good time to perform routine checks and service. Here are some examples:

- Check your oil level. Add oil if needed.
- Check the windshield washer fluid level. Add additional fluid to the reservoir, if needed.
- Clean your windshield, windows and headlights.
- Check your windshield wipers for cracks. Replace damaged blades.
- Check your tires. Do they look low? Is the tire pressure correct? Are there any visible cracks in the tire? Take care of crucial problems before you leave the gas station.

### Selecting a Qualified Technician

Vehicles are complex machines. It is important that you find a reliable service and repair location staffed with trained and certified technicians and mechanics. Talk with people you know and respect. Ask your local better business bureau. If you are a member of a motor club, ask them for recommendations.

You could also visit different automotive repair shops. Find out if the technicians and mechanics are qualified and certified. Most major dealerships have highly skilled technicians and mechanics who have passed specialized tests to obtain their certifications.

### Scheduled Service

Vehicles need periodic service. Your owner's manual shows the recommended maintenance intervals for you to follow. Save all of your service receipts. Keep a comprehensive maintenance history of your vehicle, especially for warranty-related repairs.

### State Vehicle Inspections

Some states require periodic vehicle inspections. Inspections can detect safety-related problems before they become hazards. Owners are usually required to have all serious defects repaired before the vehicle can be licensed.

While refueling, clean your windows and check wiper blades for any damage or excessive wear.

> ### Review It
> 1. List some preventive maintenance checks you should make before and after starting the vehicle, while driving, and when stopping for fuel.
> 2. List the steps you can take to find a qualified technician or mechanic.

## Background

**Oil Pressure Warning Light** Many drivers falsely believe the oil pressure warning light indicates a low oil level. They may then add oil and drive with the oil light still on, believing that the gauge is faulty. This is an expensive way to learn the real message—oil is not circulating properly within the moving parts of the engine. Circulation is necessary to reduce the heat generated by sliding friction created when metal rubs against metal. It is possible to have an adequate amount of oil without enough pressure to make it circulate properly.

## Explain

Some gasoline additives could cause damage to certain components of your fuel system. Check your owner's manual before using fuel additives.

## Explain

Explain that while fueling, you should not try to top off your tank when the pump mechanism shuts off automatically. Too much fuel in your tank can adversely affect how your engine's computer system operates.

## Explain

Motor vehicle diagnostic centers test vehicles electronically and mechanically to detect problems. A written report indicates all parts or systems that fail to work or meet acceptable standards. The vehicle owner, or a qualified technician, can refer to the report to replace defective parts or make needed repairs.

## ③ Assess

### Answers to Review It

1. Students should list some of the routine checks identified on pages 368–369.
2. Students should list steps identified on page 369.

**17.4**

# Fuel-Saving and Recycling Strategies

## 1 Focus

## Summary

This lesson presents information on innovations in design and technology that influence the ways vehicles look and perform. Lesson topics include facts about fuel efficiency, calculating miles per gallon, vehicle design, engine improvements, and recycling strategies.

## Vocabulary

*engine management system*

## 2 Teach

## Explain

Regularly checking how many miles per gallon your vehicle is using can help detect inefficiencies in the fuel system, which are costly and reduce vehicle performance. For example, a dirty air filter might cost you four or five miles per gallon.

## Objectives

1. Identify ways you can improve a vehicle's fuel efficiency.
2. Explain how to calculate miles per gallon of fuel consumption.
3. Identify strategies for recycling automotive-related materials.

Advancements in design and technology have changed the ways our vehicles look and perform. Today's vehicles are designed and built for greater fuel efficiency. The way you drive can also improve fuel efficiency.

### Facts About Fuel Efficiency

Even though vehicle designs and changes in the types of materials used in today's vehicles save fuel, drivers need to follow certain practices to help conserve resources.

### Control Your Speed

Many newer vehicles have very fuel-efficient engines that achieve maximum fuel economy at speeds between 50–55 mph. However, strong winds can reduce an engine's fuel efficiency. While driving at speeds of more than 45 mph, keep your windows closed to cut wind resistance.

Higher speeds result in more fuel being used. For every 5 mph increase in speed above 55 mph, most cars get 1.5 fewer miles per gallon.

While driving in the city, coast to a stop when possible, and moderately accelerate to your desired speed. Very fast or very slow starts waste fuel.

### Care for Your Engine

Use a vehicle with a warm engine, if you can. A warm engine is more fuel-efficient than a cold engine. The greatest fuel consumption is within the first few minutes after starting a cold engine. The most efficient way to warm up a cold engine is to drive it at moderate speeds for the first few miles. Avoid excessive idling to avoid wasting fuel and possibly damaging the engine.

### Calculating Miles Per Gallon

Most drivers want to get the most miles from each gallon of fuel. Checking your fuel economy can warn you of potential mechanical problems. Follow these simple steps to calculate miles per gallon.

1. Fill the fuel tank. Record the odometer reading, or set the trip odometer at zero.
2. Drive normally until you have about a half tank of fuel.
3. Refill the tank. Record the number of gallons it took to refill the tank. Next, record the odometer or trip odometer reading.
4. Subtract the first odometer reading from the second. Then, divide the number of miles driven by the number of gallons of fuel it took to refill the tank. The result is the number of miles per gallon (mpg).

### Vehicle Design

The designs of many vehicles have been streamlined to reduce wind resistance and help increase performance and fuel efficiency. Changes in the body shapes, wheel covers, bumpers, and headlights all have contributed to more fuel-efficient vehicles.

## Teacher's Resources

No *Drive Right* resources are needed for teaching Section 17.3.

## Cross Curricular

**Mathematics** Have students work in pairs to calculate the miles per gallon for a vehicle over a three-week period. Provide each pair with a beginning odometer reading, the amount of fuel used to fill the tank at each of three fuel stops, and the odometer readings before filling up the tank. Have students calculate the miles per gallon for the entire three-week period.

Notice how the newer vehicle is more aerodynamic.

In general, vehicles have become smaller and lighter over the years. Lighter-weight materials and plastics have replaced older, heavier steel and metal components. Smaller, lighter vehicles need less power to move. The result has been an increase in fuel efficiency.

### Engine Improvements

Because of the types of materials used in manufacturing today's vehicles, smaller engines are common. Smaller engines are designed to provide adequate power for smaller and lighter vehicles. Smaller engines also provide better fuel efficiency.

Electronic ignitions and computerized **engine management systems** help vehicles' engines operate and use fuel efficiently. A computer monitors the fuel, ignition, and emission systems. The computer collects data about each system and automatically

Chapter 17  Maintaining Your Vehicle  **371**

## Explain

If you must park outdoors when the weather is very cold, you might have an engine block heater installed. The heater, plugged into an electrical outlet, keeps your engine's oil warm and makes starting your vehicle easier.

## Discuss

Use recent magazine and newspaper articles to initiate discussion about innovations in vehicle design and engine improvements.

## Activity

**Small Group Activity** Collect fuel economy information about new vehicles from the manufacturers and magazines that publish road tests. You may also find information on the Internet. Form the class into groups of four or five students. Have each group compare miles-per-gallon figures for different kinds of vehicles and discuss reasons for differences between the figures. Have each group report their findings to the class. Then ask: why might actual miles-per-gallon figures differ from published figures?

## Explain

Used motor oil can be filtered, cleaned, and used again. It also can be recycled into other types of fuel and lubricants. If you change your own oil, take the used oil to a collection center.

## Discuss

Point out that many communities require quick-oil businesses to accept used motor oil and/or filters. Ask the *What Do You Think?* questions: Should this be a requirement? Why or why not? Encourage students to discuss the pros and cons of such requirements. Provide information about any such requirements in your community or nearby communities.

 **Assess**

## Answers to Review It

1. Control your speed and care for your engine. (p. 370)
2. Students should list steps identified on page 370.
3. Motor oil, antifreeze, and batteries can be recycled. (p. 372)

Dispose of used fluids responsibly.

makes adjustments to the respective systems. These adjustments increase operational efficiency.

For example, the air–fuel mixture introduced into the cylinders is more precise and is burned more effectively as a result of the engine management systems. Less fuel is burned, and it is burned more efficiently. The result is greater fuel efficiency and fewer hazardous gases emitted into the atmosphere.

### Recycling Strategies

Because of the concern over the environment, conservation of resources, and potential health hazards, many automotive materials are being recycled for reuse or turned into other consumer products.

Any materials meant to be used later, and not discarded, should be placed in sealed containers away from children and pets. Unused oil, gasoline, and antifreeze are just a few examples. Make sure oil and antifreeze spills or puddles are promptly absorbed and cleaned from your driveway or

**What Do You Think?** Many communities require quick-oil businesses to accept used motor oil and/or filters. Should this be a requirement? Why or why not?

garage. The sweet smell and taste of antifreeze could attract children and animals. If ingested, oil or antifreeze could poison and potentially cause death.

Many states have regulations for recycling oil and engine contaminants. Items that can be recycled, such as used motor oil, antifreeze, and batteries, should be taken to respective recycling centers, local drop-off locations, or hazardous waste collection locations.

If you have your vehicle serviced at an automotive service station or vehicle maintenance facility, you avoid the responsibility of having to handle or dispose of used parts, materials, and fluids. Businesses that service vehicles know how to properly deal with used automotive materials.

### Review It
1. What are some ways to improve the fuel efficiency of your vehicle?
2. Explain how to calculate miles-per-gallon of fuel consumption.
3. What are at least three examples of automotive-related items that can be recycled?

### Activity
**Small Group Activity** Form the class into groups of four or five students. Ask them to discuss: Where in the community are there recycling facilities? What are they likely to take to a recycling facility? Do they believe recycling is a good idea? After adequate time have them report to the class their discussions.

## Reviewing Chapter Objectives

### 1. Maintaining the Power Systems

1. What are the signs that repairs are needed for the power and drive systems, lubrication and cooling systems, and fuel and exhaust systems? (356–362)
2. What steps should you follow to start a vehicle that has a dead battery? (358–359)

### 2. Maintaining the Control Systems

3. What are the signs that repairs are needed for the steering, brake, and suspension systems? (363–369)
4. How can you maintain tires for longer wear? (366)

### 3. Preventative Maintenance

5. What are the preventive maintenance checks to make before and after starting the vehicle, while driving, and when fueling or servicing the vehicle? (368–369)
6. How can you find a qualified mechanic or technician? (369)

### 4. Fuel-Saving and Recycling Strategies

7. In what ways can you improve a vehicle's fuel efficiency? (370)
8. How do you calculate miles per gallon of fuel consumption? (370)
9. What are the strategies for recycling automotive-related materials? (372)

## Projects

### Individuals

**Interview** Make a list of certified vehicle technicians and mechanics in your area. Interview three of them to find out what their qualifications are. Ask them how long they have been in business and what they like best about their job. Determine which one you would want to repair your vehicle.

**Investigate** Use the Internet to research ways that vehicle manufacturers recycle various components of their products. Write a report based on your research and share it with the class.

### Groups

**Use Technology** Make a video about the preventive maintenance checks you should make on your vehicle. Each group member should explain a different aspect of preventive maintenance. Get an owner's permission to use an actual vehicle in your video. Present the video to your class.

**Observe** Each person in the group should check out the tires on ten vehicles in the school's parking lot. Note whether each tire is belted or radial. Note whether the tire is inflated properly and had adequate tread. Make a group spreadsheet based on each person's findings.

## Reviewing Chapter Objectives

**17.1** Maintaining the Power Systems
See Answers to Review It on page 362.
**17.2** Maintaining the Control Systems
See Answers to Review It on page 367.
**17.3** Preventive Maintenance
See Answers to Review It on page 369.
**17.4** Fuel-Saving and Recycling Strategies
See Answers to Review It on page 372.

For additional information refer to the specific page(s) in parentheses after each question.

## Projects

Some of the projects can be assigned at any time while others are more closely tied to the content presented in the student text. The page number where the topic is introduced is indicated.

**Interview:** p. 369
**Investigate:** p. 372
**Use Technology:** p. 368
**Observe:** p. 365

The results of student projects will vary.

## Teacher's Resources

### Skills and Applications Workbook
pages 65–68

### Tests and Activities
Chapter 17 Activity 17-1 and 17-2, pages 143–144
Chapter 17 Test A and Test B, pages 145–148

### TestWorks CD-ROM
Chapter 17 Test

# Answers to Check Your Knowledge

1. b
2. d
3. d
4. a
5. thermostat
6. drive shaft
7. water
8. hydraulic

# Answers to Review Vocabulary

9. carburetor (c)
10. belted tire (d)
11. radiator (a)
12. differential (b)
13. muffler (f)
14. alternator (e)

# Answers to Think Critically

Students' answers will vary. For information related to the question refer to the page(s) indicated.

1. You may fail to notice small things that are wrong with the vehicle that may later become more serious. It's less expensive to do preventive maintenance than to fix problems that arise due to neglect. Students may mention specific problems that can arise. Answers will vary. (pp. 368–369)

2. It is important to recycle automotive materials such as motor oil, antifreeze, and batteries because they are hazardous to health and the environment. You need to find out from local vehicle-service businesses how your community handles such recycling. (p. 372)

## Chapter Test

### Check Your Knowledge

**Multiple Choice** Copy the number of each sentence below on a sheet of paper. Choose the letter of the answer that best completes the statement or answers the question.

1. A vehicle's gears are housed in the
   (a) powerplant.　　(c) drive shaft.
   (b) transmission.　　(d) differential.
2. When jump starting a vehicle that has a dead battery
   (a) make sure that both batteries are the same voltage.
   (b) warm the battery up first if frozen.
   (c) start the vehicle with the good battery first.
   (d) all of the above
3. The master cylinder is found in a vehicle's
   (a) steering system.
   (b) suspension system.
   (c) traction control system.
   (d) brake system.
4. Preventive maintenance is
   (a) caring for vehicle on an ongoing basis.
   (b) caring for a vehicle once trouble begins.
   (c) overhauling the engine.
   (d) none of these

**Completion** Copy the number of each sentence below. After each number, write the word or words that complete the sentence correctly.

5. The _____ controls the flow of coolant to the radiator.
6. In rear-wheel vehicles, the _____ carries power to the differential.
7. A vehicle's catalytic converter converts harmful gases into less harmful gases and _____.
8. A power steering system uses a _____ pump and fluid to make steering easier.

### Review Vocabulary

Copy the number of each definition in list A. Match the definition in list A with the term it defines in list B.

**List A**

9. engine part that mixes air and gasoline and sends it as a fine mist to the engine cylinders
10. tire that has special layers added to a bias-ply tire for improved strength, performance, and mileage
11. part of the cooling system that holds and cools the coolant
12. arrangement of gears at the rear of the vehicle allowing one wheel to revolve faster than the opposite wheel during turns
13. device that reduces the noise from combustion sounds in the engine
14. device that generates an electrical current needed to recharge the battery and operate electrical equipment in a vehicle

**List B**

a. radiator
b. differential
c. carburetor
d. belted tire
e. alternator
f. muffler

### Think Critically

Write a paragraph to answer each question.

1. What happens if you fail to perform preventive maintenance on your vehicle?
2. Why is it important to recycle some of the automotive materials used to operate vehicles? How can you go about recycling these materials?

## Decision Making

**1.** When the driver in the car applied his brakes, the car pulled to the right. What might this indicate about the braking system?

**2.** What is wrong with this car? What would you do to correct the problem?

**3.** These two people are attempting to make a jumper cable connection to start a car that has a dead battery. What steps should they take to properly complete the connection? Which vehicle has the dead battery?

**4.** This person is shopping for a new tire. He frequently drives long distances. What guidelines should he use in selecting a replacement tire?

Chapter 17  Maintaining Your Vehicle  **375**

## Answers to Decision Making

**1.** The vehicle pulling to one side while applying the brakes is one indication that something is wrong with the braking system.

**2.** One of the headlights is burned out. Have the burned out headlight replaced as soon as possible.

**3.** The person standing by the vehicle on the right should connect the red-ended cable to the positive battery post on the right vehicle. Then the person standing by the vehicle on the left should connect the black-ended cable in her hands to the negative battery post, or an engine ground on the left vehicle. Once that person has done that, the person standing by the right vehicle should then connect the black-ended cable he is holding to a ground on the right vehicle. The vehicle on the right has the dead battery.

**4.** This person should be looking for the same size and type tire that will match the existing tires on the vehicle. Since he does a lot of interstate driving, he would want to have tires that have a good (higher) temperature and traction rating.

# Chapter 18   Planning Guide

**Student Features**

**Teacher's Edition**

| | Student Features | Teacher's Edition |
|---|---|---|
| **Chapter 18**<br>**Planning Your Travel** | You Are the Driver! *p. 377* | Projects *p. 376*<br>Special Needs *p.377* |
| **18.1  Local Travel** *pp. 378–379*<br>• State two questions you should ask yourself before making a short trip.<br>• Name three things you can do to simplify a short trip. | | Activity *pp. 378, 379* |
| **18.2  Long-Distance Travel** *pp. 380–385*<br>• Describe how to prepare for a long-distance trip.<br>• Tell what techniques you can use to stay alert while driving.<br>• Describe four things you need to be alert for when driving a rental vehicle. | Consumer Tip *p. 382*<br>What Do You Think? *p. 384* | Demonstrate *pp. 380, 381, 383*<br>Activity *pp. 380, 381, 382, 383, 384*<br>Special Needs *p. 382* |
| **18.3  Special Vehicles** *pp. 386–388*<br>• Describe some problems you might have while driving a large vehicle.<br>• Explain some special steps you need to take when pulling a trailer.<br>• Tell how to back a trailer. | | Demonstrate *p. 386*<br>Activity *p. 386* |
| **Assessment** | Reviewing Chapter<br>  Objectives *p. 389*<br>Projects *p. 389*<br>Chapter Test *p. 390*<br>Decision Making *p. 391* | Answers *pp. 390–391* |

**Teacher's Resource File**

**Videos, Overheads, and Software**

**Companion** *pp. 104–105*
**Spanish Handbook** *p. 37*

**Content Overhead 35**

**Resource Book**
Teacher's Instructions, *p. 65*
Information, *p. 76*

**Skills and Applications Workbook**, *pp. 69–72*
**Tests and Activities**
Chapter 18 Activities 18-1 and 18-2, *pp. 151–152*
Chapter 18 Test A and Test B, *pp. 153–156*
Unit 4 Test, *pp. 157–160*
Final Test, *pp. 161–166*

**TestWorks CD-ROM**
Chapter 18 Test

## Technology Resources

For: Chapter 18 online activities
Visit: PHSchool.com
Web Code: cak-9999

# Planning Your Travel

## Chapter Overview

Chapter 18 explains problems and solutions of short- and long-range travel. Students find out what knowledge and skills are needed to plan and execute driving trips. They will learn the basics of map reading, how to plan and pack for a trip, and how to operate recreational vehicles, including pulling a trailer. Alternate ways to travel and some environmental considerations relating to the use of motor vehicles also are presented.

## Chapter Vocabulary

*legend, navigating, safety chain*

376

## Teacher's Resources

For students to use as they read the chapter:

**Companion**
pages 104–105

**Spanish Handbook**
page 37

## Projects

Review the projects described on page 389. Some of the projects can be assigned at any time while others are more closely tied to the content presented in the student text.

# CHAPTER 18
## Planning Your Travel

**18.1** Local Travel

**18.2** Long-Distance Travel

**18.3** Special Vehicles and Trailers

### You Are the Driver!

You are just about to arrive at your campsite to enjoy your family vacation. You have planned your trip thoroughly. You now know that safe, smooth, stress-free travel does not happen by chance. The better your planning and attention to detail, the better the trip.

In this chapter, you will learn how to plan local travel. You'll discover how to make long trips manageable—even though the planning can be complicated. Finally, you will have a chance to learn about special vehicles and trailers and how to drive them safely.

**Go Online**
PHSchool.com
**For:** Chapter 18 online activities
**Visit:** PHSchool.com
**Web Code:** cak-9999

377

### Introducing the Chapter

Ask volunteers to describe driving trips they have taken. Encourage them to share with the class how the trip was planned, what vehicle preparation was included, and any problems that occurred during the trip. Have students suggest ways to avoid the problems mentioned.

### You Are the Driver

Let students suggest and discuss places to which they would like to travel. Encourage them to discuss what kind of planning they think they would need to do for various trips.

# Local Travel

##  Focus

### Summary

This lesson focuses on short trips and how to plan for them. Students are encouraged to ask two questions before each trip. Advanced planning, even for local travel, is emphasized.

##  Teach

### Discuss

Discuss the importance of asking these questions: Is the trip needed? Do I have enough time?

### Discuss

Relate the wear and tear on a cold engine to something students might understand. Compare driving a vehicle that has a cold engine to exercising your body without warming up. Ask students why warming up properly is important before doing strenuous exercise. Then discuss how warming up a vehicle is similar.

### Discuss

Point out the importance of allowing enough time for local trips. Ask students how this relates to their daily lives.

---

## Objectives

1. State two questions you should ask yourself before making a short trip.
2. Name three things you can do to simplify a short trip.

Most of your driving will be short, local trips. Therefore, it is important to plan carefully for local travel. If you do, you will save yourself time, money, and fuel.

### Short Trips

A short trip can be as simple as driving to a neighborhood store. Or it can mean driving to the other side of a large city. In any event, you want to arrive safely and on time. Before you start this kind of trip, ask yourself the following two questions.

### Is This Trip Needed?

Since driving can be costly, you need to ask yourself if the trip is needed. If you can answer "yes," then ask yourself if there is a less expensive, more efficient way to make the trip. Could you use public transportation or share a ride with others? Simply driving around wastes money and fuel!

Another way to save yourself time, money, and fuel is to combine several small trips into one. You will also help yourself by extending the life of your vehicle. Short trips mean you will be driving a vehicle with a cold engine. Driving with a cold engine increases the wear on your vehicle and dramatically increases its fuel use.

### Do I Have Enough Time?

If a trip is needed, will you have enough time for it? To be sure you do, make these smart decisions:

- **Allow Time** No matter how well you plan, if you don't leave on or

**How to Save Fuel**

**Use good driving habits.**

**Turn off engine.** If you are waiting in line for more than one minute, shut off the engine.

**Carry less weight.** Clean out your trunk and interior. Overloaded cars use more fuel.

**Keep engine cool.** Keep radiator filled with coolant. Excess heat increases engine wear and reduces gas mileage.

**SPEED LIMIT 50**

**Slow down.** You use less fuel if you drive at 50 mph instead of 60 mph.

**Close windows.** At high speeds, use air conditioner. At lower speeds, turn off air conditioner and open windows.

378  Unit 4  Being a Responsible Driver

---

## Teacher's Resources

No *Drive Right* resources are needed for teaching Section 18.1.

## Activity

**Class Activity** Ask students to investigate at home how cold temperatures affect oil. Have students place a plastic cup containing a tablespoon of cooking oil into the freezer overnight. Ask students to take note of the consistency of the oil when they remove it from the freezer. Ask them to note the consistency after the oil has been at room temperature for an hour. In class, discuss what the students observed. Point out that warm oil flows between the moving parts of an engine more easily than cold oil. This is necessary for proper lubrication.

ahead of time, you will not reach your destination on time. It is very difficult and often dangerous to try to make up time as you drive. Allow extra time for delays caused by bad weather or heavy traffic.

- **Listen to Weather and Traffic Reports** Local weather and traffic reports are very useful for planning local travel.
- **Choose the Best Travel Time** In many cities, normal rush-hour traffic will test your patience and waste time and fuel. When possible, travel when traffic is light.

### Planning Ahead

Have you ever watched skilled drivers? The reason they make driving look so smooth is that they think ahead. Following are three key ways you can make your travel smooth and stress free.

**Vehicle Preparation** Running out of windshield-washer fluid, driving on an underinflated tire, or having a turn-signal light fail might not sound like a big problem. However, each of these small problems could trigger a collision.

Be alert when you approach your vehicle. Before you drive, check your vehicle's tires, lights, and controls. If you detect the slightest problem, fix it before it becomes a bigger problem.

Each time you fill your vehicle's fuel tank, make a routine check of your oil, water, and windshield fluid levels. By following the points in the picture to the left, you can save fuel on every trip.

You can help plan the route as a passenger.

**Route Selection** Consider the travel time and the possible hazards when you select a route. In many cities, it is easier to drive a few more miles to take interstate expressways than it is to take local roads. You can save time and eliminate potential hazards by avoiding uncontrolled intersections and heavy traffic.

**Know Your Route and Addresses** Have you ever really been lost? It can be frightening, perhaps even dangerous. You can usually avoid this by planning your route ahead of time. Write down directions and have a map. If you have a passenger, let that person help to identify street names, directions, and addresses.

> ### Review It
> 1. What two questions should you answer before starting a short trip?
> 2. What three things can you do to simplify a short trip?

## Discuss

Ask students to offer their thoughts about why some individuals do not like to ask for directions when they are lost.

## Discuss

Have students describe how they, as passengers, have helped the driver. They might list map reading, helping to manage others in the car, and alerting the driver to possible conflicts ahead.

### 3 Assess

## Answers to Review It

1. The two questions a driver should answer before driving are: (1) Is this trip needed? and (2) Do I have enough time? (p. 378).
2. Before leaving on a short trip, you should (1) check your vehicle, (2) select your route, and (3) know streets and addresses. (p. 379)

## Activity

**Class Activity** This activity will help students see the value of planning ahead for trips. Plan two scavenger hunts for items located in your classroom. The first involves having students find five items one at a time with students returning to their desks between items. The second involves having students find all five items before returning to their desks. You will need to time both scavenger hunts. Ask students to compare the times and walking distances for the two scavenger hunts.

## Activity

**Small Group Activity** This activity will help students learn how to plan for a trip to prevent getting lost and to determine the best way to cope with being lost. Have students form into groups of four. Tell them that they are going to visit a friend in a nearby town or suburb for the first time. Have groups plan how they would prepare the vehicle, select a route, and find address directions so they will not get lost. Ask them to list what actions they would take if they did become lost. After adequate time, have the groups discuss their plans.

# Long-Distance Travel

## ① Focus

## Summary

This lesson focuses on long trips and how to plan for them. Topics presented include map reading, using the Internet to plan a trip, Global Positioning System, advance preparation, special equipment, and vehicle load. Rental vehicles also are discussed.

## Vocabulary

*legend, navigating*

## ② Teach

## Demonstrate

Use **Content Overhead 35** to demonstrate the various elements included in the legend of a typical map. Have students find an example of each legend element on the map on page 381.

## Apply

Have students identify the legend and legend elements using individual maps from a road atlas.

### Objectives

1. Describe how to prepare for a long-distance trip.
2. Tell what techniques you can use to stay alert while driving.
3. Describe four things you need to be alert for when driving a rental vehicle.

A well-planned trip can be a satisfying, memorable experience. There are many tools available to help you plan the details of your trip in advance.

### Maps and Tour Books

The basic trip-planning tool is a road map. Maps are available at service stations, auto clubs, bookstores, and chambers of commerce. Make sure the map is the most current one available.

Good maps include a **legend** that explains the markings and symbols used on the map. For example, major highways and secondary roads are usually printed in different colors. Generally, major highways will allow you to reach your destination more quickly and directly. Travel on secondary roads might take more time, but it may allow you to visit interesting places along the way.

Another valuable trip-planning tool is a tour book. Tour books are published by auto clubs and other publishers. The books list hotels, motels, inns, restaurants, and popular places of interest, organized by city or town. By using a map in combination with a tour book, you can plan how many miles you will drive each day, what sites you will see, and where you will eat and sleep.

### Internet Trip Planning

There are many Web sites that provide free trip-planning services. Some of the most useful services are sites that provide maps and directions from your starting point to your destination. These Web sites allow you to enter the address of where you are starting and where you wish to go. The software powering the Web site then maps out a route for your trip and provides step-by-step directions. You can print out the route map and directions and quickly be on your way. There are also trip-planning software packages that you can install on your computer that provide similar features.

When using Internet route-planning services or software, keep in mind that they don't always identify the most efficient routes and directions. It's always a good idea to confirm the directions on a road map or with a person who is familiar with the route.

In addition to route planning, the Internet can provide other information to help you plan your trip. You can learn more about your destination, make reservations, check the local weather forecast, and read reviews about attractions, hotels, and restaurants written by people who have used those services.

## Teacher's Resources

**Content Overheads**
Overhead 35

## Activity

**Small Group Activity**  Divide the class into groups of four students. Provide a map of your community and a telephone directory to each group. Give each group a list of places to locate on their maps. Include familiar and unusual places. Have the groups calculate the distance from school to each place they locate.

### Map Legend

**Roads and Related Symbols**

| | |
|---|---|
| ———— | Free Limited Access Highways |
| - - - - | Under Construction |
| ———— | Toll Limited-Access Highways |
| - - - - | Under Construction |
| ———— | Other Four-Lane Divided Highways |
| ———— | Principal Highways |
| ———— | Other Through Highways |
| 90 190 80 90 | Interstate Highways |
| ALT 17 183 18 | U.S. Highways |
| 8 18 14 13 | State and Provincial Highways |

Miles (red) between arrows
One mile or less not shown

Interchanges and Numbers
(For most states, mileages between
interchanges may be determined by
subtracting one number from the other)

**Cities and Towns**

| | |
|---|---|
| ▨▨▨ | Urbanized Areas |
| ▰▰▰▰ | Separate cities within metro area |
| ⊛ ★ | National Capital; State Capital |
| ● ● ○ | Cities, Towns and Recognized Places; County Seats; Neighborhoods (Size of type indicates relative population) |

A map's legend explains the map's markings and symbols.

---

### Virginia

**Population:** 6,216,568 (1990 Census)
**Land Area:** 39,598 sq. mi.
**Capital:** Richmond

**Cities and Towns**

Abingdon ..................................1-4
Accomac...............................G-13
Alexandria............................D-11
Altavista ...............................H-8
Amherst................................G-8
Appalachia............................H-2
Appomattox...........................G-8
Arlington...............................D-11
Ashland................................G-10
Bassett ...................................1-7
Bedford .................................H-7
Berryville..............................D-10
Big Stone Gap .......................H-2
Blacksburg............................H-6
Blackstone ...........................H-10
Bluefield...............................H-5
Bowling Green .......................F-11
Boydton ................................I-9
Bristol ....................................1-3
Broadway ..............................E-8
Brookneal .............................H-8
Buchanan ..............................G-7
Buckingham...........................G-9
Buena Vista ...........................G-8
Cape Charles........................H-13
Cedar Bluff............................H-4
Centreville............................D-10
Charlotte Court House ............H-9
Charlottesville.........................F-9
Chase City.............................I-9
Chatham................................I-8
Chesapeake..........................H-12
Chincoteague.........................F-14
Christiansburg........................H-6
Clarksville.............................I-9
Clifton Forge..........................G-7
Clintwood..............................H-3
Coeburn................................H-3
Colonial Beach.......................F-11
Colonial Heights....................H-11
Covington...............................G-7
Crewe ...................................H-9
Culpeper...............................E-10
Cumberland...........................G-9
Danville.................................I-8
Dublin...................................H-6
Elkton ...................................E-9
Emporia................................I-10
Exmore .................................G-13
Fairfax ..................................D-11
Falls Church..........................D-11
Falmouth...............................E-10
Farmville...............................H-9
Floyd ....................................H-6
Franklin.................................I-11
Fredericksburg ......................F-10
Front Royal............................D-9
Galax ....................................1-5
Gate City...............................I-3
Gloucester............................G-12
Goochland.............................G-10
Gordonsville..........................F-9
Gretna...................................H-8
Grottoes................................F-8
Grundy..................................H-3
Halifax ..................................I-8
Hampton...............................H-12
Harrisonburg..........................E-8
Hillsville................................I-6
Hopewell...............................H-11
Independence ........................1-5
Jarratt...................................1-11
Kenbridge .............................H-9
Lawrenceville.........................1-10
Lebanon................................H-3
Leesburg...............................D-10
Lexington ..............................G-7

---

## Explain

Stress that map reading is a form of literacy vital to operating in today's society. With this ability and the right maps, a person can go almost anywhere.

## Demonstrate

Have students follow along on the map as you explain how to use the map's index and coordinates to locate these Virginia towns and cities: Bowling Green, Exmore, and Hopewell. Then have students use the map scale to estimate the distance between Accomac and Exmore (about 16 miles or 25 kilometers).

---

## Activity

**Small Group Activity** This activity will help students develop map-reading skills. Divide the class into groups of three. Have each group plan a round trip from Wilmington, Delaware, to Williamsburg, Virginia. Between Wilmington and Williamsburg they should plan to use the most direct route. On the return, they should use a different route. Have the groups calculate the mileage for both legs of their trip.

## Cross Curricular

**Geography** Have students work in groups of three or four and use a road map or atlas to plan a driving route between their home and a national park located in another state. If possible, have them use a highlighter to mark their planned route on the map(s). Have the students write a brief description of the planned trip, including the major cities along the way and the type of roads on which they would travel. Students should calculate the mileage and estimate how long it would take to get to their destination.

## Explain

Explain to students that the fuel gauge is not a precision instrument. When the gauge indicates the tank is half full, it might not be exactly half full. For example, if you have a 10-gallon fuel tank, you might have 5 gallons, but you might have 4 or 6 gallons. It is also important to note that you cannot depend on getting the same mileage from the last third of the tank as you did from the first third. The last third usually drops more rapidly than the first third. It is a good idea to fill up when the gauge indicates that you have no less than one-third of a tank of fuel.

## Explain

Remind students to pull completely off of the road in an emergency. You should be 10 feet off the paved lanes if possible.

GPS receivers can provide detailed driving directions to your destination.

**CONSUMER**

There are numerous styles and manufacturers of GPS receivers. Before making a purchase, be sure to compare features, warrantees, and prices. In addition, there are Internet resources where you can read reviews and opinions from other consumers. These reviews can help you make an informed decision.

### Global Positioning System (GPS)

Since 1994 there has been a network of navigation satellites orbiting Earth. This network of satellites is called the *Global Positioning System*. Originally launched by the military, this navigation network is now available to the general public.

The satellites transmit radio signals that can be received by devices called GPS receivers. Each GPS receiver is capable of using those radio signals to calculate its exact position on, or above, Earth's surface. Once the current position is calculated, the GPS receiver can then map out a route to the intended destination. GPS devices are available for automobiles, boats, and airplanes. There are even handheld devices ideal for hikers.

Some vehicles come equipped with factory-installed GPS receivers. Receivers can also be purchased as an accessory and installed in just about any vehicle.

GPS-equipped vehicles enable the driver to input a destination and

receive real-time directions based on the vehicle's actual location at any point in time. If you make a wrong turn, or a detour appears unexpectedly, the GPS device automatically calculates a new route to your intended destination.

### Preparing Your Vehicle

An important part of trip planning is making sure your vehicle is serviced before you take a long trip. Let the service technician know you will be driving a long distance. This can reduce the risk of service problems while traveling.

Here are the basic systems you should have checked:

- **Brake System** Make sure all parts are in good working order.
- **Exhaust System** There must be no leaks in this system.
- **Steering System** Wheels should be aligned. Shock absorbers should be ready for heavy loads. Tires should have ample tread and be properly inflated. Do not forget to check your spare tire and carry a tire gauge for on-road checks.
- **Engine Systems** All fluids, belts, and hoses need to be ready for heavy use. The engine should be tuned. Air-conditioning coolant also should be checked.

### Special Equipment

Long-distance travel requires that you pack special equipment for use in emergencies or severe weather. This is equipment you may not normally carry.

382  Unit 4  Being a Responsible Driver

### Activity

**In-Class Activity** This activity will help students understand and relate to maps by using streets and addresses around the school. Create a map on the board or overhead projector using the streets in each direction from the school. Ask students to identify buildings and points of interest and place them on the map.

### Special Needs

Have students create a three-dimensional map of the area around your school. Have them use school supplies and household items to represent buildings and points of interest. Have them create a legend.

### Emergency Equipment

For emergency situations, you should consider packing the following items:

- cellular phone or CB radio to call for help (if available)
- containers of the right oil for your vehicle, antifreeze, and windshield-washer fluid
- A-B-C type fire extinguisher
- first-aid kit
- flashlight
- jumper cables
- spare fuses
- basic tools like an adjustable wrench, screwdriver, and pliers
- flares or reflectors

### Winter Gear

If traveling in remote or mountain areas in winter weather, you will want to pack these additional items:

- blankets and additional warm clothing including gloves
- sleeping bags
- tire chains and/or snow tires
- high-energy food such as granola bars, nuts, and dried fruit
- window scraper and snow brush
- shovel
- tow line
- sand for extra traction

### Personal Preparation

To complete your planning for the trip, make sure you have packed the following items:

- a variety of coins for tolls
- all maps and travel guides
- a spare set of vehicle keys
- all necessary medications
- telephone numbers for motor club, road emergencies, and anticipated stops

- traveler's checks, credit cards, and phone calling cards

Finally, set lights in your home on timers and stop regular deliveries. It is also a good idea to let a neighbor know when you are leaving, where you plan to be, and when you will return.

### Vehicle Load

The best rule to keep in mind when traveling is to travel light. Added weight will increase your fuel consumption and affect the way your vehicle handles. If you do travel with a full load, follow these steps:

- Use the highest tire pressure listed in your owner's manual. However, do not overinflate the tires.
- Load the heaviest items on the bottom forward part of your trunk, if you are traveling in a car.
- Keep loose items in the trunk of your car.

Tire chains can make the difference in bad weather.

## Demonstrate

Use items from the driver education car or your own vehicle to illustrate the emergency equipment outlined on this page. Drivers should consider keeping some of these items in their vehicle at all times—fire extinguisher, first aid kit, flashlight, jumper cables, and flares or reflectors.

## Discuss

Winter gear is important for long-distance travel, but it can also be helpful for short trips. Ask: How might you use the items on the list when taking a short trip? Encourage students to share experiences where these items were used or where they could have been used.

## Explain

Remind students that vehicle load increases your braking distance (as explained in Chapter 5).

### Activity

**Small Group Activity** After groups have completed the Cross Curricular activity on page 381, have them formulate a trip plan. Instruct students to use the questions listed in the textbook on page 382 as a guide. Have them make a list of what emergency equipment, possible winter gear, and personal preparations are needed. After adequate time, have groups compare plans.

## Explain

Point out the list of things a driver can do to stay alert. Remind students that it is important to look to the sides often to reduce eye fatigue. Explain that talking with passengers, not just listening, also helps the driver stay alert. If you are traveling with more than one passenger, ask the passengers to take turns staying awake.

## Discuss

Ask: How do you know when you are getting drowsy? What are the physical symptoms? Point out the importance of knowing your personal reactions to fatigue. When you recognize the symptoms, you know that it is time to find a safe place to pull over and rest.

## Explain

When a driver begins to feel drowsy, the eyes will become lazy. Explain that a person can have a built-in technique to serve as a cue when fatigue is setting in. One technique is to become sensitive to when there is internal resistance to making mirror checks. When it gets to the point that a driver is straining to move the eyes for a mirror check, it is time to find a safe place to pull over.

## Discuss

Ask students the *What Do You Think?* question: Why do you think teen drivers are at higher risk when driving at night? (Have discussion include lack of sleep, drinking alcohol, reduced visibility, and inexperience for new drivers.)

### What Do You Think?

Statistics show that teens have more collisions per mile at night than older drivers. Why do you think teen drivers are at higher risk when driving at night?

### Enjoying Your Travel

Over the years, experienced long-distance travelers have learned the subtle secrets that make traveling long distances enjoyable. Here are some tips that will help you enjoy your travel more.

**Share Navigation** Following a route by reading a map is called **navigating.** When you share driving, have your passenger navigate. Make sure you give each other directions well in advance. If you are alone, pull over to read maps, make calls, or ask directions at a service station.

**Stay Alert** Drowsy drivers are the cause of a great many collisions and near-misses. To stay alert, use a regular routine that includes the following:

- Drive only during the hours you are normally awake. Do not try to drive through the night. Avoid night driving when possible.
- Take regular breaks every two hours or so. Rotate drivers and get out of the vehicle to stretch.
- Keep fresh air circulating in the vehicle at all times.
- Drive with headlights on at all times, as shown here. This assures that you will always "see and be seen."
- Eat light.
- Maintain your focus on driving. Concentrate in heavy traffic or confusing situations.
- If your eyes are heavy and your concentration is not good, it is time to stop and rest.

### Rental Vehicles

Many of your trips will be a combination of flying and driving. You will fly to your destination, and then rent a vehicle for transportation as shown on the opposite page. Use the same rules you would when shopping for any service as you look for a rental vehicle.

Decide these points before you rent a vehicle:

- What size and type of vehicle do you want? Compare prices.
- How long do you need it? A weekly rental may be cheaper than a daily rental.
- Will it be a round-trip or one-way rental? One-way rentals usually cost more.

Daytime headlight use makes for safer driving, especially with other drowsy drivers.

### Activity

**Small Group Activity** Form the class into groups of four or five. Have students discuss situations that may lead to one becoming a drowsy driver. Then, have them formulate techniques that can be used to minimize or eliminate the drowsy condition.

- How will you handle insurance? Your regular home, vehicle, or credit card insurance policy may provide part of the needed coverage.
- Will you fill the gas tank on return, or will you buy a full tank of gas with your rental agreement?
- Don't forget to bring a child seat if needed.

Also be aware that most companies will not rent a vehicle to individuals under age 21, and sometimes 25. But young drivers usually can become part of a rental plan for an added daily fee.

Rental companies can provide a range of services for customers. They will advise you on local laws and requirements, provide maps and directions, and give you the channel numbers of local radio stations that carry traffic reports. In addition, you should stick to these basics:

- Orient yourself to your vehicle before you drive out. Know where controls and devices are ahead of time. Make sure the jack and spare tire are in good shape. When driving in a strange area, keep your windows up and your doors locked.
- If you are bumped by another vehicle or asked to stop for advice or assistance, *don't stop*. Instead, drive to the nearest well-lit service area and ask for police assistance. If necessary, use your hazard flashers to signal a need for help.

Get oriented to your rental vehicle before you begin driving.

- Know the rental company's toll-free service number in case you need help with the vehicle.
- Store all valuables out of sight in the trunk or glove compartment. At night, take valuables with you.
- Park only in well-lit, secure areas.

## Review It

1. How should you prepare in advance for a long-distance trip?
2. What steps can you take to stay alert while driving?
3. Name four things you should keep in mind when driving a rental vehicle.

## Discuss

Ask: What information provided on this page applies to all driving situations, not just when you are renting a vehicle?

 **Assess**

### Answers to Review It

**1.** To prepare for a long-distance trip, you can (1) check routes and lodging, (2) check your vehicle, (3) make sure you have emergency and winter driving equipment as needed, and (4) take steps to secure your home. (p. 382)

**2.** To stay alert while driving, drive normal daytime hours, take breaks at two-hour intervals, keep fresh air circulating, use headlights, eat light, and work at staying focused. (p. 384)

**3.** When driving a rental vehicle, orient yourself to the vehicle before driving, be prepared to ask for police assistance if harassed, know the company's service number, store all valuables out of sight, and park in well-lit areas. (pp. 384–385)

## Background

**Electronic Features** As electronics advance, new features appear on vehicles. You can now buy or rent some vehicles that will automatically dial a 911 emergency number in a collision or notify an emergency operator in the event of air bag deployment. Some new vehicles have map-reading systems. With some systems, you can use a remote control to lock your car or turn off the motor. Some systems can even help police locate your car if it's stolen.

Chapter 18
Planning Your Travel | **385**

# Special Vehicles

## 1 Focus

## Summary

This lesson presents information about driving recreational vehicles, rental trucks, and pulling a trailer.

## Vocabulary

**New:** *safety chains*

**Review:** *recreational vehicle*

## 2 Teach

## Explain

Having someone act as a backing guide can be very helpful to the driver of a large vehicle. However, anyone acting as a backing guide should use the following precautions. The guide should never stand directly to the rear of the vehicle. The driver should always keep the guide in sight in the vehicle's mirrors. Establish a clear form of communication between driver and guide. See **Resource Book,** p. 65 for more information.

## Demonstrate

Arrange for students to sit in the driver's seat of a large vehicle such as a panel truck or recreational vehicle. Have other students stand outside the vehicle in various locations to illustrate what you can and cannot see in the mirrors.

## Objectives

1. Describe some problems you might have while driving a large vehicle.
2. Explain some special steps you need to take when pulling a trailer.
3. Tell how to back a trailer.

Driving a recreational vehicle, using a rental truck, or pulling a trailer are three other ways you can travel. You will have to use additional precautions when driving these vehicles or pulling a trailer.

### Large Vehicles

A vehicle used primarily for vacations and travel is called a *recreational vehicle.* A camper on a pickup truck or a large motor home are both examples of recreational vehicles.

Rental trucks are another type of large vehicle you might use. When renting one of these trucks, be aware that special insurance protection is needed.

As you drive large vehicles, you need to be alert to the following special performance aspects.

**Seeing** The minute you get behind the wheel of a large vehicle, you will see how difficult it is to get a full view of the driving scene. Your forward field of vision is open and easy to see. But your view to the sides and rear is severely limited. In short, your ability to use the IPDE Process to the front is better, but your ability to turn and back is restricted.

Look at the illustrations below. Notice how far ahead you can see over the tops of cars. Notice how hard it is to see to the rear left. It is just as difficult to see to the right and center rear. You can see how important it is for other drivers to give a large vehicle extra room to maneuver.

**Backing** Whenever possible, avoid backing. Instead, drive around the block or turn around in a large, open parking lot. When backing, get another person to stand beside and behind your vehicle to guide you.

Drivers of large vehicles can see more ahead but less to the rear.

## Teacher's Resources

**Resource Book**
Teacher's Instructions, page 65
Information, page 76

## Activity

**Small Group Activity** Use the activity from **Resource Book** page 76 to have students learn how to discover reference points to accurately judge the fender clearance of a large vehicle.

**You Are the Driver!**
If you were driving this rental truck, how would you handle the situation?

**Maneuvering** Because your vehicle is large and heavy, it will not maneuver like a car. It will take longer to accelerate, brake, and turn.

**Crosswinds** The size of your vehicle will make it more difficult to control in high winds. If you encounter windy conditions of more than 30 mph, slow down or stop. Anticipate driving difficulty, and be ready to correct your steering. Under extremely windy conditions, some bridges or expressways may close temporarily.

**Remember Your Size** Hitting an overhead object like a roof at a drive-through restaurant is one of the most frequent collisions experienced. You must remember your large size when you project your path of travel, like the driver in the picture is doing.

**Following Distance** Because large vehicles are heavy, *your following distance must be four or more seconds.* This distance will allow more time for you to use the IPDE Process.

**Fatigue** It takes more effort to drive a large vehicle than a car. The ride can be rough and noisy. Plus, if driving a large vehicle is a new

experience, it will require more concentration over a longer period of time. Plan frequent rest stops and change drivers when possible.

### Trailers

Pulling a trailer will put an additional strain on your car. When pulling a trailer, you can count on

- doubling the time and space you need to accelerate, slow, and turn
- cutting your fuel economy almost in half

**Making Sure You're Set** Make these checks before pulling a trailer:

- Check your vehicle owner's manual to see how much weight you can tow.
- Check all fluids. Check your coolant level daily.
- Make sure all filters are clean.
- Inflate your rear tires to their maximum recommended level.
- Double-check all vehicle and trailer lights.
- Check your owner's manual to see if any special equipment is recommended.

**Special Equipment** To pull a trailer safely, you will need the appropriate size and strength trailer hitch, safety

Make sure safety chains are in place before moving.

Chapter 18  Planning Your Travel  **387**

## Explain

When driving a large profile vehicle during windy conditions, anticipate that crosswinds will be greatest when the terrain changes. For example, in the area where a large hill flattens out, a driver should expect an increase in the crosswind. This is a result of the wind being funneled around the hill. A driver should focus on the target area to be prepared for correcting the steering deviations.

## Discuss

Draw students' attention to the *You Are the Driver!* photograph. Ask: If you were driving this rental truck how would you handle the situation? Encourage discussion. Make sure that students understand that the best plan might be to park out in the lot and walk in.

## Explain

When driving a large vehicle that is rented or that you do not drive regularly, write the vehicle's height on a small, bright-colored card. Tape the card to the top of the windshield or on the dashboard to remind you of the vehicle's height when overhead clearance is low.

## Explain

When driving a large vehicle, you should use the slow lane or truck lane. Remember that your vehicle creates a line-of-sight restriction for others. Plan on longer travel times to your destination because of slower speeds and special speed limits in some states.

## Explain

You can create a simple early-detection system to identify a flat tire or a hitch problem when towing a trailer. With the trailer properly hitched, have a friend draw a circle on the front of the trailer in a location that you can see in your rearview mirror. While you are still looking in the mirror, have your friend place a dot on the rear window of your vehicle so that it appears inside the circle on the trailer. The dot will remain inside the circle when the trailer is properly hitched and all tires are correctly inflated. If the trailer loses tire pressure or there is a hitch problem, the dot will move out of the circle.

## Explain

Explain that there is an easy way to avoid becoming confused as to which way to turn the steering wheel while backing a trailer. When the driver holds his or her hand at the bottom of the steering wheel, the wheel is turned in the direction he or she wants the trailer to travel.

## 3 Assess

### Answers to Review It

**1.** Students should list from the special conditions listed on pages 386–387.

**2.** Students should list from the steps highlighted on page 388.

**3.** See illustration and instructions for backing a trailer on page 388.

As you start to back to the left, turn the wheel clockwise.

As you start to back to the right, turn the wheel counterclockwise.

Take it slow and easy while backing a trailer.

chains, and extended mirrors on both sides of your vehicle. **Safety chains,** as shown in the picture on page 387, provide a backup link to your vehicle in case the hitch fails.

**Load** Check these points when loading your trailer:

- Place heavy items low over the trailer's axle.
- If your load is more than 1,000 pounds, you should get a trailer equipped with special brakes.
- Make sure that about 10 percent of the trailer's loaded weight is on the trailer's hitch.
- Secure the load with ropes.

### Towing Techniques

When towing a trailer, remember, it will take you about twice as long to pass, stop, accelerate, and turn. Follow these rules when towing a trailer:

- Use a following distance of four or more seconds.
- Travel at the posted speed limit.

- Make turns slow and wide.
- If your trailer starts to sway or "fishtail," steer straight down the center of your lane, and let off the accelerator. Once the trailer stops swaying, use all brakes carefully.
- Allow twice as much distance to pass or stop.
- Shift to a lower gear before going up or down a steep hill.
- Be ready to slow or correct steering for crosswinds created by other vehicles.
- *Never carry passengers in a trailer.*
- If your vehicle overheats, turn off your air conditioner and turn on your heater.

**Backing** Look at the picture above to get an idea of what it's like to back a trailer. To back left, turn the wheel clockwise with your left hand. Turn the wheel counterclockwise to start your trailer backing right. Back slowly and make small steering corrections. If you cannot see out the back window, use your right and left mirrors. Always have a person outside your vehicle to help guide you.

### Review It
1. What are three potential problems you might have while driving a large vehicle?
2. What steps should you follow when towing a trailer?
3. What procedure should you use when backing a trailer?

## Reviewing Chapter Objectives

### 1. Local Travel
1. What two questions should you ask yourself before making a short trip? (378)
2. What three things can you do to simplify a short trip? (379)

### 2. Long-Distance Travel
3. What can you do to prepare for a long-distance trip? (380–382)
4. What techniques can you use to stay alert while driving? (384)
5. What four things should you be alert for when driving a rental vehicle? (384)

### 3. Special Vehicles
6. What potential problems might you have while driving a large vehicle? (386)
7. What special steps should you take when pulling a trailer? (387–388)
8. How do you back a trailer? (388)

## Projects

### Individuals

**Observe** Count the number of short vehicle trips all the drivers in your family make during a one-week period. Note which trips are necessary and which are optional. For the optional trips, list other ways in which the goal of the trip could have been accomplished.

**Demonstrate** Choose an out-of-state attraction at least 500 miles away from your school (theme park, national park, museum, etc.) Using a map and other travel information, determine the best way to reach this destination. Make a presentation to your class about how you would arrive at the destination. Include facts such as how many miles away it is, how much time it would take, and where you would stay overnight.

### Groups

**Use Technology** Choose a destination at least 500 miles from your school. Each group member should use a different Internet search engine to find information about this destination. Write a group report that combines all the information found.

**Practice** Choose a destination within 20 to 40 miles of your school. Each group member should individually plan a route to this destination. Compare the routes. Which routes are quickest, easiest, and safest? (These will not necessarily be the same.)

Chapter 18 Planning Your Travel **389**

## Reviewing Chapter Objectives

**18.1** Local Travel
See Answers to Review It on page 379.
**18.2** Long-Distance Travel
See Answers to Review It on page 385.
**18.3** Special Vehicles
See Answers to Review It on page 388.

## Projects

Some of the projects can be assigned at any time while others are more closely tied to the content presented in the student text. The page number where the topic is introduced is indicated.

    **Observe:** p. 378
    **Demonstrate:** p. 380
    **Use Technology:** p. 380
    **Practice:** p. 378
The results of student projects will vary.

## Teacher's Resources

**Skills and Applications Workbook**
pages 69–72

**Tests and Activities**
Chapter 18 Activities 18-1 and 18-2
pages 151–152
Chapter 18 Test A and Test B
pages 153–156

**TestWorks CD-ROM**
Chapter 18 Test

## Answers to Check Your Knowledge

1. d
2. b
3. c
4. a
5. route
6. GPS receiver
7. twice
8. recreational vehicle

## Answers to Review Vocabulary

9. safety chain (b)
10. legend (c)
11. navigating (a)

## Answers to Think Critically

Students' answers will vary. For information related to the question refer to the page(s) indicated.

1. With short trips you will be driving with a cold engine, which increases the wear on your vehicle and increases fuel use. (pp. 378–379)

2. Students' answers will vary but should include the steps listed on pp. 380–384.

3. When driving a large vehicle, your view of the roadway to the sides and rear is limited. It is more difficult to back, maneuver, and steer in wind. It also takes more effort and concentration to drive a large vehicle. (pp. 386–387)

## Chapter Test

### Check Your Knowledge

**Multiple Choice** Copy the number of each sentence below on a sheet of paper. Choose the letter of the answer that best completes the statement or answers the question.

1. Driving with a cold engine
   (a) occurs on short trips.
   (b) increases the wear on your vehicle.
   (c) increases fuel use.
   (d) all of the above
2. Routes mapped out by Web sites or software should always be
   (a) reliable.　　　(c) ignored.
   (b) confirmed.　　(d) inaccurate.
3. For trips in winter weather, carry extra equipment, including
   (a) a complete set of tools.
   (b) flares or reflectors.
   (c) sand for extra traction.
   (d) a flashlight.
4. When driving a recreational vehicle, your blind spots are usually
   (a) larger than with a car.
   (b) only affected at night.
   (c) the same as with a car.
   (d) lower than with a car.

**Completion** Copy the number of each sentence below. After each number, write the word or words that complete the sentence correctly.

5. To avoid getting lost, plan your _____ ahead of time.
6. A _____ reads signals from navigation satellites.
7. When towing a trailer, it will take about _____ as long to pass, stop, or turn.
8. A large vehicle used primarily for vacations and travel is called a _____.

### Review Vocabulary

Copy the number of each definition in list A. Match the definition in list A with the term it defines in list B.

**List A**
9. backup link used in case a trailer hitch fails
10. chart that explains the markings and symbols on a map
11. following a route by reading a map

**List B**
a. navigating
b. safety chain
c. legend

### Think Critically

Write a paragraph to answer each question.

1. Why is it important to have a good reason for every short trip you make in your vehicle?
2. You are planning a ski trip in January with your friends. You will be driving your family's six-month-old sport utility vehicle. What should you do in advance to be prepared for the trip and for any emergencies that might occur?
3. Why is driving a large vehicle more difficult than driving a smaller vehicle?

## Decision Making

**1.** What can you do to find out weather and traffic conditions before you begin a trip?

**2.** What main route would you take to go from Seattle to Redmond? What other routes are available?

**3.** What should you know about your rental car before driving it?

**4.** If you were pulling a trailer on this road and the trailer began to fishtail, what actions would you take?

## Answers to Decision Making

**1.** To find out about weather and traffic conditions before you travel, you can listen to a news report on radio or television. For long trips you can also gather travel information from the Internet.

**2.** You can take State Highway 520 East to State Highway 202 to Redmond. You can also take Interstate 90 East to State Highway 202 North to Redmond.

**3.** See list of pointers about rental cars on page 384.

**4.** If the trailer begins to fishtail, steer straight down the center of your lane.

Chapter 18 Planning Your Travel **391**

**acceleration lane** lane that permits drivers entering an expressway to accelerate to the speed of expressway traffic (225)

**accelerator pedal** controls the flow of fuel to the engine and regulates speed (43)

**active restraint device** restraint device that you have to engage (100)

**advisory speed limit** speed limit set for special conditions such as sharp curves (22)

**alternator** device that generates an electrical current needed to recharge the battery and operate electrical equipment in a vehicle (357)

**alternator warning light** light or gauge on the instrument panel warning that the battery is being drained (41)

**angle parking** parking the vehicle diagonally to the curb (120)

**antilock braking system (ABS)** computer-controlled braking system that keeps the wheels from locking if the driver brakes hard (41)

**assigned-risk insurance** provides minimum bodily injury and property damage liability coverage to high-risk drivers for a higher premium (346)

**backup lights** white lights at the rear of the vehicle that tell other drivers you are backing up (81)

**banked curve** curve higher on the outside than it is on the inside that helps overcome a vehicle's tendency to move to the outside of the curve (97)

**basic speed law** law stating that you may not drive faster than is safe and prudent for existing conditions, regardless of posted speed limits (22)

**belted tire** tire that has special layers added to a bias-ply tire for improved strength, performance, and mileage (365)

**blind-spot area** area that rearview mirrors cannot show (44)

**blood-alcohol concentration (BAC)** amount of alcohol in the blood expressed as a percentage of alcohol in the bloodstream (318)

**blowout** sudden loss of tire air pressure while driving (95, 268)

**blue-book price** average market value for a specific model and age of a used vehicle (339)

**bodily-injury insurance** covers the driver who is at fault against claims (342)

**brake fade** loss of braking effectiveness caused by the brakes overheating after long, continuous, hard braking (270)

**braking distance** distance your vehicle travels from the time you apply the brake until your vehicle stops (99)

**car pooling** several individuals sharing transportation to one or more destinations in a car (349)

**carbon monoxide** colorless, odorless, tasteless gas contained in the exhaust fumes of gasoline engines (261)

**carburetor** engine part that mixes air and gasoline in the proper proportion and sends it as a fine mist to the engine cylinders (361)

**catalytic converter** part of a vehicle's emission system that converts harmful gases into less harmful gases and water (361)

**center of gravity** point around which an object's weight is evenly distributed (92)

**central vision** cone-shaped area of up to 10 degrees in your field of vision in which you can see clearly while looking straight ahead (68)

**closed zone** space not open to you because of a restriction in your line of sight or intended path of travel (66)

**clutch pedal** pedal in a manual transmission vehicle that enables a driver to shift gears (43)

**collision** contact between two or more objects, as when two vehicles collide into each other (9)

**collision insurance** provides coverage to pay the costs of repair or replacement of your vehicle from a collision (344)

**color-blindness** inability to distinguish colors (298)

**commentary driving** system of thinking out loud as you practice the IPDE Process (83)

**common speed** speed used by most drivers on an expressway (231)

**comprehensive insurance** provides coverage for replacement or repair of your vehicle from damage other than from a collision (344)

**compromise space** reduce risk by giving as much space as possible to the greater of two or more hazards (79)

**console** compartment mounted between the front seats in a vehicle (42)

**controlled-access highway** highway that vehicles can enter and exit only at interchanges (222)

**controlled braking** reducing speed as quickly as possible while maintaining steering control of your vehicle (258)

**controlled intersection** intersection at which traffic signals or signs determine the right of way (134)

**controlled railroad crossing** railroad crossing controlled by flashing red lights and/or crossing gates (138)

**countersteer** steer in the opposite direction (277)

**cover the brake** take your foot off the accelerator and hold it over the brake pedal to be ready to brake quickly (184)

**crossbuck** large white X-shaped sign located beside an uncontrolled railroad crossing (141)

**cruise control** device that lets you maintain your desired speed without keeping your foot on the accelerator (42)

**deceleration lane** expressway lane used to slow your vehicle without blocking vehicles behind you (235)

**decide** third step of the IPDE Process in which the driver selects the best actions as well as when and where to take them to avoid conflicts (6)

**deductible** amount an insurance policyholder agrees to pay toward vehicle repair or replacement (344)

**defensive driving** protecting yourself and others from dangerous and unexpected driving situations (7)

**delayed green light** indicates that one side of an intersection has a green light while the light for the oncoming traffic remains red (137)

**depreciation** decrease in the value of a vehicle over time (336)

**depressant** drug that can slow down the central nervous system (321)

**depth perception** ability to judge distance between yourself and other objects (300)

**designated driver** person who decides ahead of time not to drink alcoholic beverages and is appointed to drive others who do drink (320)

**differential** arrangement of gears at the rear of the vehicle allowing one wheel to revolve faster than the opposite wheel during turns (356)

**downshifting** shifting from a higher to a lower gear (56)

**drive shaft** in rear-wheel vehicles, long metal tube turned by the transmission that carries power to the differential (356)

**driving task** all social, physical, and mental skills required to drive (6)

**driving under the influence (DUI)** an offense for which a driver can be charged in some states if the driver's blood-alcohol concentration is above 0.05 (323)

**driving while intoxicated (DWI)** an offense for which a driver can be charged in all states if the driver's blood-alcohol concentration is above a certain level (323)

**emotion** strong feeling such as anger, fear, and joy (292)

**energy of motion** kinetic energy or the energy an object has because it is moving (93)

**engine-management system** computerized system that monitors and adjusts the fuel, ignition, and emission systems (371)

**entrance ramp** ramp leading onto an expressway (225)

**euphoria** false sense of well-being developed as a result of alcohol or drug consumption (315)

**execute** fourth step of the IPDE Process in which a driver performs proper vehicle control responses to avoid possible conflicts (7)

**exit ramp** ramp leading off an expressway (235)

**field of vision** all the area a person can see while looking straight ahead (67)

**field sobriety test** series of on-the-spot, roadside tests that help an officer detect impairment of a driver suspected of DUI or DWI (324)

**financial responsibility law** law that requires you to prove that you can pay for collision damages you cause that result in death, injury, or property damage (342)

**fishtail** sliding of the rear of a vehicle from side to side (258)

**flashing signal** traffic signal that alerts drivers to dangerous conditions or tells them to stop (29)

**force of impact** force with which one moving object hits another object; varies according to speed, weight, and distance between impact and stop (100)

**4–6 second range** area where you will be traveling during the next 4 to 6 seconds, and where you get the final update of how you are controlling your intended path of travel (67)

**fresh green light** light that has just turned from red to green (136)

**friction** force that keeps each tire from sliding on the road (94)

**friction point** in shifting, the point at which you feel the engine take hold and the vehicle start to move (53)

**fringe vision** the part of your peripheral vision that is closest to your central vision and helps you monitor zone changes (300)

**fuel-injection system** fuel-combustion system (replacing a carburetor) in which vaporized fuel is pumped under pressure to the engine cylinders (361)

**full stop** a complete stop as required at a STOP sign or red light (20)

**gap** distance between vehicles (144)

**glare recovery time** time your eyes need to regain clear vision after being affected by glare (301)

**glare resistance** ability to continue seeing when looking at bright lights (301)

**graduated driver licensing program** program requiring young drivers to progress through a series of licensing stages with various restrictions (11)

**gravity** force that pulls all things to earth (92)

**ground viewing** making quick glances to the roadway in front of your vehicle (70)

**guide sign** sign that gives directions, distance, services, points of interest, and other information (25)

**hallucinogen** mind-altering drug that tends to distort a person's perceptions of direction, distance, and time (322)

**hand-over-hand steering** pulling the steering wheel down with one hand while the other hand crosses over to pull the wheel farther down (113)

**hazard flasher** device that flashes front turn-signal lights and taillights to warn others the vehicle is a hazard (44)

**head restraints** padded devices on the backs of front seats that help reduce whiplash injuries in a collision (44)

**highway hypnosis** drowsy or trancelike condition caused by concentration on the roadway ahead and monotony of driving (238)

**highway transportation system (HTS)** complex system made up of people, vehicles, and roadways (4)

**hydroplaning** occurs when a tire loses road contact by rising up on top of water (252)

**identify** first step in the IPDE Process in which the driver locates potential hazards (6)

**ignition switch** switch operated by a key which starts or stops the engine (42)

**implied-consent law** states that anyone who receives a driver's license automatically consents to be tested for blood-alcohol content and other drugs if stopped for suspicion of drug use while driving (323)

**inhibitions** inner forces of personality that restrain or hold back impulsive behavior (316)

**international symbols** symbols used on traffic signs that give a message without using words (26)

**intoxilyzer** breath-test machine most commonly used for determining blood-alcohol content (324)

**IPDE Process** organized process of seeing, thinking, and responding that includes the steps of identifying, predicting, deciding, and executing (6–7)

**jack** hand-operated device used to lift and hold one corner or side of the vehicle (268)

**joining traffic** turning right or left into lanes of other vehicles (144)

**lane signal** signal, usually overhead, that tells whether a lane can or cannot be used at a specific time (30)

**leasing** alternative to purchasing a vehicle (338)

**legend** chart that explains the markings and symbols used on a map (380)

**liability insurance** provides compensation for damages to a third party for which the insured is legally obligated to pay; covers others when you are at fault (342)

**line of sight** distance you can see ahead in the direction you are looking (65–66)

**lug nuts** devices that hold the wheel to the vehicle (269)

**mass transportation** involves moving large numbers of people together from place to place (349)

**master cylinder** device in the brake system from which brake fluid is forced to the wheel cylinders when a driver steps on the brake pedal (363)

**median** area of ground separating traffic moving in opposite directions (202)

**merging area** stretch of roadway at the end of an acceleration lane on an expressway where vehicles join the flow of traffic (225)

**minimize a hazard** reduce the possibility of conflict by putting more space between your vehicle and the hazard (78)

**minimum speed limit** speed limit to keep traffic moving safely by not allowing drivers to drive slower than a certain speed (22)

**moped** two-wheeled vehicle that can be driven with either a motor or pedal (160)

**motor scooter** low-powered, two-wheeled vehicle that is more powerful than a moped (161)

**muffler** device that reduces the noise from combustion sounds in the engine (362)

**navigating** following a route by reading a map (384)

**night blindness** not being able to see well at night (300)

**no-fault insurance** covers an insured's losses and expenses associated with a collision regardless of who is at fault (342)

**no-zones** large blind-spot areas where truck drivers cannot see other vehicles (168)

**nystagmus** involuntary jerking of the eyes as a person gazes to the side (325)

**odometer** device on the instrument panel indicating the total number of miles the vehicle has been driven (40)

**oil pump** device that forces oil from the oil pan to parts of the engine that need lubrication (359)

**open zone** space where you can drive without a restriction to your line of sight or intended path of travel (65)

**orderly visual search pattern** process of searching critical areas in a regular sequence (67)

**overdriving headlights** driving at a speed that makes your stopping distance longer than the distance lighted by your headlights (248)

**oversteer** turning the steering wheel too much (110)

**overtake** pass the vehicle ahead (186)

**over-the-counter (OTC) medicine** drug that can be obtained legally without a doctor's prescription (321)

**parallel parking** parking the vehicle parallel to the curb (121)

**passive restraint device** restraint device, such as an air bag or an automatic seat belt, that works automatically (100)

**path of travel** space your vehicle will occupy as you travel ahead (65)

**pedestrian signal** signal used at heavy traffic intersections that tells pedestrians whether they should walk or wait (30)

**peer education** process in which young people help other young people make decisions and determine goals (327)

**peer pressure** influence of others of a similar age (326)

**perception distance** distance your vehicle travels during perception time (98)

**perception time** length of time you take to identify, predict, and decide to slow for a hazard (98)

**peripheral vision** area a person can see to the left and right of central vision (68)

**perpendicular parking** parking the vehicle at a right angle to the curb (120)

**personal reference point** adapting the standard reference point to one's own vehicle (119)

**point-of-no-return** point beyond which a driver can no longer stop safely without entering the intersection (132)

**powerplant** vehicle's engine or motor that generates power (356)

**power steering** system that uses a hydraulic pump and fluid to make steering easier (363)

**predict** second step of the IPDE Process in which the driver anticipates possible conflicts (6)

**premium** specified amount of money paid to an insurance company for insurance coverage over a specified period of time (342)

**prescription medicine** drug that can be purchased legally only when ordered by a doctor (321)

**preventive maintenance** routine care and attention to your vehicle (368)

**principal driver** person who will drive a certain vehicle most often (345)

**property-damage insurance** protects the driver who is at fault against claims for damages to another person's property, up to specified limits (342)

**protected left turn** left turn made on a left-turn light, green arrow, or delayed green light while oncoming traffic is stopped (137)

**protective equipment** items a motorcyclist wears to protect head, eyes, and body (156)

**pull-out area** additional right lane on narrow mountain roadways for slower-moving vehicles (214)

**push-pull steering** pushing the steering wheel up with one hand and pulling it down with the other (113)

**radial tire** tire that has plies that run straight across under the tread and strengthening belts of steel or other materials that circle the tire (365)

**radiator** part of cooling system that holds and cools the coolant (360)

**reaction distance** distance your vehicle travels while you react (99)

**reaction time** length of time you take to execute your action (98)

**recreational vehicle** large vehicle such as a van, motor home, camper, travel trailer, pickup truck, or sport utility vehicle, used mainly for pleasure and travel (165)

**reference point** a part of the outside or inside of the vehicle, as viewed from the driver's seat, that relates to some part of the roadway (119)

**regulatory sign** sign that controls traffic (20)

**restraint device** any part of a vehicle that holds an occupant in the seat during a collision (100)

**ride the brake** resting your foot on the brake pedal while driving (184)

**riding the clutch** resting your foot on the clutch pedal while driving (54)

**right of way** privilege of having immediate use of a certain part of a roadway (21, 142)

**right-turn-on-red** turning right when the red signal is on unless specifically prohibited to turn (137)

**risk** in driving, possibility of having a conflict that results in a collision (4)

**roadway marking** marking that gives you a warning or direction (31)

**roadway users** people who use the HTS by walking, driving, or riding (4)

**rocking a vehicle** repeating the sequence of driving forward a little and then back a little to move your vehicle out of deep snow, mud, or sand (254)

**rumble strips** sections of rough pavement intended to alert drivers of approaching roadway construction, tollbooth plaza, or other traffic conditions (33)

**runaway vehicle ramp** place on mountain roads for vehicles to safely get out of traffic when their brakes are not effective (214)

**safety chains** backup link used in case a trailer hitch fails (388)

**scanning** glancing continually and quickly with very brief eye fixations through your orderly visual search pattern (68)

**school zone** portion of a street or highway near a school that is subject to special speed limits (24)

**selector lever** device in an automatic transmission vehicle used to select gears (42)

**selective seeing** identifying and selecting only those clues and events that restrict your line of sight or can change your intended path of travel (69)

**separate the hazards** process of adjusting the speed of a vehicle to handle one hazard at a time when two or more hazards threaten a driver (78)

**shared left-turn lane** lane on a busy street that helps drivers make safer mid-block left turns into business areas from a center lane (31, 115)

**skid** when tires lose part or all of their grip on the road (256)

**slow-moving vehicle** vehicle unable to travel at highway speed (209)

**Smith System** organized method designed to help drivers develop good seeing habits by using five rules for safe driving (7, 64)

**solar-powered vehicle** vehicle that captures light from the sun and transforms it into electrical power (350)

**space cushion** open area around a vehicle consisting of adequate following distance between it and the vehicles ahead and behind, plus swerve paths to left and right (76)

**speed smear** occurs when objects off to your sides become blurred and distorted as your speed increases (302)

**stale green light** light that has been green for a long time (136)

**standard reference point** point on the vehicle typical for most drivers (119)

**stimulant** drug that speeds up the central nervous system (322)

**switchback** turn in a road that bends sharply in the opposite direction (213)

**tailgate** to follow another vehicle too closely (180)

**target** stationary object that appears in the distance in the center of the path you intend to occupy (50)

**target area** section of roadway where the target is located and the area to the left and right of the target (66)

**target area range** space from your vehicle out to target area (66)

**thermostat** part of cooling system that opens and shuts to control the flow of coolant to the radiator (360)

**total stopping distance** distance your vehicle travels while you make a stop (98)

**traction** friction or gripping power between the tires and the roadway surface (74, 94)

**tractor-semitrailer** type of tractor-trailer that pulls one trailer; commonly called an "eighteen wheeler" (167)

**tractor trailer** truck that has a powerful tractor that pulls a separate trailer (167)

**traffic circle** intersection that forms when several roadways meet at a circle (130)

**traffic signal** any signal used to control the movement of traffic (27)

**transaxle** device in a front-wheel drive vehicle that carries power to the front wheels via two half-shafts (356)

**transmission** mechanism in a vehicle that delivers power from the engine to the drive wheels (356)

**tread** outer grooved surface of a tire that grips the road (94)

**tunnel vision** being able to see in a narrow field of vision of 140° or less (300)

**turnabout** maneuver for turning your vehicle around to go in the opposite direction (116)

**12–15 second range** area you will be traveling in during the next 12 to 15 seconds, and where you need to identify changes in your path of travel (66–67)

**uncontrolled intersection** intersection that has no signs or signals to regulate traffic (139)

**uncontrolled railroad crossing** railroad crossing that does not have flashing red lights or crossing gates (140)

**underinsured motorist insurance** covers costs that exceed what the other person's insurance company will pay as a result of a collision (344)

**understeer** not turning the steering wheel enough (110)

**uninsured motorist insurance** covers costs up to a certain amount if you are struck by another vehicle whose driver has no insurance (344)

**unprotected left turn** left turn made at a signal-controlled intersection without a special left-turn light (137)

**van pooling** several individuals sharing transportation to one or more destinations in a van (349)

**vehicle code** federal and state laws that regulate the HTS (5)

**velocitation** condition of unconsciously driving too fast as a result of driving for long periods at high speeds (238)

**visual acuity** ability to see things clearly both near and far away (298)

**warning sign** sign that alerts you to possible hazards and road conditions (23)

**warranty** written guarantee that the seller will make certain repairs for a stated period of time (339)

**water pump** part of cooling system that draws coolant from the radiator and forces it through the engine's cooling passages (360)

**wolf pack** group of vehicles traveling together in a bunch on an expressway (231)

**yield** to allow another vehicle or roadway user to proceed first (21, 142)

**zero-tolerance law** law stating it is illegal for persons under the age of 21 to drive with any measurable amount of alcohol in the blood (324)

**zone** one of six areas of space around a vehicle that is the width of a lane and extends as far as the driver can see (65)

**Zone Control System** organized method for managing the space—or six zones—around your vehicle (7, 64)

Index **399**

**Downshifting,** 56, 114
  in automatic transmission vehicle, 213
  with total brake failure, 270
**Drinking and driving,** 314–320. *See also* Alcohol
**DRIVE (D) gear position,** 48–49, 51
**Driver**
  altitude and, 214–215
  condition of, 291–333
  cooperating with other, 224
  designated, 320
  errors, 276–278
  heat and, 215
  looking out for problem, 70
  motorcycle. *See* Motorcyclist
  older, 307–308
  as pedestrian, 163–164
  risk factors contributed by, 62–63
  skills needed by, 6
**Driver's license,** 11–14
  for moped and motor scooter, 161
  suspension for DUI/DWI, 323
**Drive shaft,** 356
**Drive system,** 356–357
**Drive-train system,** 356
**Driveway**
  backing into for turn, 116–117
  pedestrians in, 162–163
  pulling into for turn, 117
  on rural roads, 200
  yield coming from, 143
**Driving habits,** 6. *See also* Habits
**Driving task,** 6–7
**Driving under the influence (DUI),** 323
**Driving while intoxicated (DWI),** 323
**Drowsy drivers,** 305
  on long trips, 384
  *See also* Fall asleep collisions; Fatigue
**Drugs**
  alcohol, 314–315. *See also* Alcohol
  depressants, 321
  hallucinogens, 322
  medicines, 321
  stimulants, 322
**Drum brake,** 364
**Dust storm,** 216

**Education programs**
  alcohol-related, 314
  court, 329
  driver education, 13
  peer education, 327–328
**Electrical system,** 40–41, 357–359
**Emergency equipment,** 383
**Emergency flasher.** *See* Hazard flasher
**Emergency situations**
  dialing 911 to report, 283
  handling, 267–287
  swerving in, 277–278
**Emergency vehicles,** 143, 166
**Emission system,** 361–362
**Emotions,** 292–297
**Energy of motion,** 93
**Engine**
  caring for, 370
  checking before long trip, 382
  cold, 261
  failure, 272–273
  fire in, 274
  flooded, 272
  fuel-efficient, 371
  overheated, 272–273, 360
  routine checks for, 368
  size and types of, 337
  starting, 42, 49, 54
**Engine-management systems,** 358, 371
**Entrance ramp,** 225–228
**Environment**
  drivers helping, 348–350
  responsibility for, 10
  vehicles' affect on, 347–348
**Euphoria,** 315
**Execute (IPDE Process),** 6, 63, 75, 79–82, 177, 229–230
**Exhaust, leaking,** 261
**Exhaust gases,** 347, 361
**Exhaust system,** 361, 382
**Exit ramp,** 235–237
**Expressways,** 221–243
  advantages of, 222
  clues in, 69
  applying IPDE Process on, 229–230, 234–235, 240
  changing lanes on, 232–234
  disabled vehicles on, 239
  driver condition and, 238–239

  entering, 225–228
  exiting, 235–237
  following distance on, 231–232
  interchanges on, 222–223
  lane choice on, 230
  passing and being passed on, 234
  roadway conditions, 239
  safe driving strategies for, 223–224
  safe use of, 240
  signs, signals, and roadways markings on, 230–231
  special problems, 238–240
  speed limits on, 231
  strategies for driving on, 229–234
  tailgaters on, 232
  through cities, 239
**Eye contact,** 82

**Fall-asleep collisions,** 238. *See also* Drowsy drivers; Fatigue
**Farm machinery, slow-moving,** 165
**Fatigue,** 304–305, 387. *See also* Drowsy drivers; Fall-asleep collisions
**Field sobriety test,** 324
**Field of vision,** 67–68, 299
**FIFTH (5) gear position,** 53, 55–56
**Financial responsibility,** 10
**Financial responsibility law,** 342, 345
**Fire,** 274–275
**Fire hydrant,** 33
**FIRST (1) gear position,** 53–54
**Fishtailing,** 258, 268
**Flashers, hazard,** 81
**Flashing signal,** 29
**Floods**
  driving and, 253
  flash, 216
**Fluids, disposal of,** 348, 372
**Fog,** 207, 249–250
**Following distance,** 178
  on expressways, 231–232
  for large vehicle, 387
  measuring, 178
  motorcycles and, 154, 156
  for rural driving, 201
  in urban traffic, 178
**Foot-brake pedal,** 43
**Force of impact,** 100–104
**FOURTH (4) gear position,** 53, 55–56

interstate highways, 239–240
*See also* Rural roads; Rural traffic

**Rural roads**
being passed on, 208
divided roadways, 202
hazards on, 197
hills on, 200
multilane, 201–203
passing on, 204–207
two-lane, 199–201
visual search pattern on, 199
*See also* Rural driving; Rural traffic

**Rural traffic**
animals and, 209
characteristics of, 196–197
oncoming, 210–211
roadside hazards, 197
roadways, 196
slow-moving vehicles in, 209, 211–212
speed, 196
traffic controls, 197
*See also* Rural driving; Rural roads

**Rush-hour traffic**
on expressways, 224, 227
lane signals for, 30
special lanes for, 187

**SADD (Students Against Dangerous Decisions),** 329
**Safe driving,** 8, 63, 72–73
**Safety, devices for,** 43–45
**Safety belt,** 43–44, 51
automatic, 104
collisions and, 100
fastening, 47
how to wear, 100–101
inventor of, 101
warning light, 41
**Safety chains,** 387–388
**Salting roads,** 254
**Sandstorms,** 216
**Scanning,** 68
**School bus,** 165–166
**School zone,** 23–24, 33
**Searching range,** 65–67, 199
**Seat adjustment,** 45, 47
**SECOND (2) gear position,** 53–54
**Seeing**
driving and, 298

in large vehicle, 386
*See also* Vision; Visual acuity
**Selective seeing,** 69
**Selector lever,** 42, 48, 53
**Separate the hazards,** 78, 210
**Service, scheduled,** 369
**Shared left-turn lane,** 31–32, 114–115
**Shift indicator,** 48
**Shifting gears,** 54–56
**Shock absorber,** 96, 365
**Side-impact collision,** 281–282
**Signaling,** 111
**Signals.** *See* Traffic signals
**Signs.** *See* Traffic signs
**Skidding,** 256–258
**Skills,** 6
**Slow-moving vehicles,** 165, 209, 211–212
**Smell, sense of,** 302–303
**Smith, Harold L.,** 64
**Smith System,** 7, 63–64, 68, 76–77, 83
**Smoking**
near fuel pumps, 369
while driving, 307
**Snow**
clearing from vehicle, 46
driving techniques for, 254–255
moving in, 262
no passing in, 207
reduced traction with, 253–255
reduced visibility with, 250–251
removal areas, 33
**Social skills,** 6
**Solar-powered vehicle,** 350
**Space**
compromise, 79
predicting, 73
in urban traffic, 182–187
zones of, 64
**Space cushion,** 76, 178
**Special-purpose vehicles,** 164–165
**Speed**
adjusting for city driving, 185
braking distance and, 99
common, 231
control and, 74
controlling, 79–80, 370
for curves, 97
changing, 75

drinking drivers' judgment of, 317
energy of motion and, 93
force of impact and, 100
fuel efficiency and, 370
minutes saved and, 185
for rural driving, 196, 198
shifting, 53, 55
vision and, 302
for winter driving, 262
**Speed limit**
advisory, 22
for expressway driving, 231, 223
maximum, 197, 230
minimum, 22, 231
on rural roads, 196
signs, 22
**Speedometer,** 40
**Speed smear,** 302
**Split traction,** 95–96
**Stale green light,** 136
**Standard reference point,** 119
**Staring,** 67–68, 316
**Starter switch,** 42
**Steering,** 49–51
aiming high in, 64, 68
executing and, 80
failure, 273
hand-over-hand, 113
power, 273, 363
push-pull, 113
straight, 110–111
through tunnel, 260
**Steering system,** 363, 382
**Steering wheel,** 42
adjustment lever, 42
air bag in, 102
energy-absorbing, 104
hand position on, 47, 49–50
**Stickshift transmission**
clutch pedal, 43
driving with, 53–56
starting on hill using, 124
turning, 114
*See also* Manual transmission
**Stimulant,** 322
**STOP line,** 21, 28, 33
**Stopping**
automatic transmission vehicle, 52
at intersection, 132–133

## Acknowledgments

Unless otherwise acknowledged, all photographs are the property of Prentice Hall. Page abbreviations are as follows: (t) top, (c) center, (b) bottom, (l) left, (r) right.

Grateful acknowledgment is made to the following for copyrighted material:

The Smith System marks, "Smith System®," "Aim High In Steering®," "Get The Big Picture®," "Keep Your Eyes Moving®," "Leave Yourself An Out®," and "Make Sure They See You®," are registered service marks of Smith System Driver Improvement Institute, Inc., Arlington, TX USA. Used with Permission.

Note: Every effort has been made to locate the copyright owner of material reproduced in this component. Omissions brought to our attention will be corrected in subsequent editions.

**Cover** David Epperson/Tony Stone Images; automobile console courtesy of Bredemann Ford, Glenview, IL
**1** H. Abernathy/H.Armstrong Roberts, Inc.
**2–3** David Young-Wolff/PhotoEdit
**5** (br) Jonathan Naurok/PhotoEdit
**5** (tr) Mark Burnett/Stock Boston
**5** (l) Alan Carey/Image Works
**10** Tony Freeman/PhotoEdit
**17** (bl) Superstock, Inc.
**18–19** Colin Young-Wolff/PhotoEdit
**28** (t) Tony Freeman/PhotoEdit
**37** Charles Feil/Stock Boston
**38–39** Robert Llewellyn/Corbis
**41** Courtesy, Jennings Chevrolet
**42** Courtesy, Jennings Chevrolet
**45** Courtesy, Jennings Chevrolet
**48** Courtesy, Jennings Chevrolet
**50** Courtesy, Bredemann Ford, Glenview, IL
**60–61** Siri Schwartzman
**70** Mark Richards/PhotoEdit
**88–89** David R. Frazier Photolibrary
**90–91** SuperStock, Inc./SuperStock
**103** David J. Sams/Texas Imprint/Stock Boston
**107** (tl) Courtesy, Bredemann Ford, Glenview, IL

**113** Courtesy of American Driver and Traffic Safety Education Association
**123** (all) Jim Brady
**127** (r) SuperStock/Alamy
**128–129** Mark Gibson
**138** Frank Rossotto/Stock Market
**148–149** Michael Newman/PhotoEdit
**151** Ron Davis Photography
**154** D. H. Hessel/Stock Boston
**155** Motorcycle Safety Project/Courtesy, Northern Illinois University
**160** (t) Robert Brenner/PhotoEdit
**163** Ulrike Welsch/PhotoEdit
**165** Gabe Palmer/Stock Market
**166** Courtesy, Glenview, IL Fire Department
**171** (bl) Courtesy, Glenview, IL Fire Department
**172–173** SuperStock, Inc.
**174–175** Neil Lukas/Dorling Kindersley
**187** David Young-Wolff/PhotoEdit
**193** (bl) Alex Segre/Alamy
**194–195** Jeff Greenberg/PhotoEdit
**202** Bill Horsman/Stock Boston
**214** SPECTRUM EuroStock/Robertstock
**215** Kent Knudson/Stock Boston
**216** Tony Freeman/PhotoEdit
**220–221** Tony Freeman/PhotoEdit
**222** Alex MacLean/Landslides
**223** (t) Alex MacLean/Landslides
**223** (c) Alex MacLean/Landslides
**223** (b) Alex MacLean/Landslides
**231** Momatiuk & Eastcott/Stock Boston
**238** Mark Burnett/Stock Boston
**244–245** Chuck Keeler, Jr./Corbis
**249** Mark C. Burnett/Stock Boston
**250** Mulvehill/Image Works
**251** Frank Siteman/Stock Boston
**252** Robert W. Ginn/PhotoEdit
**254** (b) Chris Sorensen/Stock Market
**257** (tl) Jim Brady
**257** (bl) Jim Brady
**262** David Epperson/Tony Stone Images
**266–267** Ingram Publishing/SuperStock
**274** Jonathan Naurok/PhotoEdit

**283** Bob Daemmrich/Stock Boston
**288–289** A&L Sinibaldi/Tony Stone Images
**290–291** Ron Chapple/PictureQuest
**304** Cindy Charles/PhotoEdit
**307** Felicia Martinez/PhotoEdit
**308** John Neubauer/PhotoEdit
**312–313** Park Street/PhotoEdit
**314** (cap inset) Tony Freeman/PhotoEdit
**321** Steve Skjold/PhotoEdit
**326** Steve Skjold/PhotoEdit
**333** (br) Cleve Bryant/PhotoEdit
**334–335** Nick Vedros/SuperStock
**337** (tl) Ron Kimball Stock Photography/Ron Kimball
**337** (tr) Ron Kimball Stock Photography/Ron Kimball
**337** (bl) Photo by Business Wire via Getty Images
**337** (br) Carphotos/Alamy
**347** Mark Burnett/Stock Boston
**349** David Young-Wolff/PhotoEdit
**350** (t) John Hillery/Reuters/Corbis
**350** (b) Michael Klinec/Alamy
**353** (tl) Vincent DeWitt/Stock Boston
**353** (bl) Tony Freeman/PhotoEdit
**353** (br) Tony Freeman/PhotoEdit
**354–355** Tony Freeman/PhotoEdit
**371** (t) Ron Perry/Transtock
**371** (b) Donald Dietz/Stock Boston
**375** (br) Rhoda Sidney/Image Works
**375** (bl) David R. Frazier Photolibrary, Inc./Alamy
**376–377** Jim Conaty/Omni-Photo Communications, Inc.
**381** "Map © by Rand McNally R.L. #98-S-135"
**382** allOver photography/Alamy
**383** Charles Feil/Stock Boston
**384** Spencer Grant/PhotoEdit
**385** Michael Newman/PhotoEdit
**391** (tl) Tony Freeman/PhotoEdit
**391** (tr) Courtesy, Washington State Department of Transportation
**391** (bl) Kathy Ferguson/PhotoEdit
**391** (br) Bill Ross/H. Armstrong Roberts, Inc.